COMPUTING WITH C# AND THE .NET Framework

Art Gittleman

California State University Long Beach

JONES AND BARTLETT PUBLISHERS

Sudbury, Massachusetts

BOSTON TORONTO LONDON SINGAPORE

World Headquarters

Jones and Bartlett Publishers
40 Tall Pine Drive
Sudbury, MA 01776
978-443-5000
info@jbpub.com
www.jbpub.com

Jones and Bartlett Publishers
Canada
6339 Ormindale Way
Mississauga, ON L5V 1J2
CANADA

Jones and Bartlett Publishers
International
Barb House, Barb Mews
London W6 7PA
UK

Library of Congress Cataloging-in-Publication Data

Gittleman, Art.
Computing with C# and the .NET framework / Arthur Gittleman.
p. cm.
ISBN 0-7637-2339-8
1. C# (Computer program language) 2. Microsoft .NET Framework. I. Title.
QA76.73.C154 G58 2003
005.13'3--dc21 2002040703

ISBN-13: 978-1-4496-1448-5
ISBN-10: 1-4496-1448-5

Editor-in-Chief, College: J. Michael Stranz
Production Manager: Amy Rose
Associate Editor: Theresa DiDonato
Associate Production Editor: Karen C. Ferreira
Senior Marketing Manager: Nathan J. Schultz
Production Assistant: Jenny L. McIsaac
Cover Design: Kristin E. Ohlin
Composition: Northeast Compositors
Design: Anne's Books
Printing and Binding: Courier
Cover Printing: Courier

This book was typeset in QuarkXpress 4.1 on a Macintosh G4. The font families used were Times, Frutiger, and Impress. The first printing was printed on 45# Highland Plus.

6048

Printed in the United States of America
12 11 10 09 08 10 9 8 7 6 5 4 3

To Charlotte with love

Contents

Appendices

Preface

C# and the .NET Framework support a new, integrated, powerful Internet programming model. We no longer need to use Visual Basic for rapid application development and forms, C++ for object-oriented applications, and ASP for the Web. We can use C# for all, and with the .NET Framework we have a platform with a huge library that can integrate applications across the Internet.

This text teaches C# from the beginning, but includes enough material for a two-term course covering more advanced topics. It teaches the concepts of computing necessary for a CS-1 course, but allows those with prior experience programming in another language to proceed quickly over the earlier chapters to learn the exciting C# language and .NET Framework in depth.

Core topics include C# basics, control structures, types, object-oriented programming, and arrays. Next come event-driven programming, user interfaces, and inheritance. Additional topics include exception handling, files, data structures, threads, animation, networking, databases, web programming with ASP.NET, and XML and web services. The later chapters can, for the most part, be studied independently, so an instructor has flexibility in the choice of topics for a more advanced course.

I believe one learns best from example, and, therefore, each chapter has many complete programs. As programmers we learn to add comments to our code, but for pedagogical purposes where comments would be so detailed as to clutter the code, I prefer to use notes. Each note contains a longer explanation of a key line of code, and appears just after the code, allowing easier reading of the code itself. By using notes in this way, I also avoid cluttering the text with detailed code explanations and can focus on explaining concepts.

One also learns by doing. To facilitate learning I include many varied exercises. Test Your Understanding Exercises at the end of each section give readers a chance to assimilate the material immediately. Answers to the odd-numbered exercises appear at the end of the text, and answers to the even-numbered exercises are available with code for all program examples on a Student Resource CD included with the text. This CD also includes the .NET framework SDK.

I include Skill Builder and Critical Thinking exercises at the end of most chapters to allow readers to master new concepts. Answers to these appear at the end of the book. A debugging exercise at the end of most chapters helps develop this necessary skill.

Program Modification exercises allow readers to tackle this common task. Program Design exercises provide practice including the entire development process.

One can debate endlessly the best way to introduce objects. I like to present objects early, but using a spiral approach so students build a sound foundation before delving into the details. Thus I start with an intuitive example in Chapter 5 and continue to show, using UML, how to design a class and code it in C#. I defer some concepts to Chapter 6, and the more difficult inheritance concepts to Chapter 9.

I thank reviewers

Gerald Baumgartner, The Ohio State University

David Binkley, Loyola College

Corinne Hoisington, Central Virginia Community College

Kenrick Mock, University of Alaska Anchorage

for their many perceptive comments and suggestions that did much to improve the manuscript. It has bee a great pleasure working with the very helpful and amiable CS team at Jones and Bartlett, including Michael Stranz, Theresa DiDonato, Amy Rose, Jenny McIsaac, and Karen Ferreira.

The web site for this book is

http://computerscience.jbpub.com/csharp

I will post errata as soon as I become aware of them. Please email any corrections to me at

artg@csulb.edu.

1 An Introduction to Computing with C#

Once upon a time, giant digital computers filled large rooms with their thousands of vacuum tubes. They were slow beasts, but looked awesome. In the years since electronic digital computers were first developed in the 1940s, computers have dramatically decreased in size and increased in computing power. Starting as a tool for science and engineering, computers have become an essential part of our society.

Studying computing challenges us to keep up with rapid technological change. With C# (pronounced *C sharp*) we can learn the basic techniques of programming that have brought us to this point, and go forward with object-oriented, interactive, graphical, event-driven programming, networking, and web services that take us to the future.

OBJECTIVES

- Introduce basic computing concepts
- Survey C# history, its features, and how it works
- Introduce the elements of a C# program
- Introduce the program development process

1.1 INTRODUCTION TO COMPUTING

Hardware

A computer has several basic components (see Figure 1.1). The processor executes programs stored in memory, using the memory to store data needed in computations. External storage, including disk drives, holds programs and data. Input devices such

FIGURE 1.1
A computer system

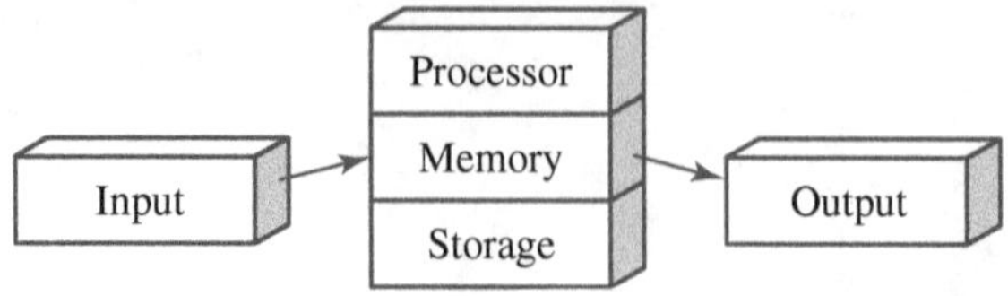

as a keyboard and a mouse allow user interaction. Output devices display results. Changing technology improves the performance of these components and provides new types, but current commercial computers have this organization.

Software

Software consists of the programs the computer executes. The operating system software makes it much easier for us to use the computer. It provides an interface to the hardware for us, so that each of us does not have to write programs to read input from the keyboard, write output to the screen, or create files on the hard disk. An operating system can be relatively simple, providing few services, or it can be a huge program with many bells and whistles for us to use.

Programmers appreciate utility programs such as editors that allow us to create or modify programs and compilers that translate programs from one language to another to facilitate their execution. End users run word processors, spreadsheets, games, browsers, and many other applications. Businesses rely on computer software to serve customers and for the businesses' accounting, payroll, and other management needs.

The processor executes software using its specially designed instruction set. Each instruction is simple so that it may take hundreds, thousands, or millions of instructions to implement the tasks we want our software to perform. Each instruction has several parts. These parts specify the operation (`addition`, for example) that the instruction performs, and any operands that it uses, such as the numbers to add. Each memory location has a numerical address. High-level languages such as C# provide instructions to perform the equivalent of many low-level machine instructions.

High-Level Languages

Each processor has its own instruction set that uses numerical codes for the operators and numerical addresses for the operations. Each instruction performs one basic step such as an addition, a load, or a store. Programming using a processor's instruction set would make it difficult to accomplish any but the simplest tasks. Moreover, we would have to write such a program all over again for the instruction set of a different processor. A program using processor ABC's instruction set will not run on processor XYZ, and vice versa.

A high-level language allows us to express the computation in a more understandable form, combining several steps into one expression, and to write a program that we can implement on many types of processors. For example, we can express an addition as

```
totalSalary = baseSalary + bonus;
```

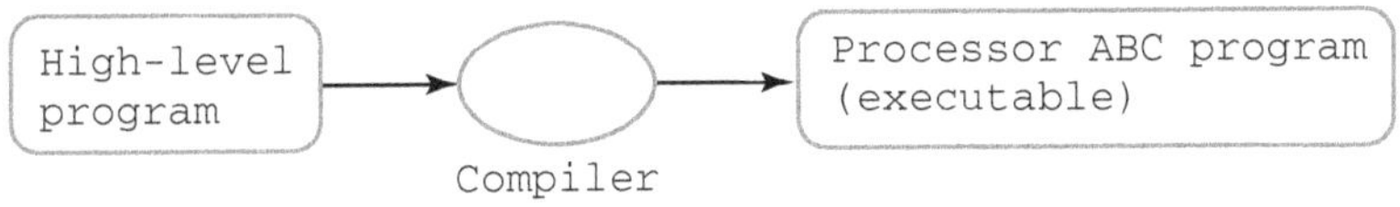

FIGURE 1.2
Translating a high-level program

and write more complicated statements such as

```
totalScore =
     (judge1Score + judge2Score + judge3Score) * difficulty;
```

which represents the total score obtained by first adding the scores of three judges, and then multiplying that sum by a difficulty factor. We use the asterisk, *, to denote multiplication.

Compilers

A compiler translates a program from one language to another. If we want to write a program in a high-level language and run it on processor ABC, we can use a compiler to translate our high-level program to an equivalent program using the instruction set of processor ABC. Each high-level statement will usually translate to several processor ABC instructions. Figure 1.2 shows this process.

To run the same program on processor XYZ we would need another compiler that translates from the high-level language to the instruction set of processor XYZ. The high-level program is called the source code, and the translated program is called the executable code or the binary code (reflecting its use of the binary number system to represent operators and operands.) Implementations of the C and C++ languages usually use compilers to produce executable code for specific processors.

Compilers are indispensable tools for program developers, but end users have no desire to use them. A player of a game wants a program that will run—an executable program. The vendor of that game must provide executable versions of the game for each processor.

Interpreters

An interpreter is a program that executes the code rather than translating it to another language. For example, an interpreter would execute the statement

```
totalSalary = baseSalary + bonus;
```

by finding the values of `baseSalary` and bonus, adding them, and storing the result in `totalSalary`. In this example, the interpreter executes a high-level language statement. The BASIC language, used on early personal computers that had insufficient memory to support the compilation process, was typically implemented by an interpreter.

We could also use an interpreter to allow one machine to simulate the instructions of another, as shown in Figure 1.3. For example, we could write a program that executes, on processor XYZ, programs written using processor ABC's instruction

FIGURE 1.3
An interpreter executing each high-level statement

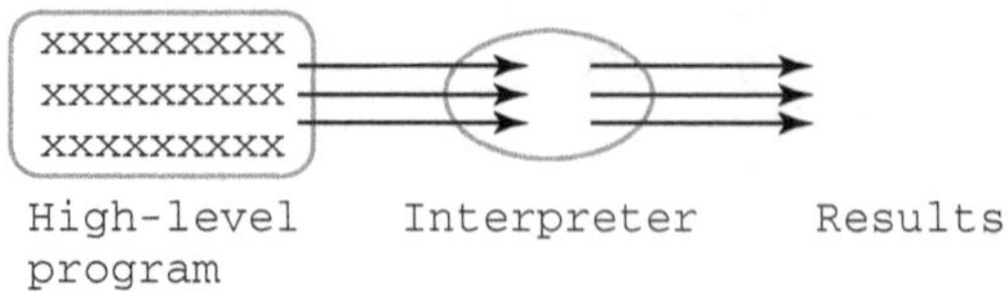

set. Many Java implementations use a combination of compilation and interpretation, as did the first implementations of the Pascal language.

Networks

Thus far we have focused on the software and hardware for a single computer. With the advent of the Internet, computers easily communicate with other computers in the same office, the same company, or at remote sites all over the world. Many of us use email more than we use regular mail or the telephone. A computer may be connected by cable to other computers in a network, or use a modem to connect over telephone lines.

The Internet is a vast network of networks over which we use familiar services such as email and file transfer. The World Wide Web, a rapidly growing part of the Internet, uses hypertext to create a web of links from one computer to another. Hypertext, which we discuss later in the text, allows us to include images, sounds, formatted text, and links to other computers in web pages which we display using a browser. Many use browser software as their primary access to computers. Web services allow computers to communicate with one another.

The BIG Picture

Operating system software handles the details of input, output, and files. Each hardware processor uses its own low-level instruction set. Higher-level languages allow programmers to write statements that are more meaningful. A compiler translates a program in a high-level language to the instruction set for a specific processor. An interpreter executes the high-level code directly.

✓ Test Your Understanding

1. Describe each component of the computer that you will be using to program in C#. What is the function of each?
2. List several software applications you have used or would like to use. Identify each as an operating system, word processor, game, etc.
3. What do we call the type of program that translates a program in a high-level language to an equivalent program in another language?
4. What do we call the type of program that executes another program?

1.2 THE .NET FRAMEWORK

Microsoft developed the C# language along with the .NET Framework, a new computing platform that simplifies application development in the distribution environment of the Internet. They designed the .NET Framework to fulfill the following objectives[1]:

- To provide a consistent object-oriented programming environment whether object code is stored and executed locally, executed locally but Internet-distributed, or executed remotely.
- To provide a code-execution environment that minimizes software deployment and versioning conflicts
- To provide a code-execution environment that guarantees safe execution of code, including code created by an unknown or semitrusted third party
- To provide a code-execution environment that eliminates the performance problems of scripted or interpreted environments
- To make the developer experience consistent across widely varying types of applications, such as Windows-based applications and Web-based applications
- To build all communication on industry standards to ensure that code based on the .NET Framework can integrate with any other code

The .NET Framework objective meets the needs of professional developers. This text presents only a small part of the .NET Framework, but we cannot climb the mountain until we take the first steps.

The two main parts of the .NET Framework are the Common Language Runtime and the .NET Framework class library.

The Common Language Runtime

The Common Language Runtime (CLR) manages the execution of code and provides services that make the execution of code easier. "Runtime" means that code is running, which is another way of saying it is being executed. "Common Language" means that this runtime manages the execution of code written in several languages that share the services provided.

Microsoft developed C# to take advantage of the CLR. Its features work especially well with the CLR. The popular Visual Basic language evolved to Visual Basic .NET, which is an object-oriented language that takes advantage of the CLR. Visual Basic programmers have to learn many new features to take advantage of the CLR using Visual Basic .Net. C++, like its C predecessor, has many capabilities that do not fit into the new approach. A version of C++, called managed C++, adapts C++ to work with the CLR, so C++ programmers can integrate code with other CLR users.

---

[1]"Overview of the .NET Framework," from the .NET Framework Developer's Guide. See `http://msdn.microsoft.com/library/`.

We call code that uses the CLR *managed code*. The Common Type System defines the types of data that managed code can use. A Common Language Specification (CLS) defines features that every language for developing managed code must provide. Programmers who use only features in the Common Language Specification can build an application combining programs in different languages. They will know that if they use a feature in one language, a program in another language will also be able to use that same construct.

To give a simplified example, consider numbers. Suppose we have space for only 10 numbers. If we use only nonnegative numbers, we can use 0, 1, 2, 3, 4, 5, 6, 7, 8, and 9. If we need to include both positive and negative values, we would choose −5, −4, −3, −2, −1, 0, 1, 2, 3, and 4. The unsigned type allows us to use larger values, but the signed type allows us to use negative values. In an analogous situation, the Common Type System provides both unsigned and signed types, but only requires that languages provide signed types to satisfy the Common Language Specification.

A developer who uses only signed types can expect every language that follows the CLS to interoperate with the code produced. A developer who uses unsigned types may produce code that another language that follows the CLS is not required to support.

A big problem facing developers is the many different types of processors that run code. Windows, Macintosh, and Unix machines use a wide variety of hardware, as do personal digital assistants, cell phones, large computers, and other platforms. One way to make a program work on each of these devices is to translate the program to the native instruction set for that device. Say we have 10 programming languages and 10 devices. Using this approach, in the worst case[2] we would need 100 compilers to translate programs in each of the 10 languages to native code for each of the 10 devices. Figure 1.4 diagrams this jumble of compilers.

Another approach, used by the CLR, is to provide an intermediate language that is much like the native languages of devices. This language is called MSIL, Microsoft Intermediate Language. We compile each language to MSIL. During runtime the CLR uses a JIT (Just In Time) compiler to compile the MSIL code to the native code for the device used.[3] This requires one JIT compiler for each device to translate MSIL code to the native code for that device. This translation process is not as difficult as translating a high-level language to native code, because the MSIL code is similar to native code.

FIGURE 1.4
Compiling three languages to native code for three machines

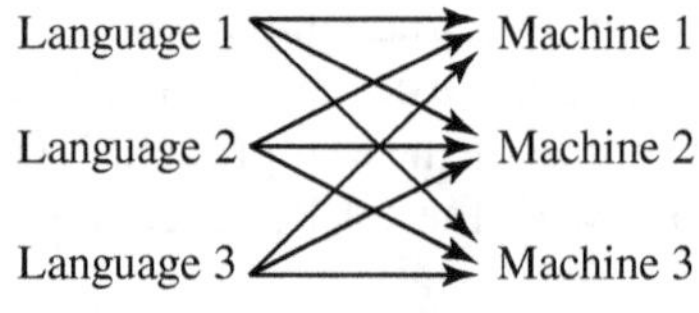

---

[2]Modern compilers use similar techniques to reduce the number needed to support multiple platforms.

[3]Java also uses a JIT compiler.

FIGURE 1.5
Compiling using an intermediate language

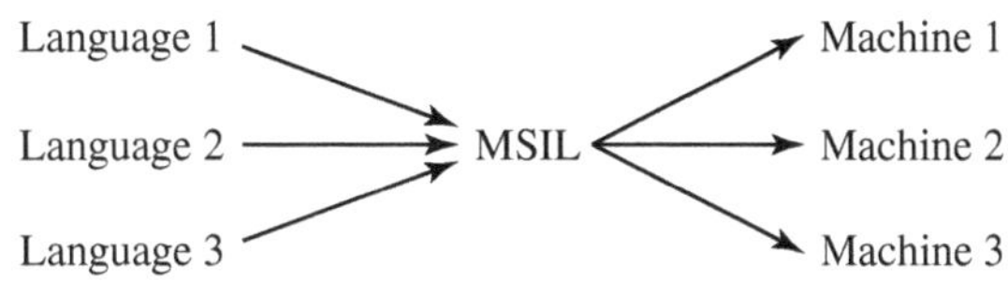

Moreover, using MSIL greatly reduces the number of compilers we need. For 10 languages and 10 devices, we need one compiler for each language to translate it to MSIL, and one JIT compiler for each device to translate MSIL code to native code for that device. Thus we need 20 compilers instead of 100. Figure 1.5 illustrates this approach.

The .NET Framework Class Library

The .NET Framework Class Library provides a large and very useful set of types that expedite the development process. The library groups the types in namespaces that combine related types. It contains about 100 namespaces of which we use only a small number in this text. Some of the namespaces from the library that we use are:

System
 Contains fundamental types

System.Collections
 Defines various collections of objects

System.Data
 Manages data from multiple sources including databases

System.Drawing
 Provides graphics

System.IO
 Allows reading and writing

System.Net
 Provides an interface computers use to communicate over networks

System.Runtime.Remoting
 Supports distributed applications

System.Text
 Handles character encoding

System.Threading
 Enables multithreaded programming

System.Web
 Enables browser–server communication

System.Web.Services
 Enables the building and use of web services

System.Windows.Forms
For user interfaces in Windows-based applications

System.Xml
Provides support for processing XML

The BIG Picture

The .NET Framework helps developers build applications for the diverse Internet environment. The Common Language Runtime and .NET Framework Class Library provide services and types to make programmers more productive.

✓ Test Your Understanding

5. What do we call code that targets the Common Language Runtime?

6. What are the two main parts of the .NET Framework?

1.3 OVERVIEW OF C#

History

FORTRAN and COBOL were among the first high-level languages, introduced in the late 1950s. Both are still used today, FORTRAN for scientific applications and COBOL for business. Smalltalk, released around 1980, is a fully object-oriented language that influenced its successors, including Java and C#.

Systems programmers who needed access to the machine hardware used assembly languages, which are very low-level and specific to the hardware. The C language, developed in the mid 1970s, is sometimes described as a portable assembly language. It is a high-level language, like FORTRAN and COBOL, but provides access to machine hardware. The UNIX operating system, developed for the then-new minicomputers, was mostly written in C, and both C and UNIX rapidly grew in popularity.

Although it is good for systems programming, C is a small language that does not facilitate the development of large software systems. Introduced in the later 1960s, object-oriented programming started to become popular in the mid 1980s. Languages that support object-oriented programming do facilitate the development of large software systems. C++ extends C to include constructs that support object-oriented programming, while still including those that access machine hardware. Consequently, C++ grew in popularity.

BASIC was developed in the 1960s as an easier way for students to learn to program. It used an interpreter so students could immediately see the results of execution. Originally, personal computers had very limited memory chips in which to hold programs, so BASIC, which did not require compilation to a larger low-level representation, became the main language used on early PCs. As memory became cheaper and graphics capabilities grew, BASIC morphed to Visual Basic, an extremely popular language for the rapid development of user applications.

With the introduction of the .NET Framework, Visual Basic evolved to Visual Basic .NET, a cousin of C#. One way we might describe C# is as a language that tries to combine the rapid application development of Visual Basic with much of the power of C++.

With the rise of desktop computers and the rapid growth of the Internet in the mid 1990s came the need for a language to support programming to enable users on vastly different systems to interact in a secure way. Java, introduced in 1995, uses a Java Virtual Machine to provide security and enable programs developed on different systems to interact. A large library extends its capabilities for Internet programming. Because it suited the new demands on developers, Java has become very popular.

The goals of C# are similar to those of Java. Those versed in one of these languages can rapidly convert to using the other. C# had the advantage of seeing the Java approach and how it might enhance it. C# adds features for the easy development of components to make it easier for developers to combine programs written on different systems. One can annotate a C# program with attributes that become part of the runtime used by the CLR. This metadata describes the program so that other programs can use it. C#, newly developed in the twenty-first century, promises to become very popular as the primary .NET programming language.

C# Features

Microsoft[4] identifies C# as a modern object-oriented language that allows programmers to quickly build .NET components from high-level business objects to system-level applications. These components can easily be converted to web services to be used over the Internet. Important characteristics are:

- Productivity and safety: C# uses the .NET platform supporting web technologies. C# works well with XML, the emerging standard to pass structured data over the Internet.

  The C# design eliminates many costly programming errors. It includes automatic memory management and initialization of variables. It checks types to avoid runtime errors.

  C# reduces updating costs by supporting versioning in the language, making it easier and less costly to introduce new versions of a product.

- Power, expressiveness, and flexibility: C# allows a close connection between the abstract business process and its software implementation. The developer can associate metadata with a program that will allow tools to determine that a component is correctly identified as part of a business object or to create reports.

  To avoid the need to use C++ to access basic machine functions, C# permits carefully identified low-level access to machine resources.

[4]`http://msdn.microsoft.com/vstudio/techinfo/articles/upgrade/Csharpintro.asp.`

C# uses a compiler, but does not immediately translate a high-level program to the machine instructions of each specific processor. The C# compiler takes as input the high-level C# program and outputs an equivalent program written using the Microsoft Intermediate Language. During runtime the CLR uses a JIT compiler to translate the MSIL code to the instruction set of the processor. Figure 1.6 shows the compilation of a C# program to MSIL followed by the JIT compilation to native code on two different processors.

The advantage of producing MSIL code instead of code for each different processor is that the same intermediate code will run on any processor that has a CLR. We can download a C# program which has been compiled to intermediate code on one type of machine and run it on a much different type of machine. For networking, this feature of C# is invaluable.

In December, 2001 ECMA (European Computer Manufacturers Association, a body that promulgates information technology standards) released the ECMA-334 standard for C#.

The BIG Picture

C# was created in the twenty-first century, basing much syntax on C and C++ and using concepts from several other languages. It combines the rapid productivity of Visual Basic with the power of C++.

C# source compiles to intermediate code. The CLR uses a JIT compiler to translate the intermediate code to code for the processor used. The .NET Framework makes C# very useful for Internet applications in which diverse machines communicate.

✓Test Your Understanding

7. Name three languages that were major influences in the development of C#.

8. List the features of C# as portrayed by its developers.

9. The C# compiler usually translates C# programs to what type of code?

FIGURE 1.6
Compiling a C# program

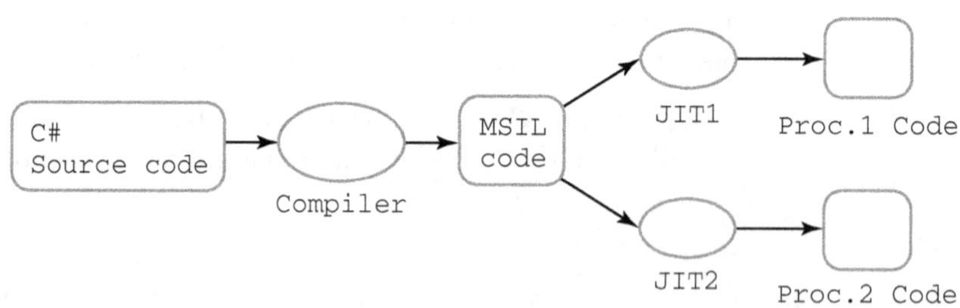

1.4 ■ THE ELEMENTS OF A C# PROGRAM

We can describe natural language on many levels. For example, this text, written in the English language, uses the Latin character set. So, at the lowest level, we see letters 'a', 'b', 'c', ... We also see punctuation, including commas and periods, and blank spaces. Characters group into words, words form sentences, and sentences form paragraphs. On a higher level, we can discuss the parts of speech: nouns, verbs, adjectives, adverbs, and so on. Moreover, the text has content that it is trying to communicate.

Programming languages have basic components that we form into larger units to build useful applications. Example 1.1 shows a simple C# program that will illustrate some of the elements of the C# programming language.

EXAMPLE 1.1 ■ Square.cs

```
/* Computes the square of a number.
 * Displays the result in a message.
 */

public class Square {
   // Execution starts here.

  static void Main() {
    int number = 345;
                                        // '=' denotes assignment
    int squared = number * number;
                                        // '*' denotes
                                        // multiplication
    System.Console.WriteLine
          ("The square of {0} is {1}", number, squared);
  }
}
```

Output

```
The square of 345 is 119025
```

■

Lexical Structure

The lexical structure identifies C# rules for dividing the program text into a sequence of input elements. Input elements include comments, whitespace, identifiers, keywords, literals, punctuators, and operators. Whitespace and comments help people to read programs but are omitted from the compiled program. We discuss each type of input element briefly.

Example 1.1 uses the familiar Latin characters, although C# can handle much larger character sets. C# is case sensitive, meaning that it distinguishes lowercase characters from uppercase. In the early days of computing character sets were small, and languages such as FORTRAN did not make that distinction.

Whitespace includes spaces, tabs, and carriage returns that we use to format the text. Formatting programs nicely makes them much easier to read and modify, but C# does not require it. Example 1.1 would be correct if none of the lines were indented, but it would be very unpleasant for humans to read. Line structure is not important in C#. The line

```
int number = 345;
```

could have been replaced by

```
int number
         = 345;
```

without changing its meaning.

A **comment** provides information for the human reader, but is not part of the executable code. Example 1.1 uses two styles of comments. Two forward slashes, `//`, mark the remaining text on that line as a comment. For comments that span multiple lines, we use `/*`, with no space between the two characters, to start the comment, and `*/` to end it. Programmers use comments to clarify the program for human readers. A general-purpose programming language like C# must use very general constructs that programmers can apply to build diverse applications. Comments help to identify what the C# code is trying to accomplish.

Example 1.1 uses **punctuators** such as the left brace, `{`, the right brace, `}`, and the semicolon, `;`. The full list of punctuators is

```
( ) { } [ ] ; , . :
```

Operators symbolize operations such as addition and multiplication. C# includes many operators, some of which require two or three characters to represent. Example 1.1 uses the `*`, `+`, and `=` operators. The asterisk, `*`, represents the multiplication operator.

Literals represent specific values. In Example 1.1, the literal `345` represents an integer. The literal `"The square of {0} is {1}"` represents a character string.

Identifiers are like the words of the program. Some identifiers are names chosen by the programmer, and others are **keywords**, reserved for special uses. Keywords in Example 1.1 include `public`, `static`, `class`, `int`, and `void`. Identifiers include `Square` and `number`. Figure 1.7 shows the lexical analysis phase

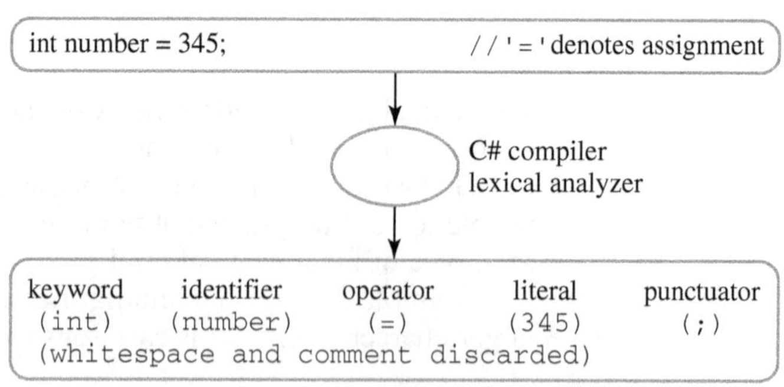

FIGURE 1.7 **Lexical analysis of a single line of Example 1.1**

of compilation. The lexical analyzer takes each line of the C# program and divides it into **tokens**, which are identifiers, keywords, literals, punctuators, or operators. It discards comments and whitespace.

Syntax

Syntax describes the grammatical rules for combining tokens into programs. In English, we form sentences from words. The sentence

```
I like to program
```

makes a declaration, and the sentence

```
Do you like to program?
```

asks a question.

C# syntactic structures include declarations, statements, and expressions. A **declaration** defines a part of a program. **Statements** control the sequence of execution of the program. **Expressions** compute values and have other effects. Figure 1.8 shows the overall syntactic structure of Example 1.1.

Example 1.1 declares a **class** named `Square`. Ignoring the outer comment, we see that, at the top level, the structure of Example 1.1 is this class declaration. `Class` is a key concept in C# and we shall have a lot to say about it. Programming languages use words in precise ways, in contrast to natural language, which can be vague. Nevertheless, C# uses the word `class` in ways that remind us of the English word `class` in the concept of classification. A class in that sense identifies a concept or type. We might classify animals into dogs, cats, horses, and so on.

A bacterium is a very simple type of animal compared to an elephant. We do not go to the zoo to see bacteria. Similarly, the `Square` class of Example 1.1 is a very limited example of a C# class. We shall later see C# classes that do define types that are more interesting. Roughly speaking, Example 1.1 does illustrate that a C# program often consists of a class declaration at its outer level.

A class contains member declarations. The `Square` class contains a **method** declaration for a method named `Main`. A method is a way of accomplishing something. We often name methods to signify what the method will accomplish. For example,

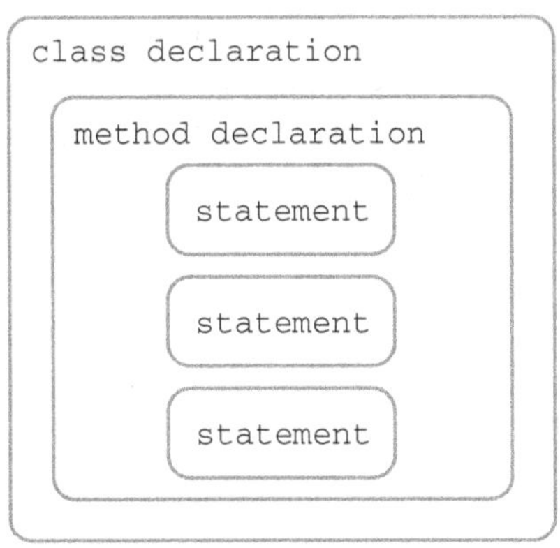

FIGURE 1.8
The overall syntactic structure of Example 1.1

Shuffle might name a method to shuffle a deck of cards. The name Main signifies the method that C# executes first.

The declaration of the Main method in Example 1.1 contains several parts. The Main method starts with "static void". The modifier static means that the Main method is part of the class definition. To understand the contrasting choice, consider the definition of an elephant, which describes a type of large animal. The Latin name for the African elephant, Loxodonta africana, is part of the definition of an elephant, but it is not part of an actual elephant. Later, when we declare more interesting classes, we shall see the analog of actual elephants, called instances or objects.

The modifier void indicates that the Main method does not return a value to its caller. Other methods may return to their callers a result of what they have accomplished.

The parentheses that immediately follow the method name, (), contain the names and types of any data that the method uses to accomplish its goal. The Main method in Example 1.1 does not use any additional data, so we leave this part of the declaration empty.

The remainder of Example 1.1 consists of the **body** of the Main method, which is a **block** of code. The body contains the code that enables the Main method to accomplish its purpose of computing and displaying the square of a number. A block contains a sequence of statements within braces, { }. The block in Example 1.1 contains three statements. We will discuss the details of the construction and meaning of these three statements later. At first glance, the first statement introduces a value of 345, the second statement squares that value, and the third statement displays the squared value. These statements contain expressions.

An **expression** specifies the computation of a value. For example, the expression

```
7 * 7
```

specifies a computation which produces the result 49. Example 1.1 uses the multiplication operator.

Example 1.1 includes a Main method. Executing Example 1.1 displays the message

```
The square of 345 is 119025
```

A class declaration does not need to include a Main method. For example, it may declare a method that can be executed from another program. Example 1.2 declares a class SquareIt. The class SquareIt declares a Square method. We do not need to look at each element of this program. It illustrates that some programs may not declare a Main method. We use the Square method of Example 1.2 in the next example.

EXAMPLE 1.2 ■ SquareIt.cs

```
/* Declares a method that computes the square of a
 * and returns its value.
 */
```

```
public class SquareIt {

  // Returns the square of its argument.

  public static int Square(int number) {            // Note 1
     return number * number;
  }
}
```

Note 1: `public static int Square(int number) {`

We need to prefix the `Square` method with the keyword `public` to make it available outside the program in which it is declared. We discuss access modifiers later in the text.

Example 1.3 contains a `Main` method that calls the `Square` method from the `SquareIt` class of Example 1.2. Because the `Square` method is in another class, we need to prefix it with the name of the class and invoke it as

```
SquareIt.Square(24);
```

for example.

EXAMPLE 1.3 ■ UseSquare.cs

```
/* Declares a method that computes the square of a
 * and returns its value.
 */

public class UseSquare {
  static void Main() {
    System.Console.WriteLine("The square of 24 is {0}",
                               SquareIt.Square(24));    // Note 1
  }
}
```

Output

```
The square of 24 is 576
```

Note 1: `System.Console.WriteLine("The square of 24 is {0}", SquareIt.Square(24));`

Computational methods like `Square` belong to the class in which they are defined. We prefix them with the class name to invoke them. Classes can also define instance methods associated with objects, as we shall later see.

The BIG Picture

Lexically, the text of a C# program is composed of a sequence of tokens. We use comments and whitespace to make the program easier to read and understand. Identifiers, keywords, operators, and punctuators make up other kinds of tokens. At the top level, a C# program may consist of a class declaration. A class declaration may contain a method declaration. C# starts executing the code of the `Main` method. A method body is a block that may contain a sequence of statements.

✓Test Your Understanding

10. List the various types of input elements C# uses.

11. Identify each of the first four input elements of Example 1.1, other than comments or whitespace, as an identifier, a keyword, an operator, or a punctuator.

12. Identity the each of the input elements of the statement

```
int number = 345;
```

13. Identify each of the operators in Example 1.1.

1.5 COMPILING AND RUNNING C# PROGRAMS

We now show how to compile and run C# programs from the command line, and how to use Visual Studio .NET.

Using the Microsoft .NET Framework Software Development Kit

The .NET Framework Software Development Kit (SDK) is available at no cost at `http://msdn.microsoft.com/library`. We include this SDK on the CD bundled with this text. It contains the C# compiler and the .NET Framework Class Library. It does not provide a development environment. We use the Notepad editor to create programs.

To run Example 1.1 we can either use the code on the disk included with this text or use an editor such as Notepad, which is included with Windows operating systems, to enter the program and save it. A window in Notepad is shown in Figure 1.9.

To compile and run Example 1.1 using Sun's tools, we first get a command window.

- On Windows NT 4.0 systems, click on the *Start* button, *Programs*, and *Command Prompt* to get the console window from which to enter the compilation command.

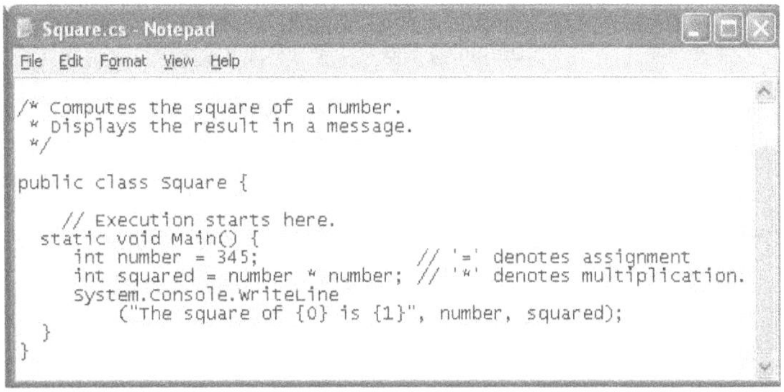

FIGURE 1.9 A Notepad window

- On Windows 2000 or XP systems, click on the *Start* button, *Programs*, *Accessories*, and *Command Prompt* to get the console window from which to enter the compilation command.

Then locate the directory containing the program. On the author's machine, the `Square.cs` code is in the `c:\booksharp\gittleman\ch1` directory, so the command

```
cd \booksharp\gittleman\ch1
```

will change to the correct directory.

Because we installed the .NET Framework SDK in the C:\WINDOWS\Microsoft.NET\Framework\v1.0.3705 directory, the C# compiler, called `csc.exe`, will be found there. To compile, we can use the command

```
\WINDOWS\Microsoft.NET\Framework\v1.0.3705\csc Square.cs
```

To avoid having to type the full path, `C:\WINDOWS\Microsoft.NET\Framework\v1.0.3705\csc`, when compiling we can set the PATH environment variable,[5] which lists all the directories the system should look in for executable files. After setting the path, we can use the command

```
csc Square.cs
```

Figure 1.10 shows the command window with the commands used to compile and run Example 1.1.

---

[5]Check the operating system help to see how to set the path for the platform you are using. Try searching "change the values of environment variables".

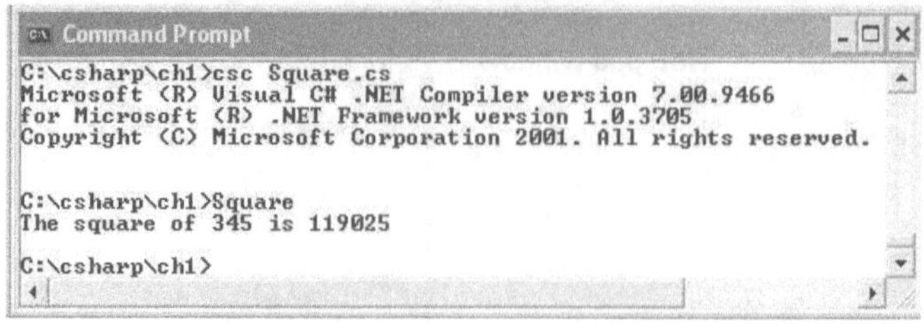

FIGURE 1.10
Compiling and running Example 1.1

The name `csc` represents the C# compiler, which translates the C# program `Square.cs` to an equivalent MSIL program. The file csc.exe produced by the compiler is an assembly in the CLR. When we run this code the JIT translates it to machine code, which is then executed to produce the result. Once we have compiled Example 1.1 we can execute the code. To run this program using the SDK, we enter the command

```
Square
```

in the console window.

Example 1.2 does not have a `Main` method. It has a `Square` method which we can call from other programs. We compile it using the command

```
csc /t:library SquareIt.cs
```

where the `/t` option, short for `/target`, tells the compiler to produce a library file, `SquareIt.dll`. We do not execute the library file directly, but reference it from other programs that call the `Square` method.

Example 1.3 uses the `Square` method from Example 1.2. We compile it using the command

```
csc /r:SquareIt.dll UseSquare.cs
```

where the option `/r`, short for `/reference`, indicates that the `UseSquare` program references the `SquareIt` assembly.

Using Visual Studio .NET

Visual Studio .NET provides a powerful development environment with tools that raise the productivity of professional developers. We illustrate the debugger in Chapter 3. Before relying on these tools, we believe one should learn the basics of C# and the .NET Framework Class Library. We could use Visual Studio .NET for all the examples in the book, but we use it only for debugging and the complex user interface at the end of Chapter 15.

After opening Visual Studio .NET, clicking on *File*, *New*, *Project* produces the screen shown in Figure 1.11. We select `Visual C# Projects` and `Console Application` and enter `Example 1.1` as the project name and `c:\csharp\ch1` as the location.

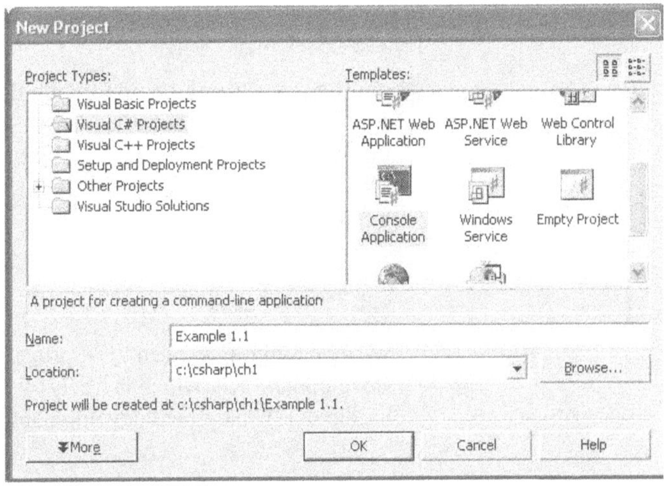

FIGURE 1.11 **Creating the Example 1.1 project**

FIGURE 1.12 **Code generated by Visual Studio .NET for Example 1.1**

```
using System;

namespace Example1_1
{
    /// <summary>
    /// Summary description for Class1.
    /// </summary>
    class Class1
    {
        /// <summary>
        /// The main entry point for the application.
        /// </summary>
        [STAThread]
        static void Main(string[] args)
        {
            //
            // TODO: Add code to start application here
            //
        }
    }
}
```

Clicking OK causes Visual Studio .NET to generate a code template for us to complete. This code, shown in Figure 1.12, is on the left in the Visual Studio .NET screen. On the right, the Solution Explorer lists the project files it has created.

All we need to do is add the lines

```
int number = 345;
int squared = number * number;
```

```
Console.WriteLine("The square of {0} is {1}", number,
squared);
```

where the TODO mark occurs inside the Main method. We can also change the name of the class from the default Class1 to Square. We click on *Debug, StartWithout Debugging* to compile and run the program.

When compiling Example 1.3 using Visual Studio .Net we need to add a reference to SquareIt.dll.

The BIG Picture

We can compile and run a C# program using either the .NET Framework Software Development Kit, which is freely available from Microsoft, or we can use the Visual Studio .NET integrated development environment.

✓Test Your Understanding

Try It Yourself ➤ **14.** Compile and run the Square.cs program of Example 1.1.

Try It Yourself ➤ **15.** Compile and run the UseSquare.cs program of Example 1.3.

1.6 DEVELOPING A C# PROGRAM

Before we can write C# programs, we must learn the structure of the C# language. However, knowing the correct C# forms only provides the basic tool for program development. Learning the correct and effective use of this tool is both more important and more difficult.

Levels of Abstraction

Our bodies have muscles, nerves, and many other parts. How many of us know much about these parts? We do not need to know which nerves and muscles are activated when we raise an arm. Raising an arm is a high-level operation that we learn to perform. It incorporates many low-level operations.

Similarly, an engineer needs to know the details of engines, fuel, and electrical systems in order to design a car. However, car drivers have a high-level interface. Starting the car is a simple operation that activates these complex systems to start the engine.

As program developers, we must create high-level operations that are easy to understand and use. We want a program that says

```
Raise arm
```

not one that has a thousand steps to activate each nerve and muscle needed to raise an arm. We want a program that says

```
Start car
```

not one that lists all the steps taken by the electrical and fuel systems (see Figure 1.13).

FIGURE 1.13
Raising an arm?

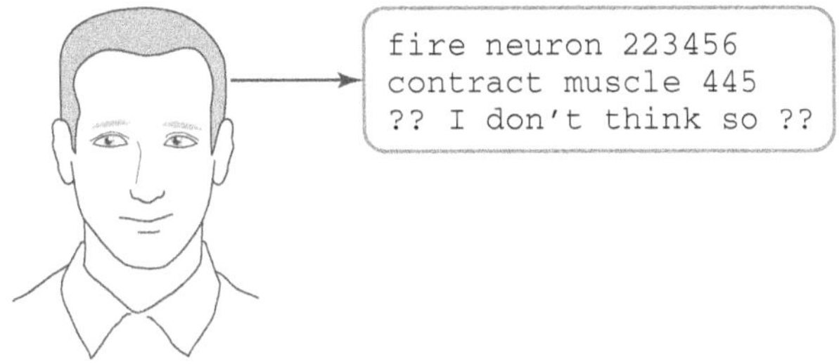

Of course, the high-level operations use the low-level details to perform their work, but we need to group low-level steps into high-level abstractions to make good, useful programs.

The Steps of Software Development

No one has yet devised the perfect method of software development. Moreover, the development process can be much simpler for a small, single-developer program than for a large software system that may involve hundreds of developers and have a lifetime of decades. Nevertheless, we can state some general principles that apply to many projects. Some keys steps are:

- Identifying the requirements of the system
- Designing a system that meets the requirements
- Implementing the system
- Testing that the system operates correctly and meets the requirements
- Making improvements as needed

Listing these steps in the order shown does not imply that we fully complete each step before we begin the next one. A good plan often is to design, implement, and test part of the system. This simplifies the problem and provides some useful capabilities in a timely manner. Some current methodologies involve testing along with the code development rather than after the code is completed.

We illustrate some of these software development steps with a simple example involving test scores from a class of students.

Requirements

A short problem description is, "Each student receives a test score between 0 and 100. The objective is to provide the class average and the number of students who receive each grade, A, B, C, D, or F." We need to make this short description more precise to understand what we need to do.

How many test scores are there? Will we know in advance, or do we have to count them during processing? How will we receive the data? Will we receive a file of scores separated by commas (76, 58, 92, for example)? Will we receive a file of scores with one score on each line? Will the user enter the scores when the program is running? If we obtain the test scores from a file, we can process them without further input from the user (see Figure 1.14).

FIGURE 1.14
Processing data without user interaction

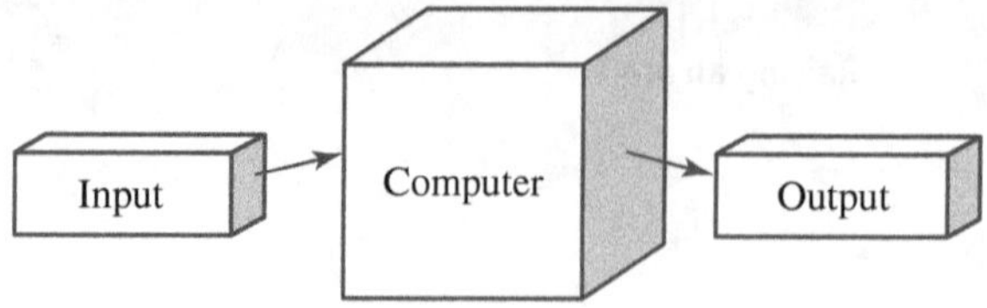

FIGURE 1.15
Processing data with user interaction

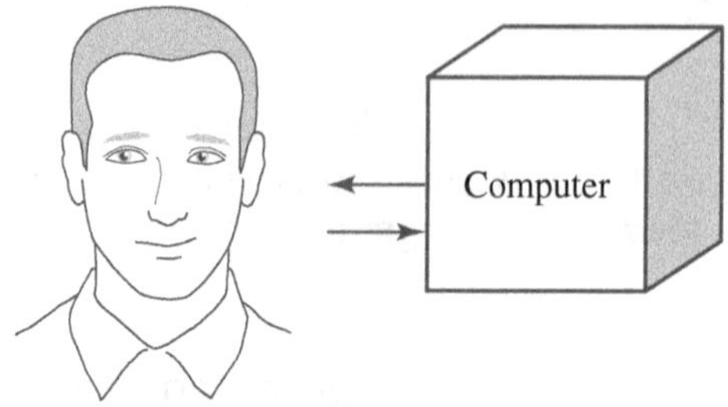

If the user enters scores while the program is running, we have a continuing interaction that might require a graphical user interface (see Figure 1.15).

What is the grading scale? Does a score of 90 or above receive an A grade, for example? Another choice would be to grade "on a curve," as shown in Figure 1.16.

How should we format the output? Can we write it to a file? Should we present it on a web site? Do we display the result in a user window?

Even with this simple problem, there is a lot to understand about the requirements. Imagine how immense the task would be to specify the requirements for an air traffic control system.

Design

We want to design a system to meet the requirements specified. Let us assume that the user will enter test scores interactively and will indicate when the entry process is complete. Grading will use a fixed scale, as follows.

```
90-100   A
80-89    B
70-79    C
60-69    D
 0-59    F
```

We will display the results in a user window.

FIGURE 1.16
Grading "on a curve"

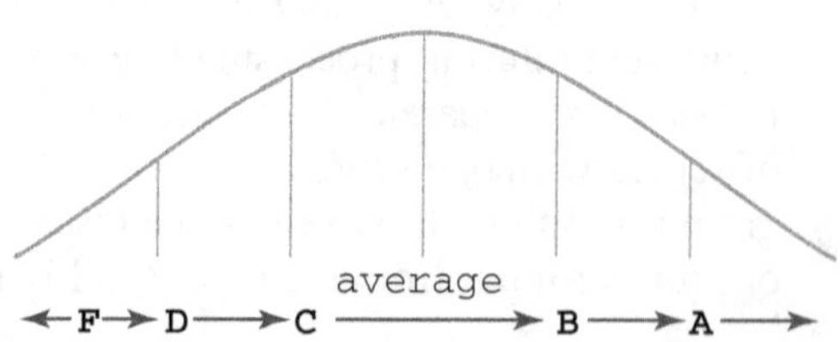

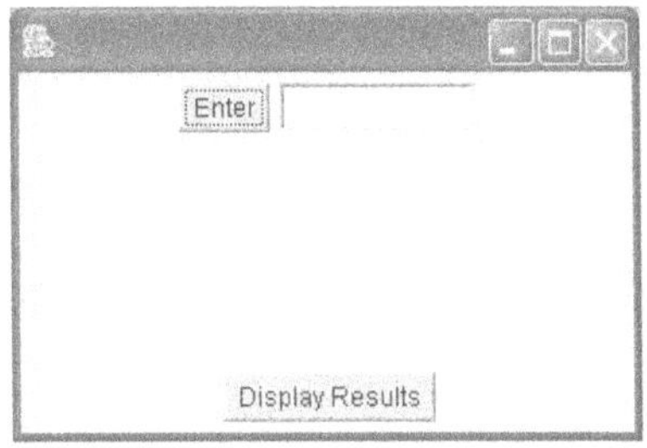

FIGURE 1.17 **A user interface to enter test scores**

Figure 1.17 shows a simple user interface to enter the scores and display the result. The user presses the *Enter* button on the left after entering a test score in the text field on the right. The user presses the *Display Results* button to display the class average and the number of students with each grade. Figure 1.18 shows the results of entering 28 test scores.

To make our program understandable, we define high-level operations that reflect the use of the system. The user performs two types of actions: adding a score, and requesting the results. When the user adds a score, we want to add the score to the sum of scores so we can compute the average. We want to assign the score a grade and update the grade tabulation to include the new grade. This leads us to define the following operations:

- `updateTotal`
- `assignGrade`
- `tabulateGrade`

When the user requests results, we want to compute the average and display the grade distribution, so we define the operations

- `computeAverage`
- `displayGrades`

The complementary aspect to defining operations is defining the data structures on which the operations operate. We need to make an important choice about whether to integrate the data with the operations or to keep it separate. Roughly speaking, keeping the data separate emphasizes the operations the program performs. We call this approach **procedural programming**, because it emphasizes the

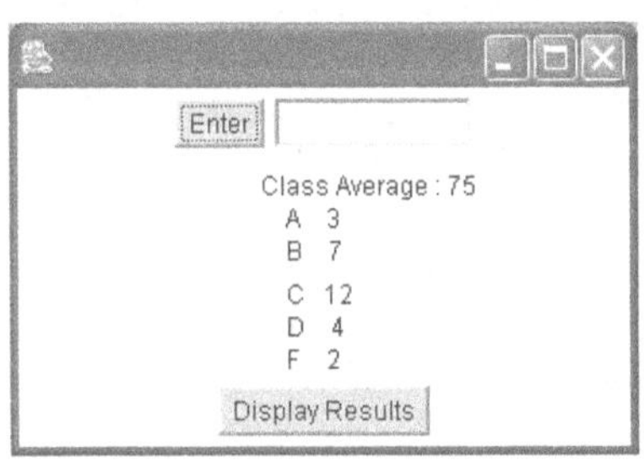

FIGURE 1.18 **Display the results**

operations of procedures we perform. Integrating the data emphasizes objects that combine data and operations. We call this approach **object-oriented programming**, because it emphasizes the encapsulation of data and operations in objects.

We will use both procedural and object-oriented programming in this text. We leave to later chapters the discussion of the details of each. We do not need to continue the design of this example any further because we have illustrated the main point: we need to define high-level understandable operations.

Implementation

We can easily see some of the constructs we will need to implement our design in C#. We have identified several high-level operations. In the implementation, these will become methods. Example 1.1 declares the `Main` method in which C# starts execution. Example 1.2 declares the `Square` method, which computes the square of a number passed to it. Our implementation might declare an `UpdateTotal` method to add the latest score to the total.

When we implement the `AssignGrade` method, we will need to make a selection of a grade that depends on the test score. C# provides several selection statements we might use. We also need to store the number of students who receive each grade. C# provides an array data structure that we might use for this purpose.

Naturally, we cannot do any implementing until we learn the relevant C# language constructs we will need. If we do some careful thinking about requirements and design, the coding part can be quick and effective. By contrast, if we write a lot of code with a good analysis of the problem and a good design, then we will probably have great difficulty completing the project successfully.

C#, like other general-purpose languages, can solve many diverse problems. If we code using only low-level C# code directly, we would have great difficulty determining what it does. Analogously, neurons and muscles can combine in untold ways to provide diverse actions. We would be unlikely to determine the ultimate action represented by a sequence of neuron firings and muscle contractions. Good analysis and design will make the high-level operations visible and the low-level operations relegated to their implementation.

Testing

Every program provides many opportunities for making errors. Programmers are not constrained by the laws of physics or chemistry the way bridge designers are. We can create an infinite variety of code. Testing checks that the program is correct and that it meets its requirements. Testing cannot prove correctness, but it can identify errors. A good testing process can greatly increase the probability that the released product will perform satisfactorily.

For this example, we would test first with simple input, computing the correct answer by hand, and checking that the program produces what we expect. We also need to check special cases that the programmer may have overlooked. What if the user asks for results before entering any data? What if the user enters invalid data, such as negative scores, or values such as "tutti frutti" that do not represent test scores? Does a score of 100 get the correct grade? How about 0?

Our test score example is quite simple. Careful testing is even more essential when the problem is complex. On a large project, teams of programmers combine to produce the software. Each programmer must check his or her code and then integrate it with that of other programmers, testing the integrated system.

Making Improvements

The world changes. Business conditions change. Tax laws change. Successful software needs to adapt to changes. One of the great benefits of well-designed software is that it can be enhanced as time goes on. In our simple example, we may wish to add a graph of the grade distribution. We may want to provide the highest and the lowest scores. Large systems need to be especially well-designed to allow them to be modified without introducing many new errors in the process.

The BIG Picture

Developing a C# program involves understanding its requirements and providing a good design that introduces meaningful operations. The C# implementation can proceed using the elements of the language covered in the text. Good testing increases the quality of the final product. A good design makes it easier to add new features or make changes.

✓Test Your Understanding

16. List the steps of software development.

17. How might we define the requirement to grade "on a curve" in the example discussed in this section?

SUMMARY

- Computers, composed of processors, memory, disk drives, and various input and output devices, run a variety of software from operating systems (which make computers easier to use) to sophisticated business, engineering, and personal applications that have made the computer an essential part of our lives.
- Each processor has its own instruction set, which uses numerical codes to represent operations and numerical addresses to represent memory locations. High-level languages allow us to program more expressively with greater ease than is possible when using the processor's instruction set directly. A compiler is a program that translates a high-level language program to an equivalent program in another language so that it can be executed more easily. An interpreter is a program that executes a program directly rather than translating it to another language.
- The .NET Framework includes the Common Language Runtime and the .NET Framework Class Library. The CLR provides an execution environment that can integrate programs from several languages. Programs reside in intermediate code format. A JIT compiler translates code to machine code during execution. The class library facilitates

the rapid development of Internet applications including web services used by applications on other systems.

- C# maintains many features of earlier languages, modeling its basic syntax on the C++ language syntax, but simplifies and extends earlier languages in useful ways. C# developers describe C# as a modern object-oriented language that allows programmers to quickly build .NET components from high-level business objects to system-level applications. Its development coincided with a rapid growth of the Internet. C# is designed to be especially useful for this diverse Internet environment.
- The lexical structure identifies C# rules for dividing the program text into a sequence of input elements. Input elements include comments, whitespace, identifiers, keywords, literals, punctuators, and operators.
- We can compile and run C# programs using either the .NET Framework Software Development Kit or Visual Studio .NET.
- As program developers, we must create high-level operations that are easy to understand and use. Some keys steps are
  - Identifying the requirements of the system
  - Designing a system that meets the requirements
  - Implementing the system
  - Testing that the system operates correctly and meets the requirements
  - Making improvements as needed

2 C# Programming Basics

In this chapter we will learn about the basic elements of a simple C# program. We use integer values and variables to represent storage locations. Identifiers name variables and other program elements. The assignment statement lets us assign a value to a variable. Expressions compute values. We study arithmetic expressions built using arithmetic operators. Precedence rules permit less use of parentheses in expressions. Input and output methods communicate between the user and the computer. A method implements a computation or an action. We learn to create our own methods, passing parameters and returning values.

OBJECTIVES

- Learn C# syntax
- Use integer variables and constants
- Use the assignment statement
- Use arithmetic expressions
- Understand operator precedence
- Use methods and parameters

2.1 VARIABLES

A variable represents a storage location. Every variable has a name and a type that determines what kind of data it holds. In this section, we look at the rules for creating names and introduce the `int` type, which represents a range of integer values.

We use a simple output statement to display the value of a variable. Example 2.1 represents a very simple C# program containing a variable.

EXAMPLE 2.1 ■ AVariable.cs

```
/* Declares and initializes an integer variable.
 * Outputs its value;
 */

public class AVariable {
  public static void Main( ) {
    int age = 19;                                        // Note 1
    System.Console.WriteLine("Age is {0}", age);
  }
}
```

Output

```
Age is 19
```

■

Note 1: `int age = 19;`

age is a local variable, defined inside the Main method for use there. Later we shall see other types of variables.

Example 2.1 has a structure similar to that of Example 1.1. It declares the AVariable class. This class declaration contains a declaration for the Main method. The Main method contains two statements. This section discusses the first statement,

```
int age = 19;
```

which is a local variable declaration, stating that age is a variable of type int with an initial value of 19.

The variable age represents a memory location that holds the value 19 initially. Figure 2.1 shows the effect of this declaration. The box signifies a location in the computer's memory. Putting 19 inside the box indicates that this location holds the value 19.[1]

Each variable has a name and a type. We discuss each of these features.

Identifiers

An **identifier** names program elements. The identifier age names an integer variable. The identifier AVariable names the class containing our program. We chose

FIGURE 2.1 **A variable representing a memory location**

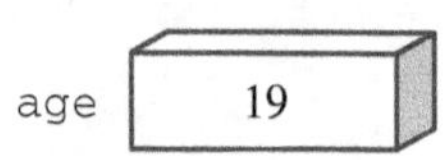

[1]The computer stores 19 in the binary number system (see Appendix A), but it is easier for us to use the base 10 system.

these names. Notice that these identifiers include both uppercase and lowercase characters. C# is case sensitive, so identifiers `age`, `Age`, and `AGE` are all different although they each use the same three letters of the alphabet in the same order.

Style

Start variable names with a lowercase character. Start method and class names with an uppercase character.

Digits occur in identifiers but cannot be the first character. Identifiers may also use the underscore character and even start with it. For example, `_hat`, `hat_box`, and `My______my` are all valid identifiers.

Style

Use underscores or uppercase letters to make identifiers easier to read. For example, use `a_big_car` or `aBigCar` rather than `abigcar`. Use meaningful names such as `age` rather than arbitrary names such as `xyz`.

Keywords

Keywords are identifiers that are reserved for special uses. In Example 2.1, `public`, `class`, `static`, `void`, and `int` are keywords. Figure 2.2 shows the complete list of C# keywords.

FIGURE 2.2
Keywords

abstract	as	base	bool	break
byte	case	catch	char	checked
class	const	continue	decimal	default
delegate	do	double	else	enum
event	explicit	extern	false	finally
fixed	float	for	foreach	goto
if	implicit	in	int	interface
internal	is	lock	long	namespace
new	null	object	operator	out
override	params	private	protected	public
readonly	ref	return	sbyte	sealed
short	sizeof	stackalloc	static	string
struct	switch	this	throw	true
try	typeof	uint	ulong	unchecked
unsafe	ushort	using	virtual	void
volatile	while			

Some valid C# identifiers are

```
savings
textLabel
rest_stop_12
B3
_test
My____my
```

Some invalid identifiers are

```
4you        // Starts with a number
x<y         // Includes an  illegal character, <
top-gun     // Includes an illegal character, -
int         // Reserved keyword
```

The Character Set

The character set defines the characters we can use in a program. The ASCII (pronounced as′-key) character set contains 128 printing and nonprinting characters shown in Appendix D. The ASCII characters include uppercase and lowercase letters, digits, and punctuation. For worldwide use, a programming language must have a much bigger character set to include the many characters of the various major languages. C# uses the Unicode character set which contains thousands of characters, including all the ASCII characters. For example, Unicode includes the Greek letter gamma, Γ. We will use only the ASCII characters in this book.

Type `int`

We must declare every variable, indicating its type. A **type** defines the values that a variable can have. In Example 2.1, the variable `age` has type `int`. In C#, type `int` represents a range of integer values. C# implements it using 32 binary digits (called bits). Example 2.2 displays the largest and smallest values of the `int` type.

EXAMPLE 2.2 ■ MaxMinInt.cs

```
/* Outputs the largest and smallest int values.
 */

public class MaxMinInt {

    // Execution starts here
  public static void Main() {
    int max = int.MaxValue;                             // Note 1
    int min = int.MinValue;
    System.Console.WriteLine
          ("The largest int value is {0}", max);
```

```
        System.Console.WriteLine
              ("The smallest int value is {0}", min);
    }
}
```

Output

```
The largest int value is 2147483647
The smallest int value is -2147483648
```

Note 1: `int max = int.MaxValue;`

The keyword `int` is another name for the type `System.Int32` in the .NET framework. Type `Int32` declares constants `MaxValue` and `MinValue`. We could have referred to this value as `System.Int32.MaxValue`.

Example 2.2 shows that the `int` type represents values from −2,147,483,648 to 2,147,483,647. C# has many other predefined types, both numerical and nonnumerical, which we will introduce in later chapters. See Appendix E for a list.

Initialization

Notice that we specified initial values for each of the variables in Examples 2.1 and 2.2. For example, the statement

```
int age = 19;
```

declares that the variable `age` has type `int` and has an initial value of 19. C# does not initialize variables declared inside methods (called local variables). Making the declaration

```
int age;
```

without initializing `age` would leave the contents of the variable unknown, as Figure 2.3 shows.

The C# compiler will not allow us to use a local variable that has an unknown value. It is a good practice always to initialize local variables.

Some characteristics of variables in a programming language are

- Variables can vary in value as the program runs.
- Each variable usually has a single purpose in a program.

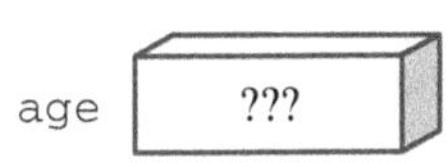

FIGURE 2.3
Memory location for the `age` variable

So far, we have not allowed our variable to vary. Using the assignment operator in the next section, we will give our variables new values.

The BIG Picture

A variable represents a storage location. It has a name and type. We use an identifier to name variables and other program elements. Keywords are reserved and may not be used as identifiers. The `int` type represents a range of integer values, both positive and negative. We refer to variables we declare inside a method as local variables because they are for use only within that method.

Good practice includes an initialization in a variable declaration statement. `print` and `println` statements allow us to display results.

✓ Test Your Understanding

1. Which of the following are valid identifiers? For each nonvalid example, explain why it is not valid.

   a. `Baby` **b.** `_chip_eater` **c.** `any.time`

   d. `#noteThis` **e.** `&car` **f.** `GROUP`

   g. `A103` **h.** `76trombones` **i.** `float`

   j. `intNumber` **k.** `$$help`

2. A variable represents a ________________.
3. A variable has a ____________ and a ____________.
4. The largest value the _____ type can hold is 2,147,483,647.
5. How can we improve the following declaration?

   ```
   int number;
   ```

2.2 ASSIGNMENT

We initialize a variable only once, in its declaration. To change the value of a variable after we have declared it, we can use the assignment operator. This, as its name suggests, assigns a value to a variable. C# uses the equal sign, =, for the assignment operator. An example of a simple assignment statement is

```
age = 10;
```

in which we assign the value 10 to the variable `age`. This assignment statement assumes that we have already declared the variable `age`. The compiler would report an error if we had not declared `age`.

We declare and initialize a variable only once, but we can assign it a value many times in a program. Later in the program we may wish to change the value of `age`, say to 20, using the assignment statement

```
age = 20;
```

FIGURE 2.4 **Declaring and assigning values to a variable**

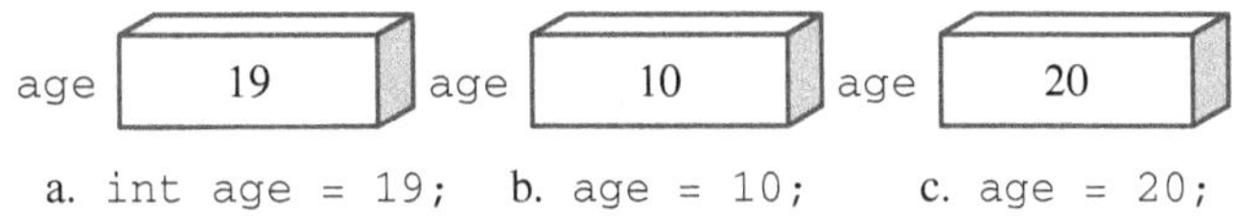

Remember that the variable, `age`, has one location. Each assignment replaces the old value with the newly assigned value. Figure 2.4 shows the changes resulting from the assignments to `age`.

So far we have only assigned constant values to variables, but we can also assign the value of one variable to another, as in

```
int mySize = 9;
int yourSize = 10;
mySize = yourSize;
```

The assignment takes the value of `yourSize`, which we initialized to 10, and assigns it to `mySize`. Figure 2.5 shows the locations for `yourSize` and `mySize` before and after the assignment.

We can write an arithmetic expression such as `y + 2` on the right-hand side of an assignment. The computer will then evaluate the expression and assign that value to the variable on the left-hand side of the assignment. We will learn about arithmetic expressions in Section 2.4. The assignment

```
mySize = yourSize + 2;
```

would give `mySize` a value of 12, given that `yourSize` still has the value of 10, with which it was initialized.

FIGURE 2.5 **The result of an assignment**

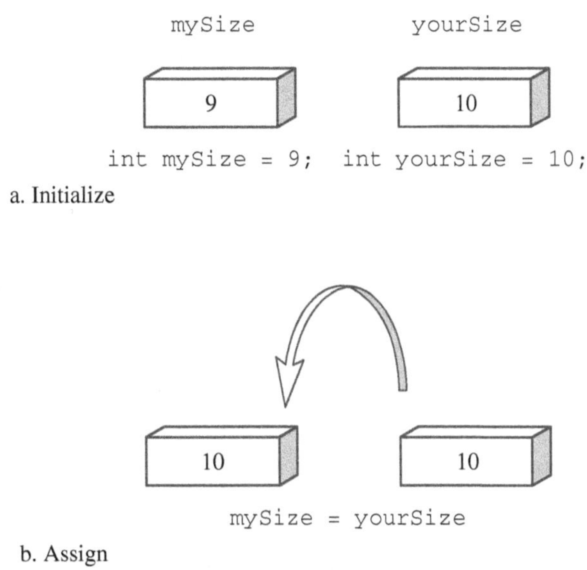

Notice that when a variable occurs on the right-hand side of an assignment we use its value that we find in its storage location. When a variable occurs on the left-hand side of an assignment, we store a value in its memory location. Variables perform this very important function of storing values for later use in our program.

Constructing a Simple Program

Now we have the tools to write a simple C# program. We can store values in variables using initialization and assignment; we can use the values of variables and constants on the right-hand side of assignments and in `Write` and `WriteLine` statements. In a program, we might group several of these statements together for C# to execute one after the other, as in

```
int number1 = 25;
Console.WriteLine(number1);
```

which declares an integer variable, `number1`, initializes it to 25, and displays its value on the screen.

A C# program consists, roughly speaking, of one or more class definitions. To write a C# program, we pick a name for a class. Example 2.3 uses the name `AssignIt`, which starts, in good C# style, with a capital letter. The program structure will then look like

```
public class AssignIt {

    //  The program code goes here

}
```

All the code will go inside the curly braces after the class name. For now we include a comment using the double forward slash, `//`. C# ignores anything on the line after the `//`; it is just a comment for human readers. We declare our class `public` so everyone can use it. We must always use the `public` modifier when declaring the `Main` method. We will discuss different types of access later in the text.

C# organizes executable code by placing it into methods.[2] A method contains code to perform an operation. We often name methods to represent their function. For example, in Section 2.4 we define a `MultiplyBy4` method to multiply a value by 4. As we have seen, C# uses a special method named `Main` to start processing a program. The `Main` method might be better named as `StartUp`, but it retains the name `Main` used in the C and C++ programming languages.

Because C# starts up an application using a `Main` method, we add a `Main` method to our class, so it now looks like this:

```
public class AssignIt {
  public static void Main() {
```

[2]We discuss methods later in this chapter, and again when we introduce arrays.

```
        /*   code goes
             here
          */
    }
}
```

C# also ignores anything between `/*` and the next `*/`, so we can use these symbols to enclose comments that take more than one line. We place the code for the `Main` method between braces, `{}`, which contain the code comprising the body of the method.

The `Main` method is itself inside a class named `AssignIt`. Figure 2.6 shows a class diagram for the `AssignIt` class. We use the Unified Modeling Language (UML).[3] The class diagram has three parts. The top section contains the class name. The middle section contains state variables, which we discuss in Chapter 5. The bottom section contains method names.

We use the modifier `static` to indicate that the `Main` method stays with the class. Following UML notation, we underline (or italicize) static methods to distinguish them from methods that will be part of object instances.

Now that we have the framework, we write some code that we insert in the `Main` method. Let us declare and use some integer variables, trying out initialization, assignment, and displaying our results. Example 2.3 shows this program.

Every C# program must have the `.cs` extension, so we use the filename `AssignIt.cs` for Example 2.3.

Style

Formatting programs nicely makes them easier to understand and modify. Example 2.3 contains a comment prefacing the `AssignIt` class and a comment before the `Main` method. We should comment each class and each method. We should comment any section of code that needs explanation of its purpose or the way it works. Because the text examples are for teaching purposes, the comments include more details than might otherwise occur. To avoid including cumbersome comments directly in the code, the text examples include a simple `Note` comment with the text of the comment appearing after the program.

Example 2.3 indents the `Main` method with respect to the class containing it. It indents the code within the `Main` method. It has no long lines. We break long lines as needed to preserve the margins and the indentation.

FIGURE 2.6 **The `AssignIt` class**

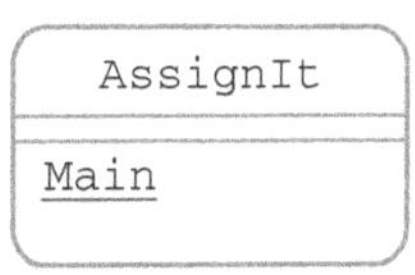

[3]See `www.rational.com/uml/` for more information on the UML.

EXAMPLE 2.3 ■ AssignIt.cs

```
/*   Declares two integer variables with initial values.
 *   Assigns a new value to the second variable.
 *   Outputs the new value.
 */

public class AssignIt {

      // Illustrates assignment
  public static void Main() {                            // Note 1
    int  number1 = 25;                                   // Note 2
    int  number2 = 12;
    number2 = number1 +  15;                             // Note 3
    System.Console.WriteLine("Number2 is now {0}", number2);
  }
}
```

Output

```
Number2 is now 40
```

Note 1: `public static void Main() {`

C# starts execution of a program with the code in the `Main` method. We must have a method named `Main`. We discuss the choice of parameters and return type for the `Main` method later in the text.

Note 2: `int  number1 = 25;`

We use the keyword `int` to declare an integer variable. Here we declare `number1` to be an integer variable and give it an initial value of 25.

Note 3: `number2 = number1 +  15;`

This is an assignment statement. We compute the value of the expression, `number1 + 15`, on the right side of the equals sign and assign it to the variable, `number2`, on the left side. This value, 40, will replace whatever previous value `number2` had, which was 12 in this example.

Constants

We changed the value of variable `number2` in Example 2.3. We can define constants, which we cannot change. For example, the declaration

```
const int FIXED = 25;
```

declares a constant named `FIXED`. Trying to assign a value to `FIXED` would generate a compilation error. The modifier `final` means that the value of `FIXED` is final and cannot be changed. We use a constant to highlight an important difference between computing and mathematics in Example 2.4.

Style

Using uppercase letters for constants makes them easy to distinguish from variables in our code.

EXAMPLE 2.4 ■ Overflow.cs

```
/*   Declares a very large constant.
 *   Adding this large number to itself produces
 *   an incorrect value due to overflow.
 */

public class Overflow {

     // Declares a constant BIG
  public static void Main( ) {
    const int BIG = int.MaxValue - 10;              // Note 1
    int  number1 = BIG;
    int number2 = number1 + number1;
    System.Console.WriteLine
           ("Twice the large number is {0}", number2);
  }
}
```

Output

```
Twice the large number is -22
```

Note 1: `const int BIG = int.MaxValue - 10;`

This value is `2147483637`. The compiler will generate an error if we try to assign a value to `BIG` later in the program.

Mathematically, the output should be 4,294,967,274, but the `int` type cannot represent a number this large, just as in Figure 2.7, two chairs cannot seat three people. We do not need to understand the details of what happens when we compute a number too large to represent. We call this phenomenon **overflow** because the number overflows the space available for it. An `int` variable holds 32 bits and

FIGURE 2.7
Overflow—Who does not get a seat?

some integers require more than 32 bits. The moral is that not everything the computer produces is necessarily correct. One must inspect results carefully.

The BIG Picture

An assignment statement assigns a value to a variable. We retrieve the value of a variable used on the right side of an assignment statement. We store a value in the location represented by a variable on the left side of an assignment.

A C# program consists of one or more class definitions. C# starts execution with an application's `Main` method. In our examples so far, the `Main` method contains a sequence of statements. These are declaration, assignment, or output statements.

We cannot change a constant.

✓ Test Your Understanding

Try It Yourself ➤ **6.** Compile and run Example 2.3 to check that it works properly.

7. In Example 2.3, what is the largest value we can use for the variable `number1`? What is the smallest?

Try It Yourself ➤ **8.** Try omitting the declaration of the variable `number1` in Example 2.3 and see what error you get.

2.3 INPUT AND OUTPUT

The programs in the last section specify the values for variables and constants in the program. To change the initialization

```
int number1 = 25;
```

to use the number 30 instead, we would have to edit the program, making the change from 25 to 30, and recompile it again. In this section, we learn to enter values from the keyboard so we can run the program again with different input values without the need to recompile. We used the `WriteLine` statement without much explanation in the last section, but here we will explore possibilities for output.

Inputting from the Console

The term **console** reminds older veterans of the early computers that could only display characters and not graphics. We use it now to refer to a window that only displays characters and not graphics.

We wish to enter data from the keyboard into the console. A good program will prompt the user with a message describing the data to enter. For example, the statement

```
System.Console.Write("Enter your name: ");
```

displays the message

```
Enter your name:
```

and remains on the same line, where the user will enter his or her name.

The statement

```
String name = System.Console.ReadLine();
```

returns a line of text that the user enters by typing the characters on the keyboard and pressing the *Enter* key. When the executing program reaches this `ReadLine` method, it waits for the user to enter a line of text, which it returns to the program, assigning it to the variable `name`. The `String` type represents text. We will learn more about it later. Just to verify that we have received the data, we use the `WriteLine` method to display it in the console.

EXAMPLE 2.5 ■ InputName.cs

```
// Inputs text from the keyboard.
using System;                                        // Note 1
public class InputName {
  public static void Main( ) {
    Console.Write("Enter your name: ");              // Note 2
    String name = Console.ReadLine();                // Note 3
    Console.WriteLine("    Your name is {0}", name);
  }
}
```

Output

```
Enter your name: Art
    Your name is Art
```

■

Note 1: `using System;`

The `System` namespace includes the `Console` class containing the `Write`, `ReadLine`, and `WriteLine` methods which we use in this example. This line is a `using` directive. It lets us use the classes in the `System` namespace without the `System` prefix. We can use the `Console` class without prefixing it with `System`. Without this directive, we must use `System.Console` to refer to the `Console` class in the `System` namespace. Using the directive, we have less keyboarding to do and shorter lines.

Note 2: `Console.Write("Enter your name: ");`

The `Write` statement leaves the cursor on the current line. By contrast, the `WriteLine` statement moves the cursor to the beginning of the next line. The cursor signals the position for the next input or output operation.

Note 3: `String name = Console.ReadLine();`

When execution reaches the `ReadLine` statement it waits for the user to enter text and press the *Enter* Key.

Inputting an Integer

The `ReadLine` method inputs text. If we enter 23, it will return the string "`23`". We are used to reading base 10 numerals, and readily understand this as a symbol for three more than the normal number of fingers and toes combined. Ancient Romans would have written `XXIII` to represent the same number. A C# program does not use either of these representations for integers. The `int` type has a `Parse` method that converts a base 10 representation to the 32-bit binary representation it uses.

EXAMPLE 2.6 ■ InputInteger.cs

```
/*   Inputs a base 10 numeral from the console.
 *   Converts to an int and outputs twice its value.
 */

using System;
public class InputInteger {
  public static void Main( ) {
    Console.Write("Enter an integer: ");
    int  number1 = int.Parse(Console.ReadLine());
                                                   // Note 1
    int number2 = number1 + number1;
    Console.WriteLine
          ("    Twice the number  is {0}", number2);
  }
}
```

Output

```
Enter an integer: 23
    Twice the number is 46
```

Note 1: `int  number1 = int.Parse(Console.ReadLine());`

Type `int` is a shorthand for `System.Int32`, so we could have written this method as `Int32.Parse`.

When we cover user interfaces later, we will have many other ways for the user to input and interact.

Output to the Console

We have used the `WriteLine` and `Write` methods to write to the console. The invocation

```
System.Console.WriteLine("The number is: {0}", number1);
```

has two arguments. The first is a string and the second is a value that C# will convert to a string for display. The format specifier, `{0}`, indicates the position where the second argument will appear in the string.

To output more than one number we use additional format specifiers, `{0}`, `{1}`, `{2}`, and so on. For each specifier, we include an argument to replace it in the output string. Thus if `number1` is 35 and `number2` is 70, the statement

```
Console.WriteLine("The number is {0} and twice it is {1}.",
                  number1, number2);
```

will output

```
The number is 35 and twice it is 70.
```

We can output the data in any order. For example,

```
Console.WriteLine
        ("Twice the number is {1} and the number is {0}",
          number1, number2);
```

outputs

```
Twice the number is 70 and the number is 35.
```

The numbers 0 and 1 in `{0}` and `{1}` indicate an argument position after the format string in the `WriteLine` invocation. We can also specify a specific format. For example, `{0:C}` would display as currency. In the United States, 35 dollars displays as $35.00.

EXAMPLE 2.7 ■ OutputFormat.cs

```
// Outputs to the console.
using System;
public class OutputFormat {
  public static void Main( ) {
    int number1 = 35;
```

```
      int number2 = number1 + number1;
      Console.WriteLine
              (“The number is {0} and twice it is {1}.”,
                number1, number2);
      Console.WriteLine
              (“{0} is the number and {1} is its double.”,
                number1, number2);
      Console.WriteLine
              (“Twice the number is {1} and the number is {0}”,
                number1, number2);
      Console.WriteLine
              (“The first is {0:C} and twice it is {1:C}.”,
                number1, number2);
  }
}
```

Output

```
The number is 35 and twice it is 70.
35 is the number and 70 is its double.
Twice the number is 70 and the number is 35.
The first is $35.00 and twice it is $70.00.
```

■

Outputting a Table

We would like to output a table in which the columns have a fixed width. We might want to align names to the left of the column and numbers to the right. To achieve this format we use the specification {0, -10} to left-align names in a field of length 10, and {1, 10} to right-align numbers in a field of size 10.

EXAMPLE 2.8 ■ OutputTable.cs

```
/*  Formats a table with fixed column lengths and
 *  either right or left alignment.
 */

using System;
public class OutputTable {
  public static void Main( ) {
    Console.WriteLine(“{0,-10}{1,10}”, “Names”, “Numbers” );
    Console.WriteLine
            (“{0,-10}{1,10}”, “Sheila”, 12345);
                                                      // Note 1
    Console.WriteLine(“{0,-10}{1,10}”, “Frances”, 241);
    Console.WriteLine(“{0,-10}{1,10}”, “Michael”, 4141);
  }
}
```

```
Names        Numbers
Sheila         12345
Frances          241
Michael         4141
```

Note 1: `Console.WriteLine`

```
("{0,-10}{1,10}", "Sheila", 12345);
```

We can output literals as well as values of variables. A **literal** is a source code representation of a value. Here "Sheila" is a string and 12345 is an integer.

The BIG Picture

Inputting from the console allows us to rerun the same program with different data. We can format output to make it more useful and visually appealing.

✓ Test Your Understanding

9. Enter *hat* instead of an integer when Example 2.6 requests a number. What happens?
10. Rewrite Example 2.5 without the `using` directive. Compile and run the modified version.
11. If *x* is 53 and *y* is 8786, what will the method display?

    System.Console.WriteLine("You owe {1:C} which is {0} days overdue", x, y);

2.4 ARITHMETIC EXPRESSIONS

In the process of solving problems, we perform operations on the data. Each type of data has suitable operations associated with it. Integer data in C#, which we use in this chapter, has the familiar arithmetic operations addition, subtraction, multiplication, division, negation, and a remainder operation.

A **binary** operator such as '+' takes two operands, as in the expression `3 + 4`, where the numbers 3 and 4 are the operands. C# supports these binary arithmetic operators:

```
+    addition
-    subtraction
*    multiplication
/    division
%    remainder
```

A **unary** operator takes one operand as in the expression `-3`. C# supports these unary arithmetic operators:

```
-    negation
+    (no effect)
```

If the operands are integers, then the result of an arithmetic operation will be an integer. Addition, subtraction, and multiplication behave as we expect from ordinary arithmetic. Some examples are:

Operation	**Result**
`32 + 273`	`305`
`63 -  19`	`44`
`42 *  12`	`504`

Integer division produces an integer result, truncating toward zero if necessary, meaning that it discards the fractional part, if any.

Operation	**Result**	
`12 / 3`	`4`	Exact
`17 / 5`	`3`	Discards the 2/5
`-17 / 5`	`-3`	Discards the -2/5

The operation `x%y` computes the remainder when `x` is divided by `y` (see Figure 2.8). The remainder operation obeys the rule

```
(x/y)*y + x%y = x
```

Operation	**Result**	**(x/y)*y + x%y = x**
`17 % 5`	`2`	`3 *5 + 2 = 17`
`-17 % 5`	`-2`	`(-3)*5 + -2 = -17`

Examples of the unary operations are `-7`, which negates the seven, and `+3`. In summary, Figure 2.9 shows the C# arithmetic operations for integers.

FIGURE 2.8 **Integer division and remainder**

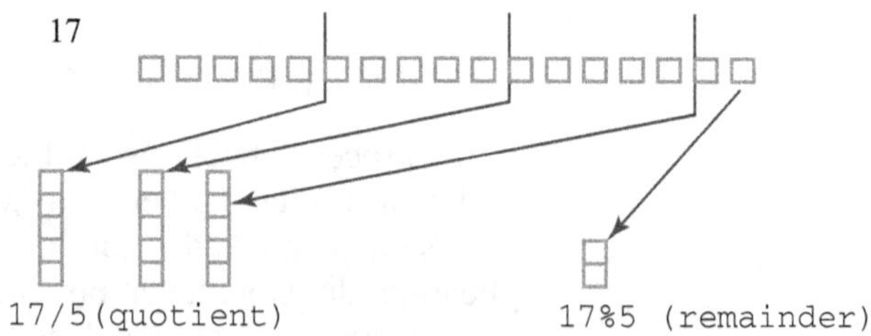

FIGURE 2.9 **C# arithmetic operations**

Operation	**Math notation**	**C# (constants)**	**C# (variables)**
Addition	a + b	3 + 4	score1 + score2
Subtraction	a - b	3 - 4	bats - gloves
Multiplication	ab	12 * 17	twelve * dozens
Division	a/b	7 / 3	total / quantity
Remainder	r in a=qb+r	43 % 5	cookies % people
Negation	-a	-6	-amount

EXAMPLE 2.9 ■ Arithmetic.cs

```
/* Try out arithmetic operators on integer data.
 */

public class Arithmetic {

    // Illustrates +, -, *, /, and %
  public static void Main () {
    int x = 25;
    int y = 14;
    int z = x + y;                                      // Note 1
    int w = x - y;
    int p = -y;
    System.Console.WriteLine
     ("x + y = {0}       x - y = {1}          -y = {2}",
       z, w, p);
    z = x * y;                                          // Note 2
    w = x / 7;                                          // Note 3
    p = x % 7;
    System.Console.WriteLine
     ("x * y = {0}      x / 7 = {1}        x % 7 = {2}",
       z, w, p);
  }
}
```

Output

```
x + y = 39     x - y = 11    -y = -14
x * y = 350    x / 7 = 3      x % 7 = 4
```

■

Note 1: `int z = x + y;`

We initialize `z` with the value of the expression `x + y`. Because we have already initialized `x` and `y`, the value of `x + y` is well defined.

Note 2: `z = x * y;`

In the next three lines we reuse the variables z, w, and p, giving them new values and illustrating the use of the operators `*`, `/`, and `%`.

Note 3: `w = x / 7;`

Recall that integer division produces an integer result, so `25 / 7 = 3`.

✓ Test Your Understanding

12. If a=4, b=23, c=-5, and d=61, evaluate

a. b/a	b. b%a	c. a%b
d. b/c	e. c*d	f. d%b
g. c/a	h. c%a	

Try It Yourself ➤ 13. Change the variable initializations in Example 2.9 to x=12 and y=5. What output do you expect from this modified program? Compile and run it to see if your expectations are correct.

✓

Precedence of Arithmetic Operators

In mathematics we apply some common rules to decide how each operation gets its operands. For example, in the expression `3 + 4*5` we would multiply `4*5`, giving 20, and then add `3+20` to get the result of 23. We say the multiplication has higher precedence than addition, meaning that it gets its operands first. In Figure 2.10 we show that * gets its operands first by drawing a box around the expression `4*5`.

If we want to do the addition first, we would need to use parentheses, as in `(3+4)*5`, as shown in Figure 2.11. We compute everything inside parentheses first, so we would add `3+4`, giving 7, and then multiply `7*5`, giving 35. By remembering the rules of precedence, we can often avoid using parentheses. We could have written parentheses in the original expression, which would then be `3+(4*5)`, but these parentheses are not needed because we know that multiplication goes first.

Higher Precedence

```
-, +        Unary Negation and Plus
*, /, %     Multiplication, Division, and Remainder
+, -        Binary Addition and Subtraction
=           Assignment
```

We evaluate `x-3/y` as `x-(3/y)` because '/' has higher precedence than '-'. We evaluate `-7+10` as `(-7)+10` or 3, because negation has higher precedence than

FIGURE 2.10
Multiplication gets its operands first

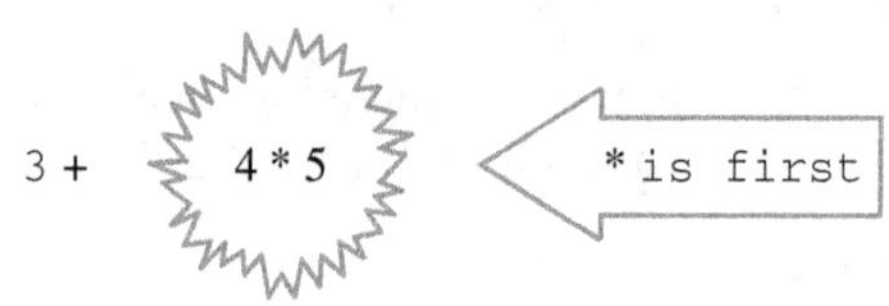

FIGURE 2.11
Compute within parentheses first

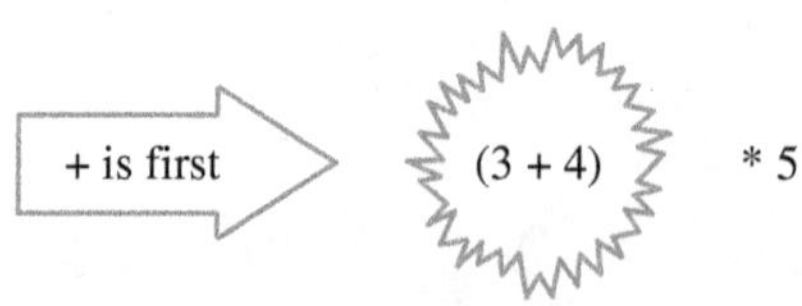

addition. In the case of arithmetic operators of equal precedence, we evaluate from left to right. Thus, we compute `3+x+7` as `(3+x)+7` and `10-7-5` as `(10-7)-5`, which is `-2`. We say that the *associativity* of the binary arithmetic operators is from left to right.

EXAMPLE 2.10 ■ Precedence.cs

```
/* Illustrates precedence rules for arithmetic operators.
 */

public class Precedence {

      /* Computes expressions three ways
       *    Without parentheses --- uses precedence rules
       *    With parentheses the same as precedence rules
       *    With parentheses different than precedence rules
       */
  public static void Main() {
    int a = 3;                                          // Note 1
    int b = 4;
    int c = 5;
    int noParen = a + 7 * b;
    int sameParen = a + (7 * b);
    int changeParen = (a + 7) * b;
    System.Console.WriteLine
      ("noParen = {0,3} sameParen = {1,3} changeParen = "
           + "{2,3}", noParen, sameParen, changeParen);
    noParen = c / a + 4;                                // Note 2
    sameParen = (c / a) + 4;
    changeParen = c / (a + 4);
    System.Console.WriteLine
      ("noParen = {0,3} sameParen = {1,3} changeParen = "
           + "{2,3}", noParen, sameParen, changeParen);
    noParen = c - a % b - a;                            // Note 3
    sameParen = (c - (a % b)) - a;
    changeParen = (c - a) % (b - a);
    System.Console.WriteLine
      ("noParen = {0,3} sameParen = {1,3} changeParen = "
           + "{2,3}", noParen, sameParen, changeParen);
  }
}
```

Output

```
noParen =  31 sameParen =  31 changeParen =  40
noParen =   5 sameParen =   5 changeParen =   0
noParen =  -1 sameParen =  -1 changeParen =   0
```

Note 1: `int a = 3;`

We use the variable `noParen` to compute the value of an expression without parentheses. The precedence order will determine which operation to perform first. The variable `sameParen` shows the expression fully parenthesized, but computed in the same order specified by the precedence. Thus the values of `noParen` and `sameParen` should be equal. The variable `changeParen` computes the same expression, but now with parentheses placed to change the order of evaluation to be different than the order specified by precedence. Thus, the value of `changeParen` may be different from `noParen`.

Note 2: `noParen = c / a + 4;`

Recall that integer division gives an integer value so `5/3 = 1`.

Note 3: `noParen = c - a % b - a;`

Recall that '`%`' is the remainder operator, so `3%4 = 3`.

✓ Test Your Understanding

Try It Yourself ➤

14. Change the variable initializations in Example 2.10 to `a=7`, `b=3`, and `c=-2`. What output do you expect from this modified program? Compile and run it to see if your expectations are correct.

15. Evaluate the following C# expressions, where `x=2`, `y=3`, `z=-4`, and `w=5`.

a. `x + w / 2` **b.** `z * 4 - y`

c. `y + w % 2` **d.** `x + y - z`

e. `x * z / y` **f.** `x + z * y / w`

g. `y * x - z / x` **h.** `w * x  % y - 4`

i. `14 % w % y`

16. Insert parentheses in each expression in problem 15, following the C# operator precedence order. This will show what you would have to write if C# did not use precedence rules. For example, inserting parentheses in `x+w*z+3` gives `(x+(w*z))+3`, because '`*`' has the highest precedence, and C# evaluates the left '`+`' first.

Combining Assignment and Arithmetic[4]

Suppose we want to add 5 to a variable x. We could do that with the assignment statement

```
x = x + 5;
```

C# has an operator that combines the assignment and the addition into one operator, +=. We can write the preceding statement more simply as

```
x += 5;
```

C# also has operators that combine assignment with the other arithmetic operators: -=, *=, /=, and %=. We must enter these two-character operators without any space between the two symbols. Some examples are in the following list.

Combined Form	Equivalent Form
`y -= 7;`	`y = y - 7;`
`a *= x;`	`a = a * x`
`x /= y;`	`x = x / y;`
`w %= z;`	`w = w % z;`
`b *= z + 3;`	`b = b*(z + 3);`

Note in the last example that we put parentheses around the entire right-hand side expression, z + 3, and multiplied that entire expression by the left-hand side variable, b.

EXAMPLE 2.11 ■ AssignOps.cs

```
/*  Uses the operators that combine arithmetic and
 *  assignment
 */

using System;
public class AssignOps {

     // Illustrates -=, *=, /=, and %=
  public static void Main() {
    int a = 2;                                           // Note 1
    int b = 4;
    int x = 3;
    int y = 5;
    int z = 6;
    int w = 14;
    y -= 7;
    Console.WriteLine("y = {0}", y);
```

[4]Although these operators provide no new functionality, they do make it easier for the compiler to generate efficient code.

```
            a *= x;
            Console.WriteLine("a = {0}", a);
            x /= y;                                      // Note 2
            Console.WriteLine("x = {0}", x);
            w %= z;
            Console.WriteLine("w = {0}", w);
            b *= z + 3;                                  // Note 3
            Console.WriteLine("b = {0}", b);
        }
    }
```

Output

```
y = -2
a = 6
x = -1
w = 2
b = 36
```

Note 1: `int a = 2;`

We initialize all variables.

Note 2: `x /= y;`

The program changed the value of `y`, so the value of `y` used here is its current value of −2, rather than its initial value, 5.

Note 3: `b *= z + 3;`

Recall that the equivalent expression is `b*(z+3)`, because the entire right-hand side expression is multiplied by the left-hand side variable, `b`.

✓ Test Your Understanding

17. What value would C# assign each variable if, for each expression, `j=7`, `k=11`, and `n=-4`?

a. `j += 31;` **b.** `k *= n;`

c. `k -= n + 7;` **d.** `k %= j`

e. `k /= n - 1`

Try It Yourself ➤

18. Change the variable initializations in Example 2.11 to `a=7`, `b=2`, `x=12`, `y=4`, `z=-6`, and `w=8`. What output do you expect from this modified program? Compile and run it to see if your expectations are correct.

Increment and Decrement Operators

C# has simple forms for the frequent operations of adding 1 to a variable (incrementing) or subtracting 1 from a variable (decrementing). To increment the variable

FIGURE 2.12
Expression (a) and equivalent expressions (b)

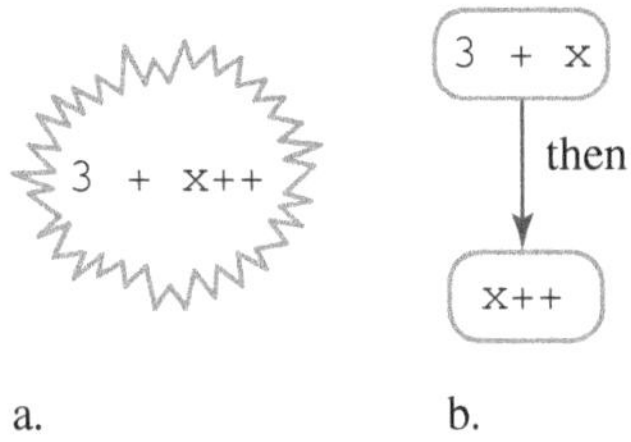

x using the postfix form of the increment operator, we write x++. If x had a value of 5, executing x++ would give it a value of 6.

There is significance to putting the plus signs after the variable (postfix). If you use this postfix increment in an expression, the computation uses the old value of the variable, and then increments it. So if x is 5, evaluating the expression 3 + x++ will give 8, and then the value of x changes to 6. Figure 2.12 shows that evaluating 3 + x++ is like evaluating two expressions, first 3 + x, and then x++.

The prefix form of the increment operator, ++x, also increments the variable by 1, but it does it before the variable is used in an expression. If x had a value of 5, evaluating the expression 3 + ++x would increment x to 6 and then evaluate the expression, giving a value of 9. Figure 2.13 shows that evaluating 3 + ++x is like evaluating two expressions, first ++x, and then 3 + x.

C# has two forms of the decrement operator. The postfix decrement, x--, uses the value of x and then decrements it, so if x is 3, then 2 + x-- evaluates to 5, and x changes to 2. The prefix decrement, --x, decrements x and then uses that new value of x, so if x is 3, then 2 + --x evaluates to 4, because x was decremented to 2 before the expression was evaluated.

TIP

We illustrate the use of the increment and decrement operators in expressions such as 3 + x++. For clarity, it is better to limit their use to variables not part of larger expressions. We could replace 3 + x++ with the two statements

```
3 + x;
x++;
```

FIGURE 2.13
Expression (a) and equivalent expressions (b)

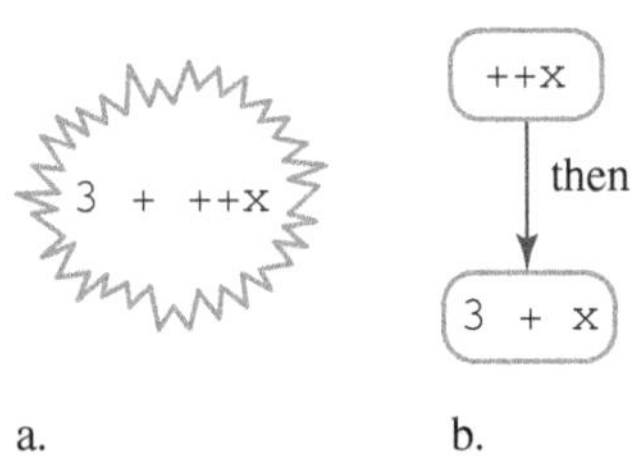

EXAMPLE 2.12 ■ Increment.cs

```
/* Uses the prefix and postfix increment and decrement
 * operators
 */

using System;
public class Increment {
  public static void Main() {
    int x = 5;
    int y = 5;
    int a = 3;
    int b = 3;
    int j = 7;
    int k = 7;
    int result = 0;
    j++;                                              // Note 1
    ++k;
    Console.WriteLine("j = {0} and k = {1}",  j, k);
    j--;
    --k;
    Console.WriteLine("j = {0} and k = {1}",  j, k);
    result = 3 +  x++;
    Console.WriteLine("result = {0} and x = {1}", result, x);
    result = 3 + ++y;                                 // Note 2
    Console.WriteLine("result = {0} and y = {1}", result, y);
    result = 2 + a--;
    Console.WriteLine("result = {0} and a = {1}", result, a);;
    result = 2 + --b;
    Console.WriteLine("result = {0} and b = {1}", result, b);
  }
}
```

Output

```
j and k are 8 and 8
j and k are 7 and 7
result and x are 8 and 6
result and y are 9 and 6
result and a are 5 and 2
result and b are 4 and 2
```

■

Note 1: `j++;`

We could have put this and the next statement on a single line as in

`j++; ++k;`

Usually, the better style puts each statement on a separate line.

Note 2: `result = 3 + ++y;`

We leave a space after the first plus sign. Otherwise, if we wrote 3 `+++ y`, C# would try to evaluate `3++ +y` which would give a compiler error, because we can only increment a variable, not a number like 3, which is constant.

The BIG Picture

Arithmetic expressions use precedence rules that model those of mathematics. These allow us to use fewer parentheses, making expressions easier to read and write. Like C and C++, C# can combine arithmetic and assignment operators and includes simple increment and decrement operators.

✓Test Your Understanding

19. Evaluate each of the following C# expressions, where for each, `x=5`, `y=7`.

a. `x--` **b.** `y++ + 6`

c. `y * --x` **d.** `x++/3`

e. `++x/3` **f.** `++y + --x`

Try It Yourself ➤ **20.** Initialize the variables in Example 2.12 to `x=7`, `y=6`, `a=5`, `b=-2`, `j=4`, and `k=3`. What output do you expect from this modified program? Compile and run it to see if your expectations are correct.

2.5 METHODS AND PARAMETERS

So far, our programs have had exactly one method, named `Main`. The system that executes a compiled C# program looks for the method named `Main` to start its execution of our program.

In order to raise the level of abstraction of our program, we should define additional methods, as we discussed in Section 1.6 on software development. In this section, we show how to define methods and revise some of our earlier examples to use methods. We use class methods here, but will study instance methods when we introduce objects in Chapter 5.

Methods

We can create programs with more than one method. A method can contain the code for an operation we need to repeat. The method name serves as the name of a new operation we have defined. As a simple example, let us define a method to multiply a value by four.[5]

[5]We would not ordinarily use a method for this simple operation, but do here as a simple first example.

Of course, we have to tell our method which value we want to multiply. Let us name this method `MultiplyBy4` and name the value `aNumber`. Our method declaration is

```
public static int MultiplyBy4(int aNumber) {
  return 4*aNumber;
}
```

The modifier `static` indicates that this is a **class method**. A class method is part of the class in which it is declared.[6] Figure 2.14 shows the class diagram for the `Multiply` class we will use in Example 2.13.

FIGURE 2.14 **The Multiply class**

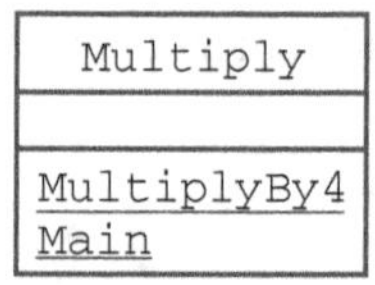

We use parameters to communicate with methods and to make them more flexible. The `MultiplyBy4` method has one parameter, the integer `aNumber`. We call the parameter `aNumber` a formal parameter. It specifies the form of the data we will pass to the method when we call it. Each parameter functions as a local variable inside the method.

A method can return a value, the result of the operation. We use the `return` statement to specify the result. Here we return four times the parameter, `aNumber`, that we pass into the method. Note the type name, `int`, just before the method name `MultiplyBy4`. It specifies the type of the result the `MultiplyBy4` method returns.

To use the `MultiplyBy4` method we pass it a value of the type specified by the formal parameter, which is an `int`. For example,

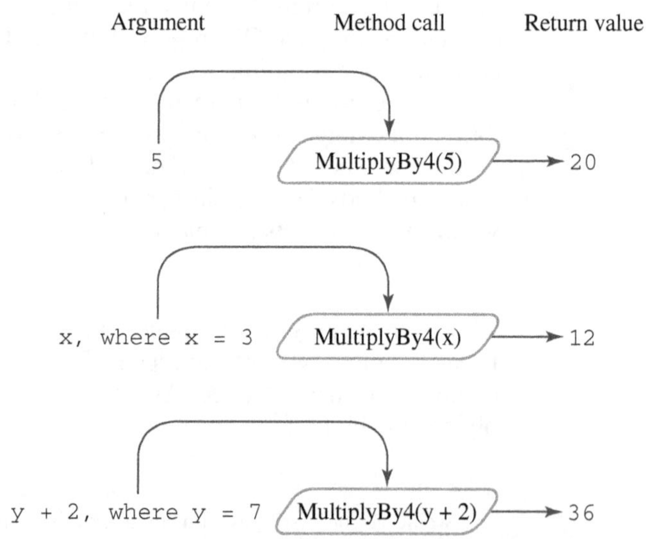

[6]In Chapter 5 we will contrast class methods with instance methods, which are part of objects.

In this text, we use the term argument to denote the actual value passed when we call a method, reserving the term parameter for the formal parameter we use in the definition of the method.

We can think of arguments as the raw materials of the method, which is like a machine that uses the raw materials to produce a product, the return value. Figure 2.15 shows this view of the `MultiplyBy4` method. We show the method as a black box because we can use it without having to look inside to see how it works.

EXAMPLE 2.13 ■ Multiply.cs

```
/*  Defines a multiplyBy4 method and uses it in a program
 */

using System;
public class Multiply {

        // Multiplies its argument by four
  public static int MultiplyBy4(int aNumber) {      // Note 1
    return 4*aNumber;
  }

      // Shows various ways of passing arguments to a method
  public static void Main() {
    int x = 7;
    int y = 20;
    int z = -3;
    int result = 0;
    result = MultiplyBy4(x);                         // Note 2
    Console.WriteLine
            ("Passing a variable, x: {0}", result);
    result = MultiplyBy4(y+2);                       // Note 3
    Console.WriteLine
            ("Passing an expression, y+2: {0}", result);
    result = 5 + MultiplyBy4(z);                     // Note 4
    Console.WriteLine
      ("Using MultiplyBy4 in an expression: {0}", result);
    result = MultiplyBy4(31);                        // Note 5
```

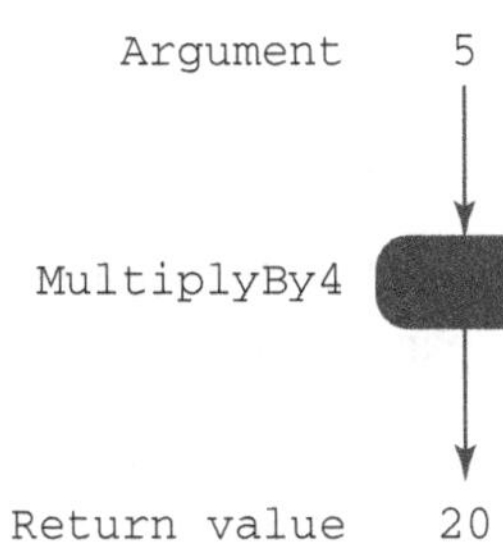

FIGURE 2.15 **The `MultiplyBy4` "machine"**

```
    Console.WriteLine
            ("Passing a constant, 31: {0}", result);
    Console.WriteLine
           ("Passing an expression to WriteLine: {0}",
             MultiplyBy4(y));                          // Note 6
  }
}
```

Output

```
Passing a variable, x: 28
Passing an expression, y+2: 88
Using MultiplyBy4 in an expression: -7
Passing a constant, 31: 124
Passing an expression to WriteLine: 80
```

Note 1: `public static int MultiplyBy4(int aNumber) {`

We declare the method `MultiplyBy4` with integer parameter `aNumber` and integer return value. The body of the method contains the code to implement the operation and compute the return value. Here we compute an expression, `4*aNumber`, and return this value. Note the semicolon we use to terminate the `return` statement.

Note 2: `result = MultiplyBy4(x);`

We call the method, passing it an argument x of type `int`, the same type we specified in the declaration. The `MultiplyBy4` method multiplies the value, 7, of `x` by 4 and returns the value 28.

Note 3: `result = MultiplyBy4(y+2);`

We can substitute an expression, `y+2`, for the parameter. Because `y` is 20, `y+2` is 22, and the return value will be 88.

Note 4: `result = 5 + MultiplyBy4(z);`

If a method returns a value, we can use that method in an expression. Here `z` is −3, so the return value from `MultiplyBy4` will be −12 and the result will be −7.

Note 5: `result = MultiplyBy4(31);`

The argument we pass to a method can be a constant value. Here we pass 31, so the result is 124.

Note 6:

```
Console.WriteLine
       ("Passing an expression to WriteLine: {0}",
         MultiplyBy4(y));
```

The return value does not necessarily need to be saved in a variable. Here it is part of the argument to the `WriteLine` method. Because `y` is

20, `MultiplyBy4(y)` returns 80, so this `WriteLine` statement will output

```
Passing an expression to WriteLine: 80
```

A method may not have any parameters, and it may not return a value. Example 2.14 shows a method, `PrintBlurb`, that has no parameters and has no return value; it simply prints a message.

EXAMPLE 2.14 ■ NoArgsNoReturn.cs

```
/*  Shows that a method may not have any parameters, and may
 *  not return a value.
 */

using System;
public class NoArgsNoReturn {

     // Displays a message
  public static void PrintBlurb()  {                  // Note 1
    Console.WriteLine("This method has no arguments, "
                  + "and it has no return value."); // Note 2
  }                                                   // Note 3

         // Execution starts here
  public static void Main( ) {
    PrintBlurb();                                     // Note 4
  }
}
```

Output

```
This method has no arguments, and it has no return value
```

■

Note 1: `public static void PrintBlurb()  {`

Even when a method has no parameters, we still use the rounded parentheses, but with nothing between them. We use `void` to show that the method has no return value.

Note 2:

```
Console.WriteLine("This method has no arguments, "
            + "and it has no return value.");
```

When we use the plus sign with string arguments it represents string concatenation, which joins the two strings into one longer string.

Note 3: `}`

We do not need a `return` statement because `PrintBlurb` does not return any value.

Note 4: `PrintBlurb();`

When calling a method with no arguments, use the empty parentheses. Because `PrintBlurb` has no return value, we cannot use it in an expression the way that we did with the `MultiplyBy4` method.

A Little Extra

Methods and Functions

Methods in C# are similar to functions in other languages. In mathematics, a function gives a correspondence between the argument passed to the function and the resulting function value. The function `f`, given by `f(x)=2x+1`, computes values as follows:

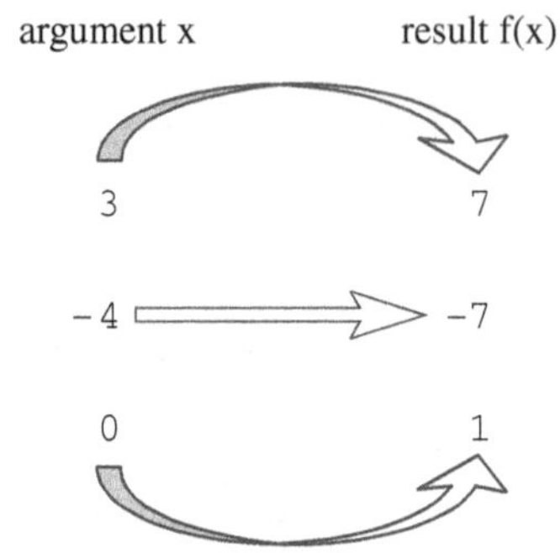

We could program a C# method

```
int F(int x) {
  return 2*x + 1;
}
```

which computes the same values, in its range, as the mathematical function `f`. We call the C# implementation a method instead of a function because we must declare it inside a class. We will cover more about classes later in this text. Other languages use the name function for a similar program that is not declared within a class.

Passing by Value

By default, C# passes arguments by value, meaning that the called method receives the value of the argument rather than its location. Figure 2.16 illustrates what happens in Example 2.13 when we call `MultiplyBy4(x)`. `Main` has a variable `x` whose value is 7. The `MultiplyBy4` method has a parameter `aNumber`, which

FIGURE 2.16
Passing by value

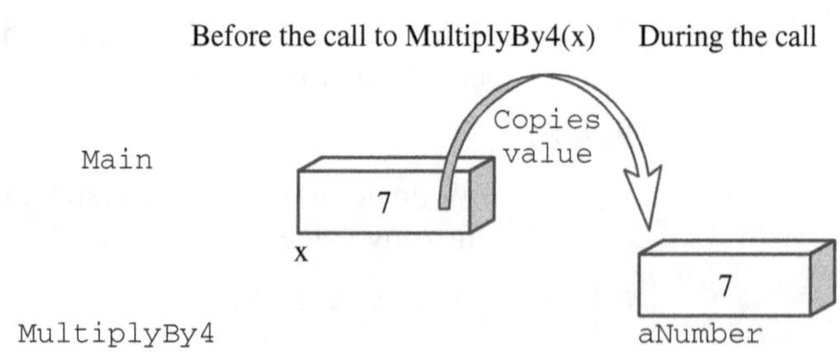

functions as a local variable. The call MultiplyBy4(x) causes C# to copy the value 7 to the variable aNumber in the MultiplyBy4 method.

Example 2.15 illustrates the effect of passing by value. We create a method that returns the cube of the argument passed to it. Passing x, which has a value of 12, will cause the Cube method to return 1728 which equals 12*12*12. We named the parameter to the Cube method, aNumber. Inside the Cube method, we add 5 to the value of aNumber, but this has no effect on the argument x, defined in the Main method, which remains 12.

We added a local variable, result, to the Cube method. We declare local variables inside a method. They may be used only inside the method in which they are declared. The **scope** of a variable signifies the region of code in which it is visible. The scope of a local variable is the method in which it is declared. The variables we declared in our previous examples in this chapter are all local variables because we declared them inside the Main method.

EXAMPLE 2.15 ■ PassByValue.cs

```
/*  Illustrates pass by value
 */

using System;
public class PassByValue {

    // Returns the cube of its argument
  public static int Cube(int aNumber) {
    int result = aNumber*aNumber*aNumber;          // Note 1
    aNumber += 5;                                  // Note 2
    return result;
  }

   /* Shows that the value in the caller
    * does not change.
    */
  public static void Main() {
    int x = 12;
    int value = Cube(x);
    Console.WriteLine("The cube of {0} is {1}",
                               x, value);          // Note 3
  }
}
```

Output

```
The cube of 12 is 1728
```

Note 1: `int result = aNumber*aNumber*aNumber;`

The variable `result` is local to the `cube` method and may only be used there.

Note 2: `aNumber += 5;`

We add 5 to `aNumber` to show that this change affects only `aNumber`, and not the variable `x` which we pass to it from `Main`.

Note 3:
```
Console.WriteLine("The cube of {0} is {1}",
                                    x, value);
```

When we pass `x` to the `Cube` method, C# copies its value, 12, to the parameter `aNumber`, which functions as a local variable of the `Cube` method. Changing `aNumber` has no effect on the value of the variable `x`, which remains 12.

Figure 2.17 illustrates the operations of Example 2.15. We see that local variables and parameters are alive only during the method call. They do not exist before or after the call. We see that C# copies the value of the argument, so the change to the parameter `aNumber` inside the `Cube` method has no effect on the value of the argument `x` in the `Main` method.

Programming with Methods

In Section 1.4 we discussed abstracting operations to make our programs rise above the level of general-purpose C# constructs. Putting a big block of low-level C# code in a `Main` method does not present our design in a meaningful way to the reader of the program. Our programming examples in this chapter illustrate basic concepts, and are not meant to provide a useful application. Nevertheless, even here we can introduce some abstraction and organize our code using methods.

FIGURE 2.17
Memory usage for parameter passing

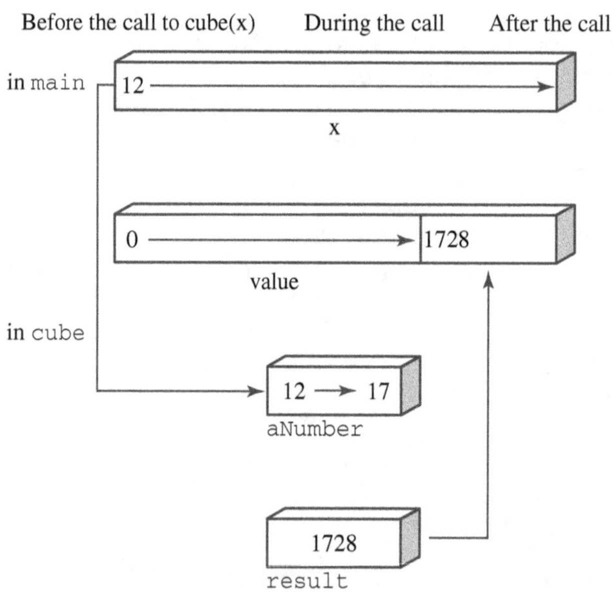

For example, let us reconsider Example 2.9, `Arithmetic.cs`. Code in the `Main` method illustrates C# arithmetic operations. Example 2.16 organizes this code into two methods, called `Additive` and `Multiplicative`. Each has two integer parameters. `Additive` illustrates the `+`, `-`, and negation operators, and `Multiplicative` illustrates `*`, `/`, and `%`. The `Main` method simply calls each of these methods. It would be easy to call these methods with different data, something that would require us to copy the code again using the approach of Example 2.9.

EXAMPLE 2.16 ■ ArithmeticMethods.cs

```
/* Uses methods to try out arithmetic operators on
 * integer data.
 */

using System;
public class ArithmeticMethods {

     /*  Illustrates the addition, subtraction,
      *  and negation operators
      */
  public static void Additive(int x, int y) {
    int z = x + y;
    int w = x - y;
    int p = -y;
    Console.WriteLine
       ("x + y = {0,3}   x - y = {1,3}      -y = {2,3}",
                  x + y, x - y, -y);
  }

      /* Illustrates the multiplication, division,
       * and remainder operators
       */
  public static void Multiplicative(int x, int y) {
    int z = x * y;
    int w = x / 7;
    int p = x % 7;
    Console.WriteLine
       ("x * y = {0,3}   x / 7 = {1,3}   x % 7 = {2,3}",
                     x * y, x / y, x % y);
  }

     // Call the methods, which organizes the code.
  public static void Main () {
    int x = 25;
    int y = 14;
```

```
        Additive(x, y);
        Multiplicative(x, y);
    }
}
```

Output

```
x + y =  39   x - y =  11      -y = -14
x * y = 350   x / 7 =   1   x % 7 =  11
```

Similarly, we can reorganize Example 2.10, `Precedence.cs`, to abstract meaningful methods. We define a `NoParen` method to evaluate three expressions without parentheses. A `SameParen` method evaluates the same expressions, which have parentheses inserted according to the precedence rules. If we insert parentheses correctly, the results from `SameParen` should be the same as the results from `NoParen`.

Finally, the `ChangeParen` method inserts parentheses to make C# evaluate the expressions in an order different from that following the precedence rules. Results from this method may differ from those obtained from the previous two methods. Again, it would be easy to call the methods with different input.

EXAMPLE 2.17 ■ PrecedenceMethods.cs

```
/* Uses methods to illustrate precedence rules
 * for arithmetic operators.
 */

using System;
public class PrecedenceMethods {

    // Uses no parentheses
  public static void NoParen(int a, int b, int c) {
    int expr1 = a + 7 * b;
    int expr2 = c / a + 4;
    int expr3 = c - a % b - a;
    Console.WriteLine("a+7*b = {0}", expr1);
    Console.WriteLine("c/a + 4 = {0}", expr2);
    Console.WriteLine("c-a % b-a = {0}", expr3);
    Console.WriteLine();
  }

    // Inserts parentheses following precedence rules
  public static void SameParen(int a, int b, int c) {
    int expr1 = a + (7 * b);
    int expr2 = (c / a) + 4;
    int expr3 = (c - (a % b)) - a;
    Console.WriteLine("a+(7*b) = {0}", expr1);
    Console.WriteLine("(c/a) + 4 = {0}", expr2);
```

```
    Console.WriteLine("(c-(a%b))-a = {0}", expr3);
    Console.WriteLine();
  }

    // Inserts parentheses to change the normal
    // evaluation order
  public static void ChangeParen(int a, int b, int c) {
    int expr1 = (a + 7) * b;
    int expr2 = c / (a + 4);
    int expr3 = (c - a) % (b - a);
    Console.WriteLine("(a+7)*b = {0}", expr1);
    Console.WriteLine("c/(a + 4) = {0}", expr2);
    Console.WriteLine("(c-a) % (b-a) {0}", expr3);
    Console.WriteLine();
  }

     // Calls each method to compare results
  public static void Main() {
    NoParen(3,4,5);
    SameParen(3,4,5);
    ChangeParen(3,4,5);
  }
}
```

Output

```
a+7*b = 31
c/a + 4 = 5
c-a % b-a = -1

a+(7*b) = 31
(c/a) + 4 = 5
(c-(a%b))-a = -1

(a+7)*b = 40
c/(a + 4) = 0
(c-a) % (b-a) = 0
```

The BIG Picture

A method contains code for an operation. We use parameters to pass values to a method, and may return a value from the method. When we change the value of a parameter inside a method, it has no effect on the value of the variable passed from the caller. We declare local variables inside a method, and can use them only there.

Using methods to abstract operations helps to organize code into meaningful units.

✓ Test Your Understanding

21. What value will the method `MultiplyBy4` return given that `x=-11`, `y=23`, and `z=6`, and that `MultiplyBy4` is called with the following argument?

    a. `x` b. `y-5`

    c. `-5` d. `z*x+10`

    e. `y-x`

Try It Yourself ➤

22. Initialize the variables in Example 2.13 to `x=-5`, `y=14`, and `z=7`. What output do you expect from this modified program? Compile and run it to see if your expectations are correct.

Try It Yourself ➤

23. Change Example 2.13 to use a method `Add4` instead of `MultiplyBy4`. The method `Add4` will add 4 to the parameter `aNumber` and return that value. Compile and run the new version in which `Add4` replaces `MultiplyBy4`, checking that the results are what you expect.

24. Consider the method declaration

```
int MyAgeIs (int myAge) {
  return  39;
}
```

    a. What is the name of this method?

    b. What is the type of its return value?

    c. What is the name of its formal parameter?

    d. What is the type of its formal parameter?

    e. Write a statement that calls the method with the argument 55.

SUMMARY

- To begin writing C# programs, we need to know the basic elements of the C# language. We name our data and other items using identifiers, which must start with a letter (or underscore, _), followed by letters or digits or both, and can be of any length. C# is case sensitive, distinguishing between identifiers fruit and Fruit, for example. Keywords such as `int` are reserved for special uses and cannot be used as identifiers. C# uses the Unicode character set, which contains thousands of characters, including all the commonly used ASCII characters.
- A variable holds data that the program uses. Every C# variable has a type and a name that the programmer must declare. C# uses the keyword `int` for an integer data type. Declaring an `int` variable specifies its type as integer. Integer variables can hold values of up to 10 decimal digits. We can initialize a variable in its declaration, which will give that variable an initial or starting value. We use the assignment statement to change a variable's value during the execution of the program.
- To perform computations, C# provides the binary arithmetic operators `+`, `-`, `*`, `/`, and `%`, and the unary arithmetic operators `+` and `-`. C# uses precedence rules to evaluate arithmetic expressions without having to clutter them with too many parentheses.

Multiplication, division, and remainder have higher precedence than addition and subtraction. C# has operators +=, -=, *=, /=, and %= that combine assignment with the other arithmetic operators, and increment and decrement operators, ++ and --, which come in either prefix or postfix forms.

- We can use the `WriteLine` and `Write` statements to display our results. `Write` leaves the cursor on the same line, and `WriteLine` moves it to the beginning of the next line. We format output using a format string with format specifiers. In the format string, {0} indicates the position of the first argument, {1} indicates the position of the second argument, and so on for additional arguments. The specifier {0,5} indicates that the argument should appear right-aligned in a field of length five. {0, -5} specifies left-alignment. Using {0:C} specifies a currency output for the first argument.
- The simplest form for a program puts the code in a `Main` method. The `Main` method is `static`, meaning that it is part of the class, not part of any object. The system begins execution with the code in our `Main` method.
- In addition to the `Main` method we can use other `static` methods in our programs. A method contains the code for an operation. We use parameters to communicate with methods and to make them more flexible. A method can return a value, the result of the operation. We use the `return` statement to specify the result. Programming with methods raises the level of abstraction of our program, making it easier to understand and modify.
- The `using` directive lets us use classes from a namespace without prefixing them with the namespace name.

SKILL BUILDER EXERCISES

1. Find the mistakes in each of the following (and correct them if possible):

a. `integer x;`

b. `public void main () { // code goes here }`

c. `z + y = 17;`

d. `public Class MyClass { // put code here }`

2. What will be the output when the following code fragment is run?

```
int x = 12, y = 14, z;
z = y / x +7;
x = z * z;
System.Console.WriteLine(x);
```

3. Match each term on the left with its meaning on the right.

a. `Main`	i. the type for integer variables
b. `return`	ii. the startup method
c. `void`	iii. a C# statement
d. `int`	iv. denotes the absence of a return value

CRITICAL THINKING EXERCISES

4. Which of the following expressions, if any, have the same value for integers *x*, *y*, and *z*?

   a. `(x + y) * z`

   b. `x + y * z`

   c. `x + (y * z)`

5. Which of the following statements, if any, have the same result for integers *x* and *y*?

   a. `x += y;`

   b. `y += x;`

   c. `x = x + y;`

6. Fill in the blanks in the following:

   a. If `x++` evaluates to 3, the value of `x` before the evaluation was _____, and its value after the evaluation will be ______.

   b. If `++x` evaluates to 3, the value of `x` before the evaluation was _____, and its value after the evaluation will be ______.

7. Which of the following uses of the `MultiplyBy4` method of Example 2.13 are incorrect? The variable `r` has type `int`.

   a. `r = MultiplyBy4(r);`

   b. `r = MultiplyBy4(12);`

   c. `System.Console.WriteLine(MultiplyBy4(12));`

   d. The above are all correct.

PROGRAM DESIGN EXERCISES

8. Write a program that displays a letter T like the one following.

```
***********
    *
    *
    *
    *
```

9. Write a program that initializes three integer variables to 35, 67, and 452, and outputs their sum and their product.

10. Write a program that reads three integers from the keyboard and outputs their sum and product.

11. Write a static method with three integer parameters that returns the product of these parameters. Call this method from the `main` method and output the result.

12. Write a program to enter the height and width of a rectangle from the keyboard and output the area of the rectangle.

13. Write a static method with two integer parameters, the height and the width of a rectangle, which returns the perimeter of that rectangle. Call this method from the `Main` method twice, each time with different arguments, and output the results.

14. Write a static method with one integer parameter and let it return the remainder of that integer when divided by 7. For example, `FindRemainder(19)` should return 5. In the `Main` method, initialize two variables, `x` and `y`, with values 73 and 16. Call the `FindRemainder` method three times, with the arguments `x`, `y`, and `x+y`, each time displaying the result returned by `FindRemainder`.

15. Write a program that reads an integer number of miles, converts it to an equivalent number of feet, and outputs the result. (There are 5280 feet in a mile.)

16. Write a program to convert degrees Fahrenheit to degrees Celsius. Input an integer Fahrenheit temperature and convert to an integer Celsius temperature using the formula Celsius = 5(Fahrenheit − 32) / 9. Output the result.

17. Write a static method with one integer parameter, `x`, that returns the value of the polynomial $3x^2 - 7x + 2$. Call this method twice from the `Main` method, each time reading in the value of `x` and displaying the result.

18. Write a static method with one integer parameter, `x`, that returns the value of the polynomial $4x^2 + 3x - 5$. Call this method twice from the `Main` method, each time reading in the value of `x` and displaying the result.

19. Write a program to convert an integer number of seconds to an equivalent number of hours, minutes, and seconds. For example, an input of 52,400 should give 14 hours, 33 minutes, and 20 seconds. (Dividing 52,400 by 3600 gives a quotient of 14 hours, and the remainder is 2000 seconds. Dividing the remainder of 2000 by 60 gives a quotient of 33 minutes with a remainder of 20.)

3 Software Engineering with Control Structures

Our C# programs so far have been simple. All we have learned to do is execute one statement after another in order. We have not had any choices. If we lived life like that, we would get up every day, get dressed, and have breakfast no matter how we felt. In reality, we make decisions among alternatives. If we are very sick we might stay in bed and not get dressed. (If we are very lucky, someone might bring us breakfast in bed.) We might not be hungry one morning, so we would get up, get dressed, but skip breakfast. Here is a description of our morning, with decisions:

```
if (I feel ill)
     stay in bed;
else  {
     get up;
     get dressed;
     if (I feel hungry)
         eat breakfast;
}
```

In this "program," what I do depends on whether "I feel ill" is true or false. We will see in this chapter how to write C# expressions that are either true or false, and how to write C# statements that allow us to choose among alternatives based on the truth or falsity of a test expression.

Making choices gives us more flexibility, but we need even more control. For example, if I am thirsty, I might drink a glass of water, but one glass of water might not be enough. What I really want to do is to keep drinking water as long as I am still thirsty. I need to be able to repeat an action. The kind of program I want is

```
while (I feel thirsty)
     drink a glass of water;
```

We will see in this chapter how to write C# statements that allow us to repeat steps in our program.

We think of C# as flowing from one statement to the next as it executes our program. The `if` and `while` statements allow us to specify how C# should flow through our program as it executes its statements.

Controlling the flow of execution gives us flexibility as to which statements we execute, but we also need some choices about the type of data we use. So far, we have declared variables only of type `int`, representing whole numbers. In this chapter we will introduce the type `double` to represent decimal numbers.

With the `if-else` and `while` statements and the type `double`, we have the language support to create more complex programs,[1] but how do we use these tools to solve problems? In this chapter we introduce a systematic process we can use to develop problem solutions.

OBJECTIVES

- Use relational operators and expressions
- Learn the basic sequence, selection, and repetition statements necessary for a general-purpose programming language
- Design solutions to problems
- Introduce simple debugging techniques, including a debugger
- Use the `double` type

3.1 RELATIONAL OPERATORS AND EXPRESSIONS

Arithmetic operators take numeric operands and give numeric results. For example, the value of `3+4` is an integer, 7. By contrast, an expression such as `3<4`, stating that 3 is less than 4, gives the value `true`, and the expression `7<2` gives the value `false`. Type `bool`, named for the British mathematician and logician, George Boole (1815–1864), provides two values, `true` and `false`, which we use to express the value of relational and logical expressions.

C# provides relational and equality operators, listed in Figure 3.1, which take two operands of a primitive type and produce a `bool` result.

[1]For pedagogical purposes we introduce a basic set of control structures and the type `double` in this chapter, leaving the variations and additional features to Chapter 4, in preference to putting all selection structures in one chapter and loops in another, with a third chapter for types.

Symbol	Meaning	Example	
`<`	`less than`	`31 < 25`	`false`
`<=`	`less than or equal`	`464 <= 7213`	`true`
`>`	`greater than`	`-98 > -12`	`false`
`>=`	`greater than or equal`	`9 >= 99`	`false`
`==`	`equal`	`9 == 12 + 12`	`false`
`!=`	`not equal`	`292 != 377`	`true`

FIGURE 3.1 **C# relational and equality operators.**

TIP The operators `<=`, `>=`, `==`, and `!=` are two-character operators which must be together, without any spaces between the two characters. The expression `3 <= 4` is fine, but `3 < = 4` will give an error. (The compiler thinks we want the '<' operator and cannot figure out why we did not give a correct right-hand operand.) ■

We can mix arithmetic operators and relational operators in the same expression, as in

```
643 < 350 + 450
```

which evaluates to `true`. We can omit parentheses because C# uses precedence rules, as we saw in Section 2.3. Arithmetic operators all have higher precedence than relational operators, so C# adds `350 + 450` giving 800, and then determines that 643 is less than 800. We could have written the expression using parentheses, as in

```
643 < (350 + 450)
```

but in this case we can omit the parentheses and let C# use the precedence rules to evaluate the expression.[2] Some programmers prefer to include parentheses for clarity, even when they are not necessary.

We can use variables in relational expressions, and can declare variables of type `bool`. For example, if `x` is an integer variable, the expression

```
x < 3
```

is true if the value of `x` is less than 3, and false otherwise. The expression

```
x == 3
```

evaluates to `true` if `x` equals 3, and to `false` otherwise.

TIP Be careful not to confuse the equality operator, `==`, with the assignment operator, `=`. If `x` has the value 12, then `x == 3` evaluates to `false`, but `x = 3` assigns the value 3 to `x`, changing it from 12. ■

---

[2]See Appendix C for the operator precedence table.

EXAMPLE 3.1 ■ Relational.cs

```
/*  Use relational expressions and boolean variables
 */

using System;
public class Relational {
  public static void Main( ) {
    int i = 3;
    bool result;                                          // Note 1

    result = (32 > 87);                                   // Note 2
    Console.WriteLine(" (32 > 87) is {0}",  result);
    result = (-20  == -20);                               // Note 3
    Console.WriteLine(" (-20 == -20) is {0}", result);
    result = -20 == -20;                                  // Note 4
    Console.WriteLine(" -20 == -20 is {0}", result);
    result = -20 == -10 - 10;                             // Note 5
    Console.WriteLine(" -20 == -10 - 10 is {0}", result);
    Console.WriteLine(" 16 <= 54 is {0}", 16 <= 54);     // Note 6
    Console.WriteLine(" i != 3 is {0}", i != 3);         // Note 7
  }
}
```

Output

```
(32 > 87) is False
 (-20 == -20) is True
 -20 == -20 is True
 -20 == -10 - 10 is True
 16 <= 54 is True
 i != 3 is False
```

Note 1: `bool result;`

We can declare variables of type `bool`, which will have the values `True` or `False`.

Note 2: `result = (32 > 87);`

For clarity we use parentheses, but we could have omitted them because the greater than operator, >, has higher precedence than the assignment operator, =. The value of the `bool` variable result is `false`, a literal of the `bool` type.

Note 3: `result = (-20  == -20);`

We could omit the parentheses because the equality operator, ==, has higher precedence than the assignment operator, =.

Note 4: `result = -20 == -20;`

We do not need parentheses, because == has higher precedence than =.

Note 5: `result = -20 == -10 - 10;`

This expression uses the equality operator, the subtraction operator and the negation operator. Again, we do not need parentheses.

Note 6: `Console.WriteLine(" 16 <= 54 is {0}", 16 <= 54);`

We can use a relational expression in a `WriteLine` statement without assigning it to a variable. C# will evaluate the expression and display its value. Here we do not need to enclose `16<=54` in parentheses.

Note 7: `Console.WriteLine(" i != 3 is {0}", i != 3);`

Here we used a variable, `i`, in a relational expression, `i != 3`. Because `i` has the value 3, the value of this expression is `false`.

The BIG Picture

The relational operators <, >, <=, >=, ==, and != return `bool` values. The last four are two-character operators that we must type without any space between the two characters. They have lower precedence than the arithmetic operators, but higher precedence than assignment.

✓Test Your Understanding

1. Write a relational expression in C# for each of the following:
   - **a.** 234 less than 52
   - **b.** 435 not equal to 87
   - **c.** −12 equal to −12
   - **d.** 76 greater than or equal to 54
2. Evaluate the following relational expressions:
   - **a.** `23 < 45`
   - **b.** `49 >= 4 + 9`
   - **c.** `95 != 100 - 5`

3. What is wrong with the expression `(3 < 4) < 5` in C#?
4. If `x` has the value 7, and `y` is 12, evaluate each of the following:
   a. `y == x + 5`
   b. `x >= y - 7`
   c. `2 * x  < y`
   d. `y + 3 != x`
5. Explain the difference between `x = 5` and `x == 5`.
6. Explain why the expression `x >= 3` is not a correct C# expression to state that `x` is greater than or equal to 3.

3.2 `if` AND `if-else` STATEMENTS[3]

We are now ready to make choices about which statements to execute. Three C# statements permit us to make choices. We cover the `if` and `if-else` statements in this section. We cover the `switch` statement, which allows a choice among multiple alternatives, in the next chapter.

The `if` Statement

The `if` statement is essential because

- It allows us to make choices.
- It allows us to solve more complex problems.

The `if` statement has the pattern

```
if (condition)
    if_true_statement
```

as in the example

```
if (x > 2)
    y = x + 17;
```

The condition is an expression such as `x > 2` that evaluates to true or false. The `if_true_statement` is a C# statement such as `y = x + 17`. If the condition is true, then execute the `if_true_statement`, but if the condition is false, skip the `if_true_statement` and go on to the next line of the program. In this example, if `x` happened to have the value 5, we would assign `y` the value 22, but if `x` had the value 1, we would skip the statement `y = x + 17`.

[3] We cover the basic form of the `if` and `if-else` statements in this section, leaving nested `if`s and the `switch` statement until Chapter 4. In this way we can develop a basic set of control structures in this chapter, including both selection and repetition, and discuss problem-solving methods earlier.

EXAMPLE 3.2 ■ Overtime.cs

```
/*  Uses the if statement */

using System;
public class Overtime {
  public static void Main( ) {
    Console.Write("Enter the hours worked this week: ");
    int hours = int.Parse(Console.ReadLine( ));
    if (hours > 40)                                   // Note 1
      Console.WriteLine("You worked overtime this week");
    Console.WriteLine
                ("You worked {0} hours", hours);    // Note 2
  }
}
```

First run

```
Enter the hours worked this week: 76
You worked overtime this week
You worked 76 hours
```

Second run

```
Enter the hours worked this week: 8
You worked 8 hours
```

■

Note 1:

```
if (hours > 40)
  Console.WriteLine("You worked overtime this week");
```

The condition, `hours > 40`, is `true` if the number we enter is greater than 40, in which case C# executes the `WriteLine` statement to display the message, `You worked overtime this week`. If the number we enter is not greater than 40, then C# skips this `WriteLine` statement.

Note 2:

```
Console.WriteLine
        ("You worked {0} hours", hours);
```

No matter what number we enter, C# executes this `WriteLine` statement, displaying the value we entered.

Style

Indent all lines after the first to show that these lines are part of the `if` statement, and to make it easier to read.

Do

```
if (myItem > 10)
  Console.WriteLine("Greater than ten");
```

Do Not

```
if (myItem > 10)
Console.WriteLine("Greater than ten");
```

Control Flow

Control flow refers to the order in which the processor executes the statements in a program. For example, the processor executes the three statements

```
int item1 = 25;
int item2 = 12;
item2 = item1 + 15;
```

one after the other. These three statements are in a sequence. We call this type of control flow, executing one statement after another in sequence, the **sequence** control structure. We can visualize the sequence structure in Figure 3.2, in which we write each statement inside a box and use directed lines to show the flow of control from one statement to the next.

The `if` statement allows us to make a choice about the control flow. In Example 3.2, if the hours worked is greater than 40, we print a message about overtime, otherwise we skip this message. We use a diamond shape to represent a decision based on the truth or falsity of a condition. One arrow, called the true branch, shows what comes next if the condition is `true`. Another arrow, called the false branch, shows

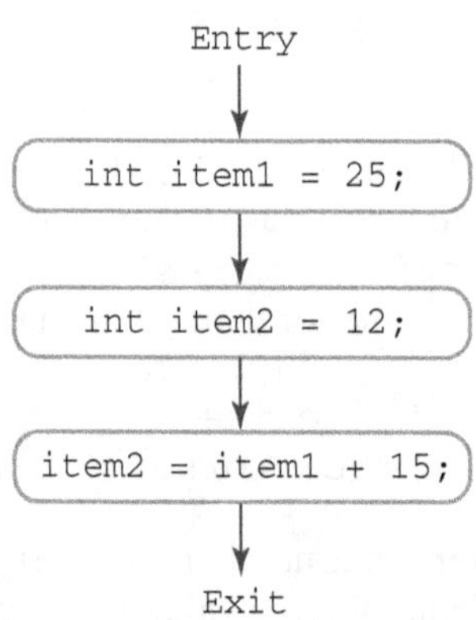

FIGURE 3.2
The sequence control flow

FIGURE 3.3
Control flow for the `if` statement

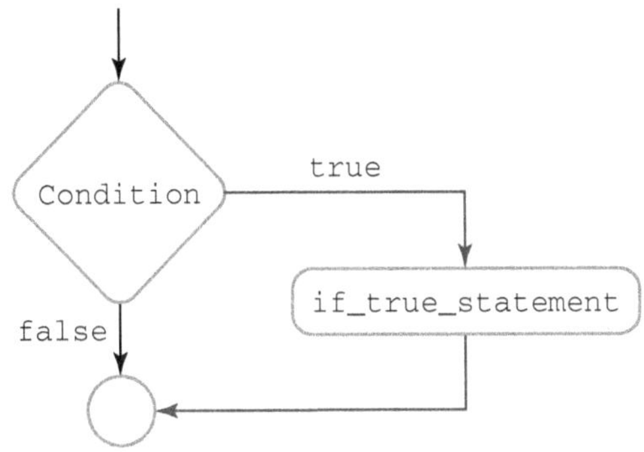

what comes next if the condition is `false`. Figure 3.3 shows the control flow for an `if` statement. When the condition is `true`, C# will execute an additional statement.

Figure 3.4 shows the control flow for the program of Example 3.2.

The `if-else` Statement

The `if` statement allows us to choose to execute a statement or not to execute it depending on the value of a test expression. With the `if-else` statement we can choose between two alternatives, executing one when the test condition is true and the other when the test condition is false.

FIGURE 3.4 **Control flow for Example 3.2**

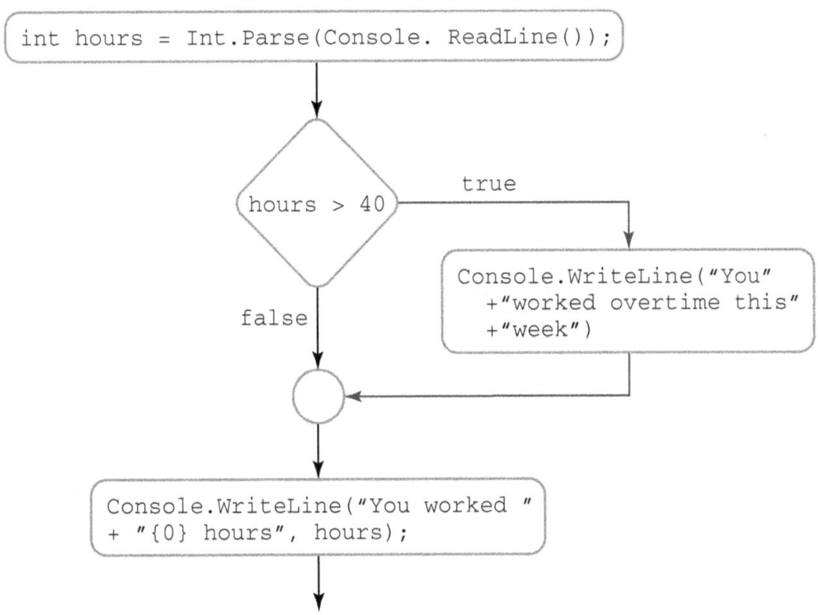

The `if-else` statement has the form

```
if  (condition)
     if_true_statement
else
     if_false_statement
```

For example,

```
if (x <= 20)
   x += 5;
else
   x += 2;
```

If x is less than or equal to 20, then we add 5 to it, otherwise we add 2 to it. The `if-else` statement gives us a choice between two alternatives. We choose `if_true_statement` if the condition is `true` and `if_false_statement` if the condition is `false`.

EXAMPLE 3.3 ■ RentalCost.cs

```
 /* Computes the cost of a car rental.
 */

using System;
public class RentalCost  {

    /* Cost is $30 per day for the first three days
     * and $20 for each additional day.
     * Input: number of days
     * Output: cost of rental
     */
  public static int Cost(int days) {
    int pay;
    if (days <= 3)
      pay = 30*days;                                   // Note 1
    else
      pay = 90 + 20*(days - 3);                        // Note 2
    return pay;
  }

       // Enters number of days. Calls the cost method.
  public static void Main()  {
    Console.Write("Enter the number of rental days: ");
    int days = int.Parse(Console.ReadLine( ));
    Console.WriteLine("The rental cost is {0:C}", Cost(days));
  }
}
```

First run

```
Enter the number of rental days: 7
The rental cost is $170
```

Second run

```
Enter the number of rental days: 2
The rental cost is $60
```

Note 1:
```
if (days <= 3)
    pay = 30*days;
```
If we rent for up to three days, the cost is $30 times the number of days.

Note 2:
```
pay = 90 + 20*(days - 3);
```
If we rent for more than three days, the cost is $90 for the first three days plus $20 for each additional day.

Figure 3.5 shows the flow chart for the `if-else` statement.

Blocks

We can group a sequence of statements inside curly braces to form a **block**, as in

```
{
  x = 5;
  y = -8;
  z = x * y;
}
```

FIGURE 3.5
Flow chart for the `if-else` statement

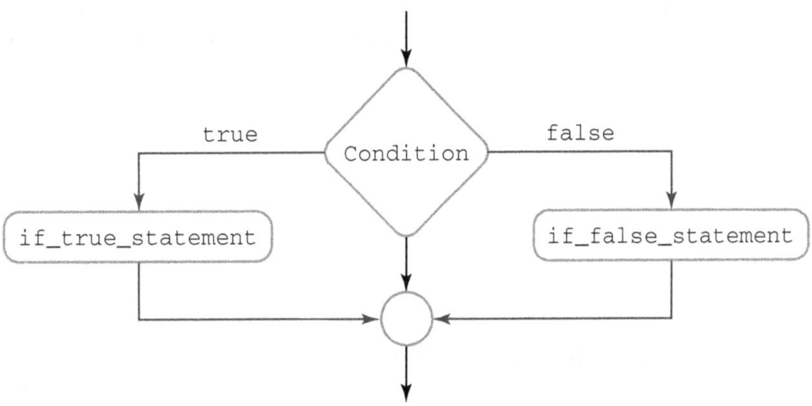

We can use a block as a statement in an `if` or an `if-else` statement, as in

```
if (y > 5) {
    x = 5;
    y = -8;
    z = x * y;
}
```

By using a block, we can perform more than one action if the test condition is `true`. In this example, if `y` is greater than 5, we want to set `x`, `y`, and `z` to new values.

TIP

Do not forget to enclose in curly braces the statements that you want to execute if a condition is `true`. Just indenting them, as in

```
if (y > 5)
  x = 5;
  y = -8;
  z = x * y;
```

will not group the three statements together. We indent to make the program easier to read; indenting does not affect the meaning of the program. Without the braces, C# will interpret the code as

```
if (y > 5)
  x = 5;
y = -8;
z = x * y;
```

If `y` is greater than 5, then C# will set `x` to 5. Whether or not `y` is greater than 5, C# will always set `y` to −8, and `z` to `x*y`. This is quite a different result than we would get if we grouped the three statements in a block, and changed the values of `x`, `y`, and `z` only if the condition is true. ■

Style

Use a consistent style for blocks to help you match the opening brace, `{`, with the closing brace, `}`. One choice is to put the left brace on the same line as the `if` or `else`, and to align the right brace with the `if` or `else`, as in

```
if (x < 10){
  y = 5;
  z = 8;
}
else  {
  y = 9;
  z = -2;
}
```

Using this style, we can match the keyword `if` with the closing brace, `}`, to keep our code neatly organized. Another choice is to align the left brace with the `if` or `else`, as in

```
if (x < 10)
{
   y = 5;
   z = 8;
}
else
{
   y = 9;
   z = -2;
}
```

Either of these styles allows us to add or delete lines within a block without having to change the braces. The latter style makes it easier to match opening with closing braces, but uses an extra line to separate the opening brace from the code. We could make the code more compact by putting the braces on the same line as the code, but this is harder to read and modify, and is not recommended.

A Little Extra

Flow Charts for `if` Statements with Blocks

Figure 3.3 shows the flow chart for the `if` statement. If the condition in the diamond is `true`, then the control flows to the statement in the box on the right. Remember that this statement can be a block, such as

```
{
   x = 2;
   y = 7;
}
```

which has the flow chart

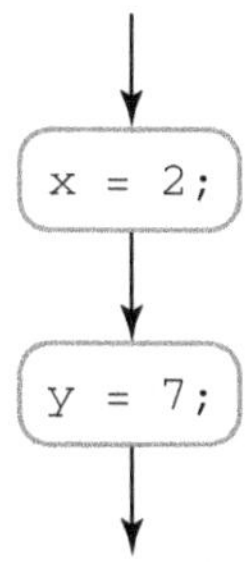

When the statement in the box is a block, we replace the box by the flow chart for that block. We find the flow chart for the `if` statement

```
if (z <= 10) {
    x = 2;
    y = 7;
}
```

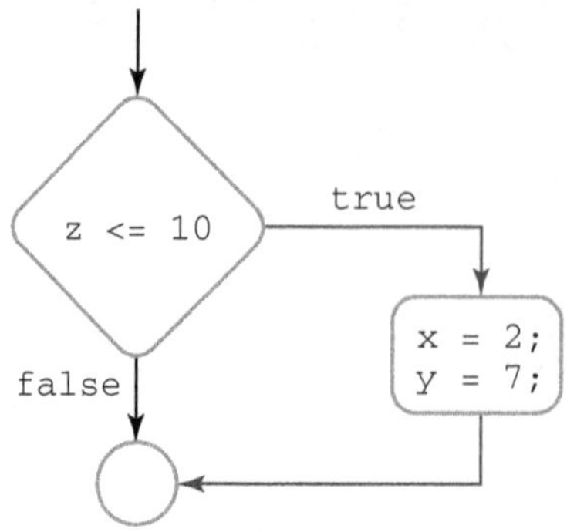

FIGURE 3.6 **Flow chart for `if` statement with block, step 1**

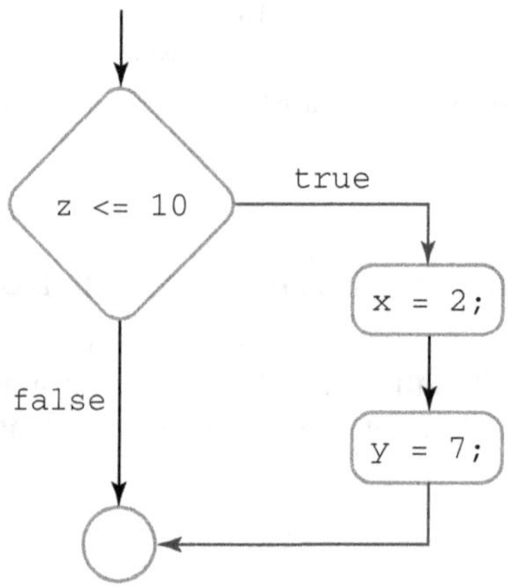

FIGURE 3.7 **Flow chart for `if` statement with block, step 2**

in two steps. First, Figure 3.6 applies the pattern of Figure 3.3 to this example. Second, in Figure 3.7 we replace the block statement by its flow chart.

The BIG Picture

The `if` statement allows us to make a choice to execute a statement or not. The `if-else` statement lets us choose between two alternatives. Each alternative may be a simple statement or a block, which uses curly brackets to enclose C# code. Flow charts show the flow of control in diagram form.

✓Test Your Understanding

7. Correct the error in each of the following:

a. `if {x == 12} y += 7;`

b. `if (x=12) y += 7;`

c. `if (x == 12) then y += 7;`

8. Correct the error in each of the following:

a.
```
if (y > 5)
  z = 7;
  x = 5;
else
  w = 4;
```

b.
```
if  y > 5
     z = 3;
else
     x = y + 2;
```

c.
```
if (y > 5)
     z= 3;
else   (
     s = y + 7;
     z = s - 2;
);
```

9. How would you improve the style in each of the following?

a.
```
if (y <= 6)
z += 5;
```

b.
```
if (x != 0)
y+=5;
else
z = y + 9;
```

10. Draw the flow chart for each of the following `if` statements:

a.
```
if (x == 17)
  y += 6;
```

b.
```
if (s > 12)
     z = 52;
```

11. Draw the flow chart for each of the following `if-else` statements.

a.
```
if (z <= 10)
  y -= 11;
else
  y += 10;
```

b.
```
if (x == 0)
     z = 3*x;
else
     y = 4 + x;
```

A Little Extra

12. Draw the flow chart for each of the following `if` statements with blocks.

a.
```
if (s > 4) {
   y = s - 30;
   z = 2;
}
```

b.
```
if (r != 0) {
      x = 4*r + 3;
      w = 3;
      y = x + w;
}
```

3.3 THE TYPE `double`[4]

In this section, we introduce the type `double` for decimal values. In the next chapter we will cover other numeric types.

[4] We deferred type `double` to this chapter to allow Chapter 2 to introduce programming without presenting any more concepts than were needed to get started writing programs.

Scientific Notation

In many applications, we need to use decimal numbers such as 2.54, the number of centimeters in an inch. Small decimal numbers like .00000003937, the number of inches in a nanometer, are harder to read, but we can use floating-point notation, 3.937E-8, to simplify them. The number following the E, -8 in this example, tells us that we need to move the decimal point eight places to the left to get the value .00000003937. We can write 5,880,000,000,000, the number of miles in a light-year, more conveniently as 5.88E12. The positive exponent, 12, in 5.88E12 informs us that we need to shift the decimal point twelve places to the right to get the number 5880000000000.0.

The number following the E, called the exponent, tells us how many places to shift the decimal point. To write very large or very small numbers in a way that is easier to read, we float the point to a more convenient location, to the right of the first non-zero digit, and adjust the exponent to keep the value of the number unchanged.

We often call this notation using exponents *scientific notation*, because of its usefulness in expressing the varied sizes of numbers used in scientific calculations. Options in scientific notation are to use a lowercase `e`, as in 5.88e12, and to use a plus sign with a positive exponent, as in 5.88E+12. Of course, we can use both options, as in 5.88e+12.

We can express the same number in many ways using scientific notation. For example, each of the following expresses the value .00000003937

```
3.937E-8       393.7E-10     .03937E-6     .00000000003937E+3
```

The usual choice is to float the decimal point just to the right of the first non-zero digit, as in 3.937E-8.

For display purposes, we write numbers that are not too small or too large without exponents, as in 2.54 or 2755.323 or .01345. Very small or very large numbers are easier to read in scientific notation, as in 5.88E+12.

✓Test Your Understanding

13. Express the following without using exponents:

a. 345.22E-2

b. −2.98765e4

c. .000098765E+8

d. 435e-2

14. Express the following in scientific notation with the decimal point to the right of the first non-zero digit:

a. 893.454

b. .000345722

c. 98761234

d. .090909

15. Which of the following express the same value?

   a. .6789E+2
   b. 6.789e-2
   c. 67.89
   d. 678.9e-2
   e. 0.006789

double Values

Now that we have seen how to write decimal numbers using scientific notation, we can introduce the type `double`, which C# provides for decimal numbers. Numbers of type `double` provide 15 decimal digits accurately. If you are using scientific notation, the exponents for `double` values can range from -324 to 308. A literal of type `double` may have a decimal point or an exponent or both, and it must have at least one digit. Some valid values of type `double` are:

```
22.7
 4.123E-2
36e2
 3.
 0.54296
  .1234
```

When we write a decimal literal such as 2.54, C# treats it as a value of type `double`. We can declare variables of type `double` as, for example

```
double length;
double height;
```

and we can initialize variables in the declaration as, for example

```
double length = 173.24E5;
double height =   1.83;
```

We can use the arithmetic operators, `+`, `-`, `*`, and `/`, with `double` operands. For example,

Expression	Value
`6.2 + 5.93`	`12.13`
`72.34 - 2.97`	`69.37`
`32.3 * 654.18`	`21130.014`
`3.0 / 2.0`	`1.5`

TIP

When dividing numbers of type `double`, be sure to include the decimal points. The expression `3/2` will use integer division, which will truncate the value to 1. Writing `3.0/2.0` gives the decimal value 1.5.

Output

If we output values of type `double` using the `WriteLine` method, we have several choices for the format specification. Example 3.4 illustrates some of the possibilities. We illustrate the E, F, and G formats,

```
E   Scientific
F   Fixed-point
G   General
```

We can use these formats alone or with a precision specifier. For example, F3 specifies a fixed-point format with three places after the decimal point.

EXAMPLE 3.4 ■ DoubleOut.cs

```
/* Illustrates output formatting for type double.
 */

using System;
public class DoubleOut {

    /* Creates double values using formats to see
     * how C# WriteLine statements display them.
     */
  public static void Main( ) {
    double five3rds = 5.0/3.0;                              // Note 1
    Console.WriteLine
      ("Default precision     {0}", five3rds);              // Note 2
    double threeHalves = 3.0/2.0;
    Console.WriteLine
      ("No trailing zeros     {0}", threeHalves);           // Note 3
    Console.WriteLine
      ("Default               {0}", 1234567890.987);        // Note 4
    Console.WriteLine
      ("Fixed, two places     {0:F2}", 1234567890.987);// Note 5
    Console.WriteLine
      ("Exponent              {0:E}", 1234567890.987); // Note 6
    Console.WriteLine
      ("Exponent, two places  {0:E2}", 1234567890.987);// Note 7
    Console.WriteLine
      ("General               {0:G}", 1234567890.987); // Note 8
    Console.WriteLine
      ("Changes to fixed      {0}", 1234567.890987E2); // Note 9
    Console.WriteLine
      ("Changes to scientific {0}", .0000123456789);   // Note 10
  }
}
```

```
Default precision      1.66666666666667
No trailing zeros      1.5
Default                1234567890.987
Fixed, two places      1234567890.99
Exponent               1.234568E+009
Exponent, two places   1.23E+009
General                1234567890.987
Changes to fixed       123456789.0987
Changes to scientific  1.23456789E-05
```

Note 1:
```
double five3rds = 5.0/3.0;
```

C# treats decimal literals such as 5.0 as type `double`.

Note 2:
```
Console.WriteLine
  ("Default precision     {0}", five3rds);
```

A `double` value is accurate to 15 decimal digits. C# converts the internal binary number to the closest decimal equivalent.

Note 3:
```
double threeHalves = 3.0/2.0;
 Console.WriteLine
    ("No trailing zeros     {0}", threeHalves);
```

C# does not print zeroes at the end of a number. Every `double` value has 15 digits, but C# does not display the trailing zeroes.

Note 4:
```
Console.WriteLine
   ("Default                 {0}", 1234567890.987);
```

C# uses the General (G) format when we do not include any format specifier. Thus `{0}` has the same effect as `{0:G}`. The G (or default) specifier will use the scientific format if the exponent the number would have when written in scientific notation is less than −4. Writing such a number in fixed-point format would require a number of leading zeroes. It will also use scientific notation if the exponent is greater than or equal to the number of significant digits in the number. The G specifier will use a fixed-point format if neither of these two conditions applies, which is the case here.

Note 5:
```
Console.WriteLine
 ("Fixed, two places     {0:F2}", 1234567890.987);
```

F2 specifies fixed-point notation with two places after the decimal point.

Note 6:
```
Console.WriteLine
   ("Exponent                {0:E}", 1234567890.987);
```

The E format uses scientific notation. It uses six places after the decimal point when no precision is specified. The exponent uses three places, filled with zeroes if necessary.

Note 7:
```
Console.WriteLine
  ("Exponent, two places  {0:E2}", 1234567890.987);
```

The E2 format specifies two places after the decimal point using scientific notation.

Note 8:
```
Console.WriteLine
    ("General                  {0:G}", 1234567890.987);
```

The G format is the default if no format is specified.

Note 9:
```
Console.WriteLine
    ("Changes to fixed       {0}", 1234567.890987E2);
```

Here the exponent is less than the number of significant digits, so the display is in fixed-point.

Note 10:
```
Console.WriteLine
    ("Changes to scientific {0}", .0000123456789);
```

Here the exponent is less than −4, so the display is in scientific notation.

Input

In C#, we can use the `double.Parse` method to convert the input `String` to a `double` value. Example 3.5 inputs hot and cold Celsius temperatures and converts them to Fahrenheit.

EXAMPLE 3.5 ■ Temperature.cs

```
/* Converts degrees Celsius to degrees Fahrenheit.
 */

using System;
public class Temperature {
  public static void Main() {
    double  hotC, coldC;
    double  hotF, coldF;
    Console.Write("Enter a hot temperature in Celsius: ");
    String input = Console.ReadLine();
    hotC = double.Parse(input);
    hotF = 9.0*hotC/5.0 + 32.0;                          // Note 1
    Console.WriteLine
       ("The Fahrenheit temperature is {0:F1}", hotF);
    Console.Write("Enter a cold temperature in Celsius: ");
    input = Console.ReadLine();
    coldC = double.Parse(input);                         // Note 2
    coldF = 9.0*coldC/5.0 + 32.0;
```

```
    Console.WriteLine
        ("The Fahrenheit temperature is {0:F1}", coldF);
  }
}
```

Run

```
Enter a hot temperature in Celsius: 56
The Fahrenheit temperature is 132.8
Enter a cold temperature in Celsius: -19.33
The Fahrenheit temperature is -2.8
```

Note 1: `hotF = 9.0*hotC/5.0 + 32.0;`

To convert degrees Centigrade to degrees Fahrenheit, we use the formula

F = 9C/5 + 32.

We write the constants with decimal points to show that they have type `double`. In the next subsection, we will discuss mixed-type expressions, in which the constants might be integers.

Note 2: `coldC = double.Parse(input);`

Type `double` is a shorthand for `System.Double`, so we could have written this method as `Double.Parse`.

Mixed-type Expressions

Usually a numeric expression uses all variables and literals of type `int`, or all type `double`. For example, `2.54 + 3.61` is a `double` addition and `254 + 361` is an `int` addition. The addition operator, `+`, looks the same in both cases, but `int` addition is quite different from `double` addition because, in the computer memory, `int` and `double` values are stored differently. For convenience, we use the same `+` symbol to represent these two kinds of addition.

When we mix types in an expression, as in `2.54 + 361`, which type of addition does C# use, `int` or `double`? As they say, it is like adding apples and oranges. We cannot just add a `double` to an `int` because they are different types. We cannot convert real apples to real oranges, or oranges to apples, but in the numeric case we have better luck. We cannot convert a `double` such as 2.54 to an `int` without losing information. Rounding it to `3` probably is not a good choice. But we can convert an `int` to a `double` without losing information, for example, by changing 361 to 361.0.

Although we do not lose any information by converting 361 to 361.0, it does require a change inside memory, because 361 has an internal representation that is a lot different from that for 361.0. Because we can always convert an `int` to a `double` without losing information, C# will do it for us automatically. If we write

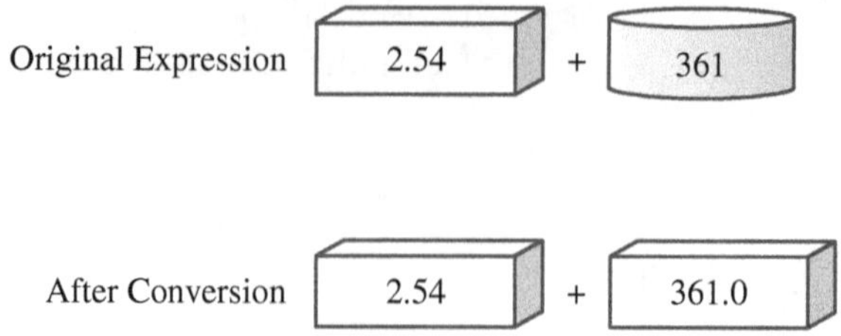

FIGURE 3.8 **Conversion of a mixed-mode expression**

`2.54 + 361`, C# will convert 361 to 361.0, and use type `double` addition to get the result 363.54. Figure 3.8 illustrates this conversion process.

We could have used this automatic conversion in Example 3.5, where we used the expression

```
9.0*c/5.0 + 32.0
```

in which we wrote all the literals as double values, 9.0, 5.0, and 32.0. Letting C# do the conversion from `int` to `double`, we could instead have written

```
9*c/5 + 32
```

where `c` has type `double`.

TIP

C# converts from `int` to `double` only in a mixed-mode expression where one operand has type `int` and the other has type `double`. The expression

```
9/5*c + 32
```

will not give the result we expect. The division `9/5` has both operands, 9 and 5, as integers, so C# uses integer division, obtaining the integer quotient of 1, not the value 1.8 that we want. Writing the expression as

```
9*c/5 + 32
```

where `c` has type `double`, works because `9*c` is a mixed-mode expression in which one operand, 9, has type `int` and the other, `c`, has type `double`. The result, `9*c`, is a `double` value, so `(9*c)/5` is a mixed-mode expression and C# will convert the 5 from `int` to `double`. Finally, `(9*c)/5` has type `double`, so C# will convert `32` from an `int` to a `double` before doing the addition. ■

C# will also convert from `int` to `double` in an assignment statement. For example, in

```
double d = 4;
```

C# will assign the `double` value 4.0 to the variable `d`. However, C# will not automatically convert a `double` to an `int` to assign it to an integer variable, because a `double` value may be out of the range of values an `int` variable can hold.

The general rule C# follows for these implicit conversions of one primitive type to another is that we can assign any numeric value to any numeric variable whose type supports a larger range of values.

A Little Extra

Type Casts

As we saw, C# will do an implicit conversion from `int` to `double` in a mixed-type expression. We could explicitly cast the type from `int` to `double` by putting the desired type, `double`, in parentheses to the left of the `int` literal or variable we wish to convert. For example, in the expression

```
2.54 + (double)361
```

C# converts the value 361 to type `double` before adding it to 2.54.

By using an explicit cast, we show that we really want C# to convert from one type to another. If we always use explicit type casts, then when checking our code we would recognize an implicit mixed-type expression, such as `2.54 + 361`, as an error, say, of omission of a decimal point in 361. We might have meant to write `2.54 + 3.61`, but instead wrote a mixed-type expression. Because C# does not treat such a mixed-type expression as an error, we would have to inspect our results carefully to see that they are not correct.

TIP

Just because your program compiles and runs does not mean that the results are correct. Always check that your results are reasonable. Make a prediction before you run your program. If you expect the result to be positive, do not accept a negative value without further investigation. If you expect the result to be about 10, do not accept a value of 17,234 without more checking.

The BIG Picture

Floating-point notation allows us to write large and small numbers conveniently. The type `double` provides 15-place accuracy. By default, C# will use the G format for output. We can use the E format to specify scientific notation or the F for fixed-point. Each format allows a precision specification for the number of decimal places. C# lets us use some forms of mixed-type expressions.

✓Test Your Understanding

16. What will be the result of each division?

a. `5.0 / 2.0`

b. `5 / 2`

c. `12 / 5`

d. `12.0 / 5.0`

17. Suppose that the `double` variable, `x`, has the indicated value. Show the result of `Console.WriteLine("{0}",x)`.

a. 3456.789

b. .0000023456

c. .09876543

d. 1234567890.987

e. −234567.765432

18. Suppose that the `double` variable, `x`, has the indicated value. Show the result of `Console.WriteLine("{0:E2}",x)`.

a. 3456.789

b. .0000023456

c. .09876543

d. 1234567890.987

e. −234567.765432

Try It Yourself ➤

19. In Example 3.5, change the formula

```
9.0*c/5.0 + 32.0
```

to

```
9*c/5 + 32
```

Do you think the program will still work correctly? Rerun Example 3.5 with this change to verify that your answer is correct.

Try It Yourself ➤

20. In Example 3.5, change the formula

```
9.0*c/5.0 + 32.0
```

to

```
9/5*c + 32
```

Do you think the program will still work correctly? Rerun Example 3.5 with this change to verify that your answer is correct.

A Little Extra

21. Rewrite each of the following to use explicit type casts:

a. `72 + 37.5`

b. `23.28 / 7`

c. `double d = 874;`

3.4 PROGRAM DESIGN WITH THE `while` LOOP[5]

The `if` and `if-else` statements give us the ability to make choices. In this section we will see how the `while` statement enables us to repeat steps.

Repetition

The `while` statement follows the pattern

```
while (condition)
  while_true_statement
```

[5]We cover the `while` loop here, deferring the `for` and `do-while` loops until Chapter 4. In this way we can develop a basic set of control structures in this chapter and discuss problem-solving methods earlier.

FIGURE 3.9 **Flow chart for the `while` loop**

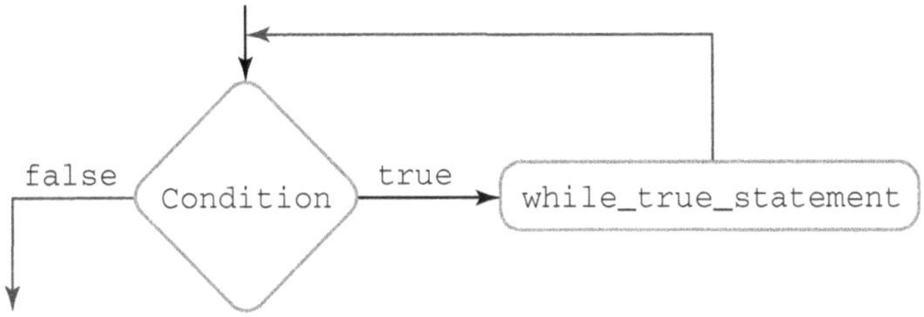

with the flow chart shown in Figure 3.9, where the condition evaluates to true or false, and the `while_true_statement` can be any C# statement including a code block. If the condition is true, C# executes the `while_true_statement` and goes back to check the condition again. If the condition is still true, C# executes the `while_true_statement` and goes back to check the condition again, and so on. This process repeats until the condition is false.

For example, suppose that the variable `x` has the value 7 just before C# starts to execute the `while` statement

```
while (x < 10)
   x += 2;
```

Because `7 < 10` is true, C# executes the statement `x += 2`, which changes the value of `x` to 9. Remember, this is a `while` statement, so C# again checks the condition, `x < 10`. Because `9 < 10` is still true C# again executes, `x += 2`, giving `x` the value 11. Now checking the condition `x < 10`, C# finds that `11<10` is false, so the execution of the `while` statement is finished.

The `while` statement is a type of **loop**, so called because execution keeps looping back to check the condition after every execution of the `while_true_statement`, which we call the **body** of the loop. The body of the loop could be a block, in which case C# executes every statement in the block while the condition is true. For example, if `x` had the value 5 before the loop, the `while` statement

```
while (x < 10) {
   Console.WriteLine("x is now {0}", x);
   x += 2;
 }
```

would output

```
x is now 5
x is now 7
x is now 9
```

The condition in a `while` statement may evaluate to `false` on the first entry to the loop, in which case C# never executes the body of the loop. For example, if `x` has the value 3 before executing the loop

```
while (x >= 5)
  x -= 4;
```

then the condition, `3 >= 5`, is false, and the loop body, `x -= 4`, is never executed.

Planning Programs Using Pseudocode

With the `while` statement we can solve more interesting problems. However, as problems get more complex, we need to plan our solutions carefully. In this section, we develop a program, Example 3.6, which uses a `while` loop to find and display the sum of test scores inputted by the user.

Before coding, we need to plan our approach. The user will keep entering test scores, which are nonnegative. To signal to the program that no more scores are available the user can enter a negative number, which cannot be a valid score. We call this value a **sentinel**. The program checks each value the user inputs. If it is the sentinel, the program exits the `while` loop and outputs the total of all the scores. If it is not the sentinel the program adds the score to the total. We can use a `while` loop to code these repetitive steps. Informally, we could write the loop as

```
Read the first score;
while (the score is not the sentinel) {
  Add the score to the total so far;
  Read the next score;
}
Output the total of all the scores.
```

We call this informal way of writing the program **pseudocode**. Pseudocode helps us design the C# program. It is easier to understand than the very specific programming language statements, so we can correct logical errors before they get into the actual program.

We can use a flow chart in the same way as pseudocode to show the structure of a program as we develop the detailed solution. For small programs both techniques work well, but for larger programs it becomes cumbersome to manage the flow charts, making pseudocode a better choice.

Pseudocode makes sense. We can execute it mentally with some test data as a further check. Suppose the scores are `56`, `84`, and `75`, and that the user follows them with the sentinel, `-1`. Let us number each line and trace, line by line, how the pseudocode would execute.

Pseudocode

```
1       Read the first score;
2       while ( the score is not the sentinel) {
3            Add the score to the total so far;
4            Read the next score;
5       }
6       Output the total of all the scores.
```

Trace of the pseudocode:

Line Number	Action
1	Read the first score: **56**
2	56 is not the sentinel.
3	Add score to total: total is 56
4	Read the next score: **84**

2	84 is not the sentinel.
3	Add score to total: total is 140
4	Read the next score: **75**
2	75 is not the sentinel.
3	Add score to total: total is 215
4	Read the next score: **−1**
2	−1 is the sentinel.
6	Output the total of 215.

This trace looks correct. We should also check our pseudocode when the user has no scores to enter.

Line Number	Action
1	Read the next score: **−1**
2	−1 is the sentinel.
6	Output the total of ???.

Here we get to line 6 without ever adding any scores to the total. The pseudocode always displays the total, whether or not the user entered any scores. We need to make sure that whenever we get to line 6, we have a total to display. If the user has no scores to enter, we could display zero. To set this initial value for the total, we could add a line at the beginning of the pseudocode, say line 0,

```
0.Initialize the total to zero.
```

that sets the total to zero. Then, if we do not read any scores, we will still have a total to display. Actually, we implicitly use the initial value of total in line 3 after we read the very first score. Line 3 states `add the score to the total so far`, but before reading any scores the total does not have a value unless we give it an initial value in line 0.

If we want to be meticulous, we might want to distinguish between the case when the total is zero because no scores were entered and when it is zero because a bunch of zero scores were entered. More broadly, we might want to keep track of the number of scores entered. Should we do these things or not? In this example, the problem does not explicitly ask to keep track of the number of scores, and for simplicity we will not add this feature now. The problem does not say what to do if no scores are available, but we assume that displaying zero is sensible, and to be sure, we check with the proposer of the problem, who agrees.

We have taken a lot of trouble to design a solution to a simple problem. Because we have been careful, we should be able to convert the pseudocode to a C# program that solves the problem. In this chapter we use a procedural approach. When we start object-oriented programming in Chapter 5, we shall see how to design a solution using an object.

We want to abstract operations that model our understanding of the problem. Looking at the pseudocode, we identify three operations

```
Input a score from the user.
Add the score to the total.
Output the total.
```

If we define a method to implement each of these operations, we can easily translate our pseudocode into an understandable C# program.

We could use any valid identifiers, not keywords, for our method and variable names. To make our program as readable as possible, we choose meaningful names, `GetScore` and `UpdateTotal` for our method names. The `GetScore` method will have a `String` prompt as a parameter. It will return the value the user enters. We will pass the new score and the current total to the `UpdateTotal` method. It will return the updated total.

EXAMPLE 3.6 ■ ScoreSum.cs

```
/*  Uses a while loop to compute the sum of
 *  test scores.
 */

using System;
public class ScoreSum  {

     // returns a score entered by the user
  public static int GetScore(String prompt) {
    Console.Write(prompt);
    return int.Parse(Console.ReadLine());
  }

     /* Input:    The new score and the total so far
      * Output:  The updated total
      */
  public static int UpdateTotal(int newValue, int subTotal) {
                                                         // Note 1
    subTotal += newValue;
    return subTotal;
  }

      // loops until the users enters -1
  public static void Main(String [] args) {
    int total = 0;                              // Sum of scores
                                                         // Note 2
    int score = GetScore("Enter the first score, -1 to quit: ");
    while (score >= 0) {
      total = UpdateTotal(score, total);
      score =  GetScore("Enter the next score, -1 to quit: ");
    }
    Console.WriteLine("The total is {0}", total);
  }
}
```

Run

```
Enter the first score, -1 to quit: 34
Enter the next score, -1 to quit: 45
Enter the next score, -1 to quit: 56
Enter the next score, -1 to quit: -1
The total is 135
```

Note 1: `public static int UpdateTotal(int newValue, int subTotal){`

We choose variable names, `newValue` and `subTotal`, that remind us of the role these quantities play. Our program is easier to understand than if we had used variable names `x` and `y` for these quantities.

Note 2: `int total = 0;`

We initialize `total` to 0, representing the sum of scores before the user has entered any scores. If the user enters the sentinel, −1, before entering any scores, the output will be 0. The C# code closely follows the steps of the pseudocode.

Having completed this program nicely, we might ask about alternative solutions in case another approach might allow us to improve our program. Instead of using a sentinel to signify the end of the input, the user might specify how many scores are available. Then we can have our loop condition check to see if all scores have been entered. If not, the body of the loop reads the next score and adds it to the total. The pseudocode for this approach is

```
Read the quantity of scores to read;
while (number of scores read so far < quantity to read) {
  Read the next score;
  Add the score to the total so far
}
Display the total;
```

Each time around the loop we need to check the condition

```
number of scores read so far < quantity to read.
```

We know how many scores the user will enter. If we have not read that many, there are more scores; otherwise, we have read them all. But how many scores have we read? Let us keep track as we read. We could include another variable, `count`, to hold the number of scores read so far. We initialize `count` to `0`, and each time we read a score, we increase `count` by 1. The revised pseudocode is shown in Figure 3.10.

We leave the next steps in this solution process, which include tracing the execution of the pseudocode with sample data and converting it to a C# program, to the exercises. Note that to solve the problem using this approach, we had to know the quantity of test scores, so we added that to the output to make it more informative.

```
Read the quantity of scores;
while (count < quantity) {
     Read the next score;
     Add the score to the total so far;
     Increment the count of scores;
}
Display the quantity and the total;
```

FIGURE 3.10 **Pseudocode for the sum of test scores problem**

TIP

Think carefully when writing the condition (often called the test) for the `while` loop. Getting it correct can be tricky. In the preceding example we might easily have written `count <= quantity`, which is incorrect because when `count` equals `quantity`, then we have already read all the scores and should terminate the loop rather than ask for another score.

A Little Extra

Input Validation

In Example 3.6, we assumed that the user would enter correct data. Entering a value such as `34.5` or `hat` will cause the program to abort. Later we will introduce exception handling, which we can use to recover from such input errors. Even if the user enters a correct `int` value, that value could be `312017` or `-52`, neither of which is likely to be a test score. We could have prompted the user to enter a value from `0` to `100`, as in

```
Enter a score between 0 and 100
```

Even then a careless user could enter an invalid value.[6]

Style

Do declare each variable on a separate line and use a comment to specify the use of that variable in the program.

Do use meaningful variable names that remind us of the purpose of that variable.

Do precede the program with a comment that describes the intent of the program, and the input and output. This comment is a good place to put the programmer's name and the date. Precede each method with a descriptive comment.

Do include comments to explain any parts of the code that might be difficult to understand. (In our examples, we use Notes at the end of the code for this purpose.)

[6]In the next chapter we will see how to add error-checking code to make our programs more robust.

Loop Termination

Each time the loop condition is `true`, C# executes the loop body. In order for the loop to terminate, something must change that causes the condition to fail. In the loop

```
while ( x < 10)
      x += 2;
```

we add 2 to `x` each time we execute the body. Eventually `x` will become greater than or equal to `10`, so the condition `x < 10` will fail and the loop will terminate.

If we were just to display the value of `x`, and not increase it, then the loop might never stop. For example, if `x` has the value 5 when C# executes the loop

```
while (x < 10)
      Console.WriteLine("x is now {0}", x);
```

the result will be an unending sequence

```
x is now 5
x is now 5
x is now 5
...
```

and so on until someone aborts the program. (Holding the *Control* key down and pressing the *C* key will interrupt the program on Windows systems.)

The last example, repeatedly displaying `x is now 5`, made it easy to spot that something was very wrong. Sometimes an unending loop (often called an **infinite loop**) may have the opposite behavior, showing nothing at all to the user while it goes on computing. For example, if `x` has the value 5, the loop

```
while (x < 10)
  x -= 2;
```

keeps subtracting 2 from `x`, never terminating. The value of `x` is `5`, `3`, `1`, `-1`, `-3`, `-5`, and so on. The condition, `x < 10`, is always true, so the loop keeps on executing, but displays nothing to the user. The programmer's first response is to blame the computer for being very slow, because nothing seems to be happening, but that eerie stillness could be a symptom of an infinite loop. If so, the user must interrupt, aborting the program.

Remember when writing a `while` statement that something must eventually cause the condition to be `false`.

TIP

Beware of loops that never terminate. We use loops because we want repetition, but we must make sure that the repetition stops. Check each loop you write to make sure that it will terminate. ■

Finding the Maximum

We close this section by solving the following problem: "Find the largest of the prices entered. The user will input a sequence of prices, and input a negative item as a sentinel to indicate that input has ended. The program will output the maximum of the prices."

First, let us try to solve the problem informally, supposing that the user inputs 49.23, 16.78, 92.14, 32.75, and −1.00. We want to compare each new price to the maximum price entered so far, to see if the new price is larger. When we get the first price, we have no previous maximum to compare with. But because all the prices are positive numbers, we can initialize our maximum to zero, which is a value smaller than any price.

By initializing the maximum to zero, we can perform the same steps with each price the user inputs. We compare the first price, 49.23, to the initial maximum of 0.0. Because 49.23 is larger than 0.0, we save it as the new maximum. Looking at the second price, 16.78, we see that it is smaller than the current maximum, so we go on. The third item, 92.14, is greater than the current maximum, so we save it as the new maximum. Finding that the fourth item, 32.75, is smaller than the maximum so far, we go on and find that the fifth invoice item is negative, so we stop and output the maximum, which is 92.14.

Our solution works for this example, but will it work for other inputs? Let us try the boundary case, when the user just inputs −1.00, signaling the end of the data. Our first step was to look at the first item and compare it to the initial maximum. We neglected to specify that we first need to check if the value the user input is negative, in which case we quit. Here, if we look at the first item, −1.00, we see that we should quit, perhaps displaying a message that no positive items were input.

The pseudocode is

```
Initialize the maximum to zero.
Input the first price.
while (the price is not the sentinel) {
  Update the maximum.
  Input the next price.
}
Output the maximum.
```

From the pseudocode, we identify three operations:

```
input a price
update the maximum
display the maximum
```

EXAMPLE 3.7 ■ Max.cs

```
/*  Finds the maximum of prices that the user enters.
 *  The user enters a negative value to indicate that
 *  no more data is available. The program displays the
 *  maximum value.
 */

using System;
public class Max {

     /* Input:    The new price and the current maximum price
      * Output: The updated maximum
      */
  public static double UpdateMax
     (double newPrice, double maxSoFar) {
```

```
    if (newPrice > maxSoFar)                              // Note 1
      return newPrice;
    else
      return maxSoFar;
  }

     // returns a double entered by the user
  public static double GetDouble(String prompt) {
    Console.Write(prompt);
    return double.Parse(Console.ReadLine());
  }

     /* Inputs prices until the users enters -1
      * Outputs the maximum of all prices entered.
      */
  public static void Main() {
    double maxSoFar = 0;   // Max of prices entered
                                                           // Note 2
    double price = GetDouble
     ("Enter the first price, -1 to quit: ");    // Note 3
    while (price >=0 ) {
      maxSoFar = UpdateMax(price, maxSoFar);
      price = GetDouble("Enter the next price, -1 to quit: ");
    }
    Console.WriteLine("The maximum is {0}", maxSoFar);
  }
}
```

First run

```
Enter the first price, -1 to quit: 49.23
Enter the next price, -1 to quit: 16.78
Enter the next price, -1 to quit: 92.14
Enter the next price, -1 to quit: 32.75
Enter the next price, -1 to quit: -1
The maximum is 92.14
```

Second run

```
Enter the first price, -1 to quit: -1
The maximum is 0
```

Note 1:
```
if (newPrice > maxSoFar)
   return newPrice;
```

`UpdatePrice` returns the new price if it is greater than the maximum found so far. Otherwise, it returns the current maximum unchanged.

Note 2:

```
double maxSoFar = 0;
```

We initialize `maxSoFar` to 0 because the prices are all nonnegative, so the maximum must be at least 0.

Note 3:

```
double price =
  GetDouble("Enter the first price, -1 to quit: ");
```

We get the first price before entering the loop because the `while` loop checks the price to see if it is the sentinel before trying to update the maximum. We could have simply initialized the price to zero with the declaration

```
double price = 0;
```

The first time we evaluate the loop condition, it would harmlessly check the zero value and go on to read the prices the user enters. By doing this, we would only need to call the `GetDouble` method once in the body of the loop.

The BIG Picture

The `while` statement enables us to repeat steps. We use pseudocode to plan problem solutions carefully. When writing `while` loops, we must make sure that the condition becomes false so the loop terminates.

✓Test Your Understanding

22. How many times will the body of each of following `while` loops be executed if `x` has the value 5 at the start of the loop?

a.
```
while (x <= 10)
  x +=3;
```

b.
```
while (x == 2)
  x -= 7;
```

c.
```
while (x > 1)
  x--;
```

23. Find any errors in the following `while` loops:

a.
```
while (x != 9}
  x +=4;
```

b.
```
while (x)
  x *= 2;
```

c.
```
while (x =! 7)
  x++;
```

24. Trace the execution of the pseudocode in Figure 3.10, assuming test scores of:

a. `95, 46, 68,` and `79`

b. `14, 87, 35, 76,` and `80`

25. Which of the following loops terminate? Assume that `x` has the value `12` at the start of the loop.

a.
```
while (x != 5)
    x++;
```
b.
```
while (x != 5)
    x--;
```
c.
```
while (x != 5)
    x = 5;
```

26. Draw the flow chart for each of the following `while` loops.

a.
```
while(y < 7)
    y += 4;
```
b.
```
while(y > 5) {
    x = y + 10;
    y --;
}
```
c.
```
while (z != 0) {
    x = 4 * z;
    z++;
}
```

27. Develop a solution in pseudocode to the problem of looking up a number in the telephone directory.

28. Develop a solution in pseudocode to the problem of finding the minimum of a sequence of nonnegative numbers entered by the user, where the user enters a negative number to terminate the input.

29. Trace the execution of the pseudocode preceding Example 3.7 for finding the maximum of numbers input by the user, with the input data `49.23`, `16.789`, `92.145`, `32.7`, and `-1`.

30. Develop a solution in pseudocode to the problem of finding the maximum of a sequence of nonnegative numbers entered by the user. In this solution, before reading the numbers, ask the user to enter how many numbers will be input.

31. Develop a solution in pseudocode to the problem of finding both the maximum and the minimum of a sequence of nonnegative numbers entered by the user. In this solution, before reading the numbers, ask the user to input how many numbers will be input.

32. Develop a solution in pseudocode to the problem of counting the number of negative numbers in a sequence of numbers the user inputs. In this solution, before reading the numbers, ask the user to input how many numbers will be input. (Example: For input `32`, `76`, `-12`, `49`, `-11`, and `-3` the output should be that there are three negative numbers.)

3.5 DEBUGGING

Following the careful problem-solving methods described in the last section will help us to produce programs free from errors. Hasty coding before developing a careful solution is much more likely to lead to errors. In this section, we discuss some simple approaches to debugging, finding, and correcting any errors in the program.

We seek to correct errors in logic in a program that compiles but either aborts with an error message while running or produces incorrect results. Those learning a new language or with little prior programming experience make many syntax errors, writing C# statements and expressions incorrectly, as part of the learning process. The compiler catches these syntax errors and provides messages to help the programmer correct the syntax.

Our examples in this section compile but do not produce the desired results. We suggest some simple techniques for finding and correcting the observed errors. We take a simple problem to sum the squares of the integers from 1 to a high value entered by the user. Example 3.8 is an attempted solution.

EXAMPLE 3.8 ■ Mistake1.cs

```
/* Incorrect attempt to sum the squares of
 * numbers from 1 to a high value entered
 * by the user
 */

using System;
public class Mistake1 {

    // Use a loop to compute a sum of squares
  public static void Main() {
    int sum = 0;                // Current value to square and add
    int count = 1;
    Console.Write("Enter the number of squares to sum: ");
    int high = int.Parse(Console.ReadLine());
    while (count <= high)
       sum += count*count;
    Console.WriteLine("The sum of the first {0} squares is {1}",
                       high, sum);
  }
}
```

■

Getting Information

When we run Example 3.8, we find that there is no output. Nothing happens, and the program does not terminate. We must abort the program. Reading the code, we see that the `WriteLine` statement comes after the `while` loop. Because the `WriteLine` statement never is executed, it seems like the `while` loop is not terminating. To see more clearly what is happening we add a `WriteLine` statement in the body of the loop.

EXAMPLE 3.9 ■ Mistake2.cs

```
/* Adds a WriteLine statement in the body of
 * the while loop of Example 3.8
 */

using System;
public class Mistake2 {
```

```
    // Use a loop to compute a sum of squares
  public static void Main() {
    int sum = 0;
    int count = 1;     // Current value to square and add
    Console.Write("Enter the number of squares to sum: ");
    int high = int.Parse(Console.ReadLine());
    while (count <= high) {                            // Note 1
      sum += count*count;
      Console.WriteLine("Sum is {0}", sum);
    }
    Console.WriteLine("The sum of the first {0} squares is {1}",
                      high, sum);
  }
}
```

Run

```
Sum is 1
Sum is 2
Sum is 3
.....(nonterminating)
```

Note 1: `while (count <= high) {`

We make the `while` loop body a block, enclosing the two statements in curly braces. We did not need the curly braces in Example 3.8 because the `while` loop body was a single assignment statement.

The output of Example 3.9 continues until we abort the program. It is clear that the `while` loop does not terminate. Looking more closely at the code, we see that we forgot to increment `count` after adding the next square to the sum.

EXAMPLE 3.10 ■ Mistake3.cs

```
/* Modifies Example 3.9 to increment the count.
 */

using System;
public class Mistake3 {

    // Use a loop to compute a sum of squares
  public static void Main() {
    int sum = 0;
    int count = 1;         // Current value to square and add
    Console.Write("Enter the number of squares to sum: ");
```

```
      int high = int.Parse(Console.ReadLine());
      while (count <= high) {
        sum += count*count;
        count++;
      }
      Console.WriteLine("The sum of the first {0} squares is {1}",
                        high, sum);
    }
  }
```

Run

```
Enter the number of squares to sum: 5
The sum of the first 5 squares is 55
```

■

Testing Carefully

The output looks correct. Checking it by hand, we see that the sum of the first five squares, `1 + 4 + 9 + 16 + 25`, is indeed 55. It is tempting to conclude that our program is correct, but we should never make such a conclusion based on one test case. Let us do some more testing, trying larger high values such as 100, 1000, and 10,000. The output of these tests is

```
Enter the number of squares to sum:  100
The sum of the first 100 squares is 338350

Enter the number of squares to sum:  1000
The sum of the first 1000 squares is 333833500

Enter the number of squares to sum:  10000
The sum of the first 10000 squares is -1624114088
```

Surely, something is wrong here. The sum of the first 10,000 squares is certainly not negative. Remember that the `int` type can hold values up to 2,147,483,647. Trying to store values larger than 2,147,483,647 will give spurious results.

We leave it to the exercises to determine the largest number of squares we can sum correctly using the program of Example 3.10. The debugging techniques we illustrated in these examples are:

- `Read the code carefully to determine where the error might be located`. In Example 3.8 we could tell from reading the code that the error was in the `while` loop.
- `Add WriteLine statements to get more information`. The added `WriteLine` statement in Example 3.9 clearly demonstrated the error.
- `Test thoroughly`. Even though our first result was correct, more extensive testing of Example 3.10 found an error.

Using the Visual Studio .Net Debugger

Many development environments include a debugger, which is an application used to debug a program. We illustrate with the Visual Studio .Net debugger using Example 3.8.

After opening Visual Studio .Net, we click on *File*, *Open*, *File* and select `Mistake1.cs`. We click on *File, Add Project, New Project* choosing `Visual C# Project` as the project type and `Empty Project` as the template. We enter a project name, choose a directory, and click *OK*. We click on *File, Move Mistake1.cs into Project* to enter our file in the project.

To compile, we click on *Build*, *Build Solution*, enter *Mistake* as the file name, and click *Save*. To see in detail how the program is executing, we execute it one step at a time, by clicking on *Debug*, *Step Over*. Choosing *Step Over* executes a method call without executing each line of the method. To execute each line of the method we would use *Step Into* instead. The *Step Into* choice is useful if the error occurs inside a method call. Hovering the mouse over a variable name in the code will pop up a box containing the current value of that variable.

Figure 3.11 shows the Visual Studio display after we first press *Debug*, *Step Over*. The lower-left section shows the values of the variables. The upper-left section shows the source code with an arrow pointed to the line to be executed next.

We can set a breakpoint by clicking in the margin next to the line at which we want to interrupt execution. We can then execute until we reach the breakpoint without having to execute each line up to that point. In this example we click to the left of the statement

```
sum += count*count;
```

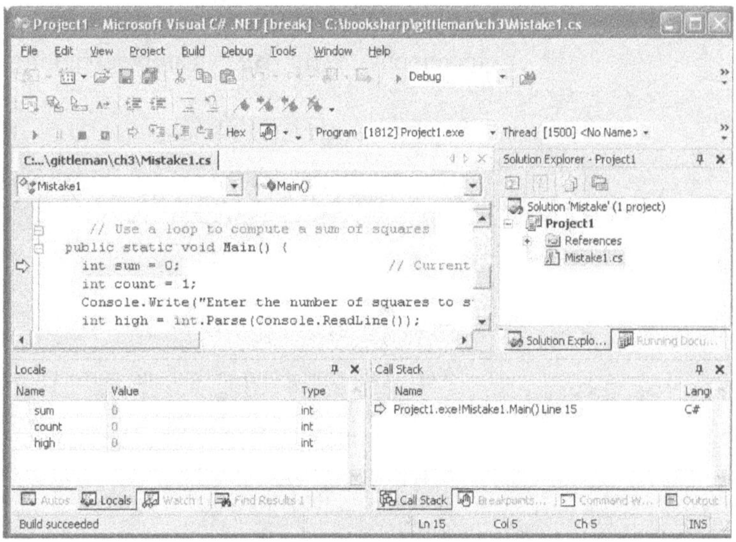

FIGURE 3.11 **Debugging Mistake1.cs**

FIGURE 3.12
Corrected Mistake1.cs

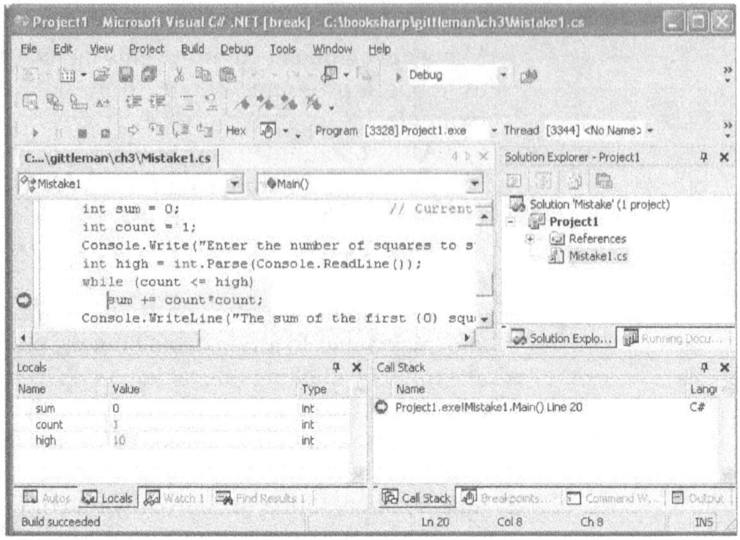

Then we click on *Debug*, *Continue* to continue executing until we reach the breakpoint. A console window opens and we enter 10 as the number of squares to sum. Execution stops at the screen shown in Figure 3.12. The upper-left window shows that the next line to execute is our breakpoint. The value of sum is 0, count is 1, and high is 10.

We now click on *Debug*, *Step Over* repeatedly to continue executing the program one line at a time. The first click changes sum to 1 and returns to the `while` test. Clicking *Debug*, *Step Over* two more times has the `while` test succeeding and sum changing to 2. We see that the program is not executing properly because we did not increment `count`. We can stop debugging and edit our program to add the line

```
count++;
```

to the `while` loop. When we recompile and rerun the program we see that it now computes the sum as we expected.

> **The BIG Picture**
>
> We debug a program to find and correct errors. Simple techniques include reading the program carefully, adding `WriteLine` statements to display values, and testing the program thoroughly. A debugger allows us to execute one statement at a time so we can watch changes in the values of variables. We can set a breakpoint to stop execution at a particular point.

✓Test Your Understanding

Try It Yourself ➤ **33.** Run Example 3.10 to find the largest value, *n*, such that Example 3.10 finds the sum of the first *n* squares correctly.

Try It Yourself ➤ **34.** Modify Example 3.10 to inform the user of the largest acceptable input in the prompt and to reject any input greater than that value.

SUMMARY

- In this chapter we develop the tools to solve problems using C#. To make our programs more flexible, we need to make decisions based on the value of a test condition that can be either true or false. C# provides the `bool` type, which has values `True` and `False`. We write our test conditions as relational or equality expressions. The relational expressions use the operators <, >, <=, and >= and produce `bool` values. The equality expressions use the operators == and != and also produce `bool` values. We can include arithmetic operators in our test conditions. C# will use precedence rules to help evaluate such expressions, with arithmetic expressions having higher precedence than relational expressions.
- Once we know how to write a test condition, we use the `if` and `if-else` statements to make choices based on the result of a test condition. In the `if` statement we execute the next statement if the condition is true and skip it if the condition is false. The `if-else` statement gives us two alternative statements, one to execute if the test condition is true and the other to execute if the test condition is false. Each of these statements can be a simple statement or a code block enclosed by curly braces. Flow charts give a visual representation of the control flow.
- The `if` and `if-else` statements give us choices in control flow. We discuss decimal numbers and the type `double` to add a choice of data in addition to the `int` type covered in Chapter 2. We can use scientific notation to express decimals, so we can write .000000645 as 6.45E-7. The type `double` represents decimal numbers with 15-digit accuracy. We can declare variables of type `double` and perform the usual arithmetic operations of +, -, *, and /.
- C# displays numbers of type `double` using the F format for fixed-point notation and the E format for scientific notation. The G, or general, format chooses one or the other depending on the size of the number. We can specify the number of places after the decimal point.
- If an operator, say +, has one `int` operand and one `double` operand, then C# will convert the `int` operand to a `double`, and add, producing a result of type `double`. C# will not automatically convert a `double` to an `int`, but we can use an explicit type cast should we need this conversion.
- To complete our set of basic control structures we have the `while` loop to handle repetition. While the test condition is true, C# repeats the body of the `while` loop, which can be either a simple C# statement or a block enclosed by curly braces.

- With the ability to do one statement after another in sequence, the `if` and `if-else` statements to make choices, and the `while` statement for repetition, we can solve complex problems. For clarity, we use pseudocode, a program-like notation showing the three control structures of sequence, choice, and repetition, but expressing the refinements informally in English.
- To debug our programs, finding and correcting any errors, we read our code carefully, inserting `WriteLine` statements to get more information, and testing our code thoroughly. A debugger lets us single-step execution and set breakpoints.

SKILL BUILDER EXERCISES

1. What will the following program fragment output?

```
int x=10, y=12, r;
if (y > x) {
   int t = y;
   y = x;
   x = t;
}
while (y != 0) {
    r = x % y;
    x = y;
    y = r;
}
Console.WriteLine(x);
```

2. Select the output on the right produced from the statement on the left.

a. `Console.WriteLine(3.0/2);`	**i.** 67.5
b. `Console.WriteLine(30*45E-1/2);`	**ii.** 1.5000000000000000
c. `Console.WriteLine(3*.000045/2)`	**iii.** 6.75E1
	iv. 6.75E-05
	v. 1.5
	vi. .0000675

3. Write C# statements that will

a. write `x > y` if `x` is greater than `y` and write `y >= x` otherwise.

b. loop while `x` is greater than 10, each time decreasing `x` by `2`.

CRITICAL THINKING EXERCISES

4. Which of the following correctly lists the sequence of statements that C# executes given the following code fragment?

```
1.     int  x = 1, y = 4;
2.     if (x >= 2)
```

```
3.      x = 7;
4.      y = 9;
5.      x = 8;
```

   a. 1, 2, 3, 4, 5
   b. 1, 2, 5
   c. 1, 2, 4, 5
   d. 1, 2, 3, 5
   e. none of the above

5. Removing which of the following lines will make the result a legal C# program fragment?

```
1.      int  x = 7;
2.      int  y;
3.      if (x <= 10)
4.        x = 9;
5.        y = 3;
6.      else
7.        x = 12;
```

   a. 5 and 6
   b. 5
   c. 2 and 5
   d. all of the above
   e. none of the above

6. How many times does the body of the following `while` statement get executed?

```
int x = 3;
while (x < 9)
  x += 2;
x++;
```

   a. 6
   b. 3
   c. 4
   d. 9
   e. none of the above

7. The following program is supposed to output the sum of the integers 1 through 10. Choose the statement that best describes the result.

```
public class Sum  {
  public static void Main() {
    int x = 0;
    int total = 0;
```

```
    while ( x < 10) {
      total += x;
    }
    Console.WriteLine
        ("The sum of 1 through 10 is {0}", total);
  }
}
```

a. The output will be correct.

b. The output will be correct, but an extra zero was added at first.

c. There will be no output.

d. The output will be too small.

DEBUGGING EXERCISE

8. The following program is supposed to find the total sales tax paid when making purchases in county A, in which the total sales tax is 4%, and in county B, in which the sales tax is 5.5%. The user first inputs the prices, excluding sales tax, of all purchases in county A, terminated by a negative value, then inputs the prices of all purchases in county B, excluding sales tax, terminated by a negative value. The program should output the total sales tax paid. Find and fix any errors in this program.

```
public class SalesTax {
  public static void Main() {
    double taxA = .05, taxB= .04;
    Console.Write
       ("Enter a purchase price in County A, -1 to quit");
    double priceA = double.Parse(Console.ReadLine());
    double totalA = 0.0, totalB = 0.0;
    while (priceA >= 0) {
      totalA += priceA;
      Console.Write
       ("Enter a purchase price in County A, -1 to quit");
      priceA = double.Parse(Console.ReadLine());
    }
    while (priceB >= 0) {
      totalB += priceB;
      Console.Write
       ("Enter a purchase price in County B, -1 to quit");
      priceB = double.Parse(Console.ReadLine());
    }
    double tax = priceA*taxA + priceB*taxB;
    Console.WriteLine
          ("The total sales tax is {0:C}", tax);
  }
}
```

9. Write a C# program that computes the weekly pay for an employee. Input the number of hours worked. The employee receives $7.50 per hour for the first 40 hours and $11.25 per hour for each additional hour. Create test data before coding and running the program.

10. Write a C# program that checks a grade point average the user inputs, and outputs `Congratulations, You made the honor roll` if the average is 3.5 and above, but outputs `Sorry, You are on probation` if the average is below 2.0.

11. Write a C# program that inputs the prices of a box of cereal and a quart of milk at store A and the prices of the same items at store B. The program should output the total cost of three boxes of cereal and two quarts of milk at whichever store has the lower cost. Either store is acceptable if the cost is the same at both.

12. Write a C# program to make change. Enter the cost of an item that is less than one dollar. Output the coins given as change, using quarters, dimes, nickels, and pennies. Use the fewest coins possible. For example, if the item cost 17 cents, the change would be three quarters, one nickel, and three pennies.

13. Write a C# program to convert kilograms to pounds or ounces. There are .45359237 kilograms in one pound, and 16 ounces in one pound. If the weight is less than one pound, just report the number of ounces. Thus 3.4 kilograms converts to 7.4957 pounds, and .4 kilograms converts to 14.1096 ounces.

14. Write a C# program to convert meters to feet or inches. There are 39.37 inches in one meter and 12 inches in a foot. If the length is less than 1 foot, just report the number of inches. Show two digits after the decimal point. Thus 3.4 meters converts to 11.15 feet, and .2 meter converts to 7.87 inches.

15. Write a C# program to find the sum of the test scores input by the user. Use the pseudocode of Figure 3.10, in which the user inputs the number of test scores and each score.

16. Write a C# program to find the minimum of a sequence of nonnegative numbers entered by the user, where the user enters a negative number to terminate the input. (Use the pseudocode from Test Your Understanding, question 28.)

17. Write a C# program to find the maximum of a sequence of nonnegative numbers entered by the user. In this solution, before reading the numbers, ask the user to input how many numbers will be input. (Use the pseudocode from Test Your Understanding, question 30.)

18. Write a C# program to find both the maximum and the minimum of a sequence of nonnegative numbers entered by the user. In this solution, before reading the numbers, ask the user to input how many numbers will be input. (Use the pseudocode from Test Your Understanding, question 31.)

19. Write a C# program to count the number of negative numbers in a sequence of numbers the user inputs. In this solution, before reading the numbers, ask the user to input how many numbers will be input. For example: For input 32, 76, −12, 49, −11, and −3 the output should be that there are three negative numbers. (Use the pseudocode from Test Your Understanding, question 32.)

20. Write a C# program to find the average of a sequence of nonnegative numbers entered by the user, where the user enters a negative number to terminate the input.

21. Suppose you have an account that earns 5% interest that is credited to your account at the end of each year. Write a C# program to calculate the number of years it will take before the account balance is at least $2000 if the initial account balance is $1000.

22. Generalize Exercise 21 by having the user enter the interest rate, the initial balance, and the final balance. Write a C# program to calculate the number of years it will take before the account balance reaches the specified final balance.

23. Suppose an annual inflation rate of 4%. Because of inflation, an item that costs $1.00 today will cost $1.04 one year from now. (We assume, for simplicity, that the item we consider will rise in price exactly at the rate of inflation.) Write a C# program that inputs the cost of an item and outputs its cost three years from now.

24. Generalize Exercise 23 by having the user input the annual inflation rate, the cost of the item, and the number of years. Write a C# program that outputs the cost of that item after the specified number of years.

25. Suppose you borrow $1000 at 12% annual interest and make monthly payments of $100. Write a C# program to calculate how many months it will take to pay off this loan. (Each month you pay interest on the remaining balance. The interest rate is 1% per month, so the first month you pay $10 interest and $90 goes to reduce the balance to $910. The next month's interest is $9.10, and $90.90 is applied to reduce the balance, and so on. The last month's payment may be less than $100.)

26. Generalize Exercise 25 by having the user input the loan amount, the annual interest rate, and the monthly payment.

4 More Control Structures and Types

In Chapters 2 and 3 we covered the essential concepts needed to start solving problems with C#. With the types `int` and `double`, the assignment, and `if-else` and `while` statements we can solve complex problems. But this is a bare bones set of tools. A good carpenter can do some fine construction with a few tools, but will be much more productive with a variety of tools to make the job easier. In this chapter, we will add some tools to build C# programs more easily.

Logical operators make it easier to use tests that are more complex, such as

```
I am hungry and I am thirsty
```

which is true if `I am hungry` and `I am thirsty` are both true.

The `if-else` statement lets us choose between two alternatives. Nested `if` statements and `switch` statements expand our choices to multiple alternatives. The `while` statement repeats while a condition is true. The `for` statement and the `do` statement make it easier to handle repetition.

We use the `int` and `double` types most frequently, but C# provides additional primitive types, including `long`, `float`, `decimal`, and `char`, which can sometimes be useful.

In addition to the statements and types in the C# language, C# libraries provide a wide range of methods to create user interfaces, connect across a network, and generally make C# a more powerful tool. In this chapter we look at the collection of methods in the Math library, which allow us to find powers, roots, maxima, minima, and evaluate natural logarithms and other functions.

Our problem-solving case study uses these topics to design a program to convert lengths between the English and Metric systems. We use this case study to introduce good software engineering techniques.

OBJECTIVES

- Use logical operators
- Learn useful selection and repetition statements
- Use additional primitive types and operators
- Use the Math library
- Build software using an iterative development cycle

4.1 THE AND, OR, AND NOT OPERATORS

The C# conditional operators express the familiar AND and OR operations, which we can use to write conditions such as

```
John's age is greater than 20 AND John's age is less than 35.
John's height is greater than 78.5 OR John's weight is
greater than 300.
```

Figure 4.1 shows the C# symbols for the conditional operators.

Note that the operands of the conditional operators have type `bool`. The expression `age > 20` is either true or false, and so is `age < 35`.

TIP: The `&&` and `||` operators use two-character symbols that must be typed without any space between them. Using `& &` instead of `&&` would give an error.

Conditional AND

The conditional AND expression `(age > 20) && (age < 35)` will be true only when both of its operands are true, and false otherwise. If the variable `age` has the value 25, both operands are true, and the whole `&&` expression is true. If age has the value 17, the first operand, `age > 20` is false, and the whole `&&` expression is false. Figure 4.2 shows some sample evaluations of a conditional AND expression, illustrating how the value of an `&&` expression depends on the values of its arguments.

Note that when the first operand is false, as it is when `age` is 17, we know that the conditional AND is false without even checking the value of the second operand.

FIGURE 4.1
Conditional operators

Symbol	*Meaning*	*Example*
`&&`	conditional AND	`(age > 20) && (age < 35)`
`||`	conditional OR	`(height > 78.5) || (weight > 300)`

FIGURE 4.2
Evaluating an example of a conditional AND expression

age	*age > 20*	*age < 35*	*age > 20 && age < 35*
10	false	true	false
25	true	true	true
40	true	false	false

Conditional OR

The conditional OR expression `(height > 78.5) || (weight > 300)` is true if either one of its operands is true, or if both are true. If height has the value 72 and weight has the value 310, then the first operand is false and the second operand is true, so the `||` expression is true. Figure 4.3 shows some sample evaluations of a conditional OR expression, illustrating how the value of an `||` expression depends on the values of its arguments.

Logical Complement

C# uses the symbol `!` for the logical complement, or NOT, operator, which has only one operand. The logical complement negates the value of its operand, as Figure 4.4 shows.

If the `bool` variable, `on`, has the value `true`, then `!on` is false, but if `on` is false, then `!on` is true. Example 4.1 allows the user to enter different values of height and weight and displays the value of conditional AND, conditional OR, and logical complement expressions.

To make our programs easier to read, we abstracted some input and output methods in an IO class. We used several of these methods in Chapter 3 examples. We include the code for the IO class that contains these methods in an addendum

FIGURE 4.3
Evaluating an example of a conditional OR expression

height	*weight*	*height > 78.5*	*weight > 300*	*(height>78.5) || (weight>300)*
62	125	false	false	false
80	250	true	false	true
72	310	false	true	true
80	325	true	true	true

FIGURE 4.4
Evaluating a logical complement expression

A	*!A*
true	false
false	true

at the end of this chapter. Using the IO class is just a convenience. With a loss of readability, we could copy the code for each method instead.

When using the .NET Framework SDK, we compile `Measure.cs` using the command

```
csc /r:IO.dll Measure.cs
```

where the `/r` option indicates that `Measure.cs` references the file `IO.dll` containing the compiled code for the `IO` class. When using Visual Studio .NET, we first create a new project. Then click on *Project, Add, Add Existing Item* to add `Measure.cs` to the project. We click on *Project, Add Reference* to add the `IO.dll` file containing the IO library.

EXAMPLE 4.1 ■ Measure.cs

```
/*  Evaluates AND, OR, and NOT expressions
 *  involving height and weight measurements.
 */

using System;
public class Measure {

     /* Inputs a height and a weight.
      * Computes boolean-valued expressions.
      */
  public static void Main() {
    double height =
      IO.GetDouble("Enter a height in inches: ");       // Note 1
    double weight = IO.GetDouble("Enter a weight in pounds: ");
    Console.Write("height < 65 && weight < 130 is ");  // Note 2
    Console.WriteLine((height < 65) && (weight  < 130));
    Console.Write("height < 65 || weight  < 130 is ");
    Console.WriteLine((height < 65) || (weight  < 130));
    bool heavy = (weight > 250);                        // Note 3
    Console.WriteLine("heavy is " + heavy);
    Console.WriteLine("!heavy is " + !heavy);
  }
}
```

First run

```
Enter a height in inches: 68
Enter a weight in pounds: 125
height < 65 && weight < 130 is False
height < 65 || weight  < 130 is True
heavy is False
!heavy is True
```

Second run

```
Enter a height in inches: 70
Enter a weight in pounds: 260
height < 65 && weight < 130 is False
height < 65 || weight  < 130 is False
heavy is True
!heavy is False
```

Note 1:

```
double height = \
  IO.GetDouble("Enter a height in inches: ");
```

We can enter a decimal number such as 62.5 or an integer such as 68, which C# will convert to a `double`. See the addendum at the end of this chapter for the code for the `IO.getDouble` method.

Note 2:

```
Console.Write("height < 65 && weight < 130 is ");
```

This statement displays the description of the expression, and the next statement displays the value of the expression.

Note 3:

```
bool heavy = (weight > 250);
```

The variable `heavy` holds the value of the condition, `weight > 250`. This is often how we use the NOT operator. We call these conditions **flags**, meaning that they send a signal. In this example, the flag `heavy` signals that the weight is over 250.

Short-circuiting

Both A and B must be true in order for `A && B` to be true. If A is false, C# knows that `A && B` is false without even evaluating B. Thus when A is false, C# does not bother to evaluate B, so we do not care what the value of B is. We say that C# short-circuits the evaluation by not evaluating the second argument when it already knows the value of the expression.[1] In general, Figure 4.5 shows how the value of a conditional AND expression, `A && B`, depends on the value of its operands, A and B.

FIGURE 4.5
Evaluating a conditional AND expression

A	*B*	*A && B*
true	true	true
true	false	false
false	(don't care)	false

[1]This short-circuiting behavior is the reason this operator is called the `conditional` AND, not simply AND. It evaluates the second argument on the condition that the first is true.

FIGURE 4.6
Evaluating a conditional OR expression

A	*B*	*A* || *B*
true	(don't care)	true
false	true	true
false	false	false

Either A or B, or both, must be true for `A || B` to be true. If A is true, C# knows that `A || B` is true without even evaluating B. Thus when A is true, C# does not bother to evaluate B, so we do not care what the value of B is. As with the conditional AND operator, C# short-circuits the evaluation by not evaluating the second argument when it already knows the value of the expression. In general, Figure 4.6 shows how the value of a conditional OR expression, `A || B`, depends on the value of its operands, A and B.

Operator Precedence

The conditional AND and conditional OR operators have lower precedence[2] than the relational and equality operators, as shown in Figure 4.7, where we show operators of equal precedence on the same line.

Remember that C# follows precedence rules in evaluating expressions, with the higher precedence operators getting their arguments first. In the expression

```
(age > 20) && (age < 35)
```

FIGURE 4.7
Operator precedence

Highest	
NOT	!
multiplicative	* / %
additive	+ -
relational	< > <= >=
equality	== !=
conditional AND	&&
conditional OR	||
assignment	= += -= *= /= %=
Lowest	

[2]See Appendix C for the complete operator precedence table.

we can omit the parentheses, writing it as

```
age > 20  && age < 35
```

The < and > operators have higher precedence than the `&&` operator, so C# will first evaluate `age > 20`. If `age > 20` is false, C# will short-circuit the evaluation, knowing that the result of the `&&` operation must be false. If `age > 20` is true, then C# will evaluate `age < 35` to determine the value of the `&&` expression.

Similarly, we can omit the parentheses in

```
(height > 78.5) || (weight > 300)
```

writing it as

```
height > 78.5 || weight > 300
```

The operator > has higher precedence than `||`, so C# will evaluate `height > 78.5` first. If `height > 78.5`, then the result of the `OR` operation, `||`, will be true, and C# will short-circuit the evaluation. If `height > 78.5` is false, C# will evaluate `weight > 300` to determine the value of the `||` expression.

The logical complement operator has higher precedence than the arithmetic, relational, equality, and conditional operators. We must include parentheses in the expression

```
!(x < 10)
```

because we want C# to evaluate the relational expression `x < 10`, and then apply the `NOT` operator, `!`. If we write

```
!x < 10
```

then, because `!` has higher precedence than <, C# will try to evaluate `!x` which will give an error, because the variable `x` is an integer, and NOT operates on `bool` values, not on integers.

Style

Use parentheses, even when not necessary, if they help to make the steps in the evaluation of the expression clearer, but omit them if they add too much clutter, making the expression harder to read. In Example 4.1, we chose to include the parentheses for clarity. Some programmers find it helpful to use parentheses always.

To show the use of the conditional `AND` in a program, we modify Example 3.6, which computes the sum of test scores, to add only those scores between zero and 100.

EXAMPLE 4.2 ■ Zero100.cs

```
/*  Uses a while loop to compute the sum of
 *  valid test scores.
 */
```

```
using System;
public class Zero100  {

    /* Input:   The new score and the total so far
     * Output:  The updated total
     */
  public static int UpdateTotal(int newValue, int subTotal) {
    subTotal += newValue;
    return subTotal;
  }

     /* Sums scores between 0 and 100.
      * Exits when the user enters a value
      * out of that range.
      */
  public static void Main() {
    int total = 0;                              // Sum of scores
    int score =
      IO.GetInt("Enter the first score (0-100), -1 to quit: ");
    while (score >= 0  && score <= 100) {               // Note 1
      total = UpdateTotal(score, total);
      score =  IO.GetInt
               ("Enter the next score (0-100), -1 to quit: ");
    }
    Console.WriteLine("The total is {0}", total);
  }
}
```

Run

```
Enter the first score (0-100), -1 to quit: 72
Enter the next score (0-100), -1 to quit: 65
Enter the next score (0-100), -1 to quit: 122
The total is 137
```

■

Note 1: `while (score >= 0  && score <= 100) {`

We check that the score is between zero and 100 before adding it to the total.

TIP

Using an `OR` instead of an `AND` in Example 4.2 would not give the desired result. The expression `(score >= 0)||(score <= 100)` is true whenever either the score is greater than zero or less than 100, so any score makes it true. ■

Combining AND with OR

We can use both the && and || operators in the same expression, as in:

```
age > 50 && (height > 78.5 || height < 60)
```

where we need the parentheses because the AND operator has higher precedence than the OR operator. Without parentheses, as in

```
age > 50 && height > 78.5 || height < 60
```

C# will evaluate the expression as if we had written it as:

```
(age > 50 && height > 78.5) || height < 60
```

which is not what we intended.

A Little Extra

De Morgan's Laws

Two useful rules for working with logical expression are named after a British mathematician, Augustus De Morgan (1806–1871). They state

```
!(A && B) = !A || !B
```

and

```
!(A || B) = !A && !B
```

The BIG Picture

The &&, ||, and ! operators allow us to use logical expressions in our programs. Conditional AND and OR short-circuit, only evaluating their second arguments when necessary to determine the value of the expression.

✓Test Your Understanding

1. For each expression, find values for x and y that make it true.
   a. `(x == 2) && (y > 4)`
   b. `(x <= 5) || (y >= 5)`
   c. `x > 10 || y != 5`
   d. `x > 10  &&  y < x + 4`
2. For each expression in question 1, find values for x and y that make it false.
3. For each expression in question 1, find values for x that allow C# to short-circuit the evaluation and not evaluate the right-hand argument. What is the value of the conditional expression?
4. For each expression in question 1, find values for x that require C# to evaluate the right-hand argument.
5. For each expression, find a value for x that makes it true.

a. `!(x == 5)`

b. `! (x <= 10)`

c. `!(x > 10 && x < 50)`

d. `!(x == 5 || x > 8)`

6. For each expression in question 5, find a value for x that makes it false.
7. Omit any unnecessary parentheses from the following expressions.

a. `((a > 1) || (c == 5))`

b. `((x < (y+5)) && (y > 2))`

c. `!((x >2)||(y != 8))`

4.2 NESTED ifS AND THE switch STATEMENT

With the `if-else` statement, we can choose between two alternatives. In this section we show two ways to choose between multiple alternatives, nested `if` statements and the `switch` statement.

Nested if Statements

Suppose we grade test scores so that 60–79 earns a C, 80–89 earns a B, and 90–100 earns an A. Given a test score between 60 and 100, we can determine the grade by first checking if the score is between 60 and 79 or higher, using the `if-else` statement of Figure 4.8.

This `if-else` statement only chooses between the two alternatives, grades C and B or better. To choose between the three alternatives, grades A, B, or C, we nest another `if-else` statement as the body of the `else-part` of our original `if-else` statement.

The code in Figure 4.9 has a problem. If we assume that a score is always between 60 and 100, then the code does what we expect, but let us trace the code if the score has a value of 40. Then the first test, `score >=60 && score < 80`, fails, so we execute the `else-part`, which is a nested `if-else` statement. Its condition, `score >= 80 && score < 90`, also fails, so we execute the `else-part`, which indicates that a score of 40 receives an A grade, not what we expect.

We can improve the code of Figure 4.9 by nesting an `if` statement in the last `else-part` to check that the score is really between 90 and 100, as shown in Figure 4.10.

```
if (score >= 60 && score < 80)
  Console.WriteLine("Score " + score + " receives a C");
else
  Console.WriteLine("Score " + score + " receives a B or an A");
```

FIGURE 4.8 **`if-else` statement to choose between two alternatives**

```
if (score >= 60 && score < 80)
  Console.WriteLine("Score " + score + " receives a C");
else if (score >=80 && score < 90)
   Console.WriteLine("Score " + score + " receives a B");
else
   Console.WriteLine("Score " + score + "receives an A");
```

FIGURE 4.9 **Nested `if-else` statement to choose among three alternatives**

```
if (score >= 60 && score < 80)
  Console.WriteLine("Score " + score + " receives a C");
else if (score >=80 && score < 90)
   Console.WriteLine("Score " + score + " receives a B");
else if (score >= 90 && score <= 100)
   Console.WriteLine("Score " + score + "receives an A");
```

FIGURE 4.10 **Improved version of Figure 4.9**

We see that using nested `if-else` statements allows us, in this example, to choose among three alternatives:

```
scores between 60 and 79
scores between 80 and 89
scores between 90 and 100
```

Figure 4.10 illustrates the style for nested `if-else` statements to choose from multiple alternatives. Figure 4.11 shows the general pattern.

```
if ( Is it the first alternative? ){
    First alternative code
} else if ( Is it the second alternative? ) {
    Second alternative code
}
  ...
}else if ( Is it the last alternative? ) {
     Last alternative code
}else {
     Code when none of the above alternatives is true
}
```

FIGURE 4.11 **Choosing from multiple alternatives**

FIGURE 4.12
Flow chart for nested `if-else` statements

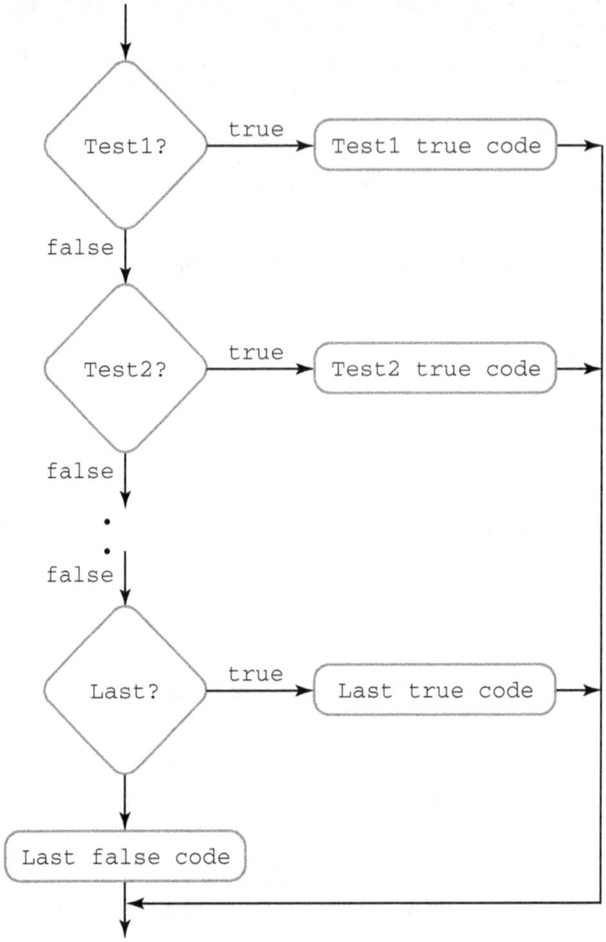

Figure 4.12 shows the flow chart for the nested `if-else` statement with the optional `else-part` at the end.

TIP

If you use code like that in Figure 4.9, having a final `else` with no nested `if`, then be sure that the code in the final `else` does handle everything else, that is, every case that does not come under one of the tested alternatives in the preceding `if` statements. ■

Pairing `else` with `if`

Without an additional rule, we cannot always determine how to read nested `if` statements. For example, contrast Figure 4.13 with Figure 4.14.

In Figure 4.13 we would like to pair `else` with the first `if`, but in Figure 4.14 we would like to pair the `else` with the second `if`. Unfortunately, aligning the `else` under the first `if` in Figure 4.13 will not achieve the outcome we want. As we know, C# does

```
if (score >= 60)
  if (score >= 80)
    Console.WriteLine("You got a B or an A");
else
  Console.WriteLine("You got a D or an F"); // Wrong pairing
```

FIGURE 4.13 **Incorrect attempt to pair an `else` with an `if`**

```
if (score >= 60)
  if (score >= 80)
    Console.WriteLine("You got a B or an A");
  else
    Console.WriteLine("You got a C");    // Correct pairing
```

FIGURE 4.14 **Corrected pairing of `else` and `if`**

not consider spacing significant, so both examples will produce the same result. C# uses the rule that pairs an `else` with the nearest `if`. Figure 4.14 is the correct version, and would be correct even if we typed the `else` under the first `if`, as in Figure 4.13.

Both Figures 4.13 and 4.14 are `if` statements with nested `if-else` statements. What we tried to do in Figure 4.13 was write an `if-else` statement whose `if-part` contained a nested `if` statement. To do that, we need to enclose the nested `if` statement in braces, as in Figure 4.15.

Remember the rule: Pair an `else` with the nearest preceding `if`. Trace each branch of nested `if` statements, checking carefully to determine which values of the data will cause execution to flow to that branch. ■

Example 4.3 uses nested `if-else` statements to assign letter grades to test scores. We use the sentinel idea introduced in Example 3.6, where the user terminates the input of scores with a negative value.

```
if (score >= 60) {
 if (score >= 80)
  Console.WriteLine("You got a B or an A");
}else                              // Paired to first 'if'
  Console.WriteLine("You got a D or an F");
```

FIGURE 4.15 **Figure 4.13 rewritten as an `if-else` with nested `if`**

EXAMPLE 4.3 ■ Score.cs

```
/*  Uses nested if-else statements to choose among alternatives
 *  to assign letter grades to test scores.
 */

using System;
public class Score {

      /*  Inputs scores, assigning grades, until the user
       * enters a negative value.
       */
  public static void Main() {
    int score = IO.GetInt("Enter a test score or -1 to quit: ");
    while (score >= 0) {
      if (score < 50)                                    // Note 1
        Console.WriteLine("Score {0} receives an F", score);
      else if (score < 60)
        Console.WriteLine("Score {0} receives a D", score);
      else if (score < 80)
        Console.WriteLine("Score {0} receives a C", score);
      else if (score < 90)
        Console.WriteLine("Score {0} receives a B", score);
      else if (score <= 100)
        Console.WriteLine("Score {0} receives an A", score);
      else                                               // Note 2
        Console.WriteLine
             ("Score can't be greater than 100, try again");
      score = IO.GetInt("Enter a test score or -1 to quit: ");
    }
  }
}
```

Run

```
Enter a test score or -1 to quit: 67
Score 67 receives a C
Enter a test score or -1 to quit: 82
Score 82 receives a B
Enter a test score or -1 to quit: 35
Score 35 receives an F
Enter a test score or -1 to quit: 98
Score 98 receives an A
Enter a test score or -1 to quit: 58
Score 58 receives a D
```

```
Enter a test score or -1 to quit: 123
Score can't be greater than 100, try again
Enter a test score or -1 to quit: -1
```

Note 1: `if (score < 50) {`

We extend the `if-else` statement from Figure 4.10 to interpret all test score values. Counting out-of-range values, we choose among six alternatives.

Note 2: `else`

This `else-part` catches any score not included by any previous alternative. Because the score has to be nonnegative for the `while` test to not fail, the only values not included are those greater than 100.

TIP Be sure to test each alternative of nested `if-else` statements, as we did in Example 4.3.

The `switch` Statement

Choosing among six alternatives is stretching the use of nested `if-else` statements. The efficiency of this construction declines as we add more alternatives. For example, to interpret a score of 98, Example 4.3 tests five conditions, the first four of which fail. The `switch` statement allows us to check a large number of alternatives more efficiently.

A `switch` statement chooses alternatives based on the value of a variable. In this section, we use an `int` variable in our switch statement. In Section 4.4 we introduce character variables, which may also be used to indicate choices in a `switch` statement. We may also use the `string` type or other integer types to indicate `switch` choices.

The `switch` statement has the form

```
switch (test_expression)  {
  case expression1:
                    statement1;
  case expression2:
                    statement2;
   .....
  default:
                    default_statement;
 }
```

We can use a `switch` statement to replace the nested `if-else` statements of Example 4.3. Computing `score/10` will give a number from 0 to 10 because each score is between 0 and 100. For example, 87/10 is 8 and 35/10 is 3. We can assign `score/10` to a variable `mark`, as in

```
int mark = score/10;
```

and use `mark` in the `switch` statement of Figure 4.16 to determine the grade for that score.

In Figure 4.16, C# evaluates the variable `mark`, jumping directly to one of 12 cases, depending on the value of `mark`. We specify each case with a case label such as `case 5:` which is made up of the word *case* followed by the number 5, followed by a colon. The label marks the place in the code to jump to when the `switch` variable value matches that case label. If `mark` is 5, C# executes the code following the label `case 5:`, which displays the grade of D; the `break` statement then causes a jump out of the `switch` statement, to the code following the closing brace, `}`.

If `mark` is 10, then C# jumps to the code at the label `case 10:`, which displays an A and breaks to the end of the switch. If mark is any integer other than 0 through 10, then C# jumps to the `default` case and displays an error message. The `default` case is optional. Had we omitted the `default` case in Figure 4.16, then C# would simply do nothing if the variable `mark` had any value other than 0 through 10. Note that several labels can refer to the same code, as for example, `case 6` and `case 7`, which both label the statement that displays a C.

FIGURE 4.16 **An example of a `switch` statement**

```
switch(mark) {
  case 0:
  case 1:
  case 2:
  case 3:
  case 4:  Console.WriteLine("F");
           break;
  case 5:  Console.WriteLine("D");
           break;
  case 6:
  case 7:  Console.WriteLine("C");
           break;
  case 8:  Console.WriteLine("B");
           break;
  case 9:
  case 10: Console.WriteLine("A");
           break;
  default: Console.WriteLine("Incorrect score");
           break;
}
```

We must include the `break` statement after each case. C# does not allow code to "fall through" to the code for the next case. However, as in Figure 4.16, several case labels may mark the same location.

Example 4.4 illustrates a good use for `switch` statements, which is to provide a menu to input choices from the user. We convert our programs from Examples 3.6 and 3.7 to methods to use as two of the menu choices.[3]

EXAMPLE 4.4 ■ UserMenu.cs

```
/*  Uses a switch statement to input a user's selection of
 *  an alternative. Uses code from Examples 3.6 and 3.7.
 */

using System;
public class UserMenu {

    //  Sums scores until user enters -1
  public static void Sum() {                                    // Note 1
    int total = 0;                // Sum of scores
    int score =
      IO.GetInt("Enter the first score, -1 to quit: ");
    while (score >= 0) {
      total += score;
      score = IO.GetInt("Enter the next score, -1 to quit");
    }
    Console.WriteLine("The total is {0}", total);
  }

     /* Inputs prices until the users enters -1.
      * Outputs the maximum of all prices entered.
      */
  public static void Max() {                                    // Note 2
    double maxSoFar = 0;    // Max of prices entered
    double price =
      IO.GetDouble("Enter the first price, -1 to quit: ");
    while (price >=0 ) {
      if (price > maxSoFar)
        maxSoFar = price;
      price =
        IO.GetDouble("Enter the next price, -1 to quit: ");
    }
    Console.WriteLine("The maximum is {0:C}", maxSoFar);
  }
```

[3]Section 2.4 introduced methods.

```
    // Loops until user chooses 4
  public static void Main() {
    int choice =
      IO.GetInt("Choose: 1-Sum, 2-Max, 3-To Do, or 4-Quit: ");
    while (choice != 4) {                                    // Note 3
      switch (choice) {
        case 1:
                Sum();                                       // Note 4
                break;                                       // Note 5
        case 2:
                Max();
                break;
        case 3:
                Console.WriteLine("Fill in code here");// Note 6
                break;
      }                                                      // Note 7
      choice =
        IO.GetInt("Choose: 1-Sum, 2-Max, 3-To Do, 4-Quit: ");
    }
  }
}
```

Run

```
Choose: 1-Sum, 2-Max, 3-To Do, or 4-Quit: 3
Fill in code here
Choose: 1-Sum, 2-Max, 3-To Do, 4-Quit: 4
```

■

Note 1: `public static void Sum() {`

This is the code from Example 3.6 to sum test scores entered by the user. We put it in a method, `Sum`, to call if the user selects choice 1.

Note 2: `public static void Max() {`

This is the code from Example 3.7 to find the maximum of the values input by the user. We put it in a method, `Max`, to call if the user selects choice 2.

Note 3: `while (choice != 4) {`

If choice has the value 1, 2, or 3, then the switch jumps to the code for that case. For a choice of 4, the `while` condition fails and the program finishes without executing the `switch` statement. If choice has any other value, then the switch does nothing, and execution continues after the switch by reading the user's next choice.

Note 4: `Sum();`

If choice has the value 1, then call the `Sum` method to add test scores. We can execute any C# statements, including `if-else` and `while` statements as well as method calls, after a `case` label.

Note 5: `break;`

This `break` statement causes execution to jump to the end of the `switch` statement, so the next statement will be the call to display the menu.

Note 6: `Console.WriteLine("Fill in code here");`

We have not really specified what to do if the user selects 3. We want to get the whole program working without adding any more code for additional choices. This illustrates a principle of program design, to solve the problem in stages, getting one stage right before going on to the next. We build a good framework and can fill in the details later.

Note 7: `}`

We do not need a `default` case in this example. If the user enters any value but 1, 2, 3, or 4, then the switch does nothing, the menu displays again, and C# asks the user for another choice. This is just what we want to happen, so there is no need for a `default` case.

Example 4.4 is longer than any of the previous examples, but much of it contains code developed in Chapter 3. In addition to illustrating the `switch` statement, it uses methods to satisfy user requests.

The BIG Picture

Nested `if` statements work for a choice among a few alternatives. With the `switch` statement, we can choose among many. `switch` statements can implement a menu of choices.

✓ Test Your Understanding

8. A charity designates donors who give more than $1,000 as Benefactors, those who give $500–$999 as Patrons, and those who give $100–$499 as Supporters. Write a nested `if-else` statement that, given the amount of a contribution, outputs the correct designation for that contributor.

9. Write a nested `if-else` statement that includes the categories from question 8 and identifies donors of $1–$99 as Contributors.

10. What value will the variable x have after executing

```
x = 6;
if (k < 10)
  if (k < 5)
    x = 7;
  else
    x = 8;
```

if k has the value

a. 9

b. 3

c. 11

d. −2

11. What value will the variable x have after executing

```
x = 6;
if (k < 10)
  if (k < 5)
    x = 7;
else
  x = 8;
```

if k has the value

a. 9

b. 3

c. 11

d. −2

12. What value will the variable x have after executing

```
x = 6;
if (k < 10)   {
   if (k < 5)
       x = 7;
}else
     x = 8;
```

if k has the value

a. 9

b. 3

c. 11

d. −2

13. What value will the variable x have after executing

```
x = 5;
switch(k) {
   case 2:
```

```
    case 3:  x = 6;
             break;
    case 5:  x = 7;
             break;
    case 9:  x = 8;
             break;
    default: x = 9;
             break;
}
```

if k has the value

a. 1

b. 3

c. 5

d. 6

e. 9

f. −5

g. 10

14. Answer question 13 for the code

```
x = 5;
switch(k) {
  case 2:
  case 3: x = 6;
          break;
  case 5: x = 7;
          break;
  case 9: x = 8;
          break;
}
```

4.3 THE for AND do LOOPS

In this section we introduce the `for` and `do` statements. The `for` statement makes it easy to repeat a block of code a fixed number of times. The `do` statement is like the `while` statement, with the difference that it tests the condition after executing a block of code rather than before. These new statements help us to write programs requiring repetition.

The for Statement

The `for` statement provides a powerful iteration capability. It works well when we know the number of repetitions. Technically, we could use a `while` statement instead of a `for` statement in these cases, but it is much more convenient to say

```
Do this calculation 10 times.
```

than it is to write

```
Declare and initialize a count variable to zero.
while (count < 10) {
    doSomething;
     count ++;
}
```

The `for` statement performs the same steps but packages them more conveniently, following the pattern

```
for (initialize; test; update)
  for_statement
```

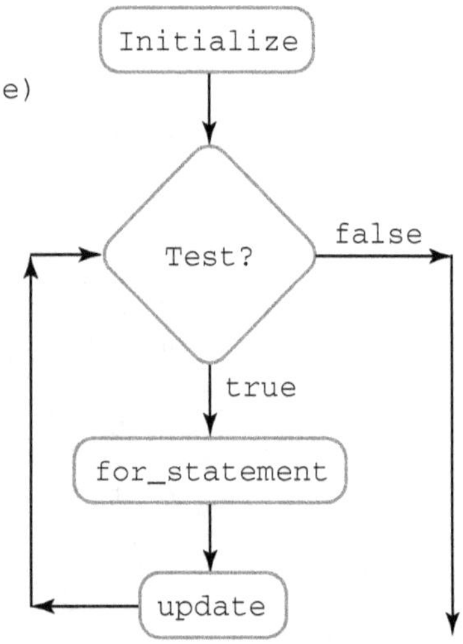

where `for_statement` can be a simple statement or a block. The code in Figure 4.17 uses a `for` statement to add the numbers from 1 to 4. The initialize part declares and initializes a variable, `i`, called the index or counter, which will count the repetitions.

The test expression, `i <= 4`, checks to determine if we need more repetitions. C# will execute the statement `sum += i` of the `for` loop body if the test condition is true—in this case, if the count, `i`, is less than or equal to 4. The loop terminates when the test condition becomes false—in this case, when `i` is greater than 4. The update expression, `i++` in this example, increments the count, `i`, by 1. C# executes the update expression after executing the `for` loop body. Figure 4.18 traces the execution of the `for` loop of Figure 4.17.

The update expression can be more general than the increment in Figure 4.17. In Figure 4.19 we find the sum of the positive odd numbers less than 10.

FIGURE 4.17 A `for` statement for the sum 1 + 2 + 3 + 4

```
int sum = 0;
for (int i = 1; i <= 4; i++)
  sum += i;
```

```
initialize      i = 1
test            1 <= 4 is true
execute body    sum += 1            (result:  sum = 0 + 1 = 1)
update          i++                 (result:  i = 2)
test            2 <= 4 is true
execute body    sum += 2            (result:  sum = 1 + 2 = 3)
update          i++                 (result:  i = 3)
test            3 <= 4 is true
execute body    sum += 3            (result:  sum = 3 + 3 = 6)
update          i++                 (result:  i = 4)
test            4 <= 4 is true
execute body    sum += 4            (result:  sum = 6 + 4 = 10)
update          i++                 (result:  i = 5)
test            5 <= 4 is false
```

FIGURE 4.18 **Trace of execution of the `for` loop of Figure 4.17**

FIGURE 4.19 **A `for` statement for the sum 1 + 3 + 5 + 7 + 9**

```
int sum = 0;
for (int i = 1; i < 10; i += 2)
  sum += i;
```

In each iteration we add 2 to the index variable, `i`, which gets the values 1, 3, 5, 7, and 9, each of which is added to `sum`, whose final value is 25.

Normally, the index variable increases at each iteration, as in the code of Figures 4.17 and 4.19. However, we can initialize the index to its highest value and decrement it at each iteration, as in Figure 4.20, which also computes the sum of the first four positive integers.

Now that we have seen how to write a `for` statement, we will use it in Example 4.5 to find out how much our money will grow in a bank account. The account earns interest at a certain rate over a specified time, assuming that interest is compounded yearly (at the end of the year the interest due for that year is added to the principal).

FIGURE 4.20 **A `for` statement for the sum 4 + 3 + 2 + 1**

```
int sum = 0;
for (int i = 4; i >= 1; i--)
   sum += i;
```

To develop a solution, let us start with a simple case, $1000 at 5% for 3 years. For each year, we have to find the interest earned and add it to the account balance, as the following table shows.

Year	*Interest*	*New Balance*
1	`1000 * .05 = 50`	`1000 + 50 = 1050`
2	`1050 * .05 = 52.50`	`1050 + 52.50 = 1102.50`
3	`1102.50 * .05 = 55.13`	`1102.50 + 55.13 = 1157.63`

From this example, we see that each year we find the interest and add it to the balance to get the new balance. We will put these two steps in the body of our `for` statement.

EXAMPLE 4.5 ■ Growth.cs

```
/*
 * Input: Rate, a double value giving the yearly percent
 *              interest rate
 *        Balance, a double value giving the amount deposited
 *        Years, an int value giving the time period for the
 *               deposit
 *
 * Output: Amount, the total amount in the account at the end of
 *                the time period.
 */

using System;
public class Growth {

    // Illustrates a for statement
  public static void Main() {
    double rate =
      IO.GetDouble("Enter the percent interest rate: ");
    double balance =
      IO.GetDouble("Enter the initial balance: ");
    int years =
      IO.GetInt("Enter the time period for the deposit: ");
    for (int i = 1; i <= years; i++)
       balance += balance * rate/100;                     // Note 1
    Console.WriteLine
        ("The balance after {0} years is {1:C}",
                                  years, balance);
  }
}
```

Run

```
Enter the percent interest rate: 5.0
Enter the initial balance: 1000
Enter the time period for the deposit: 3
The balance after 3 years is $1,157.63
```

Note 1: `balance += balance * rate/100;`

The rate is input as a percentage, which we divide by 100 to get the multiplier needed to compute the interest. Because `rate` has type `double`, C# will use floating-point division to compute the quotient, converting 100 to a type `double` value.

A Little Extra

Loop Indices

Declaring the index variable in the initialize part of the `for` statement makes it visible only within the `for` loop. For example, the index variable `i` in Figure 4.20 can be used only within the `for` loop. Any reference to it outside of that loop would be an error.

We could declare the index variable before the loop, as in Figure 4.21, in which case we could use the variable, `i`, before or after the `for` loop. In most instances, we prefer to declare the index variable inside the `for` loop and use it only as an index inside the loop. Using a variable for more than one purpose can obscure the program.

The `do` Statement

The `while` statement lets us repeat a block of code; it checks the condition before executing the loop body. In some problems, when we know we will execute the body at least once, it is more natural to check the condition after executing the body. The `do` statement, having the syntax shown in Figure 4.22, lets us do that. C# executes the statement, and then checks the condition. If the condition is true, C# executes the statement again; otherwise, it proceeds to the next statement after the loop. The statement in the body of the `do` loop can be

FIGURE 4.21
Declaring an index variable before the `for` loop

```
int i;                          // declare loop index
int sum = 0;
for (i = 4; i >= 1; i--){       // initialize loop index
    sum += i;
}
 ...
 i += 17;                       // use loop index variable i
```

FIGURE 4.22 **Syntax for the do statement**

```
do
   statement
while (condition) ;
```

a simple statement, but most often it is a **block**, a group of statements enclosed in curly braces.

- Use a `do` statement when the loop body will always be executed at least once.
- Use a `while` statement when the loop body may (possibly) never be executed.

As an example, notice that Example 4.5 terminates after one test. Instead of rerunning the program from the operating system, suppose we add another loop to ask the user whether to rerun the example with different data, while we are still executing the program. Figure 4.23 shows the pseudocode for this enhancement.

EXAMPLE 4.6 ■ DoGrowth.cs

```
/* Enhances Example 4.5 to ask if the user wants to
 * repeat the calculation.
 */

using System;
public class DoGrowth {

    // Illustrates a do statement
  public static void Main() {
    int repeat = 0;           // 1 to repeat, 0 to quit
    do {
      double rate =
        IO.GetDouble("Enter the percent interest rate: ");
                                                      // Note 1
      double balance =
        IO.GetDouble("Enter the initial balance: ");
      int years =
        IO.GetInt("Enter the time period for the deposit: ");
      for (int i = 1; i <= years; i++)
         balance += balance * rate/100;
```

FIGURE 4.23 **Pseudocode for Example 4.5 enhancement**

```
do {
    Compute balance as in Example 4.5
    Ask the user -- Repeat or Quit?
} while (User chooses to repeat);
```

```
        Console.WriteLine("The balance after {0} years is {1:C}",
        years, balance);
        repeat = IO.GetInt("Enter 1 to repeat, 0 to quit: ");
                                                          // Note 2
      } while (repeat == 1);                              // Note 3
    }
  }
```

Run

```
Enter the percent interest rate: 5.5
Enter the initial balance: 100
Enter the time period for the deposit: 12
The balance after 12 years is $190.12
Enter 1 to repeat, 0 to quit: 1
Enter the percent interest rate: 7.9
Enter the initial balance: 250
Enter the time period for the deposit: 6
The balance after 6 years is $394.52
Enter 1 to repeat, 0 to quit: 0
```

Note 1: `double rate =`

```
  IO.GetDouble("Enter the percent interest rate: ");
```

The code starting here comes from Example 4.5.

Note 2: `repeat = IO.GetInt("Enter 1 to repeat, 0 to quit: ");`

Having finished the code from Example 4.5, we ask the user whether to repeat the calculation.

Note 3: `} while (repeat == 1);`

The `do` statement works very well here. We check the user's response after each execution of the calculation.

Style

In all loops, indent the body relative to the keywords.

Good

```
do {
  statements
} while (condition);
```

Bad

```
do {
statements
} while (condition);
```

The BIG Picture

The `for` statement and the `do` statement provide useful options for repetition. The `for` statement is especially useful for a fixed number of repetitions, and the `do` works when we wish to test the condition after executing the loop body rather than before.

✓Test Your Understanding

15. Write a `for` statement that will display the numbers from 1 through 10.

16. Write a `for` statement that will display the numbers from 7 through 12.

17. Write a `for` statement that will display the numbers from 9 through 3, in that order.

18. Write a `for` statement that will display the even numbers from 4 through 20.

19. What value will the variable `sum` have after the execution of the following code?

```
int sum = 0;
for (int i = 0; i < 8; i++)
 sum += i;
```

20. What value will the variable `sum` have after the execution of the following code?

```
int sum = 100;
for (int i = 2; i < 6; i++)
 sum -= i;
```

21. What value will the variable `sum` have after the execution of the following code?

```
int sum = 100;
for (int i = 20; i > 16 ; i--)
 sum -= i;
```

22. What value will the variable `sum` have after the execution of the following code?

```
int sum = 0;
for (int i = 1; i <= 20 ; i += 3)
 sum -= i;
```

23. What value will the variable `sum` have after the execution of the following code?

```
int sum = 100;
for (int i = 20; i > 6 ; i -= 5)
 sum -= i;
```

24. Find the value of the variable `i` after the execution of the following code.

```
int i = 1;
int total = 0;
do {
 total += i;
```

```
  i++ ;
} while (total < 25);
```

25. Find the value of the variable `i` after the execution of the following code.

```
int i = 10;
int total =100;
do {
  total -= i;
  i += 5;
} while (total > 25);
```

26. Find the value of the variable `total` after the execution of the following code.

```
int i = 1;
int total = 10;
do {
  total += i;
  i++ ;
} while (i < 5);
```

27. Find the value of the variable `total` after the execution of the following code.

```
int i = 1;
int total = 100;
do {
  total -= i;
  i++ ;
} while (i <= 7);
```

28. Draw the flow diagram for the `do` statement.

4.4 ADDITIONAL TYPES

So far we have used the `int` type for integers and the `double` type for decimal numbers. In this section we introduce the `char` type for characters, the `long` type for long integers, and the `float` type for decimal numbers, which uses less precision than the type `double`.

The `char` Type

C# represents characters using single quotes, as in, for example, 'a', 'A', 'b', 'B' for letters, '0', '1' for numerals, '+','-' for operators, and '?', ',' for punctuation. Internally, C# uses the Unicode® character set, which has thousands of characters, including those needed for the world's major languages.[4] We will need only the ASCII (American Standard Code for Information Interchange) character set, which has 128 characters. (See Appendix D for a table of the ASCII characters.) Each ASCII character has an equivalent Unicode character. C# converts from ASCII

[4]See `http://unicode.org` for more information about Unicode.

input to Unicode, and from Unicode to ASCII output. We will not need to use Unicode explicitly, because internationalizing C# is beyond the scope of this text.

We call the first 32 ASCII characters *control characters*; they are nonprinting, but control functions such as formatting, including tab, newline, and return. For example, the *Enter* key and the *Tab* key have no visible symbol, but they control the position of the next input. To represent these control characters and other special characters in our program we use the escape character, the backslash, '\'. When C# sees the backslash, it escapes from its normal reading of printing characters and interprets the following character as a special character. Figure 4.24 shows some of these special characters.

Double quote and backslash are printing characters, but they have special functions in C#. Normally we enclose strings within double quotes, as in `"The result is "`. Occasionally, we want to use a string that itself uses double quotes, as in

```
"Do you like the movie \"Gone With The Wind\"? "
```

Using the backslash in `\"`, tells C# that the double quote is part of the string and not the terminating double quote.

EXAMPLE 4.7 ■ Special.cs

```
/*  Shows the effect of the special characters.
 */

using System;
public class Special {
  public static void Main()  {
    Console.WriteLine("Use \n to go to the next line");
                                                        // Note 1
    Console.WriteLine
    ("*************************\r back to start");// Note 2
    Console.WriteLine("1234\b\b5678");               // Note 3
    Console.WriteLine("***\t tab here");             // Note 4
```

FIGURE 4.24 Escape sequences for special characters

Special Character	Meaning
\n	newline, move to the start of the next line
\t	tab
\b	backspace
\r	return, move to the start of the current line
\"	double quote
\\	backslash

```
        Console.WriteLine
        ("Do you like \"Gone With the Wind\"?");        // Note 5
        Console.WriteLine("The directory is c:\\newstuff");
                                                         // Note 6
    }
}
```

```
Use
 to go to the next line
 back to start************
125678
***      tab here
Do you like "Gone With the Wind"?
The directory is c:\newstuff
```

Note 1: `Console.WriteLine("Use \n to go to the next line");`

The newline, '`\n`', positions the next output at the start of the next line. The blank space after the newline shows up as the first character on the next line.

Note 2: `Console.WriteLine`
`("*************************\r back to start");`

The return, '`\r`', positions the next output at the start of the current line.

Note 3: `Console.WriteLine("1234\b\b5678");`

The backspace, '`\b`', positions the next output one character to the left. The backspaces here position the next output to write over the preceding digits, 3 and 4.

Note 4: `Console.WriteLine("***\t tab here");`

The tab, '`\t`', positions the next input at the next tab position.

Note 5: `Console.WriteLine`
`("Do you like \"Gone With the Wind\"?");`

Uses double quotes inside the quoted string.

Note 6: `Console.WriteLine("The directory is c:\\newstuff");`

We want to indicate that the directory is `c:\newstuff`. But C# treats the backslash as the escape character, so it would interpret the '`\n`' as a newline character. To use the backslash itself inside a string we treat it as a special character '`\\`'.

We can declare variables of type `char`. Using `char` variables, we could improve Example 4.6 to allow the user to input `Y` or `y` to repeat, and `N` or `n` to quit, instead of 1 or 0. We leave this improvement as an exercise and will use this technique in Example 4.8.

The `long` Type

The range of values for `int` variables is from –2,147,483,648 to 2,147,483,647. C# provides the type `long` to represent integer values outside of this range. `Long` values range from −9,223,372,036,854,775,808 to 9,223,372,036,854,775,807. By default, when we use a whole number such as 25 in a program, C# assumes it is an `int`. We can specify a `long` value by adding an `l` or `L` suffix, as in `25L`. We can declare variables of type `long`, but would use `long` variables instead of `int` only when we needed values that the `int` type cannot handle. It takes more space to hold `long` values, and more time to process them.

To illustrate the use of the `long` type, we solve the problem suggested by a folk tale from India. In that story, a young girl greatly helped a rich rajah who was reluctant to offer her any reward. Coming from a poor village, the girl wanted to help her people, and seeing a chessboard nearby, she asked the rajah just to give her some grains of rice as her reward. She asked that on the first day the rajah place one grain of rice on the first square of the chessboard, on the second day he place two grains on the second square, on the third day four grains on the third square, each day doubling the number of grains until all 64 squares were filled.

Example 4.8 attempts to find out the size of the reward placed on any one of these squares. We will see that even the `long` type is not quite able to handle all the values we need. The `ulong` type mentioned in the next section would handle the values we need.

EXAMPLE 4.8 ■ Reward.cs

```
/* How many grains of rice does the rajah place on square n
 * if the rajah places one grain on the first square of a
 * chessboard, and places double the amount of the previous
```

```
 * square on the next square, and so on. Allow the user to
 * repeat for different n.
 */

using System;
public class Reward {

    // Uses long and char types.
  public static void Main() {
    char repeat = 'N';    // Y to repeat, N to quit

    do {
      long amount = 1;                                   // Note 1
      int squarenum = IO.GetInt("Which square, 1-64? ");
      if (squarenum == 1)
        Console.WriteLine("The reward on square 1 is 1");
                                                         // Note 2
      else {
        for (int i = 2; i <= squarenum; i++)
          amount += amount;                              // Note 3
        Console.WriteLine
          ("The reward on square {0} is {1}",
            squarenum, amount);
      }
      repeat =
          IO.GetChar("Enter 'Y' to repeat, 'N' to quit: ");
                                                         // Note 4
    } while (repeat == 'Y' || repeat == 'y');
  }
}
```

Run

```
Which square, 1-64? 4
The reward on square 4 is 8
Enter 'Y' to repeat, 'N' to quit: Y
Which square, 1-64? 63
The reward on square 63 is 4611686018427387904
Enter 'Y' to repeat, 'N' to quit: Y
Which square, 1-64? 64
The reward on square 64 is -9223372036854775808
Enter 'Y' to repeat, 'N' to quit: N
```

Note 1: `long amount = 1;`

We assign the `int` value, 1, to the `long` variable, amount. C# converts the `int` value to a `long` value. We could have specified a `long` value by writing `amount = 1L;`

Note 2:

```
if (squarenum == 1)
   Console.WriteLine("The reward on square 1 is 1");
```

For square one, we know the reward is 1.

Note 3: `amount += amount;`

We could use the expression `2*amount` to double the amount, but the expression `amount+amount` is more efficient, because addition executes much more quickly than multiplication.

Note 4:

```
repeat =
  IO.GetChar("Enter 'Y' to repeat, 'N' to quit: ");
```

We only do the repeat if the character typed is `Y` or `y`. The prompt says to type an `N` or an `n` to quit, but actually any character other than `Y` or `y` will cause the program to quit. Following English usage, we might be tempted to say `while (repeat == 'Y' || 'y')`, but that is incorrect because each operand of an `OR` operator must have type `bool`.

In testing Example 4.8, we first tried day four. It is always a good idea to try some small values that we can check by hand to see that our program is correct. The reward on square 63 is 4611686018427387904. This is reaching the limit on the size of values that a `long` variable can hold. The reward on square 64 is −9223372036854775808. Now we have passed the limit of 9,223,372,036,854,775,807 that a `long` variable can hold, so we get an erroneous negative value. Actually, we were very close here. Multiplying the previous value for square 63 by 2, we see that the correct answer is just one greater than the largest value that a `long` variable can hold.

TIP

Always check your result for reasonableness. Just because the computer gives you some output does not mean that it is correct. ■

Other Predefined Types

C# has the types `sbyte`, `byte`, `short`, and `ushort` for small integers that are used for specialized purposes. `sbyte` represents 8-bit integers between −128 and 127. `byte` is unsigned, representing 8-bit integers with values between 0 and 255. The `short` type represents 16-bit integers with values ranging between −32768 and 32767. `ushort` represents 16-bit integers between 0 and 65535. We do not use these types in this text.

C# provides a `float` type for decimal numbers, which uses less precision than the type `double`. In contrast to the integer types, where the smaller type `int` is the default and the bigger type `long` is less often used, for floating-point types, the larger type `double` is the default, and `float` is less often used. In the modern world, we often deal with decimal numbers requiring a wide range of values and high precision, whether in scientific calculations or financial transactions, and need the values that type `double` provides.

`float` values are accurate to seven digits and range from 1.4E-45 to 3.4028235E38. To represent a `float` literal add an F or an f, as in 3.14f. We can declare variables of type `float`, but must initialize them with `float` values. The declaration

```
float good = 4.25f;      // Valid
```

is fine, but the declaration

```
float bad = 4.25;        // Invalid
```

will cause an error, because the value 4.25 has type `double` by default. C# will not automatically convert from type `double` to type `float`, because, in general, a `double` value may be out of the range that a `float` variable accepts.[5] We will use `float` variables when we want to output values of seven digits rather than the 15 digits of the type `double`.

C# provides the unsigned types `uint` and `ulong`, which can be useful when we know that the represented values are all nonnegative. `uint` represents values between 0 and 4294967295. `ulong` represents values between 0 and 18446744073709551615. It would be ideal for use in Example 4.8.

The 128-bit `decimal` type is suitable for financial calculations that must be exact. It can represent values ranging from 1.0E-28 to approximately 7.9E+28 with 28–29 significant digits.

Enumerations

We can define a type that provides convenient names for values, so we do not have to use arbitrary numbers to represent nonnumerical data. For example,

```
enum Color {Red, Green, Blue}
```

defines a `Color` type with three values. We can declares variables, as for example

```
Color c = Color.Red;
```

[5]C# will not automatically convert an `int` to a float either. Integers of more than seven digits could not be represented precisely in the float format.

and we can test, as in

```
if (c == Color.Green)
    // do something
```

> **The BIG Picture**
>
> With the 16-bit `char` type, C# can handle the character sets of most of the world's languages. The 64-bit `long` type holds integers of up to 19 digits. The 32-bit `float` type provides seven decimal places. Other predefined types have special uses.

✓ Test Your Understanding

29. Show the output from each of the following statements.

a. Console.WriteLine("I like \n\nto write C# programs.");

b. Console.WriteLine("Ali Baba said, \"Open, Sesame!\"");

c. Console.WriteLine("12345\r678");

d. Console.WriteLine("Find 3\\4 of 24");

30. Show the output from each of the following statements.

a. Console.WriteLine("Descartes said, \"I think\ntherefore\nI am\"");

b. Console.WriteLine("set path=c:\\C#\\bin");

c. Console.WriteLine("12345\b678");

d. Console.WriteLine("'i' before 'e' except after 'c'");

Try It Yourself ➤

31. Change the declaration of the variable amount in Example 4.8 to have type `ulong`. Rerun the program and determine the largest square number for which the reward is computed correctly. How much is that reward?

32. Variables of type `long` can hold much larger values than variables of type `int`. Would it be a good idea to declare all integer variables as type `long` and not use type `int`? Why or why not?

4.5 USING THE MATH LIBRARY

The C# language provides the basic arithmetic operations of addition, subtraction, multiplication, and division, but not exponentiation, max, min, and other mathematical functions. As we shall see, C# adds many resources as classes that we can use in our programs.

In this section we introduce methods of the `Math` class to compute square root, absolute value, powers, max, min, random numbers, and other mathematical functions which we can use to solve problems in the remainder of the text. To use these methods, we prefix the method name with the class name, `Math`, as in `Math.Sqrt(2.0)`, which computes the square root of 2.0.

TIP

When calling class methods (methods that use the `static` modifier) from a method of the same class, as in Example 4.4, where we call `Sum` and `Max` from `Main`, we do not need to use the class prefix. Optionally, we could use the class prefix, calling the `sum` method as `UserMenu.Sum()`. When calling class methods from a method of a different class, as in Example 4.8, where we call `IO.GetInt`, we must use the class prefix. ■

Powers and Roots

The power method, `Pow`, takes two arguments of type `double` and returns a `double` value, which is the result of raising the first argument to the exponent given by the second argument. Some examples follow:

`Math.Pow(2.0,3.0)  returns 8.0` $(2.0^{3.0})$
`Math.Pow(3.0,2.0)  returns 9.0` $(3.0^{2.0})$

The square root method, `Sqrt`, takes a `double` argument and returns a `double` value, the square root of its argument. Some examples are

```
Math.Sqrt(2.0)    returns 1.4142135623730951
Math.Sqrt(16.0)   returns 4.0
```

Maximum, Minimum, and Absolute Value

C# provides `Max`, `Min`, and `Abs` methods for each of the numeric types, including `int`, `long`, `float`, and `double`. For each type, the `Max` method returns the maximum of its two arguments of that type, and the `Min` method returns the minimum of its two arguments. Some examples are

```
Math.Max(3, 4)             returns 4
Math.Max(17.32, 5.8567)    returns 17.32
Math.Max(-9, -11)          returns -9
Math.Min(3, 4)             returns 3
Math.Min(17.32, 5.8567)    returns 5.8567
Math.Min(-9, -11)          returns -11
```

For each type, the `Abs` method returns the absolute value of its argument, which, by definition, is

```
Math.Abs(x) =  x, if x >= 0
            = -x, if x <  0
```

Informally, the `Abs` method removes the minus sign, if any. Some examples are

```
Math.Abs(-10)     returns 10
Math.Abs(12.34)   returns 12.34
```

Floor and Ceiling

Informally, just as the absolute value removes the minus sign, the floor removes the fractional part of its `double` argument, returning the largest `double` value that is not greater than the argument and is equal to a mathematical integer. Some examples follow:

```
Math.Floor(25.194)  returns 25.0
Math.Floor(-134.28) returns -135.0
```

The ceiling also removes the fractional part, but it returns the smallest `double` value that is not less than the argument and is equal to a mathematical integer. Some examples include

```
Math.Ceiling(25.194)    returns 26.0
Math.Ceiling(-134.28)   returns -134.0
```

Pi and E

In addition to methods, the `Math` class contain two important constants, `Math.PI`, the circumference of a circle of diameter one, and `Math.E`, the base for natural logarithms. We will use `Math.PI` in our calculations of areas and volumes.

EXAMPLE 4.9 ■ Library.cs

```
/* Uses methods from the Math class.
 */

using System;
public class Library {
  public static void Main()  {
     Console.WriteLine("Two cubed is {0}", Math.Pow(2.0,3.0));
     Console.WriteLine("Three squared is {0}",
                                       Math.Pow(3.0,2.0));
     Console.WriteLine("The square root of two is {0}",
                                       Math.Sqrt(2.0));
     Console.WriteLine("The square root of 16 is {0}",
                                       Math.Sqrt(16.0));
     Console.WriteLine("The max of 2.56 and 7.91/3.1 is {0}",
     Math.Max(2.65,7.91/3.1));                          // Note 1
     Console.WriteLine("The min of -9 and -11 is {0}",
                            Math.Min(-9,-11));
     Console.WriteLine("The absolute value of -32.47 is {0}",
                            Math.Abs(-32.47));
     Console.WriteLine("The floor of 25.194 is {0}",
                            Math.Floor(25.194));
     Console.WriteLine("The ceiling of 25.194 is {0}",
                            Math.Ceiling(25.194));
     Console.WriteLine("Pi is {0}", Math.PI);
     Console.WriteLine
        ("Pi, to six decimal places, is {0:F6}", Math.PI);
                                                        // Note 2
```

```
        Console.WriteLine
            ("The base of natural logarithms, e, is {0}", Math.E);
    }
}
```

Output

```
Two cubed is 8.0
Three squared is 9.0
The square root of two is 1.4142135623730951
The square root of 16 is 4.0
The max of 2.56 and 7.91/3.1 is 2.65
The min of -9 and -11 is -11
The absolute value of -32.47 is 32.47
The floor of 25.194 is 25
The ceiling of 25.194 is 26
Pi is 3.14159265358979
Pi, to six decimal places, is 3.141593
The base of natural logarithms, e, is 2.71828182845905
```

Note 1: `Math.Max(2.65,7.91/3.1)`

The argument can be an expression that evaluates to a `double`, as here for the second argument of `Max`.

Note 2:

```
Console.WriteLine
("Pi, to six decimal places, is {0:F6}", Math.PI);
```

We format the output to show only the first six decimal places of pi.

A Little Extra

Math Functions

The `Math` class has methods to compute the trigonometric functions, sine, cosine, and tangent. These methods each take a `double` argument representing an angle in radians, and produce a `double` result. Some examples are

```
Math.Sin(Math.PI/6.0) returns  0.5
Math.Cos(Math.PI)     returns -1
Math.Tan(Math.PI/4.0) returns  1
```

The exponential function computes e^x, where *e* is the base of natural logarithms. The `exp` method of the `Math` class computes the exponential function. The `log` method computes the natural logarithm function, `log x`. Some examples include

```
Math.Exp(1.0)     returns 2.71828182845905
Math.Exp(2.0)     returns 7.38905609893065
Math.Log(Math.E)  returns 1
Math.Log(10.0)    returns 2.30258509299405
```

The BIG Picture

The `Math` class contains the commonly used mathematical methods for powers, maximum, minimum, absolute value, floor, ceiling, square root, and other useful functions.

✓ Test Your Understanding

33. Use methods from the `Math` class to compute each of the following.

- **a.** Seven to the fourth power.
- **b.** The square root of 43.
- **c.** The maximum of 476.22 and −608.90.
- **d.** The minimum of 58.43 and 6.32*8.87.
- **e.** The absolute value of −65.234.
- **f.** The floor of −43.99.
- **g.** The ceiling of −3.01.

34. Use methods from the `Math` class to compute each of the following.

- **a.** Four to the seventh power.
- **b.** The square root of 117.45.
- **c.** The maximum of 32.1*33.9 and 1000.2.
- **d.** The minimum of the square root of 32 and 5.613.
- **e.** The absolute value of 1089.9.
- **f.** The floor of 43.99.
- **g.** The ceiling of 3.01.

35. Using `Math.PI`, write a C# expression for the area of a circle of radius *r*.

36. Using `Math.PI`, write a C# expression for the circumference of a circle of radius *r*.

37. Use `Math` methods to write an expression showing that squaring a number and then taking the square root of the result returns the original number.

4.6 SOLVING PROBLEMS WITH C#: ITERATIVE DEVELOPMENT

In this section we develop the solution of a problem from original statement to C# code. Figure 4.25 shows the steps of the iterative process we use.

We use an iterative development cycle, designing part of the program, implementing that part, and testing it. The goal is to keep control of the design and implementation, so we can have confidence that we are producing a correct, well-designed solution to the problem.

In this case study we use many concepts from this and earlier chapters, including the `do` statement, the `switch` statement, nested `if` statements, a conditional expression, a `Math` library method, and type casting. We reuse designs from earlier examples and think about reuse for this design, because it is much more productive to build on earlier work than to start every project from scratch.

FIGURE 4.25
Iterative problem-solving process

```
Formulate the problem;
do {
   Develop pseudocode;
   Implement some pseudocode in C# program;
   Test program;
}while (More pseudocode to implement);
```

Defining the Problem

Let us develop a program to convert distances from the metric system to the English system or from the English system to the metric system. We start with some examples of uses of the system. A user may choose which conversion to do. If the user chooses to convert from the metric system, the input might be 1222.32 meters, which our program will convert to an equivalent number of yards, feet, and inches. If the user chooses to convert from the English system, input might be 793 yards, 2 feet, 6 inches, which our program will convert to an equivalent number of meters. We use the conversion factors of .9144 meters in one yard and .0254 meters in one inch. Each yard has three feet, and each foot has 12 inches.

We should think about valid inputs and outputs. In converting to the English system, the number of feet should satisfy `0 <= feet < 3`, and the number of inches should satisfy `0 <= inches < 12`. Converting from the English system, we can accept as input any nonnegative values of yards, feet, and inches. For example, 10.3 yards, 4.5 feet, 17 inches would be an acceptable, though unlikely, input.

Toward a Solution: The Iterative Process—Develop Pseudocode, a C# Program, and Test

Following the process of Figure 4.25, we repeat the three steps of developing pseudocode, implementing that pseudocode in a C# program, and testing the program, until we have completed the solution to the problem. In this example we use three iterations of the development steps to attain the solution.

Toward a Solution: First Iteration—Pseudocode, Program, Test

It is always a good idea to reuse techniques that have worked before. In solving this problem, we can reuse the idea introduced in Example 4.4 of providing a menu from which the user can choose the type of conversion. By using the `do` statement, instead of the `while` statement we used in Example 4.4, we can avoid printing the menu from two different places in our program. Figure 4.26 shows the pseudocode for the overall solution.

FIGURE 4.26
Top-level pseudocode

```
do {
  Display the menu and get the user's choice;
  Execute the user's choice;
} while (user does not choose to quit);
```

```
do {
  choice = IO.GetInt("Choose: \n"
            + "1.  Convert from meters to yds,ft,in \n"
            + "2.  Convert from yds,ft,in to meters \n"
            + "3.  Quit: ");
  switch (choice) {
    case 1: MetricToEnglish();
            break;
    case 2: EnglishToMetric();
            break;
    case 3: Console.WriteLine("Bye, Have a nice day");
            break;
  }
} while (choice != 3);
```

FIGURE 4.27 **Pattern for a menu-driven application**

The pseudocode of Figure 4.26 is actually a general pattern for a menu-driven application; we can reuse it in solving other problems. We use a `switch` statement to execute the user's choice. Figure 4.27 shows the overall operation of the menu before getting into the details of the conversion operations. We can reuse this basic design for other menu-driven applications.

In Figure 4.27 we have a reusable design for a menu-driven application, with choices designed for our length-converting application. To handle the details of the conversion we use two methods, `MetricToEnglish` and `EnglishToMetric`. Before trying to design these two methods, we can execute and test the design we have so far. Of course, we cannot do any conversion of lengths yet, but we can test the overall structure of the program. Because we have not yet designed the `MetricToEnglish` and `EnglishToMetric` methods, we will use **stubs**, methods that execute in a trivial way, just printing a message. Example 4.10 tests our high-level design before our program gets too large for us to manage.

TIP

Do not try to write the whole program and then test it. Even smaller programs provide many opportunities to introduce errors. Our defense against errors is to develop code in small pieces that we can test and debug. Use stubs to test before all methods have been coded. ■

EXAMPLE 4.10 ■ ConvertMenu.cs

```
/* Tests the structure of the program to convert using a menu to
 * get the user's choice. Uses stubs for the actual conversion
 * methods.
 */
```

```
using System;
public class ConvertMenu {                                    // Note 1

    // Uses stub for now
  public static void MetricToEnglish() {
    Console.WriteLine("Converting from meters to yds,ft,in");
  }

    // Use stub for now
  public static void EnglishToMetric() {                      // Note 2
    Console.WriteLine("Converting from yds,ft,in to meters");
  }

     // Gives the user three choices
  public static void Main() {
    int choice = 3;
    do {
      choice = IO.GetInt("\nChoose: \n"
                    + "1.  Convert from meters to yds,ft,in \n"
                    + "2.  Convert from yds,ft,in to meters \n"
                    + "3.  Quit \n");
      switch (choice) {
        case 1:
                MetricToEnglish();
                break;
        case 2:
                EnglishToMetric();
                break;
        case 3:
                Console.WriteLine("Bye, Have a nice day");
                break;
      }
    } while (choice != 3);                                    // Note 3
  }
}
```

Run

```
Choose:
1.  Convert from meters to yds,ft,in
2.  Convert from yds,ft,in to meters
```

```
3.  Quit
1
Converting from meters to yds,ft,in

Choose:
1.  Convert from meters to yds,ft,in
2.  Convert from yds,ft,in to meters
3.  Quit
4

Choose:
1.  Convert from meters to yds,ft,in
2.  Convert from yds,ft,in to meters
3.  Quit
3
Bye, Have a nice day
```

Note 1: `public class ConvertMenu {`

This stub for the `MetricToEnglish` method just prints a message. We will implement this method later.

Note 2: `public static void EnglishToMetric() {`

This stub for the `EnglishToMetric` method just prints a message. We will implement this method later.

Note 3: `} while (choice != 3);`

If the user chooses a number other than 1, 2, or 3, the `switch` statement does nothing, and because the choice is not 3, the menu prints again, giving the user another chance to enter a correct choice.

Toward a Solution: Second Iteration—Pseudocode, Program, Test

The output from Example 4.10 shows that the menu structure works well, so we proceed to design the `MetricToEnglish` and `EnglishToMetric` methods. Let us try a hand example to review how to convert. The 100-meter dash is one of the highlights of the Olympic Games. We convert 100 meters to yards, feet, and inches. There are exactly .9144 meters in one yard. The calculations are

```
(100 meters) (1 yard / .9144 meters)   =   109.36133 yards
        giving 109 yards and an excess of .36133 yard
(.36133 yards) (3 feet / yard)  = 1.08399 feet
        giving 1 foot and an excess of .08399 foot
(.08399 foot) (12 inches / foot) = 1.00788 inches
```

which gives an output of 109 yards, 1 foot, 1.00788 inches.

Try another case close to the boundary; say a small value such as .05 meter. The calculations are

```
(.05 meter) (1 yard / .9144 meters) = .0546806 yard
        giving 0 yards and an excess of .0546806 yard
(.0546806 yard) (3 feet / yard) = .1640419 foot
        giving 0 feet and an excess of .1640419 foot
(.1640419 foot) (12 inches / foot) = 1.9685039 inches
```

which gives an output of 1.9685039 inches.

Looking at our calculations, we find that we may or may not have non-zero values for yards and feet. For the output, we have to distinguish between the singular forms, "`inch`", "`foot`", "`yard`", and the plural forms, "`inches`", "`feet`", and "`yards`". Figure 4.28 expresses the conversion process in pseudocode.

On output, we want to be sure not to display zero of any unit, so we will check to see that each value is greater than zero before displaying it. Any value between zero and 1 should use the singular form of the unit name. Figure 4.29 shows this refinement.

FIGURE 4.28
Pseudocode for the `MetricToEnglish` method

```
Input the number of meters, x, to convert;
Convert x meters to y yards;
Separate y into yInteger yards and yFraction yards;
Convert yFraction yards to f feet.
Separate f into fInteger feet and fFraction feet.
Convert fFraction feet to i inches.
Display the output.
```

FIGURE 4.29
Refinement: Display the output

```
if (yInteger > 0)
  if (yInteger  <= 1)  Display yInteger yard;
  else Display yInteger yards;
if (fInteger > 0)
  if (fInteger <= 1) Display fInteger foot;
  else Display fInteger feet;
if (i > 0)
  if (i <= 1) Display i inch;
  else Display i inches;
if (yInteger == 0 && fInteger == 0 && i == 0)
  Display 0 yards;
```

Example 4.11 adds to Example 4.10 the code for the `MetricToEnglish` method, based on the pseudocode of Figure 4.28 and 4.29. We just show the added part here, but the complete program is on the disk included with this book. We test the conversion from meters to yards, feet, and inches.

EXAMPLE 4.11 ■ ConvertFromMetric.cs

```
/*  Adds the implementation of the MetricToEnglish
 *  method to the code of Example 4.10.
 */

public class ConvertFromMetric {

      // Follows pseudocode steps
  public static void MetricToEnglish() {
    const double yardsPerMeter = .9144;                    // Note 1
    double meters =
      IO.GetDouble("Enter the number of meters to convert: ");
    double toYards = meters / yardsPerMeter;
    int yards = (int)toYards;                              // Note 2
    double excessYards = toYards - yards;                  // Note 3
    double toFeet = 3 * excessYards;
    // excessYards converted to feet
    int feet = (int)toFeet;
    // integer part of toFeet
    double excessFeet = toFeet - feet;
    // fractional part of toFeet
    float toInches = (float)(12 * excessFeet);             // Note 4
    String output = "";
    // Concatenate output for message dialog
    if (meters <= 1)                                       // Note 5
      output += meters+ " meter converts to";
    else
      output += meters+ " meters convert to";
    output += "\n   ";
    if (yards > 0)                                         // Note 6
      if (yards  <= 1)  output += yards + " yard  ";
      else output += yards + " yards  ";
    if (feet > 0)
      if (feet <= 1) output += feet + " foot  ";
      else output += feet + " feet  ";
    if (toInches > 0)
```

```
      if (toInches <= 1) output += toInches + " inch";
      else output += toInches + " inches";
    if (yards == 0 && feet == 0 && toInches == 0)      // Note 7
      output += 0 + " yards";
    Console.WriteLine(output);
  }
     //  The rest of the program is the same as Example 4.10
}
```

Run

```
Choose:
1.  Convert from meters to yds,ft,in
2.  Convert from yds,ft,in to meters
3.  Quit
1
Enter the number of meters to convert: 100
100 meters convert to
   109 yards  1 foot  1.007874 inches

Choose:
1.  Convert from meters to yds,ft,in
2.  Convert from yds,ft,in to meters
3.  Quit
1
Enter the number of meters to convert: .05
0.05 meter converts to
   1.968504 inches

Choose:
1.  Convert from meters to yds,ft,in
2.  Convert from yds,ft,in to meters
3.  Quit
1
Enter the number of meters to convert: 1.02
1.02 meters convert to
   1 yard  4.15748 inches

Choose:
1.  Convert from meters to yds,ft,in
2.  Convert from yds,ft,in to meters
3.  Quit
1
Enter the number of meters to convert: 0
```

```
0 meter converts to
   0 yards

Choose:
1.  Convert from meters to yds,ft,in
2.  Convert from yds,ft,in to meters
3.  Quit
3
Bye, Have a nice day
```

Note 1: `const double yardsPerMeter = .9144;`

There are .9144 meters in one yard.

Note 2: `int yards = (int)toYards;`

We cast `toYards` to an `int`, using the type cast, (int). See Section 3.3 for examples of type casts.

Note 3: `double excessYards = toYards - yards;`

We get the fractional part of `toYards` by subtracting its integer part.

Note 4: `toInches = (float) (12 * excessFeet);`

We will display the remaining inches as a decimal number. Using the type `double` would show 16 digits, so we cast the `double` value to a `float`, which will display seven digits. We need the parentheses in (`12*excessFeet`), because we want to convert the result to a `float` value, not the number 12.

Note 5: `if (meters <= 1)`

If `meters` is less than or equal to 1, we use the singular "meter," otherwise we use the plural "meters."

Note 6: `if (yards > 0)`

We want to print only nonzero values. Thus .05 meters converts to 1.968504 inches, not to 0 yards 0 feet 1.968504 inches.

Note 7: `if (yards == 0 && feet == 0 && toInches == 0)`

This makes sure that we display the result when the input is zero.

Completing the C# Code: Third Iteration

We have yet to design the `EnglishToMetric` method. Let us try an example to see how it should go. To convert 7 yards, 2 feet, 5 inches to meters we could convert to inches computing

```
(7 yards)*(36 inches / yard) + (2 feet)*(12 inches / foot) +
5 inches = 281 inches
```

and then convert to meters using the conversion factor of exactly .0254 meters per inch, giving

```
(281 inches)*(.0254 meters / inch) = 7.1374 meters
```

Figure 4.30 shows the pseudocode for the `EnglishToMetric` method.

Example 4.12, the complete conversion program, adds the code for the `EnglishToMetric` method to Example 4.11. We show only the added part here, but the complete program is on the disk included with this book.

EXAMPLE 4.12 ■ Convert.cs

```
/*  Adds the implementation of the EnglishToMetric
 *  method to the code of Example 4.11
 */

public class Convert {
    // MetricToEnglish same as Example 4.11

  public static void EnglishToMetric() {
    const double inchesPerMeter = .0254;
    double yards = IO.GetDouble("Enter yards: ");
    double feet = IO.GetDouble("Enter feet: ");
    double inches = IO.GetDouble("Enter inches: ");
    double total = 36*yards + 12*feet + inches;     // Note 1
    double meters = (float)( inchesPerMeter *total);
    if (meters <= 1)                                // Note 2
      Console.WriteLine
          ("Your input converts to {0:F4} meter", meters);
    else
      Console.WriteLine
          ("Your input converts to {0:F4} meters", meters);
  }
     // The rest is the same as Example 4.11
}
```

```
Input yards, feet, and inches to convert;
Convert to inches;
Convert inches to meters;
Output the result;
```

FIGURE 4.30
Pseudocode for the `EnglishToMetric` method

Run

```
Choose:
1.  Convert from meters to yds,ft,in
2.  Convert from yds,ft,in to meters
3.  Quit
2
Enter yards: 7
Enter feet: 2
Enter inches: 5
Your input converts to 7.1374 meters

Choose:
1.  Convert from meters to yds,ft,in
2.  Convert from yds,ft,in to meters
3.  Quit
1
Enter the number of meters to convert: 7.1374
7.1374 meters convert to
   7 yards  2 feet  5 inches

Choose:
1.  Convert from meters to yds,ft,in
2.  Convert from yds,ft,in to meters
3.  Quit
3
Bye, Have a nice day
```

■

Note 1: `double total = 36*yards + 12*feet + inches;`

This expression converts the yards, feet, and inches input to inches.

Note 2: `if (meters <= 1)`

We use the singular "meter" if the value is between zero and one, and the plural "meters" otherwise. We do not display the user's input of yards, feet, and inches to avoid dealing with singular and plural. See the `MetricToEnglish` method, which handles singular and plural unit names.

Testing the C# Code

This conversion problem allowed us to use our own program to provide a check on our results. In the first test, 7 yards, 2 feet, 5 inches converted to 7.1374 meters. In the second test, we converted 7.1374 meters, noting that it did in fact convert back to 7 yards, 2 feet, 5 inches. To save space, we do not include any other tests, but leave such testing to the exercises.

TIP

Whenever possible, do some tests in which you know the expected result and can check that your program produces that result. Test each feature of your program, and include unusual input as well as typical cases. Test input errors to see how your program behaves when confronted with erroneous data.

We have been testing the program at each iteration. Rerunning the previous tests as we implement more features will allow us to check that the newly incorporated features have not affected the functioning of the previously tested code.

The BIG Picture

Using the iterative method for software development lets us test the overall structure with stubs. We then develop one piece at a time, testing carefully at each iteration. We try to get one piece of the program correct before going on to the next.

✓Test Your Understanding

Try It Yourself ➤ **38.** Test Example 4.14 thoroughly. For each test case determine whether or not the program is performing properly.

39. Modify the pseudocode of Figure 4.23 to provide pseudocode for a menu-driven program to convert between British currency of pounds and pence, in which 1 pound contains 100 pence, and U.S. currency in dollars and cents. Do not compile or execute any code.

Try It Yourself ➤ **40.** Add a section to the `EnglishToMetric` method in Example 4.12 to display the user's input before displaying the result of the conversion. Use the correct singular or plural form of the unit names. You may use the code in the `MetricToEnglish` method as a model.

Try It Yourself ➤ **41.** Using stubs for the conversion functions, implement and test the high-level menu program for converting currencies between British pounds and pence and U.S. dollars and cents. Use the pseudocode from question 39, and follow the model of Example 4.10, which implements the pseudocode of Figure 4.27.

SUMMARY

- This chapter covers C# operations, statements, and types that facilitate the writing of good programs. The conditional `AND`, conditional `OR`, and `NOT` operators take `bool` operands and produce a `bool` value. An `AND` expression is true only when both its operands are true; an `OR` expression is true when either or both of its operands is true; and a `NOT` expression is true when its operand is false. We use these operators to write complex conditions, which are useful as tests in `if-else` and `while` statements.
- To choose among multiple alternatives we can use nested `if-else` statements. We can use a final `else` without any following conditional test to handle the case when all the previous conditions are false. Ambiguity can arise when nesting `if` and `if-else` statements. C# uses a rule that pairs each `else` with the preceding `if`, but programmers can override this rule by enclosing a nested `if` statement in curly braces.

- A `switch` statement is a better choice than nested `if-else` statements to handle more than a few alternatives. We mark each alternative in the code with a `case` label. When C# executes a `switch` statement, it jumps to the code at the `case` label specified by the value of the switch variable, and continues executing code from that point on. `break` statements separate one alternative from the other. A `break` statement causes C# to jump to the end of the `switch` statement, bypassing the code associated with any cases that follow that break. The default label will handle any alternatives not covered by other `case` labels. We often use the `switch` statement to provide a menu of choices for the user.

- The `for` statement and the `do` statement make it easier to write programs requiring repetition. The `for` statement has four parts: initialize, test, update, and body. The initialize part initializes, and may declare, an index variable that identifies each repetition. The test condition evaluates to true or false. C# repeats the execution of the body, a simple statement, or a block enclosed in curly braces, as long as the condition is true. After each repetition, C# evaluates the update expression, which often increments the value of the index variable. The flexible `for` statement allows a number of variations in its use. It is ideal when we have a fixed number of repetitions.

- The `do` statement is like the `while` statement, but it checks the test condition after executing the loop body instead of before; the loop body will be executed at least once. C# executes the body of a `do` statement, then terminates the loop if the test condition is false, but evaluates the body again if the test is true. The repetition will terminate only when the test condition becomes false. In writing a `do` statement, as well as in writing a `for` statement or a `while` statement, we must be very careful to make sure that the test condition eventually fails or the loop will never terminate.

- The `switch`, `for`, and `do` statements give the programmer options to design the program control flow. C# has data types, `char`, `long`, and `float`, which add choices for the program's data. The character type, `char`, internally uses Unicode to represent the many characters used in different locales. In this text we use the ASCII character set, which includes lowercase and uppercase letters, numerals, punctuation, various operators, and special characters, some of which are nonprinting control characters. C# uses single quotes to represent characters such as '`A`'. The backslash, '`\`', is an escape character, signaling to C# that the next character is a special character such as '`\n`', the newline character. We can declare variables of type `char` and input character data from the keyboard.

- The `long` type allows us to use integers of up to 19 digits, roughly twice as many as the 10-digit maximum for type `int`. The `long` type has the arithmetic operators +, -,*, /, and %. We represent literals of type `long` using the suffix L or l to distinguish these values from those of type `int`. For decimal numbers, the type `float` uses less precision (seven digits) than the type `double`, and uses less space internally. We suffix each `float` literal with an F or an f to distinguish it from a value of type `double`.

- The `Math` class contains methods to compute a number of mathematical functions including powers, square roots, absolute value, maxima, minima, floor, and ceiling. There are methods for evaluating the natural logarithm, exponential, and trigonometric functions. In using any of the methods from the `Math` class we prefix the method name with the class name, `Math`, as in `Math.Sqrt(2.0)`, which computes the square root of 2.

- We apply these statements, data types, operations and `Math` functions to solve problems, using an iterative process that repeats the steps of developing pseudocode, translating the pseudocode to a C# program, and testing that program, until the solution is complete. In the early stages of development we use stubs for methods that we will design later in the development process. By building our program in stages, we keep control of the design, clearly thinking through the steps that will lead to a correct, efficient, and maintainable solution.

Addenum to Chapter 4: IO.cs

`IO.cs` contains three input methods which for convenience and reuse we group in the `IO` class. We will compile this code to a library that we can use in other programs. To avoid using this library, we could just copy these methods directly into the classes that use them.

Using the .NET Framework SDK, we compile `IO.cs` using the command

```
csc /target:library IO.cs
```

The result is the file `IO.dll`, a dynamically linked library that we can use, as we did in the examples in this chapter, by including a reference to it in the compilation, as in

```
csc /r:IO.dll Reward.cs
```

which compiles Example 4.8.

To compile `IO.cs` to a library using Visual Studio .NET, we click on *File*, *Add Project*, *New Project*, and select *Class Library* as the project type. We add `IO.cs` to the project and build the project, which produces the `IO.dll` library file.

When using Visual Studio .NET to run a program that uses the IO library, we first create a new project. Then we can click on *Project*, *Add*, *Add Existing Item* to add `Reward.cs` to the project. We then click on *Project*, *Add Reference* to add the `IO.dll` file containing the IO library.

EXAMPLE 4.15 ■ IO.cs

```
/*  Input methods we use to make examples easier to read.
  */

using System;
public class IO {

     // Returns an int value from the console
  public static int GetInt(String prompt) {
    Console.Write(prompt);
    return int.Parse(Console.ReadLine());
  }

        // Returns a double value from the console.
  public static double GetDouble(String prompt) {
    Console.Write(prompt);
```

```
        return double.Parse(Console.ReadLine());
      }

          // Returns a char value from the console.
      public static char GetChar(String prompt) {
        Console.Write(prompt);
        return Console.ReadLine()[0];                        // Note 1
      }
    }
```

Note 1: `return Console.ReadLine()[0];`

When `s` is a `String`, `s[0]` returns the first character of that `String`. Later we will study strings and the array notation used here.

SKILL BUILDER EXERCISES

1. Rewrite the following `switch` statement using `if-else` statements.

```
switch(i) {
    case 1:
          j += 2;
          break;
    case 3:
          j -= 5;
          break;
    case7:
    case10:
          j *= 17;
          break;
    default:
          j = 0;
          break;
}
```

2. Rewrite the following `for` loop using a `while` loop.

```
for (int i = 0; i <= 20; i++)
    sum += i * i;
```

3. Rewrite the following fragment using a `do` loop instead of a `while` loop.

```
int sum = 0;
int i = IO.GetInt("Enter an integer");
while (sum < 100) {
    sum += i;
    i = IO.GetInt("Enter an integer");
}
```

4. Which of the following expressions is equivalent to

```
((x + 3) < (y - 10)) && ((!(x > 4)) == (y + (2 * x)))
```

where `x` and `y` are of type `int`?

a. `x + 3 < y - 10 && !x > 4 == y + 2 * x`

b. `(x + 3 < y - 10) && (!x > 4 == y + 2 * x)`

c. `x + 3 < y - 10 && !(x > 4) == y + 2 * x`

d. all of the above

e. none of the above

5. Which of the following statements is equivalent to this `switch` statement?

```
switch(x) {
    case 2:  y = 3;
             break;
    case 5:  y = 7;
             break;
    case 7:  y = 9;
             break;
  }
```

a.
```
if (x == 2)
  y = 3;
else if (x == 5)
  y = 7;
else if (x == 7)
  y = 9;
```

b.
```
if (x == 2 || x == 5)
  y = 7;
else if (x == 7)
  y = 9;
```

c.
```
if (x == 2)
  y = 7;
else if (x == 5)
  y = 7;
else  y = 9;
```

d. none of the above

6. Which of the following `for` statements computes the same value for `sum` as this?

```
for (int x = 0; x < 15; x+=2) sum += x + 5;
```

a. `for (int x = 5; x < 20; x+=2) sum += x;`

b. `for (int x = 5; x < 20; sum += x-2) x += 2;`

c. `for (int x = 0; x < 15; sum += x+3) x += 2;`

d. all of the above

e. none of the above

7. Which of the following do statements is equivalent to this?

```
y = x + 7;
x++;
while (x < 9) {
  y = x + 7;
  x++;
}
```

a.
```
y = x + 7;
x++;
do {
    y = x + 7;
    x++;
} while (x < 9);
```

b.
```
do {
  y = x + 7;
  x++;
} while (x < 9);
```

c.
```
do {
  y = x + 7;
  x++;
} while ( x < = 9);
```

d. none of the above

DEBUGGING EXERCISE

8. The following program attempts to calculate the total commission received by a salesperson who earns 7% on sales of product A which total less than $40,000 and 10% on the amount of sales above $40,000. For example, a sale of $50,000 would earn a commission of $3800. The salesperson receives a commission of 5% on sales of product B under $20,000, 6.5% on the amount of sales over $20,000 but under $50,000, and 7.5% on the amount over $50,000. Find and correct any errors in this program.

```
public class Commission {
  public static void main(String [] args) {
    Console.Write("Enter the amount of Product A sales: ");
    double salesOfA = double.Parse(Console.ReadLine());
    Console.Write("Enter the amount of Product B sales: ");
    double salesOfB = double.Parse(Console.ReadLine());
    double amount = 0;
    if (salesOfA < 40000.00)
       amount += .07 * salesOfA;
    else
       amount = .1 * (salesOfA - 40000.0);
    if (salesOfB < 20000.00)
       amount += .05 * salesOfB;
    else if (salesOfB > 20000.00 || salesOfB < 50000.00)
       amount += 1000  + .065 * (salesOfB - 50000.00);
    else
       amount = .075 * (salesOfB - 50000.00);
    Console.WriteLine("The commission is {0}",amount);
  }
}
```

PROGRAM MODIFICATION EXERCISES

Putting It All Together ➤ **9.** Do Exercise 9 of Chapter 3 (Write a C# program that computes the weekly pay for an employee. Input the number of hours worked. The employee receives $7.50 per hour for the first 40 hours and $11.25 per hour for each additional hour.) with the added condition that the number of hours worked is between 0 and 80.

Putting It All Together ➤ **10.** Do Exercise 10 of Chapter 3 (Write a C# program that checks a grade point average the user inputs, and outputs "`Congratulations, You made the honor roll`" if the average is 3.5 and above, but outputs "`Sorry, You are on probation`" if the average is below 2.0.) with the added condition that the grade point average is between 0.0 and 4.0.

11. Modify Example 4.6 to let the user type 'Y' or 'y' instead of 1 and 'N' or 'n' instead of 0 to indicate whether or not to repeat the calculation.

12. Modify Example 4.3 to use the `switch` statement of Figure 4.13 instead of nested `if-else` statements.

PROGRAM DESIGN EXERCISES

13. Write a C# program that inputs the radius of a circle and outputs its area. Allow the user to repeat the calculation as often as desired. Use `Math.PI` for the value of pi. The area of a circle is pi times the square of the radius.

14. Write a C# program that inputs the radius of a circle and outputs its circumference. Allow the user to repeat the calculation as often as desired. Use `Math.PI` for the value of pi. The circumference of a circle is pi times the diameter. The diameter of a circle is twice the radius.

15. Write a C# program that inputs the radius of the base of a circular cylinder and its height and outputs its volume. Allow the user to repeat the calculation as often as desired. Use `Math.PI` for the value of pi. The volume of a cylinder is the height times the area of the base.

16. The ancient Babylonians used a divide and average method for computing the square root of a positive number *x*. First estimate the square root by some value *r*; any positive estimate will do. Then compute the quotient, *x/r*. Averaging *r* and *x/r* gives a better estimate, so continue the process, dividing and averaging until the estimates agree to the desired number of places. For example, to compute the square root of 2

```
estimate 1   divide 2/1 = 2       average (1+2)/2 = 1.5
estimate 1.5 divide 2/1.5 = 1.33 average (1.5+1.33)/2 = 1.415
estimate 1.415 .... and so on.
```

Write a C# program to compute the square root of a number input by the user. Use the divide and average method and stop after 10 repetitions of the divide and average steps. Compare your result with the value produced by the Sqrt method of the Math class.

17. Write a C# program to compute square roots, as described in Exercise 16, but stop the repetitions when two successive estimates differ by less than 1.0E-6. Also output the number of repetitions of the divide and average process.

18. The greatest common divisor (gcd) of two integers is the largest positive number that divides evenly into both numbers. For example, `gcd(6,9) = 3`, `gcd(4,14)=2`, and `gcd(5,8) = 1`. The Euclidean algorithm computes the `gcd` by a repetitive process. Find the remainder resulting from dividing the smaller number into the larger. Repeat this process with the smaller number and the remainder until the remainder is zero. The last non-zero remainder is the greatest common divisor. For example, to find the `gcd` of 54 and 16, the steps are

```
54 % 16 = 6
16 %  6 = 4
 6 %  4 = 2
 4 %  2 = 0
```

so `gcd(54,16) = 2`. Write a C# program to compute the greatest common divisor of two integers.

19. When we convert a fraction of the form `1/n`, where neither 2 nor 5 divide *n*, to a decimal, we find that the digits repeat a pattern over and over again. For example,

```
1/3     = .333333333333...          repeat pattern      3
1/7     = .142857142857142857...    repeat pattern 142657
1/37   = .027027027 ....            repeat pattern    027
```

The number of digits in the pattern for `1/n`, called the period, is equal to the number of zeros in the smallest power of 10 that has a remainder of one when divided by *n*. For example, to find the number of digits on the pattern for 1/37, we calculate

```
  10 % 37 = 10
 100 % 37 = 26
1000 % 37 =  1
```

Write a C# program to find the length of the repeating pattern for fractions `1/n`, where neither 2 nor 5 divide *n*.

20. Write a C# program that converts currencies between British currency of pounds and pence, in which 1 pound contains 100 pence, and U.S. currency in dollars and cents. Assume an exchange rate of 1.6595 U.S. dollars per British pound. Give the user a menu to choose the type of conversion. Allow the user to repeat as often as desired. (See Test Your Understanding questions 39 and 41.)

21. Write a C# program to perform geometric calculations. Let the user choose whether to find the area of a circle (see Exercise 13), the circumference of a circle (see Exercise 14), or the volume of a cylinder (see Exercise 15). Allow the user to repeat as often as desired.

22. Suppose you are able to pay $400 per month to buy a car. Write a C# program to determine if you can afford to buy a car that costs $15,000 if the interest rate is 6% and you make payments for 48 months. (Hint: Each month, determine how much of the $400 payment will be used to pay interest, then deduct the remaining payment from the principal.)

23. Generalize Exercise 22 to have the user input the size of the payment, the price of the car, the interest rate, and the number of monthly payments.

24. The Sturdy company invests \$100,000 in a project that earns 10% interest compounded annually. If the interest is allowed to compound, what is the value of the investment after seven years? Use the formula

$$V = P(1 + r/100)^N$$

where *r* is the interest rate, *N* is the number of years, *P* is the initial investment, and *V* is the value after *N* years.

25. The Sturdy company is evaluating an investment that will return \$400,000 at the end of five years. The company wants to earn an interest rate of 20% compounded annually. How much should they pay for this investment? Use the formula

$$P = V \; / \; (1 + r/100)^N$$

where *V* is the investment's value after *N* years and *r* is the interest rate.

26. Calculate pi using the series

```
pi / 4 = 1 - 1/3 + 1/5 - 1/7 + 1/9 - ...   and so on.
```

Output the estimate of pi after computing 100, 1000, 10,000, and 100,000 terms of the series.

27. Compute e^x where

$$e^x = 1 + x/1! + x^2/2! + x^3/3! + \ldots \quad \ldots + x^n/n! + \ldots$$

and `n! = n(n-1)(n-2)...   ...1`, the product of the integers from 1 to *n*. (We pronounce the expression `n!` as "n factorial.") Let the user input the value of *x*, of type `double`. Continue adding terms until the difference of successive terms is less than 1.0 E-6. Compare your answer with the C# method `Math.Exp(x)`. (Hint: Compute each term from the previous one. For example, the fourth term is `x/3` times the third term.)

5 Getting Started with Object-Oriented Programming

Abstracting objects makes us more successful. Life would be much more difficult if we only saw blotches of color everywhere or heard unclassified sounds, but instead we see a tree or hear a bell. In programming, too, objects help to organize our programs in ways we can understand and modify. Not every application benefits from object-oriented programming, but for many it is very effective. We first define the object concept without using C#. We illustrate objects by developing a simple vending machine.

Next, using two simple examples, a restaurant and an automated teller, we introduce object-oriented design with use cases and scenarios, which lets us identify the objects in the system. An object-oriented program shows that control and interactions are found in each object rather than in a master controller.

Looking at these design examples shows us the need for class definitions to define the state and responsibilities of our objects. Writing a simple `BankAccount` class introduces the basic concepts of instance variables and methods, constructors, and overloading.

The `BankAccount` class defines a type of object. Users of this type want to create `BankAccount` objects and invoke their services. After illustrating the use of `BankAccount` objects, we modify the definition to include a class variable and method, contrasting them with instance variables and methods. We then complete the restaurant code to show a complete object-oriented program, and also introduce some UML diagrams.

In later chapters, we continue with object-oriented concepts, including composition, interfaces, inheritance, polymorphism, abstract classes, and design with use cases and scenarios to complete the ATM example.

OBJECTIVES

- Understand the definition of an object
- Understand the difference between a concept and its instances
- Begin object-oriented design with use cases, scenarios, and UML diagrams
- Understand that a class defines a type of object
- Write a class, including instance variables and methods, and constructors
- Create and use objects
- Understand that C# primitive type variables hold values, and object variables hold references
- Understand the difference between class variables and methods and instance variables and methods

5.1 THE OBJECT CONCEPT

We introduce the object concept with an intuitive analogy to a vending machine. This section does not use any C#. We prefer to introduce these important ideas before delving into coding specifics in later sections.

Objects

An **object** has state, behavior, and identity. We sometimes speak of our state of mind as happy, sad, or angry to describe a particular condition we are in. Humans are rather complex objects. For simplicity, let us deal with inanimate objects such as vending machines (see Figure 5.1), or even conceptual objects such as bank accounts or character strings.

FIGURE 5.1 **A vending machine object**

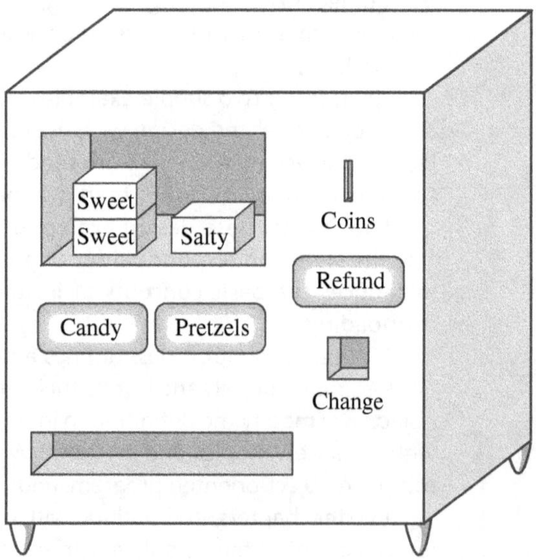

A vending machine has a state. It may be operational or broken. It may have plenty of candy or be out of candy. It may be able or unable to make change. Some information about its state may be public. For example, a big sign may state that it is out of order, or we may be able to see the number of candy bars available. Other information may be private, such as the amount of available coffee or change.

A vending machine has behavior. It does not initiate behavior, but it does provide services that we think of as its behavior. For example, we may select coffee or candy, or may ask for a refund. Most of the vending machine's behavior is public. After all, the purpose of a vending machine is to provide services. However, there might be some private behavior, used only internally, such as filling with water from a pipe when needed.

A vending machine has an identity. Another vending machine may have exactly the same state and provide the same services, but it is a different machine.

Vending machines provide an instructive model for object-oriented programming. When we select coffee, we do not need to know the details of how the vending machine provides the coffee. The coffee may be brewed in a big urn, instant coffee may be mixed with hot water, or (as young children may think), little people in the machine may make it.

As customers, we use the vending machine's services without needing to know the details of the construction of the machine. The buttons or levers of the vending machine provide an interface to its behavior. Vending machine users do not have to manage the details of how to make the coffee or of how to dispense the candy.

Using Objects

To make a vending machine work, we put money in a coin slot or press a button to make a selection. We describe this process generically as sending a message to an object. Because each vending machine has an identity, we can refer to it by a name, say `bigRed`. The machine provides a coin slot to enter money. We think of entering money in the slot as sending a message to `bigRed` to invoke its `EnterMoney` behavior. We say

```
Send the EnterMoney message with 75 cents to the bigRed
machine
```

to enter 75 cents in the `bigRed` vending machine.

Our vending machine provides a button to select candy. We say

```
Send the DispenseCandy message to the bigRed machine
```

suggesting that we would like to have `bigRed` drop a candy bar into the tray for us to take and eat.

What responses do we get from sending these messages? The response depends on the state of the machine. Ideally, we will get our candy, but what if candy costs 80 cents? Our actions are likely to get us candy only when the price is not greater than 75 cents. What if the vending machine is out of candy?

The response also depends on which machines get the messages. If `hotStuff` is another machine and we say

FIGURE 5.2 **Sending the `DispenseCandy` message to the `bigRed` vending machine**

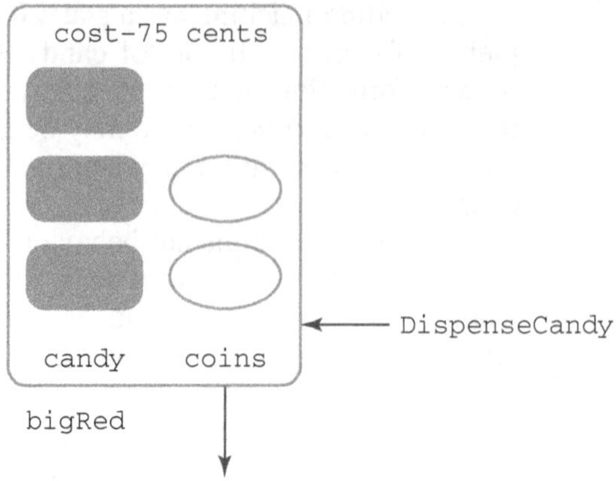


```
Send the EnterMoney message with 75 cents to the hotStuff
machine
Send the DispenseCandy message to the bigRed machine
```

we are unlikely to get candy, because we entered the money in a different machine.

These examples show that the state of a vending machine must represent the amount of money deposited, the quantity of candy it contains, and the cost of candy. The result of the `DispenseCandy` message will depend on these variables, and perhaps others, as Figure 5.2 illustrates.

With objects, the result of sending a message depends on both the object we send it to and the message we send. This contrasts with a computational method such as square root, which always gives the same result. For example, the square root of 9.0 is always 3.0. Calling

```
Math.Sqrt(9.0);
```

always returns 3.0, as Figure 5.3 illustrates. The square root computation does not need or use objects.

Defining an Object Type

We looked at vending machines as examples of objects, each having state, behavior, and identity. Our vending machines are very simple. Let us try to describe this type of vending machine. First we give it a name, say `SimpleVender`.

FIGURE 5.3 **The square root of 9.0 is always 3.0**

Next we abstract SimpleVender behavior. For our SimpleVender type, we can enter money and we can dispense candy. We think of these as two services, or operations, that a SimpleVender object will provide. Other objects can invoke these services. Together these services represent the behavior we can expect from each SimpleVender object.

Finally, we abstract the state that each SimpleVender object has. Often an object keeps its state hidden from users. Users send messages to an object, invoking its operations. As we have seen, the object's response to a message depends on its state. For SimpleVender, we have identified the amount of candy, the cost of candy, and the amount of money deposited as the quantities that define the state. It contains only one kind of candy.

We now have the equivalent of a dictionary definition for a type of vending machine. It might look like this:

SimpleVender: A type of simple vending machine. Provides two operations, EnterMoney and DispenseCandy. Maintains a state consisting of the amount of candy it contains, the amount of money deposited, and the cost of candy.

Now that we have defined the SimpleVender type, we can instantiate objects of that type.

Instantiating Objects

Identity is the third characteristic of an object. We construct real objects out of various materials. In the computer each object gets a certain location in memory. When we construct an object, we initialize its state. We initialize the state of a SimpleVender object just as we would stock and set up a real vending machine. Each object is an instance of its type, so we speak of instantiating an object when we create a new object instance.

To construct bigRed, we might specify that bigRed has type SimpleVender. We initialize bigRed with 10 candy bars, no money deposited, and with candy costing 65 cents.

Once we have created an object, we can invoke its operations, which represent its behavior. We shorten the message sending description to the notation

```
objectName.messageName(messageData);
```

Each message is directly associated with the object to which we send it. Objects of type SimpleVender accept two messages, EnterMoney and DispenseCandy. The response to

```
bigRed.DispenseCandy()
```

may be a message or silence, but it will not be candy because we have not entered any money. However, we expect candy in response to

```
bigRed.EnterMoney(65)
bigRed.DispenseCandy()
```

because we have entered enough money to cover the cost of the candy and the machine is not out of candy.

We would like to receive candy and 10 cents change from

```
bigRed.EnterMoney(75)
bigRed.DispenseCandy()
```

but the `SimpleVender` type of machine requires exact change. We could define other types that include more capabilities.

Once we have defined a type we can construct many instances of that type. For example, let us construct `highPrice`, a `SimpleVender` instance with five candy bars, no money deposited, and an 80-cent cost for candy. For this object, the sequence

```
highPrice.EnterMoney(75)
highPrice.DispenseCandy()
```

does not produce candy. The `SimpleVender` type says nothing about refunds and does not provide a service to request a refund. This is another feature we could design in a more detailed type.

The BIG Picture

An object has state, behavior, and identity. We define an object type by giving it a name and identifying the operations that each object of that type will have. We also specify the variables that each object will use to define its state. The state is usually hidden.

We can send a message to an object, asking it to perform one of its operations. Its response will depend on its state. We can create many instances of a given object type.

✓ Test Your Understanding

1. Suppose we construct an object, `myVender`, of type `SimpleVender`. What operations does `myVender` have?
2. Which state variables should we initialize when we construct an object of type `SimpleVender`?
3. Which is correct, `bigRed.EnterMoney(50)` or `SimpleVender.EnterMoney(50)`, and why?

5.2 INTRODUCTION TO OBJECT-ORIENTED DESIGN

Computer programmers must develop ever larger systems with more capabilities. They seek programming techniques that allow them to be highly productive and achieve quality programs. The procedural approach, used since the first high-level languages were introduced in the late 1950s, is complemented by object-oriented programming, an approach first discussed in the 1960s, but which became popular in the late 1980s and the 1990s.

In fiction, each story has a point of view. A single person can tell the entire story from his or her point of view, with the thoughts of the other characters never appearing. Another approach is to have each character express his or her thoughts and feelings and show their actions. Procedural programming is programming from a single point of view, using a controller that orchestrates all the action while the data acted on is passive. Object-oriented programming puts the data inside objects that actively manage that data by providing services to other objects. Rather than having a single controller manipulating passive data, an object-oriented program lets the objects interact with each other, each meeting its responsibilities. Object-oriented programming combines the data and its operations into objects.

A Definition

Bertrand Meyer gives an example of a payroll program, which produces paychecks from timecards.[1] Management may later want to extend this program to produce statistics or tax information. The payroll function itself may need to be changed to produce weekly checks instead of biweekly checks, for example. The procedures used to implement the original payroll program would need to be changed to make any of these modifications. Meyer notes that any of these payroll programs will manipulate the same sort of data, employee records, company regulations, and so forth.

Focusing on the more stable aspect of such systems, Meyer states a principle: "Ask not first what the system does: Ask WHAT it does it to!"[2]; and a definition: "Object-oriented design is the method which leads to software architectures based on the objects every system or subsystem manipulates (rather than "the" function it is meant to ensure)."[3]

Use Cases and Scenarios

In this section we model a customer order at a fast-food restaurant, showing how objects interact and call one another's services, leading to a true object-oriented simulation. We first need to identify the types of objects we will need. We do this by considering typical uses of the system, called **use cases**, and various **scenarios** which show, in a step-by-step manner, the interactions among objects that take place relating to that use case.

When designing using objects, we may start by identifying the use cases. In our example, one use case would be a customer placing an order. To understand each use of the system, we describe typical scenarios. For each use case, we develop a primary scenario showing the normal interactions and several secondary scenarios, which list the interactions that take place in more unusual or error situations.

For our restaurant example, a normal scenario (shown in Figure 5.4) would involve a customer entering the restaurant, walking up to the counter, and placing an order.

---

[1]Bertrand Meyer, *Object-Oriented Software Construction*, Second Edition, Prentice-Hall, 1997, p. 105.

[2]Ibid., p. 116.

[3]Ibid., p. 116.

```
The customer orders a burger, soda, and fries from the waiter.
The waiter asks the cook to make a burger.
The waiter serves the soda to the customer.
The waiter asks the cook to make the fries.
The cook gives the waiter the burger to serve.
The cook gives the waiter the fries to serve.
The waiter asks the customer to pay.
```

FIGURE 5.4 **A scenario for a fast-food order**

From this scenario, we identify three objects: a customer, a waiter, and a cook. The scenario also shows the responsibilities of each object. The customer places an order and pays for the food. The waiter takes an order and serves food. The cook makes burgers and fries.

Once we have identified the responsibilities of an object, we can determine the state each object needs to maintain to meet its responsibilities. The customer has money to pay for food, the waiter has cash received, and the cook has a supply of burgers and fries.

The scenario of Figure 5.4 led us to abstract the three object types of Figure 5.5. In Section 5.4 we will write a C# program that uses instances of these types to simulate a customer placing an order. We will use instances of the `Customer`, `Waiter`, and `Cook` classes, which will send each other messages according to the scenario of Figure 5.4 to complete the ordering process.

A good way to visualize each instance is as a black box with a handle for each service it provides. In design, a black box signifies that we cannot see the workings of the object but must use its services (see Figure 5.6).

An object-oriented program to simulate this use of a restaurant would create the `Customer`, `Waiter`, and `Cook` objects and let them interact as the scenario indicates. We start by sending the `PlaceOrder` message to the customer. The customer sends the `TakeOrder` message to the waiter. The waiter sends the `MakeBurger` message to the cook, and so on, following the scenario of Figure 5.4.

FIGURE 5.5 **State and responsibilities for Customer, Waiter, and Cook**

	Customer	**Waiter**	**Cook**
State	Money	Cash	Burgers and fries
Responsibilities	place order	take order	make burgers
	pay	serve item	make fries

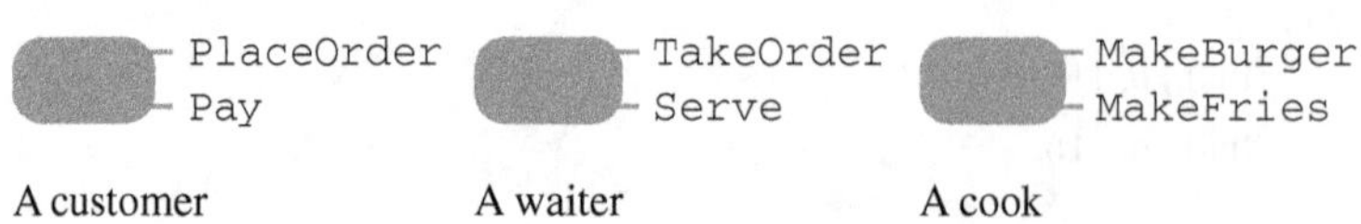

FIGURE 5.6 **Objects showing only available services**

Where do we define these services and the items that make up the state of the objects? In C# each object is an instance of a class, which defines the state variables and service methods for that type of object. For example, a `Customer` class defines the state and behavior for `Customer` objects, as do the `Waiter` and `Cook` classes for `Waiter` and `Cook` objects. In the next section we go carefully over the coding of classes. In Section 5.6 we write the `Customer`, `Waiter`, and `Cook` classes to define the services and states for the objects we used in the restaurant ordering example. First, we introduce another example of analysis and design to which we shall return several times in this text.

Scenarios for an ATM System

Before getting into the details of object-oriented programming in C#, we start another design, previewing the automated teller machine simulation we design in Section 10.5. The familiar situation is that a user inserts a card into the teller machine, the machine asks the user for a personal identification number (PIN), the user enters his or her PIN, and so on until the transaction is complete. Going through complete scenarios of typical uses of the system helps us to find the objects and identify their responsibilities. Figure 5.7 shows such a scenario for a deposit transaction.

Looking at the scenario of Figure 5.7, we identify four objects: user, teller, bank, and bank account. From this scenario, we can identify the responsibilities of each object as shown in Figure 5.8.

By writing scenarios for other types of transactions, we would find other responsibilities for our objects, and perhaps other objects. For example, an account object will have the additional responsibilities

```
Withdraw an amount
Get the account balance
```

We will look more closely at such an account object in the next section.

```
The user asks the teller to accept an ATM card.
The teller asks the user to enter a PIN.
The user asks the teller to accept a PIN.
The teller asks the user to select a transaction type.
The user asks the teller to accept a deposit.
The teller asks the user to select an account type.
The user asks the teller to accept a savings account type.
The teller asks the bank to find the bank account of the chosen
    type for the user with the specified PIN.
The bank gives the teller a reference to the account.
The teller asks the user to specify an amount.
The user asks the teller to accept an amount.
The teller asks the account to deposit the specified amount.
The teller asks the user to select another transaction....
```

FIGURE 5.7 **A scenario for a successful deposit**

FIGURE 5.8
Responsibilities derived from the scenario of Figure 5.7

```
User             Specify a PIN
                 Select a transaction type
                 Select an account type
                 Specify an amount

Bank             Find a specified account

BankAccount      Deposit an amount

Teller           Accept an ATM card
                 Accept a PIN
                 Accept a transaction type
                 Accept an account type
                 Accept an amount
                 Accept an account
```

To implement the ATM system, we need to create `User`, `Bank`, `Account`, and `Teller` objects, which we identified using a use case and scenarios, and let them interact. The `Main` method for the ATM system will be very short, because rather than a single controller manipulating data, each object keeps its own data and invokes services of other objects.

Now we are ready to see how C# lets us define and create objects, which leads us to the classification process.

Classification

Many of our everyday concepts involve a classification of objects. When we sit on a chair, we are sitting on a specific instance of the `Chair` concept. The particular chair may be hard or soft, expensive or inexpensive. It provides a service, a place to sit, and has a state, occupied or unoccupied. A lamp, an instance of the lamp class, is not a chair. Its service is light and its state is on or off. We use language to categorize groups of objects. Natural language is imprecise, but we all generally agree on what we call a chair or a lamp.

In C#, we must be more precise, but the idea is similar. C# uses a class to define the state and behavior of a type of object. The word *class* evokes the idea of classification. To understand how to build a class to define a type of object, we focus first on the `BankAccount` class.

A `BankAccount` class must describe the components of the state and behavior for the various `BankAccount` objects we create. In C#, variables save the state of an object, and methods implement its behaviors. Informally, Figure 5.9 shows how the `BankAccount` class implements the state and behaviors for each of its instances.

The Unified Modeling Language (UML) has become the standard for object-oriented modeling; we will use UML diagrams in this text.[4] Figure 5.10 represents the class of all bank accounts, showing their common structure.

[4]See `http://www.rational.com/uml/` for more information on the UML.

```
balance
   A decimal value representing the dollar amount
      of the current balance for that account.

deposit an amount
   Add the amount to the current balance.

withdraw an amount
   If the amount is not greater than the current balance,
      subtract the amount from the current balance.

get the balance
   Return the current balance.
```

FIGURE 5.9 **Implementing `BankAccount` state and behavior**

FIGURE 5.10 **The `BankAccount` class**

BankAccount
balance
GetBalance Deposit Withdraw

The top section in Figure 5.10 gives the class name, the middle section lists the variables used to represent the state of an account, and the bottom section lists each account's operations used to provide its services. We say each `Bank Account` object is an instance of the `BankAccount` class. The class describes the state (data) and behavior (operations) each object instance possesses; it is like a pattern or template specifying the state and behavior of each of its instances.

Just as we may point to a favorite chair, confident that it fully exemplifies the `Chair` concept, we create each `BankAccount` object to instantiate the `BankAccount` class. In the UML notation, objects, as pictured in Figure 5.11, also have three-part diagrams. In the top part we name the object and indicate the class that defines it, underlining both, as in

```
myAccount : BankAccount
```

The middle section shows the balance with a specific value, for example

```
balance = 24.50
```

The `BankAccount` class specifies that each account must have a balance. In the object itself, the balance has a specific value. This is analogous to the concept of a chair, which specifies a seat and legs, contrasted with an actual chair object that has a hard seat and curved legs.

The third part of the object diagram lists the services the object provides. Each `BankAccount` object can deposit, withdraw, or get its balance.

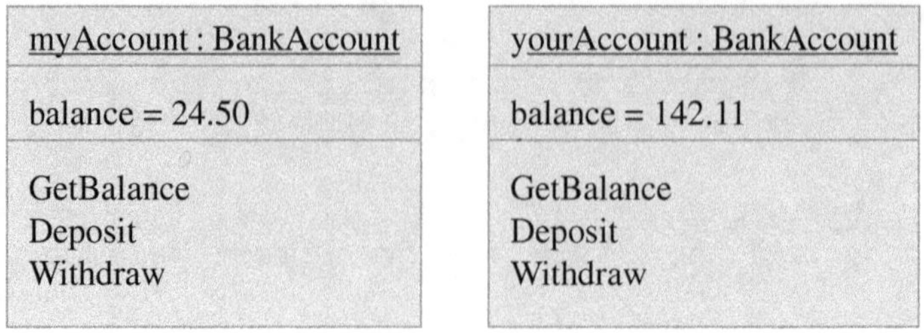

FIGURE 5.11
Two `BankAccount` objects

The objects `myAccount` and `yourAccount` of Figure 5.11 are instances of the `BankAccount` class. In the next section we will write the C# code that implements the `BankAccount` class.

The BIG Picture

In designing an object-oriented program, we write use cases listing the desired uses of the system. For each use case, scenarios show the steps for successful and unsuccessful interactions with the system. We identify objects and their responsibilities from these scenarios.

Just as a particular chair exemplifies the properties of the `Chair` concept, objects are instances of a class that defines their state and behavior. We define a class, to implement a type for each object, that specifies the data and implements operations for each object of that type.

The Unified Modeling Language (UML) is the standard notation for object-oriented design.

✓ Test Your Understanding

4. Write a scenario in which the customer orders a burger, fries, and a soda, but the drink machine is broken.
5. As a start for an object-oriented program, write a scenario describing the interactions when a customer rents a car. What objects, with what responsibilities, do you identify from this scenario?

5.3 CLASSES IN C#

Our scenarios from the previous section showed objects invoking each other's services. In order to use objects in a program, we need to define the object types we need. The type definition includes the parts necessary to create objects of that type. In Section 5.1, we defined a `SimpleVender` type informally and constructed some objects of that type. In this section, we develop a C# definition for the `BankAccount` type. In the next section, we show how to construct and use `BankAccount` objects.

We leave the full development of an ATM system, which uses inheritance and other object-oriented concepts discussed in Chapter 10, until Section 10.5.

The Structure of the `BankAccount` Class

Our analysis in the last section used a `BankAccount` object in the scenarios for the ATM system. In discussing classification, we saw that a class in C# defines the state and behavior of its object instances. To use `BankAccount` objects we need to specify them in a `BankAccount` class. The `BankAccount` class we will develop in this section will have the structure shown in Figure 5.12.

This `BankAccount` class specifies the account `balance` to represent the state of each account, and `Deposit`, `Withdraw`, and `GetBalance` as an account's behavior. The UML notation allows us to specify the type of the state variables; here `balance` is of type `double`. For simplicity we do not show the arguments to the methods or their return types. The overall structure of the `BankAccount` class in C# is

```
public class BankAccount {
    // put code to specify BankAccount objects here
}
```

A class is like a dictionary entry. The dictionary entry for *chair* defines what it means to be a chair. The `BankAccount` class defines what it means to be a bank account object. Each bank account has state, behavior, and identity. In C#, we use instance variables to hold the state of an object, and instance methods to implement the services needed to meet its responsibilities, which is what we call its behavior. We also have constructor operators to create bank accounts, each with its own memory location distinct from other objects. Thinking of the `BankAccount` class as a definition of bank account objects, it will have the structure:

```
public class BankAccount {

  // instance variables go here   (for state)
  // constructors go here         (for identity)
  // instance methods go here     (for behavior)

}
```

We now discuss each of the three parts of the `BankAccount` class: instance variables, instance methods, and constructors.

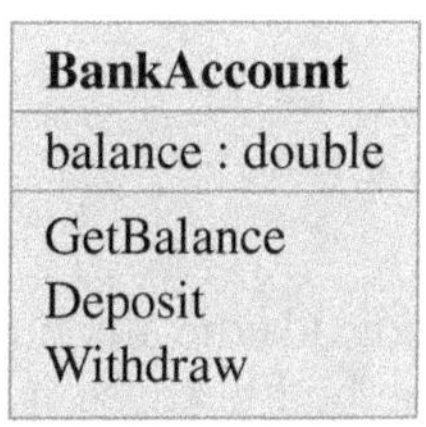

FIGURE 5.12
The `BankAccount` class

Instance Variables

An **instance variable**, also called a **field**, is a variable declared inside the class but outside of any method. The name, *instance variable,* reminds us that these variables will be part of object instances. Analogously, the `Chair` concept includes mention of legs, but the concept does not have legs, only actual chair instances do.

Our programs have used variables, but we have always declared these variables inside the `Main` method. We call these variables local variables because they are declared inside one method and cannot be used outside that method.

In C#, we declare instance variables to hold the state of an object. For a bank account we might declare

```
double balance;
```

to hold an account balance. The declaration (incomplete) for the bank account class shows how we declare the account balance outside of any method.

```
public class BankAccount  {
  private double balance;

    //  fill in the rest of the declaration here
}
```

In contrast to local variables, instance variables are available to all services of an object. Making a deposit to a bank account will increase its balance, and making a withdrawal will reduce it.

Note the use of the modifier `private`. Using `private` signifies that we want to keep the account balance data hidden within the object, accessible only by the services the object provides. The object appears as a black box to a user of its services. The user of an account can inspect its balance only by calling the object's `GetBalance` method and can change its balance only by making a deposit or a withdrawal.

Instance Methods

To specify an object's behavior we declare methods inside the class, such as a `Deposit` method in the `BankAccount` class.

```
public class BankAccount  {
  private double balance;

  public void Deposit(double amount) {
    balance += amount;
  }

    //  fill in the rest of the declaration here
}
```

The `Deposit` method adds the amount passed in as a parameter to the balance. We call it an instance method because it is part of a specific bank account instance. Each bank account will have its own `balance` and its own `Deposit` method. To put it simply, when I make a deposit into my account I want the money to increase my balance, not yours.

Our `BankAccount` class defines the concept of a bank account. Analyzing the ATM system with use cases and scenarios shows us that each bank account should provide services to get its balance and to make a withdrawal, in addition to the deposit service. Thus we must add `GetBalance` and `Withdraw` operations to the `BankAccount` class.

The code for `GetBalance()` simply returns the balance.

```
public double GetBalance() {
  return balance;
}
```

The `Withdraw` method uses an `if-else` statement to check whether the account balance is large enough to make the withdrawal. If successful, it returns the new balance, otherwise it returns –1.0, a value that is never a valid balance. We can test for a negative return value to determine if the `Withdraw` method failed because of insufficient funds.

```
public double Withdraw(double amount) {
  if (balance >= amount) {    // check for sufficient funds
    balance -= amount;
    return balance;
  }else
    return -1.0;
}
```

With the addition of the `GetBalance` and `Withdraw` methods the `BankAccount` class now has the structure

```
public class BankAccount  {
  private double balance;

  public void Deposit(double amount) {
    balance += amount;
  }
  public double GetBalance() {
    return balance;
  }
  public double Withdraw(double amount) {
    if (balance >= amount) {
      balance -= amount;
      return balance;
    }else
      return -1.0;
  }
     //  fill in the rest of the declaration here
}
```

Constructors

Our `BankAccount` class now defines the concept we identified in the analysis of the ATM system. It provides an instance variable, `balance`, for the state, and `GetBalance`, `Deposit`, and `Withdraw` methods for the services. However, we do need to add code to enable us to create and initialize `BankAccount` objects. These special methods, called **constructors**, always have the same name as the class, and never have a return value.

Every bank account has a `balance`. We can use the constructor to initialize the balance of a new account. The `BankAccount` constructor

```
public BankAccount () {
    balance = 0.0;
}
```

initializes the balance of a new `BankAccount` object to zero. Because we do not pass any values to this constructor, it must initial the balance to a default value of 0.0. If we do not include any constructors in a class, C# will create this constructor automatically. For these reasons, we call a constructor with no arguments a **default constructor**.

We would also like a constructor to create a bank account with a specified initial balance. Using method overloading, which we discuss in the next section, we can use the constructor

```
public BankAccount(double initialAmount) {
   balance = initialAmount;
}
```

to create a bank account with a balance initialized to `initialAmount`.

Figure 5.13 shows the class diagram for the `BankAccount` class as we developed it in this section.

We usually do not show this amount of detail in our class diagrams. The UML notation uses a different style from the C# style for specifying method parameters and return values. Whenever possible, we omit parameters and return values from class diagrams to avoid confusion.

Example 5.1 shows the C# code for our `BankAccount` class. This class has no `Main` method. We can compile it, but not execute it. Using the .NET Framework SDK, we create a library using the command

FIGURE 5.13
The revised `BankAccount` class

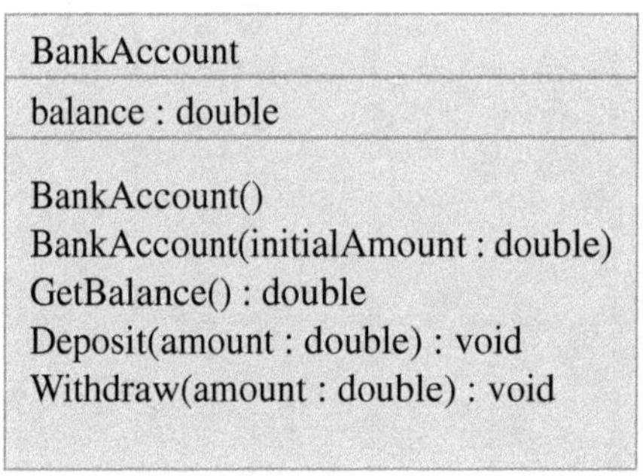

```
csc /target:library BankAccount.cs
```

We will use this library in the next example, where we create and use `BankAccount` objects. Remember that the `BankAccount` class defines the `BankAccount` object type. In the next section we will learn how to create and use `BankAccount` objects.

EXAMPLE 5.1 ■ BankAccount.cs

```
/* Declares a BankAccount class with an account balance,
 * two constructors, and GetBalance, Deposit, and
 * Withdraw operations.
 */

public class BankAccount {
  private double balance;                              // Note 1

     // Creates a Bank Account with a balance of 0
  public BankAccount()    {                            // Note 2
    balance = 0;
  }

      // Creates a Bank Account with a balance of initialAmount
  public BankAccount(double initialAmount) {           // Note 3
    balance = initialAmount;
  }

  // Returns the balance
  public double GetBalance() {                         // Note 4
    return balance;
  }

    // Increases balance by amount

  public void Deposit(double amount) {                 // Note 5
    balance += amount;
  }

   // Reduces balance by amount, if possible
  public double Withdraw(double amount) {
    if (balance >= amount) {
      balance -= amount;
      return balance;
    }else
      return -1.0;
  }
}
```

■

Note 1: `private double balance;`

We declare the variable `balance` outside of any method. Each object has its own `balance` variable that stores the balance for that specific account. We declare `balance` as `private` so only `BankAccount` operations can use it.

Note 2: `public BankAccount() {`

`BankAccount()` is a constructor. A constructor has no return value, not even `void`. It has the same name as the class, in this case, `BankAccount`. We need a `BankAccount` constructor to initialize `balance` because `balance` is a private field, and can be changed only by `BankAccount` operations. A constructor is a special operation we use when we create a new object, as in the expression `new BankAccount()`, which we will introduce in the next section.

Note 3: `public BankAccount(double initialAmount) {`

This constructor overloads the name `BankAccount`, but it has a parameter giving the initial balance for the new account, so C# can tell the difference between it and the `BankAccount` constructor with no parameters. We discuss overloading briefly in the next section.

Note 4: `public double GetBalance() {`

We include the `GetBalance` method to tell us the account balance. Because `balance` is a `private` variable, we can access it only by using a method that is a member of the `BankAccount` class. The `GetBalance` method has no parameters but returns a `double` value that is the balance.

Note 5: `public void Deposit(double amount) {`

The `Deposit` method refers to a specific `BankAccount` object. It adds the specified `amount` to the `balance` of that specific bank account. Depositing to my account will increase my account balance, and depositing to your account will increase yours.

Style

Our `BankAccount` class declares the data first, then the constructors, and finally the other methods. Even though we cannot directly use the private data, we like to place it in an easy-to-spot location at the top of the class definition. Many programmers prefer to place the private data after the methods, which are usually public. The public methods provide the interface the programmer will use directly, and some feel that for this reason they should be at the top. For your programs, choose one of these styles and use it consistently.

The BIG Picture

The `BankAccount` class implements a programmer-defined type. It contains constructors, with the same name as the class, that initialize the private instance variable `balance` when a `BankAccount` object is created. The instance methods `GetBalance`, `Deposit`, and `Withdraw` allow a `BankAccount` object to fulfill its responsibilities. Because C# supports method overloading we were able to include two constructors with the same name.

✓ Test Your Understanding

6. Write the declaration for an integer account number instance variable in the `BankAccount` class. Restrict access to the account number to methods of the `BankAccount` class.
7. Where do we declare an instance variable of a class? Give an example of an instance variable in Example 5.1.
8. Suppose we want to add a third constructor to Example 5.1 which would have no parameters, but would set the initial balance to $25.00. We could code it as

```
public BankAccount () {
 balance = 25.00;
}
```

   Could we add this constructor to Example 5.1 or will C# not allow it? Explain.

Try It Yourself ➤

9. Try omitting both constructors from Example 5.1. Check that the revised `BankAccount` class still compiles without error. Were we to use this revised definition, C# would provide a default no-argument constructor that would initialize every `BankAccount` `balance` to 0.0.

5.4 USING C# OBJECTS

Now that we have defined the `BankAccount` class, we can create `BankAccount` objects and invoke their services. C# treats object types differently than it treats primitive types, so we look first at reference types used for objects.

Reference Types

C# uses variables for objects such as bank accounts differently than it does variables for basic data types such as integers. Let us review how we created variables to hold integers. The statement

```
int x = 4;
```

declares a variable, `x`, of type integer, and initializes it with the value of 4. Inside the computer, the variable `x` has a storage location and the computer places the value 4 into that location. Here the variable holds the value 4, as is shown in Figure 5.14.

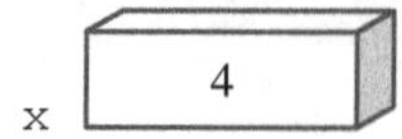

FIGURE 5.14
A primitive type variable holds a value

A real-world analogy might involve me asking at the dinner table to please pass the salt, and my wife graciously handing me the salt shaker. My wife can easily move the small salt shaker to my hand. My hand is like the variable `x`, and the salt is like the value 4.

By contrast, suppose I would like to stand next to the Grand Canyon. Even if I had a hundred helpers, they could not pass me the Grand Canyon. If I want to stand next to the Grand Canyon, I have to go there. In fact, my wife might pass me a map showing how to get to there. When I hold that map in my hand I am holding a reference to the Grand Canyon, telling me where it is.

In C#, an object is like the Grand Canyon. An object may be large, so we do not want to pass it around. We put it in one place and tell users where it is. A variable for an object holds a reference to that object, telling where to find it in the computer's memory. A variable, `myAccount`, of type `BankAccount` holds a reference to the `BankAccount` object. It does not hold the object itself. A reference tells the location of the object. Locations in the computer memory have an integer address, just as most people have an address given by a number and street name.

In Figure 5.15 the variable `myAccount` has type `BankAccount`. We shall soon see how to declare such a variable. It holds the address, which we suppose is 5000, of a `BankAccount` object. Because the actual address is an implementation detail, we often show this relationship between the variable and the object to which it refers by drawing an arrow from the variable to the object, as in Figure 5.16.

We will compare reference types with primitive types more fully in the next chapter when we introduce `String` objects. The variable `myAccount` has a refer-

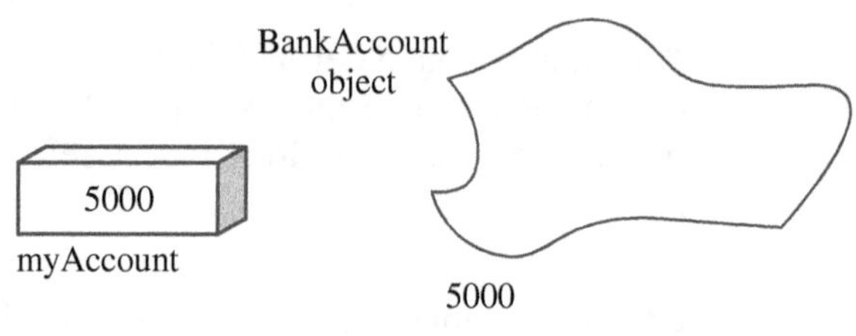

FIGURE 5.15
A variable of type `BankAccount` referring to a `BankAccount` object

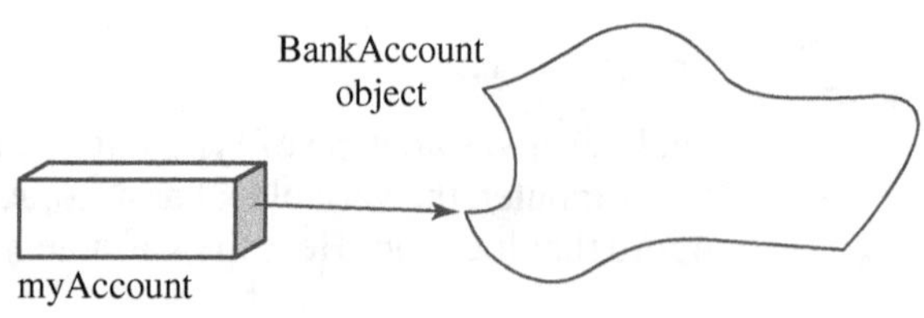

FIGURE 5.16
A variable of type `BankAccount` referring to a `BankAccount` object

FIGURE 5.17
Variables in C# do not hold objects

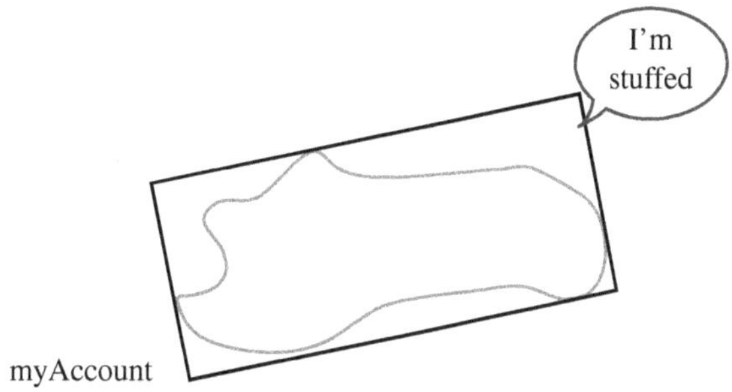

ence type because it refers to the `BankAccount` rather than trying to hold it. Figure 5.17 shows that objects may be large and unwieldy to hold in variables.

Creating Objects

C# provides an operator for creating objects, appropriately enough called **new**. We can declare a new bank account with the expression

```
new BankAccount();
```

which creates the `BankAccount` object, reserving space in memory, and calling the default `BankAccount` constructor to initialize it. This expression creates a new bank account, but does not tell anyone where it is. Figure 5.18 shows that there are no references to this new account and it has no name.

To use a `BankAccount` object we must declare a variable to refer to it, as in the statement

```
BankAccount myAccount = new BankAccount();
```

which declares the variable `myAccount` to have type `BankAccount` and to refer to a specific new `BankAccount` created with the `new` operator. The `new` operator allocates space in memory for a `BankAccount` object, calls the constructor with no arguments, and returns a reference to the object that the assignment operator stores in the variable `myAccount`. Had we used the one-argument constructor, as in

```
BankAccount myAccount = new BankAccount(50.00);
```

the account would have had an initial balance of $50.

The `myAccount` variable has a reference to the newly created `BankAccount`, so it knows where to find that account in the computer's memory. We say the account is an **instance** of the `BankAccount` type defined by the `BankAccount` class.

FIGURE 5.18
Result of new `BankAccount()`

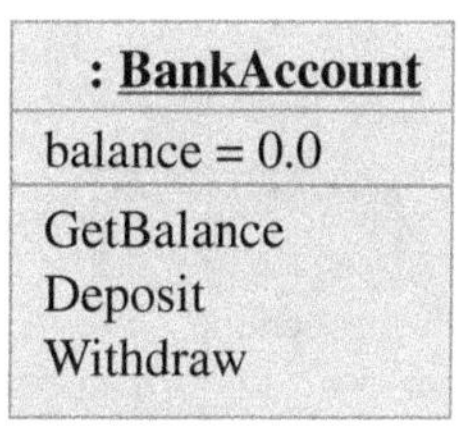

FIGURE 5.19
`myAccount` refers to a new `BankAccount`

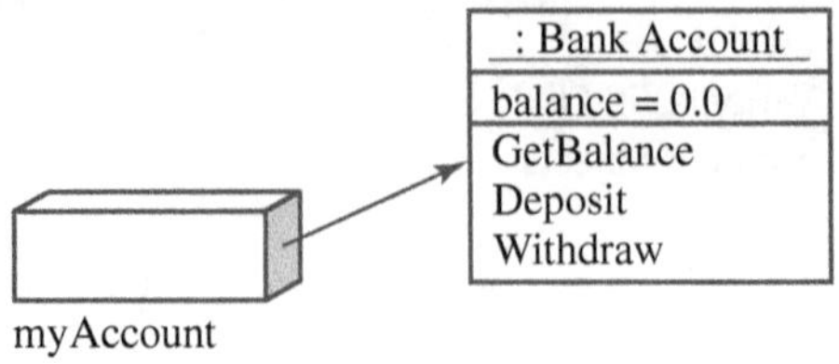

Figure 5.19 shows the variable `myAccount` referring to a newly created `BankAccount` instance. The `BankAccount` instance does not have a name. We refer to it by the name of the variable, `myAccount`.

Declaring a `BankAccount` variable without creating a `BankAccount` object for it to refer to, as in

```
BankAccount anAccount;
```

would cause `anAccount`, shown in Figure 5.20, to have the value **null**, a special value signifying that the variable does not refer to an object.

Making an Object Behave

Once we have created a new `BankAccount` object we need to get it to perform its operations. C# uses a syntax that looks like we are commanding, or sending a message to, an object to perform a service. Informally, we might command `myAccount` to deposit $100 with the command

```
myAccount deposit $100
```

In C# the code for `myAccount` to make a deposit is

```
myAccount.Deposit(100.00);
```

The bank account object referred to by `myAccount` deposits 100 dollars. The `deposit` method adds the amount of the deposit to the `balance` field of the object referred to by `myAccount`. The code for this instance method is

```
public void Deposit(double amount) {
  balance += amount;
}
```

Note that we do not refer to the object explicitly in the code. We understand the `balance` field to be the account balance of the specific `BankAccount` object that is getting the deposit, which in the statement `myAccount.Deposit(100.00)` is the object referred to by `myAccount`.

FIGURE 5.20
An object declaration without object creation

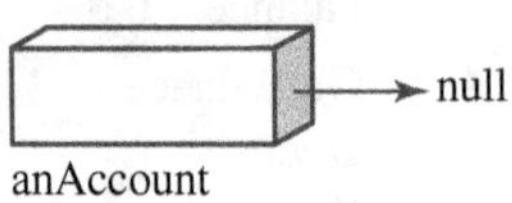

A Little Extra

The `this` Reference

C# uses this to refer to the current object whose method we are invoking. We could write the Deposit method as

```
public void Deposit(double amount) {
  this.balance += amount;
}
```

which shows explicitly that we are adding the amount to the balance field of this, referring to the current object, the account to which we are depositing.

When we invoke myAccount.Deposit(100.00), the variable this refers to the current object, the BankAccount object referred to by myAccount. When we invoke yourAccount.Deposit(100.00), the variable this refers to the BankAccount object referred to by yourAccount. English usage is similar. When I say "My book is on the table" the word *my* refers to my book, but when you say "My book is on the table" the word *my* refers to your book. When we use this inside the deposit method it refers to the account into which the deposit is being made.

The use of this is optional. We introduce it here to emphasize that instance variables and methods are always invoked by an object, even if that object is not explicitly mentioned.

As with the Deposit method, each BankAccount object has its own GetBalance method, which we invoke using the dot notation as in

```
double money = myAccount.GetBalance();
```

If the object referred to by myAccount has a balance of $24.50, the variable money will have the value 24.5.

Calling the Withdraw method, as in

```
myAccount.Withdraw(20.00);
```

will cause $20.00 to be deducted from the balance of the object referred to by myAccount if that balance is greater than or equal to $20.00, and will print a message otherwise.

Now that we have seen how to create a bank account and invoke its services, in Example 5.2 we create two accounts and use their services. Inside Main we create a BankAccount object, as in

```
BankAccount myAccount = new BankAccount(25.00);
```

and get its balance using the GetBalance method, as in

```
myAccount.GetBalance();
```

which will return the $25.00 balance with which we initialized the account. In this example, we use the BankAccount class of Example 5.1.

Using the .NET Framework SDK, the command to compile Example 5.2 is

```
csc /r:BankAccount.dll TestBankAccount.cs
```

Using Visual Studio .NET, we follow the same steps we used when compiling Example 4.1.

EXAMPLE 5.2 ■ TestBankAccount.cs

```
/* Creates and uses some BankAccount objects.
 */

using System;
public class TestBankAccount {                              // Note 1
  public static void Main () {
    BankAccount myAccount = new BankAccount(25.00);
    Console.WriteLine
      ("My balance = {0:C}", myAccount.GetBalance());
    myAccount.Deposit(700.00);                              // Note 2
    Console.WriteLine
      ("My balance = {0:C}", myAccount.GetBalance());
    if(myAccount.Withdraw(300.00) < 0)
      Console.WriteLine("Insufficient funds");
    Console.WriteLine
      ("My balance = {0:C}", myAccount.GetBalance());
    if(myAccount.Withdraw(450.00) < 0)
      Console.WriteLine("Insufficient funds");
    Console.WriteLine
      ("My balance = {0:C}", myAccount.GetBalance());   // Note 3
    BankAccount  yourAccount = new BankAccount();
    yourAccount.Deposit(1234.56);
    Console.WriteLine
      ("Your balance = {0:C}", yourAccount.GetBalance());
  }
}
```

Output

```
My balance = $25.00
My balance = $725.00
My balance = $425.00
Insufficient funds
My balance = $425.00
Your balance = $1,234.56
```

■

Note 1: `public class TestBankAccount {`

The `BankAccount` class defines a type of `BankAccount` object. We use the `TestBankAccount` class to try out the `BankAccount` type. We could have included the `Main` method in the `BankAccount` class itself. But it helps to differentiate between a class such as `BankAccount` that is used to define a type and a class such as `TestBankAccount` that tests the `BankAccount` type. Including a `Main` method in a class such as `BankAccount` is the usual way to provide testing, but including testing inside the class definition itself can be confusing when first creating class definitions.

Note 2:

```
myAccount.Deposit(700.00);
```

The variable `myAccount` invokes its `Deposit` operation. Each object has certain operations that express its behavior. A `BankAccount` can `Deposit`, and here `myAccount` deposits 700 dollars by adding that amount to its balance. We can think of `Deposit(700.00)` as a message sent to `myAccount` asking it to handle this request according to its `Deposit` method. The instance method `Deposit` always refers to a specific `BankAccount` object.

Note 3:

```
Console.WriteLine
     ("My balance = {0:C}", myAccount.GetBalance());
```

The `balance` remains the same because the previous withdrawal request was rejected for insufficient funds.

Method Overloading

We use **method overloading** to define more than one method with the same name. Such overloaded methods must have differences in their parameter lists.

We often overload constructors to provide a different way of creating objects. The `BankAccount` class of Example 5.1 has two constructors, one with no parameters and one with a single parameter specifying an initial balance. In Example 5.2 we used the constructor with no arguments to create `yourAccount` and the constructor with one argument to create `myAccount`.

When two methods have the same name, C# uses the argument types to determine which method to call. Thus C# will not let us define two methods with the same name and the same types of parameters because then it could not determine which one to call when we invoked the method in our program. We could define another `Deposit` method with an `int` argument

```
public void Deposit(int amount) { // code here }
```

but not another version of `Deposit` with the same double argument

```
public void Deposit(double amount) { // code here }
                         // cannot add another like this
```

Style

The objects referred to by `myAccount` and `yourAccount` are instances of the class `BankAccount`. Preferred style uses uppercase letters to start class and method names and lowercase letters to start object names.

The BIG Picture

Class types are reference types. A variable of type `BankAccount` refers to a `BankAccount` object, rather than holding it. A user creates a `BankAccount` object with the `new` operator, and invokes its behavior with a message sending style, as in

```
myAccount.Deposit(50.00);
```

✓ Test Your Understanding

10. What value does the variable `theAccount` have after the following declaration?

    ```
    BankAccount theAccount;
    ```

11. Rewrite the declaration

    ```
    BankAccount theAccount;
    ```

    so `theAccount` will refer to a newly created `BankAccount`.

12. Given a `BankAccount`, `myAccount`, write C# statements to
    a. deposit $35.50.
    b. get the current balance.
    c. deposit $999.

13. Which method does the `new` operator call in the following expression?

    ```
    new BankAccount();
    ```

Try It Yourself ➤

14. In Example 5.2, add a line

    ```
    Deposit(439.86);
    ```

    to the `Main` method of the `TestBankAccount` class that tries to use the `Deposit` instance method without referring to a specific `BankAccount` object. Try to compile this modified program and see what error you get.

Try It Yourself ➤

15. Replace the first `myAccount.GetBalance()` method call in the `TestBankAccount` class with a field access

    ```
    myAcccount.balance
    ```

    This will create errors because the `balance` field is private and not accessible outside the `BankAccount` class. What errors do you get when you try to compile this modified version of Example 5.2?

16. We can overload methods other than constructors. Write another `Withdraw` method, with no parameters, that will withdraw $40 if that amount is available. This method provides a quick withdrawal in which the user does not have to specify any amount.

Try It Yourself ➤

17. Add the `Withdraw` method written in question 16 to Example 5.1. Modify Example 5.2 to test the new `Withdraw` method.

5.5 CLASS VARIABLES AND METHODS

Our `BankAccount` class of Example 5.1 has only instance variables, instance methods, and constructors. It defines a new type of object, a `BankAccount`. When we use `BankAccount` methods in Example 5.2, we first create a bank account using a constructor.

```
BankAccount myAccount = new BankAcccount(25.00);
```

Only then can we perform transactions such as

```
myAccount.Deposit(700.00);
```

It would not make sense to invoke `Deposit(700.00)` without prefixing it with the object name `myAccount`. The `Deposit` method deposits into a specific account and can be called only as an operation of an account.

A class may also include **class variables** and **class methods**, which are associated with the class rather than with a particular instance of the class. They are declared using the `static` modifier. The word *static* may remind us that class variables and methods stay with the class. The `main` method is always static, a class method, because C# calls it to start the program when there are no objects.

To illustrate class variables and methods, we modify the `BankAccount` class of Example 5.1 to count the total number of `Deposit`, `Withdraw`, and `GetBalance` transactions successfully completed by all bank accounts created in a test program. We change the class name to `Acct` to avoid confusion with the unmodified `BankAccount` class.

The `Acct` class has a class variable, `transactions`,

```
public static int transactions = 0;
```

that keeps count of the number of transactions. The `Acct` class has only one copy of the `transactions` class variable, whereas each `Acct` object has its own copy of the `balance` instance variable. Thus, if `myAcct` makes a deposit and `yourAccount` performs a withdrawal, the total number of transactions will increase by two. We modify the `Deposit`, `Withdraw`, and `GetBalance` methods to increment the `transactions` variable.

We include a class method

```
public static int GetTransactions() {
  return transactions;
}
```

that returns the total number of successful transactions by all `Acct` objects.

EXAMPLE 5.3 Acct.cs

```
/* Modifies the BankAccount class to include a class variable
 * to store the total number of successful Deposit, Withdraw,
 * and GetBalance operations by any Acct object.
 */

public class Acct {
```

```
  private double balance;
  private static int transactions = 0;                                  // Note 1

  public Acct()   {
    balance = 0;
  }

  public Acct(double initialAmount) {
    balance = initialAmount;
  }

    // Increments transactions
  public void Deposit(double amount) {
    balance += amount;
    transactions++;
  }

    /* Only increments transactions if the
     * withdrawal is successful.
     */
  public double Withdraw(double amount) {
    if (balance >= amount){
      balance -= amount;
      transactions++;                                                   // Note 2
      return balance;
    }
    else
      return -1.0;
  }

  public double GetBalance() {
    transactions++;
    return balance;
  }
  public static int GetTransactionCount() {                             // Note 3
    return transactions;
  }
}
```

■

Note 1: `private static int transactions = 0;`

The `static` modifier signifies that `transactions` is a class variable. We initialize it to 0 because a test program starts with no transactions completed initially.

Note 2: `transactions++;`

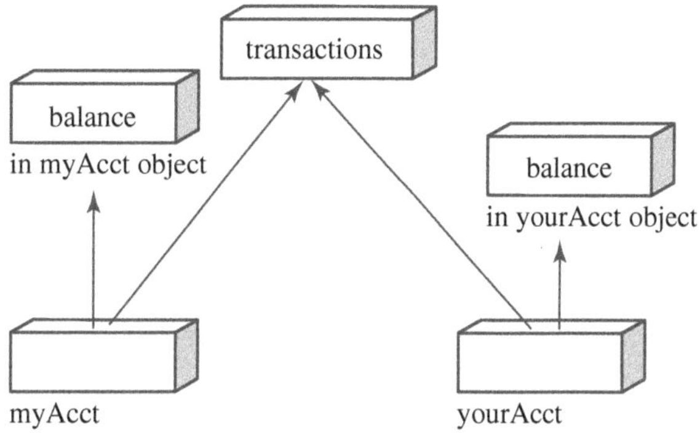

FIGURE 5.21 **The difference between class and instance variables**

We increase the count of transactions only when the withdrawal is successful.

Note 3: `public static int GetTransactionCount() {`

The `static` modifier signifies that `GetTransactionCount` is a class method.

Example 5.4 tests the `Acct` class. We create `myAcct` and execute the `Deposit`, `GetBalance`, and `Withdraw` methods. Because the last `Withdraw` is unsuccessful, we get a transaction count of 3. Creating `yourAcct` and executing the `Deposit` and `GetBalance` methods, we find that the transaction count becomes 5. The `transactions` class variable is part of the class and is incremented by all instances. Of course each object only reads or writes its own `balance` instance variable. Figure 5.21 illustrates this difference between class and instance variables.

When calling the `GetTransactionCount` method, we prefix the class name, as in

```
Acct.GetTransactions
```

reminding us that `GetTransactionCount` is a class method, not part of any instance of the `Acct` class.

EXAMPLE 5.4 ■ TestAcct.cs

```
/* Creates some Acct objects and illustrates the use of
 * class variables and methods.
 */

using System;
public class TestAcct {
  public static void Main () {
    Acct myAcct = new Acct(25.00);
    myAcct.Deposit(700.00);
    if(myAcct.Withdraw(300.00) < 0)
```

```
            Console.WriteLine("Insufficient funds");
        if(myAcct.Withdraw(450.00) < 0)
            Console.WriteLine("Insufficient funds");
        Console.WriteLine
          ("My balance after completing transactions is {0:C}",
             myAcct.GetBalance());
        Console.WriteLine
          ("The number of transactions is {0}",
             Acct.GetTransactionCount());
        Acct yourAcct = new Acct();
        yourAcct.Deposit(1234.56);
        Console.WriteLine
          ("Your balance after completing transactions is {0:C}",
             yourAcct.GetBalance());
        Console.WriteLine("The number of transactions is {0}",
             Acct.GetTransactionCount());
    }
}
```

Output

```
Insufficient funds
My balance after completing transactions is $425.00
The number of transactions is 3
Your balance after completing transactions is $1,234.56
The number of transactions is 5
```

TIP

In `Main` we cannot write

```
Deposit(100.00);
```

because `Deposit` is a method of a specific `Acct` object, and `Main` is a class method. We must write

```
myAcct.Deposit(700.00);
```

where `myAcct` refers to an `Acct` object.

The BIG Picture

Class variables and methods, declared with the `static` modifier, are part of the class but not part of any instance.

✓ Test Your Understanding

Try It Yourself ➤

18. Make `transactions` in Example 5.3 an instance variable instead of a class variable. Do you also need to convert `GetTransactionCount` to an instance method? What changes do you need to make to Example 5.4 to test this modified `Acct` class? What results do you expect from running the modified Example 5.4?

5.6 THE `QuickFood` EXAMPLE

The `BankAccount` class we wrote in Example 5.1 defines the state and services for bank account objects. The restaurant scenario of Section 5.2 uses `Customer`, `Waiter`, and `Cook` objects. We need to write the `Customer`, `Waiter`, and `Cook` classes that define the state and services for these objects. We introduce the UML class and sequence diagrams to illustrate the design.

Class Diagrams

We use the UML **class diagram** to show the associations between classes. An association represents a relationship between instances of the associated classes. For example, a customer places an order with a waiter, and a waiter asks the cook to make a burger (see Figure 5.22).

Sequence Diagrams

We can visualize the scenario of Fig 5.4 in a **sequence diagram**, another part of the UML, that shows object interactions arranged in time sequence. Each object appears at the top (see Figure 5.23), with a dashed line descending, called its **lifeline**. Time increases from top to bottom. We represent each message from one object to another using a horizontal arrow.

For ease of implementation of this introductory example, we change the model to serve each item as it is ordered. Figure 5.24 shows the new sequence diagram.

Our code for the `Customer`, `Waiter`, and `Cook` classes includes the state and responsibilities identified in Figure 5.5. For simplicity, the `PlaceOrder` method just

FIGURE 5.22
A class diagram

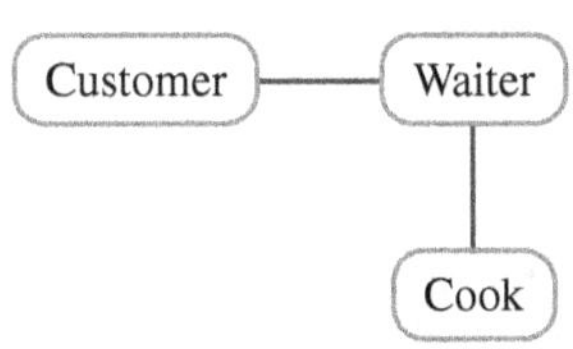

FIGURE 5.23
A sequence diagram for a food order

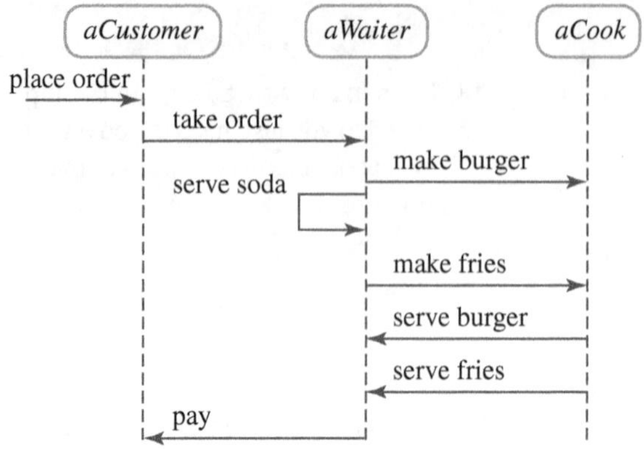

FIGURE 5.24
A revised sequence diagram for a food order

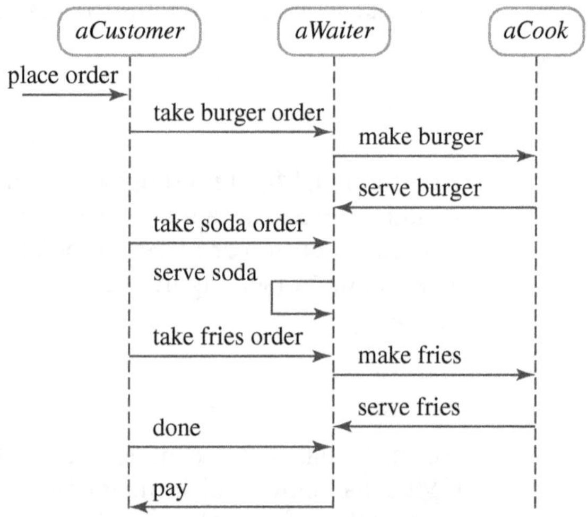

orders a burger, fries, and a soda. A more detailed implementation would provide a user interface for the customer to make selections. The `pay` method reduces the customer's money by the amount of the bill.

In implementing associations, we include a reference in one object to the object to which it is associated. The `Customer` constructor saves a reference to a `Waiter`.

```
public Customer(Waiter w) {
  waiter = w;
}
```

In taking an order, the waiter adds the price to the customer's bill and asks the cook to prepare the burger or fries, or serves the soda. The cook makes the burger or fries and asks the waiter to serve it. Example 5.5 shows the code for the simple fast-food simulation.

EXAMPLE 5.5 ■ QuickFood.cs

```
/* Defines the Customer, Waiter, and Cook classes.
 * Executes the scenario of Figure 5.4.
 */

using System;
public class Customer {                                        // Note 1
  private double money;
  private Waiter waiter;

  public Customer(Waiter w) {
    waiter = w;
  }
  public void PlaceOrder() {
    waiter.TakeOrder("Burger",this);
    waiter.TakeOrder("Soda",this);
    waiter.TakeOrder("Fries",this);
    waiter.TakeOrder("Done",this);                             // Note 2
  }
  public double Pay(double amount) {
     money -= amount;
     Console.WriteLine("Customer pays {0:C}", amount);
     return amount;
  }
}

public class Waiter {
  private double cash = 200.00;
  private Cook cook;
  private Customer customer;
  private double bill = 0;

  public Waiter(Cook c) {                                      // Note 3
    cook = c;
  }
  public void TakeOrder(String item, Customer c) {             // Note 4
    customer = c;
    if (item == "Burger"){                                     // Note 5
       Console.WriteLine("Waiter places Burger order");
       bill += 1.99;
       cook.MakeBurger(this);
    }
```

```
    else if (item == "Fries"){
       Console.WriteLine("Waiter places Fries order");
       bill += 1.19;
       cook.MakeFries(this);
    }
    else if (item == "Soda"){
       ServeFood("Soda");                                  // Note 6
       bill += .99;
    }
    else if (item == "Done")
         cash += customer.Pay(bill);;
  }
  public void ServeFood(String item) {
    Console.WriteLine("Waiter serves " + item);
  }
}
public class Cook {
  private int burgers = 10;
  private int fries = 10;

  public void MakeBurger(Waiter waiter) {                  // Note 7
    if (burgers > 0) {
      Console.WriteLine("Cook making Burger");
      waiter.ServeFood("Burger");
      burgers--;
    }
    else
      Console.WriteLine("Sorry -- No more Burgers");
  }
  public void MakeFries(Waiter waiter) {
    if (fries > 0) {
      Console.WriteLine("Cook making Fries");
      waiter.ServeFood("Fries");
      fries--;
    }
    else
      Console.WriteLine("Sorry -- No more Fries");
  }
}
public class QuickFood {
  public static void Main() {
    Cook joe = new Cook();                                 // Note 8
    Waiter suzy = new Waiter(joe);
    Customer fred = new Customer(suzy);
    fred.PlaceOrder();
  }
}
```

Output

```
Waiter places Burger order
Cook making Burger
Waiter serves Burger
Waiter serves Soda
Waiter places Fries order
Cook making Fries
Waiter serves Fries
Customer pays $4.17
```

Note 1: `public class Customer {`

For simplicity we wanted to include all the classes in the same file. Generally, classes define types that can be used in many applications, and should be declared using the `public` modifier and placed in separate files. We discuss the use of access modifiers in Section 10.4.

Note 2: `waiter.TakeOrder("Done",this);`

The customer passes "Done" to signal the order is complete.

Note 3: `public Waiter(Cook c) {`

Reflecting the association between a waiter and a cook, we pass a reference to a `cook` when we construct a `waiter`.

Note 4: `public void TakeOrder(String item, Customer c) {`

The parameter `item`, of type `String`, is the item ordered. We will discuss the `String` type in the next chapter. It represents character strings such as `"Burger"`.

Note 5: `if (item == "Burger"){`

The `==` operator returns `true` if the two strings have the same characters. We discuss `String` objects in the next chapter.

Note 6: `ServeFood("Soda");`

The `waiter` calls its own `ServeFood` method, so the object is implicit. We could have used `this.ServeFood("Soda")` to make the object explicit.

Note 7: `public void MakeBurger(Waiter waiter) {`

We do not need an explicit constructor for the `Cook` class because the `waiter` passes a reference to itself to the `cook` when it calls the `MakeBurger` method.

Note 8: `Cook joe = new Cook();`

We did not include a constructor in the `Cook` class. Even though `Cook` has an association with `Waiter`, a cook does not initiate contact with a waiter, but only responds to requests. The `cook` receives a reference to a `waiter` as an argument to its `MakeFries` and `MakeBurger` methods.

Example 5.5 illustrates, in a striking manner, how an object-oriented program leaves it to the objects to call one another's services. The `Main` method creates three objects and starts the process with one line

```
fred.PlaceOrder();
```

This one invocation gets the customer, `fred`, to communicate with the waiter, `suzy`, who then communicates with the cook, `joe`, and so on.

The `Main` method is not the master controller, but rather each object contains services called by other objects. Because there is no master controller, the `main` method of an object-oriented program is very short, just creating some objects and letting them invoke each other's services.

The BIG Picture

A large part of an object-oriented program involves writing the classes that define the state and responsibilities of its object instances. In meeting its responsibilities an object uses the services of other objects.

The UML class diagram shows the associations between classes, and the sequence diagram shows the sequence of interactions between objects, from the earliest at the top to the latest at the bottom.

✓Test Your Understanding

19. Redraw the sequence diagram of Figure 5.24 so the waiter asks the customer to take each item as it becomes available.

SUMMARY

- An object has state, behavior, and identity. In analogy with a vending machine, the services an object provides are like the buttons of the machine. Users access an object via its services, which express the behavior of that object and meet its responsibilities.
- Primitive types have small fixed sizes, so C# variables hold their values. An integer variable stores the values of an integer. By contrast, objects may be quite large and have varying sizes, so it is easier for an object variable to store a reference to an object rather than trying to hold it directly.
- Procedural programming focuses mainly on the function performed by the program and only incidentally on the data. The function performed is the aspect most likely to change, so a more stable and maintainable system results from object-oriented programming, which focuses on the objects that comprise the system. These objects have data representing their states and operations representing their behavior. The operations give each object an active role in the system. Objects communicate with each other by invoking op-

erations that allow an object to meet its responsibilities. We can use scenarios for typical uses of the system to find the relevant objects and identify their responsibilities.

- In C#, we use a class to define a type of object. Each object has state, data which we represent using instance variables that are nonstatic variables declared inside the class but outside of any method. Our `BankAccount` class defines an instance variable, `balance`, to hold the account balance. By contrast, local variables are declared inside methods and are available only inside the method in which they are declared.
- We add methods to our class to implement the behavior of its type of objects. In our `BankAccount` class we add instance methods to deposit an amount, to withdraw an amount, and to get the account balance. These methods are not static, signifying that they will be operations of each `BankAccount` object, representing that object's behaviors. Static methods such as the `GetTransactionCount` method of Example 5.3 are called class methods because they are class tools, shared by objects of that type.
- We access objects using methods, which are operations representing their behavior. C# uses the period to separate the name of the object from the operation it is invoking. This notation emphasizes that an object such as `myAccount` is performing one of its operations such as `Deposit`. Usually we make the object's data fields private, requiring that users of our objects access fields only via the object's operations.
- A special kind of method called a constructor helps the user to construct an object. Constructors have the same name as the class and no return value. We define a `BankAccount` constructor that creates a `BankAccount` object with an initial balance of zero. We create objects with the `new` operator which allocates space for the object, calls the object's constructor, and returns a reference to the object. C# uses `null` to represent an uncreated object.
- C# supports method overloading, where two methods have the same name but different parameters. One important use of overloading is to provide multiple constructors for objects of a given class. We add another constructor to our `BankAccount` class to create a `BankAccount` with a specified initial balance.

SKILL BUILDER EXERCISES

1. Match the concept name on the left with its function on the right.

a. instance variable	**i.** stores a value within a method
b. local variable	**ii.** represents a behavior of an object
c. class method	**iii.** represents an attribute of an object
d. instance method	**iv.** used by the class as a whole

2. Fill in the blanks in the following:

A variable of a primitive type holds a ______________, while a variable of a class type holds a ______________.

3. A class method is ______________ by all instances of a class.

CRITICAL THINKING EXERCISES

4. Declaring a bank account as

```
BankAccount acct;
```

and making a deposit using

```
acct.Deposit(500.00);
```

will have the following result:

   a. The compiler will generate an error message.

   b. The account acct will have a balance of $500.00.

   c. The account acct will have its previous balance increased by $500.

   d. none of the above.

5. A constructor

   a. must have the same name as the class it is declared within.

   b. is used to create objects.

   c. may be overloaded.

   d. b and c above

   e. all of the above

6. Which of the following are never part of a class definition?

   a. instance variables

   b. static methods

   c. instance methods

   d. constructors

   e. none of the above

7. Suppose `acct1` refers to an `Acct` of Example 5.3. The value returned by the `GetTransactionCount` method is the count of

   a. all successful transactions made by `acct1`.

   b. all successful transactions made by all `Acct` objects.

   c. all deposit and withdraw operations made by `acct1`.

   d. all deposit and withdraw operations made by all `Acct` objects.

DEBUGGING EXERCISE

8. The `Test` class below keeps an integer `tally`. Its `AddFive` method adds five to `tally`, and its `display` method displays the current value. The `Main` method includes a test program. Find and fix any errors.

```
public class Test {
  private int tally;
  public void Test(int start) {
    tally = start;
  }
```

```
  public void AddFive() {
    tally += 5;
  }
  public void Display() {
    Console.WriteLine("The tally is {0}", tally);
  }
  public static Main() {
    Test myTest = new Test(3);
    myTest.AddFive();
    Display();
  }
}
```

PROGRAM MODIFICATION EXERCISES

9. Modify Example 3.6, `ScoreSum.cs`, to use an object. Keep the total as an instance variable. Change the methods from class to instance methods. Create an instance in `Main` and use its methods to sum the scores.

10. Revise the `BankAccount` class of Example 5.1 to overload the `Withdraw` method. Include a `withdraw` method with no parameters, which will withdraw $40 if available, and display a message otherwise. Add tests of this new method to Example 5.2.

11. Modify Example 5.5 to add a `PickUpOrder` method to the `Customer` class, and let the `Waiter` invoke this method when each item is ready.

12. Modify Example 3.7, `Max.cs`, to use an object. Keep the current maximum as an instance variable. Change the methods from class to instance methods. Create an instance in `Main` and use its methods to find the maximum.

13. Modify the `Acct` class of Example 5.3 to add a class variable to count the number of `BankAccount` objects that have been created. Add a class method to return the number of active accounts. Modify Example 5.4 to test these added features.

PROGRAM DESIGN EXERCISES

14. Write a class for soccer game scoring. Provide a constructor that starts each team with a score of zero. Include instance variables to keep the score for both teams. Include a method to add 1 to the score of the first team and a method to add 1 to the score of the second team. Include a method that displays the score of both teams, and the `Main` method to test, creating two different soccer games. Score points so the first game is 3–2 and the second game is 0–1. Display the scores of each game.

15. Write a class that uses the soccer game class of Exercise 14. In the `Main` method create some games, score points, and display the results.

16. Write a class for a warehouse that hold radios, televisions, and computers. Provide a constructor that starts a warehouse with no items. Include instance variables to store the quantity of each item in the warehouse. Include methods to add to the stock of each item, and a method to display the contents of the warehouse. Test in a `Main` method, creating two warehouses. Add items to each and display the final contents of each warehouse.

17. Write a class to use the warehouse class of Exercise 16. In the `Main` method create some warehouses, add some items to each, and display the contents of each warehouse.

18. Write a class to keep track of the movement of a cat. Include three instance variables to hold the `x`, `y`, and `z` positions of the cat. Include a method for the cat to walk to another position. This method has two parameters specifying the change in `x` and the change in `y`. If the cat is at (3,4,5) and we ask it to Walk(1,4) then it will be at (4,8,5). (Walking is a horizontal action here.) Include a method for the cat to jump to another position. This method has one parameter specifying the change in the cat's vertical position. If the cat is at (3,4,5) and we ask it to Jump(5), it will be at (3,4,10). Include a method to display a cat's position. Test in a `Main` method, creating a few cats and having them walk and jump. Display their final positions.

19. Write a class to use the cat tracking class of Exercise 18. In the `Main` method, create some cats, make them walk and jump, and display their final positions.

20. For the `Warehouse` class of Exercise 16, overload the `Warehouse` constructor by adding another constructor to create a warehouse with specified initial quantities of radios, televisions, and computers. Revise the `Main` method to include tests of this new constructor.

21. For the `Warehouse` class of Exercise 16, add methods to remove a specified quantity of each item. If the quantity specified is greater than the amount of that item in the warehouse, then no items are removed. Add tests of the remove methods to the `Main` method.

22. Write a coffee vending machine class. Include fields giving the number of cups of coffee available, the cost of one cup of coffee, and the total amount of money inserted by the user. This machine requires exact change. Include one constructor that stocks the machine with a quantity and price of coffee specified as parameters, and another constructor with no parameters that stocks the machine with 10 cups of coffee at 50 cents each. Include the following methods:

```
Menu()                // displays the quantity and price of coffee
Insert(int quarters, int dimes, int nickels)
                      // inserts the given amount
Select()              // dispenses a cup of coffee if user has inserted enough
                      // money and coffee is available,
                      // otherwise displays a message.
Refund()              // returns the money inserted
```

Write a `Main` method to create some vending machines and test their operation.

23. Create a `Fraction` class to provide a data type for rational numbers. Each `Fraction` will have an integer numerator and denominator. Include a constructor with two integer arguments to initialize the numerator and denominator. Include methods to add, multiply, subtract, and divide, each having a `Fraction` argument and returning a `Fraction` result. Use the `Main` method to test the `Fraction` class.

6 Working with Objects

In this chapter we go further into object-oriented programming. We introduce the powerful and useful `String` class from the .NET Framework library. Strings serve as an excellent illustration of various aspects of working with objects. After introducing `String` methods, we look at the assignment and comparison of `String` objects. This requires a careful discussion of the difference between reference variables and variables of primitive types. Although we use `String` objects in our illustrations, the discussion applies to all reference types.

One of the important features of classification is that it allows us to relate different types to one another. Two important relationships are HAS-A and IS-A. Object composition, which we study in this chapter, expresses the HAS-A relationship in which one object has another object as one of its parts. For example, a computer has a CPU and memory. We discuss inheritance, in which one type is another more general type, in Chapter 10. For example, a Car is also a Vehicle.

We saw in the last chapter that a class defines a type of object. The `BankAccount` class implements the `GetBalance`, `Deposit`, and `Withdraw` services found in each `BankAccount` instance. An interface defines a reference type, but one without any implementation. The name interface suggests a view the user has of the object, without implying any particular implementation. Interfaces can be very important tools in developing good object-oriented designs.

We conclude the chapter by introducing the `Random` class, which we can use to generate random numbers useful in simulation.

OBJECTIVES

- Learn to use the `String` class
- Learn to compare reference types

- Understand the composition relationship
- Use interfaces to develop flexible designs
- Generate random numbers using `Random`

6.1 THE `String` CLASS

Instances of the class `String` represent sequences of characters. The `String` class is part of the core .NET Framework library in the `System` namespace. Inside a `String` object is a sequence of characters, such as "`C# is fun`". The state of a `String` object is private. If the letters of the string were wooden blocks numbered to indicate their position in the string, block "C" would have number 0, block "#" would have number 1, and so on. Users of `String` objects do not need to know how the characters are represented.

Visualizing a String

We visualize a `String` as an object like a vending machine with a button for each service it provides. Strings have many public operations to provide their services. We show only a few in Figure 6.1, `Length`, `IndexOf('i')`, and `ToUpper()`. The drawing of the `String` object, "`C# is fun`" in Figure 6.1 does not have a window to look inside, because strings do not show any of their state; it is all private.

When we press the `Length` button in Figure 6.1 we get the result of 9 because `"C# is fun"` has 9 characters. The result of an operation depends on the state of the object.

The `IndexOf('i')` button returns the first position in which the character `'i'` occurs in the string, or −1 if `'i'` does not occur in the string. For this object the `IndexOf('i')` operation returns 3. The first `'i'` occurs as the fourth character, but for technical reasons we start the numbering with 0, so `'i'` is at index 3.

Strings in C# never change. The `String` object in Figure 6.1 will always represent `"C# is fun"`. When we execute the `ToUpper()` operation, we do not change the object, but rather we get a new `String` object representing `"C# IS FUN"`, shown in Figure 6.2.

FIGURE 6.1 A **`String`** object for **"C# is fun"**

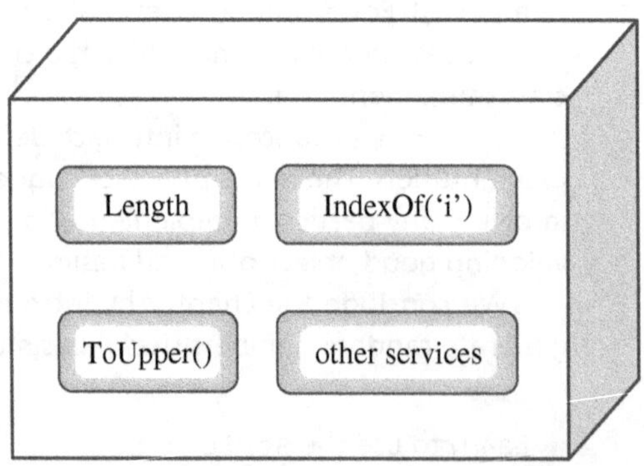

FIGURE 6.2 A `String` object for "C# IS FUN"

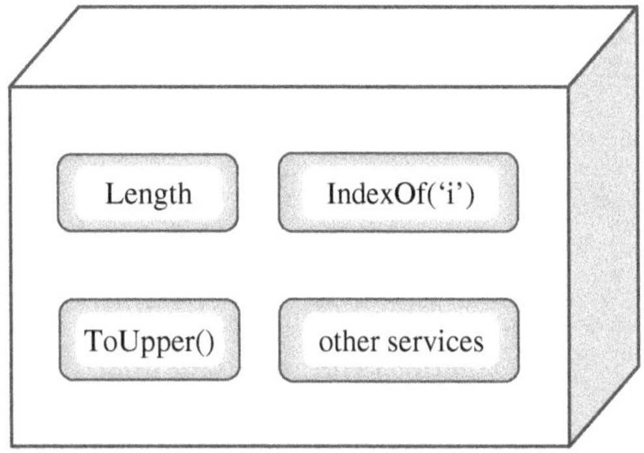

Because the state is hidden, Figure 6.2 looks just like Figure 6.1, but it operates differently. Executing the `IndexOf('i')` operation will return -1, signifying that the character `'i'` does not appear in `"C# IS FUN"`. C# is case sensitive; a lowercase `'i'` differs from an uppercase `'I'`.

Visualizing a `String` object as a vending machine in Figures 6.1 and 6.2 really helps us to keep in mind the object concepts of state, behavior, and identity. To use strings in C# programs, we need to create a string and ask it to provide one of its services.

Creating a String

C# makes a special form of declaration available for `String` objects, because we use them so frequently. C# treats a literal such as `"C# lets us use objects.  "` as an instance of the `String` class. The declaration

```
String s = "C# lets us use objects.  ";
```

creates and initializes a `String`, which we refer to as `s`. The variable `s` refers to the `String` object, as shown schematically in Figure 6.3.

String Properties

A property is like a data field, but it does not directly represent a storage location. For example, the value of a property may be computed from other values. A property provides information about an object. For example,

```
s.Length;
```

will return the number of characters in `s`—25 in this example. This string has two trailing blanks. All characters between the beginning and ending quotes are significant. We use a property like we use an instance variable, but internally it uses an

FIGURE 6.3 A `String` variable referring to a `String` object

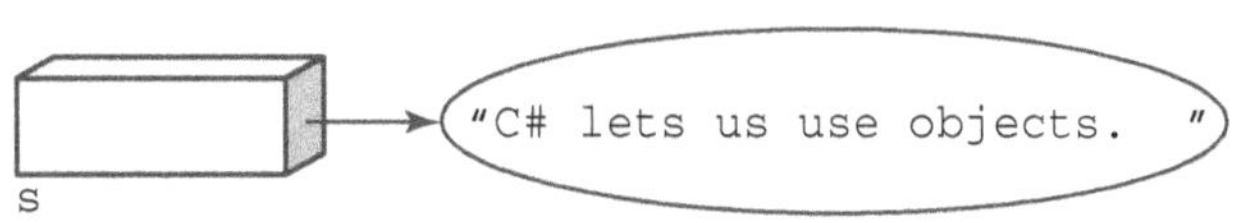

accessor method to retrieve the length. Thus we return the length using s.Length rather than s.Length(). In this text we will often use predefined properties of objects, but do not define any.

String Indexers

An indexer is like a property, but it provides access by an index, like the arrays that we will study in the next chapter. In C#, the Chars property in the String .NET Framework is an indexer for the String. It returns the character at the specified index in the string. For example,

```
s[4]
```

returns `'e'` because the character at index 4 is an `'e'`. We use square brackets, `[]`, to enclose an index rather than the round parentheses, `()`, we use for method arguments.

String Methods

The `String` class has both instance and class methods. An instance method refers to a specific `String` object. The `ToLower()` method returns a new `String` with the characters converted to lowercase. For example,

```
s.ToLower();
```

returns `"c# lets us use objects.   "`. To use this new `String`, we need to assign it to a variable, as in

```
String sLower = s.ToLower();
```

Figure 6.4 shows that we now have two `String` objects referred to by `s` and `sLower`.

The `Trim` and `Substring` methods also return new `String` objects. The `Trim` method removes leading and trailing **whitespace**, which includes blank spaces, newlines, and tabs. For example,

```
s.Trim();
```

returns `"C# lets us use objects."`

The `Substring` method has two parameters. The first gives the index at which the substring starts. The second indicates the number of characters in the substring. Thus

```
s.Substring(11,11);
```

returns `"use objects"`, composed of the characters starting at position 11 in s, and including 11 characters.

FIGURE 6.4
`s.ToLower()` returns a new `String`

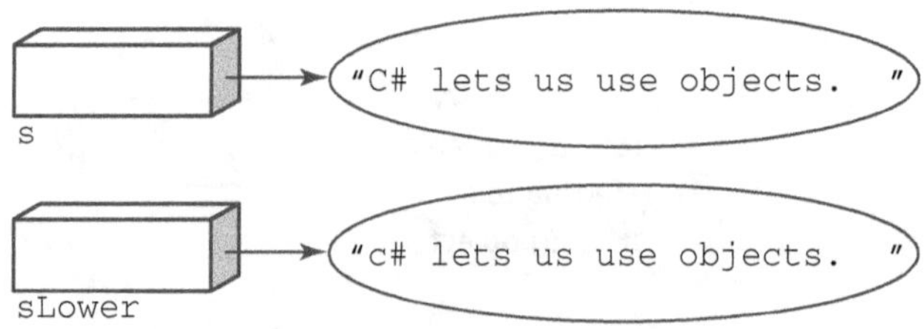

The `String` class contains overloaded methods. For example, the `IndexOf` method has six versions, which C# differentiates by the different parameters for each. The six methods are:

- `public int IndexOf(char ch)`

  returns the index of the first occurrence of `ch`
- `public int IndexOf(char ch, int from)`

  returns the index of the first occurrence of `ch` starting at index `from`
- `public int IndexOf(char ch, int from, int len)`

  returns the index of the first occurrence of `ch` starting at index `from` within the next `len` positions
- `public int IndexOf(String str)`

  returns the index of the first occurrence of `str`
- `public int IndexOf(String str, int from)`

  returns the index of the first occurrence of `str` starting at index `from`
- `public int IndexOf(String str, int from, int len)`

  returns the index of the first occurrence of `str` starting at index `from` within the next `len` positions

To illustrate,

```
s.IndexOf('e');
```

returns 4, because the leftmost `'e'` in the string occurs at index 4. The method call

```
s.IndexOf('e',8);
```

returns 13, because the first occurrence of `'e'`, starting from index 8, is at index 13. The method call

```
s.IndexOf('e',8,3);
```

returns −1, because there is no `'e'` in the next three positions starting at index 8. The method call

```
s.IndexOf("us");
```

returns 8, because the leftmost occurrence of `"us"` starts at index 8. Similarly,

```
s.IndexOf("us",11);
```

returns 11 because the first occurrence of `"us"`, starting from index 11, begins at index 11. When we try

```
s.IndexOf("us",15);
```

the result is −1, because there is no occurrence of `"us"` in `s` starting from index 15.

Programmers find it less cumbersome to use overloaded methods. For example, if the `IndexOf` method were not overloaded, we would have to use something like `IndexOfChar`, `IndexOfCharFrom`, `IndexOfCharFromLen`, `IndexOfString`,

IndexOfStringFrom, and IndexOfStringFromLen as the names for these six methods. Method overloading helps when we have methods that are similar, but operate with different arguments.

When we use an overloaded method in a program, C# can determine which method to call by looking at the type of argument we pass to it. For example, in

```
String food = "potato";
int a      = food.IndexOf('a');
int to   = food.IndexOf("to");
```

C# will call the IndexOf(char c) method to find the index of the first 'a' in "potato", because the argument 'a' passed in the call IndexOf('a') has type char. However, C# will call IndexOf(String s) to find the index of the first occurrence of "to", because the argument "to" has type String.

Replace is another overloaded method. One version replaces all occurrences of one character with another. The second version replaces all occurrences of a String with another. For example,

```
s.Replace('e', 'o')
```

returns the String

```
"C# lots us uso objocts.  "
```

and

```
s.Replace("us", "them")
```

returns

```
"C# lets them theme objects.  "
```

Class Methods

The String class has many other instance methods.[1] It also contains some class methods. The Format method returns a String like those the WriteLine method produces, but we can save a reference to it. For example,

```
double d = 3.14159265;
String w = String.Format("The price is {0:C}", d);
```

produces the String

```
"The price is $3.14"
```

Note that we prefix the Format method with the class name, String, rather than an object instance name. The Format method does not apply to a String object, in contrast to the IndexOf method and other instance methods, which only

---

[1]The documentation for the .NET Framework Class Library is available for viewing or download from http://msdn.microsoft.com/library/default.asp?url=/library/en-us/cpref/html/cpref_start.asp.

make sense when applied to a `String` instance. `Format` is a class method rather than an instance method.

To illustrate the use of objects, Example 6.1 codes our version of the `Replace` method, called `MyReplace`. We test by replacing every occurrence of the word `"fish"`, in a string entered by the user, with the word `"fowl"`.

EXAMPLE 6.1 ■ Replace.cs

```
/* Duplicates the function of the Replace method.
 */

using System;
public class Replace {
  String myString;

  public Replace(String s) {
    myString = s;
  }

    /* Replaces all occurrences of oldWord with newWord
     */
  public String MyReplace(String oldWord, String newWord) {
    String temp = myString;
    int position = temp.IndexOf(oldWord);          // Note 1
    while(position != -1) {
      temp = temp.Substring(0,position) + newWord
           + temp.Substring(position + oldWord.Length);
                                                   // Note 2
      position =
       temp.IndexOf(oldWord, position + newWord.Length);
                                                   // Note 3
    }
    return temp;
  }
     /* Replaces every occurrence of "fish" with "fowl"
      */
  public static void Main() {
    Console.Write
             ("Enter a String which includes \"fish\": ");
    Replace phrase = new Replace(Console.ReadLine());
    String changed = phrase.MyReplace("fish", "fowl");
    Console.WriteLine("The new string is: {0}", changed);
  }
}
```

First Run

```
Enter a String that includes "fish": A fish is nice
The new string is: A fowl is nice
```

Second Run

```
Enter a String that includes "fish": I like fish today and
                                        fish tomorrow
The new string is: I like fowl today and fowl tomorrow
```

Note 1: `int position = temp.IndexOf(oldWord);`

We initialize `position` with the index of the first occurrence of `oldWord`, or −1 if it does not occur in `temp`.

Note 2:
```
temp = temp.Substring(0,position) + newWord
       + temp.Substring(position + oldWord.Length);
```

When we find `oldWord` in the string `temp`, we create a new string with that occurrence of `oldWord` replaced by `newWord`. We have already used the String concatenation operator, `+`. We concatenate three pieces:

The substring before the occurrence of `oldWord`

`newWord`

The substring after the occurrence of `oldWord`

Note 3:
```
position =
  temp.IndexOf(oldWord, position + newWord.Length);
```

We continue the search from the character after `newWord`.

The BIG Picture

A `String` object hides its state, but provides many methods to access its services. The String class contains some class methods.

We ask an object to perform an operation using one of its instance methods. Such an instance method refers to that object. Thus `s.IndexOf('e')` returns the index of the first occurrence of `'e'` in a specific `String` object referred to by `s`. Just as a selection button is part of a vending machine, an instance method is part of an object.

C# overloads some string methods to provide easy-to-use operations.

✓Test Your Understanding

1. Given the `String` object `String s = "The three did feed the deer";` find

   a. `s.Length`   b. `s[5]`

   c. `s.IndexOf('e')`   d. `s.IndexOf("did")`

   e. `s.Substring(4,5)`   f. `s.ToUpper()`

2. Given the `String` object `String r = "Mississippi";` find

   a. `r.IndexOf('i')`   b. `r.IndexOf('i',4)`

   c. `r.IndexOf("is",4)`   d. `r.IndexOf("is",9)`

   e. `r.IndexOf("sip")`   f. `r.IndexOf("sissy")`

3. If String s = `"Happy days are here again"`, find

   a. `s.Replace('a', 'i')`

   b. `s.Replace("e", "xkd");`

6.2 STRING OPERATIONS

Strings are familiar objects. After all, from an early age we read texts made up of character strings. In C#, `String` is a reference type. Operating with strings gives us insight into how to work with other object types, including those we might define, such as `Employee` or `Payroll`.

C# provides many operators for primitive types. We look at assignment, equality, and relational operators to see if and how they might be used with `String` and other reference types.

Assignment

If x and y are primitive types, each variable holds a value of that type. For example, Figure 6.5 shows that x holds the value 4 and y holds the value 5.

When we assign x to y, we copy the contents of location x into location y. The assignment

```
y = x;
```

copies the contents of x, which is the value 4, into y, making a copy of the value 4. After the assignment, shown in Figure 6.6, variables x and y each have a copy of the value 4.

```
int x = 4, y = 5;
```

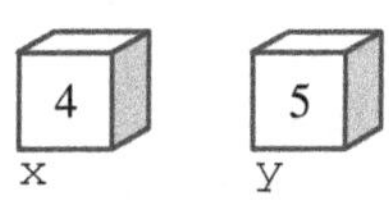

FIGURE 6.5
Variables of type `int` hold `int` values

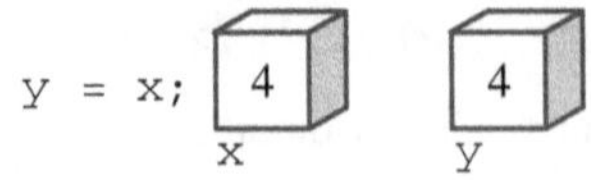

FIGURE 6.6 **Assignment of an `int` copies a value**

When we declare and initialize a `String` variable, the variable holds a reference to the `String` object. The declaration

```
String myString = "We want a big car";
```

produces the two entities shown in Figure 6.7: an object representing `"We want a big car"` and a variable, `myString`, that refers to that `String` object.

For object types such as `String`, assignment still copies the contents of one variable to another. A `String` variable holds a reference, so assignment copies that reference, as Figure 6.8 shows. After the assignment, the variable `t` has the same reference as `s`. Both refer to `"soup"`. The string `"fish"` has no references to it and is termed **garbage**. C# will automatically reclaim the memory used for `"fish"` through a process known as a **garbage collection.**

Comparing Figures 6.6 and 6.8, we see that, after the assignment, `x` and `y` each have their own copy of the value 4, but that `s` and `t` refer to the same string, `"soup"`. Figure 6.8 uses strings, but the same sharing would result from the assignment of any type of object, whereas no sharing results from assignment of primitive types.[2]

FIGURE 6.7 **A variable of type `String` holds a reference to a `String` object**

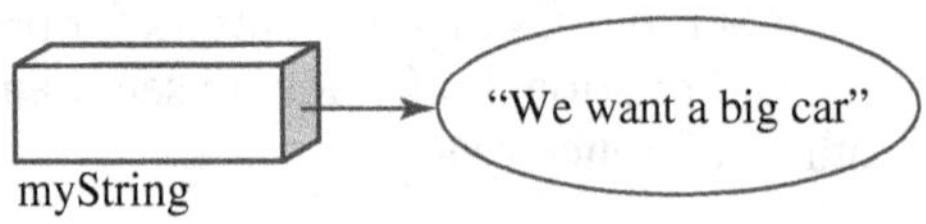

FIGURE 6.8 **Assignment of a string**

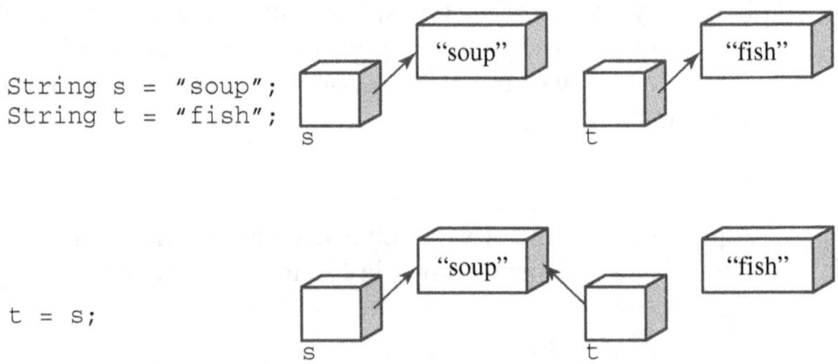

[2]Arrays, which we study in the next chapter, are reference types. Unlike strings, we can change arrays, so the sharing shown here becomes more significant.

Equality

A `String` represents a sequence of characters. We would like two `String` objects to be equal if and only if the sequences of characters they represent are the same. For example, `s` and `t` are equal if

s → "hat"   t → "hat"

but `u` and `v` are not equal if

u → "hit"   v → "hot"

For the strings `s1`, `s2`, `s3`, and `s4` given by

```
String s   = "a houseboat";
String s1 = "house";
String s2 = s.substring(2,7);
String s3 = "horse";
String s4 = s1;
```

we would like `s1` and `s2` to be equal, because each has the same characters, but expect `s1` to be unequal to `s3`, because these strings differ at index 2. Of course, `s1` and `s4` are equal, because they refer to the same string.

The equality operator, `==`, which we have used many times to test the equality of primitive values, can mislead us when applied to strings. This operator compares the contents of each variable, returning `true` if both are the same. Figure 6.9 illustrates the problem.

Object variables hold references to objects. The equality operator, `==`, compares the contents of these variables by comparing the references, not the objects to which they refer. Both `s1` and `s4` refer to the same object, so `s1==s4` evaluates to true. If we were limited to the predefined equality operator, the expression `s1==s2` would be false because the references `s1` and `s2` are not equal. They refer to different objects. Although these objects are not identical, they are equal because they each

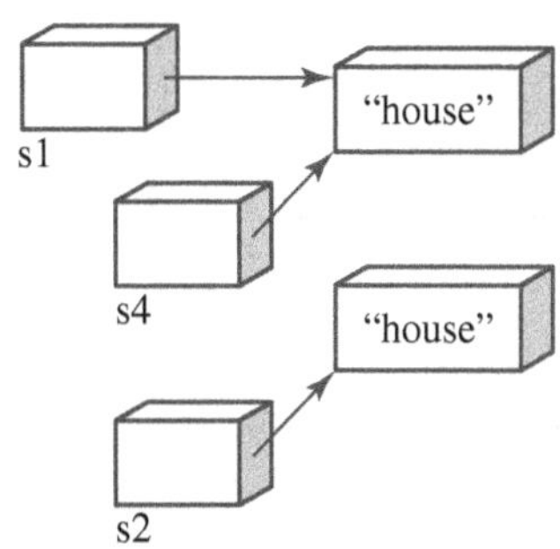

FIGURE 6.9
References s1 and s4 are equal, but s1 and s2 are not

contain the same sequence of characters. We need a replacement for the predefined equality operator that compares the objects themselves, not the references to them.

The `Equals` method, implemented in the String class, solves our problem. It returns `true` if both strings have the same sequence of characters. Thus `s1.Equals(s4)` and `s1.Equals(s2)` will both return `true`.

Operator Overloading

C# allows us to redefine operators to change how they operate on objects of a given type. The C# `String` class overloads the equality operator, `==`, to work the way we would like it to work. The `String` class includes a definition of an `operator==` method that gets invoked when we use the familiar infix notation, as in `s1 == s2`, using the example of Figure 6.9. This definition makes the `String ==` operator use the `Equals` method to compare the `String` objects rather than the references. Thus `s1 == s2` will evaluate as `true` even though the references are not equal.

To fully understand the requirements for defining an overloaded equality operator we need to consider inheritance in Chapter 10, so we defer overloading the equality operator for user-defined classes until then.

Comparing Strings

In applications such as alphabetizing we need to determine whether one string is greater than another. The `String` class provides a `CompareTo` method that returns −1 if the string is less than the string argument, returns 0 if both strings are equal, and returns 1 if the string is greater than the string argument. For strings `s1`, `s2`, and `s3` given by

```
String s1 = "house";
String s2 = s.substring(2,7);
String s3 = "horse";
```

we find that

```
s1.CompareTo(s2)   returns  0
s1.CompareTo(s3)   returns  1
s3.CompareTo(s1)   returns -1
```

The `CompareTo` method compares corresponding characters and is case sensitive. A lowercase letter is less than its uppercase counterpart. For example, ‘a’ < ‘A’. Both ‘a’ and ‘A’ are less than ‘b’.

EXAMPLE 6.2 ■ Compare.cs

```
/* Illustrates String comparisons.
 */

using System;
public class Compare {

    // Checks ==, Equals, and CompareTo
```

```
  public static void Main() {
    String s   = "a houseboat";
    String s1 = "house";
    String s2 = s.Substring(2,5);
    String s3 = "horse";
    String s4 = s1;
    Console.WriteLine("s1 == s2 is {0}", s1 == s2);
                                                      // Note 1
    Console.WriteLine
           ("s1.Equals(s2) is {0}", s1.Equals(s2));
                                                      // Note 2
    String w1 = "Apple";
    String w2 = "apple";
    String w3 = "butter";
    Console.WriteLine("{0} compared to {1} is {2}",
                         w1, w2, w1.CompareTo(w2));
                                                      // Note 3
    Console.WriteLine("{0} compared to {1} is {2}",
                         w1, w3, w1.CompareTo(w3));
                                                      // Note 4
  }
}
```

Output

```
s1 == s2 is True
s1.Equals(s2) is True
Apple compared to apple is 1
Apple compared to butter is -1
```

Note 1: `Console.WriteLine("s1 == s2 is {0}", s1 == s2);`

Because the `String` class overloads the `==` operator to check the `String` objects for equality, it functions as we expect. The default `==` operator would have checked the references `s1` and `s2`, which are not equal.

Note 2:
```
Console.WriteLine
    ("s1.Equals(s2) is {0}", s1.Equals(s2));
```

The `Equals` method compares the `String` objects. These objects have the same sequence of characters and are equal. We can use it, or the `==` operator.

Note 3:
```
Console.WriteLine("{0} compared to {1} is {2}",
                    w1, w2, w1.CompareTo(w2));
```

Corresponding uppercase letters are greater than the lowercase version, so `"Apple"` is greater than `"apple"`.

Note 4:
```
Console.WriteLine("{0} compared to {1} is {2}",
                  w1, w3, w1.CompareTo(w3));
```

Alphabetical ordering applies, so `"Apple"` is less than `"butter"`.

The BIG Picture

Using assignment with reference types such as `String` makes the variables share a reference to the same object. The default `==` operator checks equality of references. Two equal references refer to the identical object. Nonidentical objects can be equal even though the references to them are different. The `String Equals` method checks that the string objects are equal. The `String` class overloads the `==` operator to use `Equals` to check for equality of objects. The `CompareTo` method determines if its instance `String` is greater than, equal to, or less than its argument `String`.

✓Test Your Understanding

4. Given the `String` objects

```
String s = "a good time";
String s1 = "time";
String s2 = s.substring(7,11);
String s3 = s2;
```

find

a. `s1 == s2` **b.** `s1 == s`

c. `s2 == s3` **d.** `s1.Equals(s2)`

e. `s1.Equals(s3)`

5. Given the `String` objects

```
String s1 = "Happy days";
String s2 = "Hello world";
String s3 = "zebra";
```

determine whether the value returned by each of the following calls to the `CompareTo` method returns −1, 0, or 1.

a. `s1.CompareTo(s2)`

b. `s2.CompareTo(s3)`

c. `s1.CompareTo(s1)`

Try It Yourself ➤ **6.** Add tests for `s1==s3` and `s1==s4` to Example 6.2. Rerun it to see that the results confirm your expectations.

6.3 OBJECT COMPOSITION

Our BankAccount class has an instance variable balance of type double. **Composition**, a powerful object-oriented design concept, builds objects that have other objects as data fields. Our C# objects can be composed of other objects, just as a computer, for example, is composed of a CPU, a keyboard, a monitor, a disk drive, and so on. Composition models the **HAS-A** relationship in which one object contains another. An automobile has tires and an engine, for example.

We will build Name and Address objects that have String fields, and Person objects that each have a field defined as a Name and another defined as an Address. Composition and inheritance, which we cover in Chapter 10, are two ways of defining new classes using those previously defined. Composition models the whole–part relationship; that is, the whole object is composed of its parts.

We define a class Person to use in applications when we need data associated with a specific individual. We need many data items for each person, including first name, last name, street address, city, and so on. We choose to organize this data into coherent Name and Address classes rather than leaving it as an unorganized group of individual fields. Organizing our data will make our class easier to read. We can use the Name and Address classes in other applications. Figure 6.10 lists the fields for our Name, Address, and Person classes.

Each class in Figure 6.10 contains data fields that are objects. The Name class has two String objects and a char. Each Address has four String objects. The zip code, zip, uses digits, but because we do not do arithmetic on zip codes, we have no need to store it as an integer. Our Person class uses a String, a Name, and an Address. As we did with the zip code, we treat the id, usually the social security number, as a String.

Figure 6.11 illustrates composition. A Person contains references to a String, a Name, and an Address. A Name contains two String references and a character, and an Address contains four String references. We are especially interested in the fields, so we omit the operations from the class diagrams.

Each of the three classes has a constructor to initialize its fields (the Name class has two), and each has a ToString method to provide a string representation for display purposes. C# provides a ToString method for its library classes whose objects we need to display. The WriteLine method calls this ToString method when asked to display an object, as in

```
Console.WriteLine(aPerson);
```

which calls aPerson.ToString() to get the string representation for the object aPerson of type Person.

TIP

Define a ToString method for each class whose objects you need to display. Then you will be able to display your objects using the WriteLine statement. When your object is a component of another object, its string representation will be part of the string representation of the containing object. ■

```
Name
  private String first
  private char initial
  private String last
  public  Name(String f, String l)
  public  Name(String f, char i, String l)
  public  String ToString()

Address
  private String street
  private String city
  private String state
  private String zip
  public Address(String st,String cy,String se,String zp)
  public String ToString()

Person
  private String id
  private Name name
  private Address address
  public Person(String i, Name n, Address a)
  public String GetId()
  public String ToString()
```

FIGURE 6.10 **Fields for the `Name`, `Address`, and `Person` classes**

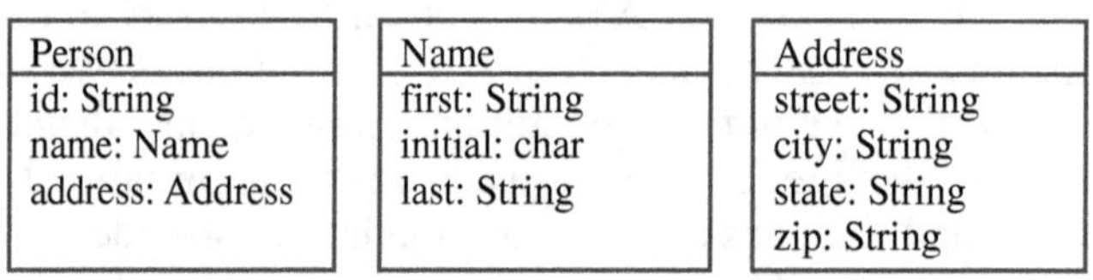

FIGURE 6.11 **Composition: The `Person`, `Name`, and `Address` classes**

Style

Do group fields into classes such as `Name` and `Address` that give meaning to the fields, help to organize your data, and can be reused in other applications.

Don't build a class with a long list of unorganized fields.

The fields listed in Figure 6.10 are instance variables. The `Name`, `Address`, and `Person` classes define the data and operations that will be part of each object of these types. Each object is an instance of its class type. For example, the object given by

FIGURE 6.12 **An instance of `Name`**

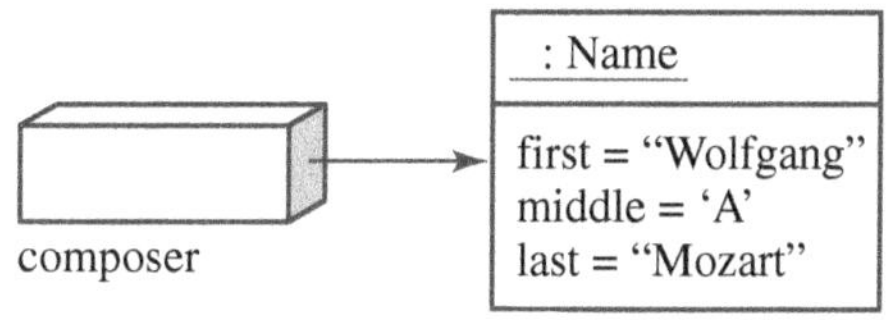


```
Name composer = new Name("Wolfgang", 'A', "Mozart");
```

shown in Figure 6.12 is an instance of the `Name` class.

The `composer` object has private data, its `first`, `initial`, and `last` fields, and a method, `ToString`, which returns its string representation. When we create an object instance of some type, we say we are **instantiating** an object of that type.

Example 6.3 creates our `Name`, `Address`, and `Person` classes, which we will use in applications later. To allow us to use each class in future applications, we make each `public` in its own file. The `TestPerson` class contains a `Main` method to test the `Person`, `Name`, and `Address` classes, also illustrating some of the `String` methods of Section 6.1.

We compile `Name.cs` to a library DLL using

```
csc /t:library Name.cs
```

We compile `Address.cs` using

```
csc /t:library Address.cs
```

We compile `Person.cs` using

```
csc /t:library /r:Name.dll,Address.dll Person.cs
```

and `TestPerson.cs` using

```
csc /r:Name.dll,Address.dll,Person.dll TestPerson.cs
```

EXAMPLE 6.3 ■ Name.cs, Address.cs, Person.cs, TestPerson.cs

Name.cs

```
/* Groups fields for a name.
 * Uses ToString to display.
 */

using System;
public class Name {
  private String first;
  private char initial;
  private String last;

  public Name(String f, String l) {                        // Note 1
    first = f;
```

```
    last = l;
  }
  public Name(String f, char i, String l) : this(f,l){ // Note 2
    initial = i;
  }
  public override String ToString() {                    // Note 3
    if (initial == '\u0000')                              // Note 4
      return first + " " + last;
    else
      return first + " " + initial + " " + last;          // Note 5
    }
  }
```

Address.cs

```
/* Groups fields for an address.
 * Uses ToString to display.
 */

using System;
public class Address {
  private String street;
  private String city;
  private String state;
  private String zip;
  public Address(String st, String cy, String se, String zp) {
    street = st;
    city = cy;
    state = se;
    zip = zp;
  }
  public override String ToString() {
    return street + "\n" + city + ", "
                          + state + " " + zip;            // Note 6
  }
}
```

Person.cs

```
/* Groups fields for a person.
 * Uses ToString to display.
 */

public class Person {
  private String id;
```

```
  private Name name;
  private Address address;
  public  Person(String i, Name n, Address a) {
    id = i;
    name = n;
    address = a;
  }
  public String GetId() {                                   // Note 7
    return id;
  }
  public override String ToString() {
    return name + "\n" + address;                           // Note 8
  }
}
```

TestPerson.cs

```
/* Tests the Person, Name, and Address classes,
 * and uses String Methods.
 */

using System;
public class TestPerson {

   /* Also illustrates some String methods.
    */
 public static void Main () {
    Name aName = new Name("Henry", "Johnson");
    Address anAddress =
    new Address("1512 Harbor Blvd.", "Long Beach",
                          "CA", "99919");
    Console.Write("Enter an id string: ");
    String anId = Console.ReadLine();
    Person aPerson = new Person(anId,aName,anAddress);
    Console.WriteLine("Our person is ");
    Console.WriteLine(aPerson);
    Console.WriteLine("   with id {0}", aPerson.GetId());
    Console.WriteLine
          ("\n And now some tests using string methods");
    String address = anAddress.ToString();
    int i = address.IndexOf("Harbor");                      // Note 9
    Console.WriteLine
           ("The index of Harbor in address is {0}", i);
    String z1 = "99919";
    int l = address.Length;                                 // Note 10
    Console.WriteLine("The length of address is {0}", l);
    String z2 = address.Substring(l-5,5);                   // Note 11
    bool same = z2.Equals(z1);                              // Note 12
```

```
      Console.WriteLine
           ("These two zip codes are the same? {0}", same);
      int less = z1.CompareTo("Harbor");                   // Note 13
      Console.WriteLine("Compare returns {0}", less);
      String hat = "   hat   ";
      Console.WriteLine(hat+"rack");
      Console.WriteLine(hat.Trim() + "rack");              // Note 14
    }
  }
```

Output

```
Enter an id string:  123456789
Our person is
Henry Johnson
1512 Harbor Blvd.
Long Beach, CA 99919
   with id 123456789

 And now some tests using string methods
The index of Harbor in address is 5
The length of address is 38
These two zip codes are the same? true
Compare returns the negative number -15
   hat   rack
hatrack
```

Note 1: `public Name(String f, String l) {`

We provide a constructor for a name without a middle initial. C# automatically initializes data fields with default values if the user does not supply any. We do not supply a value for `initial`, so C# initializes it with the default value for the type `char`, which is the character with numerical code zero. We can write this character as either `'\u0000'`, where the `'u'` stands for `Unicode`, or `'\000'`.

Note 2: `public Name(String f, char i, String l) : this(f,l){`

One constructor can call another constructor in the same class by using the name `this`, which refers to the current object. Here we call the other `Name` constructor, passing it a name and an address, and then initialize the middle initial. Note the syntax placing the call to `this(f,l)` before the body of the constructor.

Note 3: `public override String ToString() {`

When we introduce inheritance in Chapter 10, we will see that every object is a kind of `Object` and inherits a default `ToString` method. To redefine `ToString`, we need to use the `override` modifier. We will discuss overriding further in Chapter 10.

Note 4: `if (initial == '\u0000')`

We do not display the middle initial when it has the default value of `'\u0000'`, the character code with value zero, which C# assigns to the initial field when none is specified in the constructor.

Note 5: `return first + " " + initial + " " + last;`

The concatenation operator `'+'` converts any primitive type, such as `char`, to a `String` representation.

Note 6:

```
return street + "\n" + city + ", "
                          + state + " " + zip;
```

We add the string `"\n"` to include a `newline` in the string, so the street will appear on a separate line from the city, state, and zip code.

Note 7: `public String GetId() {`

We do not want to output the `id` every time we display the person's name and address. We can use this method to get the `id` when we need it.

Note 8: `return name + "\n" + address;`

The one string argument, `"\n"`, tells C# the `'+'` is the string concatenation operator rather than an arithmetic addition. The string concatenation operator uses the `ToString` methods we defined for `Name` and `Address` to get the string representations for the name and address fields without having to write `name.ToString()` or `address.ToString()`.

Note 9: `int i = address.IndexOf("Harbor");`

The `IndexOf` method returns the position of the first occurrence of its argument in the string, or −1 if the argument is not found. Here "`Harbor"` occurs starting at position five.

Note 10: `int l = address.Length;`

The `Length` property returns the length of the `String`.

Note 11: `String z2 = address.Substring(l-5,5);`

The `substring` method returns a `String` made from a range of characters of the given `String` object. Here we make a `String` from the last five characters, which is just the zip code of the address.

Note 12: `bool same = z2.Equals(z1);`

The two strings, `z1` and `z2`, are different objects but have the same characters, the zip code, so they are equal.

Note 13: `int less = z1.CompareTo("Harbor");`

Digits come before letters in the ASCII and Unicode character orderings, so a string of digits will be less than a string of letters. The `compareTo` method will return −1.

Note 14: `Console.WriteLine(hat.trim()+"rack");`

The `trim` method removes the leading and trailing whitespace from `hat`.

The BIG Picture

Composition models the HAS-A relationship between objects, in which one object contains another. We represent the contained object as an instance variable in the containing object.

✓ Test Your Understanding

7. Declare and initialize an `Address` object using your own address. List the four objects of which this `Address` is composed.
8. Declare and initialize a `Name` object using your own name.
9. Declare and initialize a `Person` object using data of your choice. List the three objects of which this `Person` is composed.

6.4 INTERFACES

A C# interface defines a reference type that has no implementation. The power of interfaces comes from the fact that users of the interface do not know anything about the implementation. A program that uses an interface will run correctly with any implementation of that interface. We can write one C# program that we can use with many different implementations.

A good example of this power comes from the .NET Framework `System.Collections` namespace. The `IList` interface provides methods such as `Add` and `Remove` for working with a list. Users of the `IList` interface write programs that work with any implementation of that interface. One program can work with many types of lists. We will introduce the `Systems.Collections` namespace in a later chapter.

Declaring an Interface

An **interface** specifies behavior but omits any implementation. The interface specifies a type for objects and can be implemented in various ways by C# classes. For example, an `IDrivable` interface might specify operations used in driving a vehicle (see Figure 6.13).

Style

Start interface names with the letter "I" to clearly distinguish them from class names.

FIGURE 6.13
The `IDrivable` interface

```
public interface IDrivable {
  void Start();
  void Stop();
  void Accelerate();
  void Decelerate();
  void Turn(String direction);
}
```

The `IDrivable` interface contains five methods. The interface states what an `IDrivable` object can do, but not how. We cannot implement any methods in an interface, nor can we include variables.

Interfaces limit the dependencies between various parts of a program, making programs easier to maintain, which is a very important consideration when developing large software systems that will be used for many years. A nice interface promotes portability. A program written using interface methods will work with any implementation of that interface.

Before we get to a C# example, consider driving an automobile. We do not have to learn a new set of skills to drive each of the many makes and models of automobiles. We usually start a car using a key, accelerate using the gas pedal, decelerate using the brake, and turn using the steering wheel. The implementation of these methods can be quite different, with a great impact on comfort and performance, but as drivers we do not need to delve into these implementation details.

In C# we can use interface methods without knowing the details of any implementation of that interface. The `GoForward` method of Figure 6.14 will work for any `IDrivable` object. It starts, accelerates to pick up speed, and decelerates to slow down.

We can pass any object that implements the `IDrivable` interface to the `GoForward` method. The developer of the `GoForward` method does not need to know about implementations of the interface.

Implementing an Interface

We can define various classes that implement `IDrivable` in their own ways. A class that implements an interface must implement each method of that interface. It may implement more than one interface and add instance variable and additional methods, as in the example on the next page.

FIGURE 6.14
Using the `IDrivable` interface

```
public static void GoForward(IDrivable d) {
  d.Start();
  d.Accelerate();
  d.Decelerate();
}
```

```
public class SportsCar : IDrivable {
    // implement Drivable methods here
}
```

In Example 6.4, we define two, `SportsCar` and `Van`, implementations of `IDrivable`. For simplicity they simply display messages that describe what each method does.

EXAMPLE 6.4 ■ SportsCar.cs, Van.cs, TestDrivable.cs

SportsCar.cs

```
/* Implements the IDrivable interface to drive
 * like a sports car.
 */

using System;
public class SportsCar : IDrivable {                    // Note 1
  public SportsCar() {
  }
  public void Start() {
    Console.WriteLine("Starting like a sports car");
  }
  public void Stop() {
    Console.WriteLine("Stopping like a sports car");
  }
  public void Accelerate() {
    Console.WriteLine("Accelerating quickly");
  }
  public void Decelerate() {
    Console.WriteLine("Decelerating rapidly");
  }
  public void Turn(String direction) {
    Console.WriteLine
          ("Turning {0} like a sports car", direction);
  }
}
```

Van.cs

```
/* Implements the IDrivable interface to drive
 * like a van.
 */

using System;
public class Van : IDrivable {
  public Van() {
  }
```

```
  public void Start() {
    Console.WriteLine("Starting like a van");
  }
  public void Stop() {
    Console.WriteLine("Stopping like a van");
  }
  public void Accelerate() {
    Console.WriteLine("Accelerating cautiously");
  }
  public void Decelerate() {
    Console.WriteLine("Decelerating gradually");
  }
  public void Turn(String direction) {
    Console.WriteLine("Turning {0} like a van", direction);
  }
}
```

TestDrivable.cs

```
/* Uses the IDrivable interface.
 */

using System;
public class TestDrivable {
  public static void GoForward(IDrivable d) {
    d.Start();
    d.Accelerate();
    d.Decelerate();
  }
  public static void Main() {
    Van mini = new Van();
    SportsCar hot = new SportsCar();
    GoForward(mini);                                   // Note 2
    Console.WriteLine();
    GoForward(hot);
  }
}
```

Output

```
Starting like a van
Accelerating cautiously
Decelerating gradually

Starting like a sports car
Accelerating quickly
Decelerating rapidly
```

Note 1: `public class SportsCar : IDrivable {`

`SportsCar` must implement all five methods of the `IDrivable` interface. It may add instance variables and methods. For example, a `SportsCar` might have a `Race` method for fast driving that other implementations of `IDrivable` would not support.

Note 2: `GoForward(mini);`

We can pass any object that implements the `IDrivable` interface to the `GoForward` method. In this example we pass two types of motor vehicle, but we could pass a `Tricycle` object if it implemented `IDrivable`.

The BIG Picture

An interface declares methods but provides no implementation. Programmers using an interface do not need to know the details of any of its implementations. A class implements an interface by implementing each of its methods.

✓Test Your Understanding

10. Describe some other classes that might implement the `IDrivable` interface.

11. Write an `AroundBlock` method with an `IDrivable` parameter. The method should enable the `IDrivable` object to traverse a rectangular city block.

6.5 RANDOM NUMBERS AND SIMULATION

Sometimes we cannot predict the outcome of an event precisely, but can specify a probability that something will occur. For example, in tossing a fair coin, we cannot predict the outcome of any one toss, but we can say that there is a 50% chance that it will be heads and a 50% chance that it will be tails. In a long series of coin tosses we expect about half of each outcome.

We can use a computer-generated sequence of numbers that appear to be random, to simulate coin tossing and many other events, such as the arrival of traffic at an intersection or customers at a bank.

The .NET Framework Class Library provides a `Random` class that we can use to generate numbers that appear to be produced randomly. We can use these random numbers in simulations of events that occur with various probabilities. In this section we simulate a simple coin toss. When we do our sorting case study in the next chapter we will generate random number data to sort.

The Random Class

The `Random` class in the `System` namespace has several methods that we can use to generate random numbers. The `NextDouble` method generates a random `double` value between `0.0` and `1.0`. The `Next()` method generates a random integer between `0` and `int.MaxValue`. The `Next(int high)` method generates a random integer between `0` and `high`. The `Next(int low, int high)` generates a random integer between `low` and `high`. In each case the upper limit is not one of the values produced. Example 6.5 illustrates these methods. Each time we run it we get different results because the methods use a seed to start the generation that depends on the current time.

EXAMPLE 6.5 ■ TryRandom.cs

```
/* Illustrates methods to generate random numbers.
 */

using System;
public class TryRandom {
  public static void Main() {
    Random r = new Random();
    Console.WriteLine(r.NextDouble());                    // Note 1
    Console.WriteLine(r.NextDouble());
    Console.WriteLine(r.Next());                          // Note 2
    Console.WriteLine(r.Next());
    Console.WriteLine(r.Next(30));                        // Note 3
    Console.WriteLine(r.Next(30));
    Console.WriteLine(r.Next(100, 125));                  // Note 4
    Console.WriteLine(r.Next(100, 125));
  }
}
```

First run

```
0.551596150524726
0.865152550332785
1999674866
768197678
3
27
124
120
```

Second run

```
0.225631200813517
0.118148481994005
1017060509
1670458154
2
29
109
122
```

Note 1: `Console.WriteLine(r.NextDouble());`

Produces a `double` randomly distributed between `0.0` and `1.0`.

Note 2: `Console.WriteLine(r.Next());`

Produces an integer randomly distributed between `0` and `int.MaxValue`.

Note 3: `Console.WriteLine(r.Next(30));`

Produces an integer randomly distributed from 0 through 29.

Note 4: `Console.WriteLine(r.Next(100, 125));`

Produces an integer randomly distributed from 100 through 124.

Simulation

We will simulate the tossing of a fair coin. We expect `Heads` and `Tails` each to occur on 50% of the tosses. To simulate this, we generate random integers chosen randomly from 0 and 1. We interpret 1 as `Heads` and 0 as `Tails`. In Example 6.6 the computer tosses the coin and the player guesses the outcome.

EXAMPLE 6.6 ■ CoinToss.cs

```
/* The player tries to guess the outcome of the
 * computer's coin toss.
 */

using System;
public class CoinToss {
  public enum Face {Heads, Tails}                        // Note 1
  private static Random r = new Random();

    /* Generates either 0 or 1 randomly. We associate 1 with
     * heads and 0 with tails. Heads and tails each occur on
     * about half the tosses, simulating a fair coin.
     */
  public static Face toss() {
    if (r.Next(2) == 1)                                  // Note 2
```

```
      return Face.Heads;
    else
      return Face.Tails;
  }

    /* Player guesses Heads or Tails
     */
  public static Face guess() {
    Console.Write("Guess? (Heads or Tails): ");
    String s = Console.ReadLine();
    if(s.ToUpper() == "HEADS")                        // Note 3
      return Face.Heads;
    return Face.Tails;
  }

    // The player wins by guessing the computer's toss
    // correctly.
  public static void Main()  {
    String repeat;

    do {
      if (guess() == toss())
        Console.WriteLine("You win!");
      else
        Console.WriteLine("Computer wins");
      Console.Write("Enter 'Y' to play again, 'N' to quit: ");
      repeat = Console.ReadLine();
    } while (repeat.ToUpper() == "Y");                 // Note 4
  }
}
```

Run

```
Guess? (Heads or Tails): Heads
Computer wins
Enter 'Y' to play again, 'N' to quit: Y
Guess? (Heads or Tails): Tails
You win!
Enter 'Y' to play again, 'N' to quit: n
```

Note 1: `public enum Face {Heads, Tails}`

We use an enumeration to represent the two outcomes, `Heads` and `Tails`.

Note 2: `if (r.Next(2) == 1)`

`r.Next(2)` generates the random numbers 0 and 1. Because the outcome is random, each occurs about half of the time.

Note 3: `if(s.ToUpper() == "HEADS")`

We convert the player's entry to uppercase to allow the player to use lowercase, uppercase, or a mixture in entering the guess.

Note 4: `} while (repeat.ToUpper() == "Y");`

The player can enter either 'Y' or 'y' to play again.

The BIG Picture

The `Random` class allows us to generate a range of either `double` or `int` values that appear to be randomly distributed. We can use these random numbers in simulations.

✓Test Your Understanding

12. How can we use random numbers to simulate rolling of a fair six-sided die? Each face of the die has a number from one to six. Each of these outcomes, one through six, is equally likely to occur.

SUMMARY

- Strings are a special class of great importance; C# provides a large library of String methods. A few, such as `Format`, are class methods which we invoke as if we were sending a message to the class; for example, `String.Format("The price is {0:C}, d)`. Most, including `CompareTo`, `Equals`, `IndexOf`, `Substring`, `ToUpper`, and `ToLower`, are instance methods, which we invoke as if sending a message to a particular object; for example `myName.ToUpper()`, where `myName` is the string given by `String myName = "Art"`. The concatenation operator, +, not only concatenates strings, but converts primitive types to a string representation and uses the `ToString` method to get the string representation for objects. We can initialize a string using a string literal such as "`house`".
- `String`, like all objects, is a reference type. A `String` variable refers to a `String` object rather than holding it. By contrast, an `int` variable holds a value rather than referring to it. The familiar operations work differently on reference types than they do on primitive types. Assignment copies the reference rather than the object to which the reference refers. Thus, assigning one `String` variable to another causes both references to refer to the same object. The default == operator compares one reference to another, not the objects to which they refer. The `String` class provides an `Equals` method to compare `String` objects. It also provides a `CompareTo` method to compare for less than and greater than. It overloads the == operator so that it checks the equality of the `String` objects rather than the references.

- We use composition, a powerful design tool, for building objects composed of other objects. Example 6.3 builds a `Name` and an `Address` from strings and a `Person` class from a `Name` and an `Address`.
- An interface specifies behavior without implementing it. A user of an interface does not need to know how it is implemented. The user may invoke any methods of the interface. Each object that implements the interface will have an implementation of that interface's methods. Using an interface allows one program to run on many different systems, each with a different implementation of that interface.
- The `Random` class provides several methods to generate numbers that seem to be randomly distributed in a given range. They include `NextDouble()`, `Next()`, `Next(int)`, and `Next(int,int)`.

SKILL BUILDER EXERCISES

1. What will be the output from the following?

```
String s = "hat";
String t = s + " rack";
Console.WriteLine(s.Substring(0,1) + t.Substring(5,3));
```

2. A `String` variable holds ____________________.

An `int` variable holds ____________________.

3. (True or False) For two `String` objects `s` and `t`,

```
if s.Equals(t) then s == t
```

CRITICAL THINKING EXERCISES

4. Which of the following can be included in an interface declaration?

a. a constant

b. a variable

c. a method declaration

d. none of the above

5. Which of the following is incorrect, where `IDrivable` is an interface and `Van` implements `Idrivable`?

a. `IDrivable d = new IDrivable();`

b. `IDrivable d = new Van();`

c. `Van v = new Van();`

d. none of the above

6. If `String s = "house"` and `String t = "domicile"`, `s.CompareTo(t)` returns

a. −1

b. true

c. 1

d. 0

e. none of the above

7. If `name` is a `Name` from Example 6.3, `Console.WriteLine(name)`

a. displays the empty `String`.

b. produces a compiler error.

c. displays the contents of the memory used by the name object.

d. displays `name.ToString()`.

e. none of the above

DEBUGGING EXERCISE

8. The following `IsEqual` method, for the `Name` class of Example 6.3, attempts to check two `Name` objects for equality. They should be equal if they have the same first name, middle initial, and last name. Find and correct any errors.

```
public bool IsEqual(Name name) {
  if (first != name.first)
    return false;
  else if(initial != name.initial)
    return false;
  else return last == name.last;
     result = true;
}
```

PROGRAM MODIFICATION EXERCISES

9. Add a `CompareTo` method to the `Name` class of Example 6.3. The `CompareTo` method should return −1 when the object is less than the argument, 0 when they are equal, and 1 when the object is greater. Compare last names first. If the last names are equal, compare first names. If the first names are equal, compare the middle initial.

10. Modify Example 5.1 to include an account holder of type `Person` in the `BankAccount` class.

PROGRAM DESIGN EXERCISES

11. Write a C# program that illustrates the use of each of the `String` methods discussed in Section 6.1.

12. Write a C# program that will find the first word, in alphabetical order, from a list of words entered by the user in an input dialog.

13. Write a C# program that counts the number of occurrences of the letter `'e'` in a `String` entered by the user.

14. Write a C# program that changes every `'p'` to a `'q'` in a `String` entered by the user.

15. Write a C# class that contains an `IDrivable` object. Include an `AroundTheBlock` method that uses `IDrivable` methods to drive the `IDrivable` object around a rectangular block. Test `AroundTheBlock` with both a `Van` and a `SportsCar`.

16. Use random numbers to simulate the repeated tossing of a fair coin. Letting the user input the number of tosses, report the percentage of outcomes that are heads. Allow the user to repeat the calculation as often as desired.

17. Calculate pi by throwing darts. In the following figure, the area of the circle divided by the area of the square is equal to pi/4. Throw darts randomly at the square, counting the total number of darts thrown and the number of darts that land inside the circle. The ratio of the latter to the former is an estimate of pi/4. Multiplying that ratio by four gives an estimate for pi. Use random numbers to simulate dart throwing. Get two random numbers for the x and y coordinates. If $(x - 0.5)^2 + (y - 0.5)^2 < .25$, then the dart landed inside the circle. Let the user input the number of dart throws.

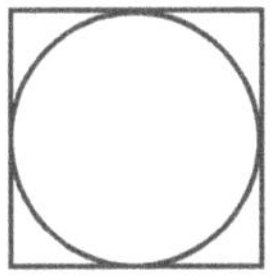

18. Create an interface, `IBendable`, with one method, `Bend`. Create two classes, `Spoon` and `Arm`, that implement `IBendable`. `Spoon` will also have an `Eat` method, and `Arm` will also have a `Raise` method. Each of these methods prints a message indicating its function. Write another class with a `Main` method, declaring two objects of type `IBendable`, one a `spoon` and another an `arm`. Call the `Bend` method.

7 Arrays

Each variable of one of the primitive types holds a single value. Using an integer variable `score` to hold a single test score, we can write a program to add a list of test scores. Once we add a score to the total we no longer need that value, and could read the next test score and save it in the same variable, `score`.

Suppose, however, that we want to arrange the scores from highest to lowest, displaying an ordered list of all scores. To sort the scores, we need to have them all available so we can compare one score with another. Using variables of type `int` would hardly be feasible. For 50 scores we would need variables `score1`, `score2`, `score3`, and so on up to `score50`. We might manage the burdensome task of typing 50 variable declarations, but suppose we had 500 scores, or 5000. Fortunately, the **array** concept solves this problem. An array provides a collection of values.

Our examples show how to use an array to handle large sets of data. We search an array for a given value, and reverse its elements. We create, input, and copy arrays. We illustrate an array of objects.

Arrays of arrays extend the array concept to multidimensional sets of data. We illustrate these concepts with an example of a class of students, each of whom has a set of test scores. Our program, using an array of arrays, computes average scores.

Our optional case study takes up the important problem of sorting, or arranging data in order. We introduce insertion sort, developing a complete sorting program. As an extra topic, we show how to add timing statements to determine the efficiency of this sorting algorithm. Those not wishing to cover sorting at this time may omit this section.

OBJECTIVES

- Know how to create and use C# arrays
- Understand that array variables hold references

- Understand memory allocation for arrays and arrays of objects
- Copy arrays and pass array arguments
- Use multidimensional arrays
- (Optional) Implement insertion sort using an array to hold the data
- (Optional) Estimate efficiency using timing statements

7.1 USING ARRAYS

As we noted in the introduction, it is not feasible to have 500 variables, `score1`, `score2`, ..., `score500`, to hold 500 test scores. The C# array lets us use one variable to refer to a collection of elements. We declare and initialize an array of type `int` that holds three integer elements as follows:

```
int[] score = {74, 38, 92};
```

Adding the square brackets to a type name, as in `int[]`, indicates an array type—in this case, a collection of `int` values. C# uses the values listed inside the curly braces to initialize the components of the array, which are called elements.

We use an integer index to access an array element. Array indices always start with zero, so we denote the three elements of the score array as `score[0]`, `score[1]`, and `score[2]`. The preceding declaration initialized `score[0]` to 74, `score[1]` to 38, and `score[2]` to 92. Figure 7.1 shows the `score` array.

The `score` array conveniently groups three integer variables, which we can use in expressions as we would any other variables. For example,

```
x = score[1] + score[2];
```

adds the values of `score[1]` and `score[2]`, storing the result in the variable `x`, and

```
score[0] = 87;
```

assigns the value 87 to `score[0]`.

Comparing Figures 7.2 and 7.3 demonstrates the advantage of using an array. Each program fragment searches for a score of 90 among the three scores.

Suppose we have 500 scores instead of three. To use integer variables we would need to add hundreds of lines to Figure 7.2, but to use an array, we need only change the test condition in Figure 7.3 to `i < 500` and the same three-line program will perform the search. We could revise Figure 7.3 to make it work no matter what the

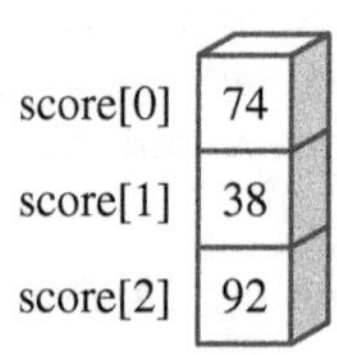

FIGURE 7.1 **The score array**

FIGURE 7.2 **Search using `int` variables**

```
if (score1 == 90)
  Console.WriteLine("It's score1");
else if (score2 == 90)
  Console.WriteLine("It's score2");
else if (score3 == 90)
  Console.WriteLine("It's score3");
```

FIGURE 7.3 **Search using an array**

```
for (int i = 0; i < 3; i++)
  if (score[i] == 90)
    Console.WriteLine("It's at index " + i);
```

FIGURE 7.4 **Search any size score array**

```
for (int i = 0; i < score.Length; i++)
  if (score[i] == 90)
    Console.WriteLine("It's at index " + i);
```

size of the array. Each array keeps its length in a field that we can access. The property `score.Length` holds the length of the score array (three in this example). Figure 7.4 shows how to rewrite the code of Figure 7.3 to use the array length to make the code work with arrays of any length.

We can declare arrays of any type. For example, we declare an array of `char`, `vowel`, to hold the five vowels,

```
char[] vowel = {'a','e','i','o','u'};
```

C# initializes the vowel array so `vowel[0] = 'a'`, `vowel[1] = 'e'`, and so on. The `double` array

```
double[] prices = {31.22,44.50,7.98,3.99,77.88,103.99};
```

has six elements, each of type `double`.

Example 7.1 searches an array for the first occurrence of a value input by the user.

EXAMPLE 7.1 ■ TryArray.cs

```
/* Searches an array for the first occurrence of a value
 * input by the user.
 */

using System;
public class TryArray {
  int[] test;
```

```
  public TryArray(int[] a) {
    test = a;
  }

    /* Returns the index in test at which testValue
     * occurs, or -1 if it does not occur
     */
  public int Search(int testValue) {
    int i = 0;
    while (i < test.Length && testValue != test[i])     // Note 1
       i++;
    if (i == test.Length)                               // Note 2
       i = -1;
    return i;
  }

    /* Inputs a test value. Calls the search method.
     * Displays the search result.
     */
  public static void Main() {
    int[] score = {56, 91, 22, 87, 49, 89, 65};         // Note 3
    TryArray t = new TryArray(score);
    Console.Write("Enter a test value: ");
    int testValue = int.Parse(Console.ReadLine());
    int i = t.Search(testValue);
    String message = " not found";                      // Note 4
    if (i != -1)
      message = " found at index " + i;
    Console.WriteLine(testValue + message);
  }
}
```

Run

```
Enter a test value: 87
87 found at index 3
```

Note 1: `while (i < test.Length && testValue != test[i])`

The loop terminates if we have either tested all elements of the array or we have found the item in the array.

Note 2: `if (i == test.Length)`

If we have tested all elements in the array, the index `i` will have been incremented to the size of the array. In that case, we set `i` to −1, a value that cannot be a valid index. If `search` returns −1, it will signify that the value was not found.

Note 3: `int[] score = {56, 91, 22, 87, 49, 89, 65};`
`score` will have elements `score[0]=56`, ..., `score[6]=65`.

Note 4: `String message = " not found";`

We initially indicate that the test value is not found, and change the message if we find it.

Changing an Array

In Example 7.1 we use an array to search for a value input by the user. We can also change individual array elements. If we executed the assignment `score[3] = 74` in the `score` array of Example 7.1, the array would be changed to

```
{56, 91, 22, 74, 49, 89, 65}
```

Let us write a program to reverse an array. Our program should change the score array of Example 7.1 to `{65, 89, 49, 87, 22, 91, 56}`. We can reverse the array by successively swapping pairs of elements. We will use symbols L and R to denote the left and right indices of the values that we will swap, starting with `L=0` and `R=score.Length-1`. After we swap two values we increment L and decrement R, repeating these steps until `L >= R`. Figure 7.5 shows the steps for the `score` array of Example 7.1.

Figure 7.6 shows the pseudocode describing this algorithm to reverse an array. Each step of the reversing process swaps two elements. We have to be very careful in doing a swap not to write over the data before we copy it. For example, if `x = 3` and `y = 4`, then the code,

```
x = y;
y = x;
```

FIGURE 7.5
Reversing an array

```
{56, 91, 22, 87, 49, 89, 65}      swap 56 and 65
 L                       R

{65, 91, 22, 87, 49, 89, 56}      swap 91 and 89
     L               R

{65, 89, 22, 87, 49, 91, 56}      swap 22 and 49
         L       R

{65, 89, 49, 87, 22, 91, 56}      reverse completed
             L
             R
```

FIGURE 7.6
Pseudocode to reverse an array

```
Initialize the array;
Initialize L to the smallest index;
Initialize R to the largest index;
while (L < R) {
  Swap the array elements at positions L and R;
  Increment L;
  Decrement R;
}
Output the reversed array;
```

which looks like it swaps x and y, causes both x and y to have the value four. The first assignment, `x = y`, erases the value of x that we need in the next assignment to assign to y. Consequently, the second assignment, `y = x`, assigns the new value of x, 4, instead of its old value, 3. To swap correctly, we need to save the value of x before we copy the value of y into it. The correct code is

```
int x = 3, y = 4, temp = 0;
temp = x;
x = y;
y = temp;
```

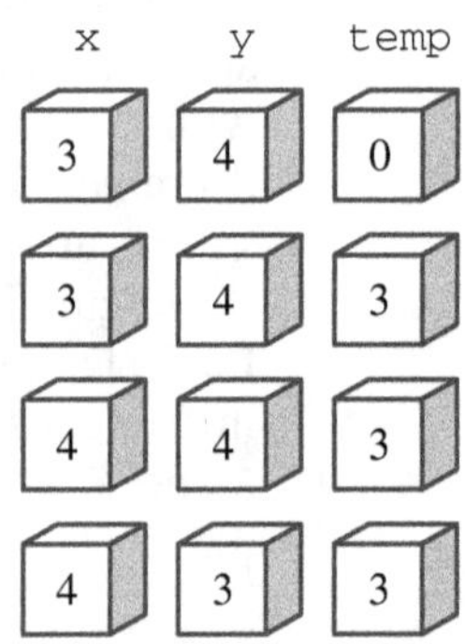

which saves the value of x in the variable temp, copies y to x, and then copies temp to y.

To output an array, we output the left brace; then each element, one at a time; then the right brace. We want to separate the values by commas, so before each element except the first we need to output a comma.

Before writing a program to reverse an array, we should check that our algorithm works for arrays with an even number of elements and for boundary cases. The array `{21,31,41,51,61,71}` has six elements. Applying our algorithm (steps omitted) will cause the `while` loop to terminate when we reach the position

```
{71,61,51,41,31,21}
      R  L
```

where R is less than L. For an array of one element, such as `{56}`, the algorithm will terminate without entering the `while` loop, because initially L starts out equal to R and the test condition fails.

Example 7.2 reverses an array. The `ReverseArray` class holds an array of integer data. A `swap` method will swap any two elements of its array. A `reverse` method will reverse a range of elements between two indices. A `Display` method will display the array between braces, on one line.

TIP Group major operations into methods, using the method names to invoke the operations. Organizing your program by naming operations make the program much easier to understand, write correctly, and change when needed. ■

EXAMPLE 7.2 ■ **ReverseArray.cs**

```
/*  Reverses an array.  Tested with
 *  an array initialized in the program.
 */

using System;
public class ReverseArray {
  private int[] data;                          // the array to reverse

  public ReverseArray(int[] d) {
    data = d;
  }

    // Swaps the array elements at indices left and right
  public void Swap(int left, int right) {
    int temp    = data[left];                               // Note 1
    data[left]  = data[right];
    data[right] = temp;
  }

    /* Reverses the order of the array elements
     * between indices left and right
     */
  public void Reverse(int left, int right) {
    while (left < right) {                                  // Note 2
      Swap(left, right);
      right--;
      left++;
    }
  }

    // Displays the array
  public void Display(String message) {
    Console.Write(message + "{");
    for (int i = 0; i<data.Length; i++) {
      if (i != 0)
           Console.Write(",");                              // Note 3
```

```
      Console.Write(data[i]);                              // Note 4
    }
    Console.WriteLine("}");
  }

    // Reverses an array and displays the result
  public static void Main()  {
    int [] score = {56, 91, 22, 87, 49, 89, 65};
    ReverseArray r = new ReverseArray(score);
    r.Reverse(0, score.Length-1);
    r.Display("The reversed array is ");
  }
}
```

Output

```
The reversed array is {65,89,49,87,22,91,56}
```

Note 1: `int temp    = data[left];`

The `temp` variable saves the value `score[left]`, so we can change `score[left]` to have the value `score[right]`, and then assign `temp` to `score[right]`, completing the swap.

Note 2: `while (left < right) {`

As long as `left < right`, there are two array elements to swap. For arrays of even length, the condition will fail with `right < left`. For arrays of odd length, it will fail with `right = left`.

Note 3: `if (i != 0) Console.Write(",");`

Before every element except the first, we output a comma to separate the next element from the preceding one.

Note 4: `Console.Write(data[i]);`

We display the array using a `for` loop to display each element. The `Write` statement keeps the output on the same line.

A Little Extra

Combining Increment with Assignment

For clarity, we adjusted the variables left and right after doing the swap, but we could have made these adjustments in the assignments themselves. The `while` loop of Example 7.2 would then read

```
while (left < right) {
  temp              = score[left];
  score[left++]     = score[right];
```

```
    score[right--]   = temp;
}
```

One defect of Example 7.2 is that we hard-coded the `score` array (initializing it with specific values in the code itself) rather than inputting it from the keyboard. In order to test other arrays, we would have to change the initialization of the score array in the program and recompile. To improve this example to let the user input array values, we need to learn more about arrays in the next section.

The BIG Picture

An array is a sequence of elements. In C#, we declare an array variable as `int[] x`, which creates an array variable `x` to refer to an array. The variable `x` has the value `null` until we refer it to an array. We can initialize an array with a sequence of values. We refer to an array element using its index. Array indices start at 0.

✓ Test Your Understanding

1. Declare and initialize an array with values 37, 44, 68, and −12. Replace the second element with 55.
2. Declare and initialize an array with values −4.3, 6.8, 32.12, −11.4, and 16.88. Copy the element from the fourth location into the first.
3. Declare and initialize an array with values 's', 'y', 't', 'c', 'v', and 'w'.
4. Write a `for` loop to find the sum of the elements of the array in question 1.
5. Show the steps of the algorithm to reverse the elements of the array `{21,31,41,51,61,71}`, as we did in Figure 7.5 for the seven-element array.

7.2 CREATING, INPUTTING, AND COPYING AN ARRAY

Like classes, arrays are reference types. We show how array variables relate to the arrays to which they refer. Then we show how to create, input, and copy an array.

Array Variables and Values

Data, like many things, comes in different sizes. Many people have cats that run around their house, and that they pick up and hold from time to time. If the cat is sitting on your lap and your sister wants to hold it, you can pass it to her. Some people have horses, but they do not give them free rein in the house, nor do they hold them on their laps. Horses are too big. Both you and your sister know where to find the horses: in the stable.

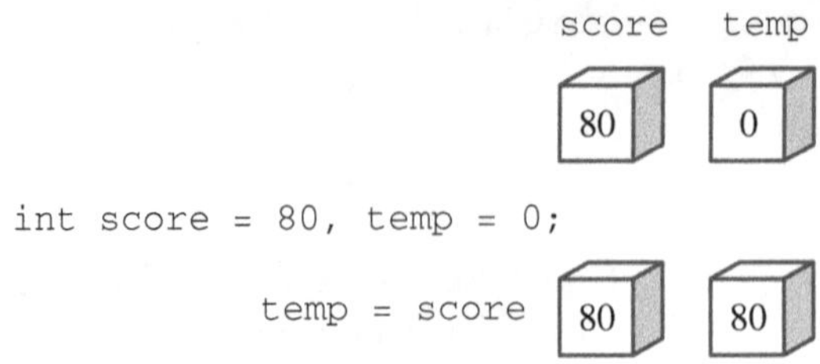

FIGURE 7.7
Primitive types hold values

Values of primitive types such as `10`, ‘`e`', or `3.14` have fixed, small sizes. Variables hold values of primitive types, and assignment copies the value from one variable to another, as Figure 7.7 shows.

Values of array types such as `{10,20,30,40,50,60,70}` can often be quite large. Variables do not hold array values, but hold references to them. A **reference** is a memory address; it tells where to find the item, in this case an array. We indicate a reference by an arrow pointing to the location of the array. Figure 7.8 shows the memory usage for the array given by

```
int[] score = {26,73,92};
```

The variable `score` holds a reference to the array of three `int` elements.

Assigning one array to another copies the reference, not the array value. For example, Figure 7.9a diagrams the memory C# uses for an array variable `x` initialized to refer to an array of five integers, and an uninitialized array variable `y`. Figure 7.9b shows the memory usage after we assign `x` to `y`.

We see that the assignment copies the reference from the variable `x` into the variable `y`. After the assignment, both variables refer to the same array. Copying a reference is more efficient than copying the whole array, which can be quite large. It takes time to copy the array values and space to hold them.

Because the variables `x` and `y` in Figure 7.9b refer to the same array, any changes made using `x` will affect `y`, and vice versa. For example, if we execute

```
y[2] = 7;
Console.WriteLine(x[2]);
```

we will see that `x[2]` has the value 7; `x` and `y` refer to the same array, so their elements must be the same. Figure 7.10 shows the effect of the assignment to `y[2]`.

Creating an Array

So far we have created each array by initializing it using an array **initializer**, which is a list of values enclosed in curly braces. Figure 7.8 shows that the array variable

FIGURE 7.8
Memory usage for `score`

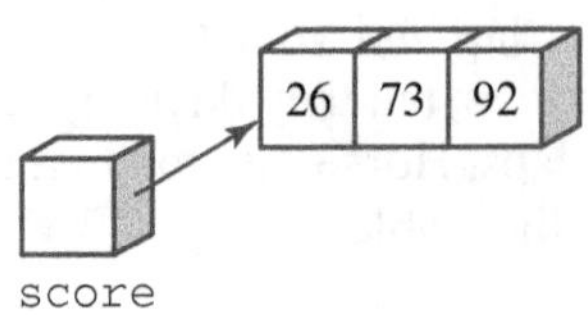

FIGURE 7.9
Memory usage for an array assignment

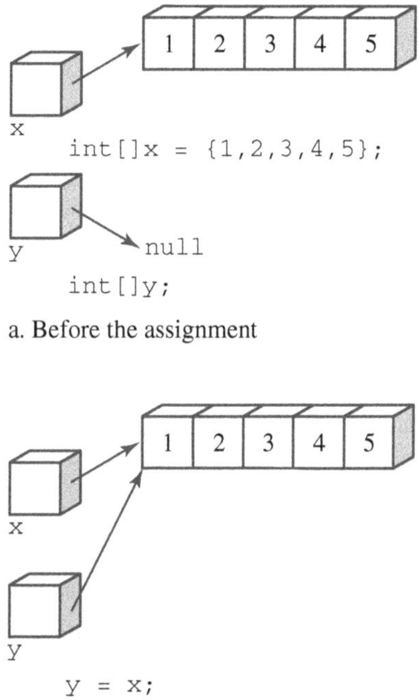

a. Before the assignment

b. After the assignment, `y = x`

FIGURE 7.10
Memory usage after the assignment `y[2] = 7`

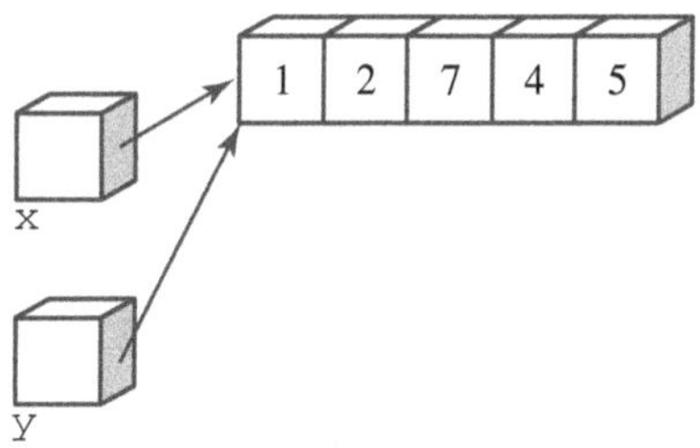

refers to the collection of array elements specified in the array initializer `{26,73,92}`. If we declare an array but do not initialize it, as in

```
int[] anArray;
```

then the memory looks like Figure 7.11, where an array variable exists but has no values to which to refer.

C# has an operator, `new`, to allocate space for the array elements. We can use the expression

FIGURE 7.11
Memory usage for `anArray`

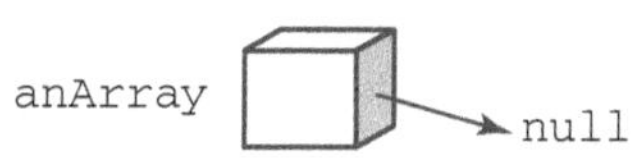

FIGURE 7.12
Memory allocation using the operator `new`

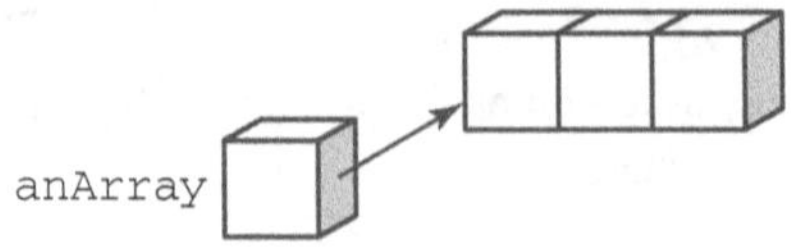


```
new int[3]
```

to allocate an array with space for three elements. Figure 7.12 shows the memory after execution of the statement `anArray = new int[3];`

Inputting an Array

Having allocated the memory for the array elements, we can assign values to them, as in

```
anArray[0] = 17;
anArray[1] =  3 + x;
anArray[2] = int.Parse(Console.ReadLine());
```

The first of these statements assigns a constant value; the second assigns the value of an expression, and the third assigns a value input by the user. Figure 7.13 diagrams the memory if the variable `x` has the value 7 and the user inputs 22.

We declared `anArray` to have three elements. By using a variable, `size`, in the declaration instead of the constant, 3, as in:

```
int[] myArray = new int[size];
```

we can declare an array `myArray` whose size depends on the value of the variable `size`. By allowing the user to input the value of `size` before making the declaration, as in

```
Console.Write("Enter the size of the array: ");
int size = int.Parse(Console.ReadLine());
int[] myArray = new int[size];
```

we can create `myArray` at runtime to have the desired size.

To summarize, an array variable holds a reference to a collection of elements. If we declare an array without initializing it, we create an array variable but no space for array elements (Figure 7.11). We create the space for the array elements either by initializing the array with a list of elements or by using the operator `new`. Initializing the array with a list of elements causes C# to allocate the memory for the array elements and initialize the memory with the specified values (Figure 7.8). Using the operator `new` allocates the memory for the array elements (Figure 7.12); we can then assign values to the elements (Figure 7.13).

FIGURE 7.13
Memory configuration for `anArray`

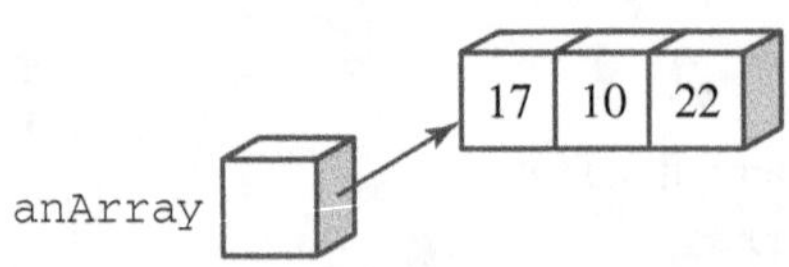

To illustrate the use of the operator `new`, Example 7.3 revises Example 7.2 to allow the user to enter the array elements from the keyboard. The user first enters the size of the array; we then create an array of that size. The `ReadIntArray` method returns the array that the user inputs.

EXAMPLE 7.3 ■ ReverseInputArray.cs

```
/*  Reverses an array.  The user inputs the
 *  size of the array and enters its components.
 */

using System;
public class ReverseInputArray {
  private int[] data;             // the array to reverse

  public ReverseInputArray(int[] d) {
    data = d;
  }

    // Uses input dialogs to input an array
  public static int[] ReadIntArray() {                    // Note 1
    Console.Write("Enter the array size: ");
    int size = int.Parse(Console.ReadLine());             // Note 2
    int[] anArray = new int[size];                        // Note 3
    for (int i=0; i<size; i++){
      Console.Write("Enter anArray["+i+"]: ");
      anArray[i] = int.Parse(Console.ReadLine());
    }
    return anArray;
  }

    // Swaps the array elements at indices left and right
  public void Swap(int left, int right) {
    int temp     = data[left];
    data[left]   = data[right];
    data[right]  = temp;
  }

    /* Reverses the order of the array elements
     * between indices left and right
     */
  public void Reverse(int left, int right) {
    while (left < right) {
      Swap(left, right);
      right--;
      left++;
    }
  }
```

```
    // Displays the array
  public void Display(String message) {
    Console.Write(message + "{");
    for (int i = 0; i<data.Length; i++) {
      if (i != 0) Console.Write(",");
      Console.Write(data[i]);
    }
    Console.WriteLine("}");
  }

    // Reverses an array and displays the result
  public static void Main()  {
    int[] score = ReadIntArray();
    ReverseInputArray r = new ReverseInputArray(score);
    r.Display("The original array is ");
    r.Reverse(0, score.Length-1);
    r.Display("The reversed array is ");
  }
}
```

Run

```
Enter the array size: 3
Enter anArray[0]: 45
Enter anArray[1]: 39
Enter anArray[2]: 67
The original array is {45,39,67}
The reversed array is {67,39,45}
```

Note 1: `public static int[] ReadIntArray() {`

`ReadIntArray` is a class method. It inputs an array and is not associated with a particular `ReverseInputArray` instance.

Note 2: `int size = int.Parse(Console.ReadLine());`

The user enters the size of the array, so we can run the program with arrays of different sizes.

Note 3: `int[] anArray = new int[size];`

The operator `new` allocates memory for an array of `int` type. Note that we can specify the number of components as the value of the `size` variable, which we input from the user. This gives much more flexibility than if we had specified a constant number of components as in the expression `new int[10]`.

In Example 7.3, the `ReadIntArray` method declares a local array variable, `anArray`, and uses the `new` operator to allocate space for an array to which `anArray` refers. It then fills the array and returns the reference to the calling method, `Main`. The `Main` method saves the reference in its local variable, `score`.

Figure 7.14 illustrates the variables and the array to which they refer while `readIntArray` is filling the array. The **heap** is an area of memory used by the `new` operator to allocate memory for reference types. Methods use a different area, called the stack, to allocate memory for local variables.

Figure 7.15 shows the memory allocation after `ReadIntArray` completes execution. The local variable, `anArray`, is no longer alive, but the `score` variable refers to the array that `ReadIntArray` created on the heap using the `new` operator.

Copying an Array

The assignment in Figure 7.9b copies the reference in the variable `x`, resulting in two variables, `x` and `y`, referring to the same array. If we want to copy the array elements, not the reference, we need to use the `new` operator to allocate space for a second array, as in

```
int[] y = new int[x.Length];
```

and write a loop to copy each element from the old array to the new array, as in

```
for (int i = 0; i < y.Length; i++)
   y[i] = x[i];
```

We can also use the `Copy` method to copy an array. The statement

```
Array.Copy(x, 0, y, 0, y.Length);
```

will copy the entire array `x` to the array `y`. The five arguments to the `Copy` method are the source array, the starting index in the source, the target array, the starting index in the target, and the number of elements to copy.

FIGURE 7.14
Memory allocation in Example 7.3 while `ReadIntArray` is active

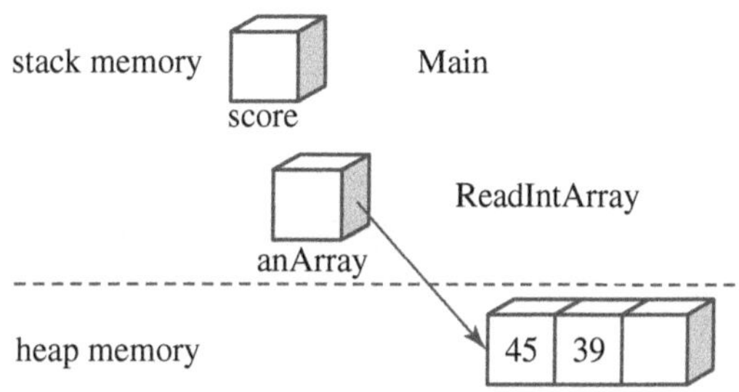

FIGURE 7.15
Memory allocation in Example 7.3 after `ReadIntArray` finishes

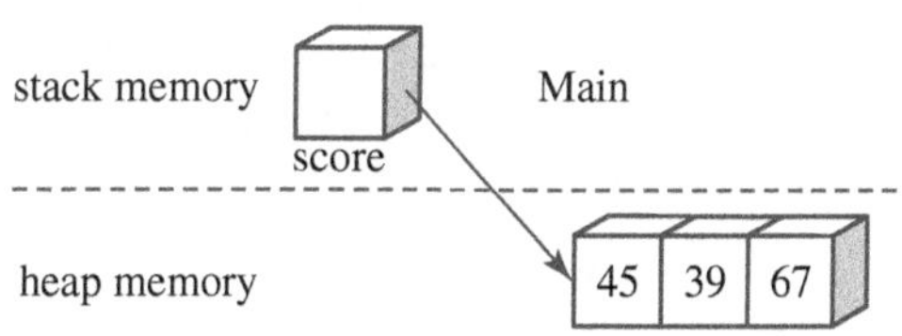

FIGURE 7.16
Copying array elements

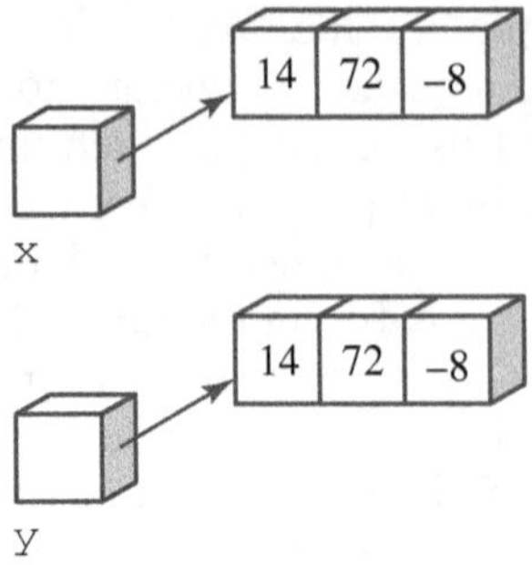

Figure 7.16 shows the result of copying the array x to the array y. If we change the x array shown in Figure 7.16, say by the assignment x[1] = 11, then the y array will not change, because y refers to a different array than x does. Example 7.4 demonstrates the difference between copying a reference and copying the array itself.

EXAMPLE 7.4 ■ ArrayCopy.cs

```
/*  Illustrates the difference between array
 *  assignment, which copies a reference to an array,
 *  and making a copy of one array in a new array.
 */

using System;
public class ArrayCopy  {

     // Displays the array
   public static void Display
                      (String message, int[] anArray) {   // Note 1
     Console.Write(message + "{");
     for (int i = 0; i < anArray.Length; i++) {
       if (i != 0) Console.Write(",");
       Console.Write(anArray[i]);
     }
     Console.WriteLine("}");
   }

   public static void Main() {
     int[] x = {4,5,6};
     int[] y = new int[x.Length];
     Array.Copy(x, 0, y, 0, x.Length);                    // Note 2
     int[] z = x;                                         // Note 3
     x[1] = 7;                                            // Note 4
     Display("The x array is now ", x);
```

```
    Display("The y array, after changing x, is ", y);  // Note 5
    Display("The z array, after changing x, is ", z);  // Note 6
  }
}
```

Output

```
The x array is now {4,7,6}
The y array, after changing x, is {4,5,6}
The z array, after changing x, is {4,7,6}
```

Note 1: `public static void Display (String message, int[] anArray) {`

We make `Display` a class method and pass it the array to display.

Note 2: `Array.Copy(x, 0, y, 0, x.Length);`

We make a copy of `x`, so `x` and `y` each refer to different arrays. There is no sharing.

Note 3: `int[] z = x;`

Assigning `x` to `z` copies the reference in `x`, so that `z` refers to the same array as `x` does.

Note 4: `x[1] = 7;`

This assignment changes the `x` array to see how it affects the `y` and `z` arrays.

Note 5: `Display("The y array, after changing x, is ", y);`

Because the array variable `y` refers to a true copy of the `x` array, changing `x` has no effect on the `y` array; it retains its original values.

Note 6: `Display("The z array, after changing x, is ", z);`

Because the array variable `z` refers to the same array the `x` does, changing the `x` array also changes the `z` array.

A Little Extra

Contrasting `int[]` and `int` arguments

When we pass an array to a method, we pass a reference, so we end up with two references to the same array—one from the actual argument passed in and one from the formal parameter. In the `change` method

```
public static void Change(int[] anArray) {
  if(anArray.Length > 1)
     anArray[1] += 2;
}
```

we add two to `anArray[1]`. This change affects the array that we pass as the argument when we call the `Change` method. For example, if we call the `Change` method with the code

```
int[] data = {3, 4, 5};
Change(data);
```

from the `Main` method, Figure 7.17 illustrates the memory configuration before the call to `Change`, and Figure 7.18 illustrates it after. Using the reference `anArray` in the `Change` method changes the `data` array in the calling method.

By contrast, when we pass a primitive type to a method, the formal parameter is a copy of the actual argument, and changing it has no effect on the actual argument. To illustrate this, consider the `Assign4` method given by

```
public static void Assign4(int someNumber) {
  someNumber = 4;
}
```

which we might call with the code

```
int x = 27;
Assign4(x);
```

When we pass the variable `x` to `Assign4`, C# copies its value, 27, to the formal parameter `someNumber`. Figure 7.19 shows the result.

When C# executes the `Assign4` method, the formal parameter changes its value to 4, but the actual argument `x` is unchanged, as Figure 7.20 shows.

■

FIGURE 7.17
Memory configuration when the `Change` method is called

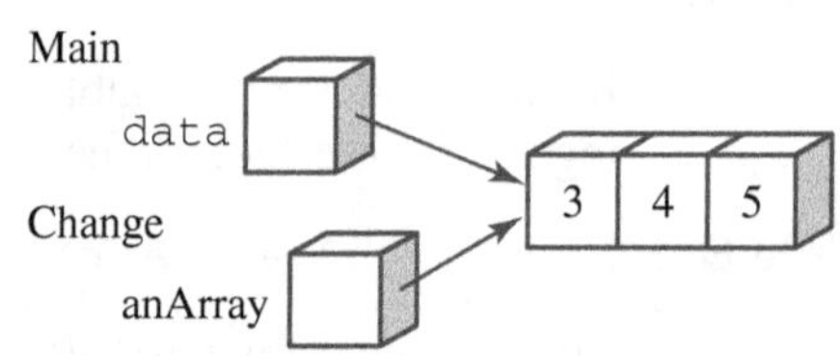

FIGURE 7.18
Memory configuration after the `Change` method is finished executing

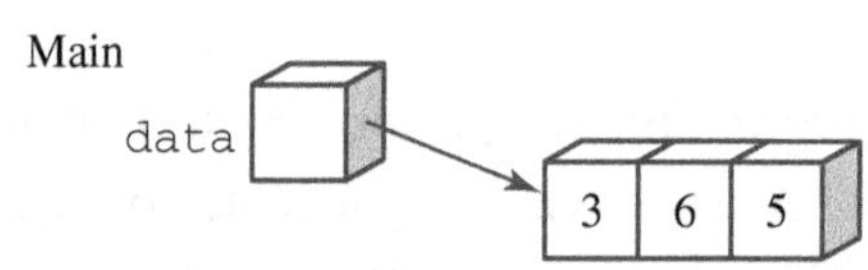

FIGURE 7.19
Memory configuration after passing `x` to `Assign4`

FIGURE 7.20 **Effect of the `Assign4` method**

> **The BIG Picture**
>
> The `new` operator allocates storage for array elements. Array variables, like object variables, are references. Assignment copies one reference to another and both variables refer to the same array. To make a copy of an array, we need to allocate storage for the new array and copy the elements. We can use the `Copy` method to copy one array to another.
>
> We can pass array arguments to and return array values from methods. The formal array parameter, used in the body of the method, refers to the array passed from the calling program, whereas for primitive types, changes to the formal parameter do not affect the value passed from the caller.

✓ Test Your Understanding

6. Diagram the memory usage for each of the following.

   a. `int[] intArray;`

   b. `char[] charArray  = {'a','b','c'};`

   c. `double[] doubleArray = new double[6];`

7. Diagram the memory usage for each of the following.

   a. `int[] intArray = {2,-4,5,9,-1};`

   b. `char[] charArray = new char[8];`

   c. `double[] doubleArray;`

8. Diagram the memory usage resulting from the execution of

```
int[] a = {36, -2, 44, 55};
int[] b = a;
```

9. Write C# code to make a copy of the array `a` of question 8.

10. Diagram the memory configuration resulting from the variables and arrays of question 9.

11. Diagram the memory configuration of the stack and heap used just before the `Display` method is called when the `Main` method of Example 7.4 is active.

12. Diagram the memory configuration of the stack and heap used when the `Display` method of Example 7.4 is active.

Try It Yourself ➤ **13.** Revise the `Main` method of Example 7.3 to reverse all components of the array but the first and last. Test with an array of size at least five.

7.3 ARRAYS OF OBJECTS AND A SIMULATION

It is important to understand the memory allocation that takes place when using arrays of objects. This section also creates a simulation of tossing dice, keeping track of the values in an array.

Arrays of Objects

When we create an array of an object type, say, in the declaration

```
BankAccount[]  account = new BankAccount[3];
```

the `new` operator creates an array of reference variables, initially with `null` values, as Figure 7.21 shows.

Figure 7.21 shows that the declaration has not created any objects. The `new` operator allocated memory for the three references to `BankAccount` objects, but did not allocate any memory for the objects themselves. To do that, we construct `BankAccount` objects using one of the `BankAccount` constructors. For example, executing

```
BankAccount account[0] = new BankAccount(25.0);
```

would add a `BankAccount` object, as Figure 7.22 shows.

Example 7.5 creates a `BankAccount` array. We compile it using the command

```
csc /r:BankAccount.dll TryObjectArray.cs
```

after we have copied `BankAccount.dll` to the current directory.

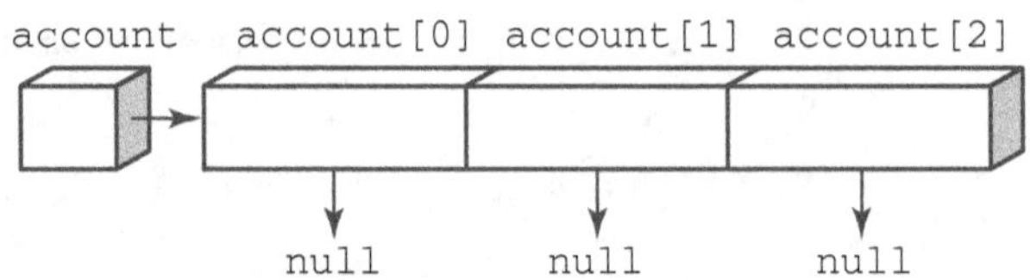

FIGURE 7.21 Declaring an array of objects

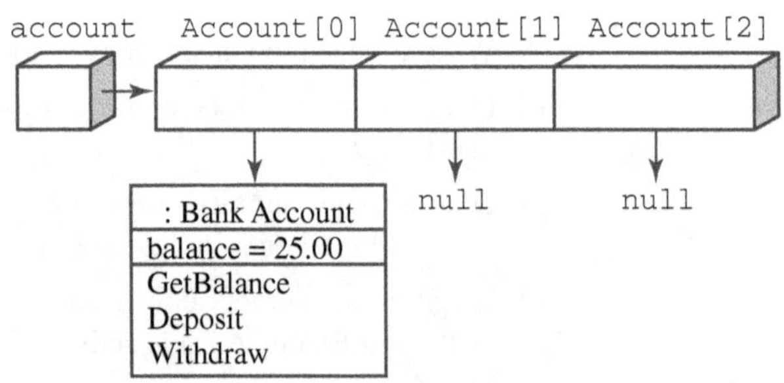

FIGURE 7.22 Adding a **`BankAccount`** element to an array

EXAMPLE 7.5 ■ TryObjectArray.cs

```
/* Illustrates an array of objects.
 */

using System;
public class TryObjectArray {

    /* Creates an array of three BankAccounts.
     * Deposits $50 in each and displays the new balance.
     */
  public static void Main() {
    BankAccount[] account = new BankAccount[3];
    account[0] = new BankAccount(25.00);
    account[1] = new BankAccount();
    account[2] = new BankAccount(470.32);
    for(int i = 0; i < account.Length; i++) {
      account[i].Deposit(50.00);
      Console.WriteLine
           ("The balance is {0:C}", account[i].GetBalance());
    }
  }
}
```

Output

```
The balance is $75.00
The balance is $50.00
The balance is $520.32
```

■

TIP

When creating an array of objects, first use the `new` operator to allocate memory for the array of references. The `new` operator then allocates memory for the objects referred to by the array references. ■

A Simulation

Before continuing with arrays of arrays, we present another example to gain further practice in using arrays. In our `Dice` class we use random numbers to simulate the tossing of two dice. Assuming that each die has an equal chance of landing so that any one of its six faces, numbered 1 through 6, will be showing, we tabulate the frequency of each of the sums, 2 through 12, of the numbers showing on each die.

We write a method, `Roll`, that simulates the roll of two dice, returning the sum of the numbers showing on each face. Calling

```
random.Next(1,7)
```

returns either 1, 2, 3, 4, 5, or 6, where `random` is a `Random` instance. Each of these should occur with equal frequency because the random numbers are distributed evenly. We toss two dice and return the sum.

The method `TossResults` tabulates the frequencies of each outcome, 2 through 12, in an array named `result`, so `result[i]` is the number of times that the sum on the two dice was `i`. We use the array elements `result[2]` through `result[12]`, leaving `result[0]` and `result[1]` unused. We simply store the outcome of the `Roll` method in the `result` array by incrementing the value in the array. For example, if the outcome is 6, we execute `result[6]++`.

Example 7.6 shows the code for this dice simulation. To find the expected frequencies, we make a `6 x 6` grid with row labels 1 through 6, and column labels 1 through 6, and enter the sum of the row and column labels in the grid, as shown in Figure 7.23.

Tabulating the 36 outcomes from Figure 7.23 gives

Sum	2	3	4	5	6	7	8	9	10	11	12
Frequency	1	2	3	4	5	6	5	4	3	2	1

showing, for example, that of the 36 outcomes, 7 occurs six times and 10 occurs three times. If the number of rolls is a simple multiple of 36, such as 36, 360, 3600, and so on, we can easily see how closely the simulation matches the prediction. For example, for 360 tosses we expect, on average, to get a distribution like

Sum	2	3	4	5	6	7	8	9	10	11	12
Frequency	10	20	30	40	50	60	50	40	30	20	10

FIGURE 7.23
Outcomes when tossing two dice

	1	2	3	4	5	6
1	2	3	4	5	6	7
2	3	4	5	6	7	8
3	4	5	6	7	8	9
4	5	6	7	8	9	10
5	6	7	8	9	10	11
6	7	8	9	10	11	12

```
/* Simulates the rolling of two dice.
 * The user inputs the number of tosses.
 * Uses arrays to tabulate the results.
 */

using System;
public class Dice {
  private Random random = new Random();

    /* Returns the sum of two random numbers
     * each between 1 and 6.
     * Simulates rolling dice.
     */
  public int Roll() {
    int die1 = random.Next(1, 7);                     // Note 1
    int die2 = random.Next(1, 7);
    return die1 + die2;
  }

    /* Returns an array of result of
     * rolling the dice a number of times
     * passed to it.
     */
  public int[] TossResults(int number) {
    int[] result = {0,0,0,0,0,0,0,0,0,0,0,0,0};       // Note 2
    for (int i = 0; i < number; i++)
      result[Roll()]++;                               // Note 3
    return result;
  }

    /* Prompts for the number of tosses.
     * Simulates the tosses.
     * Displays the results.
     */
  public static void Main() {
    Dice dice = new Dice();
    Console.Write("Enter the number of rolls of the dice: ");
    int numberOfRolls = int.Parse(Console.ReadLine());
    int[] diceThrows = dice.TossResults(numberOfRolls);
    Console.WriteLine("Sum\tFrequency");
    for (int i = 2; i <= 12; i++)
      Console.WriteLine("{0}\t{1}", i, diceThrows[i]);
  }
}
```

Run

```
Enter the number of rolls of the dice: 3600
Sum       Frequency
2            101
3            209
4            307
5            402
6            498
7            590
8            481
9            403
10           308
11           213
12            88
```

Note 1: `int die1 = random.Next(1, 7);`

This method produces values 1 through 6 with equal expected frequency.

Note 2: `int[] result = {0,0,0,0,0,0,0,0,0,0,0,0,0};`

We initialize the array with 13 components, all zero, but use only the last 11, with `result[i]` holding the number of times the sum on the two dice was `i`.

Note 3: `result[Roll()]++;`

The call to `Roll()` returns a value from 2 through 12. We increment the number stored in the array element `result[Roll()]` to indicate the occurrence of the value returned by `Roll`. For example, if `Roll()` returns five, we increment `result[5]`.

The BIG Picture

When creating an array of objects, we need to construct the array references and the objects to which they refer.

Arrays have many uses. The `Random` class has methods to generate random values to use in simulations.

✓Test Your Understanding

14. Suppose we have the situation of Figure 7.22, in which the `account` array can hold three `BankAccount` objects, but only one has been created. Would the `for` loop of Example 7.5 still execute without error? Explain.

15. Write a C# expression that generates a random integer greater than or equal to 50 but less than 500.

16. If in Example 7.6 we were to roll three dice instead of two, how many elements would we need in the `result` array? Which elements would be unused?

7.4 MULTIDIMENSIONAL ARRAYS

Arrays let us access a collection of data. An array `score` might have ten elements or 100, which we access using an array index, as in `score[9]`. An instructor might have an array of scores for each student in the class. For example,

```
student1 has scores {52, 76, 65}
student2 has scores {98, 87, 93}
student3 has scores {43, 77, 62}
student4 has scores {72, 73, 74}
```

and so on for the 30 students (or is it 300?) in the class.

We do not want to declare 30 or 300 variables. We have the same problem that we faced with one set of scores, where we had to declare variables `score1`, `score2`, `score3`, and so on, until we learned to declare an array variable score of type `int[]`. To accommodate the scores for an entire class, we can use a two-dimensional array, which we picture as a matrix with one row for each student's scores. For example, the declaration

```
int [ , ] s = new int[30][3];
```

would define a `30 x 3` array. For simplicity we reduce the class size to four, and declare

```
int [ , ] student = new int[4][3];
```

We can add initial values for the scores at the end of the declaration, as in

```
int [ , ] student = new
  int[4][3]{{52,76,65},{98,87,93},{43,77,62},{72,73,74}};
```

or in short form,

```
int [ , ] student =
  {{52,76,65},{98,87,93},{43,77,62},{72,73,74}};
```

We picture the `student` array as a two-dimensional matrix

```
52 76 65
98 87 93
43 77 62
72 73 74
```

but the array values are actually stored in a contiguous block of memory and C# computes the address of an element when it is needed.

Array indices for each dimension begin with zero, so that `student[0,0]` is 52, `student[1,2]` is 92, and `student[3,1]` is 77. Example 7.7 computes the average score for each student in the class.

EXAMPLE 7.7 ■ StudentScoreMulti.cs

```
/* Uses a multidimensional array.
 * Computes the average score of
 * each student.
 */

using System;
public class StudentScoreMulti {
  static void Main( ) {
    int [ , ]student = {{52, 76, 65},
      {98, 87, 93}, {43, 77, 62}, {72, 73, 74}};
    double sum;        // sum of the scores for each student
    for (int i = 0; i < student.GetLength(0); i++) {
                                                  // Note 1
      sum = 0;
      for (int j = 0; j < student.GetLength(1); j++)
                                                  // Note 2
        sum += student[i, j];
      Console.Write
         ("The average score for student {0} is ", i );
      Console.WriteLine
        ((sum/student.GetLength(1)).ToString("F1"));
                                                  // Note 3
    }
  }
}
```

Output

```
The average score for student 0 is 64.3
The average score for student 1 is 92.7
The average score for student 2 is 60.7
The average score for student 3 is 73.0
```

■

Note 1: `for (int i = 0; i < student.GetLength(0); i++) {`

`GetLength(0)` represents the number of elements in dimension 0—four in this example.

Note 2: `for (int j = 0; j < student.GetLength(1); j++)`

`GetLength(1)` represents the number of elements in dimension 1—three in this example.

Note 3:

```
Console.WriteLine
        ((sum/student.GetLength(1)).ToString("F1"));
```

The `ToString` method for the type `Double` accepts a formatting string as an argument. Here we format using fixed-point with one decimal place.

An Array of Arrays

If each student did not have the same number of test scores, it would be convenient to use an array of arrays. Each student would have a reference to an array of scores which might be different in size from that of other students. For example,

```
int[][] student = new int[3][];
```

shows an array of three arrays in which we do not specify the size of the array for each student. We then create an array for each student. For example, if the first student has two scores, the second has one, and the third has three, we could declare

```
student[0] = new int[2]{56, 76};
student[1] = new int[1]{83};
student[2] = new int[3]{34,78,67};
```

Figure 7.24 shows the student array of array of scores for each student.

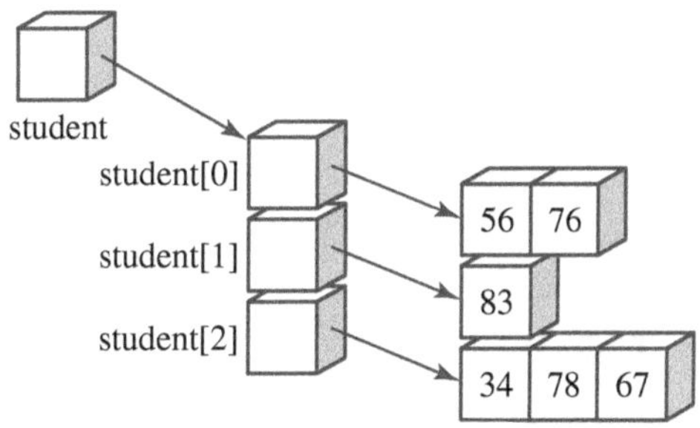

FIGURE 7.24 **The `student` array**

We can get individual scores by referring to components of these arrays, as in

```
student[1][0] is 83
student[2][2] is 67
```

The length of the `student` array, given by `student.Length`, is three. Each element of the `student` array is itself an array. The length of element `i`, `student[i]`, is given by `student[i].Length`, which in this example is three. Example 7.8 computes the average score for each student.

EXAMPLE 7.8 ■ StudentScore.cs

```
/* Uses an array of arrays.
 * Computes the average score of
```

```
 * each student.
 */

using System;
public class StudentScore {
  static void Main( ) {
    int [][]student =  new int[3][];     // scores
    student[0] = new int[2]{56, 76};
    student[1] = new int[1]{83};
    student[2] = new int[3]{34, 78, 67};
    double sum;        // sum of the scores for each student
    for (int i=0; i<student.Length; i++) {
      sum = 0;
      for (int j=0; j<student[i].Length; j++)           // Note 1
        sum += student[i][j];
      Console.Write("The average score for student {0} is ",
                                                              i );
      Console.WriteLine((sum/student[i].Length).ToString("F1"));
    }
  }
}
```

Output

```
The average score for student 0 is 66.0
The average score for student 1 is 83.0
The average score for student 2 is 59.7
```

Note 1: `for (int j=0; j<student[i].Length; j++)`

`student[i].Length` gives the number of scores for the student at index `i`.

The BIG Picture

A multidimensional array has a fixed number of rows and columns. Declaring `int [ , ] x = new int[4][3]` creates an array with four rows and three columns. We can include initial values in the declaration. `x[3,2]` refers to the element in row 3, column 2.

An array of arrays is an array whose elements are also arrays. These element arrays do not have to be the same size. Declaring `int[][] y = new int [4][]` will create an array `y` whose four elements may have different sizes. Executing `y[0] = new int[5]` will give the first element of the `y` array five elements.

✓ Test Your Understanding

17. Declare and initialize a multidimensional array of scores for two students. The first student has scores 55, 66, 87, and 76, and the second student's scores are 86, 92, 88, and 95.

18. Declare and initialize a multidimensional array of batting averages for five baseball players for each of the last three years. Batting averages are typically computed to three decimal places and range from .150 to .400.

19. Given `char[ , ] letter ={{'a','b','c'}, {'x','y','z','w'}}`, find

a. `letter[0][1]` **b.** `letter[1][0]`

c. `letter[1][3]` **d.** `letter[0][2]`

7.5 (OPTIONAL) SOLVING PROBLEMS WITH C#: INSERTION SORT

In this section we develop a program to sort an array, arranging its elements in order using insertion sort. Sorting has many uses; various algorithms have been developed to solve this important problem. Insertion sort is useful for smaller data sets, but other methods such as quicksort or merge sort work much more efficiently for larger sets of data.

Defining the Problem

To understand how insertion sort works, we start with an example. Given the values

```
54  23  78  42  26 12 41 64
```

the sorted array should be

```
12  23  26  41  42  54 64 78.
```

Insertion sort takes each element from the second element to the last element and inserts it in its proper place with respect to the preceding elements. Starting with the second element, which we underline,

54 <u>23</u> 78 42 26 12 41 64

we see that `23 < 54`, so we move 54 to the right one position in the array, and insert 23 in the beginning of the array, giving

```
23  54  78  42  26  12  41  64
```

Next we insert 78.

23 54 <u>78</u> 42 26 12 41 64

Because `78 > 23`, we compare 78 to 54. Because `78 > 54`, we know that 78 is greater than all its predecessors, so we leave it where it is in position three, and the array is unchanged. At this point we have the first three elements in order.

Next we insert the fourth element, 42.

23 54 78 <u>42</u> 26 12 41 64

FIGURE 7.25
Partially sorted array

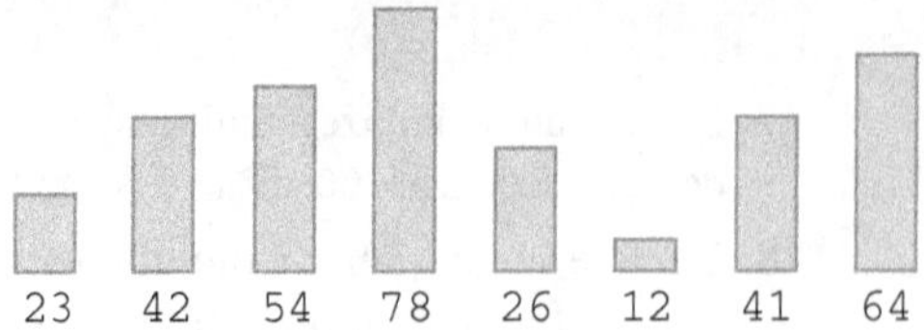

Because `42 > 23` and `42 < 54`, we move both 78 and 54 to the right by one position and insert 42 in the second position, giving

```
23  42  54  78  26  12  41  64
```

Figure 7.25 shows the array at this point, with its first four elements in order. Later we will use C# to draw such a diagram.

The fifth element, 26, is greater than 23 and less than 42, so we move the elements 42, 54, and 78 to the right and insert 26 in the second position, giving

```
23  26  42  54  78 12  41  64
```

Because 12 is smaller than 23, we move the first five elements to the right, and insert 12 at the start of the array, giving

```
12  23  26  42  54  78  41  64
```

The seventh element, 41, is greater than the first three elements, but less than 42, so we move 42, 54, and 78 to the right and insert 41 as the fourth element of the array, giving

```
12  23  26  41  42  54  78  64
```

Finally, the last element, 64, is greater than all elements but 78, so we move 78 to the right, and insert 64 as the seventh element, and the array is fully sorted.

Toward a Solution: Developing the Pseudocode

Figure 7.26 expresses the overall solution in pseudocode.

To get the data, we can allow the user to input data, or we can generate random numbers to test without requiring user input. Figure 7.27 shows this refinement.

FIGURE 7.26
Insertion sort: Top-level pseudocode

```
Get the data to sort;
Display the data to sort;
Insert each item in the correct
   position in its predecessors;
Display the sorted data;
```

FIGURE 7.27
Refinement: Get the data to sort

```
Ask if the user wants to enter data;
if (yes) Get data from the user;
else Generate random data;
```

FIGURE 7.28
Refinement: Get data from the user

```
Input the size of the data;
loop
   Get the next item;
```

In previous examples, we have used three ways to get data from the user. Because the data could be positive or negative we do not really have a convenient sentinel value that we can distinguish from a valid data value, so we will rule out the use of a sentinel. We could ask the user each time if there is more data to input, which does not require the user to know the size of the data set, but does require an extra response to input the next item. The last alternative, which we choose, is to have the user input the size of the data, as shown in the refinement in Figure 7.28, where we use `loop` to represent a loop that we will implement using one of the C# repetition statements.

To generate random data, we first ask the user to input the size of the data and then use a loop to generate the required number of random values. Having gotten this far, we see that no matter how we get the data, we will ask the user to input the size of the data. Rather than coding this request twice, we can get the data size before deciding whether to input from the user or generate random numbers. Figure 7.29 shows this revision of the refinement in Figure 7.27, including the refinements for the subproblems.

To sort the data we insert one element at a time, starting with the second element, in the correct position in its predecessors. Figure 7.30 shows this loop.

From our example, we see that to insert the item at index `i` we first find its correct position, say `j`, then move the elements at positions `j` through `i-1` to the right by one position. Finally we insert the item in the correct position. Figure 7.31 shows this refinement.

FIGURE 7.29
Revised refinement: Get the data to sort

```
Input the size of the data;
Ask if the user wants to enter the data;
if (yes)
  loop
    Get the next item;
else
  loop
    Generate the next random item;
```

FIGURE 7.30
Refinement: Insert items

```
loop, from second item to last
  Insert item i in the correct position
     in its predecessors;
```

FIGURE 7.31
Refinement: Insert item `i`

```
Find the correct position, say j, for item i;
Move elements at j to i-1 one position to the right;
Insert item i at position j.
```

To find the correct position for item `i`, we start at the leftmost element of the array, with `j` initialized to zero, and while item `i` is greater than item `j`, we increment `j`. In our example, when we insert item 6, which is 41, we do the following steps

```
41 > 12 so increment j to 1
41 > 23 so increment j to 2
41 > 26 so increment j to 3
41 < 42 so stop, finding that index 3 is the correct position
```

Figure 7.32 shows the refinement for finding the correct position.

We have to be careful to move the items starting at the right, so we do not overwrite any items before they are moved and to save item `i` before writing over it. In our example, because we found that index 3 is the correct position for 41, we need to move items 3 to 5 to the right; the steps are

```
save the 41 that we want to insert
move 78 to the right, storing it as the item at index 6
move 54 to the right, storing it as the item at index 5
move 42 to the right, storing it as the item at index 4
```

Figure 7.33 shows the `for` loop we need to move the elements at indices from `j` to `i-1` to the right by one position

FIGURE 7.32
Refinement: Finding the correct position for item `i`

```
j = 0;
while (item i > item j) j++;
```

FIGURE 7.33
Refinement: Move elements `j` to `i-1` to the right

```
Save item i;
for (int k = i; k > j; k--)
  item[k] = item[k-1];
```

FIGURE 7.34
Pseudocode for insertion sort

```
Input the size of the data;
Ask if the user wants to enter the data;
if (yes)
  loop
    Get the next item;
else
  loop
    Generate the next random item;
Display the data to sort;
loop, from second item to last {
  j = 0;
  while (item i > item j) j++;
  Save item i;
  for (int k=i; k>j; k–)
    item[k] = item[k-1];
  item[j] = item[i];
}
Display the sorted data;
```

To insert item `i` at position `j` we use the simple assignment

```
item[j] = item[i];
```

We leave the refinement to display the data until we write the C# code. We will also postpone the decision as to which random numbers to use until we write the code. We have refined all but the simplest subproblems and can put the complete pseudocode together in Figure 7.34.

Toward a Solution: Alternatives

Having completed the pseudocode for the insertion sort, we might think about other possible solutions. One alternative would allow us to combine the steps of finding the correct position and moving the elements to the right. For this alternative, when we insert element `i` we start checking at element `i-1` instead of at element `0`. We leave the development of this alternative solution to the exercises.

Completing the C# Code

The pseudocode in Figure 7.34 gives us a good basis for writing the C# program.

EXAMPLE 7.9 ■ InsertionSort.cs

```
/* Sorts an array of data using the
 * insertion sort algorithm.  Uses
 * data from the user or random data.
 */
```

```
using System;
public class InsertionSort {
  private int[] item;

  public InsertionSort(int[] i) {
    item = i;
  }

    // Returns the size of the array of data to sort
  public static int GetSize() {
    Console.Write("Enter the number of data items: ");
    return  int.Parse(Console.ReadLine());
  }

    /* Returns the data array, either
     * entered by the user, or
     * randomly selected.
     */
  public static int[] GetData(int size) {
    int[] item = new int[size];
    Console.Write
         ("Enter 'Y' to enter data, 'N' for random data: ");
    String enter = Console.ReadLine();
    if (enter.ToUpper() == "Y")
      for (int i = 0; i < size; i++) {
         Console.Write("Enter item[" + i + "]: ");
         item[i] = int.Parse(Console.ReadLine());
      }
    else {
      Random random = new Random();
      for (int i = 0; i < size; i++)
         item[i] = random.Next(100);                    // Note 1
    }
    return item;
  }

    /* Inserts the next element in the correct
     * with respect to its predecessors.
     */
  public void InsertNext(int i) {
    int current = item[i];                              // Note 2
    int j = 0;
    while (current > item[j]) j++;
    for (int k = i; k > j; k--)
      item[k] = item[k-1];
    item[j] = current;
  }
```

```
    // Inserts each element
  public void Sort() {
    for (int i = 1; i < item.Length; i++) {
      InsertNext(i);
    }
  }

    // Gets and sorts an array of integer data.
  public static void Main()  {
    int size = GetSize();
    int[] item = GetData(size);
    ArrayCopy.Display("The data to sort is ", item);   // Note 3
    InsertionSort s = new InsertionSort(item);
    s.Sort();
    ArrayCopy.Display("The sorted data is ", item);
  }
}
```

First Run

```
Enter the number of data items: 10
Enter 'Y' to enter data, 'N' for random data: n
The data to sort is {51,70,41,62,95,89,63,78,80,5}
The sorted data is {5,41,51,62,63,70,78,80,89,95}
```

Second Run

```
Enter the number of data items: 3
Enter 'Y' to enter data, 'N' for random data: y
Enter item[0]: 88
Enter item[1]: 77
Enter item[2]: 66
The data to sort is {88,77,66}
The sorted data is {66,77,88}
```

Note 1: `item[i] = random.Next(100);`

To make the display shorter, we restrict our random numbers to the range 0 to 99.

Note 2: `int current = item[i];`

We store the element at index `i` before we write over it. This store occurs in the pseudocode just before the inner `for` loop when we are about to write over item `i`. Because we refer to item `i` earlier in the code, in the `while` statement, we decided to store it earlier, before the `while` statement. This has the small advantage that, in the `while` statement, we can use the value of the variable `current` which is a little easier to look up than the array element, `item[i]`. It is like the difference between looking up a number in your personal address book or the big phone book; either way you look up a value, but one way is a little easier. For beginning programmers, we rank clarity and ease of understanding higher than efficiency concerns, but good programmers need to be aware of performance. See the following *A Little Extra* section for a more important discussion of efficiency.

Note 3: `ArrayCopy.Display("The data to sort is ", item);`

We could have included a display method in the `InsertionSort` class, but all we need is a generic method to display any array, and we already have such a display method in the ArrayCopy class. We compile using the command `csc /r:ArrayCopy.exe InsertionSort.cs` to reference the ArrayCopy code containing the Display method.

Testing the Code

We tested `InsertionSort` with two cases, one using random numbers and one with user-supplied data. The user supplied the data in reverse order, which is a special case worthy of testing. Realistically, we should provide many more tests, but because of space limitations we defer that to the exercises.

A Little Extra

Growth Rates

Polishing your code to improve efficiency is important because getting results fast is always a selling point in commercial projects. However, the best performance increases will come from using the best algorithm for the task. Data structures and algorithm analysis courses show how to analyze algorithms for efficiency and present good algorithms for important computing tasks. As an introduction to this area, we will investigate the efficiency of the `InsertionSort` algorithm of Example 7.9.

The `Environment` class has a property, `TickCount`, which returns the number of milliseconds since the system was last started. We call this method just before the loop to do the insertion sort to get the start time, and just after to get the stop time. Computing `stoptime-starttime` tells us the time spent doing the insertion sort.

Example 7.10 revises Example 7.9 to add these timing statements. We omit the output of the array because we want to run the program for very large arrays. For the same reason, we use only random number input, omitting the choice to let the user input the data.

The most interesting statistic about an algorithm is its growth rate. We want to know not just how much time insertion sort will take for a single array, but how that time grows as the size of the array grows. In our test, sorting an array of size 10,000 takes 141 milliseconds, but sorting an array of size 100,000 takes 14,391 milliseconds.[1] If we repeat with the same size arrays, we will get similar results. The size

[1]We used a Pentium 4 at 1.8 GigaHertz.

of the data increased ten-fold from 1000 to 10,000, while the time increased about 100-fold from 141 to 14,391 milliseconds.

We say that the time needed by insertion sort has a rate of growth that varies as the square of the size of the data. Based on this growth rate, we would predict that running this program on our systems with an array of size 20,000 should take about 564 milliseconds.

■

EXAMPLE 7.10 ■ InsertionSortTiming.cs

```
/* Sorts random numbers using the insertion sort algorithm.
 * Uses random data. Outputs the milliseconds taken to sort.
 * Use this program
 */

using System;
public class InsertionSortTiming {
  private int[] item;

  public InsertionSortTiming(int[] i) {
    item = i;
  }

   // Returns the size of the array of data to sort
  public static int GetSize() {
    Console.Write("Enter the number of data items: ");
    return  int.Parse(Console.ReadLine());
  }

    /* Returns the data array, either
     * entered by the user, or
     * randomly selected.
     */
  public static int[] GetData(int size) {
    int[] item = new int[size];
    Random random = new Random();
    for (int i = 0; i < size; i++)
      item[i] = random.Next(100);
    return item;
  }

    /* Inserts the next element in the correct
     * with respect to its predecessors.
     */
  public void InsertNext(int i) {
```

```
      int current = item[i];
      int j = 0;
      while (current > item[j]) j++;
      for (int k = i; k > j; k--)
        item[k] = item[k-1];
      item[j] = current;
    }

      // Inserts each element
    public void Sort() {
      for (int i = 1; i < item.Length; i++) {
        InsertNext(i);
      }
    }
      // Gets and sorts an array of integer data.
    public static void Main()  {
      int size = GetSize();
      int[] item = GetData(size);
      InsertionSortTiming s = new InsertionSortTiming(item);
      int starttime = System.Environment.TickCount;      // Note 1
      s.Sort();
      int stoptime = System.Environment.TickCount;       // Note 2
      Console.WriteLine("The time used in milliseconds is {0}",
                                 stoptime-starttime);
    }
  }
```

First Run

```
Enter the number of data items: 10000
The time used in milliseconds is 141
```

Second Run

```
Enter the number of data items: 100000
The time used in milliseconds is 14391
```

Note 1: `int starttime = System.Environment.TickCount;`

We save the time just before the loop to do the sorting.

Note 2: `int stoptime = System.Environment.TickCount;`

We save the time just after the sorting loop, so subtracting the start time from the stop time will give the time used by the sort.

The BIG Picture

Carefully developed pseudocode makes it much easier to code correctly in C#. Insertion sort is one of many algorithms that use data stored in arrays. By adding timing statements we can estimate the efficiency of the code. For insertion sort, we find that the time used grows proportionally to the square of the size of the data.

✓ Test Your Understanding

20. Show the stages of insertion sort by starting with the array 52, 38, 6, 97, 3, 41, 67, 44, 15 and showing that array after each insertion of an element in the correct position in its predecessors.

21. Change the insertion sort algorithm by providing a different refinement for the insert item `i` subproblem of Figure 7.31. In this solution, compare item `i` to item `i-1`, exchanging the two if item `i` is less than item `i-1`. Repeat this process of moving the original item `i` to the left until either that item is greater than or equal to its predecessor or there are no more predecessors.

Try It Yourself ➤ **22.** Test Example 7.9 carefully with a range of test data.

23. Using the data of question 20, show each change in that array following the revised insertion sort algorithm of question 21.

Try It Yourself ➤ A Little Extra **24.** Add timing statements before and after the call to the reverse method in Example 7.3. Try test cases to estimate the rate of growth of time taken to reverse an array as the size of the array increases. If the size of the array doubles, by what factor does the time increase? Modify Example 7.3 to use random numbers to generate data to reverse.

SUMMARY

- Arrays allow us to refer to large collections of variables conveniently. An array variable refers to the array; we use an index to refer to a specific element such as `myArray[2]`.
- To indicate an array type we add the square brackets, `[]`, to the element type. Thus `int[]` denotes the type of an array whose elements have type `int`.
- The statement `int[] myArray = {4,5,6};` declares an array variable, allocates space for three elements, and initializes the three elements to have values four, five, and six. Array indices start at zero, so `myArray[0]` has the value four.
- Array variables refer to an array of elements. The statement `int[] myArray;` declares an array variable but does not allocate space for elements to which it can refer. The statement `int[] myArray = new int[3];` uses the operator `new` to allocate space for an array of three integers to which the variable `myArray` refers. We still need to initialize this array with desired values.
- We can pass array arguments to methods and return array values from methods. A formal parameter of an array type has a copy of the reference to an array passed as the actual argument to the method, so inside the method we can change the actual array argument passed from the caller.

- A multidimensional array uses multiple indices to access an element. An array of arrays is a collection of elements which are themselves arrays.
- Many applications involve sorting. The insertion sort arranges the elements of an array in order, by inserting each element in the correct position in its predecessors. It is useful for small arrays, but gives way to more efficient methods for larger arrays. We can add timing statements to determine the time taken by an algorithm as a function of the size of the data; we call this the growth rate of the algorithm. For insertion sort, we found that the time increased as the square of the size of the data.
- Arrays, which allow us to group data, are a part of almost every major programming language.

SKILL BUILDER EXERCISES

1. Given the array

```
static int[] nums = {45,23,67,12,11,88,3,77};
```

what value does `split(0,7)` return, and how does the `nums` array change given the following C# code?

```
static void Interchange (int a, int b){
  int temp = nums[a];
  nums[a] = nums[b];
  nums[b] = temp;
}
static int Split (int first, int last) {
  int x, splitPoint;
  x = nums[first];
  splitPoint = first;
  for (int i = first;i <= last; i++)
    if (nums[i] < x) {
      splitPoint++;
      Interchange (splitPoint,i);
    }
  Interchange(first,splitPoint);
  return splitPoint;
}
```

2. Find the array that results from the execution of `f(3,4,21)` where the code for the method `f` is

```
public static int[ , ] f(int n, int m, int value) {
  int[ , ] x = new int[n][m];
  for (int i=0; i < x.GetLength(0); i++)
    for (int j=0; j < x.GetLength(1); j++)
      x[i,j] = value;
  return x;
}
```

3. Find the array that results from the execution of `g(5,34)`, where the code for the method g is

```
public static int[][] g(int n, int value) {
  int[][] x = new int[n][];
  for (int i=0; i < x.Length; i++) {
    x[i] = new int[i+1];
    for (int j=0; j < x[i].Length; j++)
      x[i][j] = value;
  }
  return x;
}
```

CRITICAL THINKING EXERCISES

4. For each of the following statements choose which of the following best describes it:
   - **i.** declares an array only
   - **ii.** declares an array and allocates space for array elements
   - **iii.** declares an array, allocates space for, and initializes its elements with values supplied by the user
   - **iv.** is incorrectly formed

   a. `int[] x;`

   b. `int y = {32, 41};`

   c. `int[] z = new int[5];`

   d. `int[] w = {5, 6};`

5. Consider the code

```
int[] x = {5,6,7,8,9};
int[] y = x;
y[2] = 3;
```

   Which of the following is correct?

   a. `x[2]` has the value 7.

   b. `x[2]` has the value 6.

   c. `x[2]` has the value 3.

   d. `y[3]` has the value 7.

6. Choose which of the following best describes the result of the statement

```
int[] myArray =
          ArrayCopy.Display("The scores are ", score);
```

   where `Display` is the method of Example 7.4.

   a. The array `myArray` will refer to the same array as `score` does.

   b. The array `myArray` will refer to a different array than `score` does.

   c. This statement is incorrectly formed.

d. None of the above

7. Given

```
BankAccount[] b = new BankAccount[5];
```

the statement `b[3].Deposit(100.00)`

a. will increase the balance by $100 of the account referred to by `b[3]`.

b. will cause a compiler error.

c. will compile, but cause a runtime error.

d. none of the above

DEBUGGING EXERCISE

8. A word is a palindrome if it reads the same backwards and forwards. For example, `dad` and `otto` are palindromes but `hat` and `boat` are not. The following program attempts to find whether a word is a palindrome. The user enters the number of characters in the word, and then enters each character, using only lowercase characters. Find and correct any errors in this program.

```
public class Pal {
  public static void Main() {
    Console.Write("How many characters? ");
    int size = int.Parse(Console.ReadLine());
    char [] a = new char[size];
    for (int i = 0; i < a.length; i++) {
      Console.Write("Enter next character");
                  a[i] = int.Parse(Console.ReadLine());
    }
    Console.Write ("The word ");
    for (int i = 0; i < a.Length; i++)
      Console.Write (a[i]);
    for (int i = 1; i < a.Length/2; i++)
      if (a[i] != a[a.Length-i]) {
        Console.WriteLine(" is not a palindrome");
        Environment.Exit(0);
      }
        Console.WriteLine(" is a palindrome");
  }
}
```

PROGRAM MODIFICATION EXERCISES

9. Modify the program to reverse an array in Example 7.3 to allow the user to repeat the code, reversing additional arrays during the same run of the program.

10. Modify Example 7.3 to make `ReadInputArray` an instance method.

11. Modify Example 7.7 to use a method to return the average score for each student.

12. Modify Example 7.7 to compute the class average for each test, rather than the average of the test scores for each student.

13. a. Modify the insertion sort program of Example 7.9 to use the insertion method described in the pseudocode of *Test Your Understanding* question 21.

A Little Extra

b. Add timing statements to the code of part a to estimate the growth rate for the insertion algorithm (See Example 7.10).

14. Modify the insertion sort algorithm of Example 7.9 to sort an array of `String` objects. Use the `CompareTo` method to replace the less than operator, <, used for integers.

15. Modify the array search program of Example 7.1 to search an array of `String` objects.

16. Modify Example 7.2 to reverse an array of `String` objects.

17. Modify Example 7.3 to reverse an array of `String` objects.

18. Modify Example 7.4 to make a copy of an array input by the user.

PROGRAM DESIGN EXERCISES

19. a. Generate an array of 20 random integers from zero to nine. Search for the first occurrence, if any, of the number 7, and report its position in the array.

b. Repeat the computation of part a 1000 times, and for each position in the array, report the number of times that the first occurrence of a 7 in the array is at that position.

20. Generate an array of 10,000 random numbers from zero to four. Report the percentage of each of the numbers, zero, one, two, three, and four in the array.

21. The standard deviation is a measure of the spread of the data with respect to the mean (average). Data with a small standard deviation will be clustered close to the mean and data with a larger standard deviation will be more spread out. To compute the standard deviation, find the mean, find the difference of each item from the mean, square those differences, find the average of those squares, and, finally, find the square root of that average, which is the standard deviation. For example, given the data 10, 20, and 30,

```
mean                 (10+20+30)/3 = 20
differences (10-20) = -10   (20-20) = 0    (30-20) = 10
squares of differences       100,  0,  100
average of the squares      (100+0+100)/3  = 66.7
square root of the average        8.2
```

Write a C# program to compute the mean and standard deviation of the elements in an array with elements of type `double`.

22. A company has five stores. Input the weekly sales for each store. Find the store with the maximum sales, the one with the minimum sales, and find the average weekly sales for the five stores.

23. A company has three regions, with five stores in the first region, three in the second, and two in the third. Input the weekly sales for each store. Find the average weekly sales for each region and for the whole company.

24. A company has five stores. Input the weekly sales for each store. Determine which stores have sales in the top half of the sales range. To find the range of sales, first find the maximum and minimum sales. The range is the maximum minus the minimum.

25. a. Write a program to partition an array. Read in `n` values to an array, and a test value `x`. Rearrange the array so the elements up to and including index `p` are less than or equal to `x` and the elements from `p+1` to `n` are greater than `x`. Elements may be repeated. The test value, `x`, may be larger than all values, smaller than all values, or in between somewhere. You may only visit each element once, and may not copy it to another array. For example, given

```
28 26 25 11 16 12 24 29 6 10
```

with test 17, the result might be

```
10 6 12 11 16 25 24 29 26 28
```

with partition index 4.

An outline of an algorithm is:

Start with markers at each end. Move markers towards each other until you find a wrongly placed pair. Allow for `x` being outside the range of array values.

While the two markers have not crossed over

exchange the wrongly placed pair and move both markers inward by one.

move the left marker to the right while elements are less than or equal to `x`.

move the right marker to the left while elements are greater than `x`.

A Little Extra

b. Add timing statements to the code of part a to estimate the growth rate of the array partitioning algorithm (see Example 7.10).

26. a. Write a C# program to perform a selection sort of an array of integers. In a selection sort, we find the smallest element of the array and interchange it with the first element. We repeat this process, finding the smallest element of the remaining elements and exchanging it with the first of the remaining elements. At each repetition the number of elements remaining decreases by one, until the whole array is sorted.

A Little Extra

b. Add timing statements to the code of part a to estimate the growth rate of the selection sort algorithm (see Example 7.10).

27. Write a `Matrix` class to operate with `NxN` matrices. For example, we represent a `3 x 3` matrix as

```
{{2.3,4.1,-1.7}, {12.4,15.0,1.2},{2.0,3.0,4.0}}.
```

Provide the addition, subtraction, and scalar multiplication operations. Adding or subtracting two matrices `x` and `y` produces a matrix with each element the sum or difference of the corresponding elements of `x` and `y`. In formulas,

```
z[i,j] = x[i,j] + y[i,j]     for the sum
z[i,j] = x[i,j] - y[i,j]     for the difference
```

The scalar multiplication of a matrix `x` by a number `n` produces a matrix with each element the product of `n` times `x[i,j]`. For example, 2.0 times the previous matrix produces the matrix

```
{{4.6,8.2,-3.4},{24.8,30.0,2.4},{4.0,6.0,8.0}}.
```

Include a constructor with parameters to specify the dimension `n` of the matrix and the array of arrays for its initial value. Use the `Main` method to test, applying `Matrix` operations to several `Matrix` objects.

8 Event-Driven Programming

Event-driven programs will respond to external events generated by the user or the operating system. In this text we introduce event-driven programming in two chapters graded according to complexity. In this chapter we cover paint, mouse, and key events. The Form can handle these events without using delegates. In Chapter 9 we cover events associated with a user interface control such as a button and introduce the delegate concept.

OBJECTIVES

- Understand the idea of event-handling code
- Respond to paint events
- Draw shapes and text
- Know .NET Framework methods needed for drawing
- Draw in color
- Respond to mouse and key events

8.1 PAINT EVENTS

Console applications use character input and output. In this section we introduce graphics applications that allow us to draw each pixel in a window. Paint events signal when the window needs to be redrawn.

FIGURE 8.1
Coordinates, in pixels, for 400 by 300 window

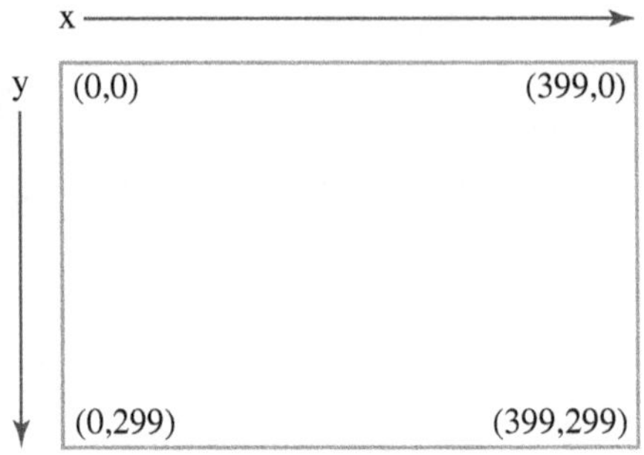

Graphics Mode

Pixels (picture elements) are dots on the screen used to create graphic images. A screen may show 25 columns of 80 characters each, for a total of 2000 characters. At a resolution of 1024 by 768, the screen displays 786,432 pixels, and at a resolution of 640 by 480, the screen displays 307,200 pixels.

We use coordinates to denote each point of the window. Figure 8.1 shows that (0,0) is the upper-left corner of the window. The x-coordinates increase in value from left to right, and the y-coordinates increase from top to bottom. We illustrate with a window that is 400 pixels wide and 300 high. Because we start numbering with 0, the bottom left corner of this window has coordinates (399,299).

Forms

The `System.Windows.Forms` namespace has classes for building Windows applications. The `Form` class represents a window. The best way to create a window is to create a class that inherits from `Form`. We can draw in the window or add controls such as buttons to it. We will cover inheritance in Chapter 10. For now we just need to know that to define our window we use a declaration such as

```
public class HelloCount : Form { // code goes here }
```

which states that our `HelloCount` class inherits from the `Form` class. `HelloCount` is a `Form`.

Example 8.1 will draw the `String "Hello Count 1"` in the window. Each time the window is redrawn the number will increase. It will count the number of times the window has been drawn. Figure 8.2 shows the initial window.

Figure 8.3 shows the window after the user minimizes it and then restores it. When restored it needs to be redrawn, and so the count increases.

FIGURE 8.2
Drawing in a Form

FIGURE 8.3 **The window after minimizing and restoring it**

By restoring the window, the user generates a `PAINT` event that Windows handles and sends to the .NET runtime, which calls the `OnPaint` method in Example 8.1

EXAMPLE 8.1 ■ HelloCount.cs

```
/* Displays the message "Hello World!" in
 * a window.
 */

using System.Drawing;                                          // Note 1
using System.Windows.Forms;                                    // Note 2
public class HelloCount : Form {                               // Note 3
  private int count = 1;                                       // Note 4

  public HelloCount() {
    Size = new Size(300,100);                                  // Note 5
    Text = "HelloCount";                                       // Note 6
  }
  protected override void OnPaint(PaintEventArgs e){           // Note 7
    Graphics g = e.Graphics;                                   // Note 8
    g.DrawString                                               // Note 9
     ("Hello " + count++, Font, Brushes.Blue, 30f, 30f);
    base.OnPaint(e);                                          // Note 10
  }
  public static void Main() {
    Application.Run(new HelloCount());                        // Note 11
  }
}
```

■

Note 1: `using System.Drawing;`

The `System.Drawing` namespace contains the classes needed for graphics programming.

Note 2: `using System.Windows.Forms;`

The `System.Windows.Forms` namespace contains classes needed for creating graphical user interfaces (GUIs).

Note 3: `public class HelloCount : Form {`

Our class, `HelloCount`, inherits from the `Form` class. We consider inheritance in Chapter 10.

Note 4: `private int count = 1;`

We initialize a state variable, `count`, to one. We will increment each time the window gets redrawn.

Note 5: `Size = new Size(300,100);`

A `Form` has properties that we can set. Here we set `Size` to a 300-by-100 pixel window. If we omit this line, .NET will use the default `Form` size.

Note 6: `Text = "HelloCount";`

We set the `Text` property to specify the title that shows in the window of Figure 8.1.

Note 7: `protected override void OnPaint(PaintEventArgs e)`

The `Form` has an `OnPaint` method that gets called when the `Form` needs to be redrawn. The runtime system calls it when it first displays the window and whenever the user generates a `PAINT` event by restoring the window or uncovering it. Because `HelloCount` inherits from `Form`, it inherits the `Form OnPaint` method. But we need to specify what we would like to appear in the window, so we do not use the inherited `OnPaint` method directly, but override it. We will discuss overriding methods in Chapter 10. The `protected` modifier makes the `Form OnPaint` method available to a class like `HelloCount` that inherits from `Form`. We discuss access modifiers in Chapter 10. The parameter of type `PaintEventArgs` describes the `PAINT` event that occurred.

Note 8: `Graphics g = e.Graphics;`

The `Graphics` class provides methods for doing Windows graphics. We use the `DrawString` method in this example, and will use others later in the chapter.

Note 9: `g.DrawString`

We pass five arguments to the `DrawString` method

The `String` to draw

The `Font` to use

The `Brush` to use

The x-coordinate of the upper-left corner of the drawn text

The y-coordinate of the upper-left corner of the drawn text

We use the default `Font` property of the `Form`. Later we will define our own `Font`. We use a `Brush` to fill the interior of shapes. The `Brushes` class is in the `System.Drawing` namespace has brushes for various colors. We will define our own `Brush` later. The coordinates of the drawn text are float values.

Note 10: `base.OnPaint(e);`

This calls the `OnPaint` method inherited from the `Form` class. We do not need to call it here, but in general it may be necessary. The `Form` `OnPaint` method calls back any registered event handlers. We will learn how to register event handlers later. If we do not call this `OnPaint` method, those event handlers would not get called.

Note 11: `Application.Run(new HelloCount());`

The `Application` class in the `System.Windows.Forms` namespace manages an application. The `Run` method processes event messages.

Redrawing a window gives a gentle introduction to event-driven programming. The operating system manages its windows, notifying .NET when a .NET window needs refreshing. In our program we write the code to execute when our window needs to be redrawn. However, we do not call this code, but rather we wait for an event such as a user resizing the window to cause the runtime to call our `OnPaint` method.

The BIG Picture

We write code in an event-driven program that is called by the system when an event occurs. A `Form` provides a window in which we do graphics. Our `OnPaint` method indicates how to redraw the window when the user restores it or uncovers it from behind another window. The `Graphics` class has drawing methods, including `DrawString`.

✓ Test Your Understanding

Try It Yourself ➤

1. Run Example 8.1 and generate `paint` events by repeatedly minimizing and restoring the window in which the form is displayed.
2. Explain how the `Graphics` class helps provide platform independence for C#.
3. We use coordinates to represent each pixel in a window or panel. What is the position of the origin `(0,0)`?
4. Give some examples of events that would cause the `OnPaint` method of Example 8.1 to be called.

8.2 DRAWING SHAPES

We introduce the methods of the `Graphics` class for drawing lines, rectangles, ovals, and arcs. Each C# implementation provides a `Graphics` class optimized for that platform. The `Graphics` methods hide the details from the C# programmer, who uses the same C# methods on all platforms.

Graphics Drawing

The `Graphics` class contains a number of methods for drawing various shapes. We will draw lines, rectangles, ellipses, rounded rectangles, and arcs. In each case, we will do our drawing in the `OnPaint` method, which the .NET runtime calls when events affecting our window cause it to need repainting.

To draw shapes, we use a `Pen`. The `Pens` class provides default pens in various colors, so we could use `Pens.Blue`, for example. But the figures look nicer with thicker lines, so we use the pen `black` created by

```
Pen black = new Pen(Color.Black, 3);
```

where we specify a thickness of three pixels for the line.

The `DrawLine` method has five parameters, a `Pen`, and four `int` parameters, the x- and y-coordinates of each endpoint of that line segment. For example,

```
g.DrawLine(black,70,80,130,230)
```

draws the line between `(70,80)` and `(130,230)` (see Figure 8.4).

The `DrawRectangle` method

```
g.DrawRectangle(Pen p, int x, int y, int w, int h)
```

draws the rectangle using `Pen p`, with upper-left corner `(x,y)`, width `w`, and height `h`. Figure 8.5 shows the rectangle produced by

```
g.DrawRectangle(black,50,50,200,100);
```

To draw an ellipse, we need to specify the rectangle that bounds the ellipse, just as we did in the `DrawRectangle` method. C# draws an oval that just touches the center points of its bounding rectangle. The arguments specify the `Pen`, the corner `(x,y)`, `width`, and `height` of the bounding rectangle. For example, Figure 8.6 shows the ellipse resulting from

```
g.DrawEllipse(black,50,50,200,100)
```

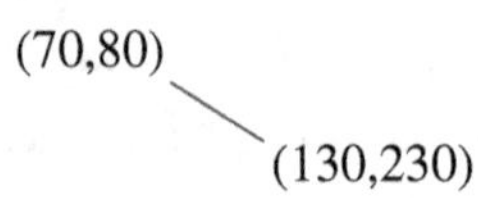

FIGURE 8.4 **Drawing a line**

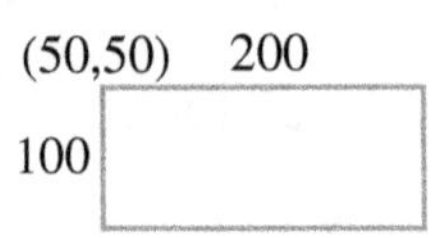

FIGURE 8.5 **Drawing a rectangle**

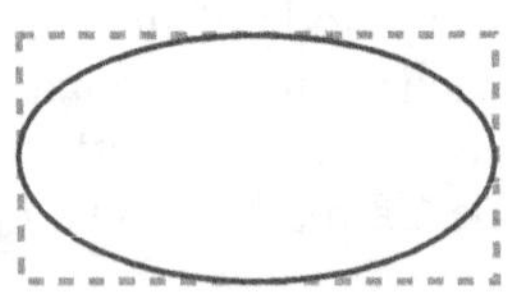

FIGURE 8.6 **An oval with its bounding rectangle**

FIGURE 8.7 Degree measures around a circle

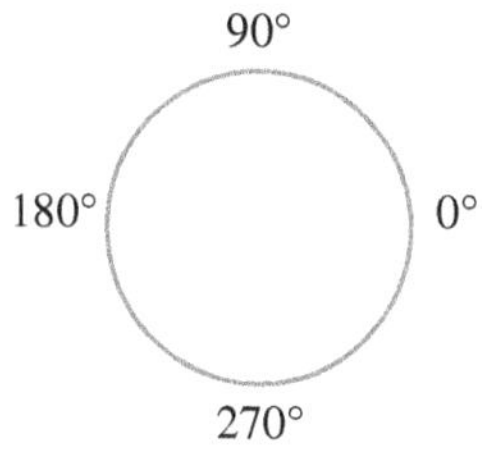

FIGURE 8.8 An arc from the oval of Figure 8.6

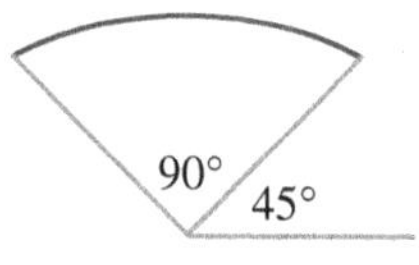

FIGURE 8.9 A polygon with three vertices

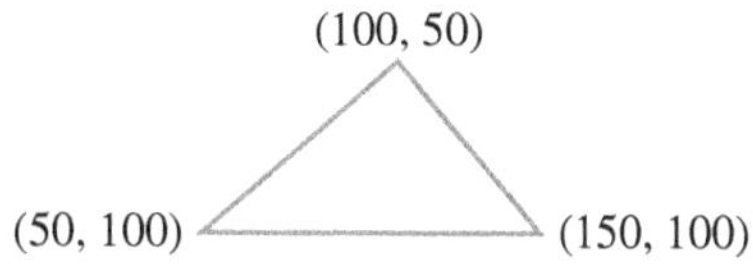

To draw a circle, we use a bounding rectangle that is a square.

An arc is a piece of an ellipse. The `DrawArc` method has seven parameters; the first is the `Pen`, the next four specify the bounding rectangle, the sixth gives the start angle for the arc, and the seventh gives the angle swept out by the arc. Referring to the face of a clock, the zero°-angle is at three o'clock, and angles increase counterclockwise with 360° in the full circle, as Figure 8.7 shows.

Figure 8.8 shows the part of the oval of Figure 8.6 that starts at 45° and sweeps out an arc of 90°, drawn by the method

```
g.DrawArc(black,50,50,200,100,45,90);
```

Positive angles sweep out an arc from the starting angle in the counterclockwise direction.

The `DrawPie` method makes an arc into a closed curve by drawing the radial lines from the center of the ellipse to each end of the arc. It has the same parameters as the `DrawArc` method. We illustrate it in Example 8.2.

We can draw a polygon of `n` sides by specifying an array of the `n` vertices. For example, to draw the triangle of Figure 8.9 we define the array

```
Point[] vertices = {new Point(50,100), new Point(100,50),
                    new Point(150,100)};
```

and use the method

```
g.DrawPolygon(black, vertices);
```

The `Point` class in the `System.Drawing` namespace represents a point.

The `DrawRectangle`, `DrawEllipse`, `DrawPie`, and `DrawPolygon` methods draw the outlines of the shapes. To draw filled ellipses, pies, rectangles, or polygons,

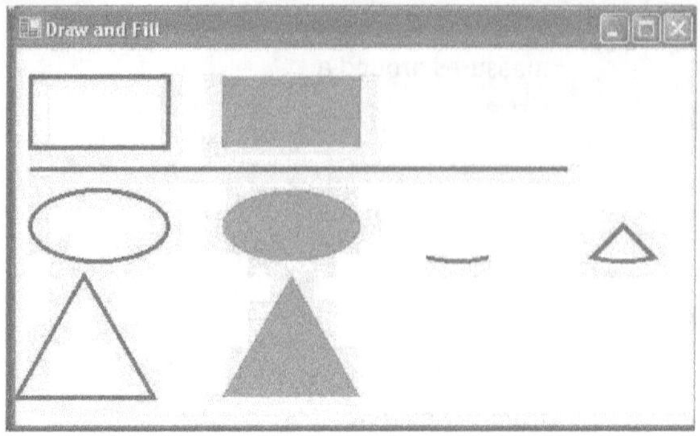

FIGURE 8.10 **The DrawFill form of Example 8.2**

we use the `FillEllipse`, `FillPie`, `FillRectangle`, and `FillPolygon` methods, which use a `Brush` instead of a `Pen`, but otherwise have the same arguments as the corresponding `Draw` methods.

Example 8.2 demonstrates these draw and fill methods. The `OnPaint` method draws various shapes when the system calls it in response to events requiring the window to be painted.

Figure 8.10 shows the window of Example 8.2.

EXAMPLE 8.2 ■ DrawFill.cs

```
/* Uses Graphics Draw and Fill methods
 * for various shapes. The runtime system calls the
 * OnPaint method when the window needs repainting
 */

using System.Drawing;
using System.Windows.Forms;
public class DrawFill : Form {
  public DrawFill() {
    Size = new Size(500,300);
    Text = "Draw and Fill";
    BackColor = Color.White;
  }
  protected override void OnPaint(PaintEventArgs e){
    Graphics g = e.Graphics;
    Pen blue = new Pen(Color.Blue, 3);
    g.DrawRectangle(blue,10,20,100,50);                    // Note 1
    g.FillRectangle(Brushes.Red,150,20,100,50);
    g.DrawLine(blue,10,85,400,85);                         // Note 2
    g.DrawEllipse(blue,10,100,100,50);                     // Note 3
    g.FillEllipse(Brushes.Red,150,100,100,50);
    g.DrawArc(blue,270,100,100,50,45,90);                  // Note 4
    g.DrawPie(blue,390,100,100,50,45,90);
    Point[] vertices = {new Point(0,246),
```

```
                    new Point(50,160), new Point(100,246)};
     g.DrawPolygon(blue, vertices);                          // Note 5
     vertices[0].X = 150;
     vertices[1].X = 200;
     vertices[2].X = 250;
     g.FillPolygon(Brushes.Red, vertices);
     base.OnPaint(e);
   }
   public static void Main() {
     Application.Run( new DrawFill() );
   }
}
```

Note 1: `g.DrawRectangle(blue,10,20,100,50);`

The rectangle has upper left corner `(10,20)`, width 100, and height 50.

Note 2: `g.DrawLine(blue,10,85,400,85);`

Draws the line from `(10,85)` to `(400,85)`.

Note 3: `g.DrawEllipse(blue,10,100,100,50);`

Draws the ellipse whose bounding rectangle has corner `(10,100)`, width 100, and height 50.

Note 4: `g.DrawArc(blue,270,100,100,50,45,90);`

Draws the arc, starting from a 45° angle and sweeping out a 90° angle counterclockwise, which is part of the ellipse whose bounding rectangle has upper left corner (270,100), width 100, and height 50.

Note 5: `g.DrawPolygon(blue, vertices);`

Draws the triangle with coordinates given by the `vertices` array.

In Example 8.2 we passed numbers as arguments to the drawing methods, drawing the pie slice, for example, starting from the point `(390,100)`. We gave the Form a width of 500, so there was space to draw this shape. Had we given the window a width of 350, the pie slice would not have appeared. Even if we create the window properly, the user can resize it to make it smaller. Our program would be more flexible if we drew the figures relative to the size of the window.

Drawing Relative to the Screen

Drawing relative to the size of the window takes more effort to implement, but will work correctly when the user changes the window's width and height. For example, to draw a rectangle whose width is one third the width of the window, whose height is one third the height of the window, and which appears at the upper-right of the window, we could use the code of Figure 8.11.

No matter what the size of the window, the rectangle of Figure 8.11 has its corner at a point two thirds of the width from the left. Its width and height are always

FIGURE 8.11
Drawing a rectangle relative to the form's size

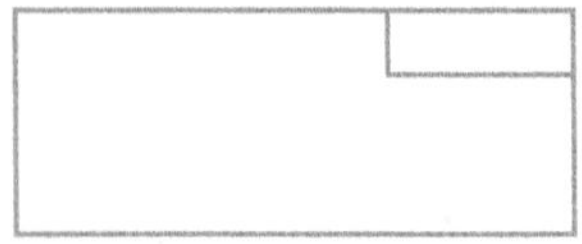

```
g.DrawRectangle (Pens.Blue, 2*Width/3, 0, Width/3, Height/3);
```

one third the width and height of the window. We leave the revision of Example 8.2 to draw figures relative to the size of the window to the exercises. We will use this technique later when we draw text.

> **The BIG Picture**
>
> Given a `Graphics` object for our platform, we draw lines, rectangles, rectangles, ellipses, arcs, pie slices, and polygons and fill all but the lines and arcs. When drawing ellipses and arcs, we specify the dimensions of their bounding rectangles. We can draw relative to the size of the window so that the figures will resize when the window does.

✓ Test Your Understanding

5. Write a statement to draw a horizontal line of length 12 whose left endpoint is (3,5).
6. Write a statement to draw a rectangle whose opposite corners are (10,10) and (100,200).
7. Write a statement to draw a square of side 50 whose upper left corner is (30,60).
8. Write a statement to draw an ellipse that touches the left side of its bounding rectangle at (100,100) and the top of its bounding rectangle at (200,50).
9. Write a statement to draw an arc of the ellipse of question 8, which starts at 90° and sweeps out an angle of 120°.
10. Write C# code to draw a triangle with coordinates (200,150), (130,80), and (50,60).

8.3 DRAWING TEXT

In this section we draw text in graphics mode, where we can choose different fonts, sizes, and styles for our text.

Fonts

The `Font` class in the `System.Drawing` namespace lets us create fonts of different types, with various sizes and a choice of styles. If we do not require a specific font, we can use one of the generic fonts available as `FontFamily` properties. They are:

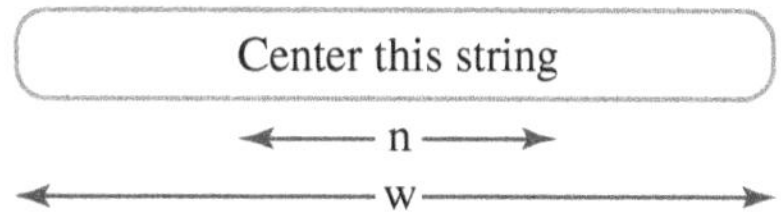

FIGURE 8.12
Centering a string

`FontFamily.GenericSerif`	The letters have hooks at the ends of the strokes.
`FontFamily.GenericSansSerif`	The letters do not have hooks.
`FontFamily.GenericMonospace`	Each character has the same width.

These font names are mapped to actual fonts available on the user's machine. Physical font names correspond to fonts installed on the user's machine. `Times New Roman`, `Arial`, and `Courier` are three commonly available fonts.

The .NET Framework provides six font styles, `FontStyle.Plain`, `FontStyle.Italic`, `FontStyle.Bold`, `Font.Regular`, `FontStyle.Strikeout`, and `FontStyle.Underline`, which are constants of the `FontStyle` enumeration. We can use the OR operator (see Appendix B) to combine styles, as in

```
FontStyle.Bold | FontStyle.Italic
```

which will be both bold and italic. We measure the character size in points; one inch is equal to 72 points.

The `Font` constructor takes three arguments—the name, size, and style—as in

```
Font arialBold24 = new Font("Arial", 24, FontStyle.Bold);
```

Notice that the three arguments are all constants. We need to construct the font `serifBold24` only once, but if we put the call to the constructor in the `OnPaint` method, we will construct the same font again each time .NET calls our `OnPaint` method.

We will draw all our text at positions defined in terms of the dimensions of the window, so if the window's size changes our text will still be displayed at the same relative position.

Suppose we want to center a string horizontally in the window. If we know the number of pixels, `n`, that a string will use when displayed in a given font, we can easily center it horizontally. If the window's width is `w`, then `w-n` gives the number of pixels on both sides of the string. Dividing `w-n` in half gives the number of pixels needed on each side of the string to make it centered, as shown in Figure 8.12.

In Example 8.3, we will center the first line horizontally and start each of the other four lines one fourth of the way in from the left. Vertically, we will position the five lines so they always divide the window into six equal parts. Figure 8.13 shows the window of Example 8.3.

EXAMPLE 8.3 ■ Text.cs

```
/* Draws the different fonts, trying all the
 * styles, and using various point sizes.  Draws
```

FIGURE 8.13 **The `Text` window of Example 8.3**

```
 * all text relative to the form's size.
 */

using System.Drawing;
using System.Windows.Forms;
public class Text : Form {
   private Font arialBold24 =
          new Font("Arial", 24, FontStyle.Bold);
   private Font timesItalic14 =
          new Font("Times New Roman", 14, FontStyle.Italic);
   private Font courierPlain18 =
     new Font("Courier New", 18, FontStyle.Strikeout); // Note 1
   private Font genericSerifBI20 =
                 new Font(FontFamily.GenericSerif,
              20, FontStyle.Bold | FontStyle.Italic);
   private Font verdanaPlain18 = new Font("Verdana", 18,
            FontStyle.Regular | FontStyle.Underline);

   public Text() {
      Size = new Size(400,200);
      Text = "Text";
      BackColor = Color.White;                           // Note 2
   }
   protected override void OnPaint(PaintEventArgs e){
     Graphics g = e.Graphics;
     int w = (int)g.MeasureString
              (arialBold24.Name, arialBold24).Width;  // Note 3
     int arialStart = (Width - w)/2;                  // Note 4
     int otherStart = Width/4;                        // Note 5
     int h = DisplayRectangle.Height;                 // Note 6
     g.DrawString(arialBold24.Name, arialBold24,
                         Brushes.Blue, arialStart,0);  // Note 7
     g.DrawString(timesItalic14.Name, timesItalic14,
                      Brushes.Blue, otherStart, h/5);  // Note 8
     g.DrawString(courierPlain18.Name, courierPlain18,
                      Brushes.Blue, otherStart, 2*h/5);
```

```
    g.DrawString(genericSerifBI20.Name, genericSerifBI20,
                    Brushes.Blue, otherStart, 3*h/5);
    g.DrawString(verdanaPlain18.Name, verdanaPlain18,
                    Brushes.Blue, otherStart, 4*h/5);
    base.OnPaint(e);
  }
  public static void Main() {
    Application.Run(new Text());
  }
}
```

Note 1: `new Font("Courier New", 18, FontStyle.Strikeout);`

The `Strikeout` style draws a line through the text.

Note 2: `BackColor = Color.White;`

We use the `BackColor` property to set the background color to white.

Note 3:
```
int w = (int)g.MeasureString
        (arialBold24.Name, arialBold24).Width;
```

The `Name` property gives the name of the font, which we will display. We need its width in order to center it. The `MeasureString` method returns the size of the `String`, passed as its first argument, in the `Font` passed as its second. Its `Width` property gives the `float` width of that size, which we cast to round down to an integer.

Note 4: `int arialStart = (Width - w)/2;`

We calculate the x-coordinate of the starting position of the String we wish to center horizontally.

Note 5: `int otherStart = Width/4;`

We will position the other strings at one fourth of the width.

Note 6: `int h = DisplayRectangle.Height;`

The `DisplayRectangle` property of the `Form` gives the size of the display area. Its `Height` will be less than the total height of the window because the title at the top takes some space.

Note 7:
```
g.DrawString(arialBold24.Name, arialBold24,
                Brushes.Blue, arialStart,0);
```

We draw the first line at `arialStart` to center it.

Note 8:
```
g.DrawString(timesItalic14.Name, timesItalic14,
                Brushes.Blue, otherStart, h/5);
```

We draw the other lines at an x-position, `otherStart`. We divide the display height into five parts to display one line in each.

The BIG Picture

Using the graphics mode we can draw text in different fonts, with italics, boldface, underline, or strikeout, and in different sizes. We can find properties of a particular font, which we can use to position text.

✓ Test Your Understanding

11. Declare and initialize a monospaced, italic, 30-point font.
12. Declare and initialize a 12-point sans serif font that is both bold and italic.
13. Write a statement to draw a string `s` of width 50 centered horizontally in a window of width 400 and height 200.
14. Write a statement to draw a string `s` of width 100 centered both horizontally and vertically in a window of width 300 and height 200. The font height is 20.

8.4 USING COLOR

Creating Colors

Using C#, we can easily draw in any of over 16,000,000 colors. The `Color` structure,[1] found in the `System.Drawing` namespace, defines the many color properties, including common ones such as `Color.Black` and `Color.Red`, and less familiar colors such as `Color.DarkOrchid` and `Color.DeepPink`.

We can construct other colors using their red, green, and blue components. The `FromArgb` method has a version that takes three integer arguments representing the red, green, and blue components of the color. We could pass any integer value, but the method uses only the first eight bits to get a value between 0 and 255. For example,

```
Color itsRed = Color.FromArgb(255,0,0);
```

constructs a color, `itsRed`, that is equal to the `Color.Red`, and

```
Color itsGreen = Color.FromArgb(0,255,0);
```

constructs another `Color.Green`.

Example 8.4 makes a 10-by-10 grid with each cell colored with a color chosen at random. Figure 8.14 shows a black and white version of this form. Run it to get the effect of the color.

EXAMPLE 8.4 ■ ColorChips.cs

```
/* Draw each of 100 cells with randomly
 * chosen colors.
```

[1] A structure is like a class but is a value type like `int` and `double` rather than a reference type.

FIGURE 8.14 **The window of Example 8.4**

```
 */

using System;
using System.Drawing;
using System.Windows.Forms;
public class ColorChips : Form {
  public ColorChips() {
    Size = new Size(300,200);
    Text = "Color Chips";
  }
  protected override void OnPaint(PaintEventArgs e){
    Graphics g = e.Graphics;
    int h = DisplayRectangle.Height;                    // Note 1
    int w = DisplayRectangle.Width;
    Random r = new Random();
    for (int i = 0; i < 10; i++)                        // Note 2
      for (int j = 0; j < 10; j++) {
        Color color = Color.FromArgb
             (r.Next(256), r.Next(256), r.Next(256));  // Note 3
        Brush brush = new SolidBrush(color);
        g.FillRectangle
               (brush, i*w/10, j*h/10, w/10, h/10);    // Note 4
      }
    base.OnPaint(e);
  }
  static void Main() {
    Application.Run(new ColorChips());
  }
}
```

Note 1: `int h = DisplayRectangle.Height;`

We use the `DisplayableRectangle` property to get the size of the display area of the window.

Note 2: `for (int i = 0; i < 10; i++)`

We use one `for` loop to divide the width of the window into 10 parts and another to divide its height into 10 parts.

Note 3:
```
Color color = Color.FromArgb
      (r.Next(256), r.Next(256), r.Next(256));
```

We use `r.Next(256)` to get a random number between 0 and 255 for each of the red, green, and blue components of the color.

Note 4:
```
g.FillRectangle
          (brush, i*w/10, j*h/10, w/10, h/10);
```

Each cell is a rectangle of width `w/10` and height `h/10`.

The BIG Picture

The `Color` class has many predefined colors. We can define others using red, green, and blue values, which are integers from 0 to 255.

✓ Test Your Understanding

15. Construct a color that is the same as `Color.Blue`.

16. Construct a color that is the same as `Color.Blue`, using the `FromKnownColor` method of the `Color` structure.

17. What are the red, green, and blue components for `Color.Black`?

18. What are the red, green, and blue components for `Color.White`?

8.5 MOUSE AND KEY EVENTS

Just as we use the `OnPaint` method to handle `Paint` events, we can use `Form` methods to handle `Mouse`, `Key`, and `KeyPress` events. Our forms will respond to the user's mouse presses or keyboard entries.

Using the Mouse

The user generates a `MouseDown` event by pressing the mouse, and a `MouseUp` event by releasing it. The `Control` that receives the mouse press will call the `OnMouseDown` method, which can handle the event and relay it to other registered handlers. Similarly, the `OnMouseUp` method handles and relays mouse releases. We will look at various controls such as buttons in the next chapter. Here we continue using a `Form`, which is itself a type of `Control`.

Example 8.5 displays a red triangle. When the user presses the mouse inside the triangle and drags the mouse outside the triangle, releasing it in a new position, the triangle moves to the new position (see Figures 8.15 and 8.16).

FIGURE 8.15
Example 8.5 initially

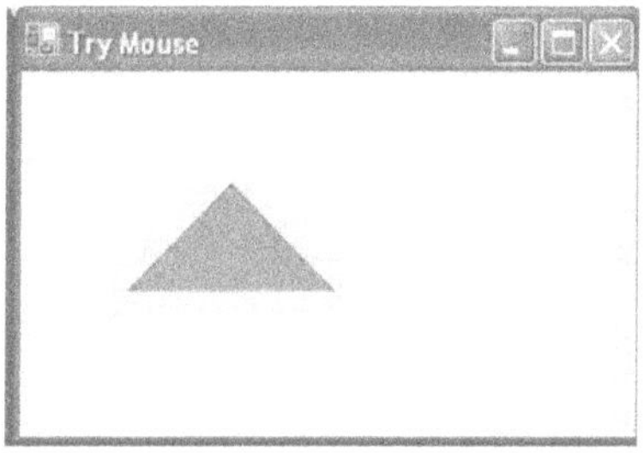

FIGURE 8.16
Example 8.5 after moving the triangle

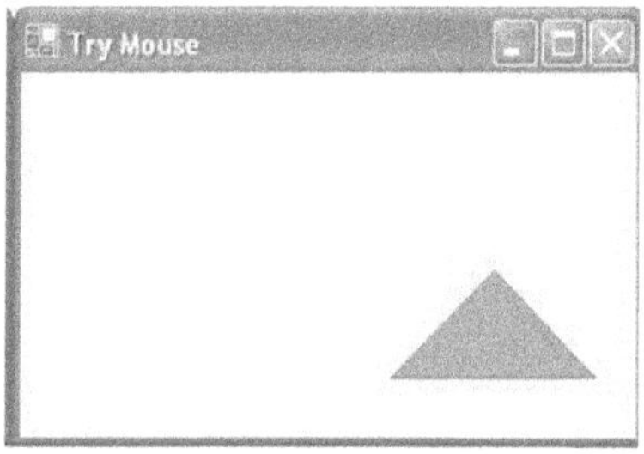

EXAMPLE 8.5 ■ TryMouse.cs

```
/* Moves a red triangle by pressing the mouse inside
 * the triangle, dragging the mouse, and releasing it
 * at the new location.
 */

using System.Drawing;
using System.Drawing.Drawing2D;                          // Note 1
using System.Windows.Forms;
public class TryMouse : Form {
  private Point[] vertices = {new Point(50,100),
             new Point(100,50), new Point(150,100)};    // Note 2
  private GraphicsPath p = new GraphicsPath();           // Note 3
  private Region region;                                 // Note 4
  private int oldX = 100;                                // Note 5
  private int oldY = 75;                                 // Note 6

  public TryMouse() {
    Size = new Size(300,200);
    Text = "Try Mouse";
    BackColor = Color.White;
    p.AddPolygon(vertices);                              // Note 7
    region = new Region(p);                              // Note 8
  }
  protected override void OnPaint(PaintEventArgs e) {
```

```
    Grpahics g = e.Graphics;
    g.FillRegion(Brushes.Red, region);                    // Note 9
    base.OnPaint(e);
  }
  protected override void
                    OnMouseDown(MouseEventArgs e){    // Note 10
    if (region.GetBounds(CreateGraphics())
                         .Contains(e.X, e.Y)){    // Note 11
      oldX = e.X;                                         // Note 12
      oldY = e.Y;
    }
    base.OnMouseDown(e);                                  // Note 13
  }
  protected override void OnMouseUp(MouseEventArgs e){
    region.Translate(e.X-oldX, e.Y-oldY);                 // Note 14
    oldX = e.X;                                           // Note 15
    oldY = e.Y;
    Invalidate();                                         // Note 16
    base.OnMouseUp(e);
  }
  public static void Main() {
    Application.Run(new TryMouse());
  }
}
```

Note 1: `using System.Drawing.Drawing2D;`

The `System.Drawing.Drawing2D` namespace contains the `GraphicsPath` class that we use to create a triangle.

Note 2:
```
private Point[] vertices = {new Point(50,100),
       new Point(100,50), new Point(150,100)};
```

These are the vertices of the triangle of the initial display.

Note 3: `private GraphicsPath p = new GraphicsPath();`

A `GraphicsPath` represents a series of connected lines and curves. We will use it to represent a triangle.

Note 4: `private Region region;`

A `Region`, in the `System.Drawing` namespace, describes the interior of a graphics shape composed of rectangles and paths. We use it because it has a `Translate` method that we can use to move the shape.

Note 5: `private int oldX = 100;`
`oldX` is the x-position of the triangle before we move it.

Note 6: `private int oldY = 755;`

`oldY` is the y-position of the triangle before we move it.

Note 7: `p.AddPolygon(vertices);`

We add the triangle to the `GraphicsPath`.

Note 8: `region = new Region(p);`

We initialize a region with the `GraphicsPath`.

Note 9: `g.FillRegion(Brushes.Red, region);`

This displays the filled triangle.

Note 10:
```
protected override void
            OnMouseDown(MouseEventArgs e){
```

The `OnMouseDown` method invokes any registered event handlers for the `MouseDown` event. We do not have any here. Because this `Form` is a `Control` that has an `OnMouseDown` method, it can handle the `MouseDown` event without using an event handler. The `MouseEventArgs` parameter provides information about the event. We use the `X` and `Y` properties that give the position of the mouse press. The `Button` property tells which mouse button was pressed, and the `Click` property gives the number of clicks.

Note 11:
```
if (region.GetBounds(CreateGraphics())
                    .Contains(e.X, e.Y)){
```

The `GetBounds` method returns a bounding rectangle for the region. The `Contains` method determines if the point passed to it is inside the rectangle. We test the point at which the user presses the mouse. Using the bounding rectangle for the test is accurate enough to determine if the user has chosen the triangle to move.

Note 12: `oldX = e.X;`

We save the position of mouse press as the old position of the triangle.

Note 13: `base.OnMouseDown(e);`

We call the `OnMouseDown` method in the `Control` class, which will invoke any registered event handlers.

Note 14: `region.Translate(e.X-oldX, e.Y-oldY);`

We translate the triangle to the position at which the user released the mouse.

Note 15: `oldX = e.X;`

After we move the triangle, we save the current position as the old position with respect to the next move the user might make.

Note 16: `Invalidate();`

The user can cause a `Paint` event by manipulating the window in various ways. We use the `Invalidate` method to have our program cause

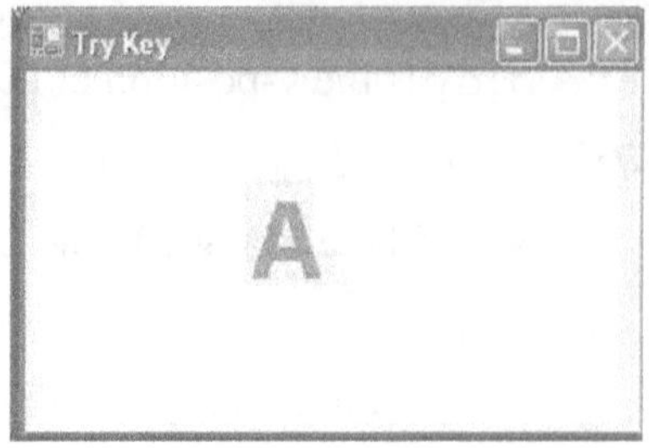

FIGURE 8.17 **The initial window of Example 8.6**

FIGURE 8.18 **Using keys**

the window to be redrawn. It causes a paint message to be sent to invoke the `OnPaint` method.

Using Keys

The `KeyDown` and `KeyUp` events represent the physical pressing and releasing of a key. The `KeyPress` event represents the character that was typed. It could represent multiple keystrokes. For example, to enter an uppercase `'G'` we hold the *Shift* key while pressing the *G* key.

The mouse has a natural association with a control. We can associate the position of the mouse with the control it is over. A key press or release does not have any natural association with a control. The key event will be sent to the control that has the focus. Because the `Form` is our only control in this chapter, there is no ambiguity about where to send any key events.

Example 8.6 displays a letter. When the user presses the *Left Arrow* key, it moves the letter slowly to the left. If the user holds the *Control* key down while pressing the *Left Arrow* key, the letter will move more quickly to the left. The *Right Arrow* key works similarly. When the user hits a letter or a number key, the display changes to that letter or number. Figure 8.17 shows the window of Example 8.6 initially, and Figure 8.18 displays it after the user has changed the letter and moved it to the right.

EXAMPLE 8.6 ■ TryKey.cs

```
/*  Displays a key pressed by the user.  Moves the
 *  character to the right if the user presses the right arrow
 *  key and to the left if the user presses the left arrow
```

```
 *  key.  Moves ten pixels if the user holds down the
 *  control key and two pixels otherwise.
 */

using System.Drawing;
using System.Windows.Forms;
public class TryKey : Form {
  public const int SLOW = 2;
  public const int FAST = 10;
  private int x = 100, y = 50;      // initial position
  private char theKey = 'A';        // initial character
  private Font f = new Font("Arial", 36, FontStyle.Bold);
  private int deltaX = SLOW;        // amount to move

  public TryKey() {
    Size = new Size(300,200);
    Text = "Try Key";
    BackColor = Color.White;
  }
  protected override void OnPaint(PaintEventArgs e) {
    Graphics g = e.Graphics;
    g.DrawString(theKey.ToString(), f, Brushes.Red, x, y);
    base.OnPaint(e);
  }
  protected override void OnKeyDown(KeyEventArgs e){
    if (e.Control)                                      // Note 1
      deltaX = FAST;
    if (e.KeyCode == Keys.Right)                        // Note 2
      x += deltaX;
    else if (e.KeyCode == Keys.Left)
      x -= deltaX;
    Invalidate();                                       // Note 3
    base.OnKeyDown(e);                                  // Note 4
  }
  protected override void OnKeyUp(KeyEventArgs e) {
    if (e.Control)
          deltaX = SLOW;                                // Note 5
    base.OnKeyUp(e);
  }
  protected override void OnKeyPress(KeyPressEventArgs e) {
    if (char.IsLetterOrDigit(e.KeyChar))                // Note 6
      theKey = e.KeyChar;
    Invalidate();
    base.OnKeyPress(e);
  }
  public static void Main() {
```

```
      Application.Run(new TryKey());
   }
}
```

Note 1: `if (e.Control)`

The `Control` property returns `true` if the `Control` key was pressed. We increase the increment we use at each *Arrow* key press.

Note 2: `if (e.KeyCode == Keys.Right)`

The `Keys` enumeration defines values for each of the keys. The `KeyCode` property gives the `Keys` value of the key that the user pressed. We increase the x-coordinate when the user presses the *Right Arrow* key.

Note 3: `Invalidate();`

The `Invalidate` method creates a `Paint` event so the window will be redrawn with the character in the new position.

Note 4: `base.OnKeyDown(e);`

We call the `Control OnKeyDown` method to pass the event to any registered event handlers.

Note 5: `if (e.Control) deltaX = SLOW;`

When the user releases the `Control` key, we reduce the size of the increment used to move the character.

Note 6: `if (char.IsLetterOrDigit(e.KeyChar))`

We want to display only letters or numbers.

The BIG Picture

The `MouseDown` and `MouseUp` events let us respond to the mouse in our program. The `KeyDown`, `KeyUp`, and `KeyPress` events let us respond to key presses.

✓Test Your Understanding

Try It Yourself ➤

19. Explain the result of removing the call to the `Invalidate` method in Example 8.5.

20. List the key events that occur if the user presses the `G` key without holding down the `Shift` key.

FIGURE 8.19 **The seven tangram pieces**

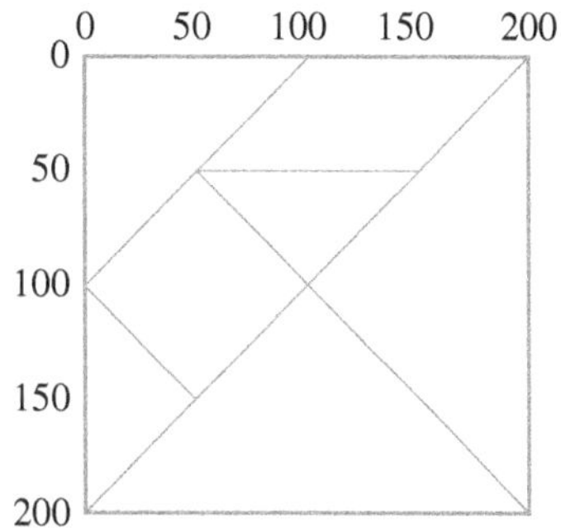

Try It Yourself ➤

21. Add `WriteLine` statements to the `OnKeyPress`, `OnKeyDown`, and `OnKeyUp` methods of Example 8.6 to see in what order these events are generated when the user presses the `R` key. Try this with and without holding down the *`Shift`* key.

8.6 (OPTIONAL) SOLVING PROBLEMS WITH C#: THE TANGRAM PUZZLE

The traditional tangram puzzle uses seven plastic or wooden pieces that fit nicely into a square shape, but can also be moved to create other figures. In this section we computerize the tangram puzzle.

Defining the Problem

In the ancient Chinese tangram puzzle, a square is cut into five triangles, a square, and a parallelogram. The object of the puzzle is to reassemble the pieces into various fanciful shapes. Figure 8.19 shows the seven pieces in the square, and Figure 8.20 shows a cat into which they can be arranged.

To solve tangram puzzles on the computer we need to drag polygons to new locations and rotate them. We use the mouse to drag polygons and key presses to rotate them. We use the *B* key (for back) to rotate a polygon counterclockwise and use the *F* key (for forward) to rotate the polygon clockwise. With these translation and rotation operations we can move the puzzle pieces to form other designs. We leave to the exercises the implementation of an operation to reflect the parallelogram, in effect flipping it over, to allow the user to form even more shapes.

Completing the C# Code

As we did in Example 8.5, we create a `GraphicsPath` and a `Region` for each polygon. But the bounding rectangle is not a close enough approximation to each polygon when we have several polygons that may be close together. To get a better approximation we use the `GetRegionScans` method to return an array of rectangles that as a group approximate the polygon.

FIGURE 8.20
The Cat

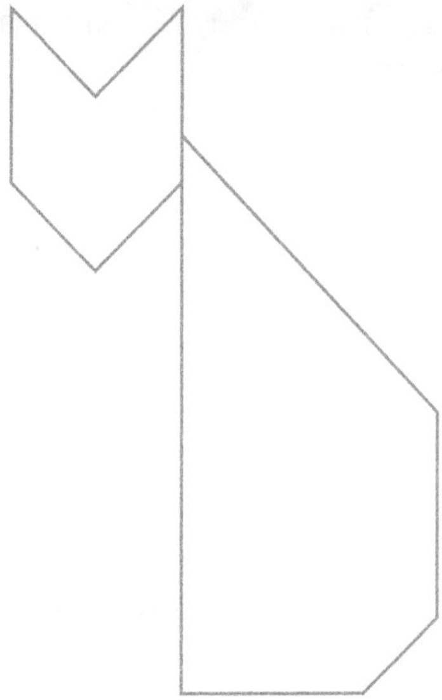

FIGURE 8.21 **The tangram puzzle**

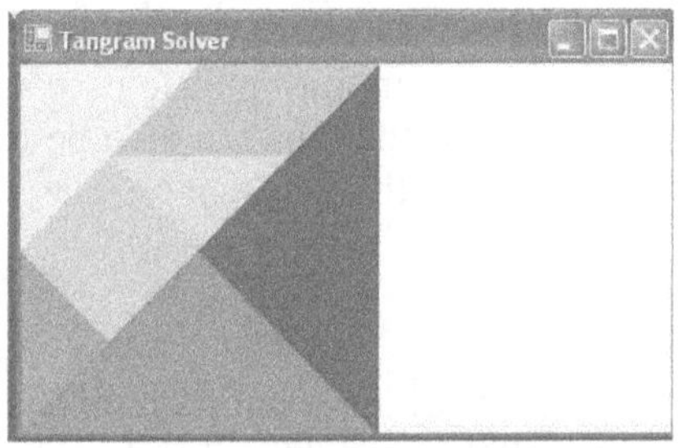

As in Example 8.5, we store the current location of the polygon when the user presses the mouse in it, but here we have to loop through the seven polygons to find in which one, if any, the user pressed the mouse.

If the user drags one of the polygons, we translate it to the new position. Pressing the *B* key will rotate that polygon counterclockwise (back) by three degrees. Pressing *B* will rotate counterclockwise by 30°. For forward rotations, we use the *F* and *F* keys. Figure 8.21 shows the initial tangram in the form of a square. Figure 8.22 shows the pieces moved to form a cat.

EXAMPLE 8.7 ■ TangramSolver.cs

```
/*  Start with the seven polygons forming
 *  a square. Drag them with the mouse and rotate
 *  them with the F and B keys to form other shapes.
 */
```

FIGURE 8.22
Making a cat

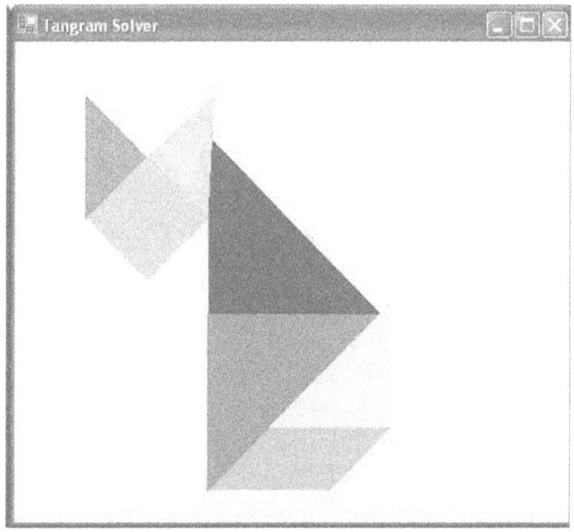


```
using System;
using System.Drawing;
using System.Drawing.Drawing2D;
using System.Windows.Forms;
public class TangramSolver : Form {
  private PointF[][] vertices = new PointF[7][];        // Note 1
  private Brush[] color = {Brushes.Red, Brushes.Blue,   // Note 2
     Brushes.Yellow, Brushes.Magenta, Brushes.Cyan,
     Brushes.Pink, Brushes.Orange};
  private GraphicsPath[] polygon = new GraphicsPath[7];
  private Region[] region = new Region[7];
  private float[] oldX = new float[7];
  private float[] oldY = new float[7];
  private int index;     // polygon to translate or rotate

  public TangramSolver() {
    Size = new Size(500,500);
    Text = "Tangram Solver";
    BackColor = Color.White;
    vertices[0] = new PointF[3]{new PointF(0,200),
            new PointF(100,100), new PointF(200,200)}; // Note 3
    vertices[1] = new PointF[3]{new PointF(100,100),
               new PointF(200,0), new PointF(200,200)};
    vertices[2] = new PointF[3]{new PointF(0,0),
               new PointF(100,0), new Point(0,100)};
    vertices[3] = new PointF[3]{new PointF(0,100),
                new PointF(50,150), new PointF(0,200)};
    vertices[4] = new PointF[3]{new PointF(50,50),
              new PointF(150,50), new PointF(100,100)};
    vertices[5] = new PointF[4]{new PointF(0,100),
                                new PointF(50,50),
```

```
             new PointF(100,100), new PointF(50,150)};
  vertices[6] = new PointF[4]{new PointF(100,0),
                              new PointF(200,0),
              new PointF(150,50), new PointF(50,50)};
  for (int i = 0; i < vertices.Length; i++) {
    polygon[i] = new GraphicsPath();
    polygon[i].AddPolygon(vertices[i]);
    region[i] = new Region(polygon[i]);
  }
}
protected override void OnMouseDown(MouseEventArgs e){
  bool found = false;
  int i = 0;
  while(!found && i < region.Length){
    RectangleF[] scans =
        region[i].GetRegionScans(new Matrix());      // Note 4
    int j = 0;
    while(!found && j < scans.Length){               // Note 5
      if (scans[j].Contains(e.X, e.Y)){
        oldX[i] = e.X;
        oldY[i] = e.Y;
        index = i;
        found = true;
      }
      j++;
    }
    i++;
  }
  base.OnMouseDown(e);
}
protected override void OnMouseUp(MouseEventArgs e){ // Note 6
  region[index].Translate(e.X-oldX[index], e.Y-oldY[index]);
  oldX[index] = e.X;
  oldY[index] = e.Y;
  Invalidate();
  base.OnMouseUp(e);
}
protected override void OnPaint(PaintEventArgs e){
  Graphics g = e.Graphics;
  for (int i = 0; i < region.Length; i++)
    g.FillRegion(color[i], region[i]);               // Note 7
  base.OnPaint(e);
}
protected override void OnKeyPress(KeyPressEventArgs e){
  float angle = 0;
  switch(e.KeyChar){
```

```
      case 'b'     : angle = -3;                              // Note 8
                     break;
      case 'B'     : angle = -30;
                     break;
      case 'f'     : angle =  3;
                     break;
      case 'F'     : angle =  30;
                     break;
    }
    Matrix m = new Matrix();                                  // Note 9
    m.RotateAt(angle,
          new PointF(oldX[index],oldY[index]));              // Note 10
    region[index].Transform(m);                              // Note 11
    Invalidate();
    base.OnKeyPress(e);
  }
  public static void Main() {
    Application.Run(new TangramSolver());
  }
}
```

Note 1: `private PointF[][] vertices = new PointF[7][];`

We create an array of arrays, with one array for the vertices of each polygon.

Note 2: `private Brush[] color = {Brushes.Red, Brushes.Blue,`

We pick a different color for each polygon.

Note 3:
```
vertices[0] = new PointF[3]{new PointF(0,200),
    new PointF(100,100), new PointF(200,200)};
```

We create each polygon using the coordinates shown in Figure 8.19.

Note 4:
```
RectangleF[] scans =
        region[i].GetRegionScans(new Matrix());
```

When the user presses the mouse, we check each polygon to find if the user pressed the mouse in it. The `GetRegionScans` method returns a `RectangleF` array of rectangles that together approximate the polygon. We use an identity matrix for the argument, because we are not transforming the polygon now.

Note 5: `while(!found && j < scans.Length){`

We check if the mouse was pressed in the polygon by checking whether it was pressed in one of the rectangles of the scan. If it was, we save the coordinates and the index to use for translating and rotating.

Note 6: `protected override void OnMouseUp(MouseEventArgs e)`

When the user releases the mouse, we translate the polygon selected with the mouse down and save the coordinates for the next operation.

Note 7: `g.FillRegion(color[i], region[i]);`

We draw each polygon in a different color.

Note 8: `case 'b'     : angle = -3;`

Pressing the *b* key causes a rotation of 3° counterclockwise.

Note 9: `Matrix m = new Matrix();`

A `Matrix` represents a transformation. We do not need to know the details of this representation because the `Matrix` class provides operations that encapsulate them. This is the identity matrix we will transform by rotation.

Note 10:
```
m.RotateAt(angle,
   new PointF(oldX[index],oldY[index]));
```

We adjust the matrix to represent a rotation by the specified angle around the point where the mouse was released.

Note 11: `region[index].Transform(m);`

We apply the rotation to the selected polygon.

Testing the Code

Figure 8.22 shows the polygons dragged and rotated into the shape of a cat. *Test Your Understanding* questions 23 and 24 provide other tests of the tangram solver.

> **The BIG Picture**
>
> We use the mouse to drag polygons and the keyboard to rotate them. With these operations, we can solve tangram puzzles.

✓Test Your Understanding

Try It Yourself ➤ **22.** In Example 8.7, in the `OnMouseUp` method, save the coordinates (e.X, e.Y) before translating the polygon. Run the modified program to see what happens.

Try It Yourself ➤ **23.** Run the tangram solver of Example 8.7 to transform the seven polygons into the duck shown in Figure 8.23.

Try It Yourself ➤ **24.** Run the tangram solver of Example 8.7 to transform the seven polygons into the boat shown in Figure 8.24.

FIGURE 8.23
The duck

FIGURE 8.24
The boat

SUMMARY

- In the `OnPaint` method we include statements describing what text and shapes we want to draw, but our program does not call the `paint` method. The .NET system calls our `OnPaint` method when events cause our window to need repainting. For example, if the user minimizes and restores the window, it needs to be redrawn. The operating system handles the events from the user, passing them to .NET, which calls our `OnPaint` method to redraw our window. Because we use only a Form and no other controls, we can handle the paint event directly. In the next chapter we will learn to respond to button clicks, checkbox selections, and other user-interface-generated events.
- The `Graphics` class has methods to draw lines, rectangles, ellipses, arcs, pie shapes, and polygons, and to fill any of them (except the line and arc). We specify

  A line with the coordinates of its endpoints

  A rectangle with its upper left corner, width, and height

  An ellipse with the arguments for its bounding rectangle

  An arc with the arguments for an oval, a start angle, and a sweep angle

  A polygon with an array of vertex points
- We use a pen for drawing and a brush for filling shapes.
- The `DrawString` method of the `Graphics` class has five parameters: the string to draw, the font, a brush, and the x and y positions at which to draw it. We can construct a font, specifying a font name, point size, and style. C# uses several generic font names and

any installed font. The style can be combinations of regular, bold, italic, underline, or strikeout.

- The `Color` class provides many predefined colors and allows us to construct other colors specifying their red, green, and blue components as integers from 0 to 255.
- We handle the `MouseDown` event in the `OnMouseDown` method and the `MouseUp` event in the `OnMouseUp` method. The `MouseEventArgs` provides the `X` and `Y` values at which the mouse was pressed or released. We handle the `KeyDown`, `KeyUp`, and `KeyPress` events in the `OnKeyDown`, `OnKeyUp`, and `OnKeyPress` methods. The `Keys` enumeration provides a value for each key. The `KeyCode` property of `KeyEventArgs` provides the key that was down or up. The `KeyChar` property of `KeyPressEventArgs` provides the logical character denoted, perhaps by more than one physical key press. The tangram puzzle demonstrates the use of keys and the mouse.

SKILL BUILDER EXERCISES

1. The following code, showing the key events generated when the user types an uppercase T, does not list these events in the order in which they occur. Rearrange the list to reflect the order in which they are generated.

```
KeyPress, KeyDown, KeyUp, KeyDown, KeyUp
```

2. Describe what the following program will display.

```
using System.Drawing;
using System.Windows.Forms;
public class Skill : Form {
  public override void OnPaint(PaintEventArgs e) {
    int h = DisplayRectangle.Height;
    int w = DisplayRectangle.Width;
    Graphics g = e.Graphics;
    g.DrawRectangle(Pens.Blue, w/4, h/4, w/2, h/2);
  }
}
```

3. Identify any errors in the following `Font` constructor.

```
new Font("FontFamily.GenericSansSerif",
          Font.Italic);
```

CRITICAL THINKING EXERCISES

4.

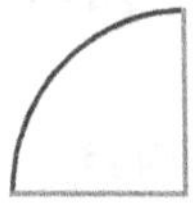

(40,40)

Which of the following will draw the arc shown above with center at (40,40) and radius 40?

a. `g.DrawArc(Pens.blue,0,0,40,40,0,90);`

b. `g.DrawArc(Pens.blue,40,40,0,0,0,90);`

c. `g.DrawArc(Pens.blue,0,0,80,80,90,90);`

d. `g.DrawArc(Pens.blue,0,0,80,80,90,180);`

e. `g.DrawArc(Pens.blue,40,40,0,0,90,90);`

5. Invoking `event.KeyCode`, where event is a `KeyEventArgs`, will return

   a. the character that the user typed, even if it required pressing two keys; for example, typing an uppercase `G`.

   b. an integer representing the character typed, so a lowercase `g` will be distinguished from an uppercase `G`.

   c. an integer representing the physical key generating the event.

   d. None of the above.

6. In a 500 × 300 window, where is the point (50,150) relative to the point (50,50)?

   a. 100 pixels above it

   b. 100 pixels to the right of it

   c. 100 pixels below it

   d. 100 pixels to the left of it

7. To draw a String, we use

   a. a Pen.

   b. a Brush.

   c. a Pen and a Brush.

   d. None of the above.

DEBUGGING EXERCISE

8. The following program attempts to center a string horizontally. Find and fix any errors in it.

```
using System.Drawing;
using System.Windows.Forms;
public class Center : Form {
  Font f;
  String s;
  int x, w;

  public Center() {
    f = new Font(FontFamily.GenericMonospaced,
                 18,FontStyle.Regular);
    s = f.GetName();
  }
  public void OnPaint(PaintEventArgs e) {
    w = (int)g.MeasureString(f.Name, f).Width;
    int h = DisplayRectangle.Height;
```

```
        int x = w-h;
        g.DrawString(f,s,x,50);
    }
}
```

PROGRAM MODIFICATION EXERCISES

9. Modify Example 8.3 so each line of text is centered horizontally.

10. Modify Example 8.5 to use an array of `RectangleF` rather than using the bounding rectangle to see if the mouse is pressed inside the triangle.

11. Modify Example 8.2 to draw each figure relative to the size of the window, so that when the window is resized, the figures will be resized proportionally.

12. Modify the tangram solver of Example 8.7 so that the parallelogram flips over, as shown, when the user presses the *R* key.

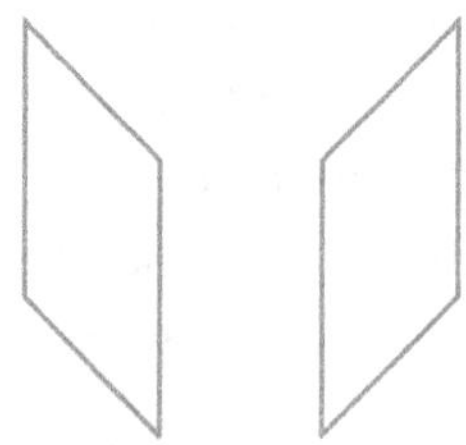

13. Modify Example 8.6 to move the character using the *Up* and *Down Arrow* keys in addition to moving it with the *Left* and *Right Arrow* keys.

PROGRAM DESIGN EXERCISES

14. Write a program to draw a chessboard that has 64 squares alternating in color.

15. Write a method, `GetPointSize`, that has formal parameters, a string, a font, a window width, and a window height and returns the largest point size at which drawing the string just fits within the window. Write a program that draws the string using that point size.

16. Write a program that causes a blue rectangle to appear where the user clicks the mouse and to disappear when the user double-clicks the mouse inside it. (Use the `Click` property to get the click count. A double-click is two mouse clicks in quick succession.)

17. Write a program that centers your name both vertically and horizontally.

18. The Tomato Soup Company wants a new logo on its website. Write a program containing a design for the logo that includes a nice red tomato with a green stem. Include the name of the company in the design.

19. Write a program that draws a happy face of your design. Use colors as desired.

20. Draw the happy face of Exercise 19 so it resizes when the window is redrawn.

21. Write a program that draws a clock (the old-fashioned kind with an hour hand, a minute hand, and numerals for each hour.)

22. Write a program that draws a maze of your own design.

23. Write a program that prints the user's name wherever the user clicks the mouse.

24. Write a program that displays a circle that changes its color to red when the user presses the *R* key, to yellow when the user presses the *Y* key, to blue when the user presses the *B* key, and to green when the user presses the *G* key.

25. Write a program that draws a pentagon inscribed in a circle. Connect the diagonals of the pentagon to form a star (which will contain a smaller pentagon in its center). Use the `sine` and `cosine` methods from the `Math` class with arguments `0`, `2pi/5`, `4pi/5`, `6pi/5`, and `8pi/5` to get the coordinates of the points as `(r*cos x, r*sin x)` where `r` is the radius of the circle, and `x` is one of the five angles listed.

26. Write a program that displays a store's daily sales over the period of one week in a bar graph. It should look like the following figure.

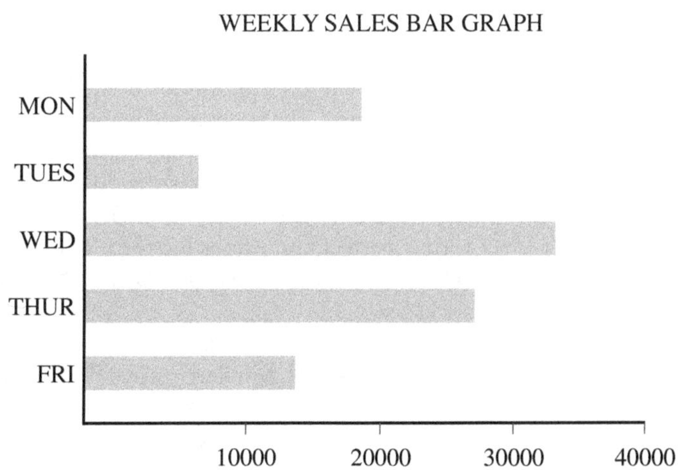

27. Write a program to draw a stick figure of the following form (more artistically if you like).

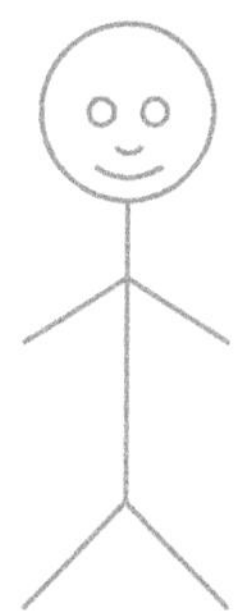

28. Write a program to draw a stick figure. Combine hair, face, and body to make the figure. Create `Hair`, `Face`, and `Body` classes to draw each of these parts. Each class will

have a `Draw` method that accepts a `Graphics` parameter. Use that `Graphics` object to draw that part. Do the drawing relative to the size of the window. If the window gets larger, the figure should get larger also.

One approach might be to use a round face and locate all three parts of the figure using the center and radius of the face. The hair might use a line of random length from each point of the upper semicircle of the face. The equation of a circle is:

$$(x - xCenter)^2 + (y - yCenter)^2 = radius^2$$

The following figure shows how the hair might look.

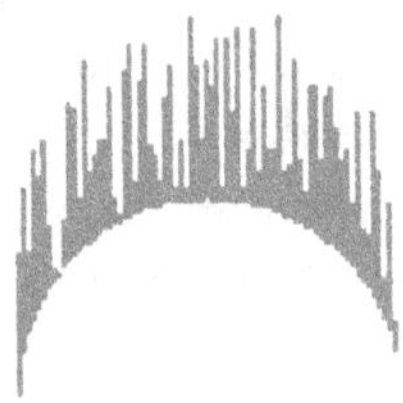

29. Write a program to move a piece around the following board. The piece starts at the lower-left corner. The squares are numbered from 0, counterclockwise from the lower left. The piece moves one to six spaces, randomly, at each turn. It scores three if it lands on a square whose number is divisible by three and five if it lands on a square whose number is divisible by five. Generating a paint event, say by covering and uncovering the window, causes the piece to move. Continue playing until the piece travels all the way around the board. Display the total score after each move, and the final score at the end.

Note that, when drawing the rows, each square has the same y, and the x increases by the same amount. Similarly, when drawing the columns, each square has the same x, and the y increases by a fixed amount. We can use simple loops to draw the board. This regularity allows us to compute the score given the square number. Each row or column has simple equations to determine (x,y) given the square number.

Use a class to provide the operations for the piece. The program will create and move the piece.

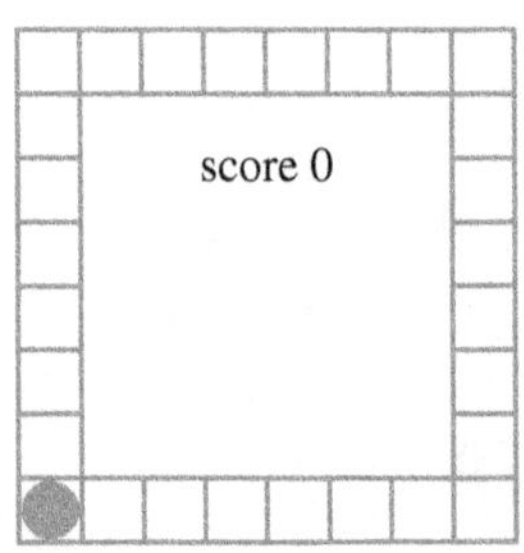

30. Write a program that displays a string, change it to bold if the user presses the *B* key, to italics if the user presses the *I* key, to all uppercase if the user presses the *Shift* key, and to all lowercase if the user presses the *Ctrl* key.

31. Write a program to play the game of Nim with the computer. To play Nim, start with 15 tokens. Each player takes from one up to a maximum of three tokens at each turn, and the player taking the last token loses. Randomly choose whether the user or the computer moves first. At startup, display all the tokens. Let the user select a token with a mouse click, which should cause that token to be erased. When finished selecting tokens, the user should press the *N* key. The computer should print a message stating how many tokens it chooses, and these tokens should be erased. When the game is over, display a message announcing the winner. Use colors to enhance the display.

32. Write a program to play a game of Tick Tack Toe with the computer. Let the player move by clicking the mouse in an available square.

    a. For an easier version, let the computer make its move in any available square.

    b. For a more challenging program, have the computer find its best move.

33. Develop a simplified Blackjack game. Create a deck of 51 cards, 17 each of threes, sevens, and tens. Deal two cards face down to the player and two cards to the computer, one face up and one face down. Allow the user to turn over the player's cards by clicking on them. The user will hit the *H* key to get another card and the *S* key to stop drawing cards. The player loses if his total is greater than 21. If not, the dealer draws cards until the dealer's total is greater than 16. The dealer loses if her total is over 21. Otherwise, the one with the greater score wins.

9 User Interfaces

Graphical user interface components such as buttons and text boxes let the user communicate directly with our program. We first introduce delegates and the various user interface controls, and next show how the C# event model allows `TextBox`, `ComboBox`, `Button`, `CheckBox`, `RadioButton`, and `ListBox` event sources to communicate with event handlers. An optional section uses Visual Studio .NET to create a `Form`. The concluding optional case study uses exploratory programming to develop a GUI for insertion sorting. We defer menus to a later chapter after we have introduced files.

We show the displays from our examples and the code, but running these highly interactive programs will give the best sense of how they work.

OBJECTIVES

- Know important `Control` subclasses
- Understand the C# event model
- Use buttons, text boxes, and labels
- Use checkboxes, combo boxes, list boxes, picture boxes, and radio buttons
- (Optional) Use Visual Studio .NET to develop a GUI
- (Optional) Try exploratory programming to develop a GUI

9.1 CONTROLS AND EVENT HANDLING

After presenting the user interface controls that we will study, we demonstrate how the .NET Framework handles events.

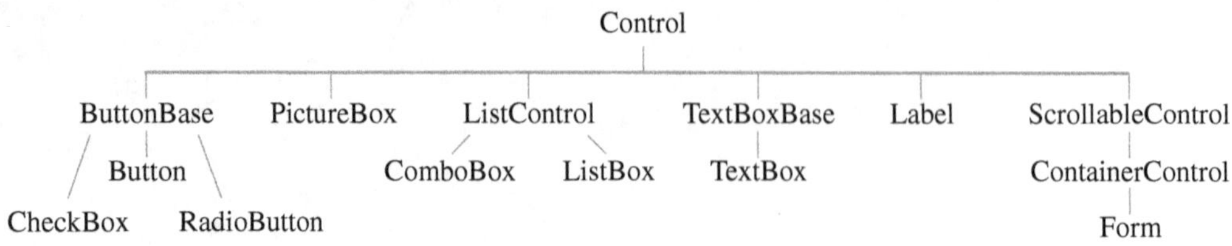

FIGURE 9.1 **Some types of `Control`**

The Control Hierarchy

A **control** is a component with a visual representation. The `Control` class, in the `System.Windows.Forms` namespace, is the base class for the graphical objects on the screen that provide the interface to the user. We will study inheritance carefully in the next chapter. For now, all we need to know is that a derived class is like a specialization of the parent class. For example, a Dog is a type of Animal. Figure 9.1 shows the derived classes of `Control` that we will treat in this text.

Buttons

A `Form` is a type of `ContainerControl`, meaning that it can contain other controls, and we can add controls to it. For example, we may add several buttons to a form. When the user presses a button, we want something to happen, such as displaying a message. We use methods to encapsulate code to do something, so we can write a method to display the message. The method we write is the event handler that we want to be called when the user presses the button.

Here is the problem we face. The .NET Framework contains a `Button` class. When a user presses a button in our `Form`, that `Button` code needs to find the method we wrote to display a message. Obviously, the .NET Framework never heard of us or our program, but it did establish a way for us to communicate with it. It tells us the type of method we need to write, and lets us register our methods of that type. Before we define the new concepts needed, we should look at an example to see how it works. Example 9.1 defines a `Form` with two `Button` objects and a `Label`. A *Print* button displays a message in the label, and a *Clear* button erases it. Figure 9.2 shows the form after the user presses the *Print* button.

FIGURE 9.2 **Pressing *Print* in Example 9.1**

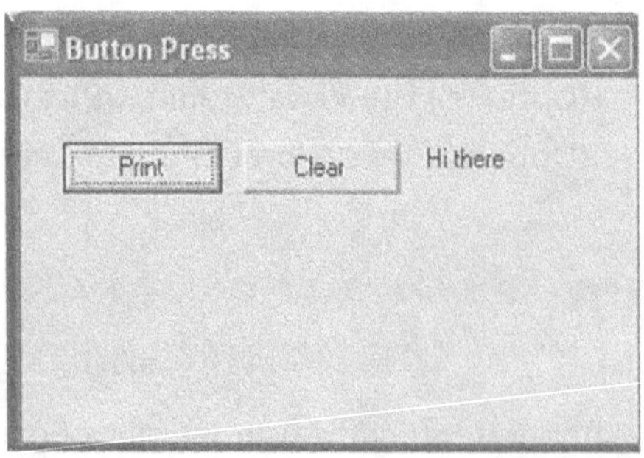

We wrote the code for Example 9.1 using the .NET Framework, without Visual Studio .NET. Using Visual Studio .NET we can position the buttons and label by dragging the control onto the form and letting Visual Studio generate the code. But it is easy and instructive to do it ourselves. It allows us to use the .NET Framework, which is freely downloadable. Those who wish to use Visual Studio .NET could easily produce this form, as we illustrate in Section 9.3.

Part of the code of Example 9.1 involves creating the controls and adding them to the form at the desired locations. Another part involves setting up the event handling.

EXAMPLE 9.1 ■ ButtonPress.cs

```
/* A print button prints a message.
 * A clear button erases the message.
 * We use a Label to hold the message.
 */

using System;
using System.Drawing;
using System.Windows.Forms;
public class ButtonPress : Form {

    // Create the controls
  private Button print = new Button();                        // Note 1
  private Button clear = new Button();
  private Label message = new Label();

  public ButtonPress( ) {

        // Captions
      Text = "Button Press";
      print.Text = "Print";                                   // Note 2
      clear.Text = "Clear";
      message.Text = "Message goes here";

        // Sizes
      Size = new Size(300,200);
      message.Size = new Size(message.PreferredWidth,
                             message.PreferredHeight); // Note 3

       // Locations
      print.Location = new Point(20,30);                      // Note 4
      clear.Location = new Point(30 + print.Width, 30);// Note 5
      message.Location =
         new Point(40 + print.Width + clear.Width, 30);// Note 6

       // Add them to the form
```

```
        Controls.Add(print);                                  // Note 7
        Controls.Add(clear);
        Controls.Add(message);

          // Tell the Click events which methods to call
        print.Click += new EventHandler(Print_Click);         // Note 8
        clear.Click += new EventHandler(Clear_Click);
    }

      // method to make the Print button work
    protected void
            Print_Click(Object sender, EventArgs e){         // Note 9
       message.Text = "Hi there";
    }

      // method to make the Clear button work
    protected void Clear_Click(Object sender, EventArgs e) {
       message.Text = "";
    }
    static void Main() {
       Application.Run( new ButtonPress() );
    }
}
```

Note 1: `private Button print = new Button();`

We create the three controls that we add to the form in this example.

Note 2: `print.Text = "Print";`

We use the `Text` property to set the captions for the title of the form, the names on the buttons, and the initial message in the label.

Note 3:
```
message.Size = new Size(message.PreferredWidth,
                        message.PreferredHeight);
```

We want the `Label` to display our entire initial message. The `PreferredHeight` and `PreferredWidth` properties give the height and width necessary to display the text in the chosen font. We use these values to set the size. The button automatically adjusts them to the size of the caption we specify, so we do not need to set their size.

Note 4: `print.Location = new Point(20,30);`

We position the *Print* button 20 pixels across from the upper-left corner of the form and 30 pixels down.

Note 5: `clear.Location = new Point(30 + print.Width, 30)`

We add 10 pixels plus `print.Width` to the position of the *Print* button. This positions the *Clear* button 10 pixels to the right of the *Print* button.

Note 6: `message.Location = new Point(40 + print.Width + clear.Width, 30);`

```
message.Location =
      new Point(40 + print.Width + clear.Width, 30);
```

We add 10 pixels plus `clear.Width` to the position of the *Clear* button. This positions the `Label` 10 pixels to the right of the *Clear* button.

Note 7:

```
Controls.Add(print);
```

We add each control to the `Form`. The `Controls` property of the `Form` control represents a `ControlCollection` that contains the controls for this `Form`. The `Add` method adds a control to the collection.

Note 8:

```
print.Click += new EventHandler(Print_Click);
```

Any `Control`, including this `Print` button, defines a `Click` event that occurs when the user clicks the control. This line of code tells the `Click` event for the `Print` button that we want the `Print_Click` method to be called when the `Click` event occurs. We are saying that our `Print_Click` method has the same type as the `EventHandler` delegate associated with the `Click` event. We introduce delegates later in this section. The overloaded `+=` operator adds our `Print_Click` method to the registered handlers for the `Click` event. There can be more than one handler, and they will all be called when the `Click` event occurs. This is how we communicate our newly written `Print_Click` method to the .NET Framework `Button` code that raises the `Click` event.

Note 9:

```
protected void
    Print_Click(Object sender, EventArgs e)
```

The `EventHandler` delegate defines the type that our method must have. It specifies a `void` return type and two parameters, the `Object` that is the source of the event and an `EventArgs` object that describes the event. We declare our `Print_Click` method to fit the `EventHandler` delegate type. The method displays the message `"Hi there"` when the user clicks the *Print* button. The `Click` event causes an `OnClick` method to be called. The `OnClick` method calls any registered delegates. When the user presses the *Print* button, `OnClick` will call our `Print_Click` method.

Events

A class may contain an **event** that allows it to provide notifications. For example, the `Control` class declares the `Click` event that allows it to notify an event handler when the user clicks the control. When the user presses a `Button`, which is a type of `Control`, the `Click` event will notify any registered event handlers.

To perform event notification, an event uses a delegate type, which is associated with the event when it is declared. A **delegate** defines a class that encapsulates one or more methods. The `Click` event uses an `EventHandler` delegate. The event causes the system to call the `OnClick` method, which calls the registered `EventHandler` delegates. These delegates make the button do what we want.

To summarize:

The .NET `Button` *code:*

- Declares a `Click` event (inherited from `Control`)
- Associates an `EventHandler` delegate as the type of method needed to handle a `Click` event
- Raises the `Click` event when the user clicks the button, causing calls to all registered delegates

Our `ButtonPress` *code:*

- Declares a `Print_Handler` method for the `Print` button that fits the definition of the `EventHandler` delegate
- Registers `Print_Handler` as a new delegate to handle the `Click` event for the `Print` button

Delegates

C# uses delegates where languages such as C and C++ use function pointers. As we noted, a delegate defines a class that encapsulates one or more methods. The .NET Framework defines the `EventHandler` delegate type. We use that definition but do not see the code for it. In Example 9.2 we declare a `ComputeDelegate` type that will represent a method that has one parameter of type `double` and returns a value of type `double`. It represents a method that computes something. For example, it can represent a method that computes the square root of its argument or one that returns the square of its argument. The declaration looks like

```
public delegate double ComputeDelegate(double d);
```

We pass an argument of type `ComputeDelegate` to our `Test` method. Our `Test` method uses whatever method we pass to it. A delegate provides a way to pass a method as an argument to another method. The `Test` method requires a delegate of type `ComputeDelegate`, so we can pass it any method that has a double parameter and returns a `double` value. A delegate does not know or care about the classes of the methods it encapsulates. These methods must be compatible with the delegate's type.

EXAMPLE 9.2 ■ Compute.cs

```
/* Defines a delegate type and a method that computes
 * with that type. Computes square roots and squares
 * to illustrate.
 */

using System;
```

```
public delegate double ComputeDelegate(double d);      // Note 1

public class Compute {

    /* Returns the sum of applying the delegate
     * method to the numbers from 1.0 to n.
     */
  public double Test (int n, ComputeDelegate cd) {      // Note 2
    double total = 0.0;
    for (double i = 1; i <= n; i++)
      total += cd(i);                                    // Note 3
    return total;
  }

    /* Fits the ComputeDelegate pattern
     */
  public double Square(double d) {                      // Note 4
    return d*d;
  }

    /* Tests with Sqrt and Square */
  public static void Main() {
    Compute test = new Compute();
    ComputeDelegate compute =
                   new ComputeDelegate(Math.Sqrt); // Note 5
    Console.WriteLine(test.Test(5, compute));         // Note 6
    compute = new ComputeDelegate(test.Square);       // Note 7
    Console.WriteLine(test.Test(5, compute));         // Note 8
  }
}
```

Output

```
8.38233234744176
55
```

Note 1: `public delegate double ComputeDelegate(double d);`

This declaration says that `ComputeDelegate` can represent any method that has a parameter of type `double` and returns a `double` value. We could have placed this declaration inside the `Compute` class, but chose to put it at the top level to remind us that it declares a class derived from `System.Delegate`.

Note 2: `public double Test (int n, ComputeDelegate cd) {`

The `Test` method applies a method that we pass in as a `ComputeDelegate` argument. The `Test` method does not know the class from which the method comes. It requires only a method that fits the `ComputeDelegate` pattern of a `double` parameter and `double` return value.

Note 3: `total += cd(i);`

Calling `cd(i)` applies the method encapsulated by the delegate.

Note 4: `public double Square(double d) {`

`Square` is an instance method that fits the pattern required by the `ComputeDelegate` delegate.

Note 5:

```
ComputeDelegate compute =
            new ComputeDelegate(Math.Sqrt);
```

We instantiate a `ComputeDelegate` delegate object, passing the class method `Math.Sqrt`, which has a `double` parameter and returns a `double` result. This delegate instance represents the `Math.Sqrt` method.

Note 6: `Console.WriteLine(test.Test(5, compute));`

We pass the `compute` delegate to the `Test` method. The return value will be the sum of the `Math.Sqrt` method applied to the five values 1.0, 2.0, 3.0, 4.0, and 5.0.

Note 7: `compute = new ComputeDelegate(test.Square);`

We instantiate a `ComputeDelegate` delegate object, passing the instance method `test.Square`, which has a `double` parameter and returns a `double` result. This delegate instance represents the `test.Square` method.

Note 8: `Console.WriteLine(test.Test(5, compute));`

We pass the `compute` delegate to the `Test` method. The return value will be the sum of the `test.Square` method applied to the five values 1.0, 2.0, 3.0, 4.0, and 5.0.

Taking a second look at Example 9.1, we see that the line

```
print.Click += new EventHandler(Print_Click);
```

registers a delegate, of type `EventHandler` that represents our `Print_Click` method, with the `Click` event of the `Print` button. The `OnClick` method that calls the delegate is part of the .NET code that will be invoked when the user clicks the `Print` button. The `EventHandler` declaration in the .NET Framework looks like

```
public delegate void EventHandler(Object sender, EventArgs e);
```

The BIG Picture

We add controls to a `Form` to create a user interface. The user generates an event by interacting with a control. The event specifies a delegate type that we need to handle that event. We write a method of that type and register with the event. When the event occurs, our method will be called.

✓Test Your Understanding

1. What event occurs when the user clicks the *Print* button in the `Form` of Example 9.1?
2. Which line of code in Example 9.1 registers an event handler for the event generated when the user clicks the *Print* button?
3. Which method in Example 9.1 handles the event generated when the user clicks the *Print* button?
4. Could we create a `ComputeDelegate` in Example 9.2 using the `Math.Pow` method?

Try It Yourself ➤

5. Add a test to Example 9.2 using the `Math.Floor` method to create a `ComputeDelegate`.

9.2 USING CONTROLS

Controls are components with visual representation. We illustrate the use of various controls, including `Button`, `TextBox`, `ComboBox`, `RadioButton`, `CheckBox`, `ListBox`, and `PictureBox`.

Text Boxes

A `TextBox` lets the user enter data. By default it allows a single line, but we can configure it to allow multiple lines. In Example 9.3 we use a `TextBox` to enter prices of items. After entering a price, we can press either the *Enter* key or the *Enter Price* button to submit the new value. Pressing the *Average* button displays the average of all the prices entered. Figure 9.3 shows the `Form` of Example 9.3 after the user has entered some prices and clicked the `Average` button.

EXAMPLE 9.3 ■ EnterPrice.cs

```
/* Converts the price the user enters in the text box to a
 * double and adds it to the sum when the user hits the
 * Enter key or presses the Enter button.  Displays the average
 * in a label when the user presses the Average button.
 */
```

FIGURE 9.3 **The `Form` of Example 9.3**

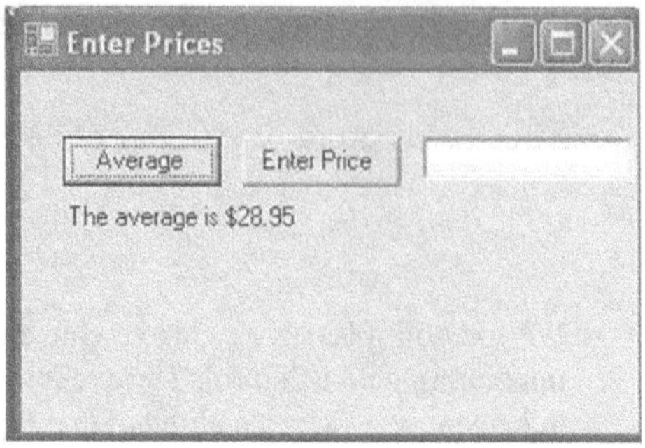


```
using System;
using System.Drawing;
using System.Windows.Forms;
public class EnterPrice : Form {

    // Create controls
  private Button average = new Button();
  private Button enter = new Button();
  private Label answer = new Label();
  private TextBox text = new TextBox( );

  private int count = 0;       // Count entries
  private double sum = 0.0;    // Sum entries

  public EnterPrice( ) {

      // Set captions
    Text = "Enter Prices";
    average.Text = "Average";
    enter.Text = "Enter Price";
    text.Text = "";
    answer.Text = "Message goes here";

      // Set sizes
    Size = new Size(300,200);
    answer.Size = new Size(200,50);                          // Note 1

      // Set locations
    average.Location = new Point(20,30);
    enter.Location = new Point(30 + average.Width, 30);
    text.Location =
       new Point(40 + average.Width + enter.Width, 30);
    answer.Location = new Point(20, 60);                     // Note 2
```

```
      // Associate Enter key with enter button
    AcceptButton = enter;                                    // Note 3

      // Add controls to the form
    Controls.Add(text);
    Controls.Add(answer);
    Controls.Add(enter);
    Controls.Add(average);

      // Register event handlers
    average.Click += new EventHandler(Average_Click);
    enter.Click += new EventHandler(Enter_Click);
  }

     // Handle a click of the Average button
  protected void Average_Click(Object sender, EventArgs e) {
    answer.Text =
        "The average is " + (sum/count).ToString("C"); // Note 4
  }

     // Handle a click of the Enter Price button
  protected void Enter_Click(Object sender, EventArgs e) {
    sum += Double.Parse(text.Text);                          // Note 5
    count++;
    text.Text = "";                                          // Note 6
    text.Focus();                                            // Note 7
  }
  static void Main() {
    Application.Run(new EnterPrice());
  }
}
```

Note 1: `answer.Size = new Size(200,50);`

We allocate the label a size large enough to hold all the messages we will display.

Note 2: `answer.Location = new Point(20, 60);`

We increase the y coordinate to move the control to the second row.

Note 3: `AcceptButton = enter;`

We use the `AcceptButton` property to set the *Enter Price* button to respond when the user hits the *Enter* key. This allows two ways to enter the data: by pressing the *Enter* key or by clicking the *Enter Price* button.

Note 4:
```
answer.Text =
      "The average is " + (sum/count).ToString("C");
```

The `Double ToString` method converts the `double` value to a `String`. We pass the currency format, `"C"`, to output the result in the local currency notation.

Note 5:
```
sum += Double.Parse(text.Text);
```

We convert the text from the `TextBox` to a `double` and add it to the sum.

Note 6:
```
text.Text = "";
```

We erase the value from the `TextBox` to make it easier for the user to enter another value.

Note 7:
```
text.Focus();
```

The `Focus` method gives the focus to the `TextBox`, so the cursor will remain there. That way the user will not have to click the mouse in the `TextBox` to give it the focus to direct key presses to it.

Radio Buttons and Combo Boxes

A `RadioButton` works like the button on a car radio. Each button on a car radio selects a station, and pushing a button deactivates the button that was previously pushed. All radio buttons in a `Form` belong to one group by default. Selecting one deselects the others. A `ComboBox` contains a list of items, but it shows only one, allowing the user to pop up the remaining items.

Our next two examples illustrate the use of radio buttons and combo boxes in two ways. In Example 9.4 (see Figure 9.4) we do not respond to any events generated by the radio buttons or combo box. We add a button to the form and make changes only when the user clicks the button. We use the radio buttons and combo

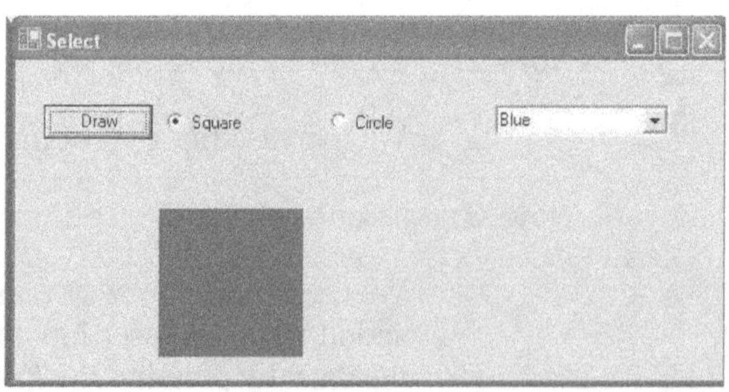

FIGURE 9.4 **The `Form` of Example 9.4**

box to make selections, but not to initiate any changes. In Example 9.5 each selection using a radio button or combo box becomes effective immediately.

EXAMPLE 9.4 ■ Select.cs

```
/* Uses a combo box to choose a color, and
 * two radio buttons to choose a shape. Uses a draw button
 * to request drawing the selected shape in the
 * selected color.
 */

using System;
using System.Drawing;
using System.Windows.Forms;
public class Select : Form {

    // Create controls
  private Button draw = new Button();
  private RadioButton square = new RadioButton();
  private RadioButton circle = new RadioButton();
  private ComboBox color = new ComboBox();

  private Color c = Color.Yellow;                          // Note 1

  public Select( ) {

      // Set captions
    Text = "Select";
    draw.Text = "Draw";
    color.Text = "Choose a color";
    square.Text = "Square";
    circle.Text = "Circle";

      // Set size
    Size = new Size(500,250);

      // Set locations
    int w = 20;
    draw.Location = new Point(20,30);
    square.Location = new Point(w+= 10 + draw.Width, 30);
    circle.Location = new Point(w += 10 + square.Width, 30);
    color.Location = new Point(w += 10 + circle.Width, 30);

      // Add items to combo box
    color.Items.Add("Red");                                // Note 2
    color.Items.Add("Green");
    color.Items.Add("Blue");
```

```
        // Add controls to form
      Controls.Add(draw);
      Controls.Add(square);
      Controls.Add(circle);
      Controls.Add(color);

        // Register event handler
      draw.Click += new EventHandler(Draw_Click);
    }

      // Display chosen shape in selected color
    protected override void OnPaint(PaintEventArgs e){
      Graphics g = e.Graphics;
      Brush brush = new SolidBrush(c);                       // Note 3
      if (square.Checked)                                     // Note 4
        g.FillRectangle(brush,100,100,100,100);
      else                                                    // Note 5
        g.FillEllipse(brush,100,100,100,100);
      base.OnPaint( e );
    }

      // Handle button click
    protected void Draw_Click(Object sender, EventArgs e){
      if (color.SelectedItem.ToString() == "Red" )            // Note 6
        c = Color.Red;
      else if (color.SelectedItem.ToString() == "Green")
        c = Color.Green;
      else
        c = Color.Blue;
      Invalidate();
    }
    static void Main() {
      Application.Run(new Select());
    }
  }
```

■

Note 1: `private Color c = Color.Yellow;`

Yellow is the color we use before the user has a chance to select a color.

Note 2: `color.Items.Add("Red");`

The `Items` property holds a collection. We use the `Add` method to add each color name to the collection the `ComboBox` will display.

Note 3: `Brush brush = new SolidBrush(c);`

FIGURE 9.5 **The `Form` of Example 9.5**

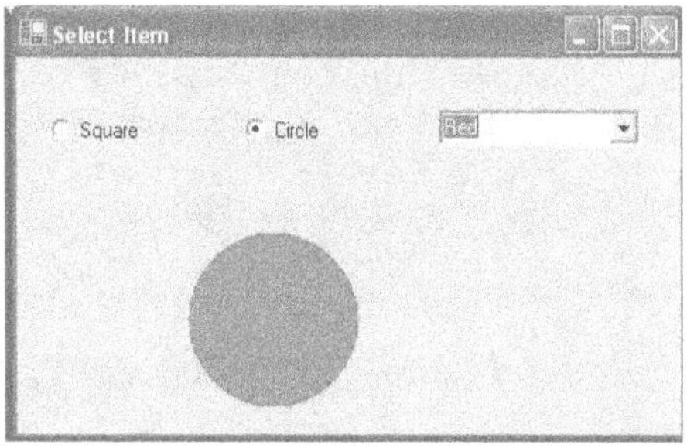

We create a `Brush` of the chosen color.

Note 4: `if (square.Checked)`

The `Checked` property returns `true` if its radio button is checked.

Note 5: `else`

Because exactly one radio button must be checked, we know that if `square` is not checked then `circle` must be, so we do not need an explicit check.

Note 6: `if (color.SelectedItem.ToString() == "Red" )`

The `SelectedItem` property has type `Object`, so we use the `ToString` method to get the string representation.

Figure 9.5 shows the `Form` of Example 9.5.

EXAMPLE 9.5 ■ SelectItem.cs

```
/* Uses a combo box to choose a color and two
 * radio buttons to choose a shape. Uses a draw
 * button to request drawing the selected shape
 * in the selected color.
 */

using System;
using System.Drawing;
using System.Windows.Forms;
public class SelectItem : Form {

    // Create controls
  private RadioButton square = new RadioButton();
  private RadioButton circle = new RadioButton();
  private ComboBox color = new ComboBox();

  private Color c = Color.Yellow;  // initial color

  public SelectItem( ) {
```

```
    // Set captions
  Text = "Select Item";
  square.Text = "Square";
  circle.Text = "Circle";
  color.Text = "Choose a color";

    // Set size
  Size = new Size(400,250);

    // Set locations
  int w = 20;
  square.Location = new Point(w, 30);
  circle.Location = new Point(w += 10 + square.Width, 30);
  color.Location = new Point(w += 10 + circle.Width, 30);

    // Add color names to combo box
  color.Items.Add("Red");
  color.Items.Add("Green");
  color.Items.Add("Blue");

    // Add controls to form
  Controls.Add(square);
  Controls.Add(circle);
  Controls.Add(color);

    // Register event handlers
  square.CheckedChanged +=
                 new EventHandler(Checked_Changed);
                                                   // Note 1
  circle.CheckedChanged +=
                 new EventHandler(Checked_Changed);
                                                   // Note 2
  color.SelectedIndexChanged +=
                 new EventHandler(Selected_Index);
                                                   // Note 3
}

  // Draw the selected shape in the selected color
protected override void OnPaint(PaintEventArgs e){
  Graphics g = e.Graphics;
  Brush brush = new SolidBrush(c);
  if (square.Checked)
    g.FillRectangle(brush,100,100,100,100);
  else
    g.FillEllipse(brush,100,100,100,100);
  base.OnPaint( e );
}
```

```
    // Change the color as soon as the user selects it
  protected void Selected_Index(Object sender, EventArgs e){
    if (color.SelectedItem.ToString() == "Red" )
      c = Color.Red;
    else if (color.SelectedItem.ToString() == "Green")
      c = Color.Green;
    else
      c = Color.Blue;
    Invalidate();                                          // Note 4
  }

    // Draw the shape as soon as the user selects it
  protected void
         Checked_Changed(Object sender, EventArgs e) {
    Invalidate();                                          // Note 5
  }
  static void Main() {
    Application.Run(new SelectItem());
  }
}
```

Note 1:

```
square.CheckedChanged +=
             new EventHandler(Checked_Changed);
```

The `CheckChanged` event occurs when the `RadioButton` is checked or becomes unchecked. We register the `Check_Changed` method to immediately cause the newly selected shape to be drawn.

Note 2:

```
circle.CheckedChanged +=
             new EventHandler(Checked_Changed);
```

We register the same event handling method for both radio buttons.

Note 3:

```
color.SelectedIndexChanged +=
              new EventHandler(Selected_Index);
```

The `SelectedIndexChanged` event occurs when the user changes the selection in the `ComboBox`. We register the `Selected_Index` method to immediately cause the shape to be drawn using the newly selected color.

Note 4:

```
Invalidate();
```

The call to `Invalidate` generates a `Paint` event so the `OnPaint` method will redraw the `Form` using the newly selected color.

Note 5: `Invalidate();`

When the user selects a shape, we need only to generate a `Paint` event. The `OnPaint` method uses the `Checked` property to determine which `RadioButton` the user selected.

List, Picture, and Check Boxes

A `CheckBox` is like a `RadioButton`, but we can select any number of them or none of them. In Example 9.6 we will illustrate this with a `CheckBox` for a drawing and another for a photo. We can display neither, either, or both.

A `PictureBox` is a control we use to display an `Image`. We provide a simple `Bitmap` drawing created using the `Paint` program included with the Windows operating system. A photo of the author in a GIF format serves as a second image.

A `ListBox` is like a `ComboBox`, but it can display more than one item. We can configure a `ListBox` to allow only one selection or to allow multiple selections. We respond immediately to the user's selection when only one selection is allowed, but we prefer not to respond to events generated by a `ListBox` when the user can make multiple selections.

Example 9.6 has a list of things, of which the user can select only one. When the user chooses a thing, we echo that choice in a `TextBox`. Example 9.6 has a list of animals. The user can select multiple animals. When the user clicks the *Choose Animals* button, a message appears saying that the selected animals jumped over the selected thing. Each of two checkboxes shows a `PictureBox` when checked.

StringBuilder

A C# `String` is immutable. It cannot be changed. The concatenation operator causes new temporary strings to be created. Creating a simple message such as

```
String message = "The cow jumped over the moon";
```

presents no problem, but suppose the animal names and the thing they jump over are stored in variables. For example, suppose we have two variables, `animal1` and `animal2`, that hold the names of animals, and a variable, `thing`, that holds the name of a thing. To construct a similar `String` we could use the statements

```
String message = "The ";
message += animal1;
message += " and ";
message += animal2;
message += " jumped over the ";
message += thing;
```

FIGURE 9.6
Concatenating strings

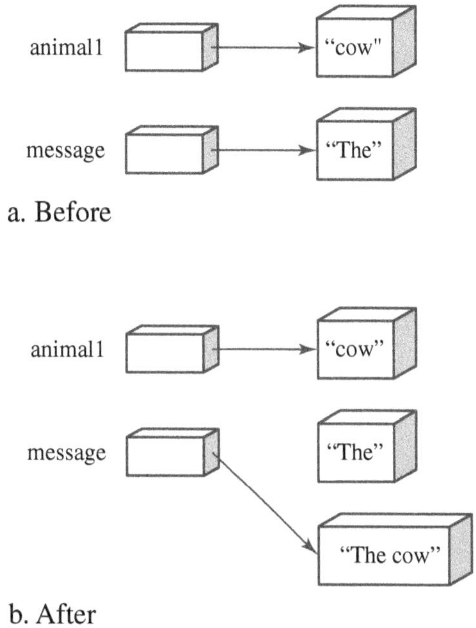

Each concatenation would create a temporary `String` and change the message variable to refer to it. Figure 9.6 shows how the first step would work.

By contrast, we can change a `StringBuilder`. The `Append` method adds a string to the existing `StringBuilder` and does not need to create a new object. Using a `StringBuilder` we could create the message with the code

```
StringBuilder mess  = new StringBuilder("The ");
mess.Append(animal1);
mess.Append(" and ");
mess.Append(animal2);
mess.Append(" jumped over the ");
mess.Append(thing);
String message = mess.ToString();
```

We use a `StringBuilder` in Example 9.6 (see Figure 9.7), where we need to make choices concerning the punctuation of the message.

EXAMPLE 9.6 ■ ListText.cs

```
/* Illustrates the ListBox, TextBox, PictureBox,
 * and CheckBox controls.
 */
```

FIGURE 9.7 **The `Form` of Example 9.6**

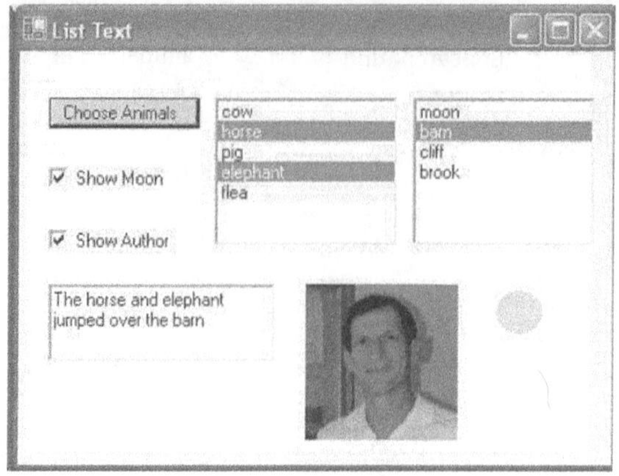


```
using System;
using System.Drawing;
using System.Text;                                              // Note 1
using System.Windows.Forms;
public class ListText : Form {

    // Create controls
  private Button choose = new Button();
  private ListBox animalList = new ListBox( );
  private ListBox things = new ListBox( );
  private TextBox text = new TextBox( );
  private PictureBox picture = new PictureBox();
  private PictureBox photo = new PictureBox();
  private CheckBox show = new CheckBox();
  private CheckBox author = new CheckBox();

  private Bitmap moon = new Bitmap("ex9-6.bmp");                // Note 2

  public ListText( ) {

      // Set captions
    Text = "List Text";
    choose.Text = "Choose Animals";
    show.Text = "Show Moon";
    author.Text = "Show Author";

      // Set sizes
    Size = new Size(400, 300);
    choose.Size = new Size(100,20);
    text.Size = new Size(150,50);                               // Note 3
    photo.Size = new Size(100,100);                             // Note 4
```

```
  // Set locations
choose.Location = new Point(20,30);
animalList.Location = new Point(30 + choose.Width, 30);
things.Location =
   new Point(40 + choose.Width + animalList.Width, 30);
text.Location = new Point(20, 150);
photo.Location = new Point(40 + text.Width, 150);
picture.Location =
      new Point(60 + text.Width + photo.Width, 150);
show.Location = new Point(20,70);
author.Location = new Point(20,110);

  // Configure controls
animalList.SelectionMode =
                        SelectionMode.MultiSimple; // Note 5
things.SelectionMode = SelectionMode.One;
text.Multiline = true;                             // Note 6
picture.Image = (Image)moon;                       // Note 7
picture.Visible = false;                           // Note 8
photo.Image = Image.FromFile("gittleman.gif");     // Note 9
photo.Visible = false;
BackColor = Color.White;
choose.BackColor = Color.Pink;

  // Configure lists
animalList.Items.Add("cow");
animalList.Items.Add("horse");
animalList.Items.Add("pig");
animalList.Items.Add("elephant");
animalList.Items.Add("flea");
things.Items.Add("moon");
things.Items.Add("barn");
things.Items.Add("cliff");
things.Items.Add("brook");

  // Add controls to form
Controls.Add(animalList);
Controls.Add(things);
Controls.Add(choose);
Controls.Add(text);
Controls.Add(picture);
Controls.Add(show);
Controls.Add(author);
Controls.Add(photo);

  // Register event handlers
choose.Click += new EventHandler(Choose_Click);
```

```
  things.SelectedIndexChanged +=
                         new EventHandler(Things_Changed);
  show.CheckedChanged += new EventHandler(Picture_Changed);
  author.CheckedChanged += new EventHandler(Photo_Changed);
}

  // Creates a message
public String BuildString(ListBox.SelectedObjectCollection
                              animals, String thing){
                                                      //Note 10
  StringBuilder message = new StringBuilder("The ");
  int length = animals.Count;                         //Note 11
  switch(length) {
    case 0: message.Append("??");                     //Note 12
            break;
    case 1: message.Append(animals[0].ToString());    //Note 13
            break;
    case 2: message.Append(animals[0].ToString());
            message.Append(" and ");                  //Note 14
            message.Append(animals[1].ToString());
            break;
    default:
       for(int i = 0; i < length-1; i++){
          message.Append(animals[i].ToString());
          message.Append(", ");                       //Note 15
       }
       message.Append("and ");
       message.Append(animals[length-1].ToString());
       break;
  }
  message.Append(" jumped over the ");
  message.Append(thing);
  return message.ToString();
}

  // Register an event handler for the Choose Animal button
protected void Choose_Click(object sender, EventArgs e) {
  text.Text = BuildString(animalList.SelectedItems,
                      (String)things.SelectedItem);
                                                      //Note 16
}

  // Registers an event handler for the list of things
protected void Things_Changed(object sender, EventArgs e) {
  text.Text = "You selected " + things.SelectedItem; //Note 17
}

  // Registers an event handler for the picture check box
```

```
  protected void Picture_Changed(Object sender, EventArgs e) {
    if (show.Checked)                                    //Note 18
      picture.Visible = true;
    else
      picture.Visible = false;
    Invalidate();
  }

    // Registers an event handler for the photo check box
  protected void Photo_Changed(Object sender, EventArgs e) {
    if (author.Checked)
      photo.Visible = true;
    else
      photo.Visible = false;
    Invalidate();
  }
  static void Main() {
     Application.Run(new ListText());
  }
}
```

Note 1: `using System.Text;`

We use the `System.Text` namespace for the `StringBuilder` class.

Note 2: `private Bitmap moon = new Bitmap("ex9-6.bmp");`

The bitmap is a Windows image format. We created the file using the Paint program included with Windows. Users of other systems can replace it with another image or convert it to another format. The files for this chapter include a conversion to JPG format.

Note 3: `text.Size = new Size(150,50);`

We set the size of the `TextBox` large enough to hold a multiline message.

Note 4: `photo.Size = new Size(100,100);`

We set the size of the photo to the dimensions of the image.

Note 5:
```
animalList.SelectionMode =
                        SelectionMode.MultiSimple;
```

The `SelectionMode` property has one of the `SelectionMode` enumeration values, which are:

MultiExtended:	Multiple items can be selected, and the user can use the *SHIFT*, *CTRL*, and *arrow* keys to make selections
MultiSimple:	Multiple items can be selected.
None:	No items can be selected.
One:	Only one item can be selected.

Note 6: `text.Multiline = true;`

We set the `Multiline` property to allow multiple lines in the `TextBox`.

Note 7: `picture.Image = (Image)moon;`

We set the `Image` property of the `PictureBox` to the moon bitmap. This configures the `PictureBox` with the `Image`.

Note 8: `picture.Visible = false;`

We use the `Visible` property to hide the `PictureBox` until the user checks the corresponding `CheckBox`.

Note 9: `photo.Image = Image.FromFile("gittleman.gif");`

For the photo `PictureBox`, we get the `Image` from a GIF file.

Note 10:

```
public String
    BuildString(ListBox.SelectedObjectCollection
                                animals, String thing)
```

A `SelectedObjectCollection` holds the currently selected animals. The `BuildString` method creates the message that the selected animals jumped over the selected thing.

Note 11: `int length = animals.Count;`

The `Count` property gives the number of items in the collection of currently selected animals.

Note 12: `case 0: message.Append("??");`

When the user has not selected any animals we add `"??"` to the message.

Note 13: `case 1: message.Append(animals[0].ToString());`

We use the array notation to get each of the selected items, starting with index 0. This works because the `SelectedObjectCollection` defines an indexer. We do not need to define indexers in our examples, but find it handy to use those defined in the .NET Framework.

Note 14: `message.Append(" and ");`

When the user selects two animals, we insert `" and "` between them.

Note 15: `message.Append(", ");`

When the user selects more than two animals, we insert a comma after all but the last animal.

Note 16:

```
text.Text = BuildString(animalList.SelectedItems,
                        (String)things.SelectedItem);
```

When the user clicks the *Choose Animals* button, we build the message passing the selections from each of the lists.

Note 17: `text.Text = "You selected " + things.SelectedItem;`

When the user selects a thing, we display a message in the `TextBox`.

Note 18: `if (show.Checked)`

If the user checks this `CheckBox` we make the drawing visible, but if the user removes the check we remove the drawing.

The BIG Picture

Controls have a visual representation. We illustrated `Button`, `TextBox`, `RadioButton`, `Label`, `ComboBox`, `ListBox`, `PictureBox`, and `CheckBox`, and the `Form` that contains them. We cannot change a `String`, but can change a `StringBuilder`. Using a `StringBuilder` avoids needless `String` creation in certain situations.

✓Test Your Understanding

6. How can we configure a `TextBox` to hold multiple lines of data?
7. Which line of code in Example 9.5 registers an event handler for an event generated by a radio button?
8. Which line of code of Example 9.5 registers an event handler for an event generated by a combo box?
9. Identify the event handling methods in Example 9.5. What delegate type does each exemplify?
10. How can we configure a `ListBox` to accept multiple selections?
11. What is the main difference between a `String` and a `StringBuilder`?

9.3 (OPTIONAL) USING VISUAL STUDIO .NET

So far in this chapter, we have written all the code for our forms without using Visual Studio .NET. This lets us fully understand all the code. If we have access to Visual Studio .NET, we can use a powerful tool that lets us drag controls onto a form and generates the configuration code. To illustrate Visual Studio .NET, we use it to create the form of Example 9.4.

Creating a Project

We first click on *File*, *New*, *Project,* and select *Visual C# Projects* from the Project Types and *Windows Application* from the Templates. We enter a folder name for the project files in the *Name* field, and browse to select the parent directory in the *Location* field. Clicking *OK* brings up a blank form.

If the Toolbox is not visible, we can click on *View, Toolbox* to pop up a list of controls that we can drag onto the form. For the form of Example 9.4, we drag a button, two radio buttons, and a combo box onto the top row. Figure 9.8 shows the Visual Studio .NET screen. The controls have default captions, such as `button1`

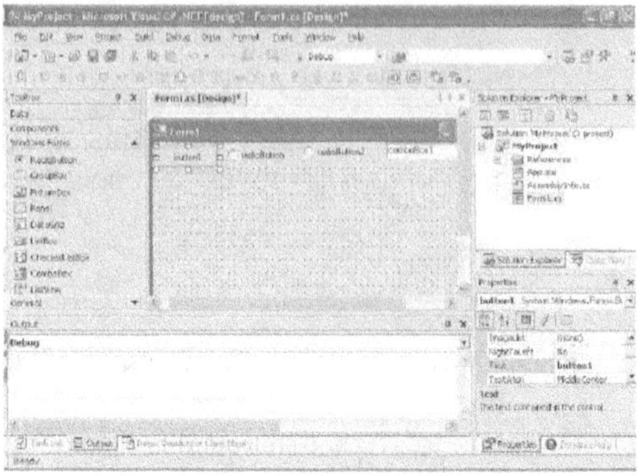

FIGURE 9.8 A `Form` created using Visual Studio .NET

for the button. A `Properties` sheet in the lower-left corner allows us to change any properties of the highlighted control, which is the button in Figure 9.8. We can change the `Text` property to `"Draw"`. Similarly, we can set the captions of the other controls.

Visual Studio writes much of the configuration code, such as setting the locations of the controls. We can add an event handler for a control by double-clicking on it, which will register an event handler and show its template for us to fill in. For example, double-clicking on the button brings up the code

```
private void button1_Click(object sender, System.EventArgs e)
{

}
```

for us to fill in the body.

We need to complete the event handling code, declare the `Color` variable `c`, and add the `OnPaint` method that we used in Example 9.4. Visual Studio .NET generated the remaining code of Example 9.7.

EXAMPLE 9.7 ■ Form1.cs

```
using System;
using System.Drawing;
using System.Collections;
using System.ComponentModel;
using System.Windows.Forms;
using System.Data;

namespace Visual
{
      /// <summary>
      /// Summary description for Form1.
      /// </summary>
```

```
public class Form1 : System.Windows.Forms.Form
{
     private System.Windows.Forms.Button button1;
     private System.Windows.Forms.RadioButton radioButton1;
     private System.Windows.Forms.RadioButton radioButton2;
     private System.Windows.Forms.ComboBox comboBox1;
     /// <summary>
     /// Required designer variable.
     /// </summary>
     private System.ComponentModel.Container components
                                                   = null;
           private Color c = Color.Yellow;

     public Form1()
     {
          //
          // Required for Windows Form Designer support
          //
          InitializeComponent();

          //
          // TODO: Add any constructor code after
                    InitializeComponent call
          //
     }

     /// <summary>
     /// Clean up any resources being used.
     /// </summary>
     protected override void Dispose( bool disposing )
     {
          if( disposing )
          {
               if (components != null)
               {
                    components.Dispose();
               }
          }
          base.Dispose( disposing );
     }

     #region Windows Form Designer generated code
     /// <summary>
     /// Required method for Designer support -
            do not modify
     /// the contents of this method with the code editor.
```

```
/// </summary>
private void InitializeComponent()
{
     this.button1 = new System.Windows.Forms.Button();
     this.radioButton1 =
              new System.Windows.Forms.RadioButton();
     this.radioButton2 =
              new System.Windows.Forms.RadioButton();
     this.comboBox1 =
                new System.Windows.Forms.ComboBox();
     this.SuspendLayout();
     //
     // button1
     //
     this.button1.Location =
                  new System.Drawing.Point(16, 16);
     this.button1.Name = "button1";
     this.button1.TabIndex = 0;
     this.button1.Text = "Draw";
     this.button1.Click +=
          new System.EventHandler(this.button1_Click);
     //
     // radioButton1
     //
     this.radioButton1.Location =
                 new System.Drawing.Point(104, 16);
     this.radioButton1.Name = "radioButton1";
     this.radioButton1.TabIndex = 1;
     this.radioButton1.Text = "Square";

     //
     // radioButton2
     //
     this.radioButton2.Location =
                 new System.Drawing.Point(240, 16);
     this.radioButton2.Name = "radioButton2";
     this.radioButton2.TabIndex = 2;
     this.radioButton2.Text = "Circle";
     //
     // comboBox1
     //
     this.comboBox1.Items.AddRange(new object[] {
                            "Red",
                              "Green",
                            "Blue"});
     this.comboBox1.Location =
                 new System.Drawing.Point(368, 16);
     this.comboBox1.Name = "comboBox1";
```

```
		this.comboBox1.Size =
				new System.Drawing.Size(121, 21);
		this.comboBox1.TabIndex = 3;
		//
		// Form1
		//
		this.AutoScaleBaseSize =
				   new System.Drawing.Size(5, 13);
		this.ClientSize =
				new System.Drawing.Size(488, 266);
		this.Controls.AddRange
			    (new System.Windows.Forms.Control[] {
			   this.comboBox1,
			   this.radioButton2,
			   this.radioButton1,
			   this.button1});
		this.Name = "Form1";
		this.Text = "Select Item";
		this.ResumeLayout(false);

	}
	#endregion

	// Display chosen shape in selected color
	protected override void OnPaint(PaintEventArgs e)
	{
		Graphics g = e.Graphics;
		Brush brush = new SolidBrush(c);
		if (radioButton1.Checked)
			g.FillRectangle(brush,100,100,100,100);
		else
			g.FillEllipse(brush,100,100,100,100);
		base.OnPaint( e );
	}

	/// <summary>
	/// The main entry point for the application.
	/// </summary>
	[STAThread]
	static void Main()
	{
		Application.Run(new Form1());
	}

	private void button1_Click
			(object sender, System.EventArgs e)
	{
		if (comboBox1.SelectedItem.ToString() == "Red" )
```

FIGURE 9.9 **The `Form` of Example 9.7**

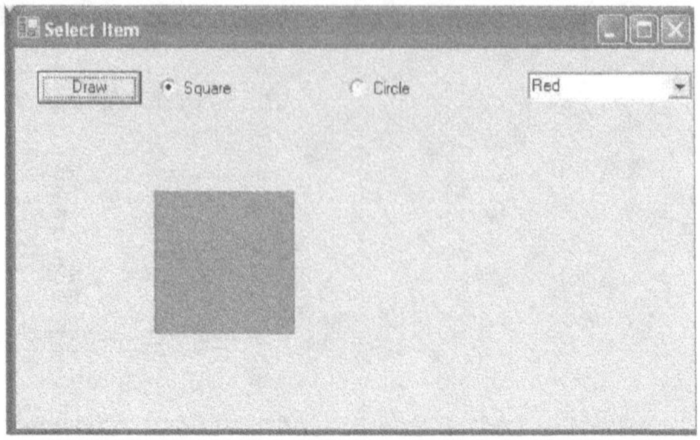


```
            c = Color.Red;
         else if(comboBox1.SelectedItem.ToString() == "Green")
            c = Color.Green;
         else
            c = Color.Blue;
         Invalidate();
        }
    }
}
```

We use Visual Studio .NET to build and run the application. Figure 9.9 shows the completed application of Example 9.9.

The BIG Picture

Visual Studio .NET provides an integrated development environment that generates code to configure controls that we drag onto a form. We can build and debug our application using this tool.

✓ Test Your Understanding

Try It Yourself ➤ **12.** If available, use Visual Studio .NET to create the GUI of Example 9.6.

9.4 (OPTIONAL) A GUI FOR INSERTION SORTING

With user interface components we can enhance our console applications, making them more user-friendly and interactive. In this optional section we develop a graphical user interface for the insertion sort application of Section 7.5. We complete one function at a time before moving on to the next, thus controlling the development process. We have something to show for our effort before we finish the entire project.

Defining the Problem

In this section we develop a graphical user interface to sort by insertion. In Example 7.8 we sorted data input by the user in a console window, displaying the sorted array in the same way, with no graphics. Here we provide a user-friendly interface that lets us see the insertion sort proceed graphically, step by step.

Designing a Solution: The Exploratory Process

Sometimes problems come to us fully formulated, our job being to develop a good solution. Other times we have a general goal, but have not yet settled on the specific requirements. For example, we have the goal of providing a GUI for insertion sort, but have not decided on a specific design. A good approach in this situation is to do a little exploratory programming, trying out some ideas on a small scale to determine what might work nicely.

We will want to display the data in a bar chart, so let us start the exploratory process by trying to display data in a chart. We can use a text box to enter the data. Our program will be event driven, getting the data and displaying when the user clicks the *Submit* button.

Designing a Solution: Making a Chart

We need to figure out how to draw the chart. We might have very large or very small values, positive or negative. The best approach is to simplify as much as possible, adding refinements later when we master the simpler cases. For now, let us use integer data between 0 and 99, which will eliminate the problem of figuring out the vertical scale; we represent a value of 59 with a bar of height 59 pixels. To find the width of each bar, we divide the width of the form by the size of the data, dividing the form into equal parts for each bar.

To use the `FillRectangle` method to draw our bars, we need the upper-left corner for each bar and its height and width. Figure 9.10 shows the chart with a few bars.

FIGURE 9.10 **Part of a bar chart**

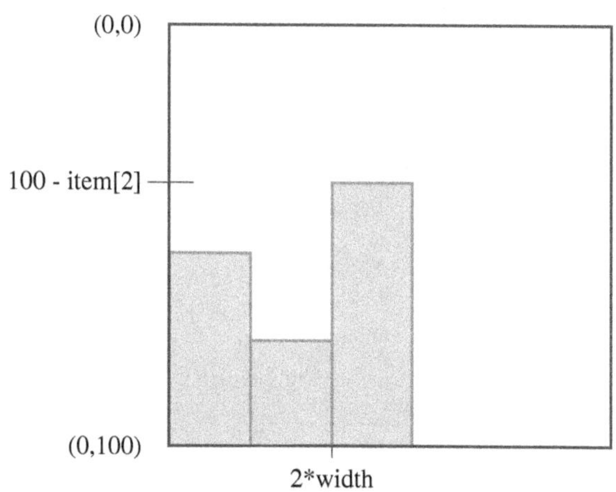

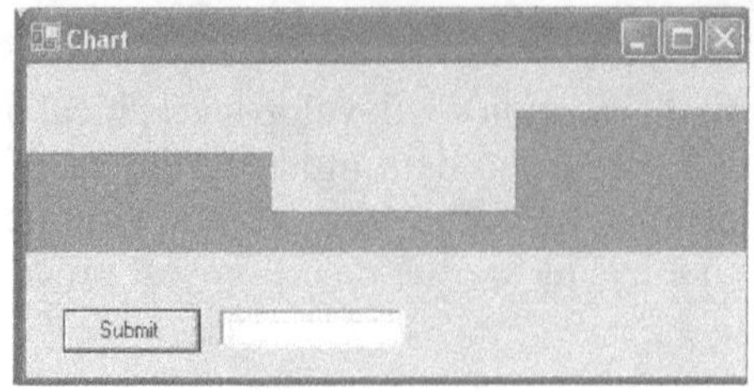

FIGURE 9.11 **The chart of Example 9.8**

Because the coordinate origin is in the upper-left corner of the canvas, the upper-left corner of the bar representing the array element `item[i]` is `(i*width,100-item[i])` where `width` is the common width of each bar, given by `CHART_WIDTH/count`, and `count` is the number of elements entered thus far.

In the `OnPaint` method, we draw a bar chart showing the values entered so far. Figure 9.11 shows the chart after the user enters the values 53, 22, and 75. Example 9.8 gives the code for this exploration.

EXAMPLE 9.8 ■ InsertA.cs

```
/* Uses a text box to enter data and a form
 * to display the chart.  This is an exploratory
 * program to develop a GUI for insertion sort.
 */

using System;
using System.Drawing;
using System.Windows.Forms;
public class InsertA : Form {
  public const int ITEM_SIZE = 10;
  public const int CHART_HEIGHT = 100;
  public const int CHART_WIDTH = 400;

  private TextBox number = new TextBox();
  private Button submit = new Button();

  int[] item = new int[ITEM_SIZE];  // Data to sort     // Note 1
  int count = 0;                    // Size of data

  public InsertA() {

      // Set captions
    Text = "Chart";
    submit.Text = "Submit";

      // Set size
```

```
    Size = new Size(400,200);

      // Set locations
    submit.Location = new Point(20,130);
    number.Location = new Point(30 + submit.Width,130);

      // Configure controls
    AcceptButton = submit;

      // Add controls to form
    Controls.Add(number);
    Controls.Add(submit);

      // Register event handler
    submit.Click += new EventHandler(Submit_Click);
  }

    /* Handles button click.  Enters new data in array.
     * Redraws the chart.
     */
  protected void Submit_Click(Object sender, EventArgs e){
    item[count++] = int.Parse(number.Text);              // Note 2
    number.Text = "";
    number.Focus();                                      // Note 3
    Invalidate();                                        // Note 4
  }

    // Draws the chart
  protected override void OnPaint(PaintEventArgs e){
    Graphics g = e.Graphics;
    if (count > 0){                                      // Note 5
      int width = CHART_WIDTH/count;                     // Note 6
      for (int i = 0; i < count; i++)
        g.FillRectangle(Brushes.Red, i*width,
              CHART_HEIGHT-item[i], width,item[i]);      // Note 7
    }
  }
  public static void Main() {
    Application.Run(new InsertA());
  }
}
```

Note 1: `int[] item = new int[ITEM_SIZE];`

We use an array of size 10 for simplicity, but later will allow different sizes of data.

Note 2: `item[count++] = int.Parse(number.Text);`

When the user clicks the *Submit* button, we get the value from the text field, convert it to an integer, save it in the next position in the array, and increment the count of the items entered so far.

Note 3: `number.Focus();`

After handling the event, we return the focus to the text box so the user will not have to click the mouse before entering another value.

Note 4: `Invalidate();`

Because the user just entered another value, we generate a `Paint` event to redraw the chart including this new value.

Note 5: `if (count > 0){`

When the application starts, .NET will call this `OnPaint` method to draw the form once before the user has a chance to enter any values. While the count is still zero, we do not want to draw a chart.

Note 6: `int width = CHART_WIDTH/count;`

To get the width of each bar, we divide the width of the chart, `CHART_WIDTH`, by the number of data items, `size`.

Note 7:
```
g.FillRectangle(Brushes.Red, i*width,
      CHART_HEIGHT-item[i], width,item[i]);
```

Figure 9.10 shows a few bars of the chart. We can see from this figure how to get the coordinates of the upper-left corner of each bar. The data value itself gives the height of the bar, because we do not need to scale the data.

Designing a Solution: Sorting

We can improve the chart later, but at least Example 9.8 shows that we are on the right track. For our next step, let us try to sort the data. Each time the user enters another value, we can insert it in the order of its predecessors. To do this we can copy the code from Example 7.8 into an `InsertNext` method to which we pass the array of data and the number of elements so far. The array holds 10 elements, but if the user entered the third element, for example, the `InsertNext` method should insert that value in the correct position with respect to its two predecessors, ignoring the array values beyond the third.

Figure 9.12 shows the chart just after the user enters the values 53, 22, and 75; as we can see, the values are sorted. Example 9.9 shows the additions to Example 9.8 needed to do the sorting.

EXAMPLE 9.9 ■ InsertB.cs

```
/* Add an InsertNext method to insert each value
 * in order as soon as the user enters it.
 */
```

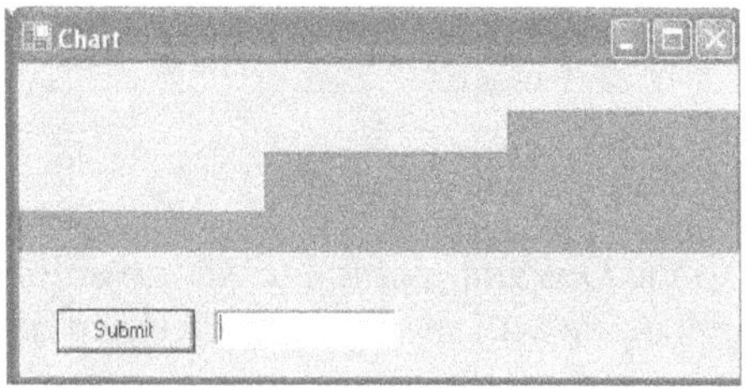

FIGURE 9.12 **The sorted chart of Example 9.9**

```
public class InsertB : Form {
       // The rest is the same as Example 9.8

  protected void Submit_Click(Object sender, EventArgs e) {
    item[count] = int.Parse(number.Text);
    InsertNext(item,count++);                          // Note 1
    number.Text = "";
    number.Focus();
    Invalidate();
  }
  public void InsertNext(int[] data, int size) {       // Note 2
    int current = data[size];
    int j = 0;
    while (current > data[j])
      j++;
    for (int k = size; k > j; k--)
      data[k] = data[k-1];
    data[j] = current;
  }
}
```

Note 1: `InsertNext(item,count++);`

We insert the next value in the correct position as soon as the user enters it in the text box and clicks the *Submit* button to generate the `Click` event.

Note 2: `public void InsertNext(int[] data, int size) {`

We copied the code for inserting the next element from Example 7.8.

We are making progress, but the chart does not look very nice with every bar the same color. We can greatly improve the appearance of the chart by drawing adjacent bars in different colors. To do this we add this simple statement

```
if (i%2==0)
  b = Brushes.Blue;
else
  b = Brushes.Red;
```

to the OnPaint method to set the color to blue if the index is even and to red otherwise. We will see this improvement in our next example.

Designing a Solution: The User Interface

Now that we are comfortable with the sorting and drawing, we can think about the user interface. We will keep the text box for the user to enter data values and add another text box for the user to specify the size of the array.

As in Example 7.8, it is nice to be able to select random input generated by the computer or manual input from the user in the text field. We add two radio buttons to make these selections. We add another button to use when sorting the random numbers.

Let us see how the GUI looks before we try to make it work. In Example 9.10 we add the new components, but do not respond to any events other than the text entry of Example 9.9. Figure 9.13 shows our new GUI.

EXAMPLE 9.10 ■ InsertC.cs

```
/* Adds controls to Example 9.9
 */

using System;
using System.Drawing;
using System.Windows.Forms;
public class InsertC : Form {
  public const int ITEM_SIZE = 10;
  public const int CHART_HEIGHT = 100;
  public const int CHART_WIDTH = 400;

    // Create controls
```

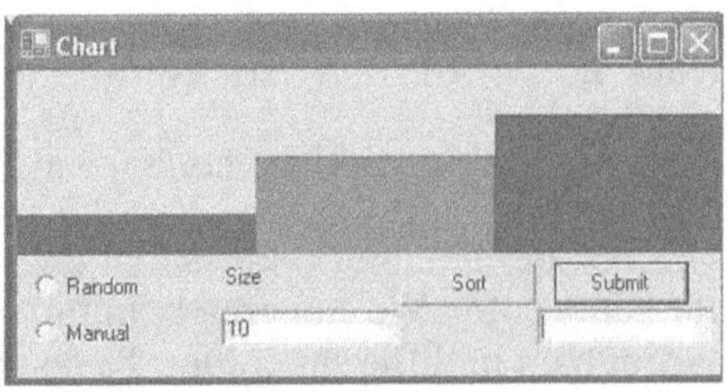

FIGURE 9.13 **The GUI of Example 9.10**

```
private TextBox number = new TextBox();
private Button submit = new Button();
private RadioButton random = new RadioButton();
private RadioButton manual = new RadioButton();
private Label size = new Label();
private TextBox getSize = new TextBox();
private Button sort = new Button();

int[] item = new int[ITEM_SIZE];  // Data to sort
int count = 0;                    // Size of data

public InsertC() {

    // Set captions
  Text = "Chart";
  submit.Text = "Submit";
  random.Text = "Random";
  manual.Text = "Manual";
  size.Text = "Size";
  getSize.Text = "10";
  sort.Text = "Sort";

    // Set size
  Size = new Size(400,200);

    // Set locations
  int w = 10;
  random.Location = new Point(w,105);
  manual.Location = new Point(w,130);
  size.Location = new Point(w += random.Width,105);
  getSize.Location = new Point(w,130);
  sort.Location = new Point(w += getSize.Width,105);
  number.Location = new Point(w += sort.Width,130);
  submit.Location = new Point(w + 10,105);

    // Configure controls
  AcceptButton = submit;

    // Add controls to form
  Controls.Add(number);
  Controls.Add(submit);
  Controls.Add(random);
  Controls.Add(manual);
  Controls.Add(size);
  Controls.Add(getSize);
  Controls.Add(sort);
```

```
        // Register event handler
      submit.Click += new EventHandler(Submit_Click);
    }
      // The rest is the same as Example 9.9
}
```

Completing the C# Code: Making the User Interface Work

Our attempt at a GUI, shown in Figure 9.13, looks reasonable enough to attempt to continue the implementation. Before getting into the details of the implementation we need to look at a few techniques we will need.

We can disable a control `c` using the statement

```
c.Enabled = false;
```

and enable it with

```
c.Enabled = true;
```

We should disable components when they should not be used. For example, when the user selects random data, we should disable the text field that allows the user to input data manually. Until we are ready to handle repeated sorting with different data, we should disable most of the components after we complete the first sort.

In addition to getting data from a text box or reading the label of a button, we can also set these strings to desired values. We can clear the text box after each data entry, so the user will not have to delete the previous value to enter a new one. After the user presses the *Sort* button to start the sorting, we can change that button's label to *Next* so the user can command that we insert the next value.

Returning to our GUI, we will start with both the *Sort* button and the data entry text box disabled. If the user selects random input we enable the *Sort* button, but if the user selects manual input we enable the data entry field. No matter what type of input the user selects, we disable both radio buttons after the first selection because we will not yet handle repeated sorting or changes in the input method.

Inputting manually, when the user submits the first number the event handler will allocate an array and get the size for it from the other text field in which the user specified the array size. We initialize this field with a default size of 10. We accept data entry only until the user has entered the specified number of elements. After processing the latest entry we set the text box text to the empty string to make it easier for the user to enter the next element.

We use the *Sort* button for random input. On the first press, when the button has its original label, *Sort*, the event handler gets the desired size of the data, creates the array, and fills it with random numbers from 0 to 99. It generates a `Paint` event to display the data, and changes the button's label to *Next* so the user can start inserting the items one by one.

Each time the user presses the *Next* button, the event handler inserts the next element in order with respect to its predecessors and generates a `Paint` event to dis-

FIGURE 9.14 **The GUI of Example 9.11**

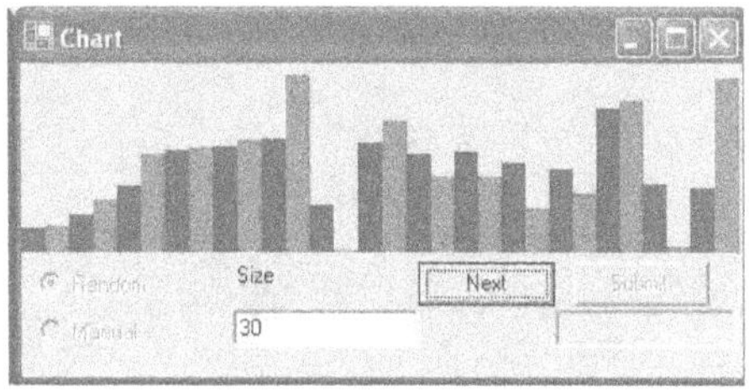

play the data. Thus we see the sorting process step-by-step. The event handler disables the button when all the elements have been inserted and the data is completely sorted.

Figure 9.14 shows the sorting partially completed. Example 9.11 shows the changes from Example 9.10 needed to make the application respond to the events generated by the user.

EXAMPLE 9.11 ■ InsertD.cs

```
/* Provides a user interface for insertion sorting.
 * The user can choose random data or input values
 * manually.  The user specifies the size of the data.
 * As the user inserts each item, the chart is redisplayed.
 */

using System;
using System.Drawing;
using System.Windows.Forms;
public class InsertD : Form {
  public const int ITEM_SIZE = 10;
  public const int CHART_HEIGHT = 100;
  public const int CHART_WIDTH = 400;

    // Create controls
  private TextBox number = new TextBox();
  private Button submit = new Button();
  private RadioButton random = new RadioButton();
  private RadioButton manual = new RadioButton();
  private Label size = new Label();
  private TextBox getSize = new TextBox();
  private Button sort = new Button();

  private int[] item;           // Data to sort
  private int count = 0;        // Size of display
  private int itemSize = 0;     // Max size of data
  private int nextCount = 1;    // Random data index
```

```
public InsertD() {

    // Set captions
  Text = "Chart";
  submit.Text = "Submit";
  random.Text = "Random";
  manual.Text = "Manual";
  size.Text = "Size";
  getSize.Text = "10";
  sort.Text = "Sort";

    // Set size
  Size = new Size(400,200);

    // Set locations
  int w = 10;
  random.Location = new Point(w,105);
  manual.Location = new Point(w,130);
  size.Location = new Point(w += random.Width,105);
  getSize.Location = new Point(w,130);
  sort.Location = new Point(w += getSize.Width,105);
  number.Location = new Point(w += sort.Width,130);
  submit.Location = new Point(w + 10,105);

    // Configure controls
  AcceptButton = submit;
  number.Enabled = false;                               // Note 1
  sort.Enabled = false;
  submit.Enabled = false;

    // Add controls to form
  Controls.Add(number);
  Controls.Add(submit);
  Controls.Add(random);
  Controls.Add(manual);
  Controls.Add(size);
  Controls.Add(getSize);
  Controls.Add(sort);

    // Register event handlers
  submit.Click += new EventHandler(Submit_Click);
  sort.Click += new EventHandler(Sort_Click);
  random.CheckedChanged += new EventHandler(Random_Changed);
  manual.CheckedChanged += new EventHandler(Manual_Changed);
}

  // The insert step in insertion sort
public void InsertNext(int[] data, int size) {
```

```
      int current = data[size];
      int j = 0;
      while (current > data[j]) j++;
      for (int k = size; k > j; k--)
        data[k] = data[k-1];
      data[j] = current;
  }

    /* Handles button click.  Enters new data in array.
     * Redraws the chart.
     */
  protected void Submit_Click(Object sender, EventArgs e) {
    if (count == 0) {
      itemSize = int.Parse(getSize.Text);
      item = new int[itemSize];
    }
    if (count < itemSize) {
      item[count] = int.Parse(number.Text);
      InsertNext(item,count++);
      number.Text = "";
      number.Focus();
      Invalidate();
    }
    if (count == itemSize)
      number.Enabled = false;
  }

    /* Generates random data with "Sort" caption.
     * Inserts nest value with "Next" caption.
     */
  protected void Sort_Click(Object sender, EventArgs e) {
    if (sort.Text.Equals("Sort")) {
      itemSize = int.Parse(getSize.Text);
      count = itemSize;
      item = new int[itemSize];
      Random r = new Random();
      for (int i = 0; i < itemSize; i++)
         item[i] = r.Next(100);
      Invalidate();
      if (itemSize == 1)                               // Note 2
        sort.Enabled = false;
      else
        sort.Text = "Next";
    }
    else if (sort.Text.Equals("Next")) {               // Note 3
      InsertNext(item,nextCount++);
      Invalidate();
      if (nextCount == itemSize)                       // Note 4
```

```
            sort.Enabled = false;
        }
    }

        // Enables Sort button to generate random numbers.
    protected void Random_Changed(Object sender, EventArgs e) {
        sort.Enabled = true;                              // Note 5
        random.Enabled = false;
        manual.Enabled = false;
    }

        // Enables text box and submit button to enter data.
    protected void Manual_Changed(Object sender, EventArgs e) {
        number.Enabled = true;                            // Note 6
        submit.Enabled = true;
        random.Enabled = false;
        manual.Enabled = false;
        number.Focus();
    }

        // Draws the chart
    protected override void OnPaint(PaintEventArgs e){
        Graphics g = e.Graphics;
        Brush b = Brushes.Red;
        if (count > 0){
          int width = CHART_WIDTH/count;
          for (int i = 0; i < count; i++) {
            if (i%2 == 0)
              b = Brushes.Blue;
            else
              b = Brushes.Red;
            g.FillRectangle
              (b,i*width,CHART_HEIGHT-item[i],width,item[i]);
          }
        }
    }
    public static void Main() {
        Application.Run(new InsertD());
    }
}
```

■

Note 1: `number.Enabled = false;`

Until the user selects either the random or the manual data entry method, we disable both the *Sort* button and the data entry text field.

Note 2: `if (itemSize == 1)`

When the user clicks the *Sort* button, we generate the indicated number of random numbers. If the size is one, we are done; otherwise, we change the button caption to *Next* so the user can sort the data.

Note 3: `else if (sort.Text.Equals("Next")) {`

When the user clicks the *Next* button, we insert the next value in order in its predecessors and redraw the data.

Note 4: `if (nextCount == itemSize)`

If we have inserted all the data, we disable the *Next* button.

Note 5: `sort.Enabled = true;`

When the user selects random input, we enable the *Sort* button.

Note 6: `number.Enabled = true;`

When the user selects manual input, we enable the data entry text box and the *Submit* button.

Testing the Code

By developing our program in stages, we are also able to test it in stages. We tested the making of the chart in `InsertA`, the sorting in `InsertB`, and the look of the user interface in `InsertC`. Finally, we test the implementation of the user interface in `InsertD`.

We should carefully test the two main use cases of this system, sorting with random input and sorting manually. When we select random input we check that the *Sort* button becomes enabled and the text field remains disabled. First we check the sorting using the default size of 10 and then check with size 1. With size 10, pressing the *Sort* button does display the chart properly and change the button label to *Next*. Pressing the *Next* button the first time inserts the second element in the correct place with respect to the first element. Pressing the *Next* button nine times results in a completely sorted array, at which time the *Next* button becomes disabled. Using size 1 causes the *Sort* button to be immediately disabled after we press it, which is what we want because there is no need to do anything further to sort one element.

When we select manual input of 10 items, we see that the *Sort* button is disabled and the *Enter* text field is enabled, so we can enter the data to sort. Entering each value causes it to be placed in the correct order with respect to the data previously entered. After entering 10 items, the *Enter* text field becomes disabled.

In industrial-strength systems, much effort is spent in validating the input to ensure the program does not crash if the user enters incorrect data.[1]

---

[1]Later, we will cover the C# exception handling facility, which helps us check for and recover from errors.

The BIG Picture

The development of a GUI for insertion sorting illustrates the exploratory development process. First we make the chart, and then we add the sorting algorithm. Next we design the user interface, and finally we make the user interface work. At each stage we have a complete program we can test.

SUMMARY

- In this chapter we created graphical user interfaces. The `Control` class is the base class of the various components we can add to a form to make a user interface. We configure controls by setting various properties such as `Size`, `Text`, and `Location`.
- The .NET event model allows methods that must be called when an event occurs to register with the event source. The event handling method implements methods required by the event. The event source will call each registered method when the event occurs.
- We use the following events with their associated delegate types:

Control	**Event**	**Delegate**
Button	Click	EventHandler
RadioButton	CheckChanged	EventHandler
CheckBox	CheckChanged	EventHandler
ListBox	SelectedIndexChanged	EventHandler
ComboBox	SelectedIndexChanged	EventHandler

The `EventHandler` delegate type is

```
public delegate void
      EventHandler(Object sender, EventArgs e);
```

- To handle an event, we write a method of the `EventHandler` type and register it with the appropriate event of the `Control`. For example, to handle a click of a `draw` button, we write a `Draw_Click` method with parameters `Object sender` and `EventsArgs e` and return type `void`. We register this method using

```
draw.Click += new EventHandler(Draw_Click);
```

When the user clicks the `draw` button, the .NET system will call our `Draw_Click` method.
- We can use exploratory programming to develop an interface step by step. At each stage we have a working program that provides some of the functionality we want, and we can focus all our attention on the next enhancement. We used this technique to provide an interface for insertion sorting, which lets us see each step of the sorting process.

SKILL BUILDER EXERCISES

1. Match the `Event` on the left with the control type on the right that generated that event type in one of the examples of this chapter.

a. `Click` i. `CheckBox`

b. `CheckChanged` ii. `Button`

c. `SelectedIndexChanged` iii. `ComboBox`

2. A control executes the ______________ method to direct keystrokes to it.
3. When we need to generate a `Paint` event from our program, we call the ________________ method.

CRITICAL THINKING EXERCISES

4. Which of the following methods could not be encapsulated by a `ComputeDelegate` instance as `ComputeDelegate` is declared in Example 9.2?
   a. `Math.Max`
   b. `Math.Ceiling`
   c. `Math.Abs`
   d. `Math.Sin`
5. The `MyClick` method of the form

```
protected void MyClick(Object o, EventArgs e) {
      // event handling code goes here
}
```

   could not be encapsulated by an `EventHandler` delegate because
   a. The declaration should be `Object sender` instead of `Object o`.
   b. The method name should be `My_Click` instead of `MyClick`.
   c. The return type should be `double` instead of `void`.
   d. None of the above.
6. The `AcceptButton` property of a `Form`
   a. specifies a button to click when the user hits the *Enter* key.
   b. is set to `true` when the form contains a button.
   c. is set to `true` when it is OK to add a button to the form.
   d. is set to `false` to disable all buttons in the form.
7. A `ListBox` can be configured to allow
   a. only one selection or multiple selections, but not no selections.
   b. no selections or one selection, but not multiple selections.
   c. no selections, one selection, or multiple selections.
   d. None of the above.

DEBUGGING EXERCISE

8. The following form attempts to draw the figure selected in a checkbox, with the name of the shape displayed inside it, when the user presses the *Draw* button. Find and fix any errors.

```
using System.Windows.Forms;
using System.Drawing;
public class NameIt : Form {
  private Button draw = new Button();
  private RadioButton square = new RadioButton();
  private RadioButton circle = new RadioButton();

  public NameIt() {    Text = "Select";
    draw.Text = "Draw";
    square.Text = "Square";
    circle.Text = "Circle";
    Size = new Size(500,250);
    int w = 20;
    draw.Location = new Point(20,30);
    square.Location = new Point(w+=10 + draw.Width, 30);
    circle.Location = new Point(w+=10+square.Width, 30);
    Controls.Add(draw);
    Controls.Add(square);
    Controls.Add(circle);
  }
  protected override void OnPaint(PaintEventArgs e){
    Graphics g = e.Graphics;
    if (square.Checked)
      g.FillRectangle(Brushes.Red,100,100,100,100);
    else
      g.FillEllipse(Brushes.Red,100,100,100,100);
    base.OnPaint( e );
  }
  static void Main() {
    Application.Run(new NameIt());
  }
}
```

PROGRAM MODIFICATION EXERCISES

9. Modify Example 9.5 to use a `ListBox` instead of a `ComboBox`.

Putting It All Together ➤ **10. a.** Example 8.3 displayed text in various fonts. Develop a GUI to allow the user to select a font from a combo box, to select a style from checkboxes, and to enter a point size in a text box. Display a message using the selected font.

b. Check that the message will fit on one line. If it does not fit in the point size that the user requested, reduce the point size until it does fit.

c. Allow the user to select a color, and display the text in that color.

Putting It All Together ➤ **11. a.** Example 8.2 displayed various shapes. Develop a GUI to allow the user to select a shape from a combo box. Use radio buttons for the user to select whether to draw the shape filled or unfilled. If the user selects a line, disable the radio buttons. Display the selected shape.

b. Allow the user to select a color, and display the shapes in that color.

12. Modify Example 9.6 to allow multiple selections in the `things List`.

13. Modify Example 9.11, the GUI for insertion sort, to indicate the number below each bar in the chart.

14. Modify Example 9.4 to center the figure in the form.

15. Modify Example 9.5 to center the figure in the form.

PROGRAM DESIGN EXERCISES

16. a. Develop a GUI for a four-function (+, -, *, /) calculator. Use a text box for the display and a grid of buttons for the input. Provide only the interface; do not try to implement the calculator functions.

b. Implement the calculator functions +, -, *, and /.

17. Write a program that lets the user input, in a text box, the number of fair coins to toss. Using random numbers to simulate the toss of a coin, repeat this experiment 100 times, and display a bar chart showing the distribution of the outcomes for each possible number of heads obtained. For example, tossing six coins 100 times might give no heads twice, one head 10 times, two heads 20 times, three heads 30 times, four heads 24 times, five heads 13 times, and six heads once.

18. a. A market sells eggs at $1.90 per dozen, milk at $1.47 per quart, and bread at $2.12 per loaf. Use a combo box to allow the user to select an item, and a text box for the user to input the quantity desired. Include an *`Order`* button to allow the user to order the specified quantity of the selected item. When the user selects an item, the price should appear in a label. When the user presses the *`Order`* button, a description and the total cost of the order should appear in the form.

b. Allow the user to order more than one type of food. Each time the user presses the *`Order`* button, describe the purchase. Add a *`Total`* button, and when the user presses this button, display the total prices of all items ordered.

19. Every brokerage firm has its own formulas for calculating commissions when stocks are purchased or sold. Many of these formulas are based on the number of round lots (groups of 100) purchased and the number of stocks in any odd lot (less than 100) purchased, as well as the price of the stock. To keep things simple, our company will charge according to the number of stocks purchased, as follows: $30 per round lot and $.50 per stock in any odd lot. Thus, for example, if the purchaser buys 110 shares of stock, he or she is charged $35 in commissions. Include three text boxes for the user to enter the name of a stock, the quantity desired, and the cost of one share. Include a *`Buy`* button, and when the user presses this button display the total cost of that stock, including the commission.

FIGURE 9.15 **User interface for Exercise 20**

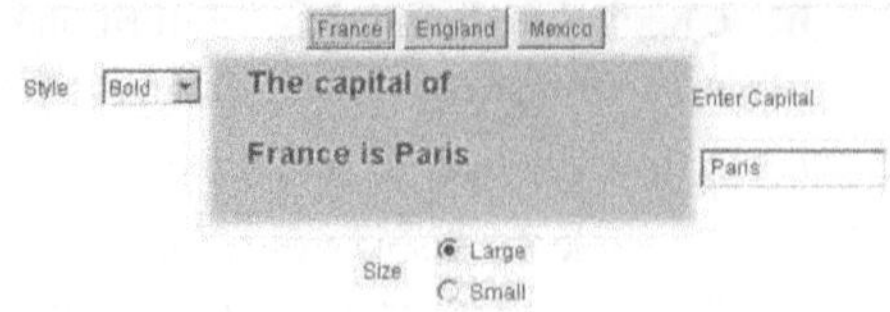

20. Write an application that prints the message listing the capital of a country using the interface shown in Figure 9.15, in which the style can be bold or italic, and the size, large or small, refers to the point size of the font.

21. Develop a GUI that reverses an array. Allow the user to choose random input or to input the array manually. Display the array in a bar chart on the left of a form. Provide a button, and when the user presses the button do one more interchange of elements, displaying the partially reversed array on the right of the form. When the reversal is complete, disable the button.

22. Make a user interface for a car rental. Include a combo box with the make of car, a text field for the number of days rented, two checkboxes for air and automatic, and a button to make the rental. Also include a label for display. When the user selects a make, indicate the price in the label. When the user indicates the number of days, indicate the total price in that label. When the user chooses air or automatic, adjust the price in the label to reflect the additional cost. Adjust the label immediately after each selection. Do not wait for the user to press the button. When the user presses the button, draw a car (not any particular model) with the price showing on its side. Change the label on the button to *Move*, and when the user presses the button, move the car to the right by 50 pixels.

10 Inheritance

C# is an object-oriented programming language. Object-oriented programming is especially useful in managing the complexity of very large software systems because it focuses on the objects, which are the most stable aspect of these systems. Designing with objects is natural for us and allows us to reuse designs in new contexts, making software less expensive to produce and easier to maintain. To get these benefits we need to use the full range of object-oriented techniques.

In this chapter we focus on inheritance and include discussions of polymorphism and abstract classes. After looking at access modes, we conclude with an optional case study illustrating the flavor of the object-oriented programming paradigm using the object-oriented design techniques of use cases and scenarios.

OBJECTIVES

- Use inheritance to relate classes
- Use polymorphism to improve design
- Use abstract classes to achieve implementation independence
- Understand the use of modifiers in specifying access
- (Optional) Develop an object-oriented design from use cases and scenarios

10.1 DERIVED CLASSES

Inheritance lets us do in C# what we do when classifying natural objects, which is to group common properties and behavior into a higher-level base class. We can talk about objects generally on a higher level or more specifically with lower-level details.

Classification Revisited

Classification organizes knowledge. We divide living things into plant and animal categories. Among animals we differentiate reptiles from mammals, and among mammals we can tell cats from bats. Finally, we recognize individual cats, Tabby and Tom.

Using these categories we can refer to the `Animal` class for behavior, such as movement, that Tabby and Tom share just by being animals. The `Mammal` class stores the common property of having hair, and all `Cat` instances are carnivorous. Finally, some properties differ from cat to cat. We have thin cats and fat cats, feisty cats and fraidy cats.

Classification reflects the **IS-A** relationship in that every `Mammal` is an `Animal`, and every `Cat` is a `Mammal`.

Class Hierarchies

C# lets us organize our classes into a hierarchy in which a class can have several **derived classes**, each of these derived classes can itself have derived classes, and so on. For example, our `BankAccount` class could specify the state and behavior common to all bank accounts. A `SavingsAccount` derived class of `BankAccount` will define accounts that earn interest. `SavingsAccount` might have a `TimedAccount` derived class to define accounts in which we deposit funds for a fixed period of time. A `CheckingAccount` derived class of `BankAccount` will define accounts with check-writing privileges. Figure 10.1 shows this hierarchy of account classes.

Constructing a Derived Class

When creating a derived class, we inherit all the attributes and behavior of that class. A declaration for a `SavingsAccount` derived class would have the pattern

```
public class SavingsAccount : BankAccount {
          .....
}
```

where the colon separator tells us that `SavingsAccount` is a derived class of the `BankAccount` class. Here `SavingsAccount` is a derived class of `BankAccount`, and `BankAccount` is the **base class** of `SavingsAccount`.

FIGURE 10.1 The account hierarchy

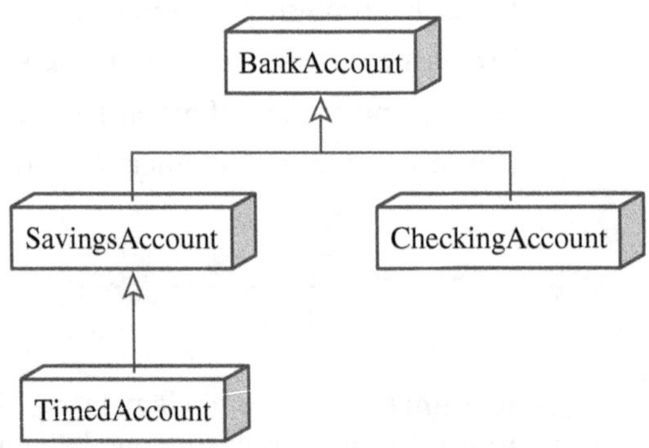

Example 10.1 creates a `SimpleSavings1` class that simply derives from `BankAccount` and does nothing more. We normally would not make such a simple extension that adds or changes nothing in `BankAccount`. We do it to illustrate that the derived class `SimpleSavings1` inherits the state and behavior from its base class `BankAccount`.

EXAMPLE 10.1 ■ SimpleSavings1.cs

```
/* Illustrates the simplest inheritance.
 */

public class SimpleSavings1 : BankAccount {      // Note 1
}
```

Note 1: The `SimpleSavings1` inherits from the `BankAccount` class. Using the .NET Framework SDK, we compile to a DLL using the command

```
csc /r:BankAccount.dll /t:library SimpleSavings1.cs
```

We make sure that `BankAccount.dll` is in the current directory.

Example 10.2 tests the `SimpleSavings1` class. We see that we can declare a `SimpleSavings1` object which has an initial balance `$0.00`. `SimpleSavings1` inherits the `GetBalance`, `Deposit`, and `Withdraw` methods from its `BankAccount` base class. Using the .NET Framework SDK, we compile with the command

```
csc /r:SimpleSavings1.dll,BankAccount.dll
UseSimpleSavings1.cs
```

EXAMPLE 10.2 ■ UseSimpleSavings1.cs

```
/* Tests the SimpleSavings1 class.
 */

using System;
public class UseSimpleSavings1 {
  public static void Main() {
    SimpleSavings1 ss1Acct = new SimpleSavings1();     // Note 1
    Console.WriteLine("Initial balance is {0:C}",
                               ss1Acct.GetBalance());
    ss1Acct.Deposit(400.00);                           // Note 2
    ss1Acct.Withdraw(50.00);
    Console.WriteLine("Current balance is {0:C}",
                               ss1Acct.GetBalance());
  }
}
```

```
Initial balance is $0.00
Current balance is $350.00
```

■

Note 1: `SimpleSavings1 ss1Acct = new SimpleSavings1();`

The `SimpleSavings1` class of Example 10.1 does not contain any constructor. When a class has no constructors, C# will create a default constructor for it. Because `SimpleSavings1` is a derived class of `BankAccount`, its constructor will call a base class constructor to initialize instance variables of its base class, `BankAccount`. Because the default `SimpleSavings1` constructor has no arguments, it will call the default `BankAccount` constructor, which also has no arguments. The `BankAccount` default constructor initializes its balance variable to $0.00.

Note 2: `ss1Acct.Deposit(400.00);`

A `SimpleSavings1` object inherits the behavior of its `BankAccount` base class. It inherits the `Deposit`, `Withdraw`, and `GetBalance` methods.

We cannot create a `SimpleSavings1` object with an initial balance different from $0.00. To do that, we need to add a constructor and pass the initial balance to it.

Derived classes do not inherit the constructors of their base classes. Even though `SimpleSavings1` does not inherit the `BankAccount` constructors, it is a `BankAccount` and, as part of its construction, must use one of the `BankAccount` constructors to initialize the `balance` field it inherits. A derived class constructor calls a constructor for its base class by calling `base` just before the body of the constructor, passing it any arguments that the base class constructor needs.

We create another class, `SimpleSavings2`, to add the constructor. The code for the `SimpleSavings2` constructor is

```
public SimpleSavings2(double amount) : base(amount) {
}
```

C# uses the keyword **base** to represent the base class. The call

```
base(amount);
```

indicates a call to a base class constructor for the `BankAccount` base class of `SimpleSavings2`. Because we pass one argument of type `double`, the `BankAccount` base class must have a constructor with one argument of type `double`.

EXAMPLE 10.3 ■ SimpleSavings2.cs

```
/* Creates a constuctor for the derived class which calls the
 * base class constructor.
 */

public class SimpleSavings2 : BankAccount       {       // Note 1
```

```
  public SimpleSavings2(double amount) : base(amount){ // Note 2
  }
}
```

Note 1: It would not work to extend `SimpleSavings1`. We leave it to an exercise to explain why not.

Note 2: Whenever a class has at least one constructor, C# will not create any others. By including only this constructor with one parameter, we have made it impossible to use a default constructor (with no arguments) for `SimpleSavings2`.

Example 10.4 tests the `SimpleSavings2` class. We create a `SimpleSavings2` object with an initial balance of $500.00.

EXAMPLE 10.4 ■ UseSimpleSavings2.cs

```
/* Tests the SimpleSavings2 class.
 */

using System;
public class UseSimpleSavings2 {
  public static void Main() {
    SimpleSavings2 ss2Acct =
                         new SimpleSavings2(500.00);    // Note 1
    Console.WriteLine("Initial balance is {0:C}",
                              ss2Acct.GetBalance());
    ss2Acct.Deposit(400.00);
    ss2Acct.Withdraw(50.00);
    Console.WriteLine("Current balance is {0:C}",
                              ss2Acct.GetBalance());
  //  ss2Acct = new SimpleSavings2();                   // Note 2
  }
}
```

Output

```
Initial balance is $500.00
Current balance is $850.00
```

Note 1:
```
SimpleSavings2 ss2Acct =
                 new SimpleSavings2(500.00);
```

The `SimpleSavings2` constructor passes the argument, `500.00`, to the `BankAccount` base class constructor to initialize the account balance.

Note 2:
```
//  ss2Acct = new SimpleSavings2();
```

We commented out this line because `SavingsAccount2` has no default constructor, and C# will not create one as it did for `SavingsAccount1`.

Adding State and Behavior to a Derived Class

A derived class inherits the state and behavior of its base class. The `SavingsAccount` class inherits the data fields and methods of the `BankAccount` class. Every `SavingsAccount` is a `BankAccount`. Our `BankAccount` class of Example 5.1 has an instance variable, `balance`, to hold the balance, and instance methods, `GetBalance`, `Deposit`, and `Withdraw`. The `SavingsAccount` class extends `BankAccount`, so it will inherit the `balance` field, and the `GetBalance`, `Deposit`, and `Withdraw` methods. The `SavingsAccount` class is a derived class of the `BankAccount` class, and the `BankAccount` class is a base class of `SavingsAcccount`.

`SavingsAccount` can add additional state and behavior, which would apply only to the derived class. The `SavingsAccount` class needs an `interestRate` field to store the interest rate for an account, and a `PostInterest` method to compute the interest and add it to the account balance. Example 10.5 shows these additions.

EXAMPLE 10.5 ■ SavingsAccount.cs

```
/* Defines a SavingsAccount class derived from BankAccount.
 */

public class SavingsAccount : BankAccount  {
  private double interestRate;                              // Note 1

  public SavingsAccount(double amount, double rate)
                                    : base(amount){  // Note 2
     interestRate = rate;                                   // Note 3
  }
  public void PostInterest()  {
    double balance = GetBalance();
    double interest = interestRate/100*balance;             // Note 4
    Deposit(interest);                                      // Note 5
  }
}
```

■

Note 1: `private double interestRate;`

We add the `interestRate` field, where we intend the user to enter 5.0 for an interest rate of 5%.

Note 2:
```
public SavingsAccount(double amount, double rate)
                              : base(amount){
```

The `SavingsAccount` constructor has two parameters, the first to pass the initial account balance and the second to pass the interest rate. We leave for the exercises the addition of additional constructors, such as a no-argument constructor or a constructor that passes an interest rate but not an initial balance.

We pass the initial account balance to the base class, `BankAccount`, constructor. This `base` invocation comes before the constructor body. It would not work to try to initialize the balance field directly using

```
balance = amount;
```

because `balance` is a private field and is not directly accessible in the derived class. Even if it were permitted, it would be less efficient. If we do not call a constructor, C# will call a default constructor and initialize `balance` to `0.0`. We would then change it to `amount`, doing a second step when only one call to the correct base class constructor is necessary.

Note 3: `interestRate = rate;`

After calling the base class constructor to initialize the base class variables, we initialize `interestRate` directly.

Note 4: `double interest = interestRate/100*balance;`

To convert a percent to a decimal, we divide by 100.

Note 5: `Deposit(interest);`

We cannot add the interest to the private `balance` field directly, so we call the `Deposit` method to deposit the interest to the savings account.

Example 10.6 tests the `SavingsAccount` class. We use the methods, `Deposit`, `Withdraw`, and `GetBalance`, that `SavingsAccount` inherits from `BankAccount` as well as the `PostInterest` method that it adds. If we create a `BankAccount`, we cannot call the `PostInterest` method.

EXAMPLE 10.6 ■ UseSavingsAccount.cs

```
/* Tests the SavingsAccount class.
 */

using System;
public class UseSavingsAccount {
  public static void Main() {
    SavingsAccount s =  new SavingsAccount(500.00, 4.5);
    s.Deposit(135.22);
    s.PostInterest();
    s.Withdraw(50);
    Console.WriteLine
          ("The balance of SavingsAccount s is {0:C}",
                                          s.GetBalance());
  }
}
```

Output

```
The balance of SavingsAccount s is $613.80
```

Overriding Behavior

Objects exhibit their unique behavior. Each type of account can handle a withdraw request, for example, in its own way. A derived class automatically inherits the public methods of its base class, but it may choose to **override** some of them to implement its own specific behavior.

The `SavingsAccount` class accepted the behavior it inherited. The `Deposit`, `Withdraw`, and `GetBalance` methods work in the same way for the `SavingsAccount` derived class as they do for its `BankAccount` base class. However, a class does not have to accept the implementations that it inherits.

We define a `CheckingAccount` class that charges a service charge for each check cashed unless the account balance is above a specified minimum balance, in which case check cashing incurs no charge. A `CheckingAccount` inherits the `balance` instance variable from `BankAccount`, and we add two additional instance variables:

`charge`	The service charge if the balance is below the minimum
`minBalance`	The minimum balance necessary to waive the check cashing charge

The `CheckingAccount` class will inherit the `GetBalance` and `Deposit` methods from `BankAccount`, but will override the `Withdraw` method to call a `ProcessCheck` method because this type of checking account only permits withdrawals by check. A `CheckingAccount` is a kind of `BankAccount`, but it handles withdrawals in its own way. Figure 10.2 contains the code for the `CheckingAccount Withdraw` method which overrides the `BankAccount Withdraw` method.

Virtual Methods

To override a base class method we must declare that base class method as a **virtual** method using the `virtual` keyword. To override the `Withdraw` method, we need to declare it in `BankAccount` as

```
public virtual double Withdraw(double amount) {
  if (balance >= amount) {
    balance -= amount;
    return balance;
```

FIGURE 10.2 **`Withdraw` method overrides `BankAccount Withdraw`**

```
public override double Withdraw(double amount) {
  return ProcessCheck(amount);
}
```

```
    } else
        return -1;
}
```

There is a slight overhead involved in accessing the correct version of an overridden method at runtime, so C# gives us the choice to allow it or not. The BankAccount class used in this chapter revises the BankAccount class of Example 5.1 to declare the Withdraw method as virtual.

The CheckingAccount class adds the ProcessCheck method. It determines whether the account contains the minimum balance necessary for free checks. If so, it withdraws the amount of the check. If not, it withdraws the amount of the check plus the service charge. To remove the funds from the account, ProcessCheck uses the Withdraw method of the BankAccount class. But there are two Withdraw methods. We need to distinguish the base class BankAccount Withdraw method from the derived class CheckingAccount Withdraw method.

When implementing CheckingAccount methods, calling

```
Withdraw(40.00)
```

refers to CheckingAccount Withdraw, but

```
base.Withdraw(40.00)
```

refers to the base class method, BankAccount Withdraw.

TIP

Do not confuse overriding with overloading. An overloaded method has the **same** name as the original method, but **different** parameters. It provides an **additional** method for a class. For example, the BankAccount class of Example 5.1 has overloaded constructors, one with no parameters and the other with a single parameter of type **double**. A user of the BankAccount class may call either constructor, new BankAccount() or new BankAccount(500.00)

An overridden method has the **same** name as the original method, and the **same** parameters. The new implementation of the method in the derived class **replaces** the old implementation of that method in the base class. For example, the CheckingAccount Withdraw method overrides the Withdraw method of the BankAccount class. Each has one parameter of type double. We could overload the Withdraw method by declaring a CheckingAccount Withdraw method of the form

```
public int Withdraw(int amount)
```

where the parameter has type int. The CheckingAccount class would then have two Withdraw methods, one inherited from BankAccount and one added with an int parameter.

If you intend to override a method, make sure to use the same parameters that are used in the method you are overriding. ■

Figure 10.3 shows the inheritance relationship between the BankAccount class and its SavingsAccount and CheckingAccount derived classes. The UML uses the unfilled arrow to denote the inheritance relationship. The derived classes inherit from their parent base class.

FIGURE 10.3
Inheritance

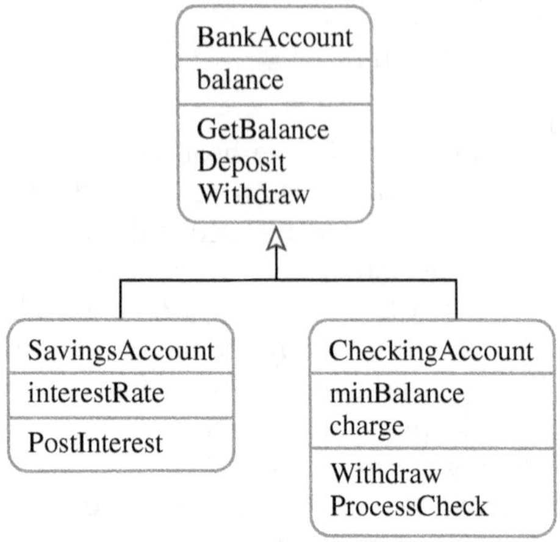

In Example 10.7 we illustrate inheritance with the code for derived class `CheckingAccount` of the `BankAccount` class.

EXAMPLE 10.7 ■ CheckingAccount.cs

```
/* Defines CheckingAccount class derived from BankAccount.
 */

public class CheckingAccount : BankAccount {
  private double minBalance;   // Balance needed to avoid charge
  private double charge;       // Per check charge

  public CheckingAccount
                (double minAmount, double charge)      // Note 1
                                     : base (){      // Note 2
    minBalance = minAmount;
    this.charge = charge;
  }
  public double ProcessCheck(double amount)  {
    double result;
    if (GetBalance() >= minBalance)
      result=base.Withdraw(amount);                     // Note 3
    else
      result=base.Withdraw(amount + charge);            // Note 4
    return result;
  }
  public override double Withdraw(double amount) {      // Note 5
    return ProcessCheck(amount);
  }
}
```

■

Note 1: `public CheckingAccount (double minAmount, double charge)`

We define only one `CheckingAccount` constructor. The arguments are the minimum balance needed for free checking and the charge per check if the balance is below the minimum. We do not pass an initial balance to the `CheckingAccount` constructor, but do pass it to the constructor for the `SavingsAccount` class to see the contrast. Each `CheckingAccount` object will start with an initial balance of `$0.00`.

Note 2: `: base (){`

Because we do not specify an initial balance, we call the default constructor (the one with no arguments that sets the balance to zero) for the `BankAccount` base class. If we omit this call C# will add it anyway, because a derived class constructor must always call some base class constructor to correctly initialize the part of the object inherited from the base class.

Note 3: `result=base.Withdraw(amount);`

To call the `BankAccount` `Withdraw` method, we use the prefix `base`. Because the balance is above the minimum needed for free checks, we withdraw the amount requested. We do not have to check whether the amount requested is available, because the `Withdraw` method performs that check.

Note 4: `result=base.Withdraw(amount + charge);`

The balance is below the minimum, so we withdraw the amount requested plus the service charge for the check.

Note 5: `public override double Withdraw(double amount) {`

We override the `BankAccount` `Withdraw` method to permit withdrawal only by check.

Example 10.8 tests the `CheckingAccount` class.

EXAMPLE 10.8 ■ UseCheckingAccount.cs

```
/* Tests the CheckingAccount class.
 */

using System;
public class UseCheckingAccount {
  public static void Main() {
    CheckingAccount c =
             new CheckingAccount(2500.00, .50);     // Note 1
    c.Deposit(1000.00);                             // Note 2
    c.ProcessCheck(200.00);                         // Note 3
    c.Withdraw(100.00);                             // Note 4
```

```
        Console.WriteLine
            ("The balance of CheckingAccount c is {0:C}",
                                         c.GetBalance());
    }
}
```

Output

```
The balance of CheckingAccount c is $699.00
```

Note 1:
```
CheckingAccount c =
  new CheckingAccount(2500.00, .50);
```

The minimum balance for free checking is $2500, and the service charge per check if the balance is below $2500 is $.50.

Note 2: `c.Deposit(1000.00);`

Because the initial account balance is zero, we first make a deposit.

Note 3: `c.ProcessCheck(200.00);`

Because the balance is below $2500, we will withdraw $200.50 to cover the amount requested and the service charge.

Note 4: `c.Withdraw(100.00);`

Because the balance is below $2500, we will withdraw $100.50 to cover the amount requested and the service charge.

The `Object` Class

The `Object` class, in the `System` namespace, is a base class of every C# class. A class such as `Person` from Example 6.3 that does not explicitly extend any class, implicitly extends `Object`. C# treats the `Person` class as if we had declared it as

```
public class Person : Object {// same as Example 6.3}
```

Our `SavingsAccount` class from Example 10.5 explicitly extends `BankAccount`, and `BankAccount` implicitly extends `Object`. The .NET library classes all directly or indirectly extend `Object`.

The `Object` class provides a default implementation of the `ToString` method that returns the class name. Because every class inherits from `Object`, every class can invoke its `ToString` method. For example, a `BankAccount` object, `myAccount`, is also an `Object`, so we can invoke the `ToString` method explicitly, as in

```
Console.WriteLine(myAccount.ToString());
```

or implicitly, as in

```
Console.WriteLine(myAccount);
```

FIGURE 10.4
Inheriting from `Object`

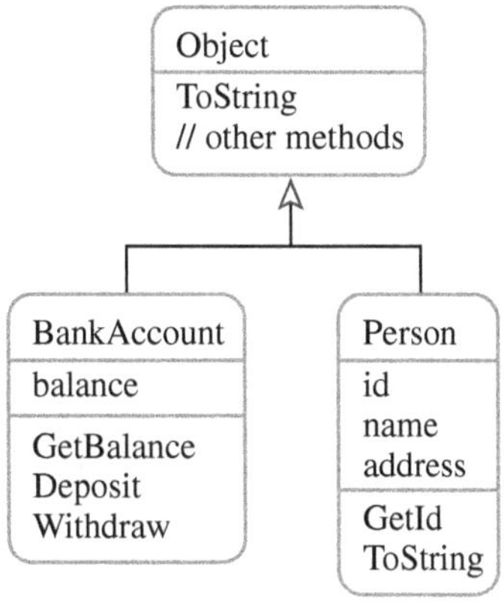

either of which will display the class name. Any class that should have a string representation should override the `ToString` method as we did in Example 6.3 for the `Name`, `Address`, and `Person` classes. Figure 10.4 shows the `BankAccount` class inheriting the `ToString` method from `Object`, while the `Person` class overrides it.

The BIG Picture

The base class contains data and operations common to all derived classes. Rather than duplicating these fields in each derived class, we let the derived classes inherit them from the base class. A derived class can override inherited virtual methods and add additional methods and data fields.

Inheritance supports the IS-A relationship in which a derived class object is also a type of base class object.

✓Test Your Understanding

1. Each class, except `Object`, derives from another class either implicitly or explicitly. For each of the following classes, from which class does it derive?
   - **a.** `SavingsAccount` **b.** `String`
   - **c.** `BankAccount` **d.** `Address`
   - **e.** `CheckingAccount`
2. Declare and initialize a `SavingsAccount`, `s`, with an initial balance of \$50.00 and an interest rate of 3.5 percent.
3. Declare and initialize a `CheckingAccount`, `c`, which requires a minimum balance of \$1500 to avoid the 35 cent service charge per check.
4. Describe the output from each of the following, where `s` is the `SavingsAccount` defined in question 2, and

```
Name president = new Name("Abraham", "Lincoln");
```

```
String s3 = "horse";
```

a. `Console.WriteLine(s);`

b. `Console.WriteLine(s3);`

c. `Console.WriteLine(president);`

5. Suppose we add a `Withdraw` method to the `SavingsAccount` class, using the pattern

```
public double Withdraw(double amount, bool receipt)
    { ... },
```

which would perform the withdrawal giving a receipt if the bool variable `receipt` is `true`. Would we be overriding the `Withdraw` method of the `BankAccount` base class or overloading it? Explain.

10.2 POLYMORPHISM

With **polymorphism** we get the benefit of letting each type of object define its own behavior. Our programs ask objects to do something, but each does that operation in its own way. Our programs are easier to create and maintain because we leave to the objects the details of how to perform their operations.

Polymorphic Operations

When we say "that animal is eating," it could mean that a lion is tearing flesh from its kill or that a giraffe is munching tree leaves. Each derived class of `Animal` has its own way of eating. The eating operation is **polymorphic**, meaning that it has many structures. A lion implements it in one way, a giraffe does something quite different, but they both eat.

Most of us do not talk to animals, but if we did, we could command `animal1 Eat, animal2 Eat,...` and so on. Each animal knows how to eat and will do so in its own way. We do not even have to know what kind of animals we are talking to, or how they eat. Our command is like a program that will execute correctly, even if other animals come along later that we had not known about. We say `animal902 Eat`, and it eats because it knows how to eat.

Our command program would not be nearly as flexible if we had to know the type of each animal. We could start commanding `lion Eat`, `giraffe Eat`, but this program only works for a lion followed by a giraffe and does not allow for any other type of animal. Our earlier command was more flexible because we used the base class type `Animal` in our command, rather than the derived class types `Lion` and `Giraffe`.

Compile-Time and Runtime Types

Our common usage shows that we talk of animals in general, but of course each animal is really a specific type such as a lion or a giraffe. In C# we distinguish between the compile-time type of an object variable and its runtime type.

- `Compile-time type` The variable's declared type
- `Runtime type` The type of the object to which the variable currently refers

FIGURE 10.5
Illustrating polymorphism

```
public void Feed(Animal[] theZoo) {
     for (int i = 0; i < theZoo.Length; i++)
          theZoo[i].Eat();
}
```

The runtime type may be the same as the compile-time type or it may be any derived class of it. For example, if we declare

```
Animal herman;
```

herman has the compile-time type Animal. After the code

```
herman = new Lion();
```

`herman` has the runtime type `Lion`, because the variable `herman` refers to a `Lion`. This assignment works because every lion is an animal. An assignment such as `Lion leo = new Animal()` would in general not be valid, because every animal is not a lion.

Inheritance allows us to assign a derived class object to a base class variable. It works because a derived class object is also a base class object. A `Lion` is an `Animal`. Later on in code we might include the lines

```
Animal zelda;
zelda  = new Giraffe();
```

`zelda` has the compile-time type `Animal`, and the runtime type `Giraffe`, which is also an `Animal`.

The power of polymorphism comes when we write code that is very general and easy to maintain. Figure 10.5 shows a `Feed` method that will feed any type of animal.

We can use the `Feed` method to feed lions or giraffes or any kind of animal. For example, we feed `herman` and `zelda` using the code

```
Animal[] two = {herman, zelda};
Feed(two);
```

When C# executes the `Feed` method it uses the runtime type of each array element to determine which method to call. If `theZoo[i]` refers to a `Lion`, it calls the `Lion Eat` method, but if it refers to a `Giraffe` it calls the `Giraffe Eat`. As programmers, we do not have to distinguish one animal from another. We let each object eat in its own way.

We must remember, however, that any method that we expect to work for each derived class must occur in the common base class.

TIP

Suppose we try another command,

```
theZoo[i].BrushTeeth();
```

If `theZoo[i]` refers to our brother, this command might be diligently executed, but if `theZoo[i]` refers to a lion, that lion might show us his teeth, but he would not be brushing them. Not every animal brushes its teeth. To use specialized methods we must declare the object to have the derived class type containing those methods. For example, to use an `attack` method that a `Lion` has but not a `Giraffe`, we use the code

```
Lion salina = new Lion();
salina.attack();
```

The `attack` method does not apply to all animals. ■

Example 10.9 illustrates polymorphism with the simplified `Animal` hierarchy for clarity. We provide a first version of an `Animal` class, which we will revise when we discuss abstract classes.

EXAMPLE 10.9 ■ Animal.cs, Lion.cs, Giraffe.cs, UseAnimals.cs

Animal.cs

```
/* A first version of the Animal class.
 */

public class Animal {
  public virtual void Eat() {                          // Note 1
  }
}
```

Lion.cs

```
/* Lions eat and attack.  The Lion class overrides the Animal
 * Eat method, and adds an Attack method.
 */

using System;
public class Lion : Animal {
  public override void Eat() {                         // Note 2
    Console.WriteLine("Eating like a lion");
  }
  public void Attack() {                               // Note 3
    Console.WriteLine("Attacking like a lion");
  }
}
```

Giraffe.cs

```
/* Giraffes eat and look around.  The Giraffe class overrides
 * Animal Eat and adds a LookAround method.
 */

using System;
```

```
public class Giraffe : Animal {
  public override void Eat() {
    Console.WriteLine("Eating like a giraffe");
  }
  public void LookAround() {
    Console.WriteLine("Looking around like a giraffe");
  }
}
```

UseAnimals.cs

```
/* Uses Animal objects polymorphically.
 */

public class UseAnimals {
  public static void Feed(Animal[] theZoo) {
    for (int i= 0; i < theZoo.Length; i++)
       theZoo[i].Eat();
  }
  public static void Main() {
    Lion herman = new Lion();
    Giraffe zelda = new Giraffe();
    Animal[] two = {herman, zelda};
    Feed(two);                                      // Note 4
    herman.Attack();                                // Note 5
  }
}
```

Output

```
Eating like a lion
Eating like a giraffe
Attacking like a lion
```

Note 1: `public virtual void Eat() {`

We implement the `Eat` method to do nothing, because `Animal` is a general category with no method of eating that applies to it.

Note 2: `public override void Eat() {`

`Lion` overrides the `Eat` method of `Animal` to eat like a lion. We omit more realistic descriptions of lions eating.

Note 3: `public void Attack() {`

We add the specialized `Attack` method to the `Lion` class. Because it does not occur in the `Animal` class we cannot invoke it for an object declared as an `Animal`.

Note 4: `Feed(two);`

The `Feed` method is very general. It runs through its array argument, invoking the `Eat` method for each `Animal`. At runtime, .NET determines what each array element refers to and calls the correct `Eat` method. Because `herman` refers to a `Lion`, .NET will call the `Lion Eat` method rather than `Animal Eat`. For `zelda`, .NET will call `Giraffe Eat`. Because .NET determines which method to call while the program is running, we call this process **dynamic binding**.

Note 5: `herman.Attack();`

Because we declared `leo` to have type `Lion`, we can call the specialized `Attack` method. We cannot call the `Attack` method for `herman`, because we declared `herman` to have type `Animal`. The compile-time type determines which method we can invoke for an object.

To appreciate the advantages of polymorphism, we show that the same `Feed` method works even if we add a new type of `Animal`. We add a `Duck` class and create a new `Animal` array including a duck. Our test program shows that the `Feed` method needs no changes to work correctly.

EXAMPLE 10.10 ■ Duck.cs, UseNewAnimal.cs

Duck.cs

```
/* A Duck eats.  The Eat method overrides Animal Eat.
 */

using System;
public class Duck : Animal {
  public override void Eat() {
    Console.WriteLine("Eating like a duck");
  }
}
```

UseNewAnimal.cs

```
/* Shows that the Feed method works unchanged
 * when ducks are included.
 */

public class UseNewAnimal {
  public static void Feed(Animal[] theZoo) {
    for (int i = 0; i < theZoo.Length; i++)
       theZoo[i].Eat();                                    // Note 1
  }
  public static void Main() {
```

```
    Animal herman = new Lion();
    Animal zelda = new Giraffe();
    Animal don = new Duck();
    Animal[] three = {herman, zelda, don};
    Feed(three);
  }
}
```

Output

```
Eating like a lion
Eating like a giraffe
Eating like a duck
```

Note 1: `theZoo[i].Eat();`

.NET will check at runtime to determine what type of `Animal` each array element references. It will call the correct `Eat` method. The programmer of the `feed` method does not have to know how each `Animal` eats. Each derived class of `Animal` implements the `eat` method in the manner appropriate for it.

The `BankAccount` Hierarchy

Now that we have illustrated polymorphism using `Animal` and its derived classes, we return to the `BankAccount` hierarchy. We cannot make our bank accounts eat, but we can make withdrawals. To use polymorphism, we refer to all our accounts using the base class type `BankAccount`. After all, every `SavingsAccount` or `CheckingAccount` is a `BankAccount`, just as every lion or giraffe is an animal.

Suppose we have several `BankAccount` objects, `b1`, `b2`, and `b3`. We can command them to withdraw $50 each with the statements

```
b1.Withdraw(50.00);
b2.Withdraw(50.00);
b3.Withdraw(50.00);
```

We do not have to know what kind of bank accounts `b1`, `b2`, and `b3` are, because every bank account knows how to withdraw, just as every animal knows how to eat. This is the beauty of object-oriented programming—each object implements its own behavior.

If `b1` happens to be a checking account, it will deduct a service charge if the balance is below the minimum for free checking; we just ask it to withdraw, and trust `b1` to know how to process a `Withdraw` request. Our little program is quite flexible. We can apply it at some future time when we have written a `TimedAccount` derived class of `BankAccount` that overrides the `Withdraw` method to prohibit withdrawals. If `b2` happens to refer to a `TimedAccount`, then .NET will execute the `Withdraw` method defined in the `TimedAccount` class.

The `Withdraw` operation has many structures, depending on which derived class of `BankAccount` is processing the withdrawal. As we saw with animals, to

FIGURE 10.6 **Two `BankAccount` objects**

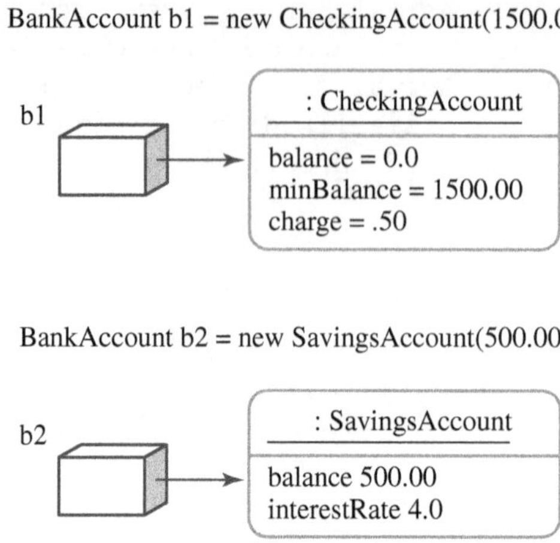

get the flexibility of polymorphism, we need to refer to objects by their base class type. We start by creating two `BankAccount` objects (see Figure 10.6).

We declare `b1` with type `BankAccount`, but actually assign it a value of type `CheckingAccount`, which is a subtype of `BankAccount`. Similarly, we declare `b2` with type `BankAccount`, but assign it a `SavingsAccount`. If we make a deposit and withdrawals

```
b1.Deposit(400.00);
b1.Withdraw(50.00);
b2.Withdraw(50.00);
```

`b1` will process the `Withdraw` using `CheckingAccount Withdraw`, deducting a service charge, but `b2` will process the `Withdraw` using `SavingsAccount Withdraw` (inherited from `BankAccount`), not deducting a service charge.

If we now change `b2` to refer to the `CheckingAccount` to which `b1` refers, and then do a withdrawal, as in

```
b2 = b1;
b2.Withdraw(50.00);
```

the account `b2` will now process the withdrawal using `CheckingAccount Withdraw`, and will deduct a service charge because, as shown in Figure 10.7, `b2` refers to a checking account.

FIGURE 10.7
Variable `b2` refers to a checking account

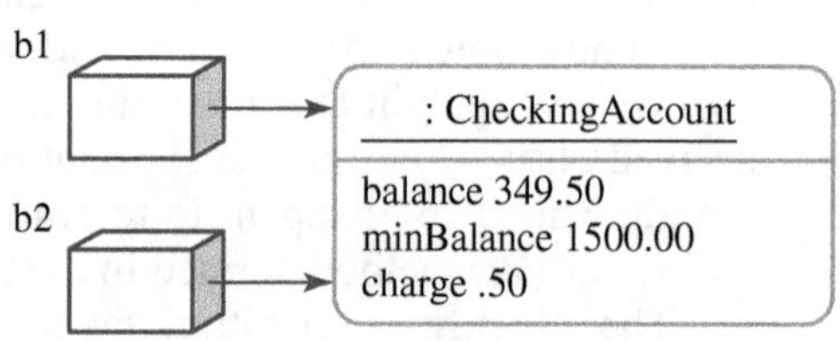

As the program is running, .NET determines to which type object the variable `b2` refers and invokes the `Withdraw` method for that type.

EXAMPLE 10.11 ■ Withdraw.cs

```
/* Uses the Withdraw operation of BankAccount and its
 * derived classes to illustrate polymorphism.
 */

using System;
public class Withdraw {
  public static void Main() {
    BankAccount b1 = new CheckingAccount(1500.00,.50); // Note 1
    BankAccount b2 = new SavingsAccount(500.00, 4.0);
    b1.Deposit(400.00);
    b1.Withdraw(50.00);                                 // Note 2
    Console.WriteLine("The balance of the BankAccount "
     + "to which b1 refers is {0:C}", b1.GetBalance());
    b2.Withdraw(50.00);                                 // Note 3
    Console.WriteLine("The balance of the BankAccount "
     + "to which b2 refers is {0:C}", b2.GetBalance());
    b2 = b1;                                            // Note 4
    b2.Withdraw(50.00);                                 // Note 5
    Console.WriteLine("The balance of the BankAccount "
     + "to which b2 refers is {0:C}", b2.GetBalance());
  }
}
```

Output

```
The balance of the BankAccount to which b1 refers is $349.50
The balance of the BankAccount to which b2 refers is $450.00
The balance of the BankAccount to which b2 refers is $299.00
```

■

Note 1: `BankAccount b1 = new CheckingAccount(1500.00,.50);`

The key to using polymorphism is to declare objects of a general base class type but assign instances of various derived classes. We do that here, declaring `b1` to have type `BankAccount`, but assigning it an object of type `CheckingAccount`.

Note 2: `b1.Withdraw(50.00);`

Because `b1` refers to a `CheckingAccount`, `Withdraw` deducts a service charge.

Note 3: `b2.Withdraw(50.00);`

Because b2 currently refers to a SavingsAccount, Withdraw does not deduct a service charge.

Note 4: `b2 = b1;`

We change b2 to refer to a CheckingAccount.

Note 5: `b2.Withdraw(50.00);`

Because b2 now refers to a CheckingAccount, the Withdraw deducts a service charge. In this example, the variable b2 refers to some bank account object, either a SavingsAccount or a CheckingAccount. This example shows that we can change this reference during the course of the program among various derived classes of BankAccount, which is the declared type of b2.

We illustrated polymorphism with animals eating and withdrawals from bank accounts. Every bank account can process a withdrawal and every animal can eat. Just as we cannot expect every animal to brush its teeth, we cannot expect every bank account to process a check. Only a CheckingAccount has a ProcessCheck method. If we declare b as a BankAccount, we can call methods only of the BankAccount class, even though b might actually refer to a CheckingAccount at some point in the code. For example, given the code

```
BankAccount b;
           . . .
b = new CheckingAccount(750.00, .75);
           . . .
b.ProcessCheck(50.00);        // rejected
```

C# will reject the ProcessCheck statement. We declared b to have type BankAccount, which cannot always process a check. At runtime b might actually refer to a CheckingAccount, which can process a check, but then again it might refer to a SavingsAccount, which cannot. The C# compiler stops us from making a fatal runtime error, allowing only a method like Deposit or Withdraw that every account can execute.

If we want to use methods that apply only to a certain type of account, then we should declare our objects to be of that type. For example, declaring b to be a CheckingAccount will allow us to execute b.ProcessCheck.

The BIG Picture

Polymorphism is one of the key benefits of object-oriented programming. A statement such as animal.Eat() will apply to objects of any derived class of animal, such as lions and giraffes, and will apply to those objects yet to be defined, such as ducks. Such code needs less modification because it is independent of the details of how each type of animal eats, which are left to the derived classes to implement.

✓ Test Your Understanding

6. If we declare `b` as in

```
BankAccount b = new CheckingAccount(1500.00,.50);
```

which of the following will generate a compiler error?

a. `b.Deposit(100.00);`

b. `b.ProcessCheck(25.25);`

c. `b.PostInterest();`

d. `b.GetBalance();`

e. `b.Withdraw(75.00);`

7. If we declare `b` as in

```
CheckingAccount b = new CheckingAccount(1500.00,.50);
```

which of the method calls of question 6 will generate a compiler error?

10.3 ABSTRACT CLASSES

Abstract classes let us talk about operations in general without creating instances. They may defer implementation details to concrete derived classes. For example, nothing is just an `Animal`. Every animal is a member of some derived class such as `Lion` or `Giraffe`. The class `Animal` has no instances, in contrast to the class `Lion`, which has various, perhaps ferocious, instances.

Declaring an Abstract Class

C# uses the modifier `abstract` to denote that a class cannot have any instances. Figure 10.8 revises the `Animal` class to be abstract. The only change we make to the `Animal` class in Example 10.9 is to add the `abstract` modifier in the class declaration.

By making `Animal` abstract, we prohibit the creation of `Animal` objects. The code

```
Animal error = new Animal();        // incorrect
```

will not compile. Remember that `Animal` is a general concept. We never want just an `Animal`, but rather we would like one of its derived classes such as `Lion` or `Giraffe`.

FIGURE 10.8
Making the `Animal` class abstract

```
public abstract class Animal {
    public virtual void Eat() {
    }
}
```

We can declare an object whose compile-time type is an abstract class. The declaration

```
Animal anAnimal;
```

is legal. Until `anAnimal` refers to an object it has the value `null`. We can assign any concrete derived class of `Animal` to `anAnimal`. For example,

```
anAnimal = new Giraffe();
```

is legal. ■

Polymorphism and Abstract Classes

Polymorphism does not require abstract classes but often works together with them. We use an abstract class to specify the behavior common to a number of concrete classes, just as the `Animal` class specifies that every `Animal` can eat. Programs that use the operations of the abstract class will work for objects of any class derived from that class. We saw in Example 10.10 that the `Feed` method continued to work with `Duck` objects that were not even created when `Feed` was first used in Example 10.9 with `Lion` and `Giraffe` objects.

In retrospect, now that we have `SavingsAccount` and `CheckingAccount` classes, our `BankAccount` class might be better defined to have no instances. We never want an object that is just a `BankAccount`; every account is either a `CheckingAccount` or a `SavingsAccount`. Declaring `BankAccount` using the pattern

```
public abstract class BankAccount { // same as before }
```

will cause the C# compiler to reject any attempts to instantiate `BankAccount` objects, as for example,

```
BankAccount b = new BankAccount(1000.00);   // rejected now
```

By using the `abstract` modifier we can make `BankAccount` an abstract class. Nevertheless, `BankAccount` implements the `Deposit`, `Withdraw`, and `GetBalance` methods, which its derived classes inherit. The `BankAccount` class implements all its methods. An abstract class can implement only some of its methods and leave others to be implemented by derived classes, as we will see when we develop the `Shape` class next.

A Shape Class

`Shape` is an abstract concept. Nothing is just a `Shape`, but `Shape` has derived classes such as `Line` and `Circle` that have instances. We define an abstract `Shape` class to allow programmers to work with shapes in general and get the advantages of polymorphism. We include in `Shape` the state and behavior that apply to all derived classes of `Shape` such as `Line` and `Circle`.

We will create every `Shape` with a point, which determines where it is located. The location point will have a specific interpretation for each derived class of `Shape`. The .NET Framework provides a `Point` class in the `System.Drawing` namespace that we can use for the location.

We want to be able to draw and move every concrete shape, so we add `Draw` and `Move` methods to the `Shape` class. To provide a `String` representation for every `Shape`, we override the `Object ToString` method in every derived class.

A `Shape` has no particular form, so we make the `draw` operation abstract, to be implemented only in derived classes of `Shape`. C# allows us to do this by using the `abstract` modifier, as in

```
public abstract void Draw();
```

which declares, but does not implement, the `Draw` method.

Declaring an abstract method is a good choice when we have no useful implementation in the base class and want to implement it only in derived classes. We could have declared the `Eat` method in the `Animal` class abstract

```
public abstract void Eat();
```

rather than implementing it with an empty body

```
public virtual void Eat() { }
```

The difference is:

- Abstract method: Concrete derived classes **must** override to provide an implementation
- Empty body: Concrete derived classes **may** override to provide an implementation **or** may inherit the empty body implementation

TIP

Any class that has an abstract method must be declared abstract using the `abstract` modifier. ■

Even though `Shape` is abstract, we can implement the `Move` method. When we move any `Shape` we must move its location. We pass two arguments to the `Move` method, the distances to move in the x- and y-directions. Every `Shape` moves by moving its `location` by the specified distances in each direction.

We use a `Point` constructor

```
public Point(int x, int y);
```

that creates a `Point`, given its `x` and `y` coordinates. The `Point` class overloads the + operator to translate itself by a given `Size`. Translating a point `p` at `(3,4)` by 2 in the x-direction and 5 in the y-direction, as in:

```
Point p = new Point(3,4);
p += new Size(2,5);
```

would move the point `p` to `(5,9)`.

We implement the `ToString` method to return the `String` representation of the location point of the `Shape` using the `ToString` method of the `Point` class. We will call this method in derived classes to display the locations of specific shapes.

FIGURE 10.9 **The abstract `Shape` class**

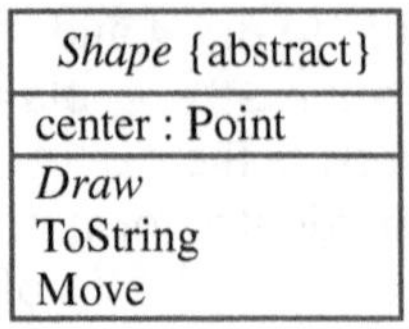

Figure 10.9 shows the diagram for the abstract `Shape` class. Using the UML notation, we italicize the class name and the abstract `Draw` method, and also designate `Shape` as abstract, using `{abstract}`.

EXAMPLE 10.12 ■ Shape.cs

```
/* Specifies state and behavior common to all shapes.
 */

using System;
using System.Drawing;
public abstract class Shape {                                  // Note 1
  protected Point location;                                    // Note 2

  public Shape() {                                             // Note 3
    location =  new Point(0,0);
  }
  public Shape(Point p) {
    location = p;
  }
  public abstract void Draw(Graphics g);                       // Note 4
  public virtual void Move(int xamount, int yamount){
    location += new Size(xamount,yamount);                     // Note 5
  }
  public override String ToString() {
    return location.ToString();                                // Note 6
  }
}
```

■

Note 1: `public abstract class Shape {`

The `abstract` modifier indicates that Shape will have no instances.

Note 2: `protected Point location;`

We use the `protected` modifier to make the location `Point` visible to derived classes. We discuss modifiers and access in Section 10.4. We could have used the `private` modifier and provided a public method, `GetLocation`, to access the location point.

Note 3: `public Shape() {`

The default constructor sets `location` to the origin, (0,0).

Note 4: `public abstract void Draw(Graphics g);`

We declare the `draw` method as abstract. Any class with an abstract method is an abstract class with no instances. Any derived class that we want to instantiate must implement the `Draw` method. We pass a `Graphics` argument to use the drawing methods it provides.

Note 5: `location += new Size(xamount,yamount);`

The overloaded `'+'` operator translates `location` by `(xamount, yamount)`.

Note 6: `location.ToString();`

Each `Shape` has a location. We return the `String` representation of `location`, which we will use in describing derived class shapes.

Because `Shape` is abstract, we cannot instantiate any `Shape` objects, but we can write a method that uses a `Shape` array. Figure 10.10 shows a `MoveDraw` method that takes a `Shape` array, the amounts to move in the x- and y-directions, and a `Graphics` object. It moves and draws each `Shape` in the array. The `MoveDraw` method will work for any derived classes of `Shape` that we choose to put into an array.

Line and Circle

The `Line` class extends `Shape`, adding an instance variable, `end`, of type `Point` to represent the other end of the line (the location point of the parent shape represents one end of the line). Because `Line` is a `Shape`, it inherits the `Shape Draw`, `Move`, and `ToString` methods. However, it overrides all three of them.

`Line` must override the abstract `Shape Draw`. It uses the `Graphics` object to draw the line from the `location` point to the `end` point. `Line` overrides the `Shape`

FIGURE 10.10
Moving and drawing shapes

```
public void MoveDraw
 (Shape[] theShapes,  int xAmount,  int yAmount,
                                       Graphics g) {
  for (int i  =  0; i < theShapes.Length; i++)  {
    theShapes[i].Move(xAmount, yAmount);
    theShapes[i].Draw(g);
  }
}
```

FIGURE 10.11 **The `UseShapes` screen**

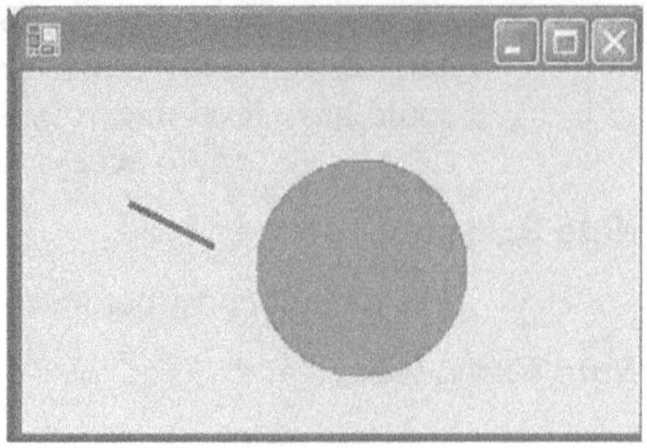

`Move` method by extending its function. To move a `Line` we must move both the `location` and the `end` points. The `Shape Move` method already moves the `location` point, so `Line Move` first calls `Shape Move` to move the `location`, and then moves the `end` point. This illustrates a common form of overriding in which the derived class extends the behavior of the base class.

The `Line` class overrides the `ToString` method to describe the line between the `location` and `end` points. It calls the base class `ToString` method to get the `String` representation of `location`, and calls the `ToString` method to display `end`. This illustrates a common technique of building on what was already done. When writing `ToString` methods, we use the `ToString` methods of the component parts of the object.

The `Circle` class extends `Shape`, adding an instance variable `radius` of type `int` to represent the radius. (The location point of the parent shape represents the center of the circle.) The `Circle` class inherits the `Shape Draw`, `Move`, and `ToString` methods. It must override `Shape Draw`. `Circle Draw` displays a circle with the given center and radius. `Circle` implements its own `ToString` method, using the base class `ToString` method in the process. The `Circle` class has no need to override the inherited `Move` method, which moves the location point by the specified amounts in the x- and y-directions.

Example 10.13 contains the `Line` and `Circle` classes and a `UseShapes` test program. To test, we create two shapes, assigning a line to the first and a circle to the second. Because the `Shape` class declares `Draw` and `Move` methods, the C# compiler lets each of our shapes invoke them. .NET, at runtime, finds the right version of each method. If we move a shape that is a line, then .NET executes the `Move` defined in the `Line` class. If we move a shape that is a circle, then .NET, realizing that circles inherit the `Move` operation from the `Shape` class, calls the `Move` method defined in the `Shape` class. Figure 10.11 shows the `UseShapes` screen.

EXAMPLE 10.13 ■ Line.cs, Circle.cs, UseShapes.cs

Line.cs

```
/*  Extends the Shape class.
 */
```

```
using System;
using System.Drawing;
public class Line : Shape {
  protected Point end;

  public Line(int x1, int y1, int x2, int y2)           // Note 1
                          : base(new Point(x1,y1)) {    // Note 2
    end = new Point(x2,y2);
  }
  public override void Draw(Graphics g) {
    Pen blue = new Pen(Color.Blue, 3);
    g.DrawLine(blue, location, end);                    // Note 3
  }
  public override String ToString() {
    return  "Line from " + base.ToString()
                             + " to " + end;            // Note 4
  }
  public override void Move(int xamount, int yamount) {
    base.Move(xamount,yamount);
    end += new Size(xamount,yamount);
  }
}
```

Circle.cs

```
/* Extends the Shape class.
 */

using System;
using System.Drawing;
public class Circle : Shape {
  int radius;

  public Circle(Point p, int r) : base(p){
    radius = r;
  }
  public override void Draw(Graphics g) {
    g.FillEllipse(Brushes.Red, location.X-radius,
          location.Y-radius, 2*radius, 2*radius);      // Note 5
  }
  public override string ToString() {
    return "Circle at " + base.ToString()
                    + " with radius " + radius;
  }
}
```

UseShapes.cs

```
/* Moves and draws an array of Shapes polymorphically.
 */

using System;
using System.Drawing;
using System.Windows.Forms;
public class UseShapes : Form{
  Shape[] s = new Shape[2];                              // Note 6

  public void MoveDraw(Shape[] theShapes, int xAmount,
                       int yAmount, Graphics g) {
    for (int i = 0; i < theShapes.Length; i++)  {
       theShapes[i].Move(xAmount, yAmount);
       theShapes[i].Draw(g);
    }
  }
  public UseShapes( ) {
    Size = new Size(300,200);
    s[0] = new Line(20,50,60,70);                        // Note 7
    s[1] = new Circle( new Point(130,80) ,50);
    Console.WriteLine(s[1]);
  }
  protected override void OnPaint(PaintEventArgs e){
     Graphics g = e.Graphics;
     MoveDraw(s, 30, 10, g);                             // Note 8
     base.OnPaint(e);
  }
  static void Main() {
     Application.Run(new UseShapes());
  }
}
```

Note 1: `public Line(int x1, int y1, int x2, int y2)`

We pass the `x`- and `y`-coordinates of the two endpoints of the line. Alternatively, we could have defined the constructor to accept two `Point` arguments.

Note 2: `: base(new Point(x1,y1)) {`

When constructing a derived class, we often call the base class constructor to construct the base class part of the object. Here we call the `Shape` constructor to initialize the `location` point. It would be a mistake to omit this call, because C# will call the default `Shape` constructor, which initializes the `location` to `(0,0)` instead of `(x1,y1)`.

Because the `Shape` constructor requires a `Point` argument, we create a `Point` from `x1` and `y1`.

Note 3:
```
g.DrawLine(blue, location, end);
```

We use an overloaded version of the `DrawLine` method that accepts `Point` arguments.

Note 4:
```
return  "Line from " + base.ToString()
                        + " to " + end;
```

When an object such as `end` appears as an argument of a `String` concatenation, C# automatically calls its `ToString` method to obtain its `String` representation.

Note 5:
```
g.FillEllipse(Brushes.Red, location.X-radius,
          location.Y-radius, 2*radius, 2*radius);
```

The point `(location.X-radius, location.Y-radius)` gives the upper-left corner of the square surrounding the circle we want to draw. The side of the bounding square is `2*radius`.

Note 6:
```
Shape[] s = new Shape[2];
```

We create an array of two references, which C# initializes to null. We declare the references to the abstract `Shape` class, but the objects we create for these references will have types that are concrete derived classes of `Shape`, such as `Line` or `Circle`.

Note 7:
```
s[0] =new Line(20,50,60,70);
```

The line has coordinates (20,50) and (60,70).

Note 8:
```
MoveDraw(s, 30, 10, g);
```

.NET determines at runtime that `s[0]` refers to a `Line` and calls the correct version of `Move` from the `Line` class. Because `s[0]` refers to a `Line`, .NET calls the `Draw` method from the `Line` class, which is no longer abstract. Because `s[1]` refers to a `Circle`, .NET uses the `Move` method inherited from `Shape`. Because `s[1]` refers to a `Circle`, .NET calls the `Draw` method defined in `Circle`.

The BIG Picture

By declaring a reference, `s`, as an abstract `Shape`, we can ask it to draw or move

```
s.Draw(g);     s.Move(30,40);
```

leaving the details of how a concrete shape, such as a line, moves or draws itself to the details of the implementation of the derived class. The same operations will apply to any derived class of `Shape`, even those, such as `Rectangle`, `Polygon`, or `Ellipse`, which we have not yet defined.

Our program will depend on the abstract class, which is less likely to change than are the details of the concrete derived classes that extend it.

Try It Yourself ➤

✓Test Your Understanding

8. What will be the result if we declare the Shape class of Example 10.12 without the abstract modifier, declaring it as shown here?

   ```
   public class Shape { // same as Example 10.12 };
   ```

   Revise Example 10.12 to omit the modifier at that position. Does the compiler allow this change?

9. Will the Shape class of Example 10.12 still be abstract if we revise that example to implement the Draw method in the Shape class to return the String representation of a Shape? Explain.

10. Where does the point p, where p = new Point(3,4), move to as a result of p += new Size(-1,6)?

✓

10.4 MODIFIERS AND ACCESS

In a library we may use reference books such as encyclopedias but not take them home, whereas we are encouraged to borrow nonreference books to read at home. Rare books may be restricted to scholars with special credentials. Just as access to library books varies, access to C# classes, data fields, and methods also can vary. C# uses the **modifiers** public, protected internal, protected, internal, and private to specify the type of access.

Class Visibility

We can declare a class using the public modifier, as in

```
public class A { ... }
```

or without any modifier, as in

```
class B { ... }
```

We can access a public class from other programs, but we can access a class that lacks the public modifier only from the program in which it is defined. We say that a class declared without the public modifier has internal visibility, meaning that it is visible only in its own program.

The significance of the public modifier shows up only if we want to use a class outside of the program it is in. For example, we used the BankAccount class in example 10.11, Withdraw.cs. Had we omitted the public modifier from the BankAccount declaration we would not have been able to reference the BankAccount class in Example 10.11. .NET library classes such as the String class are public. If they were not, we could not have used them.

Data Field and Method Visibility

We declare data fields and methods using one of the modifiers public, protected internal, protected, internal, or private to specify the type of access we

FIGURE 10.13
Access modifiers for data fields and methods

`public`	Accessible anywhere the class name is accessible
`protected internal`	Accessible in derived classes and in the program in which the data field or method is declared
`protected`	Accessible in derived classes
`internal`	Accessible in the program in which the data field or method is declared
`private`	Accessible only in the class in which the data field or method is declared

want for that data field or method. Figure 10.13 lists these modifiers with the least restrictive at the top and the most restrictive at the bottom.

Access to Data Fields

In our examples we usually make data fields private to hide the data, allowing users to access it only by means of the public methods of the class. When we define a class that we expect to be a base class of various derived classes, we have to decide how we would like these derived classes to have access to data of the base class. Had we declared the location `Point` as private in the `Shape` class of Example 10.12, then the `Draw` methods of derived classes `Line` and `Circle` would not have had access to the `location` variable.

In Example 10.12, we declared the location `Point` as `protected`. Another choice would be to declare `location` with `private` access, and include a method, `GetLocation`, as in

```
public Point GetLocation() {
  return location;
}
```

which would allow all users of shapes to get the value of `location`. The `Draw` method of the `Line` class could use `GetLocation` to find the location point, as in

```
g.DrawLine(blue, GetLocation(), end);
```

Comparing these two choices, using `protected` lets any derived class use the `location` field directly. We have no knowledge of who might write a class derived from ours. Because a class has no way to know which classes may have extended it, it has no way to communicate a change in its data representation to derived classes that have access to protected data fields. For example, if we later changed the representation to use x- and y-coordinates for the location instead of a `Point`, all derived classes of `Shape` would have to be revised.

Making the data private ensures that no other class can use the data directly. The developer can change the data without affecting any users as long as the public methods remain the same. This approach requires a method such as

GetLocation() if users need to read the data, and another method such as SetLocation() if users need to change the data.

The internal modifier would be used by the developer of a program for data needed only in development but not intended for the end user. Such data could be shared among classes in the program but would be hidden from end users. Using public has drawbacks when applied to data fields. Any user of the class can modify public data. We would like our classes to provide a carefully chosen interface using public operations, following the model of primitive types which we access using operations such as + and *, never using the representation of the primitive data.

TIP

Avoiding public or protected data fields allows you to change the representation of the data without affecting users of your class. Anyone can derive a class and access protected data. Such code would break if we changed the data type. Provide methods if users need to access the data. ■

Access to Methods

Most often we make methods public. An object's methods provide its behavior for others to use. Our public Draw, Move, and ToString methods allow users to perform these operations on any shape. Class developers might use a private method to help implement the public methods.

TIP

Make any methods private that are not intended for users of the class. Such a method might use an algorithm to help implement the public methods. You can change a private method later to use a better algorithm, knowing that no users of the class will be affected. ■

TIP

Protected methods also have their uses. For example, if we declare the location instance variable of the Shape class of Example 10.12 using the private modifier, we could declare GetCenter and SetCenter methods using the protected modifier, as in

```
protected Point GetLocation() {
  return location;
}
protected void SetLocation(Point p) {
  location = p;
}
```

which would limit access to these methods to derived classes of Shape. ■

Example 10.14 illustrates the use of the access modifiers for classes, data fields, and methods. We put classes A and B in one program. Class A is public, but B has no modifier, which gives it internal visibility by default. Inside A we declare data fields and methods with each of the five kinds of access. In the following examples we show in which classes these data fields and methods will be visible. We demonstrate the difference in visibility between the public class `A` and the internal class `B`.

The program `A.cs` contains declarations for classes `A` and `B`. Each has a `Main` method. When compiling, we need to indicate which `Main` we wish to use. To use the `Main` from class `A`, we compile with

```
csc /m:A A.cs
```

EXAMPLE 10.14 ■ A.cs

```
/* Public class A declares data fields and methods
 * with each of the five access modifiers to illustrate
 * their use. Class B, not public, will be visible only
 * in this program.
 */

using System;
public class A {                                          // Note 1
  public int d1 = 1;                                      // Note 2
  protected internal int d2 = 2;
  protected int d3 = 3;
  internal int d4 = 4;
  private int d5 = 5;

  public int get1() {
    return d1;
  }
  protected internal int get2() {
    return d2;
  }
  protected int get3() {
    return d3;
  }
  internal int get4() {
    return d4;
  }
  private int get5() {
    return d5;
  }
  public int usePrivate(){                                // Note 3
    return d5 + get5();
  }
  public static void Main() {
    A a = new A();
    B b = new B();                                        // Note 4
```

```
      int i,j;
      i = a.d1 + a.d2 + a.d3 + a.d4 + a.d5
                              + b.d6 + a.usePrivate();    // Note 5
      j = a.get1() + a.get2() + a.get3()
                              + a.get4() + a.get5();
      Console.WriteLine("i is " + i + " and j is " + j);
    }
  }
  class B {                                               // Note 6
    public int d6 = 6;
    public static void Main() {
      A a = new A();
      B b = new B();
      int i,j;
      i = a.d1 + a.d2 + a.d4 + b.d6 + a.usePrivate();     // Note 7
      j = a.get1() + a.get2() + a.get4();
      Console.WriteLine("i is " + i + " and j is " + j);
    }
  }
```

Output (using Main from A)

```
i is 31 and j is 15
```

Output (using Main from B)

```
i is 23 and j is 7
```

Note 1: `public class A {`

The public class `A` will be visible everywhere.

Note 2: `public int d1 = 1;`

We declare five variables and five methods using each of the five modifiers. We will see which we can access in classes `A`, `B`, `C`, and `D` in this and in later examples.

Note 3: `public int usePrivate(){`

We can directly access the private `d5` and `Get5` only in `A`, but we can access a public method that uses them anywhere.

Note 4: `B b = new B();`

We can access `B` here because class `A` is in the same program as class `B`.

Note 5:
```
i = a.d1 + a.d2 + a.d3 + a.d4 + a.d5
                         + b.d6 + a.usePrivate();
```

Inside class A we can access all the variables and methods of A, including those that are private.

Note 6: Declared with no modifier, the class B is visible only in its program. The public d6 is visible anywhere B is.

Note 7: `i = a.d1 + a.d2 + a.d4 + b.d6 + a.usePrivate();`

In class B we cannot access d3 because B is not derived from A. We cannot access the private field d5. Both d2 and d4 specify internal access by the class B in the same program as class A.

Example 10.15 contains a class C derived from class A to illustrate the access to protected fields in derived classes. We compile using

```
csc /r:A.exe C.cs
```

EXAMPLE 10.15 ■ C.cs

```
/* Class C derives from A.  It can use fields that
 * specify public, protected, or protected internal
 * access.
 */

using System;
public class C : A {
  public new static void Main() {
    A a = new A();
    C c = new C();
    int i,j;
    i = a.d1 + c.d2 + c.d3 + a.usePrivate();          // Note 1
    j = a.get1() + c.get2() + c.get3();
    Console.WriteLine("i is " + i + " and j is " + j);
  }
}
```

Output

```
i is 16 and j is 6
```

■

Note 1: `i = a.d1 + c.d2 + c.d3 + a.usePrivate();`

Class C can use the public fields of class A from an instance of A. It can access the protected and protected internal fields of A, but only from an instance of the derived class C.

Example 10.16 contains a class D that is neither in the same program as A nor derived from A. It can only access public fields of A.

EXAMPLE 10.16 ■ D.cs

```
/* Class D can only use public data
 * and methods from A.
 */

using System;
public class D {
  public static void Main() {
    A a = new A();
    int i,j;
    i = a.d1 + a.usePrivate();
    j = a.get1();
    Console.WriteLine("i is " + i + " and j is " + j);
  }
}
```

Output

```
i is 11 and j is 1
```

■

The BIG Picture

Classes declared internal (implicitly by omitting the public modifier or explicitly) may be used only in the same program. Instance variables and methods can have five levels of access. Usually data is private. Methods representing the behavior of the object are public, but the other access modes have their uses.

✓Test Your Understanding

11. Example 10.12 uses the `Point` class from the `System.Drawing` namespace. Without looking at the source, can you tell whether or not `Point` is declared using the `public` modifier? Why or why not?

12. In Example 10.14, what is the difference in accessibility to `d2` compared with accessibility to `d3`?

13. In Example 10.14, what is the difference in accessibility to `Get2()` compared with accessibility to `Get4()`?

14. Explain why the field `d6`, declared public in Example 10.14, is not visible in either class `C` or `D`.

10.5 ■ (OPTIONAL) OBJECT-ORIENTED DESIGN WITH USE CASES AND SCENARIOS

In object-oriented programming we solve our problem by identifying objects, each having certain responsibilities, and let these objects use each other's services. Each object's methods provide that object's services, which allow it to meet its responsibilities.

To identify the objects we analyze the system using use cases and scenarios. Each **use case** describes one function that the system should provide. For each use case, we develop several **scenarios**, which are step-by-step listings of the interactions among the user and other parts of the system, to provide the function described by that use case. Usually, for each use case there will be a primary scenario, which represents the interactions for a successful use, and several secondary scenarios representing the various errors that might occur.

Defining the Problem

For our example case study we will develop a simple automatic teller application. A user of the system should be able to choose an account, either savings or checking, and make deposits to, withdrawals from, or get the balance of that account. For simplicity, we assume that each user has at most one account of each type.

Developing Scenarios

For the automatic teller system our use cases consist of the deposit, withdrawal, and get balance transactions that the user can perform. To discover the objects we need, we can look at scenarios that represent each use case, first looking at scenarios that everything goes well, and then looking at some processing failures. Figure 10.14 describes a scenario for a successful deposit.

```
The user asks the teller to accept an ATM card.
The teller asks the user to enter a PIN.
The user asks the teller to accept a PIN.
The teller asks the user to select a transaction type.
The user asks the teller to accept a deposit.
The teller asks the user to select an account type.
The user asks the teller to accept a savings account type.
The teller asks the bank to find the account of the chosen
  type for the user with the specified PIN.
The bank gives the teller a reference to the account.
The teller asks the user to specify an amount.
The user asks the teller to accept an amount.
The teller asks the account to deposit the specified amount.
The teller asks the user to select another transaction....
```

FIGURE 10.14 **A scenario for a successful deposit**

```
The user asks the teller to accept an ATM card.
The teller asks the user to enter a PIN.
The user asks the teller to accept a PIN.
The teller asks the user to select a transaction type.
The user asks the teller to accept a get balance
  transaction.
The teller asks the user to select an account type.
The user asks the teller to accept a checking account type.
The teller asks the bank to find the account of the chosen
  type for the user with the specified PIN.
The bank gives the teller a null account.
The teller asks the user to select another transaction....
```

FIGURE 10.15 **A scenario when the specified account does not exist**

The scenario in Figure 10.14 involves four objects, `user`, `teller`, `bank`, and `account`. The user is an actor who interacts with the system via a user interface, which we model as an `AtmScreen`. We write an event-driven program that responds to user-generated events. For every successful scenario there are usually several scenarios in which something goes wrong. Figure 10.15 shows one of them, when no account exists of the type specified by the user.

We leave to the exercises the writing of other scenarios to explore possible uses (and misuses) of the automatic teller system.

Assigning Responsibilities

Using scenarios gives us an idea of the responsibilities for each object. Figure 10.16 shows these responsibilities.

Figure 10.17 shows the relationships between classes we have identified. Each line represents an association between the two classes it connects. These associations are evident from the scenarios in which one class makes a request of another.

Defining the Classes

We can define our classes and create methods to handle each of these responsibilities. The `AtmScreen` has methods to present the appropriate screen to the user to meet each of its responsibilities: entering a PIN, selecting a transaction type, selecting an account type, and specifying an amount. The `Teller` methods accept information from the user and the bank, and use the information to initiate the next step of the transaction. When the teller accepts the account from the bank, it can ask the account to execute a `GetBalance` transaction, but needs to wait for the user to enter the amount to deposit or withdraw before asking the account to execute one of these transactions. When a transaction is complete, the teller asks the user to select another transaction, until the user cancels the session.

FIGURE 10.16 **Objects and their responsibilities**

```
AtmScreen  Enter a PIN
           Select a transaction type
           Select an account type
           Specify an amount

Bank       Find a specified account

Account    Deposit
           Withdraw
           Get balance

Teller     Accept an ATM card
           Accept a PIN
           Accept a transaction type
           Accept an account type
           Accept an amount
           Accept an account
```

FIGURE 10.17 **Class associations**

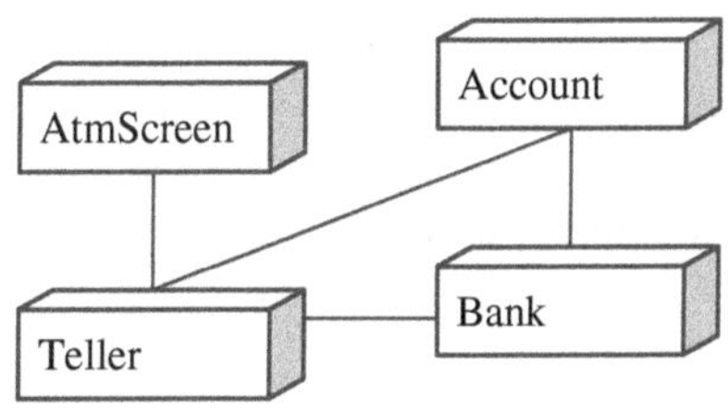

The `Account` class revises the `BankAccount` class of Example 5.1 by making `Account` abstract and adding a `Person` data field for the account holder. The `Savings` class revises class `SavingsAccount` of Example 10.5 to inherit from `Account` and accept a `Person` in its constructor. The `Checking` class revises class `CheckingAccount` of Example 10.7 to inherit from `Account` and accept a `Person` in its constructor.

Large systems use databases to hold account data. Here we simply create three accounts in the `Bank` class. When asked to find an account, the bank checks each account to see if the account ID matches the PIN specified by the user and if its type matches the type specified by the user.

We purposely avoid complicating the system. Obviously, a real ATM system would be orders of magnitude more complex. We omit any security considerations for entering PINs and greatly simplify the interactions with the bank. Normally the user would have an ID such as a social security number and a separate PIN for a bank account. We use only one identification number, which we store as the `id` field in the `Person` class. Each account has a `holder` field of type `Person`, which allows the bank to compare the PIN entered by the user to the `id` of the account holder.

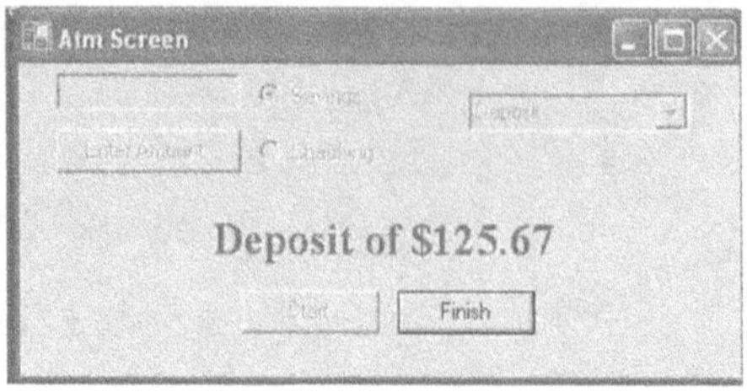

FIGURE 10.18
The `AtmScreen` application

Completing the C# Code

The event-driven, object-oriented programming style really becomes evident when we look at the event-handling methods, which provide the responses to user actions. The application waits for user actions, which cause objects to interact in fulfilling their responsibilities.

For the user interface, a text box allows the user to enter a name, a PIN, and an amount. Radio buttons let the user choose the type of account, and a combo box presents the types of transaction. *Start* and *Finish* buttons appear at the bottom.

Figure 10.18 shows the application after a user has made a deposit.

We find modeling with objects natural because it mirrors our world of objects, even though objects in our programs can also model abstractions not based on real-world analogies. The process of developing scenarios modifies the stepwise refinement process to apply to interacting objects. Traditional stepwise refinement is essential in implementing those methods of a class that use more complex algorithms.

EXAMPLE 10.17 ■ AtmScreen.cs

```
/* Illustrates event-driven object-oriented programming .
 */

using System;
using System.Drawing;
using System.Windows.Forms;
public class AtmScreen : Form {
  private Button start = new Button();
  private Button finish = new Button();
  private Button enter = new Button();
  private TextBox dataEntry = new TextBox();
  private RadioButton savings = new RadioButton();
  private RadioButton checking = new RadioButton();
  private ComboBox transaction = new ComboBox();
  private String message = "Welcome to Art's Bank";
  private Bank bank = new Bank();
  private Person[] person = Database.PersonData();
  private Teller teller;
```

```
private Font font = new Font(FontFamily.GenericSerif,
                                  18, FontStyle.Bold);

public AtmScreen() {

    // Set captions
  Text = "Atm Screen";
  start.Text = "Start";
  finish.Text = "Finish";
  savings.Text = "Savings";
  checking.Text = "Checking";
  enter.Text = "Enter Name";

    // Set sizes
  Size = new Size(400,200);
  enter.Width = 100;

    // Set locations
  int w = 20;
  dataEntry.Location = new Point(w, 5);
  enter.Location = new Point(w, 35);
  savings.Location = new Point(w += 10 + dataEntry.Width, 5);
  checking.Location = new Point(w, 35);
  transaction.Location =
                    new Point(w += 10 + savings.Width, 15);
  start.Location = new Point(120,120);
  finish.Location = new Point(130 + start.Width, 120);

    // Add transaction types
  transaction.Items.Add("Deposit");
  transaction.Items.Add("Withdraw");
  transaction.Items.Add("Balance");

    // Add controls to form
  Controls.Add(start);
  Controls.Add(finish);
  Controls.Add(dataEntry);
  Controls.Add(savings);
  Controls.Add(checking);
  Controls.Add(transaction);
  Controls.Add(enter);

  AcceptButton = enter;

    // Register event handlers
  enter.Click += new EventHandler(Enter_Click);
  start.Click += new EventHandler(Start_Click);
```

```
    finish.Click += new EventHandler(Finish_Click);
    savings.CheckedChanged += new EventHandler(Savings_Changed);
    checking.CheckedChanged
                      += new EventHandler(Checking_Changed);
    transaction.SelectedIndexChanged
                        += new EventHandler(Selected_Index);
    Clear();
  }
  protected void Enter_Click
                    (Object sender, EventArgs e){   // Note 1
    String s = enter.Text;
    if (s == "Enter Name"){                         // Note 2
      String name = dataEntry.Text;
      if (name == "John Venn")
        teller.AcceptCard(person[0]);
      else if (name == "Mabel Venn")
        teller.AcceptCard(person[1]);
      else {
        message = "Enter John Venn or Mabel Venn";
        dataEntry.Text = "";
        Invalidate();
      }
    }
    else if (s == "Enter PIN")
      teller.AcceptPIN(dataEntry.Text);
    else if (s == "Enter Amount")
      teller.AcceptAmount(double.Parse(dataEntry.Text));
  }
  protected void Finish_Click(Object sender, EventArgs e) {
    Clear();
  }
  protected void Start_Click(Object sender, EventArgs e) {
    dataEntry.Enabled = true;
    dataEntry.Focus();                              // Note 3
    enter.Enabled = true;
    start.Enabled = false;
    Invalidate();
  }
  protected void Selected_Index
                   (Object sender, EventArgs e) {   // Note 4
    teller.AcceptTransaction(transaction.SelectedIndex);
  }
  protected void Savings_Changed(Object sender, EventArgs e) {
    teller.AcceptType(Bank.SAVINGS);
  }
  protected void Checking_Changed(Object sender, EventArgs e) {
    teller.AcceptType(Bank.CHECKING);
  }
```

```
public void EnterPIN() {
  dataEntry.Text = "";
  enter.Text = "Enter PIN";
  message = "Enter your PIN number";
  Invalidate();
}
public void SelectTransaction() {
  dataEntry.Text = "";
  dataEntry.Enabled = false;                          // Note 5
  enter.Enabled = false;
  transaction.Enabled = true;
  message = "Select your transaction";
  Invalidate();
}
public void SelectType() {
  savings.Enabled = true;
  checking.Enabled = true;
  transaction.Enabled = false;
  message = "Select your account type";
  Invalidate();
}
public void SpecifyAmount() {
  dataEntry.Enabled = true;
  dataEntry.Focus();
  enter.Enabled = true;
  enter.Text = "Enter Amount";
  savings.Enabled = false;
  checking.Enabled = false;
  message = "Specify the amount";
  Invalidate();
}
public void Display(String s) {
  dataEntry.Text = "";
  enter.Enabled = false;
  dataEntry.Enabled = false;
  checking.Enabled = false;
  savings.Enabled = false;
  message = s;
  Invalidate();
}
public void Clear() {                                 // Note 6
  start.Enabled = true;
  savings.Enabled = false;
  checking.Enabled = false;
  transaction.Enabled = false;
  enter.Text = "Enter Name";
  enter.Enabled = false;
  dataEntry.Text = "";
```

```
    dataEntry.Enabled = false;
    message = "Welcome to Art's bank";
    Invalidate();
    teller = new Teller(bank,this);
  }
  protected override void OnPaint(PaintEventArgs e){
    Graphics g = e.Graphics;
    int w = (int)g.MeasureString(message, font).Width; // Note 7
    g.DrawString(message, font,
                       Brushes.Blue, (Width-w)/2, 80);
  }

  static void Main() {
    Application.Run(new AtmScreen());
  }
}

class Teller {
  public const int DEPOSIT = 0;                              // Note 8
  public const int WITHDRAW = 1;
  public const int BALANCE = 2;
  private String id;
  private int transType;
  private int  acctType;
  private Person user;
  private Bank bank;
  private Account account;
  private AtmScreen screen;

  public Teller(Bank b, AtmScreen s) {
    bank = b;                                                // Note 9
    screen = s;
  }
  public void AcceptCard(Person p) {
    user = p;                                               // Note 10
    screen.EnterPIN();                                      // Note 11
  }
  public void AcceptPIN(String s) {
    id = s;
    screen.SelectTransaction();
  }
  public void AcceptTransaction(int trans) {
    transType = trans;
    screen.SelectType();
  }
  public void AcceptType(int type) {
    acctType = type;
    bank.Find(id, acctType, this);
```

```
  }
  public void AcceptAccount(Account a) {
    account = a;
    if (account != null)                              // Note 12
      if (transType == BALANCE){
        screen.Display("The balance is {0:C}"
                + account.GetBalance());
      }
      else {
         if (transType == DEPOSIT || transType == WITHDRAW){
           screen.SpecifyAmount();
         }
      }
    else
      screen.Display("No such account -- session terminated");
  }
  public void AcceptAmount(double amount) {
    switch(transType) {
      case DEPOSIT :
        account.Deposit(amount);
        screen.Display("Deposit of " + amount.ToString("C"));
        break;
      case WITHDRAW:
        double taken = account.Withdraw(amount);
        if (taken >= 0)
          screen.Display
                   ("Withdrawal of " + taken.ToString("C"));
        else
          screen.Display("Insufficient funds");
        break;
    }
  }
}

class Database {
  public static Person[] PersonData() {
    Name n1 = new Name("John","Venn");
    Address a1 = new Address
              ( "123 Main St.", "Tyler","WY", "45654");
    Person p1 = new Person("123123123",n1,a1);
    Name n2 = new Name("Mabel","Venn");
    Person p2 = new Person("456456456",n2,a1);
    Person[] p = {p1,p2};
    return p;
  }
  public static Account[] AccountData() {
    Person[] p = PersonData();
    Account p1Savings = new Savings(1500.00,p[0],4.0);// Note 13
```

```
    Account p1Checking = new Checking(p[0],2500.00,.50);
    Account p2Savings = new Savings(1000.00,p[1],3.5);
    Account[] a = {p1Savings,p1Checking,p2Savings};
    return a;
  }
}
class Bank {
  public const int SAVINGS = 1;
  public const int CHECKING = 2;
  private Account[] accounts = Database.AccountData();
  public void Find
        (String id, int acctType, Teller teller) {   // Note 14
    for (int i = 0; i < accounts.Length; i++) {
      Account acct = accounts[i];
      if (acct.GetId() == id)
        switch(acctType) {
          case SAVINGS:
            if (acct is Savings){
              teller.AcceptAccount(acct);
              return;
            }
            break;
          case CHECKING:
            if (acct is Checking){
              teller.AcceptAccount(acct);
              return;
            }
            break;
          }
     }
     teller.AcceptAccount(null);                     // Note 15
  }
}
abstract class Account {
  private double balance;
  private Person holder;
  public Account(Person p) : this(0,p) {
  }
  public Account(double initialAmount, Person p) {
    balance = initialAmount;
    holder = p;
  }
  public String GetId() {
    return holder.GetId();
  }
  public void Deposit(double amount) {
    balance += amount;
  }
```

```
  public virtual double Withdraw(double amount) {
    if (balance >= amount){
       balance -= amount;
       return amount;
    }
    else
       return -1.0;
  }
  public double GetBalance() {
    return balance;
  }
}
class Checking : Account {
  private double minBalance;
  private double charge;
  public Checking(Person p,double minAmount, double charge)
                                                : base(p) {
    minBalance = minAmount;
    this.charge = charge;
  }
  public double ProcessCheck(double amount)  {
    if (GetBalance() >= minBalance)
      return base.Withdraw(amount);
    else
      return base.Withdraw(amount + charge);
  }
  public override double Withdraw(double amount) {
    return ProcessCheck(amount);
  }
}
class Savings : Account  {
  private double interestRate;
  public Savings(double amount, Person p, double rate)
                                            : base(amount,p) {
    interestRate = rate;
  }
  public void PostInterest()  {
    double balance = GetBalance();
    double interest = interestRate/100*balance;
    Deposit(balance + interest);
  }
}
```

■

Note 1: `protected void Enter_Click`
`(Object sender, EventArgs e){`

We respond here to enter button presses.

Note 2: `if (s == "Enter Name"){`

We use the text box to enter the name, the PIN, and the amount, so we check the `enter` button caption to determine which of these the user entered.

Note 3: `dataEntry.Focus();`

Text entry does not have a natural association with any component. Requesting the focus for the text box directs text entry to it, so the user does not need to click the mouse.

Note 4:

```
protected void Selected_Index
                    (Object sender, EventArgs e)
```

We respond here to the combo box selection.

Note 5: `dataEntry.Enabled = false;`

When we want the user to choose the transaction type, we disable the text box, which is not needed, to avoid confusion. We disable unnecessary components whenever possible.

Note 6: `public void Clear() {`

We reset the user interface initially and when the user finishes a transaction.

Note 7: `int w = (int)g.MeasureString(message, font).Width;`

We get the width of each message so we can center it in the canvas.

Note 8: `public const int DEPOSIT = 0;`

Named constants make the program easier to maintain and modify. We use the C style, naming constants with uppercase identifiers.

Note 9: `bank = b;`

The teller saves the reference to the bank so it can find accounts.

Note 10: `user = u;`

The teller saves the reference to the user, to continue communication during the execution of the transactions for that user.

Note 11: `screen.EnterPIN();`

After getting the user's name, the teller asks the screen to set up the interface for the user to enter the PIN.

Note 12: `if (account != null)`

The bank sends a `null` account to the teller if it cannot find an account of the specified type for that user.

Note 13: `Account p1Savings = new Savings(1500.00,p1,4.0);`

We create three accounts to test our program.

FIGURE 10.19
Another scenario for the application of Example 10.17

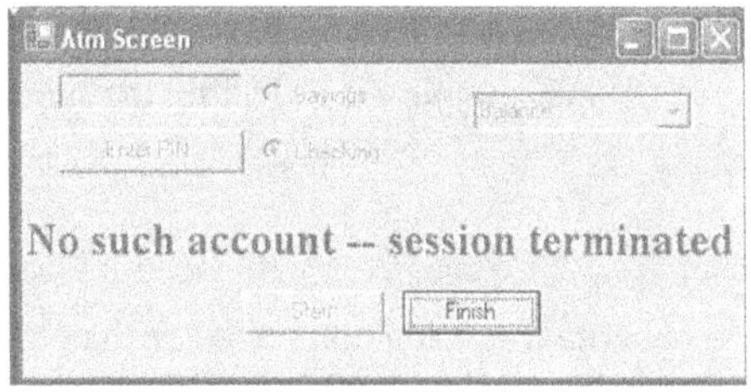

Note 14:
```
public void Find
        (String id, int acctType, Teller teller)
```

The `Find` method checks that the requested account exists.

Note 15:
```
teller.AcceptAccount(null);
```

If none of the accounts match the `id` and account type specified by the user, the bank sends the value `null` back to the teller.

Testing the Code

We test the code with the scenarios of Figures 10.14 and 10.15, leaving other tests for the exercises. The first user, John Venn, makes a deposit of $125.67 to a savings account. This transaction succeeds (Figure 10.18), because this user has a savings account. The second user, Mabel Venn, attempts to get the balance of a checking account, but this transaction fails (Figure 10.19) because this user does not have a checking account.

The use cases and scenarios express the intended functionality of the system, so testing based on these scenarios will help ensure that our system correctly provides the required behavior.

The BIG Picture

Use cases and scenarios help us to identify objects and their responsibilities. A class implementing an object type includes methods to enable objects of that type to meet their responsibilities. Rather than following a recipe, as in a procedural program, the program creates a user interface. User-generated events cause objects to interact with one another.

✓Test Your Understanding

15. Write a scenario for a successful withdrawal of $100 from a checking account.

16. Write a scenario for a user who chooses to cancel rather than input a transaction type.

17. Write a scenario for a user who cancels a deposit while specifying the account type.

18. Write a scenario for a successful `getBalance` transaction from a savings account.

Try It Yourself ➤ 19. Run Example 10.17 testing the scenarios of questions 15 through 18.

SUMMARY

- Inheritance, often contrasted with composition, is another way to relate objects. A class that extends another class, said to be a derived class of the class it extends, can add data fields and methods to those of its parent class; it can also override methods, tailoring their implementations to express its own behavior. In our bank account example, a savings account adds an interest rate field and a method to post the interest. A checking account overrides the `Withdraw` method of its bank account base class to deduct a service charge if the balance is below the minimum needed for free checking. Every class, directly or indirectly, extends the `Object` class, which provides a default implementation for the `ToString` method that returns the class name.
- Polymorphism, the many forms that operations can have, distinguishes object-oriented programming from other paradigms. A base class variable can refer to objects of any of its derived classes. A bank account variable might refer to a savings account or it might refer to a checking account; its withdraw behavior will be different in each case. As programmers, we just ask the object to execute its withdraw behavior. Our programs can have broad applicability, leaving each object to implement the specifics of its behavior. We use the same name, `Withdraw`, but the result depends on the type of object whose `Withdraw` method we invoke.
- Often the base classes we use polymorphically are abstract, not having any instances. In Example 10.12 the abstract `Shape` class implements its `Move` method, but not its `Draw` method. Derived classes `Line` and `Circle` must override `Draw`, but may either override or inherit the `Move` method from `Shape`. When we draw or move shapes, each instance will draw or move itself behaving according to its derived class type.
- C# uses modifiers to specify the type of access for classes, interfaces, data fields, and methods. We can declare a class public, making it visible everywhere, or without any modifier, restricting its visibility to the program in which it is declared. We can declare data fields and methods with the `private`, `internal`, `protected`, `protected internal`, or `public` modifiers. Using the `private` modifier restricts access to the methods of the class in which the data field or method is declared. This is the most restrictive modifier. Using the `internal` modifier restricts access to the program containing the data field or method.
- Using the `protected` modifier restricts access to the containing class or to any derived classes of the containing class. The `protected internal` modifier combines `protected` and `internal` access. Finally, the `public` modifier makes the data field or method visible anywhere its containing class is visible. Generally speaking, we declare data fields `private` or with no modifier. Methods are most often `public`, but the other access types can be useful.
- Our case study demonstrates the object-oriented programming methodology. Thinking in objects fits in with our normal experiences. To develop a system, we look at the uses of that system, giving scenarios for each use, stepping through the interactions needed to accomplish that use. We construct normal scenarios describing successful outcomes and scenarios for the many cases in which something goes wrong. From these scenarios we

identify the objects of the system and their responsibilities. We implement methods to allow objects to satisfy these responsibilities. The system runs by creating objects and letting them interact serving each other with their methods that execute their responsibilities. Our automatic teller application is quite simple, but illustrates this approach nicely.

SKILL BUILDER EXERCISES

1. Fill in the blanks in the following:

A class can extend one __________ but may implement more than one __________.
An __________ class has no instances, but it can implement some of its __________.
Redefining an operation in a derived class is called __________. The behavior expressed by that operation depends on the __________ of the object that invokes it.

2. Fill in the modifier needed to provide the desired access for the following declarations in a public class C which is defined in a program P.

a. __________ int a; access only in the program P

b. __________ double d; access in P and in derived classes of C

c. __________ String s; access everywhere C is accessible

d. __________ char c; access only within C

3. What will be the output from the following program?

```
class H {
   private int a;
   public H() {
       a = 0;
   }
   public H(int i) {
       a = i;
   }
   public void Display() {
       System.Console.WriteLine(a);
   }
}
class K : H {
   public K(int i) : base(i*i) {
   }
}
public class HK {
    public static void Main() {
        H first = new H(4);
        H second  = new K(5);
        first.Display();
        first = second;
        first.Display();
    }
}
```

CRITICAL THINKING EXERCISES

4. Using the `Name` class of Example 6.3 and the `SavingsAccount` class of Example 10.5, given

```
Name name = new Name("Ben","Franklin");
SavingsAccount savings = new SavingsAccount(500.00,4.0);
String s = "The account of " + name + " is " + savings;
```

choose the correct value of the string `s`.

a. `"The account of Ben Franklin is $500 at 4% interest"`

b. `"The account of Ben Franklin is SavingsAccount"`

c. `"The account of Franklin, Ben is $500 at 4% interest"`

d. None of the above.

5. A derived class can override a method of its base class or overload it. Choose the correct description from the following:

a. Overriding replaces the method of the base class, and overloading adds another method with the same name.

b. Overloading replaces the method of the base class, and overriding adds another method with the same name.

c. Both overriding and overloading replace the method of the base class.

d. None of the above.

6. Which of the following best describes the relationship between an abstract class and an interface?

a. An interface is another name for an abstract class.

b. An abstract class must be totally abstract, but an interface may be partially implemented.

c. Every abstract class implements an interface.

d. None of the above.

7. Given

```
BankAccount b = new SavingsAccount(500.00,4.0);
```

referring to the classes of Examples 5.1 and 10.5, choose which of the following is correct.

a. The statement `b.postInterest()` is not valid.

b. Later in the program, the variable `b` may refer to a `CheckingAccount` object.

c. The statement `b.Withdraw(100.00)` will invoke the `Withdraw` method from the `BankAccount` class.

d. All of the above.

DEBUGGING EXERCISE

8. The following program attempts to override the Shape class of Example 10.5 to create an Oval with a given center point, x-diameter, and y-diameter. Find and correct any errors.

```
using System;
using System.Drawing;
using System.Windows.Forms;
public class Oval : Shape {
  int xdiam;
  int ydiam;

  public Oval(Point p, int ma, int mi) {
    xdiam = ma;
    ydiam = mi;
  }
  public override void Draw(Graphics g) {
    g.FillEllipse(Brushes.Red, location.X-2*xdiam,
          location.Y-2*ydiam, xdiam, ydiam);
 }
}
public class Ex10_8 : Form {
  Shape s;

  public Ex10_8() {
    Size = new Size(300,200);
    s = new Oval(new Point(100,100), 70, 30);
  }

  protected override void OnPaint(PaintEventArgs e){
    Graphics g = e.Graphics;
    s.Draw(g);
    base.OnPaint(e);
  }
  static void Main() {
    Application.Run(new Ex10_8());
  }
}
```

PROGRAM MODIFICATION EXERCISES

9. Modify Example 5.1 to add a `ReadAccount` method to the `BankAccount` class that will return a `BankAccount` constructed from data input from the keyboard. Override `ReadAccount` in `SavingsAccount` to return an account that refers to a `SavingsAccount` that you construct, again initializing it with data from the keyboard. Similarly, implement `ReadAccount` in the `CheckingAccount` class.

10. Create a `TimedAccount` derived class of the `SavingsAccount` class of Example 10.5, which has an instance variable `fundsAvailable` to indicate that part of the balance is available for withdrawal. Override the `Withdraw` method to check that the amount requested does not exceed the funds available for withdrawal. Override the `Deposit` method to permit, at most, three deposits during the life of the account. Use an instance variable to hold the number of deposits made. Revise the base class to make methods virtual as needed.

11. Create a `Rectangle` derived class of the `Shape class` of Example 10.12. Let the location point of the shape represent the upper-left corner, and add another point that represents the lower-right corner of the rectangle.

12. Modify the `Line`, `Circle`, and `Shape` classes of Examples 10.12 and 10.13 to make all data fields private and add public methods such as `GetLocation` to access those fields.

PROGRAM DESIGN EXERCISES

13. Implement a set of classes for dining out that will demonstrate polymorphism. An abstract `Restaurant` class will have abstract methods such as `GetMenu`, `GetBill`, `OrderFood`, `PayBill`, and so on. Implement an `EatOut` method by calling the abstract methods in the order they would occur in a typical restaurant scenario. Implement `FastFood`, `CoffeeShop`, and `Fancy` derived classes of `Restaurant` which implement all the abstract methods, using stubs to print messages describing what would happen in that type of restaurant. For example, the `OrderFood` method in the `FastFood` class might describe talking to a machine from a car window in a drive-through line, and the `OrderFood` method in the `Fancy` class might call a method to order wine to go with the meal. To demonstrate the polymorphism, declare several restaurant objects that refer to the various derived classes. Calling the `EatOut` method for each restaurant will show that each behaves in its own way, appropriate to that type of restaurant. A derived class may override the `EatOut` method if the order of method calls defined in the `EatOut` method in the `Restaurant` class is not appropriate for that derived class.

14. Implement a set of classes for accommodations that will demonstrate polymorphism. An abstract `Accommodation` class will have abstract methods such as `Reserve`, `CheckIn`, `TipStaff`, `PayBill`, and so on. Implement a `SleepOut` method by calling the abstract methods in the order they would occur in a typical accommodation scenario. Implement `LuxuryHotel`, `Motel`, and `Campground` derived classes of `Accommodation`, and make each implement all the abstract methods, using stubs to print messages describing what would happen in that type of accommodation. For example, the `CheckIn` method in the `Campground` class might describe pitching a tent, and the `CheckIn` method in the `LuxuryHotel` class might call a method to have the luggage carried to the room.

    To demonstrate the polymorphism, declare several accommodation objects that refer to the various derived classes. Calling the `SleepOut` method for each accommodation will show that each behaves in its own way, appropriate to that type of accommodation. A derived class may override the `SleepOut` method if the order of method calls defined in the `SleepOut` method in the `Accommodation` class is not appropriate for that derived class.

15. Identify use cases and develop scenarios for a car rental system in which users may reserve a car in advance, cancel a reservation, and pick up or return a car. The company has different types of cars, such as compact cars and luxury cars. Make a list of the responsibilities of each object you identify from the scenarios. Implement the rental system using an object-oriented approach, developing methods to implement an object's responsibilities, and letting the objects interact. There is no "right" answer for this exercise. Good solutions will differ in many respects from one another.

16. Create an interface, `IBendable`, with one method, `Bend`. Create two classes, `Spoon`, and `Arm`, which implement `IBendable`. `Spoon` will also have an `Eat` method, and `Arm` will also have a `Raise` method. Write a graphics application that draws a spoon and an arm, each declared as type `IBendable`. Include a *Bend* button and a *Reset* button. Clicking the *Bend* button calls the `Bend` method for the spoon and arm. Clicking *Reset* restores them to their original positions.

17. Create a `Picture` derived class of the `Shape` class of Example 10.5. A picture contains an array of shapes, which may themselves be pictures or any other shapes. Implement the `Draw`, `Move`, and `ToString` methods for pictures. Implement an `Add` method that will add shapes to the picture. The center of a shape will be the center of the picture. When drawing a picture, draw its shapes relative to the center of the picture. For example, if a picture has center (100,100) and contains a circle with center (20,30) and radius 10, then draw that circle at center (120,130) with radius 10.

18. Create a program to display a circle and a line, and allow the user to choose which figures to move. Add text boxes to allow the user to input the amounts to move in the x and y directions, and a button for the user to request the move. Move the selected figure when the user presses the button.

19. Create an object-oriented design and implementation to play games of Match (only interesting to young children). Match uses 36 cards, with four each of values 2 through 10, and suits red and black squares and circles.

Rules

The deck must be shuffled to put the cards in random order.

The first player gets cards 1, 3, 5, 7, 9, 11, ..., 35, and the second player gets the rest.

The players do not look at the cards or change the order in which they were dealt.

There is a center pile of played cards, initially empty.

Each player plays the top card on the pile. If the number (suit is irrelevant) matches the number of the card currently on top of the pile, the player gets to add all the cards from the center pile to the bottom of his or her pile.

If a player runs out of cards, the cards of the center pile are divided evenly between both players.

The game ends when one player captures all 36 cards.

Use a button for each to play a card. Always show the top card of the center pile. It is not necessary to show the other cards. If the player's card does not match, play it on the top of the center pile. If it does match, play it next to the center pile. Each player will have a checkbox to claim the pile. Use a label for each player to show how many cards that player currently has.

11 Exception Handling and Input/Output

In this chapter we explore exceptions and input and output in C#. Exception handling enables us to manage serious errors that might occur such as trying to read from a file that does not exist. It is essential for implementing input and output operations and networking, in which errors beyond the control of the programmer may easily occur.

After we discuss exception handling, we show how to read from and write to external files. Files persist after our program is finished, keeping data for later use. Business applications, and many others, are heavily dependent on good access to external data. Because handling data carefully is important, it is not easy to do it well. We left it until this chapter to ensure that we have developed sufficient background to tackle these concepts. We first work with text and then consider binary data.

Inside our programs we have passed data as arguments to individual methods but not to the `Main` method called at the start of execution. We start this chapter by showing how to use program arguments to pass data to the `Main` method so we can use this technique in the rest of the chapter.

OBJECTIVES

- Handle exceptions
- Read and write text files
- Input and output binary files
- Pass arguments to the `Main` method of an application

11.1 EXCEPTION HANDLING

We do not want our programs to crash or to produce erroneous results. When inputting a test score we can check that the value entered was between 0 and 100. We can easily include this check on the value of the score in our program, but sometimes we have no control over circumstances that might affect our program. For example, if our program tries to read from a file that does not exist, it may abort. Someone else may have deleted that file without our knowledge, or the disk drive may have failed. C# provides an exception handling facility to allow the programmer to insert code to handle such unexpected errors and allow the program to recover and continue executing, or to terminate gracefully, whichever is appropriate.

We first show how to pass arguments to the `Main` method.

Program Arguments

In all our examples we have declared the `Main` method without any parameters. We can pass it an array of `String` parameters, in which case we declare `Main` as

```
public static void Main(String[] args)
```

When we call a method, we pass it its arguments. For example, we can pass the values 4.5, 1000.0, and 7 to the `Amount` method of Example 4.5, as in `Amount(4.5, 1000, 7)`. However, we do not call the `Main` method, the system does. The technique for passing arguments to the `Main` method depends on which environment we are using. **Program arguments**, passed to the `Main` method, are often called command-line arguments because they are placed just after the program name when a command line is used to run the program.

In Example 11.1, we adapt the temperature conversion program of Example 3.5 to use program arguments to input the temperatures to convert. Using the .NET Framework, we enter a hot temperature and a cold temperature on the command line

```
PassArguments  56.0  -19.33
```

The method to pass the arguments in to the `Main` method depends on which environment we are using, but inside the program we use the arguments in the same way, referring to the strings passed as program arguments using the `String` variable, `args`. When executing the program, C# sets `args[0]` to the hot temperature, 56.0, and `args[1]` to the cold temperature, −19.33, passing these values to the `Main` method. We can run our program again, passing different program arguments such as 49.7 and −12.44. When passed these arguments, our program will output the Fahrenheit values of the two Celsius temperatures. If the user does not pass two program arguments, we display a message and return to the operating system, terminating the program.

Each program argument is passed as a string. The arguments in our example specify `double` values. Inside the program we need to convert the strings `args[0]` and `args[1]` to type `double`.

```
/* Converts degrees Celsius to degrees Fahrenheit.
 * Uses program arguments to input values to convert.
 */

using System;
public class PassArguments {
  public static void Main(String[] args) {
    double  hotC, coldC;
    double  hotF, coldF;
    if (args.Length != 2) {                              // Note 1
      Console.WriteLine("Enter a hot and a cold "
               + "temperature as program arguments.");
      return;
    }
    hotC = double.Parse(args[0]);                        // Note 2
    hotF = 9.0*hotC/5.0 + 32.0;
    Console.WriteLine("The Fahrenheit temperature "
                    +           "is: {0:F1}", hotF);
    coldC = double.Parse(args[1]);
    coldF = 9.0*coldC/5.0 + 32.0;
    Console.WriteLine("The Fahrenheit temperature "
                          + "is: {0:F1}", coldF);
  }
}
```

Output

```
(Using  PassArguments  56.0  -19.33)

The Fahrenheit temperature is: 132.8
The Fahrenheit temperature is: -2.8
```

Note 1: `if (args.Length != 2) {`

We check that the user entered two arguments. If not, we return to the system.

Note 2: `hotC = double.Parse(args[0]);`

The program arguments are strings. Because they represent temperatures, we use the `Parse` method to convert them to `double` values.

Exception Classes

An **exception** signals that a condition such as an error has occurred. We **throw** an exception as a signal, and **catch** it to handle it and take appropriate action. We will

FIGURE 11.1
Classes of exceptions

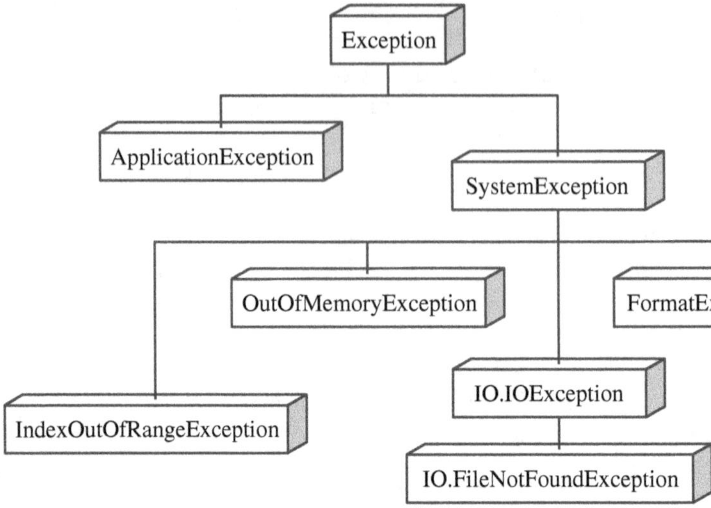

not cover all of the features of exception handling in this text, but will show how to handle exceptions that C# generates.

In C#, exceptions are instances of a class derived from `Exception`. Figure 11.1 shows the exception classes that we discuss in this chapter. All classes in Figure 11.1 are in the `System` namespace or the `System.IO` namespace. In this section we consider index out of range and format exceptions, leaving the IO exceptions to the next section.

The Index Out of Range Exception

The array

```
int[] a = {4,5,6};
```

has three elements which we can access using the indices `0`, `1`, and `2`. If we try to use an index other than these three, as, for example, in the expression `i=a[3]`, C# will throw an array out of range exception. Each exception is an instance of a class. We can write our own classes to define new types of exceptions, which we do in Section 12.3, but in this text we mostly use the C# exception classes shown in Figure 11.1.

Throwing an exception interrupts the program, transferring control to a user-defined `catch` clause, if any, which specifies how to handle the exception, or aborting if no `catch` clause is found. Example 11.2 shows the latter case when no catch clause is found. C# aborts execution with a message when it reaches the statement that uses an index that is out of range, and will not return to execute the rest of the program.

EXAMPLE 11.2 ■ Abort.cs

```
/* Shows that .NET aborts when it encounters
 * an out of bounds array index.
 */
```

```
public class Abort{
  public static void Main() {
    int[] anArray = {5,6,7};
    int badIndex = 5;                                    // Note 1
    int causesError;
    causesError = anArray[badIndex];                     // Note 2
    System.Console.WriteLine
             ("This statement never gets executed.");    // Note 3
  }
}
```

Output

```
Unhandled Exception: System.IndexOutOfRangeException:
Index was outside the bounds of the array.
   at Abort.Main()
```

■

Note 1: `int badIndex = 5;`

Only 0, 1, and 2 are valid indices for `anArray`.

Note 2: `causesError = anArray[badIndex];`

C# throws an index out of range exception when it encounters this use of the bad index 5. It prints a message naming the type of exception, with a short description of the error. Because the program does not handle this exception, .NET aborts the program.

Note 3:
```
System.Console.WriteLine
    ("This statement never gets executed.");
```

.NET aborted the program before reaching this line, thus it never gets executed.

We can easily fix Example 11.2 so it does not abort. Example 11.3 asks the user to input an index, but confirms that the index is between zero and two so the program does not abort. If the index is out of range, then we display an error message.

EXAMPLE 11.3 ■ ValidateInput.cs

```
/* Validates the index that the user inputs
 * so the program doesn't abort.
 */

using System;
public class ValidateInput{
  public static void Main(String[] args) {
    int[] anArray = {5,6,7};
    int index = int.Parse(args[0]);
    int value;
    if (index >= 0 && index <= 2){                       // Note 1
```

```
            value = anArray[index];
            Console.WriteLine
              ("Execution does not get here if index is bad");
          }
          else
            Console.WriteLine("Stick with 0, 1, or 2");
        }
      }
```

Output

(Using `ValidateInput 1`)

```
Execution does not get here if index is bad
```

Output

(Using `ValidateInput 34`)

```
Stick with 0, 1, or 2
```

Note 1: `if (index >= 0 && index <= 2) {`

We validate the user's input, accepting indices in the correct range and displaying an error message otherwise.

TIP

If there is a good way to validate the input, do so yourself. Much code in many applications is devoted to validating the data. Unsophisticated users may be unsure of the proper way to enter data, and even professionals make occasional errors.

C# does not require the programmer to handle the index out of range exception, but does allow the programmer to do so. To handle an exception, we put the code that could cause that exception to occur in a `try` block followed by a `catch` clause to handle the exception, as in

```
try {
  //some code that might generate an out of bounds exception
} catch(IndexOutOfRangeException e) {
    // some code to execute when that exception occurs
}
```

where `IndexOutOfRangeException` is the type of exception we are trying to catch. C# passes an instance, `e`, of this exception, which contains information about the index out of range exception that occurred, to the `catch` clause.

If an exception occurs in the `try` block, then C# looks for a `catch` clause that handles that exception. If it finds such a catch clause, it jumps immediately to execute that code, never returning to any code in the `try` block after the code that caused the exception. If C# does not find such a `catch` clause, it will abort the program with an error message, as happened in Example 11.2.

In Example 11.4 we put our use of the array index into a `try` block, and when C# throws the index out of range exception, we catch it and display an error message. Our program does not abort, and execution continues after the `catch` clause. With a little more effort, we could use a loop to give the user another chance to input a correct value after making an error. We leave this enhancement to the exercises.

EXAMPLE 11.4 ■ TryException.cs

```
/* Puts the array code in a try block and
 * catches the index out of range exception
 * if it occurs.
 */

using System;
public class TryException{
  public static void Main(String[] args) {
    int value;
    try {
      int[] anArray = {5,6,7};
      int index = int.Parse(args[0]);
      value = anArray[index];                        // Note 1
      Console.WriteLine
        ("Execution does not get here if index is bad");
    }catch (IndexOutOfRangeException e) {            // Note 2
      Console.WriteLine("Stick with 0, 1, or 2");
    }
    Console.WriteLine
                ("This is the end of the program");  // Note 3
  }
}
```

(Using `TryException 2`)

```
Execution does not get here if index is bad
This is the end of the program
```

(Using `TryException 89`)

```
Stick with 0, 1, or 2
This is the end of the program
```

■

Note 1: `value = anArray[index];`

C# will throw an index out of range exception if `index < 0` or if `index >2`.

Note 2: `}catch (IndexOutOfRangeException e) {`

After throwing an index out of range exception, C# jumps here to the handler, skipping any code remaining in the `try` block.

Note 3:
```
Console.WriteLine
            ("This is the end of the program");
```

After executing the code in the `catch` clause, C# continues executing here. Handling the index out of range exception allows the program to continue executing whether or not C# throws an index out of range exception.

If there is no `catch` clause for an exception immediately following the `try` block, when that exception occurs C# looks for the `catch` clause in the caller of the method in which the `try` block is contained. In Example 11.5 we use an out of range array index in the `GetAndSetValue` method, but do not include a `catch` clause in that method. When .NET encounters the invalid index during execution, it throws an index out of range exception and looks for a `catch` clause that handles that exception. Not finding one in `GetAndSetValue`, .NET looks in the caller of the `GetAndSetValue` method, the `Main` method, which does have a clause that catches the exception. .NET jumps to the `catch` clause in the `Main` method in which we display the `ToString` representation of the exception `e`, the index out of range exception that C# passes to the `catch` clause. This error message contains a list of all the methods that were active when the exception occurred. The method that threw the exception is at the top of the list, and its caller is below it. In this example we use only two methods, but in general the stack of methods can be much longer.

By reading the message, we can follow the sequence of method calls that culminated in the throwing of the exception. After executing the code in the catch clause, C# continues execution with the code following the `catch` clause. Had we omitted the `catch` clause, C# would have aborted the program with an error message, as in Example 11.2. Handling the exception allows us to recover from the error and continue executing the remainder of the program.

EXAMPLE 11.5 ■ TryExceptionTrace.cs

```
/* Shows the use of the exception object
 * to obtain the sequence of method calls that
 * culminated in the throwing of the index
 * out of range exception.
 */

using System;
public class TryExceptionTrace{
  public static int GetAndSetValue(String value) {
    int[] anArray = {5,6,7};
    int index = int.Parse(value);
    return anArray[index];                              // Note 1
  }
  public static void Main(String[] args) {
```

```
      int value;
      try {
        value = GetAndSetValue(args[0]);                    // Note 2
        Console.WriteLine
          ("Execution does not get here if index is bad");
      }catch (IndexOutOfRangeException e) {
          Console.WriteLine(e);
      }
      Console.WriteLine("This is the end of the program");
    }
  }
```

Output

(Using `TryExceptionTrace 98`)

```
System.IndexOutOfRangeException: Index was outside the
bounds of the array.
   at TryExceptionTrace.GetAndSetValue(String value)
   at TryExceptionTrace.Main(String[] args)
This is the end of the program
```

Note 1: `return anArray[index];`

This is the line that causes the exception.

Note 2: `value = GetAndSetValue(args[0]);`

This is where the `Main` method calls the `GetAndSetValue` method that produces the exception.

The Format Exception

C# allows us to construct an `int` object from a `String`, as in

```
int i = int.Parse("375");
```

If we provide a string that is not a valid integer constant, as in

```
int i = int.Parse("3.75");
```

then C# will throw a format exception. If we do not handle the exception in a catch clause, C# will abort the program with an error message.

Example 11.6 shows both valid and invalid attempts to construct an `int` and a `double` from strings. As in Example 11.5, we display the `ToString` representation of the exception that occurs. In this example the stack of method calls shows two entries, the bottom from our `Main` method and the top from the `ParseInt32` class of the .NET library.

EXAMPLE 11.6 ■ StringToNumber.cs

```
/* Illustrates the format exception thrown
 * when the string has an invalid format.
```

```
 */

using System;
public class StringToNumber {
  public static void Main() {
    try {
      int i = int.Parse("435");                              // Note 1
      Console.WriteLine("i = {0}", i);
      int j = int.Parse("45.2");                             // Note 2
      Console.WriteLine("j = {0}", j);
    }catch(FormatException e) {
      Console.WriteLine(e);                                  // Note 3
    }
    double d = double.Parse("3.14");                         // Note 4
    Console.WriteLine("d = {0}", d);
  }
}
```

Output

```
i = 435
System.FormatException: Input string was not in a correct
format.
   at System.Number.ParseInt32
      (String s, NumberStyles style, NumberFormatInfo info)
   at StringToNumber.Main()
d = 3.14
```

Note 1: `int i = int.Parse("435");`

We construct an `int` from the string "435", which represents an integer literal.

Note 2: `int j = int.Parse("45.2");`

Passing the string "45.2" to the `Parse method` causes C# to throw a format exception, as 45.2 is not a valid integer literal.

Note 3: `Console.WriteLine(e);`

The message shows that two methods were active when the exception occurred.

Note 4: `double d = double.Parse("3.14");`

After handling the exception, we do a valid conversion from `String` to `double`.

Style

Even though the `catch` clause in Example 11.7 has just one statement, we still need to enclose it in curly braces. If a `try` block contains just one statement, it needs to be enclosed in curly braces.

The BIG Picture

Enclosing code that can throw an exception in a `try` block allows us to handle that exception in a `catch` clause. When C# throws an exception it will jump to a `catch` clause for that exception in the same method if there is one, and will otherwise continue searching for a `catch` clause in the calling method. Printing a string representation of the exception shows the methods that were in progress when the exception occurred.

✓ Test Your Understanding

Try It Yourself ➤ **1.** Run Examples 11.4 and 11.5 entering a negative value for the index to see that C# throws an exception in this case.

Try It Yourself ➤ **2.** Revise Example 11.6 to remove the `try` statement and the `catch` clause for the `FormatException`. Rerun the revised code and note what happens and what code gets executed.

3. Which of the following will cause C# to throw a `FormatException`?

a. `int i = int.Parse("-7200");`

b. `double d = double.Parse("PI");`

c. `String s = new String("PI");`

d. `String s = new String("64000");`

e. `double d = double.Parse(".123");`

11.2 TEXT FILE INPUT AND OUTPUT

So far we have done our character mode input from the keyboard and our character mode output to the screen. In this section we see how to read from and write to external files.

Reading from a File

The `StreamReader` class allows us to read from an external file stored on a disk. We pass the name of the file to the constructor, as in

```
StreamReader input = new StreamReader("myFile.data");
```

Many errors can occur during the input and output process. For example, if the file `myFile.data` does not exist (it may have been accidentally deleted, or never created), then C# will throw a `FileNotFoundException`. In our file IO programs in this section we catch `IOException`, which is a superclass of all the IO exceptions, so we will be notified if any IO exception occurs, such as an unexpected end of file or a file not found.

Example 11.7 shows two attempts to construct a `StreamReader`. Both will generate a `FileNotFoundException` at runtime because there is no external file named `zxcvb.data`. The first places the constructor in a `try` block with a `catch` clause for an `IOException`. We just print a message and continue the program, but we could try something more useful such as trying to open another file. The second attempt does not use exception handling, and the program aborts when it cannot find the indicated file. We print an exception message and let the program terminate. We leave it to the exercises to improve the program by allowing the user to enter another file name if the current name causes an exception.

EXAMPLE 11.7 ■ IoError.cs

```
/* Throws an IO exception because the
 * file zxcvb.data doesn't exist.
 */

using System.IO;                                        // Note 1
public class IoError {
  public static void Main() {
    StreamReader f;
    try{
      f = new StreamReader("zxcvb.data");               // Note 2
    }catch(IOException e) {
      System.Console.WriteLine(e);                      // Note 3
    }
    f = new StreamReader("zxcvb.data");
  }
}
```

Output

```
System.IO.FileNotFoundException: Could not find file
"C:\booksharp\gittleman\ch11\zxcvb.data".
File name: "C:\booksharp\gittleman\ch11\zxcvb.data"
   at System.IO.Error.WinIOError(Int32 errorCode, String str)
   at System.IO.FileStream..ctor(String path, FileMode mode,
        FileAccess access, FileShare share, Int32
        bufferSize, Boolean useAsync, String msgPath,
        Boolean bFromProxy)
   at System.IO.FileStream..ctor(String path, FileMode mode,
        FileAccess access, FileShare share, Int32
        bufferSize)
```

```
   at System.IO.StreamReader..ctor(String path,
          Encoding encoding, Boolean
          detectEncodingFromByteOrderMarks, Int32
          bufferSize)
   at System.IO.StreamReader..ctor(String path)
   at IoError.Main()

Unhandled Exception: System.IO.FileNotFoundException: Could
not find file "C:\booksharp\gittleman\ch11\zxcvb.data".
File name: "C:\booksharp\gittleman\ch11\zxcvb.data"
   at System.IO.Error.WinIOError(Int32 errorCode, String str)
   at System.IO.FileStream..ctor(String path, FileMode mode,
        FileAccess access, FileShare share, Int32
        bufferSize, Boolean useAsync, String msgPath,
        Boolean bFromProxy)
   at System.IO.FileStream..ctor(String path, FileMode mode,
        FileAccess access, FileShare share, Int32
        bufferSize)
   at System.IO.StreamReader..ctor(String path,
          Encoding encoding, Boolean
          detectEncodingFromByteOrderMarks, Int32
          bufferSize)
   at System.IO.StreamReader..ctor(String path)
   at IoError.Main()
```

Note 1: `using System.IO;`

We tell the compiler to look for the classes used for input or output, such as `StreamReader` or `IOException`, in the namespace `System.IO`.

Note 2: `f = new StreamReader("zxcvb.data");`

If the file does not exist at runtime, .NET will throw a file not found exception. The file, `zxcvb.data`, named in this example does not exist.

Note 3: `System.Console.WriteLine(e);`

The error message shows six active methods. The label `ctor` indicates a constructor.

Reading Lines and Fields

C# provides classes for both binary and text input and output. Binary IO uses the internal representations of the data without converting them to the character representations using digits and letters that humans can more easily read. Such binary IO can be very useful for transferring data from one file to another. We will concentrate on text IO in this section and binary IO in the next.

Disk storage units have mechanical parts that make access to external data much more slow than access to data residing in the computer's memory. Reading one character at a time from a disk would be very inefficient. A better plan is to read a whole block of data from the disk, say 1024 characters, storing these characters in an area of the computer memory called a **buffer**. We then read the characters, when we need them, from the buffer. Because the buffer is in memory rather than on the disk, we can access the data much faster. When we have read all the characters in the buffer, we read another block of data from the disk.

The process works in reverse for output. We write each character into a buffer, and when the buffer is full we write the entire buffer to the external disk. C# automatically provides a buffer for `StreamReader` input. To read from the buffer, we use the `ReadLine` method, which reads a line of text, returning it as a string.

Example 11.8 reads the strings from the `messages.data` file, which we created by typing some lines of our choosing using a simple text editor (that is, not using a fancy editor with hidden formatting characters). The `while` loop terminates when the `ReadLine` method returns `null`, indicating it is at the end of the file. After reading the strings we close the file, releasing any resources used back to the operating system.

EXAMPLE 11.8 ■ FileReadStrings.cs

```
/* Reads strings from a file created in
 * a text editor.
 */

using System;
using System.IO;
public class FileReadStrings {
  public static void Main( ) {
    String line;
    StreamReader f = new StreamReader("messages.data");
    while((line=f.ReadLine()) != null)                    // Note 1
      Console.WriteLine(line);
    f.Close();                                            // Note 2
  }
}
```

Output

```
C# is fun.
The three did feed the deer.
An apple a day keeps the doctor away.
```

■

Note 1: `while((line=f.ReadLine()) != null)`

We read a line from the file, assigning it to the variable `line`. We terminate the loop when `line` is `null`, which indicates we are at the end of the file.

Note 2: `f.Close();`

We close the file to release the resources it used back to the operating system.

A Little Extra

The Finally Clause

C# provides a `finally` clause to clean up after it completes the execution of the code in the `try` clause, either normally or by throwing an exception. If we added exception handling to Example 11.8, we could use the `finally` clause to close the file `f`. The `Close()` method at the end of the `try` block will not be invoked if the `ReadLine` method throws an exception. Putting the statement `f.Close()` in the `finally` clause will make sure that it gets executed whether or not an exception occurs. The revised code fragment using the `finally` clause is:

```
public static void Main( ) {
  String line;
  try {
    StreamReader f = new StreamReader("messages.data");
    while((line=f.ReadLine()) != null)
      Console.WriteLine(line);
  }catch(IOException e) {
      Console.WriteLine(e);
  }
  finally {
    f.Close();
  }
}                                          }
```

In Example 11.8 we read one string from each line. Typically, data files contain records with several fields on each line. We will separate fields by a delimiter, which we can choose. For example, if we use the vertical bar to separate the fields, we can write the name, product number, color, and price of an item as

```
shirt|12345|blue|15.99
```

We can use the `Split` method of the `String` class to read several fields from a single line. We pass `Split` a `char` array of delimiter character. It returns a `String` array of fields in the original `String` that were delimited by one of the characters passed in the argument.

In Example 11.9 we will enter the four fields—street, city, state, and zip—of the `Address` class of Example 6.3 on a single line separating them with the vertical bar, as in

```
77 Sunset Strip|Hollywood|CA|90048
```

EXAMPLE 11.9 ■ FileReadAddresses.cs

```
/* Reads the four fields of an Address, separated by vertical
 * bars, from a single line.
 */

using System;
using System.IO;
public class FileReadAddresses {
  public static void Main( ) {
    String line;
    String street, city, state, zip;
    Address address;
    StreamReader f = new StreamReader("addresses.data");
    while ((line=f.ReadLine())!= null){
      String[] strings = line.Split(new char[]{'|'});  // Note 1
      if (strings.Length == 4) {                       // Note 2
        street = strings[0];
        city = strings[1];
        state = strings[2];
        zip = strings[3];
        address = new Address(street,city,state,zip);  // Note 3
        Console.WriteLine(address);                    // Note 4
        Console.WriteLine();
      }
    }
    f.Close();
  }
}
```

Output

```
77 Sunset Strip
Hollywood, CA 90048

222 Bridge Road
Grand Palabra, ND 58585
```

Note 1: `String[] strings = line.Split(new char[]{'|'});`

We pass a `char` array initialized with one delimiter character, the vertical bar.

Note 2: `if (strings.Length == 4) {`

We check that the line has four fields before processing it.

Note 3: `address = new Address(street,city,state,zip);`

We create an `Address` object as defined in Example 6.3. When compiling, we reference `Address.dll`.

Note 4: `Console.WriteLine(address);`

The `WriteLine` method uses the `ToString` method of the `Address` class to print the `address` object on the screen. Notice that the `address` object rearranges the fields input from the file to look like an address on two lines.

In Example 11.9 we read lines containing four strings. Often our lines may contain other types of data such as `int` or `double`. For example, we might have a line with three fields, an item that is a string, an `int` quantity, and a price of type `double`, as in

```
Milk   3    2.10
```

where for variety we separate the fields using blank spaces. Using the blank spaces to delimit the fields prevents us from including an item such as ice cream, which has an internal blank.

The `Split` method treats each field as a `String`. We must convert the string representing the quantity to an `int` and the string representing the price to a `double`. C# allows us not to handle the format exception that would be generated if, for example, our file had a value of 3.5 in the field for the quantity. In that case our program would abort, so we might include a `catch` clause to handle the format exception. We leave this improvement for the exercises.

Writing to a File

C# makes it easy to write values of different types to an external file. A `StreamWriter` has the `Write` and `WriteLine` methods familiar from the `Console` class. Using `Write` and `WriteLine` statements, we will write to the external file `totalCost.data`, overwriting its previous contents or creating the file if it does not exist.

TIP

To append to the end of `totalCost.data` instead of overwriting its contents, use the constructor

```
new StreamWriter("totalCost.data", true);
```

where the second argument is an `append` flag set to `true` to append to the file and `false` to overwrite it. ■

EXAMPLE 11.10 ■ Prices.cs

```
/* Reads records from a file, each containing an item, a
 * quantity, and a price.  Computes the total cost of each item,
 * writes a double to a file, and writes in currency format to
 * the screen.
 */
```

```
using System;
using System.IO;
public class Prices {
  public static void Main( ) {
    String line;
    String item;
    int quantity;
    double price;
    double cost;
    StreamReader f = new StreamReader("prices.data");
    StreamWriter p = new StreamWriter("totalCost.data");
    while ((line = f.ReadLine()) != null){
      String[] strings = line.Split();                    // Note 1
      if (strings.Length == 3) {
        item = strings[0];
        quantity =  int.Parse(strings[1]);                // Note 2
        price =  double.Parse(strings[2]);
        cost = price * quantity;
        Console.WriteLine("Total cost of {0} is {1:C}",
                                          item, cost);
        p.WriteLine("{0} {1:F2}", item, cost);
      }
    }
    f.Close();
    p.Close();
  }
}
```

```
Total cost of Milk is $6.30
Total cost of Coffee is $6.78
Total cost of Bread is $5.67
```

The file TotalCost.data

```
Milk 6.30
Coffee 6.78
Bread 5.67
```

Note 1: `String[] strings = line.Split();`

We use the `Split` method with no arguments. We use the default delimiters space, tab, and newline, often called **whitespace** characters, so we do not need to specify the delimiters.

Note 2: `quantity =  int.Parse(strings[1]);`

We convert the string to an `int` for the `quantity` field.

> **The BIG Picture**
>
> The `StreamReader` lets us read characters from a file using the `ReadLine` method. We can use the `Split` method to retrieve fields from a line. Similarly, a `StreamWriter` lets us write characters to a file using the familiar `Write` and `WriteLine` methods.

✓ Test Your Understanding

Try It Yourself ➤ 4. Create a `prices.data` file in which each row has a `String` naming an item, an `int` representing the quantity desired of that item, and a `double` representing the unit price for that item. Let it contain data in an invalid format, such as a value of 3.5 for the quantity. Run Example 11.10 and explain the result.

Try It Yourself ➤ 5. Write your own `messages.data` file with one string on each line, and run the code of Example 11.8, checking that the program does list the strings from your file.

Try It Yourself ➤ 6. Change the file `prices.data` used in Example 11.10 to include ice cream as an item. Run the program and explain what happens.

11.3 BINARY INPUT AND OUTPUT

We use binary input and output for data in 8-bit byte form rather than the character form needed for 16-bit Unicode characters. Such binary data can be stored in files, but it is not meant to be read by humans.

The `FileInfo` Class

The `FileInfo` class provides methods for creating, copying, deleting, moving, and opening files. It contains descriptive properties for the files. Example 11.11 illustrates these properties, whose names nicely signify their functions.

EXAMPLE 11.11 ■ FileProperties.cs

```
/* Creates a File and returns some
 * of its properties.
 */

using System;
using System.IO;
public class FileProperties {
  public static void Main(string[] args) {
    FileInfo f = new FileInfo(args[0]);
    Console.WriteLine("Name: "+f.Name);
```

```
      Console.WriteLine("Full name: "+f.FullName);
      Console.WriteLine("Creation time: "+f.CreationTime);
      Console.WriteLine("Last access time: "
                            + f.LastAccessTime);
      Console.WriteLine("Length: "+f.Length);
      Console.WriteLine("Parent directory: "
                            + f.DirectoryName);
      FileInfo output = f.CopyTo(args[1]);          // Note 1
    }
  }
```

Output

(Using `FileProperties FileProperties.cs FP.cs`)

```
Name: FileProperties.cs
Full name: C:\booksharp\gittleman\ch11\FileProperties.cs
Creation time: 5/30/2002 11:30:18 PM
Last access time: 7/19/2002 12:09:55 PM
Length: 660
Parent directory: C:\booksharp\gittleman\ch11
```

Note 1: `FileInfo output = f.CopyTo(args[1]);`

The file named in `args[1]` will be created as a copy of the file named in `args[0]`.

Reading and Writing Bytes

The abstract `Stream` class contains an abstract `Read` method. The method

```
public abstract int Read(byte[] b, int off, int len)
```

reads into an array of bytes, with the second argument specifying the starting offset in the array and the third giving the maximum number of bytes to read. It returns the number of bytes read, or 0 if it is at the end of the file. The `ReadByte` method,

```
public virtual int ReadByte( );
```

reads a single byte, returning −1 if at end of file.

In Example 11.12 we read and display bytes from standard input or read from a file by entering its name on the command line. C# declares the standard input stream, `System.Console.In`, usually the keyboard, as a `TextReader`. The `FileStream` class lets us read from a file. It buffers input and output to improve performance. Buffering involves reading a block, say 4096 bytes, from the disk to an internal memory buffer. The next reads will take bytes from the buffer rather than having to make inefficient disk accesses. When the buffer is empty, the next read will grab another block to fill it.

EXAMPLE 11.12 ■ ReadBytes.cs

```
/* Reads and displays bytes until end-of-file. Reads from a
 * file whose name is entered as a program argument,
 * or from the keyboard.
 */

using System;
using System.IO;
public class ReadBytes {
  public static void Main(string[] args) {
    if (args.Length == 1) {
      Stream input =
           new FileStream(args[0], FileMode.Open);
                                                    // Note 1
      int i;
      while((i = input.ReadByte()) != -1)
        Console.Write(i + " ");
      input.Close();
    }else {
      int i;
      while((i = Console.In.Read()) != -1)          // Note 2
        Console.Write(i + " ");
    }
  }
}
```

Output

(from `ReadBytes`)

```
a big car
97 32 98 105 103 32 99 97 114 13 10 ^Z              // Note 3
```

Output

(from `ReadBytes test.data` where `test.data` contains `á big car`)

```
225 32 98 105 103 32 99 97 114                      // Note 4
```

■

Note 1: `new FileStream(args[0], FileMode.Open);`

The FileMode second argument has several possible values.

Append	Writes at the end
Create	Creates. Overwrites existing file
CreateNew	Creates a new file
Open	Opens an existing file
OpenOrCreate	Opens existing file, or creates new
Truncate	Rewrites an existing file

Note 2: `while((i = Console.In.Read()) != -1)`

The Read method inputs a single character as an int. ASCII characters use one byte. Unicode characters other than ASCII use more than one byte. We do not use Unicode in this text.

Note 3: `97 32 98 105 103 32 99 97 114 13 10 ^Z`

The program outputs the ASCII values for the characters. The last two values, 13 and 10, represent carriage return and newline generated in Windows by pressing the *Enter* key. C# buffers the standard input so the user can backspace and make changes. Hitting the *Enter* key signals that the user is satisfied with the input. To signal the end of the input, the user enters Control Z on a separate line of input.

Note 4: `225 32 98 105 103 32 99 97 114`

We added an accented character, á, to show a value, 225, that would be negative if the return type was byte. In Notepad, entering Alt 0225 produces the character á. The Unicode value for á is 225.

Reading and Writing Primitive Types

The BinaryWriter class has overloaded Write methods for writing each of the primitive types in binary form, and BinaryReader has methods for reading these types, including readDouble and readInt32. To create a BinaryWriter, we first create a FileStream

```
new FileStream(args[0],FileMode.Create)
```

where args[0] is the name of the file to which we write. We pass this FileStream to a BinaryWriter,

```
new BinaryWriter(new FileStream(args[0], FileMode.Create))
```

In Example 11.13 we use the Write method to write the integers 0 through 9 and the decimals from 0.0 through 9.0 to a file. The binary format is not suitable for human reading. We use the ReadDouble method to read from the newly created file, displaying the values on the screen to verify that the file was written correctly.

```
/* Illustrates the BinaryWriter and BinaryReader classes
 * for the writing and reading of primitive types.
 */

using System;
using System.IO;
public class Binary {
  public static void Main(string [] args) {
    BinaryWriter output = new BinaryWriter
            (new FileStream(args[0],FileMode.Create));
    for (int i = 0; i < 10; i++)
      output.Write(i);
    for (double d = 0.0; d < 10.0; d++)                // Note 1
      output.Write(d);
    output.Close();
    BinaryReader input = new BinaryReader
             (new FileStream(args[0],FileMode.Open));
    for (int i = 0; i < 10; i++)
      Console.Write("{0} ", input.ReadInt32());
    for (int i = 0; i < 10; i++)
      Console.Write("{0:F1} ", input.ReadDouble());
    input.Close();
  }
}
```

Output

(from `Binary primitive.data`)

```
0 1 2 3 4 5 6 7 8 9 0.0 1.0 2.0 3.0 4.0 5.0 6.0 7.0 8.0 9.0
```

■

Note 1: `for (double d = 0.0; d < 10.0; d++)`

Although `for` loops usually use integer indices, using a `double` index suits this example well. We illustrate the `BinaryWriter` and `BinaryReader` classes using types `double` and `int`, leaving the use of other primitive types for the exercises.

Example 11.13 writes the `int` and `double` values in binary form, using four bytes for each `int` and eight for each `double`. Running Example 11.12 to inspect this representation, using the command

```
ReadBytes primitive.data
```

produces

```
0 0 0 0  1 0 0 0  2 0 0 0  3 0 0 0  4 0 0 0  5 0 0 0
6 0 0 0  7 0 0 0  8 0 0 0  9 0 0 0
0 0 0 0 0 0  0  0   0 0 0 0 0 0 240 63  0 0 0 0 0 0  0 64
0 0 0 0 0 0  8 64   0 0 0 0 0 0  16 64  0 0 0 0 0 0 20 64
0 0 0 0 0 0 24 64   0 0 0 0 0 0  28 64  0 0 0 0 0 0 32 64
0 0 0 0 0 0 34 64
```

The first ten entries show the 4-byte integer values, while the second ten show 8-byte doubles. The `double` format is not obvious and is not meant for human reading. It separates each number into a fraction part and an exponent and includes a sign bit.

Random Access Files

The `Seek` method for a `FileStream` enables us to move to a specific position in a file, rather than just reading or writing it sequentially. Calling `Seek(20, SeekOrigin.Begin)` sets the position at the twentieth byte from the start of the file, at which position we can either read or write. After completing a read or write operation, we can use `Seek(4,SeekOrigin.Begin)` to move the position to the location further back in the file at byte 4. To illustrate, we use the data file `primitive.data` output by Example 11.13. We will read four bytes and convert them to an integer.

EXAMPLE 11.14 ■ RandomAccess.cs

```
/* Illustrates random access to a file.
 */

using System;
using System.IO;
public class RandomAccess {
  public static void Main(String[] args) {
    FileStream raf = new FileStream(args[0], FileMode.Open);
    raf.Seek(20, SeekOrigin.Begin);                        // Note 1
    byte[] anInt = new byte[4];
    raf.Read(anInt,0,4);                                   // Note 2
    int number = anInt[3];                                 // Note 3
    for(int i = 2; i >= 0; i--){                           // Note 4
      number *= 256;                                       // Note 5
      number += anInt[i];                                  // Note 6
    }
    Console.WriteLine
      ("The number starting at byte 20 is {0}", number);
    raf.Seek(4, SeekOrigin.Begin);                         // Note 7
    raf.Read(anInt,0,4);
    number = anInt[3];
    for(int i = 2; i >= 0; i--){
      number *= 256;
      number += anInt[i];
```

```
    }
    Console.WriteLine
      ("The number starting at byte 4 is {0}", number);
    raf.Close();
  }
}
```

(Using `RandomAccess primitive.data`)

```
The number starting at byte 20 is 5
The number starting at byte 4 is 1
```

Note 1: `raf.Seek(20, SeekOrigin.Begin);`

We position the file at byte 20 from the start of the file. Each integer is 32 bits or 4 bytes, so the position at byte 20 will bypass the first five integers (0, 1, 2, 3, and 4) in the file. (The bytes are numbered 0, 1, ..., 19.) Positioning at byte 20 makes the next four bytes 5, 0, 0, and 0, representing the number five. The second argument specifies the reference point for the offset in the first argument. The choices for the second argument are

```
SeekOrigin.Begin

SeekOrigin.Current

SeekOrigin.End
```

Note 2: `raf.Read(anInt,0,4);`

The `anInt` array will hold four bytes that hold the 32-bit representation of an integer read from the data file.

Note 3: `int number = anInt[3];`

As we saw when we used `ReadBytes` to inspect `primitive.data`, the integers are stored with the low byte first. For example, the four bytes for the number five are 5, 0, 0, and 0 rather than 0, 0, 0, and 5. We want to build the integer by shifting the highest byte 24 bits to the left, the next highest 16 bits left, and the next by 8 bits. We initialize the integer with the high byte, so it will be shifted the most times in the loop.

Note 4: `for(int i = 2; i >= 0; i--){`

This loop adds the last three bytes to the resulting integer in the correct positions.

Note 5: `number *= 256;`

$256 = 2^8$, so multiplying by 256 shifts the number eight bits to the left. It would be more efficient to use the left-shift operator, <<, writing `number << 8` instead. (See Appendix B.) The low order eight bits are filled in with zeros.

Note 6: `number += anInt[i];`

Because `anInt[i]` is a byte, it fills in the eight bits vacated by the previous byte that was shifted to the left. It would be more efficient to use the bitwise or operator, `|`, writing `number |= anInt[i]` instead. (See Appendix B.)

Note 7: `raf.Seek(4, SeekOrigin.Begin);`

Going back to byte 4 will position the file after the first integer, 0, so reading an integer at this position should return the value 1.

The BIG Picture

The `FileInfo` class allows us to get file properties and to copy files. To read and write binary files we can use a `FileStream` with sequential or random access. We use a `BinaryReader` to read primitive types and a `BinaryWriter` to write them.

✓Test Your Understanding

Try It Yourself ➤

7. Modify Example 11.13 to use the `ReadInt64` method instead of `ReadDouble`.
8. Write the statement to position the `FileStream raf` of Example 11.14 to the value 5.0 in the file primitive.data output by Example 11.13.

11.4 MENUS[1] AND FILE DIALOGS

We can add menus to a `Form`. We use menus to illustrate some dialogs. The `OpenFileDialog` lets us open a file. We use `SaveFileDialog` to save a file and `FontDialog` to select a font. Menu items have a `Click` event with which we can register an event handler to make the menu item function as desired.

Figure 11.2 shows the form of Example 11.15 after the user has opened `MenuDialog.cs`.

EXAMPLE 11.15 ■ MenuDialog.cs

```
/* Illustrates some menu and dialog features.
 */

using System;
using System.Drawing;
```

[1]We could have introduced menus in Chapter 9 with the other user interface components, but it is convenient to do so now to illustrate file dialogs.

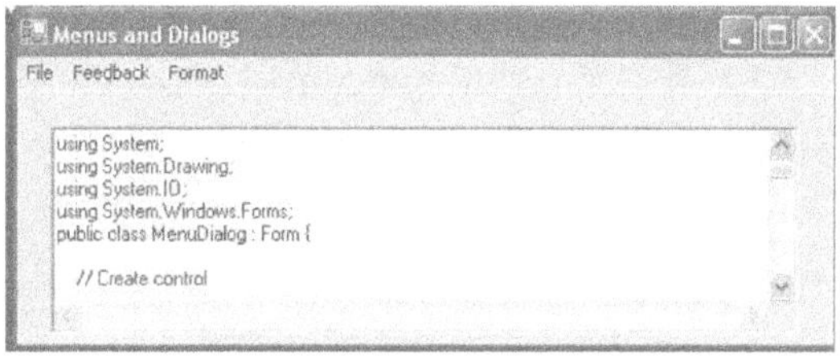

FIGURE 11.2 **The form of Example 11.15**

```
using System.IO;
using System.Windows.Forms;
public class MenuDialog : Form {

    // Create control
  TextBox text = new TextBox();

  public MenuDialog() {

      // Configure form
    Size = new Size(500,200);
    Text = "Menus and Dialogs";

      // Configure text box
    text.Size = new Size(450,120);
    text.Multiline = true;
    text.ScrollBars = ScrollBars.Both;                    // Note 1
    text.WordWrap = false;                                // Note 2
    text.Location = new Point(20,20);

      // Configure file menu
    MenuItem fileMenu = new MenuItem("File");             // Note 3
    MenuItem open = new MenuItem("Open");
    open.Shortcut = Shortcut.CtrlO;                       // Note 4
    MenuItem save = new MenuItem("Save");
    save.Shortcut = Shortcut.CtrlS;
    fileMenu.MenuItems.Add(open);                         // Note 5
    fileMenu.MenuItems.Add(save);

      // Configure feedback menu
    MenuItem feedbackMenu = new MenuItem("Feedback");
    MenuItem message = new MenuItem("Message");
    message.Shortcut = Shortcut.CtrlM;
    feedbackMenu.MenuItems.Add(message);

      // Configure format menu
    MenuItem formatMenu = new MenuItem("Format");
```

```
  MenuItem font = new MenuItem("Font");
  font.Shortcut = Shortcut.CtrlF;
  formatMenu.MenuItems.Add(font);

    // Configure main menu
  MainMenu bar = new MainMenu();
  Menu = bar;                                          // Note 6
  bar.MenuItems.Add(fileMenu);                         // Note 7
  bar.MenuItems.Add(feedbackMenu);
  bar.MenuItems.Add(formatMenu);

    // Add control to form
  Controls.Add(text);

    // Register event handlers
  open.Click += new EventHandler(Open_Click);
  save.Click += new EventHandler(Save_Click);
  message.Click += new EventHandler(Message_Click);
  font.Click += new EventHandler(Font_Click);
}

  // Handle open menu item
protected void Open_Click(Object sender, EventArgs e) {
  OpenFileDialog o = new OpenFileDialog();
  if(o.ShowDialog() == DialogResult.OK) {              // Note 8
    Stream file = o.OpenFile();                        // Note 9
    StreamReader reader = new StreamReader(file);     // Note 10
    char[] data = new char[file.Length];
    reader.ReadBlock(data,0,(int)file.Length);        // Note 11
    text.Text = new String(data);                     // Note 12
    reader.Close();
  }
}

  // Handle save menu item
protected void Save_Click(Object sender, EventArgs e) {
  SaveFileDialog s = new SaveFileDialog();
  if(s.ShowDialog() == DialogResult.OK) {
    StreamWriter writer
              = new StreamWriter(s.OpenFile());
    writer.Write(text.Text);                          // Note 13
    writer.Close();
  }
}

  // Handle message menu
protected void Message_Click(Object sender, EventArgs e) {
  MessageBox.Show("You clicked the Message menu",
```

```
                                          "My message");
  }

    // Handle font menu
  protected void Font_Click(Object sender, EventArgs e) {
    FontDialog f = new FontDialog();
    if(f.ShowDialog() == DialogResult.OK)
      text.Font = f.Font;                              // Note 14
  }

  public static void Main() {
    Application.Run(new MenuDialog());
  }
}
```

Note 1: `text.ScrollBars = ScrollBars.Both;`

We set the `ScrollBars` property to add scroll bars to the text box. The possible values from the `ScrollBars` enumeration are `Both`, `Horizontal`, `None`, and `Vertical`.

Note 2: `text.WordWrap = false;`

The horizontal scroll bar will not be added unless we set the `WordWrap` property to `false`. The default is to wrap lines when they reach the right boundary of the text box.

Note 3: `MenuItem fileMenu = new MenuItem("File");`

Menu items form a hierarchy. Each one can be the parent of nested menu items. Here we create the *File* menu item, which we will add to the main menu. The *File* menu item will contain the *Open* and *Save* menu items.

Note 4: `open.Shortcut = Shortcut.CtrlO;`

We set a shortcut for the `Open` menu item. Pressing *Control O* will have the same effect as directly clicking the `Open` menu item.

Note 5: `fileMenu.MenuItems.Add(open);`

The `MenuItems` property of the *File* menu item holds the collection of its menu items. We use the `Add` method to add the *Open* menu item to this collection.

Note 6: `Menu = bar;`

We create a `MainMenu`, which we set as the `Menu` property of the form.

Note 7: `bar.MenuItems.Add(fileMenu);`

We add some menu items to the `MenuItems` collection for the main menu.

Note 8: `if(o.ShowDialog() == DialogResult.OK)`

The `ShowDialog` method runs the dialog, in this case an open file dialog. It returns `DialogResult.OK` if the user clicks *OK* and `DialogResult.Cancel` otherwise.

Note 9: `Stream file = o.OpenFile();`

The `OpenFile` method opens the file selected by the user.

Note 10: `StreamReader reader = new StreamReader(file);`

We create a `StreamReader` because we are reading text files rather than binary files.

Note 11: `reader.ReadBlock(data,0,(int)file.Length);`

The first argument is the `char` array to read into. The second argument is the starting index in that array. The third argument is the maximum number of characters to read. Because the `Length` property is a `long` value we cast it to `int`.

Note 12: `text.Text = new String(data);`

We create a `String` from the `char` array and set the `Text` property to add it to the text box.

Note 13: `writer.Write(text.Text);`

We write the text from the text box using the file name selected by the user.

Note 14: `text.Font = f.Font;`

We change the font in the text box to the one selected by the user.

The BIG Picture

We can add menus to a form. We use a click event to enable the menu item to perform useful functions. File, save, and font dialogs let the user make selections.

✓Test Your Understanding

Try It Yourself ➤ **9.** Revise Example 11.15 to omit setting the `WordWrap` property. Describe the result.

Try It Yourself ➤ **10.** Can you make changes to the text in the `TextBox` of Example 11.15?

SUMMARY

- We can use program arguments to pass data to the `Main` method of an application. If the formal parameter to the `Main` method is `String[] args`, then `args[0]` will represent the first program argument, `args[1]` the second, and so on. These values are strings, which we may need to convert to type `int` or `double`.
- C# provides an exception handling facility with a hierarchy of predefined exception classes. Some of the methods in the .NET library packages throw exceptions when error conditions occur. C# will throw an index out of range exception when a user tries to use

an array element having an index outside the range specified in the creation of the array. The program aborts when an unhandled exception occurs.

- To handle an exception, we put the code that can throw that exception in a `try` block followed by a `catch` clause for that exception. C# passes an object representing that exception to the `catch` clause. Inside the `catch` block we can put the code we want to execute after an exception has occurred. C# jumps from the line where the exception occurred to the `catch` clause and continues execution from there, never returning to the code that caused the exception.
- If there is no `catch` clause in the method where the exception occurs, C# will look for one in the caller of that method, and so on to its caller, finally aborting the program if no `catch` clause is found. Inside the `catch` block we can display the exception to show which exception occurred and to see the sequence of method calls that led to the exception.
- To prevent the program from aborting, we can sometimes validate our data; for example, we can check that array indices are valid or that objects are non-null before we try to access their fields.
- C# has classes for binary IO, in which data is kept in an internal format not easily readable, and for text IO, in which we convert internal values to text output and text input to binary internal values. We can read from an external text file by passing the file name to the `StreamReader` constructor. The `StreamReader` is buffered to minimize the number of accesses to the external disk and do most of the reading from a buffer in memory. The `ReadLine` method reads a line from the file, returning `null` at the end of the file. We could handle the `IOException` that the constructors and methods might generate. The `Close` method releases resources back to the operating system.
- We use the `Split` class to read more than one field from a single line. The default delimiters for the `Split` method assume that whitespace separates the strings, but an optional second argument allows us to specify other delimiters, such as the vertical bar. The `Split method` returns a `String` array. We may need to convert some fields to an `int` for integer data or to a `double` for decimal values.
- To write to a text file, we pass the file name to a `StreamWriter` constructor. We can use the familiar `Write` and `WriteLine` methods to output values of any of the primitive types or use the `ToString` method to output string representations of objects.
- The `FileInfo` class has methods to obtain the properties of a file. We use the `Read and ReadBytes` methods of the `FileStream` class to read bytes from a file and the `Write` method to write bytes to a file. The methods of the `BinaryReader` and `BinaryWriter` classes allow the input and output of primitive types in binary format. We can seek a specific position using the `Seek` method.
- The `OpenFileDialog`, `SaveFileDialog`, and `FontDialog` classes in the `System.Windows.Forms` namespace are not controls. They allow the user to make useful selections. We can nest menus in a form and add them to the main menu.

SKILL BUILDER EXERCISES

1. For each code fragment in the left column, choose the exception from the right column that it might throw.

a. `r.ReadLine()` i. `IndexOutOfRangeException`

b. `a[index]` ii. `FormatException`

c. `new Integer(s)` iii. `IOException`

d. `new StreamReader("abc.data")`

2. Fill in the blanks in the code to create a reader to read `int` values in binary format from a file `values.data`.

```
____________ input
      = new ____________ (new ____________ (_____,_________));
```

3. Fill in the blanks in the code to create a writer to write `int` values in binary format to a file `values.out`.

```
__________ output
      = new ____________ (new _________ (_____, _________));
```

CRITICAL THINKING EXERCISES

4. Which of the following is not a possible `FileMode`?

   a. `OpenCreate`

   b. `Append`

   c. `Truncate`

   d. `CreateNew`

   e. None of the above.

5. If we include the statement

   ```
   StreamReader reader = new StreamReader("test.dat");
   ```

   in our program without putting it in a `try` block with a `catch` clause for the `IOException`

   a. the compiler will report an error.

   b. the program will compile, but will abort when running if there is no file named `test.dat` on the user's machine.

   c. the program will always run, using a default file if `test.dat` is not available.

   d. None of the above.

6. If we include the statement

   ```
   int i = int.Parse("3.14");
   ```

   in our program without putting it in a `try` block with a `catch` clause for the `FormatException`

   a. the compiler will report an error.

   b. the program will compile, but will abort when it reaches this statement.

   c. the program will always run, truncating the value 3.14 to 3.

   d. None of the above.

7. Given the statement

```
String[] s =
  new Split("123|abc|456","|");
```

which of the following statements will cause the `int` variable `i` to have the value `123`?

a. `int i = s[0];`

b. `int i = int.Parse(s[0]);`

c. `int i = int.Parse(s);`

d. `int i = NextToken(s);`

e. None of the above.

DEBUGGING EXERCISE

8. The following program attempts to read a fixed number of lines from a file and display them on the screen. The file name is the first program argument and the number of lines is the second. Find and correct any errors in this program.

```
using System;
public class ReadFile {
  public static void Main(String[] args) {
    String line;
    int totalLines;    // number of lines to read
    int count = 0;     // number of lines read so far
    totalLines = int.Parse(args[2]);
    StreamReader f = new StreamReader(args[1]);
    while((line = f.ReadLine()) != -1
           && count++ < totalLines)
      Console.WriteLine(line);
    f.Close;
  }
}
```

PROGRAM MODIFICATION EXERCISES

9. Modify Example 11.4 to give the user another chance to enter a correct value after .NET throws an exception.

Putting It All Together ➤ 10. Modify Example 7.7, `StudentScoreMulti`, to read the test scores from a file. The first line will contain the number of students. Put each student's scores on a separate line, with each score separated by a blank. Prompt the user to enter the file name.

11. Modify Example 11.7 to allow the user to enter another file name if an exception is thrown.

12. Modify Example 11.10, `Prices`, to catch the format exceptions that might be generated. Test with a file that includes some values that will cause the exception to be thrown.

PROGRAM DESIGN EXERCISES

13. Open your program source (the C# program you wrote) as a file. Read and display each of the next four bytes, starting at the specified byte number entered by the user on the command line.
14. Write a binary file containing five randomly generated integers. Open the file and read the second four bytes. Convert them to an integer and output the result.
15. Write a binary file containing five randomly generated double values. Open the file you wrote and read and display each of the next eight bytes, starting at the byte number entered by the user. Assume that the eight bytes are the binary representation of the double and convert them to that double using the following rules.

52 mantissa bits	11 exponent bits	1 sign

64 bits

Rules for the 8-bit representation of a double:

1. The sign bit is 0 for positive, 1 for negative.
2. The exponent's base is two.
3. The exponent field contains 127 plus the true exponent for single precision, or 1023 plus the true exponent for double precision.
4. The first bit of the mantissa is typically assumed to be 1.*f*, where *f* is the field of fraction bits. (We put the binary point after the first 1, and do not show it.)

16. Write a C# application that presents data read from a file in a bar chart.
17. Write a C# program that searches a file for a string. Pass the string and the file name as program arguments.
18. Write a C# program that reads a text file, removing any extra spaces between words, and writes the output to a file. Enter the file names to read from and write to as program arguments.
19. Write a C# program to update an inventory file. Each line of the inventory file will have a product number, a product name, and a quantity separated by vertical bars. The items in the inventory file will be ordered by product number. The transaction file will contain a product number and a change amount, which may be positive for an increase or negative for a decrease. Assume the transaction file is also ordered by product number. Use the transaction file to update the inventory file, writing a new inventory file with the updated quantities. Assume there is at most one transaction for each item in the inventory, and that no new items occur in the transaction file.

20. Write a C# program that provides a GUI to copy C# programs to the screen or to another file. List the C# programs in a combo box. Use radio buttons to indicate whether to copy the file to the console window or to another file. Use a text box to enter the name of the file receiving the copy.

12 Data Structures

Recursion is another approach to repetition. In recursion, instead of spelling out each step of the repetition the way loops do, we do one step and call the recursive method again to complete the remaining steps. We illustrate recursion with two important data processing applications, searching and sorting.

Data structures allow us to organize data for efficient processing. In this chapter we introduce several of the most important data structures: linked lists, queues, stacks, array lists, and hash tables. In contrast to an array, which stores its elements together, a linked list uses a link to refer to the location of its next item, making it easier to add and remove elements but harder to search for them. Choosing the right data structure is an engineering decision based on the requirements of the problem being solved.

The stack in computer science is like a stack of books; putting data on a stack has the last in, first out (LIFO) property that the last item placed on it is the first item removed. We implement our stack using an array, but could make a more flexible stack using a linked list to hold its elements. The model for a queue is a line of customers; the head of the line gets served first, and new customers go to the end of the line.

The .NET Library includes useful data structures. An `ArrayList` keeps elements together in a more flexible way than in an array. A `Hashtable` provides quick access to individual elements, but not to a range of elements. A `SortedList` keeps elements in order.

OBJECTIVES

- Use recursive methods
- Be familiar with binary search and merge sort algorithms
- Implement the linked list, stack, and queue data structures
- Experiment with `ArrayList`, `Hashtable`, and `SortedList` operations

12.1 RECURSION

Iteration and recursion allow us to repeat steps in a program. The `while`, `for`, and `do-while` loops use iteration to repeat steps in which continuing the repetitions is based on the value of a test condition. Using iteration, our program shows the detailed mechanics of the repetition process. By contrast, **recursion** deals with repetition at a higher level, letting C# manage the details hidden in calls to recursive methods. Some problems are much easier and more natural to solve using recursion, but in some situations using recursion can be inefficient. With experience, which comes with further study, one can judge when a recursive solution is appropriate.

An old proverb says that the journey of a thousand miles begins with the first step. This proverb captures the essence of recursion. Take one step and you start toward your goal. To achieve the goal you just have to repeat the process, beginning at your new position, taking one step farther along the road. We can express this proverb in a C# method, `travel`:

```
public void travel(int start, int finish) {
  if (start < finish) {
    takeOneStep(start);
    travel(start + 1,finish);
  }
}
```

The `travel` method is **recursive**; it recurs inside of itself. One reason recursion is an important concept is that recursive methods are easy to read. The code is like a specification of the travel process. The `travel` code says that to complete the trip from start to finish, if you are not already at the finish, then take one step and travel from that point to the finish, a method that certainly works.

Another important aspect of recursion is that recursive methods are usually short because we do not need to specify each detailed step of the solution. We call the method recursively, as in

```
travel(start+1,finish);
```

letting the `travel` method fill in one more step every time it recurs. Another old proverb says that one picture is worth a thousand words, which we modernize to "one program is worth a thousand words" (the number 1000 seems to have some significance in proverbs). Our one program is Example 12.1.

EXAMPLE 12.1 ■ Journey.cs

```
/* Use a recursive method, travel, to journey from start
 * to finish, printing messages to show its progress.
 */

using System;
public class Journey {
```

```
  private static String indent = "";                       // Note 1
  public static void TakeOneStep(int step) {
    Console.WriteLine("{0}Taking step {1}", indent, step);
  }
  public static void Travel(int start, int finish) {
    string oldIndent = indent;
    Console.WriteLine("{0}Starting travel from {1} to {2}",
                             indent, start, finish);  // Note 2
    if (start < finish) {
      TakeOneStep(start);
      indent += "   ";                                   // Note 3
      Travel(start+1, finish);                           // Note 4
      indent = oldIndent;                                // Note 5
    }
    Console.WriteLine("{0}Finishing travel from {1} to {2}",
                              indent, start, finish); // Note 6
  }
  public static void Main(String [] args) {
    int start = int.Parse(args[0]);                      // Note 7
    int finish = int.Parse(args[1]);
    Travel(start, finish);
  }
}
```

Output

from `Journey 1 4`

```
Starting travel from 1 to 4
Taking step 1
   Starting travel from 2 to 4
   Taking step 2
      Starting travel from 3 to 4
      Taking step 3
         Starting travel from 4 to 4
         Finishing travel from 4 to 4
      Finishing travel from 3 to 4
   Finishing travel from 2 to 4
Finishing travel from 1 to 4
```

Note 1: `private static String indent = "";`

We use a static field to keep the string that specifies the amount to indent the message. Each time we call the `Travel` method we increase the indent by three spaces, and each time we return we restore the previous indent three spaces to the left.

Note 2: `Console.WriteLine("{0}Starting travel from {1} to {2}", indent, start, finish);`

We print the message using the current indent.

Note 3: `indent += "    ";`

We increase the indent before calling the `Travel` method recursively.

Note 4: `Travel(start+1, finish);`

This recursive call starts executing the `Travel` method with new arguments. This new activation of the `Travel` method starts before the previous call to `Travel` has returned.

Note 5: `indent = oldIndent;`

We restore the previous indent when we finish executing the `Travel` method.

Note 6: `Console.WriteLine("{0}Finishing travel from {1} to {2}", indent, start, finish);`

We display a message to show when this call to `Travel` completes.

Note 7: `int start = int.Parse(args[0]);`

We use program arguments to specify the start and finish values.

We see from the output that `Travel(1,4)` takes the first step and calls `Travel(2,4)` to complete the trip. `Travel(2,4)` takes the second step and calls `Travel(3,4)` to complete the trip. `Travel(3,4)` takes the third step and calls `Travel(4,4)` to complete the trip. `Travel(4,4)` concludes that the trip is complete and terminates. `Travel(3,4)` terminates, `Travel(2,4)` terminates, and, finally, `Travel(1,4)` terminates.

A recursive method needs an alternative that does not involve making another recursive call, or it will never terminate. The `Travel` method terminates if `start >= finish`. At each call to `Travel` we increase the start by one, getting closer to the finish, so that eventually the program will terminate.

Before tackling the interesting binary search and merge sort problems, we use recursion to sum an array of prices. Like the `Travel` method, our recursive `sum` method adds the sum of the remaining elements of the array to the start element. We find the sum of 12.23 + 3.68 + 34.99 + 8.87 + 63.99 by adding 12.23 to the sum of 3.68 + 34.99 + 8.87 + 63.99, which we find by adding 3.68 to the sum of 34.99 + 8.87 + 63.99, and so on.

EXAMPLE 12.2 ■ SumPrices.cs

```
/* The recursive sum method sums the elements
 * from start to end of the array passed to it.
 */

public class SumPrices {
  public static double Sum(double[] p, int start, int end) {
```

```
    if (start < end)
       return p[start] + Sum(p,start+1,end);          // Note 1
    else
       return 0;                                      // Note 2
  }
  public static void Main() {
    double[] prices = {12.23, 3.68, 34.99, 8.87, 63.99};
    System.Console.WriteLine
          ("The sum is {0:C}", Sum(prices,0,prices.Length));
  }
}
```

Output

```
The sum is $123.76
```

Note 1: `return p[start] + Sum(p,start+1,end);`

This is the recursive call in which we add the start element of the array to the remaining elements.

Note 2: `return 0;`

When `start` reaches `end` we have added all the elements and no longer need to make a recursive call. We return a zero as the sum of the remaining (none) elements.

Binary Search

A simple way to search for a value in an array compares the value with each element of the array until we find the element or reach the end of the array. In the worst case, when the element sought is not an element of the array, we must check each element.

If we keep the elements in the array in order from smallest to largest, then we can find an element using binary search, a much more efficient algorithm. We can program binary search as a recursive method or using a loop. In this section we write a recursive method to perform a binary search.

The idea behind binary search is quite simple. Compare the element sought, called the key, with the middle element in the array. If the key equals the middle element, then we have found it and we are done. If the key is smaller than the middle element, we know we need only search the left half of the array; because the array is ordered, a key smaller than the middle element can be found only in the left half of the array. In this case we call the binary search method recursively to search the array elements to the left of the middle. If the key is greater than the middle element, then we need only search the right half of the array. In this case we call the binary search method recursively to search the array elements to the right of the middle.

In the journey of a thousand miles we take the first step, and then travel the rest of the way. In binary search we compare our key to the middle element of the

```
BinarySearch(data,78,0,12)
  1. Find middle element of range:    middle = (0+12)/2   = 6
  2. Find which half test, 78, is in:   78 > data[6]=56
     Conclusion:                        search right half,
                                          index 7 to index 12.

  binarySearch(data,78,7,12)
    1. Find middle element of range:    middle = (7+12)/2 = 9
    2. Find which half test, 78, is in:  78 < data[9]=123
       Conclusion:                       search left half,
                                            from index 7 to 8.

       binarySearch(data,78,7,8)
         1. Find middle element:          middle = (7 + 8)/2 = 7
         2. Find half to test, 78:        78 = data[7]=78
            Conclusion:                   return the index 7
                                                   to the caller.
```

FIGURE 12.1 **Trace of a binary search for 78 in the `data` array**

array, and if it is not the value for which we are searching, we search either the left half or the right half of the array for the key.

Figure 12.1 shows a trace of a binary search for 78 in an array, `data`, where `data = 2,5,7,12,23,34,56,78,99,123,234,345,567}`, whose leftmost element has index 0 and whose rightmost element has index 12.

Example 12.3 shows the code for a binary search. The user inputs the array elements as program arguments to the `Main` method, entering the elements in order from smallest to largest. The program prompts the user for the key to search.

EXAMPLE 12.3 ■ BinarySearch.cs

```
/* Inputs integers in order from smallest to largest on the
 * command line.  Uses a recursive method to implement binary
 * search.
 */

using System;
public class BinarySearch {
  public static int Search
       (int[] data, int key, int left, int right) {
    if (left <= right) {                                    // Note 1
      int middle = (left + right)/2;
      if (key == data[middle])
        return middle;
      else if (key < data[middle])
```

```
        return Search(data,key,left,middle-1);          // Note 2
      else                                              // Note 3
        return Search(data,key,middle+1,right);
    }
    return -1;
  }
  public static void Main(String[] args) {
    int key;        // the search key
    int index;      // the index returned
    int[] data = new int[args.Length];
    for(int i = 0; i < data.Length; i++)
      data[i] = int.Parse(args[i]);                     // Note 4
    Console.Write("Enter the search key: ");
    key = int.Parse(Console.In.ReadLine());
    index = Search(data, key, 0, data.Length-1);
    if (index == -1)
      Console.WriteLine("Key {0} not found", key);
    else
      Console.WriteLine("Key {0} found at index {1}",
                                              key, index);
  }
}
```

(Using program arguments 2 5 7 12 23 34 56 78 99 123 234 345 567)

```
Enter the search key:  78
Key 78 found at index 7
```

(Using program arguments 2 5 7 12 23 34 56 78 99 123 234 345 567)

```
Enter the search key:  8
Key 8 not found
```

Note 1: `if (left <= right) {`

We do not use a `while` loop here, because the recursive call will start the rest of the search. We just determine one of three conditions: either we found the key, it can be found in the left half of the data, or it can be found in the right half of the data. In the first case, we return the index at which we found the key. In the second and third cases, we return the result of the recursive call to the binary search method on the appropriate half of the array.

Note 2: `return Search(data,key,left,middle-1);`

We know that `data[middle]` is greater than the key, so we need to search the array only up to and including the element at index `middle-1`.

Note 3: `else`

In this third case, the only possibility remaining is that

```
key > data[middle]
```

so we call the binary search method to search the array from position `middle+1` to `right`.

Note 4: `data[i] = int.Parse(args[i]);`

We convert the program arguments to `int` values, storing them in the data array that we will search.

We can also program binary search using a `while` loop, without recursion. We leave this approach for the exercises.

Merge Sort

We introduced the insertion sorting method in Chapter 7 and developed a GUI for it in Chapter 9. The **merge sort** algorithm, easily programmed recursively, is much more efficient than insertion sort, especially for larger sets of data.

Merge sort uses the merge operation to sort the data. The merge operation takes two sorted arrays, merging them into a larger sorted array containing all the elements of the original two arrays. For example, the arrays `{2,4,6,8}` and `{1,3,5,7}` merge into the array `{1,2,3,4,5,6,7,8}`. Figure 12.2 traces a merge operation. At each step, we compare the initial elements of the first and second arrays, adding the smallest of these two elements to the merged array. When we have added all the elements of one array to the merged array, we simply copy the remaining elements in the other array to the merged array.

To make an analogy illustrating merge sort, we could say that a journey of a thousand miles ends with a single step. Given an array such as `{8,5,2,7,10,9,3,4}` to sort, we first sort each half, `{8,5,2,7}` and `{10,9,3,4}`, obtaining the two sorted arrays `{2,5,7,8}` and `{3,4,9,10}`. As the final step, we merge the two sorted halves into the final sorted array as shown in Figure 12.2.

FIGURE 12.2
Merging two sorted arrays

First Array	Second Array	Merged Array
{2,5,7,8}	{3,4,9,10}	{2}
{5,7,8}	{3,4,9,10}	{2,3}
{5,7,8}	{4,9,10}	{2,3,4}
{5,7,8}	{9,10}	{2,3,4,5}
{7,8}	{9,10}	{2,3,4,5,7}
{8}	{9,10}	{2,3,4,5,7,8}
{}	{9,10}	{2,3,4,5,7,8,9,10}

We can write the merge sort program very simply, just as described in the last paragraph. The details of sorting the two arrays {8,5,2,7} and {10,9,3,4} are hidden in further recursive calls. To sort {8,5,2,7} we first sort each half, {8,5} and {2,7}, giving the two arrays {5,8} and {2,7}, and then merge these two sorted arrays into {2,5,7,8}. To sort {8,5} we first sort each half, {8} and {5}—the recursion stops here because single-element arrays are already sorted—and then merge these two sorted arrays into the array {5,8}. We have not traced all the steps involved in the merge sort. Tracing shows how the merge sort works, but we do not need these details to write the program.

EXAMPLE 12.4 ■ MergeSort.cs

```
/* Implements the recursive merge sort
 * algorithm to sort an array that the user
 * inputs on the command line.
 */

using System;
public class MergeSort {
  public static void Sort (int[] data, int left, int right) {
    if (left < right) {
      int middle = (left + right)/2;
      Sort(data, left, middle);
      Sort(data, middle + 1, right);
      Merge(data,left, middle, middle+1, right);
    }
  }
  public static void Merge
              (int[] data, int l1, int r1, int l2, int r2) {
    int oldPosition = l1;
    int size = r2 - l1 + 1;
    int[] temp = new int[size];
    int i = 0;
    while (l1 <= r1 && l2 <= r2) {                    // Note 1
      if (data[l1] <= data[l2])
        temp[i++] = data[l1++];
      else
        temp[i++] = data[l2++];
    }
    if (l1 > r1)                                      // Note 2
      for (int j = l2; j <= r2; j++)
        temp[i++] = data[l2++];
    else
      for (int j = l1; j <= r1; j++)
        temp[i++] = data[l1++];
```

```
    Array.Copy(temp, 0, data, oldPosition, size);         // Note 3
  }
  public static void Display(String message,
                                  int[] anArray) {        // Note 4
    Console.Write(message + "{");
    for (int i = 0; i < anArray.Length; i++) {
      if (i != 0) Console.Write(",");
      Console.Write(anArray[i]);
    }
    Console.WriteLine("}");
  }
  public static void Main (String[] args) {
    int[] data = new int[args.Length];
    for (int i=0; i < data.Length; i++)
      data[i] = int.Parse(args[i]);
    Display("The original data: ", data);
    Sort(data, 0, data.Length-1);
    Display("The sorted data: ", data);
  }
}
```

Output

(Using program arguments 8 5 2 7 10 9 3 4 6 11 77 1)

```
{1,2,3,4,5,6,7,8,9,10,11,77}
```

Note 1: `while (l1 <= r1 && l2 <= r2) {`

As long as both arrays that we are merging are not empty, we copy the smallest element of both arrays into a temporary array and increment the index, either l1 or l2, to the array containing the smallest element.

Note 2: `if (l1 > r1)`

If the first array empties first, we copy the remaining elements of the second array into the temporary array; otherwise we copy the remaining elements of the first array.

Note 3: `Array.Copy(temp, 0, data, oldPosition, size);`

We want to copy the merged elements in the temporary array back to the original array that we are sorting. We use the `Copy` method of the `System.Array` class, which takes as its arguments

```
source array
starting index in the source array at which to
    start copying
destination array
```

```
starting index in the destination array for the
    copied elements
number of elements to copy
```

Note 4:
```
public static void Display(String message,
                           int[] anArray) {
```

We use the `Display` method of Example 7.4.

The BIG Picture

Iteration, used in `for` and `while` loops, manages each step of a repetition explicitly. Recursion takes a higher level approach to repetition, doing one step, which reduces the problem to a smaller size, and then asking to repeat that process. The system, behind the scenes, attends to the details. Binary search and merge sort, two important algorithms, illustrate recursion.

✓ Test Your Understanding

1. Trace all the steps of the merge sort method on the array `{8,5,2,7,10,9,3,4}`.
2. As we did in Figure 12.1, trace the steps in the binary search for `8` in the array `{2,5,7,12,23,34,56,78,99,123,234,345,567}`.
3. Run the merge sort of Example 12.4 to sort the array `{34,23,67,87,2,45,98,12,16,78,32}`. (Try It Yourself ➤)

12.2 LINKED LISTS

Data structures, ways of organizing data, are an important computer science topic because they are an important tool programmers use to develop efficient solutions to a variety of problems. Having a repertoire of data structures and the knowledge of the characteristics needed to use them effectively is essential. In this and the next section we introduce two of the most important data structures, the linked list and the stack, to add to the array that we have already introduced.

The very efficient binary search method of Example 12.3 uses an ordered array to hold the data to be searched. We can search array data efficiently, but inserting or deleting elements from an ordered array is not very efficient. For example, to insert 17 in the array `{1,3,5,9,12,15,19,23,34,36,45}`, we would have to move the elements greater than 17 one position to the right, assuming space is available in the array. If the array is full, then we have to allocate a new array and copy the whole array into the larger array.

The **linked list** data structure makes it easy to add or remove elements, which is why it is so important, but searching for an item may be less efficient than in the

FIGURE 12.3 **A linked list**

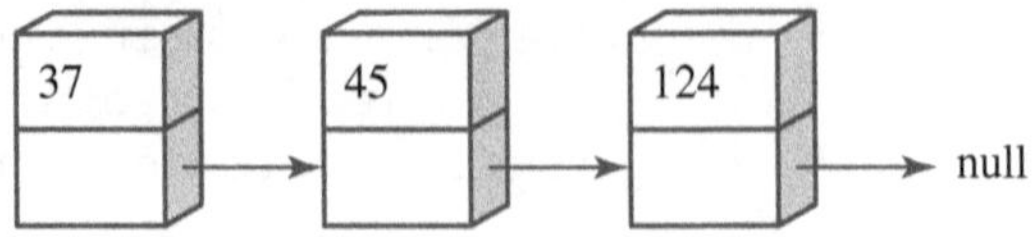

FIGURE 12.4 **Adding 40 to the linked list of Figure 12.3**

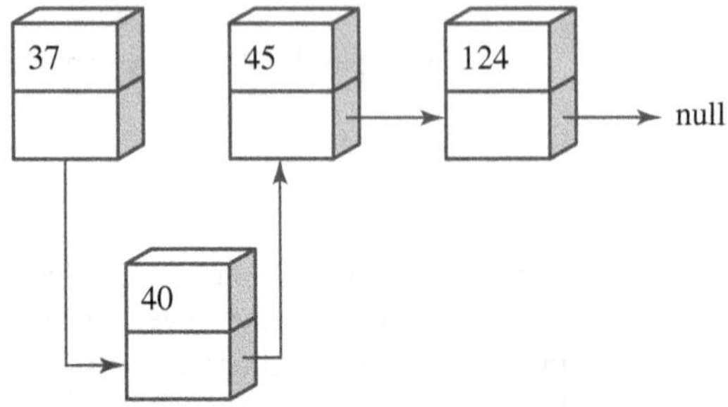

best array searches. In a linked list, we keep each data item in a node that also contains a reference to the next node in the list. Figure 12.3 shows a linked list containing integer data.

We show the reference in each node as an arrow pointing to the next node. In contrast to arrays, which store their elements contiguously, linked lists allocate each individual node as needed. No matter the size of the list, adding an element to it requires us to change only two references, which is why lists are especially useful when we have to perform many additions and deletions. For example, to add 40 to the list of Figure 12.3, we need to allocate a new node, enter 40 in its data field, enter a reference to the node containing 45, and change the node containing 37 to refer to this new node. Figure 12.4 shows these changes.

We can implement a linked list in a variety of ways. We choose to use a class, `Node`, for the individual nodes of the list. The private field `head` refers to the head node, which is the front of the list. The private field `current` refers to the current element. We can advance to the next element of a list, so at any given time we may be inspecting any of the list elements. We need the field `previous`, which refers to the list element just before the current element, when we remove the current element.

Figure 12.5 shows the list operations we include in our `LinkedList` data type. Example 12.5 shows the code for the `LinkedList` class. The `Main` method tests the class. We can use `LinkedList` objects in other classes.

EXAMPLE 12.5 ■ **LinkedList.cs**

```
/* Implements the LinkedList data structure.
 */

using System;
class Node {
  internal Object data;
  internal Node next;
```

`public LinkedList()`
Constructs an empty linked list, with the `head`, `previous`, and `current` nodes null.

`public boolean IsEmpty()`
Returns `true` if the list is empty and `false` otherwise.

`public void Insert(Object o)`
Creates a node containing the object `o`, inserting it before the current element.

`public void Remove()`
Removes the current element.

`public Object GetData()`
Gets the `data` field from the current element. Returns `null` if the current element is null.

`public boolean AtEnd()`
Returns `true` if the current element is `null`, and returns `false` otherwise.

`public void Advance()`
If `current` is not null, advances the `previous` and `current` references.

`public void Reset()`
Resets the `current` reference to refer to the head of the list.

`public void Display()`
Prints each element of the list on a separate line.

FIGURE 12.5 **The operations of the `LinkedList` class**

```
    public Node(Object o, Node n){
      data = o;
      next = n;
    }
  }
  public class LinkedList {
    private Node head;
    private Node previous;
    private Node current;

    public LinkedList() {
      head = null;
      previous = null;
      current = null;
    }
    public bool IsEmpty() {
      return head == null;
    }
    public void Insert(Object o) {                  // Note 1
      Node n = new Node(o,current);                 // Note 2
      if (previous == null)
        head = n;
      else
```

```
      previous.next = n;
    current = n;                                          // Note 3
  }
  public void Remove() {
    if (head != null){
      if (previous == null)                               // Note 4
        head = head.next;
      else
        previous.next = current.next;
      current = current.next;                             // Note 5
    }
  }
  public Object GetData(){
    if (current != null)
      return current.data;
    return null;
  }
  public bool AtEnd() {
    return current == null;
  }
  public void Advance(){
    if (!AtEnd()){
      previous = current;
      current = current .next;
    }
  }
  public void Reset() {
    previous = null;
    current = head;
  }
  public void Display() {
    Reset();                                              // Note 6
    if (head != null)
      do {
        Console.WriteLine("    {0}", GetData());
        Advance();
      }while (!AtEnd());
  }
  public static void Main() {
    LinkedList list = new LinkedList();
    Console.WriteLine("It is {0} that this list in empty",
                                          list.IsEmpty());
    list.Insert("Happy days");
    list.Insert("Pie in the sky");
    list.Insert("Trouble in River City");
    Console.WriteLine("The original list is:");
    list.Display();
    list.Reset();                                         // Note 7
```

```
    list.Advance();
    Console.WriteLine("The current list element is {0}",
                                          list.GetData());
    list.Remove();
    Console.WriteLine
     ("The list, after removing the current element, is:");
                                          list.Display();
  }
}
```

```
It is true that this list is empty
The original list is:
  Trouble in River City
  Pie in the sky
  Happy days
The current list element is Pie in the sky
The list, after removing the current element, is:
  Trouble in River City
  Happy days
```

Note 1: `public void Insert(Object o) {`

We insert the new node before the current element, passing the current element to the `next` field of the new node.

Note 2: `Node n = new Node(o,current);`

If we are inserting a node before the head node, we make `head` refer to the new node; otherwise we set the `next` field of the previous node to refer to the new node.

Note 3: `current = n;`

The node being inserted becomes the current node.

Note 4: `if (previous == null)`

If we remove the head node, then we update the `head` reference; otherwise we change the `next` field of the previous node to refer to the node following the current node. This change unlinks the current node from the list.

Note 5: `current = current.next;`

The node following the current node becomes the new current node when we remove the current node.

Note 6: `Reset();`

We reset to the beginning of the list to display the entire list.

Note 7: `list.Reset();`

After displaying the list, the current node is `null`, at the end of the list. We need to reset to the beginning of the list to process the list further.

A Little Extra **Running Out of Memory**

Whenever we use the `new` operator, as we do in creating nodes in a linked list, we are allocating memory. C# uses garbage collection to reclaim memory no longer in use by our program, but programs that use a lot of memory may cause memory to run out. If not enough memory is available, C# throws the `OutOfMemoryException`. Because our examples have been relatively small, we have not been concerned with running out of memory and have not caught this exception.

The BIG Picture

In contrast to an array, a linked list does not keep its data in neighboring locations, but, rather, each node has a field that refers to its successor. This structure makes it easier to add and delete elements because we do not have to move as many items as we would in an array. We can use an index to directly access an array element, but must traverse the list to reach a list element.

✓Test Your Understanding

4. When using the `Insert` method for a `LinkedList`, is the element inserted before or after the current element?

Try It Yourself ➤ **5.** Devise a thorough series of tests for the `LinkedList` class of Example 12.5. Run these tests and note the results.

12.3 STACKS AND QUEUES

Stack and queues carefully control access to the data. A stack allows insertion and deletion only at one end of the sequence of values. A queue deletes from the front and adds to the back.

Stacks

The stack is one of the most useful data structures. We have already seen it in Section 11.1 in the listing of the stack of method calls in progress when an exception occurs.

Often technical terms mirror familiar terms that provide good analogies to the technical concepts. *Stack* is such a term. A stack of data is similar to a stack of books or a stack of dishes. We add a book to the top of the stack and also remove a book from the

FIGURE 12.6 **A stack growing from left to right**

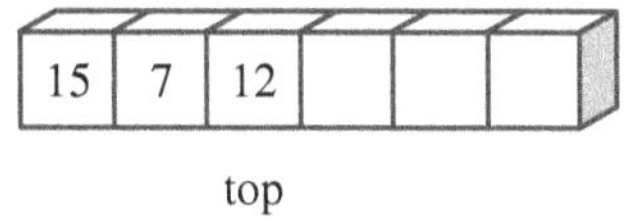

top. Sometimes we call the stack a LIFO stack, where **LIFO** stands for last in, first out. The last dish we stacked is the first that we remove, because it is on the top of the stack.

Of course computer people have to introduce some jargon, so we call the add operation **Push** and the remove operation **Pop**. In addition to the `Push` and `Pop` operations, we want an operation `IsEmpty` to tell us if the stack is empty, an operation `IsFull` to tell us if the stack is full, and an operation `Top` to tell us what is on top of the stack without removing it.

Users of stacks just need to know the stack operations to work with stacks. As implementers of the `Stack` class, we can hide the representation of the stack by using private data fields. Let us use the elements of an array to hold the stack data, which for this example will be integers such as 15, 7, or 12. Stacks of books or dishes grow vertically, but we draw our arrays horizontally, so our stack will grow from left to right. Figure 12.6 shows a stack with space for six integers, which currently contains three integers.

A field, `top`, tells us the index of the top element on the stack. In Figure 12.6, `top` has the value two. The `Top` method returns the element on the top of the stack without changing or removing it. Figure 12.7 shows an empty stack, in which case we assign `top` a value of `-1` to indicate that nothing is on the stack yet. When the stack is full, as in Figure 12.8, then `top` has the value `size-1`, where the `size` field gives the number of elements allocated for the array.

Using our array, we implement the `Push` operation with the pseudocode

FIGURE 12.7 **An empty stack**

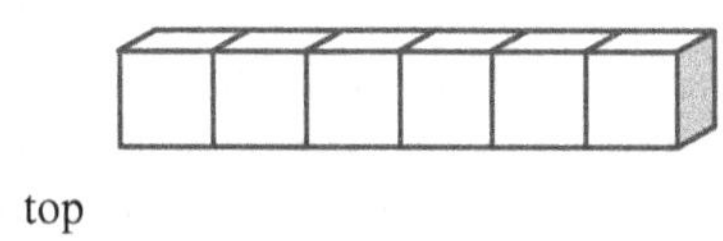

FIGURE 12.8 **A full stack**

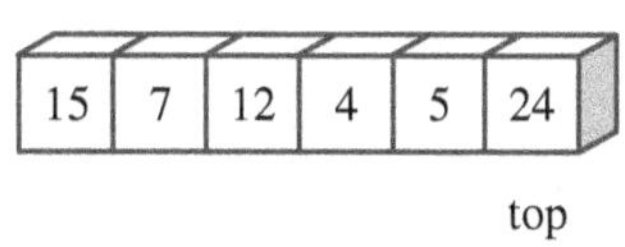

FIGURE 12.9
Pushing 4 onto the stack of Figure 12.6

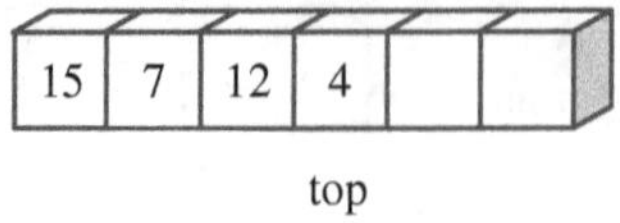


```
if (stack full)
  throw an exception;
else  {
  Increment top;
  Add item to the array at index top;
}
```

Figure 12.9 shows the result of pushing 4 onto the stack of Figure 12.6.

The `Pop` method returns and removes the element on the top of the stack, which presents a problem when the stack is empty, in which case we throw an exception. The pseudocode for the `Pop` operation is

```
if (stack empty) {
  throw an exception;
}
Return the top of the stack and decrement top;
```

Figure 12.10 shows the stack resulting from popping the stack of Figure 12.9. The integer 4 is still at index three of the array, but top is now two, so we ignore it.

When the `Push` method encounters a full stack it can throw a standard `ApplicationException`, passing it a message describing the nature of the error. Similarly, the `Pop` method can throw an `ApplicationException` when it tries to remove an element or return the top from an empty stack. We can also define our own exception classes with names specific to the error identified. For example, to handle a stack empty error, we can define a `StackEmptyException` class, which has a constructor with a string parameter that we pass to the base class. When C# throws a `StackEmptyException` we display this error message and a stack trace.

Example 12.6 shows the code for the stack data type implemented using an array for the stack data, a `size` field giving the number of elements allocated, and a `top` field that holds the index of the top element of the stack. We provide two constructors, one that allocates an array with a default size of 10 and one that allocates an array with a size passed in as an argument. Note that using an array to hold the stack values limits the size of the stack to the number of elements allocated for that array. We leave to the exercises the use of a linked list to create a stack which would remove this limitation.

FIGURE 12.10
Popping the stack of Figure 12.9

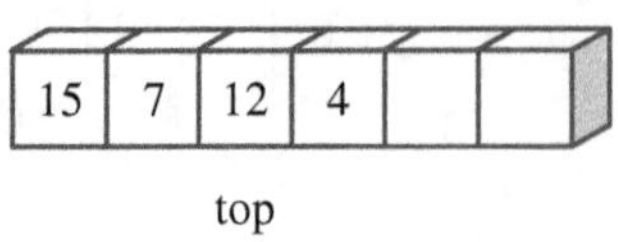

EXAMPLE 12.6 ■ Stack.cs

```
/* Implements the stack data type using
 * an array, and fields top and size.
 */

using System;
public class Stack {
  private int[] data;         // stack data
  private int size;           // size allocated
  private int top = -1;       // index of the top          // Note 1
                              //  or -1 if empty
  public Stack() {                                           // Note 2
    size = 10;
    data = new int[size];
  }
  public Stack(int size) {
    this.size = size;                                        // Note 3
    data = new int[size];
  }
  public bool IsEmpty() {
    return top == -1;                                        // Note 4
  }
  public bool IsFull() {
    return top == size - 1;                                  // Note 5
  }
  public void Push(int i){
    if (IsFull())
      throw new ApplicationException
               ("Stack full -- cannot push");               // Note 6
    else
      data[++top] = i;                                       // Note 7
  }
  public int Pop(){
    if (IsEmpty())
       throw new StackEmptyException
               ("Stack empty -- cannot pop");
    else
       return data[top--];                                   // Note 8
  }
  public int Top(){
    if (IsEmpty())
      throw new StackEmptyException
              ("Stack empty -- top undefined");
    else
      return data[top];
  }
```

```
  public static void Main(String[] args) {
    try {
      Stack stack1 = new Stack();
      Stack stack2 = new Stack(3);
      stack2.Push(4);
      stack2.Push(5);
      Console.WriteLine("The top is now {0}", stack2.Top());
      stack2.Push(6);
      Console.WriteLine
           ("Popping stack 2 returns {0}", stack2.Pop());
      Console.WriteLine("Stack 1 has size {0}", stack1.size);
      Console.WriteLine("Stack 1 empty? {0}", stack1.IsEmpty());
      stack1.Pop();
      Console.WriteLine("Throws exception before we get here");
    }catch(Exception e) {
       Console.WriteLine(e);
    }
  }
}
class StackEmptyException : ApplicationException {
  public StackEmptyException(String message) : base(message) {
  }
}
```

Output

```
The top is now 5
Popping stack 2 returns 6
Stack 1 has size 10
Stack 1 empty? true
StackEmptyException: Stack empty -- cannot pop
   at Stack.Pop()
   at Stack.Main()
```

Note 1: `private int top = -1;`

We always construct empty stacks to start, so no matter which constructor we use, the correct initial value of `top` is −1.

Note 2: `public Stack() {`

This constructor initializes the stack with a default size of 10.

Note 3: `this.size = size;`

This constructor initializes the stack with the size passed in as an argument. The formal parameter has the same name as the field, so we refer to the field as `this.size`, where the variable `this` refers to the current object. We do not often need to refer to the current object explicitly, but here is an example in which we need to use the variable `this`.

Note 4: `return top == -1;`

`top` holds the index of the top element on the stack. When the stack is empty `top` has the value `-1`.

Note 5: `return top == size - 1;`

When the stack is full, `top` holds the index, `size-1`, of the last element in the array.

Note 6:

```
throw new ApplicationException
                    ("Stack full -- cannot push");
```

When the array is full we cannot add any more elements. Trying to add more would cause C# to throw an index out of range exception and abort. We can detect this condition and throw an exception ourselves to allow users of a stack to catch the exception and continue processing. We could have written our own exception class, but for simplicity chose to throw `ApplicationException`. In the `catch` clause, we display the message we pass to the exception object.

Note 7: `data[++top] = i;`

The expression `++top` increments `top` to point to the next free space in the array and returns the new value to use as the array index. This is equivalent to the code

```
top++;
data[top] = i;
```

Note 8: `return data[top--];`

When the stack is not empty, we return the integer `data[top]` at index `top` and decrement `top`. We do not have to remove the value from the array. The index `top` tells us where the top of the stack is. We ignore any array elements with index higher than `top`.

A Little Extra

Using a Stack

Stacks have many uses, including the evaluation of expressions. To evaluate an expression, we write it in **postfix** form, sometimes called reverse Polish notation, in which the operands occur first, followed by the operator. The expression `5 + 6` has the postfix form `5 6 +`, and the expression `(7 + 8)*(4 + 5)` has the postfix form `7 8 + 4 5 + *`. Remember that the postfix form follows the pattern

```
left operand    right operand    operator
```

We will not cover methods for converting an infix expression to its postfix form. It helps to add parentheses and then follow the pattern. For example, given the expression `3 + 4 * 5`, multiplication has higher precedence, so we add parentheses to give `3 + (4*5)`. Following the pattern, the postfix is

```
3    4 5 *      +
```

or `3 4 5 * +`.

Once we have a postfix expression, we can easily evaluate it using a stack. Let us assume, for simplicity, that all operands are single digits 0 to 9, and that the operators are the binary arithmetic operators, `+`, `-`, `*`, and `/`. The algorithm for evaluating a postfix expression is

```
do {
  Read the next character;
  if (next character is a digit)
    Convert the digit to an integer
       and push the integer on  the stack;
  else if (next character is an operator) {
    Pop two operands from stack;
    Perform the operation;
    Push the result onto the stack;
  }
} while (more characters);
  Display the top of the stack;
```

Figure 12.11 applies this algorithm to the expression `7 8 + 4 5 + *`.

TIP

When evaluating subtraction, we take the top entry on the stack and subtract it from the next to the top entry. For example, when evaluating `7 5 -` we follow the steps push 7, push 5, pop 5 and 7, subtract 7-5, push 2.

When evaluating division, we take the top entry on the stack and divide it into the next to the top entry. For example, when evaluating `14 3 /` we follow the steps push 14, push 3, pop 3 and 14, divide 14/3, push 4.

We leave the writing of a program to evaluate a postfix expression using a stack to the exercises.

Queues

A **queue** is like a waiting line in that the first element added is the first removed. We term this a FIFO (First In First Out) queue. `front` and `back` fields keep track of the positions of the first and last elements in the queue. Figure 12.12 shows a queue containing three elements. It can hold six.

The `front` field holds the index of the position before the first element, and the `back` field holds the index of the position after the last element. We add an element at the `back` position and then increment `back` so it still marks the position after the last element. Before removing an element we increment `front`, and then remove the element at the `front` position. After the removal, `front` will still be the position before the first element.

Actions	**Stack**
Read '7'	
Push the integer 7	7
Read '8'	
Push the integer 8	7 8
Read '+'	
Pop 8 and pop 7	empty
Add, getting 15	
Push 15	15
Read '4'	
Push the integer 4	15 4
Read '5'	
Push the integer 5	15 4 5
Read '+'	
Pop 5 and pop 4	15
Add, getting 9	
Push 9	15 9
Read '*'	
Pop 9 and pop 15	empty
Multiply, giving 135	
Push 135	135
Pop 135 and display it.	

FIGURE 12.11 **Evaluating the expression `7 8 + 4 5 + *`**

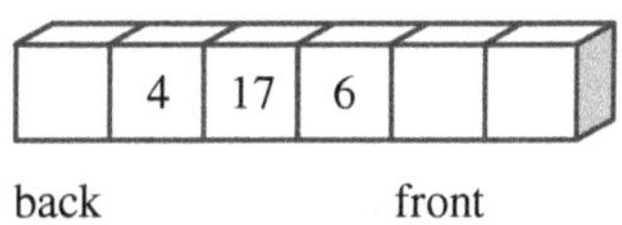

FIGURE 12.12
A queue containing three elements

We start entering queue elements at index 0 of the array, but as we use the queue, removing elements from the front and adding elements to the back, we might reach the end of the array but have free space remaining at the front where elements were removed. To make full use of the array we create a circular queue, where we treat the array as if it were arranged in a circle. In that configuration, position `0` would follow position `size-1`, as Figure 12.13 shows.

When entering elements, we cannot simply increment the `back` index using `back++`. If the array holding the data has size 5, the valid array indices are 0, 1, 2, 3, and 4. If `back` is 4, then `back++` would be 5, which is invalid. We use the expression

```
back++ % size
```

FIGURE 12.13
A circular queue

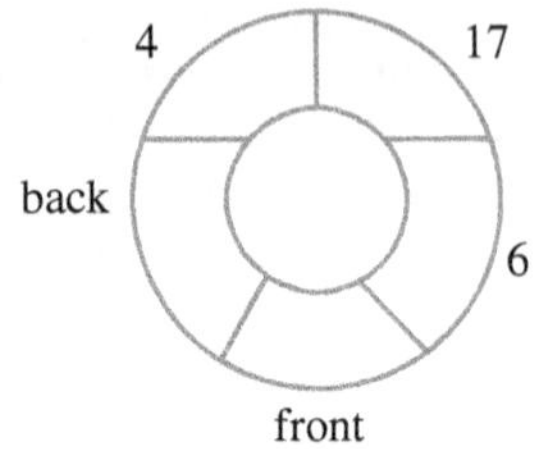

which evaluates to 5%5, which equals 0. Using this expression causes the index 0 to follow the index 4, so the array, in effect, wraps around in a circle. We use similar expressions for all the index calculations. Example 12.7 contains the code for this circular queue.

EXAMPLE 12.7 ■ Queue.cs

```
/* Implements the queue data type using
 * an array, and fields front, back, and size.
 */

using System;
public class Queue {
  private int[] data;      //  stack data
  private int size;        //  size allocated
  private int front = -1;  //  index of the front, -1 if empty
  private int back = 0;    //  index of the first free spot.
  private int count = 0;   //  number of elements in queue

  public Queue() {
    size = 10;
    data = new int[size];
  }
  public Queue(int size) {
    this.size = size;
    data = new int[size];
  }
  public bool IsEmpty() {
    return  count == 0;                                 // Note 1
  }
  public bool IsFull() {
    return count == size;                               // Note 2
  }
  public void Add(int i){
    if (IsFull())
      throw new ApplicationException
                       ("Queue full -- cannot add");
```

```
    else {
      count++;
      data[back++ % size] = i;
    }
  }
  public int Remove(){
    if (IsEmpty())
       throw new ApplicationException
                    ("Queue empty -- cannot remove");
    else {
       count--;
       return data[++front % size];
    }
  }
  public int Head(){
    if (IsEmpty()){
      throw new ApplicationException
                    ("Queue empty -- head undefined");
    }
    else
      return data[(front+1) % size];
  }
  public static void Main() {
    try {
      Queue q1 = new Queue();
      Queue q2 = new Queue(3);
      q2.Add(4);
      q2.Add(5);
      Console.WriteLine("The front is now {0}", q2.Head());
      q2.Add(6);
      Console.WriteLine
             ("Removing from q2 returns {0}", q2.Remove());
      Console.WriteLine("Queue 1 has size {0}", q1.size);
      Console.WriteLine("Queue 1 empty? {0}", q1.IsEmpty());
      q1.Remove();
      Console.WriteLine("Throws exception before we get here");
    }catch(Exception e) {
        Console.WriteLine(e);
    }
  }
}
```

Output

```
The front is now 4
Removing from q2 returns 4
Queue 1 has size 10
Queue 1 empty? True
```

```
System.ApplicationException: Queue empty -- cannot remove
   at Queue.Remove()
   at Queue.Main()
```

Note 1: `return   count == 0;`

We use a `count` field to keep track of the number of elements in the queue. The queue is empty when `count` is 0.

Note 2: `return count == size;`

When the queue is full, `count` equals `size`, the capacity of the array.

The `System.Collections` namespace contains `Stack` and `Queue` classes, but we feel it is instructive to build them ourselves. We look at `System.Collections` in the remainder of the chapter.

The BIG Picture

A stack allows us to add and remove data at the top of the stack. Because we implemented a stack using an array, we throw an exception if the user tries to pop an empty stack or to push onto a full stack. We illustrated this by throwing a standard `ApplicationException` and creating our own `StackEmptyException` class. Stacks have many uses; one is evaluating postfix expressions. A queue allows us to add at the front and remove from the back of the queue.

✓Test Your Understanding

6. Show the stack of Figure 12.6 after performing the operations `Pop()`, `Pop()`, and `Push(19)`, in that order.

7. Show the stack of Figure 12.6 after performing the operation `Push(Pop())`. What can you conclude about the relationship between the push and pop operations?

A Little Extra

8. Use a stack to evaluate the following postfix expressions:

   a. `2 3 4 * + 6 2 - +`

   b. `9 9 + 9 9 * -`

   c. `6 3 / 4 9 8 + - +`

Try It Yourself ➤

9. Run additional tests of the stack operations for the `Stack` class of Example 12.6.

10. Will a test `front  ==  back` determine when the queue of Example 12.7 is full? Explain.

12.4 COLLECTIONS: ArrayList

The System.Collections namespace contains interfaces and classes for several useful data structures. In this section we cover lists, and in the next section we cover dictionaries.

An ArrayList is like an array, but it can grow in size. It represents a sequence of values that we access by an index as we do with ordinary arrays. The ArrayList class has three constructors. Using the default

```
new ArrayList();
```

will give us a vector of capacity 16, which doubles in size when more space is needed. The constructor

```
new ArrayList(200);
```

creates a list with the capacity to hold 200 elements, which doubles in size when necessary. The third constructor initializes the ArrayList to another collection passed to it.

To add an element to the end of an ArrayList we use the Add method, which has a parameter of type Object. Because every class is, directly or indirectly, a subclass of Object, we can add any object to an ArrayList. We can also add primitive types, which C# will wrap in an object for us. This process is known as boxing. The code

```
ArrayList v = new ArrayList ();
String s = "Happy days";
v.Add(s);
```

creates an ArrayList and a string and adds the string to the ArrayList.

Using the Add method, as in

```
v.Add("A big car");
v.Add("Less is more");
```

adds the strings at the end of the ArrayList

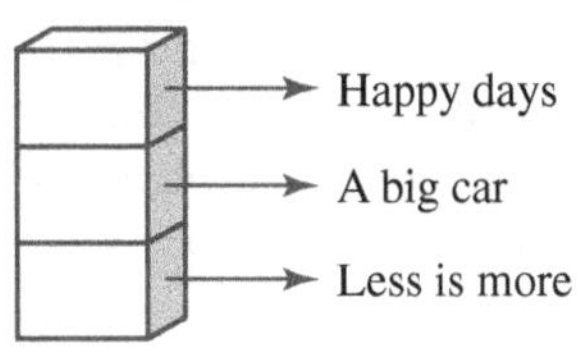

We could use the Insert method to insert an item at a given index in the ArrayList, but that is less efficient than adding at the end. For example,

```
v.Insert(1,"Candy and cake");
```

changes v to

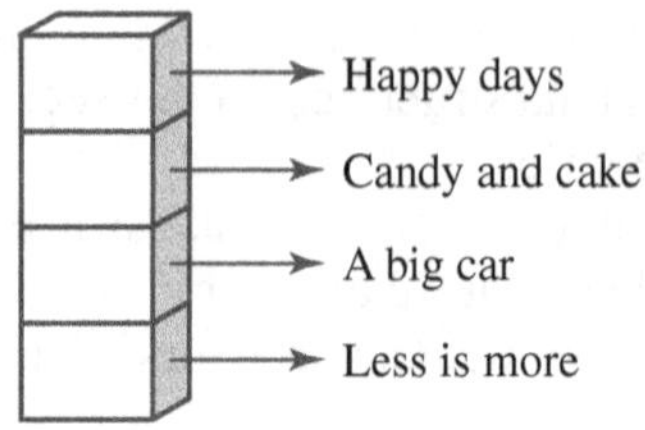

requiring the moving of two elements. In a large `ArrayList`, insertion might require moving a large number of elements.

We use array notation to get the element at a given index. For example,

```
String atTwo = (String)v[2];
```

assigns `"A big car"` to `atTwo`. We cast the `Object` value to `String`. The `ArrayList` `v` contains only string elements, so we know casting to a string will not cause an error.

The `ArrayList` class provides several methods to locate elements. The `Contains` method returns `true` if its argument is an element of the list and `false` otherwise. Thus

```
v.Contains("A big car");
```

returns `true`, but

```
v.Contains("Sweet dreams");
```

returns `false`. If we need the exact location of an element, the `indexOf` method returns the index of its first occurrence in the `ArrayList`, or −1 if it does not occur. For example,

```
v.IndexOf("A big car");
```

would return 2, and

```
v.IndexOf("Sweet dreams");
```

would return −1. The call

```
v.IndexOf("Happy days",1);
```

returns −1, because there is no occurrence in `v` of `"Happy days"` starting at index 1. Another version of `IndexOf` accepts three arguments: the object sought, the initial index to start searching at, and the number of elements to search.

The `Capacity` property gets or sets the number of elements allocated for the list and the `Count` property gets the number of its elements. Thus

```
v.Capacity;
```

returns 16, and

```
v.Count;
```

returns 4. Either

```
v.Remove("Candy and cake");
```

or

```
v.Remove(1);
```

would remove the element at index `1` from `v`.

The `foreach` Statement

The `foreach` statement enumerates the elements of a collection. It executes an embedded statement for each element of the collection. For example,

```
foreach (String  s in v)
  Console.WriteLine(s);
```

displays each `String` in the `ArrayList v`.

Example 12.8 illustrates `ArrayList` methods using the text from the Gettsyburg address, in the file `gettysburg.txt`.

EXAMPLE 12.8 ■ ListMethods.cs

```
/* Illustrates ArrayList methods.
 */

using System;
using System.IO;
using System.Collections;
public class ListMethods {
  public static void Main(String[] args) {
    StreamReader input = new StreamReader(args[0]);
    ArrayList list = new ArrayList();                         // Note 1
    String line;
    int duplicates = 0;
    while((line = input.ReadLine()) != null) {
      String[] token = line.Split(new char[]
           {'-',' ', ',', '.', '\n', '\r', '\t'});            // Note 2
      for(int i = 0; i < token.Length; i++) {
        String tok = token[i].ToLower();                      // Note 3
        if (list.Contains(tok))                               // Note 4
          duplicates++;
        else if(tok != "")
          list.Add(tok);
      }
    }
    Console.WriteLine
       ("{0} has {1} distinct words.", args[0], list.Count);
    Console.WriteLine
          ("There are {0} duplicate words.", duplicates);
    Console.WriteLine
          ("The capacity is {0}", list.Capacity);             // Note 5
    Console.WriteLine("Contains \"fourscore\"? {0}",
```

```
                          list.Contains("fourscore"));
    Console.WriteLine("Contains \"computer\"? {0}",
                                     list.Contains("computer"));
    Console.WriteLine("Index of \"ago\" is {0}",
                                 list.IndexOf("ago"));
    Console.WriteLine("Inserting \"computer\"");
    list.Insert(4,"computer");
    Console.WriteLine("Element 3 is {0} and 4 is {1}",
                                    list[3], list[4]);
    Console.WriteLine("Removing \"computer\"");
    list.Remove("computer");
    Console.WriteLine("Removing element at index 3");
    list.RemoveAt(3);
    Console.WriteLine("Element 3 is {0} and 4 is {1}",
                                    list[3], list[4]); // Note 6
    Console.WriteLine("Reversing the first four elements");
    list.Reverse(0,4);
    Console.WriteLine
         ("The first four elements are: {0} {1} {2} {3}",
                       list[0], list[1], list[2], list[3]);
    Console.WriteLine("Sorting the list");
    list.Sort();                                       // Note 7
    Console.WriteLine
         ("The first four elements are: {0} {1} {2} {3}",
                       list[0], list[1], list[2], list[3]);
    Console.WriteLine
      ("Creating an ArrayList from elements 20, 21, and 22");
    ArrayList three = list.GetRange(20, 3);            // Note 8
    Console.WriteLine("These elements are: {0} {1} {2}",
                          list[20], list[21], list[22]);
    three[1] = "potato";                               // Note 9
    Console.WriteLine
     ("Changing three[1] changes list[21] to {0}",list[21]);
    ArrayList shallow = (ArrayList)list.Clone();      // Note 10
    shallow[21] = "cause";                            // Note 11
    Console.WriteLine("Changing shallow[21] but "
                  + "list[21] remains {0}", list[21]);
    Console.WriteLine("The list contains: ");
    int k = 0;
    foreach(String s in shallow) {                    // Note 12
      Console.Write("{0,12} ", s);                    // Note 13
      if(++k % 6 == 0) Console.WriteLine();
    }
    Console.WriteLine();
    Console.WriteLine("\"fathers\" found at index {0}",
      list.BinarySearch("fathers"));                  // Note 14
  }
}
```

Output

```
gettysburg.txt has 138 distinct words.
There are 129 duplicate words.
The capacity is 256
Contains "fourscore"? True
Contains "computer"? False
Index of "ago" is 4
Inserting "computer"
Element 3 is years and 4 is computer
Removing "computer"
Removing element at index 3
Element 3 is ago and 4 is our
Reversing the first four elements
The first four elements are: ago seven and fourscore
Sorting the list
The first four elements are: a above add advanced
Creating an ArrayList from elements 20, 21, and 22
These elements are: cannot cause civil
The list contains:
          a      above          add    advanced      ago          all
 altogether        and          any         are       as  battlefield
         be     before        birth       brave  brought          but
         by        can       cannot       cause    civil         come
  conceived consecrate  consecrated   continent  created         dead
   dedicate  dedicated      detract    devotion      did         died
         do      earth       endure     engaged    equal          far
    fathers      field        final     fitting      for       forget
      forth     fought    fourscore     freedom     from         full
       gave        god   government       great   ground       hallow
       have       here       highly     honored       in    increased
         is         it       larger        last  liberty       little
       live      lives       living        long  measure          men
        met      might       nation       never      new        nobly
        nor        not         note         now       of           on
         or        our       people      perish    place         poor
    portion      power       proper proposition   rather    remaining
   remember    resolve      resting         say    sense        seven
      shall     should           so   struggled     take         task
    testing       that          the       their    these         they
       this      those         thus          to    under   unfinished
         us       vain          war          we     what      whether
      which        who         will        work    world
"fathers" found at index 42
```

Note 1: `ArrayList list = new ArrayList();`

The default size is 16. If we know the approximate size of the data it would be more efficient to pass it to the constructor to allocate the entire list now, instead of having to double the size when it gets full and copy from the smaller to the bigger list.

Note 2:
```
String[] token = line.Split(new char[]
    {'-',' ', ',', '.', '\n', '\r', '\t'});
```

We do not want to include punctuation as parts of the words, so we include these characters passed to the `Split` method to signal the end of words.

Note 3:
```
String tok = token[i].ToLower();
```

Words such as `"The"` and `"the"` would both appear in the list unless we first convert each word to lowercase.

Note 4:
```
if (list.Contains(tok))
```

If the word is in the list already, we increase the duplicate count. If not and it is not empty, we add it to the list.

Note 5:
```
Console.WriteLine
   ("The capacity is {0}", list.Capacity);
```

As we added words, the `Capacity` went from 16 to 32 to 64 to 128 to 256.

Note 6:
```
Console.WriteLine("Element 3 is {0} and 4 is {1}",
                                       list[3], list[4]);
```

This shows that the previous `list[3]` and `list[4]` elements have been removed.

Note 7:
```
list.Sort();
```

The `Sort` method uses the `QuickSort` algorithm to sort the list. To sort, we must be able to compare any two elements. The `String` class defines a comparison method that determines whether one string is greater than, equal to, or less than another, so we can sort strings.

Note 8:
```
ArrayList three = list.GetRange(20, 3);
```

We create an `ArrayList` using three elements from `list`, starting at index 20. The list `three` shares its elements with the source, `list`.

Note 9:
```
three[1] = "potato";
```

`three[1]` refers to the same element as `list[21]`. Changing one will change the other.

Note 10:
```
ArrayList shallow = (ArrayList)list.Clone();
```

The `Clone` method makes a shallow copy of the list. It copies the objects so there is no sharing. We call it a shallow copy because it does not copy any objects referred by the list elements.

Note 11:
```
shallow[21] = "cause";
```

When we change `shallow[21]` we do not change `list[21]`, because in creating `shallow` we make copies of the objects in `list`.

Note 12: `foreach(String s in shallow) {`

The `foreach` statement lets us process each element in a collection. In this case, we display each `String` in the `ArrayList shallow` in a table.

Note 13: `Console.Write("{0,12} ", s);`

The format `{0,12}` right-justifies the value in a field of width 12.

Note 14: `list.BinarySearch("fathers"));`

Because we sorted the list, we can use the `BinarySearch` method to find the index of the `String` to which we pass an argument.

To provide another illustration of `ArrayList` objects, we create a list of the Fibonacci numbers less than 2^{63}. We choose this upper limit because the `ulong` type in C# uses 64 bits to hold unsigned integers. The Fibonacci sequence starts with its first two elements, $f_1 = f_2 = 1$, and the remaining numbers are computed by

$$f_{i+1} = f_i + f_{i-1}$$

so the first 10 Fibonacci numbers are 1, 1, 2, 3, 5, 8, 13, 21, 34, and 55. The Fibonacci numbers have useful applications in numerical analysis and occur in nature, but here we use them solely to illustrate `ArrayList`.

EXAMPLE 12.9 ■ Fibonacci.cs

```
/* Uses the Fibonacci sequence to
 * illustrate ArrayList
 */

using System;
using System.Collections;
public class Fibonacci {
  public static void Main() {
    ArrayList fib =  new ArrayList();
    Console.WriteLine("The initial capacity is {0}",
                                        fib.Capacity);
    ulong previous = 1;
    ulong current = previous;
    double limit = Math.Pow(2,63);
    fib.Add(previous);
    ulong temp;
    while (current < limit) {
      fib.Add(current);
      temp = current;
      current += previous;                          // Note 1
      previous = temp;
```

```
    }
    Console.WriteLine("The fifth Fibonacci number is {0}",
                                               fib[4]);  // Note 2
    Console.WriteLine("The capacity is {0}",
                                         fib.Capacity);  // Note 3
    Console.WriteLine("The count is {0}", fib.Count);
    Console.WriteLine("Fibonacci number {0} is {1}",
                          fib.Count, fib[fib.Count-1]); // Note 4
    ArrayList divByFive = new ArrayList();
    foreach (ulong num in fib) {
       if (num % 5 == 0)
          divByFive.Add(num);                           // Note 5
    }
    Console.WriteLine
         ("The Fibonacci numbers divisible by five are:");
    foreach (ulong five in divByFive)
       Console.Write("{0} ", five);
    Console.WriteLine("\r\nThe capacity is {0}",
                                   divByFive.Capacity);
    Console.WriteLine("The count is {0}", divByFive.Count);
    Console.WriteLine("The sixth Fibonacci divisible by five"
                 + " is the {0}th Fibonacci number ",
                       fib.IndexOf(divByFive[5]) + 1); // Note 6
    int count = 0;
    Random random = new Random();
    do {
      count++;
    }while (!fib.Contains((ulong)random.Next(100)));   // Note 7
    Console.WriteLine
          ("It took {0} tries to find a Fibonacci number"
           + " less than 100 randomly", count);
  }
}
```

Output

```
The initial capacity is 16
The fifth Fibonacci number is 5
The capacity is 128
The count is 92
Fibonacci number 92 is 7540113804746346429
The Fibonacci numbers divisible by five are:
5 55 610 6765 75025 832040 9227465 102334155 1134903170
12586269025 139583862445 1548008755920 17167680177565
190392490709135 2111485077978050 23416728348467685
259695496911122585 2880067194370816120
The capacity is 32
The count is 18
The sixth Fibonacci divisible by five is the 30th
```

```
Fibonacci number
It took 4 tries to find a Fibonacci number less than 100
randomly
```

Note 1: `current += previous;`

We use two variables, `previous` and `current`, to represent the last two Fibonacci numbers computed. Each time through the loop we save the current number, add it to the previous number to get the updated `current`, and then copy the saved old `current` to get the new `previous`.

Note 2: `fib[4]`

It is always a good practice to check a computation with a known value, which we do here, checking that the fifth Fibonacci number is 5.

Note 3: `fib.Capacity`

The capacity increased from its original 16 to 32 to 64 to 128 when necessary.

Note 4: `fib.Count, fib[fig.Count-1]`

We list the largest Fibonacci number we found.

Note 5: `divByFive.Add(num)`

We create a new `ArrayList` and add to it each number from the original list that is divisible by five.

Note 6: `fib.IndexOf(divByFive[5]) + 1`

We find the index in `fib` of the sixth Fibonacci number that is divisible by five.

Note 7: `}while (!fib.Contains((ulong)random.Next(100)));`

We keep computing random numbers from 1 to 100 as long as they are not Fibonacci numbers. Because there are 11 Fibonacci numbers between 1 and 100, we expect about `100/11 = 9.09` trials, on the average, until we find a Fibonacci number.

Timing `ArrayList` Operations

The `Environment` class has a `TickCount` property that gives the number of milliseconds since the computer was last started. We can use this value to time operations to test their efficiency. However, we need to repeat the operation many times to use enough time to measure with this tool. Example 12.10 illustrates this process.

EXAMPLE 12.10 ■ ArrayListTiming.cs

```
/* Checks time needed for list operations
 * using an ArrayList implementation.
 */

using System;
using System.Drawing;
using System.Collections;
```

```
public class ArrayListTiming {
  public static void Main() {
    ArrayList arrayImp = new ArrayList();
    Point p = new Point(34, 156);                         // Note 1
    int time1, time2;
    Object o;
    time1 = Environment.TickCount;
    for(int i = 0; i < 100000; i++)
       arrayImp.Add(p);                                   // Note 2
    time2 = Environment.TickCount;
    Console.WriteLine("Time for 100,000 adds: " +
                       (time2 - time1));                  // Note 3
    time1 = Environment.TickCount;
    for(int i = 0; i < 10000; i++)
       arrayImp.Insert(50, p);                            // Note 4
    time2 = Environment.TickCount;
    Console.WriteLine
       ("Time for 10,000 adds at position 50: "
                                    + (time2 - time1));
    time1 = Environment.TickCount;
    for(int i = 0; i < 10000000; i++)
       o = arrayImp[5000];                                // Note 5
    time2 = Environment.TickCount;
    Console.WriteLine
       ("Time for 10,000,000 gets at position 5000: "
                                    + (time2 - time1));
  }
}
```

Output

```
Time for 100,000 adds: 31
Time for 10,000 adds at position 50: 2906
Time for 10,000,000 gets at position 5000: 125
```

Note 1: `Point p = new Point(34, 156);`

We choose an arbitrary value to add to the `ArrayList`.

Note 2: `arrayImp.Add(p);`

Because we are adding at the end of the array, we do not have to move any elements and the operation is very efficient.

Note 3:
```
Console.WriteLine("Time for 100,000 adds: " +
                   (time2 - time1));
```

We get the `TickCount` just before and just after we do the 100,000 `Add` operations. Subtracting these values gives the time elapsed.

Note 4: `arrayImp.Insert(50, p);`

Adding at position 50 in this array requires us to move at least 9950 elements one position to the right to make room for the added element. This is not efficient.

Note 5: `o = arrayImp[5000];`

Using the index, we can retrieve the element at position 5000 without accessing any other array elements, which is extremely efficient.

> **The BIG Picture**
>
> An `ArrayList` grows automatically to accommodate more data. The `foreach` statement allows us to process each element of a collection. Using the `TickCount` we can time code segments to estimate their efficiency.

✓ Test Your Understanding

11. Declare an `ArrayList` that initially can hold 25 elements.

12. Explain the difference between the `ArrayList` `capacity` and the `size` methods.

12.5 COLLECTIONS: `Hashtable` AND `SortedList`

In this section we look at collections of key–value pairs such as a dictionary, in which the word is the key and the definition is the value. Just as we look up a word to find its definition, we look up a key to find its value. The two implementations, `Hashtable` and `SortedList`, have contrasting strengths and weaknesses. A `Hashtable` is very efficient, but cannot easily produce a range of sorted data. A `SortedList` is generally not as efficient as a `Hashtable`, but it does allow us to find a range of ordered values. The C# `SortedList` cleverly combines features of a hash table and an array to get good performance.

`Hashtable`

A **hash table** maps keys to values. We use a hash function to compute an integer from the data that will tell us where to add or search for that item. Suppose we want to create a symbol table of identifiers in a program. Each identifier is the name of a variable or other entity. We associated various properties with a variable such as its type and memory location. For simplicity, in Figure 12.14 we associate only a type with each variable.

The idea of hashing is that we compute an integer from the key and use that integer as an array index to enter the identifier and its associated data. For example, suppose that the hash function computes 10 when given the identifier `sum`. Then we enter `sum` at index 10 in the array. When we need to look up the data for `sum`, we compute the hash value, 10, and find `sum` in position 10 without searching any other elements.

FIGURE 12.14
Identifiers and their types

Variable name	Type
sum	int
average	double
count	int
number	int
name	String
address	String
repeat	char
line	String
background	Color
g	Graphics
print	Button
text	TextBox

In this ideal case hashing is very fast, because with only a simple computation and no search we can find the data. In practice, collisions occur because hash functions produce duplicate values. If the hash value for `count` is also 10, then we cannot put `count` in position 10 because `sum` is already there. Various collision resolution algorithms find another location for `count`. When we look up `count` we first expect it to be in location 10, but not finding it there, we have to continue the search, which becomes less efficient.

A good hash function distributes the hash values with few duplicates. Ideally, the 12 entries in Figure 12.14 would have 12 different hash values, so there would be no conflicts. The worst hash function gives the 12 identifiers a single value such as 10. A typical hash function uses the features of the data it is hashing. A hash function might add the values of each character and shift bits to increase randomness.

A class whose objects might be hashed should override the `GetHashCode` method, inherited from `Object`, which returns an integer value. The hash values might be rather large numbers and we may have a relatively small table. For example, to store the 12 identifiers of Figure 12.14 we could use a table of size 23. This allows some extra space to reduce the chance of collisions. If the hash value is larger than 22, we find its remainder when divided by 23 to get its table index. For example, if `repeat` has a hash value of 12345, we compute `12345 % 23`, which gives 17 as the table index.

Figure 12.14 contains `String` data, and fortunately the `String` class has a `GetHashCode` method. Example 12.11 computes the hash values for each identifier and the table indices based on a table size of 23. We do not enter any data in a hash table until the next example.

EXAMPLE 12.11 ■ HashValues.cs

```
/* Computes the hash values of 12 identifiers, and
 * the index of each in a table of size 23.
 */
```

```
using System;
public class HashValues {
  public static void Main( ) {
    String[] identifiers = {"sum","average","count","number",
                            "name", "address", "repeat","line",
                            "background","g","print","text"};
    for(int i = 0; i < identifiers.Length; i++) {
      String id = identifiers[i];
      int hash = id.GetHashCode();
      int code = hash % 23;                          // Note 1
      Console.WriteLine("{0,-12}{1,12}{2,12}",
                             id, hash, code);        // Note 2
    }
  }
}
```

Output

```
sum            193432878           3
average        627270758          15
count          176967078          18
number        1682699846          20
name          2087876002          11
address         76895091          19
repeat        2123762162           7
line          2087656651          11
background    1383623595          14
g                 177602          19
print          187024980          20
text          2087956376           0
```

Note 1: `int code = hash % 23;`

The remainder of the hash code when divided by 23 gives a number from 0 to 22, which we use to enter the data in a hash table of size 23 in the next example.

Note 2:
```
Console.WriteLine("{0,-12}{1,12}{2,12}",
                             id, hash, code);
```

We use format specifiers to right-justify the indentifiers and left-justify the integers in fields of size 12. We use the `Add` method

```
void Add(Object key, Object value)
```

to enter data in a hash table, and array index notation to retrieve it. Example 12.12 puts all the values from Figure 12.14 into a hash table.

```
/* Enters 12 identifiers in a hash table.
 */

using System;
using System.Collections;
public class HashPut {
  public static void Main() {
    String[] identifiers = {"sum","average","count","number",
                            "name","address","repeat","line",
                            "background","g","print","text"};
    String[] types = {"int","double","int","int","string",
                      "string","char","string","Color",
                      "Graphics","Button","TextBox"};
    Hashtable table = new Hashtable(23);                // Note 1
    for(int i = 0; i < identifiers.Length; i++)
      table.Add(identifiers[i], types[i]);              // Note 2
    Console.WriteLine("The type of background is {0}",
                              table["background"]);     // Note 3
    Console.WriteLine("The keys are:");
    foreach (DictionaryEntry entry in table)            // Note 4
      Console.Write("{0} ", entry.Key);
  }
}
```

Output

```
The type of background is Color
The keys are:
average address line sum text repeat background number print
name g count
```

■

Note 1: `Hashtable table = new Hashtable(23);`

We choose a table size to be a prime number. By choosing it to be about double the size of the data, we reduce the number of collisions expected. The ratio of the number of keys in the table to the size of the table is called the **load**. In order not to degrade performance, we like to keep the load under .75.

Note 2: `table.Add(identifiers[i], types[i]);`

We put each identifier into the table and associate its type with it.

Note 3:
```
Console.WriteLine("The type of background is {0}",
                              table["background"]);
```

We use array notation to retrieve the object associated with the key `"background"`.

FIGURE 12.15
Rivers of the world and their lengths (in miles)

Amazon	4000	Indus	1800
Chang (Yangtze)	3964	Mekong	2600
Colorado	1450	Mississippi	2340
Columbia	1243	Missouri	2315
Congo	2718	Niger	2590
Danube	1776	Nile	4160
Euphrates	1700	Rio Grande	1900
Ganges	1560	Volga	2290
Huang (Yellow)	3395		

Note 4: `foreach (DictionaryEntry entry in table)`

The `foreach` statement requires the type of the elements in the collection. For `Hashtable` the type is `DictionaryEntry`, which is a `(key, value)` pair. We can use the `Key` and `Value` properties. We see that the keys do not appear in alphabetical order. A hash table is not a suitable data structure when we need to find a range of elements, such as all keys beginning with the letter '`m`'.

As another example, Figure 12.15 shows the lengths of some of the world's major rivers. The key is the name of the river, and the value is its length.

A hash table uses a hash function to map each key to a location. In our example we have 17 rivers. We will create a hash table with 37 spaces to reduce the chance of collisions. There are thousands of possible river names. A hash function associates a position in a hash table with a name. For example, a simple hash function might add up the ASCII values of the characters in the name and divide by the table size to get the remainder, which gives the table position. For `Nile` that calculation would be

```
N=78, i=105, l=108, e=101
78+105+108+101 = 392
392 = 10*37 + 22
```

so `Nile` would go in position 22 in the table.

Because C# implements the hashing function, we do not need to know the details, but it helps to see the basic concept to understand the efficiency of the operation. To enter `Nile` in the table or to search for it requires just a computation of the hash function without traversing other elements in the table, except to resolve collisions that arise when another element also hashes to the same value of 22.

The reason an alphabetical listing is difficult is that adjacent elements alphabetically may have totally different hash values. For example, to hash `Rio Grande`

```
R=82, i=105, o=111, blank=32, G=71, r=114, a=97, n=110,
   d=100, e=101
82+105+111+32+71+114+97+110+100+101 = 923
923 = 24*37+35
```

Rio Grande would go in position 35 if this hash function were used.

A SortedList represents a collection of (key, value) pairs sorted by key. We compare the efficiency of a Hashtable with a SortedList in the next example, and use sorted lists in the next section.

EXAMPLE 12.13 ■ RiverMap.cs

```
/* Illustrates Hashtable methods.  Compares
 * Hashtable with SortedList.
 */

using System;
using System.Collections;
public class RiverMap {
  public static void Main() {
    Hashtable rivers = new Hashtable(37);                    // Note 1
    int[] lengths = {4000,3964,1450,1243,2718,1776,1700,
      1560,3395,1800,2600,2340,2315,2590,4160,1900,2290};
    String[] names = {"Amazon", "Chang", "Colorado", "Columbia",
                      "Congo", "Danube", "Euphrates", "Ganges",
                      "Huang", "Indus", "Mekong", "Mississippi",
                      "Missouri", "Niger", "Nile", "Rio Grande",
                      "Volga"};
    int size = 0;
    for (int i = 0; i < names.Length; i++)
         rivers.Add(names[i], lengths[i]);
    Console.WriteLine("The size of the rivers map is: "
         + rivers.Count);                                    // Note 2
    Console.WriteLine("Rivers map contains key 'Congo': "
         + rivers.Contains("Congo"));                        // Note 3
    Console.WriteLine("Rivers map contains value 3500: "
         + rivers.ContainsValue(3500));                      // Note 4
    foreach (DictionaryEntry entry in rivers)
      Console.Write("{[leftbrace]0}, {1}] ", entry.Key,
                                          entry.Value);
    Console.WriteLine();
    SortedList riversList = new SortedList(rivers);      // Note 5
    foreach (DictionaryEntry entry in riversList)
      Console.Write("{[leftbrace]0}, {1}] ", entry.Key,
                                          entry.Value);
    Console.WriteLine();
    long starttime = Environment.TickCount;
    for (int i = 0; i < 100000; i++)
      size = (int)rivers["Columbia"];
    long stoptime = Environment.TickCount;
    Console.WriteLine
         ("Time for 100000 gets in a hashtable is {0}",
```

```
                                   (stoptime-starttime));
    starttime = Environment.TickCount;
    for (int i = 0; i < 100000; i++)
      size = (int)riversList["Columbia"];
    stoptime = Environment.TickCount;
    Console.WriteLine
       ("Time for 100000 gets in a sorted list is {0}",
                                   (stoptime-starttime));// Note 6
  }
}
```

Output

```
The size of the rivers map is: 17
Rivers map contains key 'Congo': True
Rivers map contains value 3500: False
[Columbia, 1243] [Rio Grande, 1900] [Indus, 1800] [Huang,
3395] [Volga, 2290] [Ganges, 1560] [Congo, 2718] [Niger,
2590] [Danube, 1776] [Euphrates, 1700] [Mississippi, 2340]
[Missouri, 2315] [Colorado, 1450] [Amazon, 4000] [Nile,
4160] [Mekong, 2600] [Chang, 3964]
[Amazon, 4000] [Chang, 3964] [Colorado, 1450] [Columbia,
1243] [Congo, 2718] [Danube, 1776] [Euphrates, 1700]
[Ganges, 1560] [Huang, 3395] [Indus, 1800] [Mekong, 2600]
[Mississippi, 2340] [Missouri, 2315] [Niger, 2590] [Nile,
4160] [Rio Grande, 1900] [Volga, 2290]
Time for 100000 gets in a hashtable is 16
Time for 100000 gets in a sorted list is 62
```

Note 1: `Hashtable rivers = new Hashtable(37);`

We choose a table size of 37 because it is the nearest prime to twice the size of the data. We want the data to be spread as uniformly as possible in the table to minimize the chance of collisions and a prime table size helps spread the values to each possible location using the common hash functions.

Note 2: `Console.WriteLine("The size of the rivers map is: " + rivers.Count);`

The `Count` property gives us the number of elements currently in the collection.

Note 3: `Console.WriteLine("Rivers map contains key 'Congo': " + rivers.Contains("Congo"));`

The `Contains` method behaves the same as the `ContainsKey` method. It returns `true` if the key is contained in the `Hashtable` and `false` otherwise.

Note 4:

```
Console.WriteLine("Rivers map contains value 3500: "
  + rivers.ContainsValue(3500));
```

The `ContainsValue` method returns `true` if the value is associated with some key in the `Hashtable` and `false` otherwise.

Note 5:

```
SortedList riversList = new SortedList(rivers);
```

We can construct a `SortedList`, initialized with the elements of a specified collection, by passing the collection to the `SortedList` constructor.

Note 6: We find that a `SortedList` is less efficient than a `Hashtable`.

The BIG Picture

A hash table maps keys to values. A hash function computes an integer index used to enter the key and its associated value into the table. Different keys may have the same hash value, which causes a collision that degrades performance. Keeping the load factor below .75 helps avoid collisions. A class implements the `GetHashCode` method to provide a hash value for its instances.

✓ Test Your Understanding

Try It Yourself ➤ **13.** Change the keys in Example 12.11 and rerun. Is the number of collisions about the same?

Try It Yourself ➤ **14.** Change the table size to 67 in Example 12.11 and rerun it. How many collisions are there?

15. In Example 12.13, if we make the size of the map five greater than the size of the data, would you expect more or fewer collisions to occur? Explain.

12.6 COMPARISONS AND ORDERING

Thus far in this chapter we have been adding strings to our collections. Part of the .NET library, the `String` class is well behaved in that comparison between strings works as expected. In this section we learn to make our user classes implement the necessary comparison operations properly, so we can add them to collections and arrange them in order.

Inheriting from `Object`

Class `Object` provides default implementations of the methods

```
bool Equals(Object o);
int GetHashCode();
String ToString();
```

so every class inherits these methods. However, `Object` implements these methods based on a reference to an object, not based on the state of the object itself.

FIGURE 12.16
Two `Name` instances

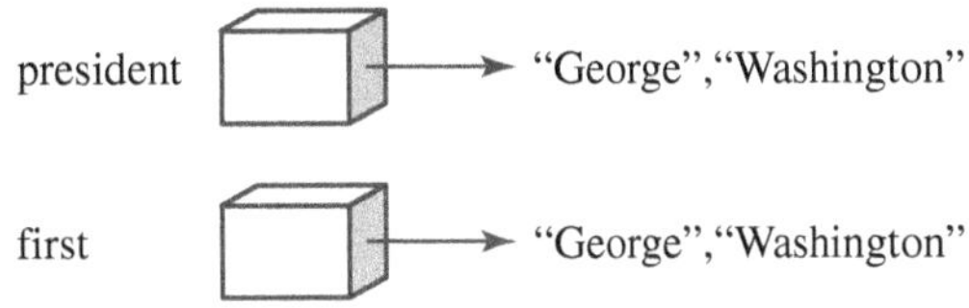

Subclasses normally must override these methods for them to work properly, as the `String` class does. To see why such overriding is necessary, we use the `Name` class of Example 6.3, with the instances of Figure 12.16.

```
Name president = new Name ("George", "Washington");
Name first = new Name ("George", "Washington");
```

Example 12.14 shows what happens when a class uses the default implementations that it inherits from `Object`.

EXAMPLE 12.14 ■ BadCompare.cs

```
/* Shows that the Name class does not behave properly
 * using inherited Equals and GetHashCode methods.
 */

using System;
using System.Collections;
public class BadCompare {
  public static void Main() {
    Name president = new Name ("George", "Washington");
    Name first = new Name ("George", "Washington");     // Note 1
    Console.WriteLine
          ("Should be equal, but Equals returns: {0}",
                                first.Equals(president)); // Note 2
    Console.Write
     ("The hash codes for first and president are: ");
    if (president.GetHashCode() == first.GetHashCode())// Note 3
       Console.WriteLine("equal");
    else
       Console.WriteLine("not equal");
    Hashtable m = new Hashtable();
    m.Add(president, "first");
    Console.WriteLine
     ("Should contain George Washington, but Contains returns: "
                                + m.Contains(first));      // Note 4
    Console.WriteLine
       ("Should find 'first', but m[first] returns: "
                                            + m[first]); // Note 5
```

```
        Console.WriteLine
            ("ToString overridden so first is: " + first); // Note 6
    }
}
```

Output

```
Should be equal, but Equals returns: False
The hash codes for first and president are: not equal
Should contain George Washington, but Contains returns: False
Should find 'first', but m[first] returns:
ToString overridden so first is: George Washington
```

Note 1: `Name first = new Name ("George", "Washington");`

Figure 12.16 shows that `first` and `president` refer to different objects.

Note 2: `first.Equals(president)`

The `Equals` method inherited from `Object` checks the equality of references. The two references, `president` and `first`, are not equal even though the names they point to are.

Note 3: `if (president.GetHashCode() == first.GetHashCode())`

The `GetHashCode` method inherited from `Object` computes a hash value based on the reference, so the two references, `president` and `first`, have different hash codes. Any implementation that uses these hash values to find locations for objects will put `first` and `president` in two different locations.

Note 4: `m.Contains(first)`

The `Hashtable` implementation uses the `GetHashCode` method to check whether an object is contained in a set. After adding `president` the table will contain the name of the first president, but the `Contains` method returns `false` because the `GetHashCode` method inherited from `Object` looks for the object referred to by `first` in a different location from the one containing the object referred to by `president`.

Note 5: `m[first]`

The `Hashtable` implementation uses the `GetHashCode` method to store and retrieve items from the map. Because `president` and `first` have different hash codes, they will be stored in different locations. Calling `m[first]` will look only in the location found using the hash code of `first` and thus will not find the name placed using the `president` reference.

Note 6:

```
Console.WriteLine
        ("ToString overridden so first is: " + first);
```

Because the `Name` class overrides the `ToString` method, we do obtain the desired result. Had `Name` not overriden `ToString`, the inherited implementation from Object would have been used, which displays an empty string.

Overriding Object Methods

To make the Name class function properly we must override the Equals and GetHashCode methods. Example 12.15 shows the rewritten class, where we rename the Name class as NewName to avoid confusion.

EXAMPLE 12.15 ■ NewName.cs

```
/* Groups fields for a name. Overrides Equals and GetHashCode.
 */

using System;
public class NewName : Name {

  public NewName(String f, String l) : base(f,l) {
  }
  public NewName(String f, char i, String l) : base(f,i,l) {
  }
  public override bool Equals(Object o) {
    if (!(o is NewName))
       return false;                                    // Note 1
    NewName name = (NewName)o;
    return first == name.first && initial == name.initial
             && last == name.last;                      // Note 2
  }
  public override int GetHashCode() {
    return first.GetHashCode() + (int)initial
                        + last.GetHashCode();           // Note 3
  }
}
```

■

Note 1: `if (!(o is NewName)) return false;`

The Equals method overrides the method inherited from Object, which of course has a parameter of type Object. The actual argument we pass to the Equals method can be any subclass of Object. Because we are checking equality of NewName objects, we use the is operator to rule out any object that is not of that type.

Note 2:
```
return first == name.first && initial == name.initial
     && last == name.last;
```

The two objects are equal if they have the same first and last names and middle initial. Because the first and last names are strings, we can use the Equals method of the String class to do these checks.

Note 3: `return first.GetHashCode() + (int)initial + last.GetHashCode();`

```
return first.GetHashCode() + (int)initial
                               + last.GetHashCode();
```

To compute a hash code for a name, we add the hash codes of the first and last names and the ASCII value of the middle initial. The first and last names are strings that implement the `GetHashCode` method properly. We could have constructed a more complex hash function, for example, by shifting the hash code for the first name right by several bits before adding the middle initial and last name hash code. Such a tweaking of the function might make the distribution of hash values more uniform, thus reducing the number of collisions and improving the efficiency of the hashing.

Example 12.16 shows that by using the `NewName` class the problems encountered in Example 12.14 using the `Name` class are corrected.

EXAMPLE 12.16 ■ GoodCompare.cs

```
/* Shows that the NewName class behaves properly
 * using overridden Equals and GetHashCode methods.
 */

using System;
using System.Collections;
public class GoodCompare {
  public static void Main() {
    NewName president = new NewName ("George", "Washington");
    NewName first = new NewName ("George", "Washington");
    Console.WriteLine
          ("Should be equal, but Equals returns: {0}",
                                   first.Equals(president));
    Console.Write
         ("The hash codes for first and president are: ");
    if (president.GetHashCode() == first.GetHashCode())
       Console.WriteLine("equal");
    else
       Console.WriteLine("not equal");
    Hashtable m = new Hashtable();
    m.Add(president, "first");
    Console.WriteLine
     ("Should contain George Washington, but Contains returns: "
                                       + m.Contains(first));
    Console.WriteLine
              ("Should find 'first', but m[first] returns: "
                                                + m[first]);
    Console.WriteLine
              ("ToString overridden so first is: " + first);
  }
}
```

```
Should be equal, but Equals returns: True
The hash codes for first and president are: equal
Should contain George Washington, but Contains returns: True
Should find 'first', but m[first] returns: first
ToString overridden so first is: George Washington
```

The IComparable Interface

Classes implement the `IComparable` interface to allow objects to be ordered. For example, the `String` class implements it. The `IComparable` interface has one method,

```
int CompareTo(Object object);
```

which returns a negative integer if the result is less, zero if equal, and a positive integer if greater.

Names do have a natural alphabetical ordering. In Example 12.17 we revise the `NewName` class to implement the `IComparable` interface.

EXAMPLE 12.17 ■ NewOrderedName.cs

```
/* Groups fields for a name. Overrides NewName and
 * implements the IComparable interface.
 */

using System;
public class NewOrderedName : NewName, IComparable {

  public NewOrderedName(String f, String l) : base(f,l) {
  }
  public NewOrderedName(String f, char i, String l)
                                         : base(f,i,l) {
  }
  public int CompareTo(Object o) {
    NewOrderedName name = (NewOrderedName)o;
    int lastResult = last.CompareTo(name.last);
    if (lastResult != 0)
      return lastResult;                              // Note 1
    else {
      int firstResult = first.CompareTo(name.first);
      if (firstResult != 0)
         return firstResult;
      else
         return (int)initial - (int)name.initial;     // Note 2
    }
  }
  public static void Main() {                         // Note 3
    NewOrderedName jAdams = new NewOrderedName("John", "Adams");
```

```
    NewOrderedName jqAdams =
            new NewOrderedName("John", 'Q', "Adams");
    NewOrderedName hAdams =
            new NewOrderedName("Henry", "Adams");
    Console.WriteLine
       ("jAdams vs. jqAdams {0}", jAdams.CompareTo(jqAdams));
    Console.WriteLine
       ("jAdams vs. hAdams {0}", jAdams.CompareTo(hAdams));
    Console.WriteLine
       ("hAdams vs. hAdams {0}", hAdams.CompareTo(hAdams));
  }
}
```

Output

```
jAdams vs. jqAdams -81
jAdams vs. hAdams 1
hAdams vs. hAdams 0
```

Note 1: `if (lastResult != 0) return lastResult;`

We first check last names using the `CompareTo` method for strings and return if the last names are unequal.

Note 2: `return (int)initial - (int)name.initial;`

If the first and last names are equal, we return the different of the ASCII values of the middle initials.

Note 3: `public static void Main() {`

It is a good idea to include some tests of the class methods in the `Main` method.

Example 12.18 shows that we can add `NewOrderedName` objects to a `SortedList`. We add the names of the first 10 presidents associated with their ages at death. We could not use a `SortedList` with `Name` or `NewName` objects because they do not implement the `IComparable` interface.

EXAMPLE 12.18 ■ Ordering.cs

```
/* Uses a SortedList with NewOrderedName keys.
 */

using System;
using System.Collections;
public class Ordering {
  public static void Main() {
    SortedList list = new SortedList();
    NewOrderedName jackson, madison;
```

```
    list.Add(new NewOrderedName("George", "Washington"), 67);
    list.Add(new NewOrderedName("John", "Adams"), 90);
    list.Add(new NewOrderedName("Thomas", "Jefferson"), 83);
    list.Add
      (madison = new NewOrderedName("James", "Madison"), 85);
    list.Add(new NewOrderedName("James", "Monroe"), 73);
    list.Add(new NewOrderedName("John", 'Q', "Adams"), 80);
    list.Add
      (jackson = new NewOrderedName("Andrew", "Jackson"), 78);
    list.Add(new NewOrderedName("Martin", "Van Buren"), 79);
    list.Add
      (new NewOrderedName("William", 'H', "Harrison"), 68);
    list.Add(new NewOrderedName("John", "Tyler"), 71);
    foreach(DictionaryEntry entry in list)
      Console.Write("{0} ", entry.Key);                    // Note 1
  }
}
```

Output

```
John Adams John Q Adams William H Harrison Andrew Jackson
Thomas Jefferson James Madison James Monroe John Tyler
Martin Van Buren George Washington
```

Note 1:

```
foreach(DictionaryEntry entry in list)
          Console.Write("{0} ", entry.Key);
```

The `foreach` statement outputs the keys in alphabetical order because we used a `SortedList`.

The BIG Picture

To add our own object types to containers we need to override the `Equals`, `GetHashCode`, and `ToString` methods inherited from `Object`. To be able to sort our own object types, we need to make them implement the `IComparable` interface and implement the `CompareTo` method. We can add types that implement `IComparable` to sorted lists, which keeps them in order.

✓Test Your Understanding

Try It Yourself ➤ **16.** What happens in Example 12.17 if you try to compare `jAdams` to the `String` "John Adams"? Explain.

Try It Yourself ➤ **17.** What happens if you change the `Hashtable m` in Example 12.16 to a `SortedList`? Explain.

SUMMARY

- Recursion deals with repetition by describing a process whose structure recurs within itself. In binary search, we compare the key with the middle element. If they are equal, we have found what we are looking for; if the key is greater than the middle element, we have only to search the upper portion of this sorted array. Calling binary search recursively, we compare our key to the middle of the upper portion, either returning if we found it or starting yet another binary search of the upper or lower half (of the upper half of the original array). Although the trace of a recursive algorithm can get complicated, the program is usually very simple.
- Merge sort is a very efficient sorting method which has a very nice recursive implementation. We call merge sort recursively to sort the left and right halves of the array, and then merge the resulting sorted arrays into the final result.
- The linked list data structure makes it easy to add and remove elements, but loses some of the advantages of arrays for searches and takes extra space to hold the node references. Each node of a linked list contains a data field and a reference to another node. When we add an item to the list or remove an item from a list, we have to change only two references. If the `Stack` class used a linked list to store its data, rather than an array, it would be able to grow in size without being restricted to the size of its internal array.
- The useful `Stack` type has operations `Push`, `Pop`, `Top`, `IsEmpty`, and `IsFull`. `Push` adds an item to the top of the stack. `Pop` removes the item on the top of the stack, and `Top` inspects the top item without removing it. `IsEmpty` and `IsFull` tell us whether the stack is empty or full. We operate on stacks using just these operations and constructors. The representation of the stack, which is hidden from the user, uses an array to hold the data, a `size` field to hold the size of the array, and a `top` field that gives the index of the top element of the stack or holds -1 if the stack is empty.
- A queue has operations `Add`, `Remove`, `Head`, `IsEmpty`, and `IsFull`. `Add` enters an item at the back of the queue. `Remove` takes it away from the front. `Head` returns the front element without removing it. We implement the queue using an array, in a way that makes it appear circular, with index `0` following index `size-1` if necessary.
- An `ArrayList` is like an array, but can grow in size. The `Add` method adds an element to the end of an `ArrayList` and increases its size, if necessary, to accommodate the added element. We get an element using its index, as in an array. Other methods help us find an element in a vector. The `foreach` statement lets us process each member of a collection.
- A hash table uses an integer computed from the key to find the index at which to enter the key and its value in the table. It can be extremely efficient.
- By default, the `Equals` method compares references and the `GetHashCode` method computes the hash value of references. Objects that we wish to add to collections must override these methods to check equality of objects and to compute a hash value based on the object data. A class must implement the `IComparable` interface, providing a `CompareTo` method, to allow its objects to be sorted or placed in a sorted collection, which keeps its elements in sorted order.

SKILL BUILDER EXERCISES

1. What is the output if 7 is passed as a program argument to the following program?

```
public class Fun {
    public static int F(int n) {
        if (n==1 | n==2) return 1;
        else return f(n-1) + f(n-2);
    }
    public static void Main(String[] args) {
        Console.WriteLine(F(int.Parse(args[0])));
    }
}
```

2. What is the output if 2, 3, and 5 are passed as program arguments to the following program?

```
public class Ack {
    public static int A(int x, int y, int z) {
        if (x == 0) return y + z;
        if (z == 0) {
          if(x == 1) return 0;
          if(x == 2) return 1;
          if(x > 2) return y;
        }
        if(x>0 && z>0)
          return A(x-1, y, A(x,y,z-1));
        return -1;
    }
    public static void Main(String[] args) {
        Console.WriteLine(a(int.Parse(args[0]),
            int.Parse(args[1]),
            int.Parse(args[2])
        ));
    }
}
```

3. A class whose objects may be entered as keys in a hash table should override the ________________ and the ________________ methods.

CRITICAL THINKING EXERCISES

4. A difference between a stack and a queue is
   - **a.** We can add to and remove from a stack, but can only add to a queue.
   - **b.** The last one in is the first one out for a queue, but is the last one out for a stack.
   - **c.** The first one in for a queue is the first one out, but is the last one out for a stack.
   - **d.** We can add to and remove from a queue, but can only add to a stack.

5. Which of the following is true about a hash table?
   a. Decreasing the load improves performance.
   b. Increasing the load improves performance.
   c. Hash tables keep data in alphabetical order.
   d. Hash values are almost always strings.
   e. None of the above.
6. Which of the following is not a linked list operation?
   a. Insert an element.
   b. Check if the list is empty.
   c. Remove an element.
   d. None of the above.
7. In the merge sort algorithm, we
   a. sort the left part of the data before the right.
   b. merge the two sorted parts of the data.
   c. may use recursion.
   d. All of the above.

DEBUGGING EXERCISE

8. The following program attempts to compute the product of the first `n` integers where `n` is passed as a program argument. For example, passing a program argument of 4 should generate a result of 24 because 4*3*2*1 = 24. Find and correct any errors in this program.

```
public class Factorial {
    public static int Product(int n) {
        return n*Product(n - 1);
    }
    public static void Main(String[] args) {
        Console.WriteLine(Product(int.Parse(args[0])));
    }
}
```

PROGRAM MODIFICATION EXERCISES

9. Modify Example 12.6 to define an `Object` stack rather than an integer stack.
10. Modify Example 12.7 to define an `Object` queue rather than an integer queue.
11. Modify the `Stack` class of Example 12.6 to use the `LinkedList` of Example 12.5, rather than an array, to hold the stack elements.
12. Modify Example 12.6 to create a graphical interface for the user to perform stack operations. Include *Push* and *Pop* buttons and a text box to enter data. After each operation, draw the current stack.

13. Modify Example 12.3, `BinarySearch`, to use a `TextBox` to input the data and display the result of the search in a `Form`.

14. Modify the merge sort program of Example 12.4 to input the numbers to be sorted from a file, rather than as program arguments. Pass the file name as a program argument.

15. Modify the merge sort program of Example 12.4 to sort `String` objects. Input the strings from a file, rather than as program arguments, and write the sorted strings to a file. Pass the file name as a program argument.

16. Modify Example 12.6 by writing an exception class `StackFullException` and throwing this exception instead of `ApplicationException`.

17. Modify Example 12.10 to also compare times for removing an element.

PROGRAM DESIGN EXERCISES

18. Create a user interface to manipulate and display a linked list. Include buttons to insert and remove a string entered in a text box, and a button to reset the list to its head. Display the list using rectangles for the nodes.

19. Write a C# program that searches a file for a string. Pass the string and the file name as program arguments.

20. Write a C# program that uses a stack to reverse an array.

21. Write a C# program that does not use recursion to perform a binary search of an array input from a file.

22. Write a C# program to search for an item in a linked list. Use the `LinkedList` class of Example 12.5. Use a recursive method to do the search.

23. Write a C# program to check if a string is a palindrome (reads the same backward and forward, as, for example, "toot"). Use a recursive method to do the checking.

24. (Towers of Hanoi) Suppose we have *n* disks on a peg, each of different sizes, stacked in order of size, with the largest on the bottom, and two other pegs, as shown in Figure 12.17.

    What is the sequence of moves needed to transfer the rings to the second peg, in the same configuration, in order from largest to the smallest, with the largest at the bottom, if we can move only one disk at a time and cannot place a larger disk on top of a smaller

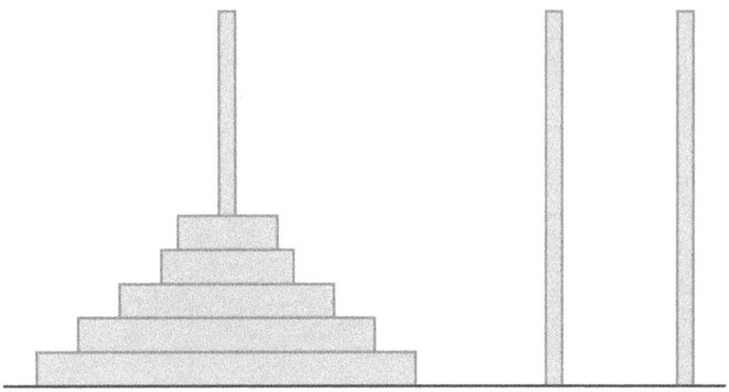

FIGURE 12.17
The Towers of Hanoi puzzle

disk? We may use the last peg to store disks, but the same rules apply. Use a recursive method to provide the solution. To move n disks from peg 1 to peg 2, move n-1 disks to peg 3, move the bottom disk to peg 2, then move n-1 disks from peg 3 to peg 2. For this problem, print out the sequence of moves, as, for example, "Move disk from peg 1 to peg 2," and so on.

A Little Extra

25. In Section 12.3 we showed how to use a stack to evaluate a postfix expression. Write a program to allow the user to input a postfix expression of the form described in Section 12.3 in a text box. Add a button for the user to ask the program to process the next character. Make a graphical display that shows the stack as it grows and shrinks, and display the result of the evaluation.

26. Draw the Towers of Hanoi configuration in Figure 12.17. Allow the user to drag the disks to new locations to solve the puzzle. Include a text box for the user to enter the number of disks.

27. Write a C# program that uses a recursive method to reverse an array.

28. Make a `Hashtable` containing the distinct words of the Gettysburg address as the keys and their frequency of occurrence as the values.

29. Create an `ArrayList` containing 1000 random numbers between 0 and 1,000,000, and sort it. Use binary search to find the index at which 500,000 occurs in the list or the index at which it should be inserted if it does not occur.

30. Create a deck of `Card` objects. Each card has a suit and a value. The suits are `Clubs`, `Diamonds`, `Hearts`, and `Spades`. The values, which can be characters, are `2`, `3`, `4`, `5`, `6`, `7`, `8`, `9`, `10`, `J`, `Q`, `K`, `A`. Shuffle the deck and deal four hands of 13 cards each. Use suitable collection methods wherever possible.

31. Keep the words `macabre`, `macaco`, `macadam`, `macadamia`, `macaque`, `macaroni`, `macaronic`, `macaroon`, `macaw`, and `maccaboy` in a `SortedList`. When the user enters a word alphabetically greater than `mac` but less than `macd` and not in the list, show the nearest four words to it and let the user choose a replacement.

13 Threads and Animation

In this chapter we introduce threads, which allow two or more pieces of a program to execute in their own threads of control, appearing to work simultaneously. Animation provides a good illustration of thread use. Running an animation in one thread allows the program to continue other processing. We can animate graphics that we draw on the screen or images that we can download from remote sites. Concurrent programming involves threads working together to accomplish a task.

OBJECTIVES

- Add threads to C# programs
- Use threads in animation
- Use images
- Introduce concurrent programming

13.1 INTRODUCTION TO THREADS

The term **thread** is short for `thread of control`. Someone who can read a book and watch television at the same time is processing two threads. For a while she concentrates on the book, perhaps during a commercial, but then devotes her attention to a segment of the TV program. Because the TV program does not require her undivided attention, she reads a few more lines every now and then. Each thread gets some of her attention. Perhaps she can concentrate on both threads simultaneously, like musicians who are able to follow the different parts of the harmony.

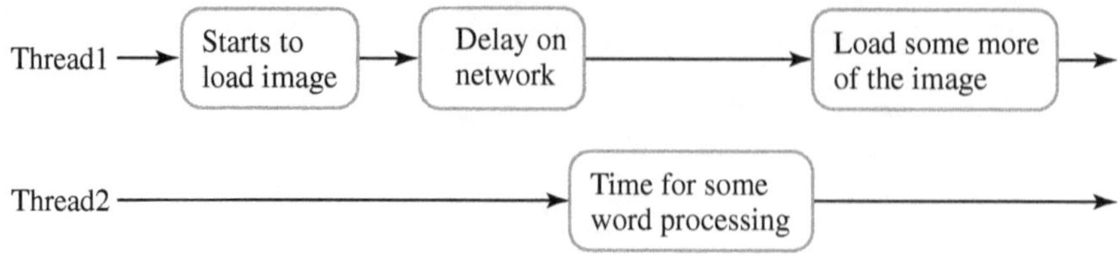

FIGURE 13.1 Two threads sharing the processor

If we have only one thread of control, then we have to wait whenever that thread gets delayed. For example, suppose our thread is downloading a picture from the Internet. It may have to wait while the system transfers all the pixels of the picture from some remote site. If our program can create a second thread to wait for the input from the remote site, it can go on with other processing while the new thread is waiting. When some new data comes in from the remote site, the new thread can receive it while the first thread waits for a while. The two threads share the processor. Figure 13.1 illustrates this sharing.

The Thread Class

C# allows us to use threads in our program. Our program can define two or more threads; the processor will divide its attention among the active threads. We use a `ThreadStart` delegate to specify the code that the `Thread` will execute. It has the form

```
public delegate void ThreadStart();
```

so we can pass any method with no arguments and no return value to the `Thread`. It will execute that method when it gets the processor.

To make a thread run, we can create a new thread and call its `Start` method, passing it the `ThreadStart` delegate, as in

```
Thread t = new Thread(new ThreadStart(Run));
t.Start();
```

`Run` is a method with no arguments and no return value that contains the code that this thread will execute when it gets the processor. When another thread gets a turn, the thread `t` will stop executing the code in its `Run` method, but will start again from where it left off, when it gets another turn.

The `Thread` class has a class method, `Sleep(int milliseconds)`, which will cause its caller to sleep (be blocked from using the processor) for the specified number of milliseconds. While one thread sleeps, another will get a turn.

In Example 13.1 we create two threads, `Bonnie` and `Clyde`, and let them write their names five times, sleeping after each writing. Processors are so fast that a thread could do a large amount of output while it has its turn. We sleep here to slow the thread down to human scale, so we have to read only a few lines of output. The `Main` method runs in a thread different from the two we create, so we will actually have three threads sharing the processor, writing their names when they get their turns.

EXAMPLE 13.1 ■ NameUsingThread.cs

```
/* Creates two threads that write their names and
 * sleep.  The Main thread also writes its name
 * and sleeps.

using System;
using System.Threading;                                    // Note 1
public class NameUsingThread  {
  private int time;
  private Thread thread;

  public NameUsingThread(String n, int t) {
    time=t;
    thread = new Thread(new ThreadStart(Run));
    thread.Name = n;                                       // Note 2
    thread.Start();
  }
  public void Run() {
    for (int i = 1; i <= 5; i++) {                         // Note 3
      Console.WriteLine(thread.Name + " " + i);
      Thread.Sleep(time);
     }
  }
  public static void Main( ) {
    NameUsingThread bonnie
             = new NameUsingThread("Bonnie",1000);
    NameUsingThread clyde
             =  new NameUsingThread("Clyde",700);
    for (int i = 1; i <= 5; i++) {
      Console.WriteLine
             (Thread.CurrentThread.Name + " " + i);        // Note 4
      Thread.Sleep(1100);
    }
  }
}
```

Output

```
 1
Bonnie 1
Clyde 1
Clyde 2
Bonnie 2
 2
Clyde 3
Bonnie 3
```

```
Clyde 4
 3
Clyde 5
Bonnie 4
 4
Bonnie 5
 5
```

Note 1: `using System.Threading;`

The `System.Threading` namespace contains the `Thread` class.

Note 2: `thread.Name = n;`

We use the `Name` property to give each thread a name.

Note 3: `for (int i = 1; i <= 5; i++) {`

Each thread will print its name five times and sleep after each time, beginning where it left off when it gets the processor again. We can see in the output that after `Bonnie` prints her name the first time, `Clyde` gets a turn and manages to print his name twice before `Bonnie` returns and prints her name the second time. `Main` started first because it had the processor first.

Note 4:
```
Console.WriteLine
    (Thread.CurrentThread.Name + "  " + i);
```

The `Main` method also writes its name five times. Because we did not create this thread in our program we get it using the static `CurrentThread` property of the `Thread` class.

Figure 13.2 helps us to understand the order in which the three threads execute in Example 13.1. Each thread spends most of its time sleeping; printing its name takes a mere fraction of the time it sleeps. By graphing the sleep times in Figure 13.2 we can get a good idea of when each thread will be ready to run.

`Main` prints its name first and then sleeps for 1.1 seconds. `Bonnie` starts next, printing her name and sleeping for 1 second. `Clyde` prints his name and sleeps for .7 second. When he wakes up, the other two threads are still sleeping, so he prints

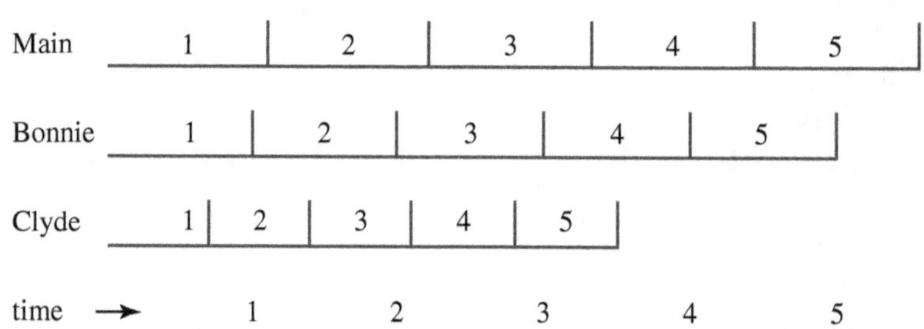

FIGURE 13.2 **Threads of Example 13.1 sleeping and waking up**

his name again (#2). Because `Bonnie` woke up before `main`, she prints her name (#2) first, followed by `Main` (#2). (Picking the thread that becomes ready first is a choice made by the thread scheduler.) When `Main` finishes, both `Bonnie` and `Clyde` are awake, but `Clyde` woke up first and executes first (#3). We leave it to the reader to continue following the diagram in Figure 13.2 to explain the results of Example 13.1.

Interrupting Computation

Example 13.1 is somewhat artificial, because each thread just sleeps after it writes its name. Typically, a thread is involved in a time-consuming computation or other process when it gets interrupted by the scheduler that allows another thread to have the processor. (Of course, on multiprocessor machines, more than one thread can run simultaneously.) To simulate such a process we revise Example 13.1 to repeat some computations, so the loop will be interrupted when the thread loses its turn and continued when the thread gets another turn.

Because of the actual computation going on when each thread gets interrupted, the system has to do some work to save and restore the state. Other processes may also be running on the same machine. So each time we run Example 13.2 we are likely to get a different order of names than that of the previous execution. This contrasts with Example 13.1, in which the fixed sleep times always determine the same ordering.

EXAMPLE 13.2 ■ NameBusy.cs

```
/* Each thread repeats computations in a loop that
 * will be interrupted when the thread loses the
 * processor and resumed when it regains it.
 */

using System;
using System.Threading;
public class NameBusy  {
  private int time;
  private Thread thread;

  public NameBusy(String n, int t) {
    time=t;
    thread = new Thread(new ThreadStart(Run));
    thread.Name = n;
    thread.Start();
  }
  public void Run() {
    for (int i = 1; i <= 5; i++) {
      Console.WriteLine(thread.Name + " " + i);
      double k = 0;
      for(int j = 0; j < 100000; j++)                // Note 1
        k = Math.Sqrt(j) * Math.Exp(j);
    }
  }
```

```
  public static void Main( ) {
    NameBusy bonnie = new NameBusy("Bonnie",1000);
    NameBusy clyde =  new NameBusy("Clyde",700);
    for (int i = 1; i <= 5; i++) {
      Console.WriteLine(Thread.CurrentThread.Name + " " + i);
      double k = 0;
      for(int j = 0; j < 100000; j++)
        k = Math.Sqrt(j) * Math.Exp(j);
    }
  }
}
```

Output

First Run

```
1
Bonnie 1
Bonnie 2
Clyde 1
Clyde 2
 2
 3
Bonnie 3
Bonnie 4
Clyde 3
Clyde 4
 4
 5
Bonnie 5
Clyde 5
```

Output

Second Run

```
1
Bonnie 1
Bonnie 2
Clyde 1
Clyde 2
 2
 3
 4
 5
Bonnie 3
Bonnie 4
Clyde 3
```

```
Clyde 4
Bonnie 5
Clyde 5
```

Note 1: `for(int j = 0; j < 100000; j++)`

We repeat an arbitrary computation 100,000 times. The size of the loop needs to be adjusted to the speed of the processor. If the loop is too small, a fast processor will finish the entire loop in one turn. Each thread will then complete before the next thread runs.

> **The BIG Picture**
>
> Threads allow two or more processes to proceed as if each had it own processor. A scheduler arranges for them to share processing time. A `ThreadStart` delegate contains the code that the thread executes when it gets its turn. The `Start` method includes the thread in the group of running threads.

✓ Test Your Understanding

Try It Yourself ➤ 1. In Example 13.1, change the sleep amounts for threads `Bonnie` and `Clyde` to `300` and `200` milliseconds respectively. How does the output change when you rerun the example?

Try It Yourself ➤ 2. In Example 13.2, find the number of iterations needed in the inner `for` loop so each thread does not terminate in one turn.

Try It Yourself ➤ 3. What do you predict the output will be if you omit all the `Sleep` statements from Example 13.1? Rerun the program with these changes and see if your supposition is correct.

13.2 ANIMATION

Animation provides an interesting application for threads. We will use a thread to show a ball moving across the screen. This thread computes the new position of the ball, asks the system to repaint the screen showing the ball in the new position, and sleeps for a fraction of a second so we can see the ball moving at human speed.

We start by exploring some possibilities for adding animation. Suppose we want to write an application to move a ball across the screen. We can add a button,

FIGURE 13.3
Handling a button press to move a ball

```
protected void Move_Click(object sender, EventArgs e) {
  x += 9;
  y += 9;
  Invalidate();
}
```

FIGURE 13.4
An attempt to move the ball 10 times with one button press

```
protected void Move_Click(object sender, EventArgs e) {
  for (int i = 0; i < 10; i++) {
    x += 9;
    y += 9;
    Invalidate();
  }
}
```

and whenever the user presses the button we can change the position of the ball, asking the system to repaint the screen. Figure 13.3 shows the `Move_Click` method that handles the button press.

Each time we press the button, the system executes the code of Figure 13.3. The call to `Invalidate` asks to paint the screen which, because `x` and `y` have increased, will show the ball in its new position. When the event-handling thread releases control, the system paints the screen. We can press the button several times, each time moving the ball farther.

Suppose we try to have the user initiate several moves with one button press; Figure 13.4 shows the `Move_Click` method with a loop to repeat the move. When the user presses the button, the system executes the `Move_Click` method. Every time around the loop, the `Move_Click` method requests the system to paint the ball in its new position, but it does not release control until the loop is finished. The system combines all the `Invalidate` requests that it could not get to while the `Move_Click` method was executing and just draws the ball in its final position.

Example 13.3 shows the complete code using the `Move_Click` method of Figure 13.3, which moves the ball once with each button press. We leave it as an exercise to modify this example to use the `Move_Click` method of Figure 13.4 and see what happens (or does not happen).

Figure 13.5 shows the ball, which the user can move by pressing the button.

EXAMPLE 13.3 ■ ButtonToMove.cs

```
/* Moves a ball when the user presses a
 * button. Modifying the Move_Click method
 * to put the code in a loop will cause the form
 * to display only the ball's final position.
 */
```

FIGURE 13.5
The ButtonToMove form of Example 13.3

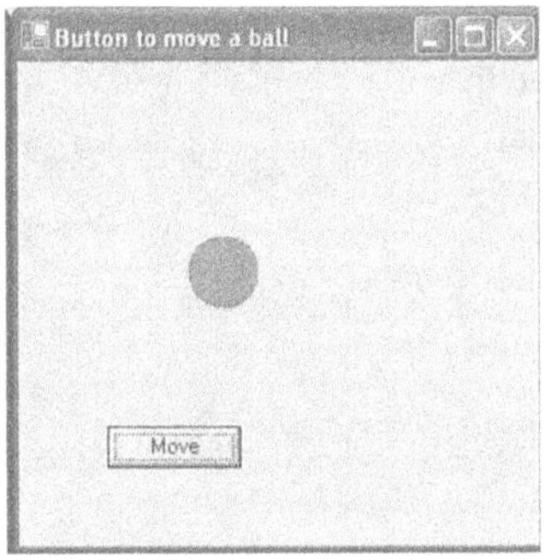


```
using System;
using System.Drawing;
using System.Windows.Forms;
public class ButtonToMove : Form {
  private int x = 50, y = 50;
  private Button move = new Button();

  public ButtonToMove() {
    Text = "Button to move a ball";
    move.Text = "Move";
    move.Location = new Point(50,200);
    Controls.Add(move);
    move.Click += new EventHandler(Move_Click);
  }
  protected void Move_Click(object sender, EventArgs e) {
    x += 9;
    y += 9;
    Invalidate();
  }
  protected override void OnPaint( PaintEventArgs e )    {
    Graphics g = e.Graphics;
    Brush red = new SolidBrush(Color.Red);
    g.FillEllipse(red ,x ,y, 40 ,40);
    base.OnPaint(e);
  }
  public static void Main( ) {
    Application.Run(new ButtonToMove());
  }
}
```

An application needs its own thread of control to do animation. By using a separate thread, other system functions can proceed in parallel, sharing the processor, so the animation will not monopolize the system's resources. The `Run` method

FIGURE 13.6 **The code executed by a thread for an animation**

```
public void Run() {
  int dx = 9, dy = 9;
  for(int i = 0; i < 10; i++) {
    x += dx;
    y += dy;
    Invalidate();
    Thread.Sleep(300);
  }
}
```

shown in Figure 13.6 will serve as the `ThreadStart` delegate that the thread will execute when it gets its turn.

Our thread changes the position of the ball, calls the `Invalidate` method to show the ball in its new location, and sleeps for 300 milliseconds to do the animation on a human scale and allow the system to paint the screen. When a thread sleeps, other threads that are waiting to run, if any, get their turn to use the processor.

When the user presses the button, the event handler creates an instance of `Thread`, passing the `ThreadStart` delegate based on the `Run` method

```
Thread t = new Thread(new ThreadStart(Run));
```

so the thread will know which method to execute. To set up the thread and make it ready to run, the event handler calls the thread's `Start` method, as in

```
t.Start();
```

As soon as it gets its turn, the thread will start executing the `Run` method, terminating when it has finished. While executing, it takes turns with the system, which paints the ball in the new position. Example 13.4 moves the ball ten times when the user presses the button. Each time the user presses the button, we return the ball to its start position and repeat the ten moves. Try it out; a static figure will not show how it works. A snapshot of the execution looks like Figure 13.5, but one button press moves the ball ten times.

EXAMPLE 13.4 ■ MoveBall.cs

```
/* Uses a thread to move a ball ten times
 * when the user presses a button.
 */

using System;
using System.Drawing;
using System.Threading;
```

```
using System.Windows.Forms;
public class MoveBall : Form {
  private int x = 50, y = 50;
  private Button move = new Button();

  public MoveBall() {
    BackColor = Color.White;
    Text = "Move a ball ten times";
    move.Text = "Move";
    move.Location = new Point(50, 200);
    move.Click += new EventHandler(Move_Click);
    Controls.Add(move);
  }
  protected void Move_Click(object sender, EventArgs e) {
    x = 50; y = 50;
    Thread t = new Thread(new ThreadStart(Run));
    t.Start();
  }
  protected override void OnPaint( PaintEventArgs e )   {
    Graphics g = e.Graphics;
    g.FillEllipse(Brushes.Red, x ,y, 40 ,40);
    base.OnPaint(e);
  }
  public void Run() {
    int dx = 9, dy = 9;
    for(int i = 0; i < 10; i++) {
      x += dx;
      y += dy;
      Invalidate();
      Thread.Sleep(300);
    }
  }
  public static void Main( ) {
    Application.Run(new MoveBall());
  }
}
```

Because the animation occurs in a thread and does not interfere with other processing, we can modify Example 13.4 to keep it going indefinitely. To move the ball continuously, we use a nonterminating loop in the `Run` method, moving the ball ten times down and to the right, followed by ten moves up and to the left. While the ball moves, notice that we can edit text in another window or run another program. The animation shares the processor rather than monopolizing it.

Example 13.5 uses a thread to move the ball back and forth until the user aborts it by pressing a button. We must terminate the thread before closing the window. We also add buttons to suspend and resume the thread to allow us to stop and start the ball.

EXAMPLE 13.5 ■ AnimateBall.cs

```
/* Animates a ball. Uses a thread to allow the system to
 * continue other processing.
 */

using System;
using System.Drawing;
using System.Threading;
using System.Windows.Forms;
public class AnimateBall : Form {
  private int x, y;
  private Button suspend = new Button();
  private Button resume = new Button();
  private Button abort = new Button();
  Thread t;

  public AnimateBall() {
    BackColor = Color.White;
    Text = "Animate Ball";
    abort.Text = "Abort";
    suspend.Text = "Suspend";
    resume.Text = "Resume";

    int w = 20;
    suspend.Location = new Point(w, 200);
    resume.Location = new Point(w += 10 + suspend.Width, 200);
    abort.Location = new Point(w += 10 + resume.Width, 200);

    abort.Click += new EventHandler(Abort_Click);
    suspend.Click += new EventHandler(Suspend_Click);
    resume.Click += new EventHandler(Resume_Click);

    Controls.Add(suspend);
    Controls.Add(resume);
    Controls.Add(abort);

    x = 50; y = 50;
    t = new Thread(new ThreadStart(Run));
    t.Start();
  }
  protected void Abort_Click(object sender, EventArgs e) {
    t.Abort();                                          // Note 1
```

```
  }
  protected void Suspend_Click(object sender, EventArgs e) {
    t.Suspend();
  }
  protected void Resume_Click(object sender, EventArgs e) {
    t.Resume();
  }
  protected override void OnPaint( PaintEventArgs e )   {
    Graphics g = e.Graphics;
    g.FillEllipse(Brushes.Red, x ,y, 40 ,40);
    base.OnPaint(e);
  }
  public void Run() {
    int dx=9, dy=9;
    while (true) {                                    // Note 2
      for(int i=0; i<10; i++) {
        x+=dx;
        y+=dy;
        Invalidate();
        Thread.Sleep(100);
      }
      dx = -dx; dy = -dy;                             // Note 3
    }
  }
  public static void Main( ) {
    Application.Run(new AnimateBall());
  }
}
```

Note 1: `t.Abort();`

The `Abort` method, as its name suggests, aborts the thread. Similarly, the `Suspend` method suspends it and the `Resume` method resumes it after it was suspended.

Note 2: `while (true) {`

Threads often run in a nonterminating loop. Because they share the processor with other threads, they can keep running until the user terminates them. By contrast, a nonterminating loop in a program without threads would monopolize the processor, not allowing the program to perform other tasks.

Note 3: `dx = -dx; dy = -dy;`

To get the ball to move back and forth, we change the direction of the increment after every ten moves.

FIGURE 13.7 **A face from the applet of Example 13.6**

We used a thread to animate a ball; we can use the same technique to do fancier animations, for example, to draw a sequence of figures that would change the appearance of each frame of the animation. To make a modest start in this direction, we animate a circular face with circles for eyes, a line for a nose, and an arc for a mouth. We use three different frames and continually draw one after the other, sleeping for 300 milliseconds between each repainting of the next frame. Example 13.6 performs this animation. Figure 13.7 shows one of the three faces we use in the animation.

EXAMPLE 13.6 ■ AnimateFace.cs

```
/* Animates a face, drawing it in three different sizes
 * with an interval of 300 milliseconds between each
 * repainting.
 */

using System;
using System.Drawing;
using System.Threading;
using System.Windows.Forms;
public class AnimateFace : Form {
  private int x = 10, y = 10;
  private int width = 200, height = 200;
  private int leftEyeX = 50, leftEyeY = 70;
  private int lwidth = 30, lheight = 30;
  private int rightEyeX = 150, rightEyeY = 70;
  private int rwidth = 30, rheight = 30;
  private int leftNoseX = 90, leftNoseY = 120;
  private int rightNoseX = 140, rightNoseY = 120;
  private int mouthX = 50, mouthY = 130;
  private int mouthWidth = 120, mouthHeight = 40;
  private Button suspend = new Button();
  private Button resume = new Button();
  private Button abort = new Button();
  private Thread t;
```

```
public AnimateFace() {
  BackColor = Color.White;
  Text = "Animate Ball";
  abort.Text = "Abort";
  suspend.Text = "Suspend";
  resume.Text = "Resume";

  Controls.Add(suspend);
  Controls.Add(resume);
  Controls.Add(abort);

  int w = 20;
  suspend.Location = new Point(w, 240);
  resume.Location = new Point(w += 10 + suspend.Width, 240);
  abort.Location = new Point(w += 10 + resume.Width, 240);

  abort.Click += new EventHandler(Abort_Click);
  suspend.Click += new EventHandler(Suspend_Click);
  resume.Click += new EventHandler(Resume_Click);

  t = new Thread(new ThreadStart(Run));
  t.Start();
}
protected void Abort_Click(object sender, EventArgs e) {
  t.Abort();
}
protected void Suspend_Click(object sender, EventArgs e) {
  t.Suspend();
}
protected void Resume_Click(object sender, EventArgs e) {
  t.Resume();
}
protected override void OnPaint( PaintEventArgs e )   {
  Graphics g = e.Graphics;
  Pen green = new Pen(Color.Green, 3);
  Brush red = new SolidBrush(Color.Red);
  g.DrawEllipse(green, x, y, width, height);
  g.FillEllipse
   (Brushes.Blue, leftEyeX, leftEyeY, lwidth, lheight);
  g.FillEllipse
   (Brushes.Blue, rightEyeX, rightEyeY, rwidth, rheight);
  g.DrawLine
   (green, leftNoseX, leftNoseY,rightNoseX, rightNoseY);
  g.FillPie(Brushes.Red, mouthX, mouthY, mouthWidth,
                                  mouthHeight, 0, 180);
  base.OnPaint(e);
}
```

```
  public void Run() {
    int dx=9, dy=9;
    while (true) {
      for (int i = 0; i < 3; i++) {
        x += dx;                                          // Note 1
        y += dy;
        width -= dx;
        height -= dy;
        leftEyeX += dx;
        leftEyeY += dy;
        lwidth -= dx;
        lheight -= dy;
        rightEyeX += dx;
        rightEyeY += dy;
        rwidth -= dx;
        rheight -= dy;
        leftNoseX += dx;
        rightNoseX -= dx;
        mouthX += dx;
        mouthY += dy;
        mouthWidth -= dx;
        mouthHeight -= dy;
        Invalidate();
        Thread.Sleep(300);
      }
      dx = -dx; dy = -dy;
    }
  }
  public static void Main( ) {
    Application.Run(new AnimateFace());
  }
}
```

Note 1: `x += dx;`

We add a small amount to the position of each of the components of the face to move it slightly to the right three times, returning it to its original position in the next three moves. We decrease the size of the face and its eyes, nose, and mouth as we move it to the right, increasing it to the original size as we move back to the original position.

The BIG Picture

We change each frame of the animation in the method passed to the `ThreadStart` delegate. The thread displays the new drawing, sleeps, and repeats this process over and over again.

✓ Test Your Understanding

Try It Yourself ➤ **4.** Change the `Move_Click` method of Example 13.3 to the method of Figure 13.4. Run the code and observe the result. Does it draw the ball 10 times?

Try It Yourself ➤ **5.** Start the animation of Example 13.5 and leave it running. Can you edit another program while the animation is running? Can you open another console window and run another C# program while the animation is running?

Try It Yourself ➤ **6.** In Example 13.6, try different values for the sleep time and decide which you think makes the animation look best. How might we make it easier to try the program with these different sleep times?

13.3 IMAGES

We can create an image object from an image file using the class method, `Image.FromFile`, as in

```
Image.FromFile("gittleman.jpg");
```

When the image is loaded we can draw it using the `DrawImage` method of the `Graphics` class, as in

```
g.DrawImage(pic,10,10);
```

where the first argument is the image and the next two arguments are the `(x,y)` coordinates of the upper-left corner of the drawn image.

The three-argument version of the `DrawImage` method draws the image in its normal size. A five-argument version of `DrawImage` lets us scale the image, as in

```
g.drawImage(pic,10,10,100,100);
```

which scales the image, drawing it in a `100 x 100` region.

Our program to animate images follows the format of our animation programs of Section 13.2. In those examples we used a loop in the `Run` method to change the location and/or the dimensions of the shapes to be drawn, to repaint, and to sleep. In Example 13.7 we load an image of the author. In the `Run` method, we keep changing the desired size of the image, repaint, and sleep for 300 milliseconds. The image expands, filling up more of the screen, and then contracts, repeating this behavior over and over again.

Double Buffering

Each time we repaint, we see a blank screen followed by the image. This alternation of blank screen and image appears as a distracting flicker. To eliminate the flicker, we do our drawing, whether of graphical shapes, text, or images, on an off-screen buffer. Only when the drawing is done do we copy it to the visible screen. Using .NET, the `SetStyle` method lets us configure our `Form` so .NET will do the double buffering for us. The correct call to `SetStyle` is

```
SetStyle(ControlStyles.DoubleBuffer
           | ControlStyles.AllPaintingInWmPaint
           | ControlStyles.UserPaint, true);
```

FIGURE 13.8 **A step in the animation of Example 13.7**

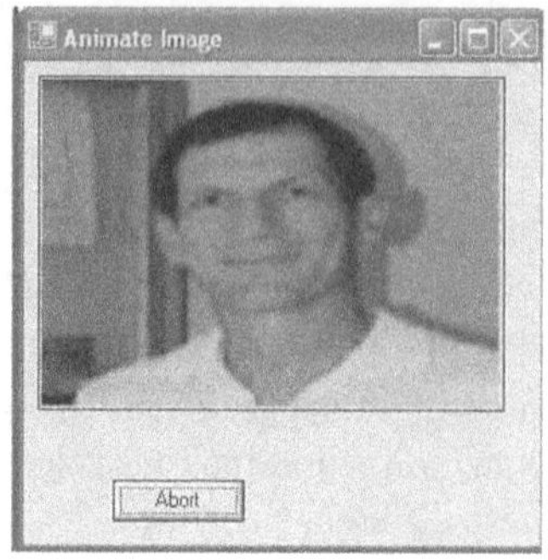

Figure 13.8 shows the distorted image of the author that occurs as part of the animation of Example 13.7.

EXAMPLE 13.7 ■ AnimateImage.cs

```
/* Animates an image. Uses a thread to allow the system to
 * continue other processing.
 */

using System;
using System.Drawing;
using System.Threading;
using System.Windows.Forms;
public class AnimateImage : Form {
  private int width = 100;
  private int height = 100;
  Image pic = Image.FromFile("gittleman.jpg");
  private Button abort = new Button();
  Thread t;

  public AnimateImage() {
    Text = "Animate Image";
    abort.Text = "Abort";
    abort.Location = new Point(50, 230);
    abort.Click += new EventHandler(Abort_Click);
    Controls.Add(abort);
    SetStyle(ControlStyles.DoubleBuffer
           | ControlStyles.AllPaintingInWmPaint
           | ControlStyles.UserPaint, true);            // Note 1
    t = new Thread(new ThreadStart(Run));
    t.Start();
  }
  protected void Abort_Click(object sender, EventArgs e) {
```

```
      t.Abort();
    }
    protected override void OnPaint( PaintEventArgs e )   {
       Graphics g = e.Graphics;
       g.DrawRectangle(Pens.Black, 8, 8, width+3, height+3);
       g.DrawImage(pic, 10, 10, width, height);
       base.OnPaint(e);
    }
    public void Run() {
        int dx=20, dy=10;
        while (true) {
          for(int i = 0; i < 10; i++) {
            width += dx;                                    // Note 2
            height += dy;
            Invalidate();
            Thread.Sleep(300);
          }
          dx = -dx; dy = -dy;
        }
    }
    public static void Main( ) {
        Application.Run(new AnimateImage());
    }
}
```

Note 1:

```
SetStyle(ControlStyles.DoubleBuffer
   | ControlStyles.AllPaintingInWmPaint
   | ControlStyles.UserPaint, true);
```

The `SetStyle` method sets style characteristics. The first argument gives the styles to set. The second argument, if true, applies the styles to the control. We use the bitwise OR operator (see Appendix B) to combine styles. To enable double buffering we need to enable the three styles from the `ControlStyles` enumeration.

`DoubleBuffer`	Draw in buffer, then to screen.
`AllPaintingInWmPaint`	Do not erase screen on repaint.
`UserPaint`	Control paints itself.

Note 2: `width += dx;`

At each iteration of the loop we change the size of our scaled image. We loop ten times, increasing the size of the display, alternating with ten iterations that decrease the size back to its original value.

The BIG Picture

We can create an image from a file, and draw it either in its original size or scaled. We can set the style to enable double buffering to eliminate flicker.

✓Test Your Understanding

Try It Yourself ➤ **7.** Describe the effect of modifying Example 13.7 to omit the call to `SetStyle`.

Try It Yourself ➤ **8.** Vary the sleep time in Example 13.7, running the example each time, and describing how the change in the sleep time affects the animation.

13.4 CONCURRENT PROGRAMMING

Having seen threads running independently in Section 13.1, we take up the interesting and difficult problem of threads that share data and need to cooperate with each other to operate correctly.

An Example Without Synchronization

To illustrate the problem, suppose that two threads are depositing to an account, and that a deposit involves two steps:

1. Get the current balance.
2. Compute and save the new balance.

A thread runs for a certain time period, and then another thread gets its turn. If each thread completes both steps when it has its turn, the balance will be consistent. But perhaps thread1 loses its turn after completing step 1.

The execution sequence of Figure 13.9 shows that after thread1 computes a balance of $100 it loses its turn to thread2, which computes a balance of $200 and records the new balance. When thread1 gets its turn again it finishes where it left off, entering $100, which is now incorrect.

To create a simple program to illustrate this phenomenon, we use a buffer that contains an integer, `balance`, that two threads share. The `Increment` method simulates an updating process. It reads `balance` and then repeats a computation 15,000 times to simulate the update computation. Finally, it adds 1 to `balance` and saves the incremented value. Using a simple increment of one makes it easier to understand the results.

FIGURE 13.9
A problem with threads

thread1	**thread2**
`balance = $100`	
	`balance = $200`
	`Compute $200 and update`
`Compute $100 and update`	

We create two threads that access the same buffer. Each thread performs 100 increments. We keep track of the total and see that it is 200 after both threads complete. However, as in Figure 13.9, when a thread gets interrupted during its computation after it saves the current balance but before it updates with the incremented value, it will cause an updating error when it resumes execution. The final balance should be 200, but it is incorrect.

Each thread writes to a file after each increment, recording the total number of increments so far and the current value of the balance. In a correct implementation these would always be the same because we increment both by 1 at each step. We show the significant lines of these files.

EXAMPLE 13.8 ■ TallyWrong.cs

```
/* Two threads occasionally err in reporting
 * values because they get interrupted before
 * finishing to execute a method.
 */

using System;
using System.IO;
using System.Threading;
class Buffer {
  private int balance = 0;  // shared data
  private int total = 0;    // total number of increments

  public void Increment() {
    int i = balance;                                  // Note 1
    total++;
    for(int j = 0; j < 15000; j++) {                  // Note 2
      double k = Math.Sqrt(j) * Math.Exp(j);
    }
    balance = ++i;                                    // Note 3
  }
  public String Result() {
    return "total = " + total + " balance = " + balance;
  }
}
class Plus {
  private Buffer buf;
  StreamWriter p;

  public Plus(Buffer b, String n) {
    buf=b;
    p = new StreamWriter(n);
    Thread t = new Thread(new ThreadStart(Run));
    t.Name = n;
    t.Start();
  }
```

```
  public void Run() {
    for(int i = 0; i < 100; i++){
      buf.Increment();
      p.WriteLine(Thread.CurrentThread.Name +
                                          " " + buf.Result());
    }
    p.Close();
  }
}
public class TallyWrong {
  public static void Main() {
    Buffer b = new Buffer();
    Plus p1 = new Plus(b, "First");                     // Note 4
    Plus p2 = new Plus(b, "Second");
  }
}
```

Output

```
First total = 1 balance = 1
...
First total = 47 balance = 47
                              Second total = 49 balance = 48
                              ...
                              Second total = 67 balance = 66
First total = 68 balance = 48
..
First total = 90 balance = 70
                              Second total = 91 balance = 67
                              ...
                              Second total = 115 balance = 91
First total = 116 balance = 71
...
First total = 139 balance = 94
                              Second total = 140 balance = 92
                              ...
                              Second total = 163 balance = 115
First total = 164 balance = 95
...
First total = 169 balance = 100
                              Second total = 169 balance = 116
                              ...
                              Second total = 200 balance = 147
```

Note 1: `int i = balance;`

We save `balance` to use in a computation to update it to a new value.

Note 2: `for(int j = 0; j < 15000; j++) {`

We repeat a computation 15,000 times to simulate some time-consuming updating of the balance. Most likely this thread will be interrupted here to allow the other thread to compute. When it returns it will still be using the old value of `balance` with which it started the loop, but the other thread already will have made that value incorrect.

Note 3: `balance = ++i;`

We increment the balance to simulate the result of a computation, and save it in the shared variable.

Note 4: `Plus p1 = new Plus(b, "First");`

We pass the same `Buffer`, `b`, to both threads so they will each update the same `balance`.

Synchronization

To correct the problem exhibited by Example 13.8, we need to enable the `Increment` method to execute completely once it has begun. Then the thread will update the `balance` field with the new value without overwriting any updating done by the other thread.

C# lets a thread request a **lock** on an object when it calls one of that object's methods. If no other thread is using that object, the request succeeds and that thread will have exclusive access to that object, allowing it to complete the method execution without interruption. If another thread is using that object, then the thread making the request must wait until the object becomes available. C# uses an attribute to synchronize access to objects.

Attributes

Attributes declare properties of the code that can be accessed at run time. In this text we will use only predefined attributes from the .NET Library. It is possible to define attributes in user-written code.

To enable locking, we annotate the `Increment` and `Result` methods in the `Buffer` class of Example 13.8 with the attribute

```
[MethodImpl(MethodImplOptions.Synchronized)]
```

The `MethodImpl` attribute specifies the details of how a method is implemented. The .NET Framework defines it using the `MethodImplAttribute` class in the `System.Runtime.CompilerServices` namespace.

Example 13.9 revises Example 13.8 to synchronize the `Increment` and `Result` methods. For example, when thread1 calls

```
buf.increment();
```

FIGURE 13.10
thread1 locks buf while thread2 waits

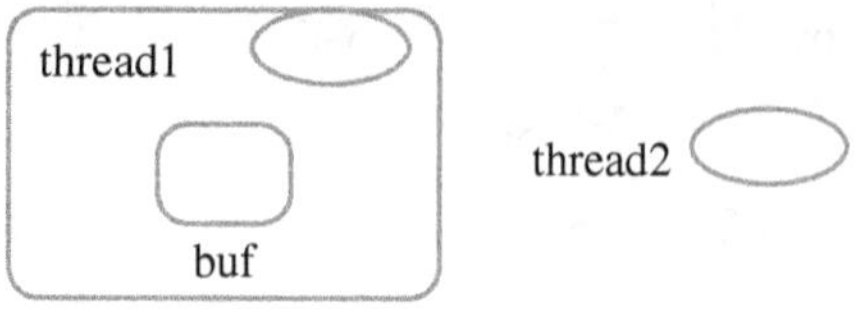

if no other thread is executing any method of `buf`, thread1 gets a lock for the object. Therefore, no other thread can use `buf` until thread1 has finished executing the `increment` method. If another thread is executing a method of `buf`, then thread1 must wait until that operation completes. If several threads are waiting to get a lock on an object, the thread scheduler determines which thread will get it when it becomes available.

With synchronized methods, behavior like that shown in Figure 13.9 cannot occur, because once a thread starts executing a synchronized method it is allowed to finish. Each time a thread enters the `Increment` method, it increments `balance` and saves the new value, so `balance` and `total` always agree.

EXAMPLE 13.9 ■ TallyRight.cs

```
/* Uses attributes to synchronize methods to correct the
 * error in Example 13.8.
 */

using System;
using System.IO;
using System.Runtime.CompilerServices;
using System.Threading;
class Buffer {
  private int balance = 0;  // shared data
  private int total = 0;    // total number of increments

  [MethodImpl(MethodImplOptions.Synchronized)]
  public void Increment() {
    int i = balance;
    total++;
    for(int j = 0; j < 50000; j++) {
      double k = Math.Sqrt(j) * Math.Exp(j);
    }
    balance = ++i;
  }

  [MethodImpl(MethodImplOptions.Synchronized)]
  public String Result() {
    return "total = " + total + " balance = " + balance;
  }
```

```
}
class Plus {
  private Buffer buf;
  private StreamWriter p;

  public Plus(Buffer b, String n) {
    buf=b;
    p = new StreamWriter(n);
    Thread t = new Thread(new ThreadStart(Run));
    t.Name = n;
    t.Start();
  }
  public void Run() {
    for(int i = 0; i < 100; i++){
      buf.Increment();
      p.WriteLine("{0} {1}",
             Thread.CurrentThread.Name, buf.Result());
    }
    p.Close();
  }
}
public class TallyRight {
  public static void Main() {
    Buffer b = new Buffer();
    Plus p1 = new Plus(b, "right1");
    Plus p2 = new Plus(b, "right2");
  }
}
```

Output

```
right1 total = 1 balance = 1
...
right1 total = 53 balance = 53
                              right2 total = 55 balance = 55
                              ...
                              right2 total = 102 balance = 102
right1 total = 103 balance = 103
...
right1 total = 149 balance = 149
                              right2 total = 149 balance = 149
                              ...
                              right2 total = 200 balance = 200
```

■

Synchronization allows threads to complete portions of code without interruption. Sometimes threads also need to communicate with one another to signal the occurrence of a condition that may affect their ability to proceed. For our example, we look at the classic **producer-consumer problem**, in which both producer threads and consumer threads access a data buffer. Producers add data to the buffer, and consumers remove it.

Assuming a fixed-size buffer, a producer cannot add more than the buffer can hold, and a consumer cannot retrieve data from an empty buffer. The `Monitor` class controls access to objects. It has `Wait` and `Pulse` class methods, which are useful in this situation. When a producer has a lock on the buffer and cannot add data because the buffer is full, it executes the `Wait` method, causing it to release the lock and wait to be notified when the state of the buffer has changed. When a consumer removes an item from a full buffer, it executes the `Pulse` method to notify a waiting thread that the buffer is no longer full. Similarly, when a consumer has a lock on the buffer and cannot remove data because the buffer is empty, it executes the `Wait` method, causing it to release the lock and wait to be notified that the state of the buffer has changed. When a producer puts an item into an empty buffer, it executes the `Pulse` method to notify a waiting thread that the buffer is no longer empty.

Example 13.10 solves this producer-consumer problem. We input sleep times for each thread to see how the behavior varies depending on which thread has more time. We use one producer and one consumer thread.

EXAMPLE 13.10 ■ PutGet.cs

```
/* Uses Wait and Pulse to enable producer and
 * consumer threads to cooperate in using a buffer.
 */

using System;
using System.Runtime.CompilerServices;
using System.Threading;
  class Buffer {
    public const int size = 3;
    int[] buffer = new int [size];
    int putpos=0;
    int getpos=0;
    int number=0;

    [MethodImpl(MethodImplOptions.Synchronized)]        // Note 1
    public void Put(int value) {
      if (number == size) {
        Console.WriteLine("Cannot put -- Buffer full");
        Monitor.Wait(this);                              // Note 2
      }
      number++;
```

```
    buffer[putpos] = value;
    Console.WriteLine("Put "+value);
    putpos = (putpos + 1) % size;                        // Note 3
    if (number == 1) Monitor.Pulse(this);                // Note 4
  }

  [MethodImpl(MethodImplOptions.Synchronized)]
  public int Get() {
    if (number == 0) {
       Console.WriteLine("Buffer empty");
       Monitor.Wait(this);
    }
    number--;
    int n = buffer[getpos];
    Console.WriteLine("Get "+n);
    getpos = (getpos + 1) % size;
    if (number == size - 1) Monitor.Pulse(this);         // Note 5
    return n;
  }
}
class Producer {
   Buffer buf;
   int time;
   public Producer(Buffer b, int t) {
      buf = b;
      time = t;
      Thread thread = new Thread(new ThreadStart(Run));
      thread.Start();
   }
   public void Run() {
     for(int i = 1; i <= 10; i++) {                      // Note 6
        buf.Put(i);
        Thread.Sleep(time);                              // Note 7
     }
   }
}
class Consumer {
   Buffer buf;
   int time;
   public Consumer(Buffer b, int t) {
     buf = b;
     time = t;
     Thread thread = new Thread(new ThreadStart(Run));
     thread.Start();
   }
   public void Run() {
     for (int i = 1; i <= 10; i++) {
```

```
            buf.Get();
            Thread.Sleep(time);
        }
      }
  }

public class PutGet {
  public static void Main(String[] args) {
    Buffer b = new Buffer();
    Producer p = new Producer(b, int.Parse(args[0]));
    Consumer c = new Consumer(b, int.Parse(args[1]));
  }
}
```

Output

from PutGet 300 500

```
Put 1
Get 1
Put 2
Get 2
Put 3
Put 4
Get 3
Put 5
Put 6
Get 4
Put 7
Get 5
Put 8
Cannot put -- Buffer full
Get 6
Put 9
Cannot put -- Buffer full
Get 7
Put 10
Get 8
Get 9
Get 10
```

Note 1: `[MethodImpl(MethodImplOptions.Synchronized)]`

We must invoke the `Pulse` and `Wait` methods from synchronized blocks of code.

Note 2: `Monitor.Wait(this);`

The argument is the object we need to wait for. We pass `this` because the thread executing the `Put` method cannot proceed until the buffer in this object has a space available.

Note 3: `putpos = (putpos + 1) % size;`

We use a circular buffer. Visualizing the array as a circle shows that after filling position 2, we move to position 0 again. This formula computes indices in this way: 0, 1, 2, 0, 1, 2, and so on.

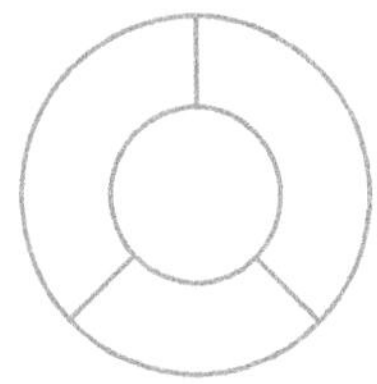

Note 4: `if (number == 1) Monitor.Pulse(this);`

After putting an item into an empty buffer, we call `Pulse`. The scheduler will notify one thread, making it ready to run. In our example, we have at most one thread waiting; if it is waiting it will be notified that the buffer is not empty. When more than one thread may be waiting, calling `PulseAll` will wake them all up.

Note 5: `if (number == size - 1) Monitor.Pulse(this);`

By removing an item from a full buffer, the consumer has just made it possible for a waiting producer to add an item. Calling `Pulse` will wake up a waiting producer.

Note 6: `for(int i = 1; i <= 10; i++)`

We let the producer produce 10 numbers and the consumer consume these 10. We could have run these threads in an unending loop and aborted the program manually.

Note 7: `Thread.Sleep(time);`

Typically there will be some extended computation to produce the value to put in the buffer. For simplicity, we sleep to simulate some computational time.

Deadlock

When threads wait for locks to be freed that cannot be freed we have **deadlock**. We can easily modify Example 13.10 to produce deadlock. If we change the condition for the producer to put only when the buffer is empty and the consumer to get only when the buffer is full, we reach a deadlocked state almost immediately.

The buffer starts out empty, so the consumer cannot get anything. The producer can put one item into it, but no more until the consumer removes that item, making the buffer empty again. The consumer cannot remove the one item in the buffer until the producer adds two more items to fill the buffer. Both the producer and consumer are stuck, each waiting for an action by the other that can never occur.

Good programming is the only prevention for deadlock. In more complicated situations it can be very difficult to determine if deadlock can occur.

EXAMPLE 13.11 ■ Deadlock.cs

```
/* Modifies Example 13.10 to illustrate deadlock.
 */

using System;
using System.Runtime.CompilerServices;
using System.Threading;
  class Buffer {
  public const int size = 3;
    int[] buffer = new int [size];
    int putpos=0;
    int getpos=0;
    int number=0;

    [MethodImpl(MethodImplOptions.Synchronized)]
    public void Put(int value) {
      if (number != 0) {                              // Note 1
        Console.WriteLine("Cannot Put -- Buffer not empty");
        Monitor.Wait(this);
      }
      number++;
      buffer[putpos] = value;
      Console.WriteLine("Put "+value);
      putpos = (putpos + 1) % size;
      if (number == size -1)                          // Note 2
         Monitor.Pulse(this);
    }

   [MethodImpl(MethodImplOptions.Synchronized)]
    public int Get() {
      if (number != size) {
         Console.WriteLine("Cannot Get -- Buffer not full");
         Monitor.Wait(this);
      }
      number--;
      int n = buffer[getpos];
      Console.WriteLine("Get "+n);
      getpos = (getpos + 1) % size;
      if (number == 0)
        Monitor.Pulse(this);
      return n;
```

```
    }
  }
  class Producer {
     Buffer buf;
     int time;
     public Producer(Buffer b, int t) {
        buf = b;
        time = t;
        Thread thread = new Thread(new ThreadStart(Run));
        thread.Start();
     }
     public void Run() {
       for(int i = 1; i <= 10; i++) {
              buf.Put(i);
             Thread.Sleep(time);
       }
     }
  }
  class Consumer {
     Buffer buf;
     int time;
     public Consumer(Buffer b, int t) {
       buf = b;
       time = t;
       Thread thread = new Thread(new ThreadStart(Run));
       thread.Start();
     }
     public void Run() {
       for (int i = 1; i <= 10; i++) {
            buf.Get();
            Thread.Sleep(time);
       }
     }
  }

public class PutGet {
  public static void Main(String[] args) {
    Buffer b = new Buffer();
    Producer p = new Producer(b, int.Parse(args[0]));
    Consumer c = new Consumer(b, int.Parse(args[1]));
  }
}
```

Output

```
Cannot Get -- Buffer not full
Put 1
Cannot Put -- Buffer not empty
```

(At this point the program hangs up because neither the producer nor the consumer can proceed.)

Note 1: `if (number != 0) {`

The producer only puts a value in the buffer when it is empty.

Note 2: `if (number == size -1)`

The producer signals the consumer when the buffer is full.

The BIG Picture

Concurrent programming coordinates multiple threads. When threads share data we can synchronize access so that a thread using the data will be able to complete its operation before another thread gets access to that data. A thread gets a lock on the object that contains the data until it finishes the synchronized method or block.

Threads can wait on a condition to be notified by other threads when changes occur that may make the condition satisfied. Deadlock occurs when threads wait for locks that can never be freed and no thread can proceed.

✓Test Your Understanding

Try It Yourself ➤ **9.** Vary the sleep times when running Example 13.10, and determine how that affects the results.

Try It Yourself ➤ **10.** Modify Example 13.10 to start two producers and two consumers, and explain the resulting behavior.

SUMMARY

- C# allows several threads of control to proceed simultaneously, sharing the processor. Each thread executes when it gets the processor. We pass it a `ThreadStart` delegate with the method to execute. Calling the `Start` method of a thread makes it ready to run. The `Suspend` method suspends it, the `Resume` method resumes it, and the `Abort` method aborts it.
- A `Thread` can `Sleep` for a specified number of milliseconds. We can construct a thread with a name, which we can get later with the `Name` property. To get a thread that we did not create ourselves, such as the thread that runs the `Main` method, we can use the static `CurrentThread` property of the `Thread` class.
- Animations run in threads, sharing the processor with the `Main` method. We can run an animation in a nonterminating loop because other activities can proceed in other threads concurrently. In a simple example, we display the same figure at different positions, allowing the thread to sleep for a fraction of a second between repaints of the screen. To make the animation more interesting, we change the figure before repainting it.

- We can use images in our C# programs. The `DrawImage` method has several versions. We use the simplest, with three arguments: the image and the `(x,y)` coordinates of the position at which to draw the image. This version of `DrawImage` draws the image in its normal size. We also use the five-argument version of `DrawImage`, which includes two arguments representing the scaled size we prefer for the image.
- The images we animate will flicker a lot because the repainting clears the screen. The alternation of clear background and image causes the flicker. We can eliminate the flicker by the technique of double buffering, doing all the drawing of graphics and images on the offscreen buffer. As the last step, we draw the offscreen buffer on the screen. We can clear the offscreen image between repaints; we do not see this background, so this does not cause flicker. We use the `SetStyle` method to enable double buffering.
- When threads share data we must be careful to ensure correct access. We annotate a method with an attribute to indicate that access to it should be synchronized. A thread must obtain a lock on an object to use its synchronized methods. It then has exclusive access. The thread holding the lock may complete the method or block of code without interruption.
- The `Wait` and `Pulse` methods help threads communicate. The `Wait` method signals that a condition is not satisfied, so the thread executing it must wait. The `Pulse` method wakes up one thread, signaling that a condition has been satisfied. Concurrent programming requires great care to avoid problems such as deadlock where threads are unable to proceed, halting the system.

SKILL BUILDER EXERCISES

1. Executing the ______________ method makes a thread ready to run.

2. Match a `Monitor` method name on the left with its description on the right.

a. `Pulse`	i. Releases the lock on an object and blocks the current thread until it reacquires the lock
b. `Wait`	ii. Notifies all waiting threads of a change in the object's state
c. `PulseAll`	iii. Notifies a thread in the waiting queue of a change in the locked object's state

3. Deadlock occurs when ____________________________________.

CRITICAL THINKING EXERCISES

4. Executing the following event handler when the user presses a button will

a. call the `OnPaint` method only when the loop completes execution.

b. call the `OnPaint` method once for each iteration of the loop.

c. do alternatives a or b depending on the implementation.

d. cause an error.

```
protected void Move_Click(object sender, EventArgs e) {
  for (int i = 0; i < 10; i++) {
    x += 9;
    y += 9;
    Invalidate();
  }
}
```

5. Adding the line

```
Sleep(150.5)
```

to a program would cause an error because

   a. the argument must be an integer.
   b. the prefix `Thread.` should be used.
   c. exception handling has not been provided.
   d. a and b.
   e. All of the above.

6. Which of the following is not one of the styles necessary to enable double buffering?
   a. `ControlStyles.DoubleBuffer`
   b. `ControlStyles.ResizeRedraw`
   c. `ControlStyles.AllPaintingInWmPaint`
   d. `ControlStyles.UserPaint`

7. In `g.DrawImage(pic,10,10,100,100)` the last two arguments represent
   a. the dimensions of `pic`.
   b. the desired size of the drawing.
   c. the lower-right corner of the rectangle whose upper-right corner is (10,10).
   d. the intensity and brightness of the colors used.

DEBUGGING EXERCISE

8. The following program attempts to draw a rectangle in colors chosen at random, changing the color every two seconds. Find and correct any errors.

```
public class ColoredBoxes : Form {
  Color c;
  public ColoredBoxes() {
    Thread t = new Thread(new ThreadStart(Run));
  }
  protected override void OnPaint(PaintEventArgs e) {
    Graphics g = e.Graphics;
    g.DrawRectangle(c, 100, 100, 30, 30);
    base.OnPaint(e);
  }
  public void Run(){
```

```
        Random r = new Random();
        while(true) {
          c = Color.FromArgb(r.Next(256),
                             r.Next(256),r.Next(256));
          Thread.Sleep(200);
        }
      }
    }
```

PROGRAM MODIFICATION EXERCISES

9. Modify Example 13.6 to specify the sleep time as a program argument.
10. Modify Example 13.7 to specify the sleep time as a program argument.
11. Modify Example 13.5 to use double buffering to remove the flicker.
12. Modify Example 13.6 to use double buffering to remove the flicker.
13. Modify Example 13.5 to draw the ball in a color of your choice.
14. Modify Example 13.5 to draw the ball in a different color for each of the ten iterations of the loop.
15. Modify Example 13.6 to draw the eyes in one color and the mouth in another, both different from black.
16. Modify Example 13.5 so that instead of arbitrarily moving the ball ten times in each direction, we use the size of the form, the size of the ball, and the size of the increment to determine how many times we can move the ball before it goes off the screen.

PROGRAM DESIGN EXERCISES

Putting It All Together ➤

17. Example 9.10 provides a user interface for insertion sorting. In that example the user inserts one element at a time, pressing a button to perform the next insertion. Write a C# program that will display the bar chart as the sorting progresses, without requiring the user to press a button to insert each item. Use a thread and let the sorting proceed, sleeping between each insertion to make it easier to view.
18. Write a C# program that uses two threads, one to animate a ball, and one to animate a face. Make sure that the ball and the face do not collide.
19. a. Write a C# program that moves a ball around the screen randomly. If the user clicks the mouse on the ball, increment a score showing in the corner of the screen. If the user reaches a score of 5, make the ball move faster so it is more difficult to catch. If the user reaches a score of 10, make the ball smaller.

    b. In part a, use an image of your choice instead of a ball.
20. Write a C# program that displays a digital clock that shows the correct time. To get the current time, use the `getInstance()` method of the `Calendar` class, in the `cs.util` package, to get a `Calendar` object, `c`. Then use the `Calendar` get method to get the hours, minutes, and seconds, as in

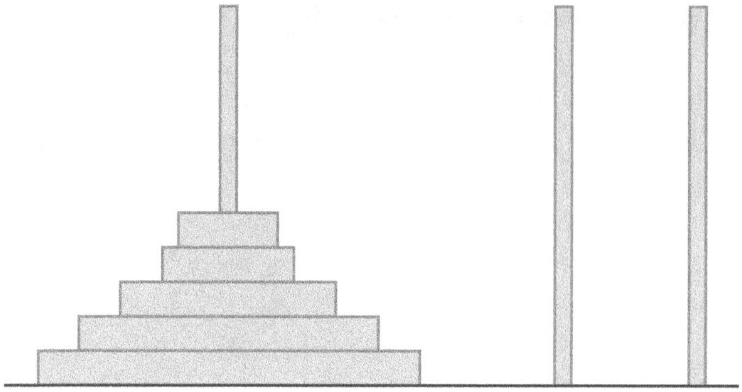

FIGURE 13.11
The Towers of Hanoi puzzle

```
int hour = c.get(Calendar.HOUR);
int minute = c.get(Calendar.MINUTE);
int second = c.get(Clandar.SECOND);
```

Use a thread to allow the clock to keep the correct time.

Putting It All Together ➤ **21.** (Towers of Hanoi) Suppose we have *n* disks on a peg, each of different sizes, stacked in order of size, with the largest on the bottom, and two other pegs, as shown in Figure 13.11.

What is the sequence of moves needed to transfer the rings to the second peg, in the same configuration, in order from largest to the smallest, with the largest at the bottom, if we can move only one disk at a time, and we cannot place a larger disk on top of a smaller disk? We may use the last peg to store disks, but the same rules apply. Use a recursive method to provide the solution. To move *n* disks from peg 1 to peg 2, move *n*-1 disks to peg 3, move the bottom disk to peg 2, then move *n*-1 disks from peg 3 to peg 2.

Use a thread to animate the solution, using various colors for the disks.

14 Networking

C# makes it easy to connect to other computers, using classes from the .NET Library. We first write client programs that connect to a server, which is a program that performs a task useful to its clients, and then write our own servers. A web server provides files such as web pages and images.

To write client programs, we first use C# classes that enable us to hide the details of the interaction between client and server. We then try classes that let us customize the connection, and present classes that give us full control of the communication, but require us then to know the details of the request and response commands.

The simplest clients connect to a server using a `WebClient` object, or for more flexibility, `WebRequest` and `WebResponse` objects. A client talks to a server using a specific protocol. We introduce HTTP, the Hypertext Transfer Protocol used to connect to a web server. Understanding HTTP allows us to customize a connection using `HttpWebRequest` methods and to write our own simple web client and web server using `TcpClient` and `TcpListener` objects. This will enable us to develop and use our own protocols for clients and servers to communicate. The `Socket` class allows a lower-level access to a network connection. We do not use it in this text.

On a higher level, Remoting allows us to invoke objects on remote machines, introducing powerful distributed computing using C#.

OBJECTIVES

- Introduce HTTP to understand how web clients and servers communicate.
- Use a `WebClient` to connect to a remote site.
- Use `WebRequest` and `WebResponse`, which encapsulate protocols.
- Use `HttpWebRequest` to customize a connection.
- Use `TcpClient` and `TcpListener` objects to have full control over the communication.

- Write a very simple browser and a very simple web server.
- Use threads to enable a server to handle multiple clients.
- Introduce distributed computing using Remoting.

14.1 REQUESTS AND RESPONSES

Computers use protocols to communicate. A client sends requests using the commands provided by the protocol in the order specified in the protocol, and the server responds similarly. The `WebRequest` and `WebResponse` classes encapsulate two popular protocols, handling their details and making it easier for C# programmers to make network connections to display a page or retrieve a file. They can provide a common interface for other protocols, as implemented. The `WebClient` class provides an easy interface to a `WebRequest`. We will describe a URL, describe the Hypertext Transfer Protocol (HTTP), and then show how to connect to remote sites.

The Uniform Resource Locator (URL)

A **URL** has four parts: the protocol name, the host address, the port, and the path to the resource file. The **port** number specifies a specific communication link between computers. For example, the full URL for Microsoft's home page is

```
http://microsoft.com:80/index.html
```

where HTTP is the protocol, `microsoft.com` is the host address, `80` is the port, and `index.html` is the path to the resource. Because `80` is the default port for the HTTP service and `index.html` is often the default file name, we can write the same URL more concisely as

```
http://microsoft.com/
```

Using the URL for Microsoft's home page, our C# client connects our machine to the web server on Microsoft's host machine. This server program must understand HTTP, which we introduce next. Using a `WebClient` to write our client programs, we let C# handle the details of the messages specified by the HTTP protocol to communicate with a web server.

The Hypertext Transfer Protocol (HTTP)[1]

We use HTTP to connect to a web site. A web client such as a browser connects to a web server on a computer at a remote site. Each protocol, including HTTP, allows a formal exchange of messages using well-specified formats.

An HTTP client sends a **request** to the server in which the first line has three parts,

```
Method used   Identifier for the resource   Protocol version
```

[1] See `http://www.w3.org/` for the complete HTTP specification.

FIGURE 14.1
Some HTTP request methods

Method	Description
GET	Retrieves the resource requested. Appends data sent to the URL.
HEAD	Returns the response headers only and not the resource.
POST	Its function depends on the resource type. It differs from GET in that it sends data after the blank line that terminates the request headers.

FIGURE 14.2
Some HTTP request headers

Field	Description
User-Agent	Identifies the client.
Host	Identifies the server.
Accept	Specifies the types[2] of files the client is prepared to accept. Each type has a preference associated with it given by the value of q (for "quality"). This value ranges from a low of 0 to the default of 1. For example, `Accept: text/html, text/plain;q=.2` indicates that text/html is the preferred format with a default quality of 1.0 and that text/plain is acceptable with a preference of .2.
Connection	Specifies the type of connection. For example, `Connection: keep-alive` expresses the client's wish to keep the connection alive for multiple requests.

The following lines of the request are various **request headers**, which provide information about the capabilities of the client. Each request header has two parts separated by a colon.

```
Name  :  Value
```

The client sends a blank line after the request headers to let the server know that there are no more request headers. The client then sends the data, if any, to the server.

In this chapter, we use the GET method when making HTTP requests. An example HTTP request is

```
GET  /TryURL.cs  HTTP/1.0
```

where the three parts are the name of the request, GET, the resource requested, /TryURL.cs, and the protocol version, HTTP/1.0. Figure 14.1 shows some HTTP request methods. Figure 14.2 describes some request headers.

[2]The type names are MIME (Multipurpose Internet Mail Extensions) types.

FIGURE 14.3
Some HTTP status codes

Type	Code	Typical Message
Success	200	OK
Redirection	301	Moved Permanently
Client Error	400	Bad Request
	404	Not Found
	406	Not Acceptable
Server Error	501	Not Implemented

FIGURE 14.4
Some HTTP response headers

Field	Description
Date	Gives the day and Greenwich Mean Time
Server	Names the web server used
Content-type	Describes the content
Content-length	Number of bytes in the file

An HTTP server responds to a request with a **status line** followed by various **response headers**. The status line has the form

```
HTTP Version      Status Code         Reason
```

For example, the status line

```
HTTP/1.0  200  Document follows
```

shows a successful request with the code 200. Figure 14.3 shows some status codes.

The response headers have the same form as the request headers,

```
Name: Value
```

Figure 14.4 describes some response headers.

Connecting from `WebClient`

The `WebClient` class provides a simple facility to make connections as shown in Example 14.1.

EXAMPLE 14.1 ■ TryURL.cs

```
/* Displays the resource specified
 * on the command line.
 */

using System;
```

```
using System.IO;
using System.Net;
public class TryURL {
  public static void Main(String [] args) {
    WebClient client = new WebClient();
    client.BaseAddress = args[0];                              // Note 1
    client.DownloadFile(args[1], args[2]);                     // Note 2
    StreamReader input =
          new StreamReader(client.OpenRead(args[1]));  // Note 3
    Console.WriteLine(input.ReadToEnd());                      // Note 4
    Console.WriteLine("Request header count: {0}",
                              client.Headers.Count);  // Note 5
    WebHeaderCollection header = client.ResponseHeaders;
    Console.WriteLine
      ("Response header count: {0}", header.Count);
    for (int i = 0; i < header.Count; i++)
      Console.WriteLine("    {0} : {1}",
                         header.GetKey(i), header[i]); // Note 6
    input.Close();
  }
}
```

Output

(Using the command

```
TryURL http://www.cecs.csulb.edu/~artg/ TryURL.cs test)
```

(We omit the file TryURL.cs)

```
Request header count: 0
Response header count: 7
   Date : Sat, 03 Aug 2002 16:50:44 GMT
   Server : Apache/1.3.9 (Unix) PHP/4.0.6 mod_perl/1.21
   Last-Modified : Sat, 03 Aug 2002 12:40:05 GMT
   ETag : "10f16c-375-3d4bcf25"
   Accept-Ranges : bytes
   Content-Length : 885
   Content-Type : text/plain
```

Note 1: `client.BaseAddress = args[0];`

We set the `BaseAddress` property with the address of the remote site. Any resources we request will have a path relative to this base.

Note 2: `client.DownloadFile(args[1], args[2]);`

The `DownloadFile` method downloads the file to the local machine. The first argument gives the path of the file to download, relative to the base address. The second argument gives the name to copy it to on the local system.

Note 3: `new StreamReader(client.OpenRead(args[1]));`

We can read the file from the remote machine. The `OpenRead` method opens a stream to download the file.

Note 4: `Console.WriteLine(input.ReadToEnd());`

The `ReadToEnd` method reads the stream from the current position to the end of the stream.

Note 5:
```
Console.WriteLine("Request header count: {0}",
                          client.Headers.Count);
```

The `Headers` property represents a collection of the request headers sent to the server. This `WebClient` does not send any.

Note 6:
```
Console.WriteLine("    {0} : {1}",
                    header.GetKey(i), header[i]);
```

The server sends seven response headers. We use the `ResponseHeaders` property to find them. We use the `GetKey` method to find the key for each header. We index the collection using array notation to find the value associated with the key. The `ETag` header is an identifier used for validation. The `Accept-Ranges` header indicates that `bytes` is the unit of measure used.

Connecting with `WebRequest` and `WebResponse`

The `WebRequest` and `WebResponse` classes encapsulate several protocols with a common interface. The .NET Library provides two derived classes, `HttpWebResponse` which implements HTTP, and `FileWebResponse` which implements the `file` protocol. Users can derive classes to implement other protocols.

We run Example 14.2 to illustrate both of the .NET implemented protocols. The file URL we test with is

```
file://c:/booksharp/gittleman/ch14/TryURL.cs
```

It represents a file on the local machine. Using Windows, `c:` indicates the C drive. The file `TryURL.cs` is on the C drive in the folder `\booksharp\gittleman\ch14`. We use forward slashes for all URLs, but on Windows systems we could use backslashes in the `file` URL.

EXAMPLE 14.2 ■ TryWebRequest.cs

```
/* Uses WebRequest and WebResponse. Tests use HTTP
 * and the file protocol.
 */

using System;
using System.IO;
```

```
using System.Net;
public class TryWebRequest {
  public static void Main(String [] args) {
    WebRequest request = WebRequest.Create(args[0]);   // Note 1
    WebResponse response = request.GetResponse();      // Note 2
    Console.WriteLine("Content length: {0}",
                        response.ContentLength);       // Note 3
    Console.WriteLine("Content type: {0}\n",
                        response.ContentType);
    Console.WriteLine("Request header count: {0}",
                        request.Headers.Count);        // Note 4
    WebHeaderCollection header = request.Headers;
    for (int i = 0; i < header.Count; i++)
      Console.WriteLine("   {0} : {1}",
                        header.GetKey(i), header[i]);
    StreamReader input =
      new StreamReader(response.GetResponseStream());  // Note 5
    Console.WriteLine(input.ReadToEnd());
    input.Close();
  }
}
```

Output

(Using the command

`TryWebRequest http://www.cecs.csulb.edu/~artg/TryURL.cs)`

```
Content length: 885
Content type: text/plain

Request header count: 2
   Connection : Keep-Alive
   Host : www.cecs.csulb.edu
```

(We omit the file TryURL.cs)

Output

(Using the command

`TryWebRequest file://c:/booksharp/gittleman/ch14/TryURL.cs)`

```
Content length: 955
Content type: binary/octet-stream

Request header count: 0
```

(We omit the file TryURL.cs)

■

Note 1: `WebRequest request = WebRequest.Create(args[0]);`

We use the `Create` method rather than a constructor to get the `WebRequest` object, because the type of the object created depends on the protocol we use for the request. It will be a class derived from `WebRequest`.

Note 2: `WebResponse response = request.GetResponse();`

The `GetResponse` method gets the `WebResponse` associated with the request.

Note 3:
```
Console.WriteLine("Content length: {0}",
                        response.ContentLength);
```

Each type of `WebResponse` has `ContentType` and `ContentLength` properties that encapsulate these headers. Derived classes may add additional header properties.

Note 4:
```
Console.WriteLine("Request header count: {0}",
                        request.Headers.Count);
```

When using HTTP the client sends two request headers, but when using the file protocol it sends none.

Note 5:
```
StreamReader input =
     new StreamReader(response.GetResponseStream());
```

The `GetResponseStream` method opens a stream to download the resource requested.

Using `HttpWebRequest` and `HttpWebResponse`

When we want to use only HTTP we can use derived classes, which expose some details of this protocol. Example 14.3 uses `HttpWebRequest` and `HttpWebResponse`.

EXAMPLE 14.3 ■ TryHttpRequest.cs

```
/* Uses HTTP specific classes to expose more of that protocol.
 */

using System;
using System.IO;
using System.Net;
public class TryHttpRequest {
  public static void Main(String [] args) {
    HttpWebRequest request =
          (HttpWebRequest)WebRequest.Create(args[0]);
    HttpWebResponse response =
             (HttpWebResponse)request.GetResponse();
    request.Accept = "text/plain";                        // Note 1
```

```
    Console.WriteLine("Request header count: {0}",
                            request.Headers.Count); // Note 2
    WebHeaderCollection header = request.Headers;
    for (int i = 0; i < header.Count; i++)
      Console.WriteLine("   {0} : {1}",
                      header.GetKey(i), header[i]);
    Console.WriteLine("Response headers");
    Console.WriteLine("  Protocol version: {0}",
                      response.ProtocolVersion);     // Note 3
    Console.WriteLine("  Status code: {0}",
                      response.StatusCode);          // Note 4
    Console.WriteLine("  Status description: {0}",
                      response.StatusDescription);
    Console.WriteLine("  Content encoding: {0}",
                      response.ContentEncoding);
    Console.WriteLine("  Content length: {0}",
                      response.ContentLength);
    Console.WriteLine("  Content type: {0}",
                      response.ContentType);
    Console.WriteLine("  Last Modified: {0}",
                      response.LastModified);
    Console.WriteLine("  Server: {0}", response.Server);
    Console.WriteLine("  Length using method: {0}\n",
       response.GetResponseHeader("Content-Length"));  // Note 5
    StreamReader input =
        new StreamReader(response.GetResponseStream());
    Console.WriteLine(input.ReadToEnd());
    input.Close();
  }
}
```

Output

(Using the command

```
TryHttpRequest http://www.cecs.csulb.edu/~artg/TryURL.cs)
```

```
Request header count: 3
   Connection : Keep-Alive
   Host : www.cecs.csulb.edu
   Accept : text/plain
Response headers
  Protocol version: 1.1
  Status code: OK
  Status description: OK
  Content encoding:
  Content length: 885
  Content type: text/plain
  Last Modified: 8/3/2002 5:40:05 AM
```

```
Server: Apache/1.3.9 (Unix) PHP/4.0.6 mod_perl/1.21
Length using method: 885
```

(We omit the file TryURL.cs)

Note 1:
```
request.Accept = "text/plain";
```

We can use properties to either get or set a value. Here we set the `Accept` request header to have the value `text/plain`, indicating to the server that we wish to accept plain text responses.

Note 2:
```
Console.WriteLine("Request header count: {0}",
                           request.Headers.Count);
```

The client sends three request headers, the two that it sent in Example 14.2 and the `Accept` header that we added.

Note 3:
```
Console.WriteLine("  Protocol version: {0}",
                      response.ProtocolVersion);
```

We use `HttpWebResponse` properties to find the response headers that the server sends to respond to this request. Blank output means that the server did not send that header.

Note 4:
```
Console.WriteLine("  Status code: {0}",
                           response.StatusCode);
```

The `StatusCode` property uses the `HttpStatusCode` enumeration to provide descriptive names for each of the numerical status codes used in the status line giving the server's response. OK represents the successful fulfillment of the request denoted by the 200 code. See the .NET Library documentation for a table of the `HttpStatusCode` enumeration values and their association with numerical codes.

Note 5:
```
Console.WriteLine("  Length using method: {0}\n",
   response.GetResponseHeader("Content-Length"));
```

The `GetResponseHeader` method returns the response header whose name is passed as its argument.

The BIG Picture

Network clients and servers communicate using protocols. A URL consists of a protocol, a server address, a port, and a path to the resource. Using HTTP to communicate with a web server, the client sends a request followed by various request headers giving information about the client. The server responds with a status line and various response headers describing the server and the response. The `WebClient`, `WebRequest`, and `WebResponse` classes hide the details of some popular protocols, letting us make connections more easily.

✓ **Test Your Understanding**

Try It Yourself ➤ **1.** Use Example 14.2 to connect to the author's home page, `http://www.cecs.csulb.edu/~artg/`. Explain the result.

2. For the `Accept` request header given by

```
Accept: text/plain; q=0.5, text/html,
        application/zip; q=0.8, image/gif
```

which two file types are most preferred, which is next, and which is least preferred?

Try It Yourself ➤ **3.** In Example 14.3 use the `GetResponseHeader` method to get the content type instead of the `ContentType` property.

Try It Yourself ➤ **4.** Use Example 14.3 to connect to five web sites, in addition to those tried in the text.

14.2 CLIENTS AND SERVERS

The `WebClient`, `WebRequest`, and `WebResponse` classes hide the details of a few common protocols, most importantly HTTP, so we can easily write programs to connect to a web server, for example. With the `TcpClient` and `TcpListener` classes we can write clients and servers using existing protocols, and develop our own protocols for communicating between client and server. After introducing ports, through which we connect, we use our own protocol, writing both a server and a client.

Server Ports

Each server listens on a numbered port. The system servers use port numbers below 1024; we can use higher numbered ports for our servers. The familiar services use standard port numbers. For example, web servers usually use port 80, **SMTP** (Simple Mail Transfer Protocol) servers for sending mail use port 25, and **POP3** (Post Office Protocol—version 3) servers for receiving mail use port 110.

We could use C# to write a client to connect to a system server. For example, we could get our email by writing a client for a POP3 server. In writing such a client we would have to follow the Post Office Protocol—version 3, which specifies the form of the communication between the client and the server. Figure 14.5 shows sample interaction between a client and a POP3 server.

Handling HTTP Explicitly

If we use a TcpClient[3] in the `System.Net.Sockets` namespace to connect, we must explicitly follow all the steps that HTTP specifies for making a request. We must send the request, any request headers, and the blank line. We read the status line, response headers, and the response data.

[3]TCP is a network protocol responsible for verifying the correct delivery of data from client to server. It works at a lower level than HTTP and other protocols we use directly.

```
Server: +OK POP3 server ready  // server sends welcome
Client: USER username          // client sends user's name
Server: +OK                    // server responds OK
Client: PASS password          // client sends the password
Server: +OK 23 messages 3040 octets
                               // server sends message info
Client: RETR 23                // asks for message 23
Server: text of message 23, ending
          with a '.' alone on a line
Client: QUIT
```

FIGURE 14.5 **Interacting with the POP3 server**

EXAMPLE 14.4 ■ TryTcp.cs

```
/* Uses a TcpClient to handle HTTP explicitly.
 */

using System;
using System.Text;
using System.IO;
using System.Net.Sockets;
public class TryTcp {
  public static void Main(String [] args) {
    TcpClient client =
         new TcpClient(args[0], int.Parse(args[1]));   // Note 1
    NetworkStream stream = client.GetStream();         // Note 2
    byte[] send = Encoding.ASCII.GetBytes
          ("GET " + args[2] + " HTTP/1.0 \r\n\r\n");   // Note 3
    stream.Write(send, 0, send.Length);                // Note 4
    byte[] bytes = new byte[client.ReceiveBufferSize]; // Note 5
    int count = stream.Read
            (bytes, 0, (int)client.ReceiveBufferSize); // Note 6
    String data = Encoding.ASCII.GetString(bytes);     // Note 7
    char[] unused = {(char)data[count]};               // Note 8
    Console.WriteLine(data.TrimEnd(unused));           // Note 9
    stream.Close();
    client.Close();
  }
}
```

Output

(Using the command

`TryTcp www.cecs.csulb.edu 80 /~artg/TryURL.cs`)

```
HTTP/1.1 200 OK
Date: Sat, 03 Aug 2002 21:37:39 GMT
Server: Apache/1.3.9 (Unix) PHP/4.0.6 mod_perl/1.21
Last-Modified: Sat, 03 Aug 2002 12:40:05 GMT
ETag: "10f16c-375-3d4bcf25"
Accept-Ranges: bytes
Content-Length: 885
Connection: close
Content-Type: text/plain
```

(We omit the file TryURL.cs)

Note 1: `new TcpClient(args[0], int.Parse(args[1]));`

The first argument to the constructor is the name of the host to which we want to connect. The second argument is the port on which the server is running.

Note 2: `NetworkStream stream = client.GetStream();`

The `GetStream` method returns a `NetworkStream` used to send and receive data.

Note 3:

```
byte[] send = Encoding.ASCII.GetBytes
  ("GET " + args[2] + " HTTP/1.0 \r\n\r\n");
```

The `Encoding` class in the `System.Text` namespace represents character encodings. The `ASCII` property provides encoding for the ASCII (7-bit) character set. The `GetBytes` method encodes the specified `String` in a byte array. The `String` we use represents an HTTP request followed by a blank line. There are no request headers. The special character sequence "`\r\n`" signals a carriage return and a newline command. The first such sequence gets to the line after the request and the second provides the blank line.

Note 4: `stream.Write(send, 0, send.Length);`

The first argument is the array containing the bytes to send to the server. The second argument is the starting index in the array. The third is the number of bytes to send.

Note 5: `byte[] bytes = new byte[client.ReceiveBufferSize];`

We need to create a byte array to hold the data we read from the server. We use `ReceiveBufferSize`, the number of bytes we expect to store in the buffer at each read operation.

Note 6:

```
int count = stream.Read
     (bytes, 0, (int)client.ReceiveBufferSize);
```

We read from the server into the `bytes` array. The second argument is the array index at which to start, and the third argument is the number of bytes to read. The return value represents the number of bytes read.

Note 7: `String data = Encoding.ASCII.GetString(bytes);`

The `GetString` method converts the bytes to a character `String` according to the `ASCII` encoding.

Note 8: `char[] unused = {(char)data[count]};`

Because we convert a whole block of data, there may be extra characters at the end that are not part of our requested resource. We use the character just beyond those at indices `0` through `count -1`, representing the data we read from the server. We make a `char` array to use when removing extraneous characters from the end of the string.

Note 9: `Console.WriteLine(data.TrimEnd(unused));`

The `TrimEnd` method returns a String with any characters in the `char` array passed to it removed from the end of the `data` String.

A Client–Server Example

If we write our own server we can use our own protocol for communicating with a client. We write a very simple server that reverses the text the client sends to it. Figure 14.6 shows the server window and Figure 14.7 shows the client window.

The .NET Framework provides a `TcpClient` class for the client to connect to a server on a specific port and a `TcpListener` class for the server to listen for clients who wish to make a connection. Once the client connects with the server, they use the stream classes to send and receive data to and from one another. Example 14.5 shows the code for a server that reverses whatever the client sends it.

We choose an arbitrary port number, 5678, on which our server will listen. The `AcceptTcpClient` method waits for a client to make a connection. When a client connects, its method returns a `TcpClient` and our server prints a message announcing the connection. The client has a `GetStream` method which the server

FIGURE 14.6 **The `ReverseServer` window**

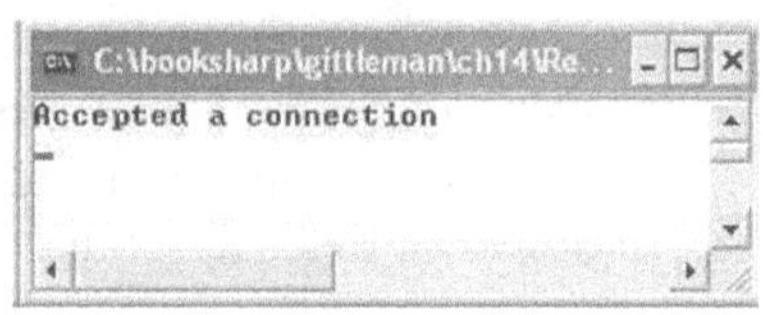

FIGURE 14.7 **The `ReverseClient` window**

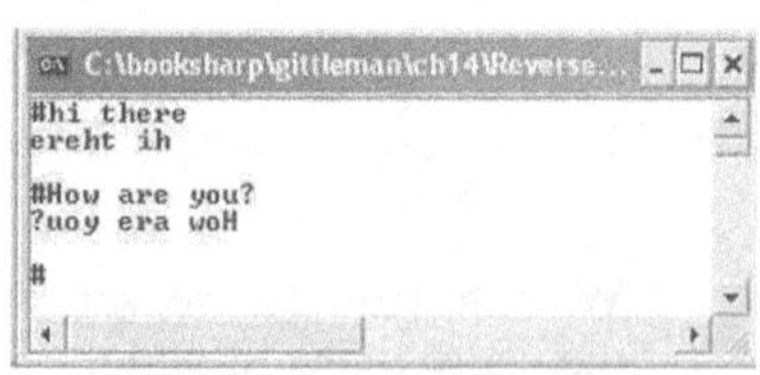

uses to create a `NetworkStream` to communicate with the client. The server reads one line at a time from the client, reversing it and sending it back.

EXAMPLE 14.5 ■ ReverseServer.cs

```
/* Listens on port 5678.  When a client connects, the server
 * reverses whatever the client sends, and sends it back.
 */

using System;
using System.IO;
using System.Text;
using System.Net.Sockets;
public class ReverseServer {
  public static void Main() {
    TcpListener server = new TcpListener(5678);        // Note 1
    server.Start();                                    // Note 2
    TcpClient client = server.AcceptTcpClient();       // Note 3
    Console.WriteLine("Accepted a connection");
    try{
      NetworkStream stream = client.GetStream();
      while(true) {
        byte[] receive = new byte[80];                 // Note 4
        int count = stream.Read(receive, 0, 80);
        if (count == 0)
           break;                                      // Note 5
        String s = Encoding.ASCII.GetString(receive);
        char[] unused = {(char)s[count]};
        int size = s.TrimEnd(unused).Length;
        char[] c = new char[size];                     // Note 6
        for (int i = 0; i < size; i++)
          c[i] = s[size-1-i];                          // Note 7
        byte[] send = Encoding.ASCII.GetBytes(c);      // Note 8
        stream.Write(send, 0, send.Length);
      }
    }catch(Exception e) {                              // Note 9
       Console.WriteLine(e);
    }finally {                                         //Note 10
       client.Close();
       server.Stop();                                  //Note 11
    }
  }
}
```

Note 1: `TcpListener server = new TcpListener(5678);`

The `TcpListener` class builds on the `Socket` to provide TCP services at a higher level of abstraction. We create a server to listen for connections on port 5678.

Note 2: `server.Start();`

`Start` initializes the underlying socket. It listens for network requests.

Note 3: `TcpClient client = server.AcceptTcpClient();`

The `AcceptTcpClient` method blocks any further progress in the program until a client connects; it then returns the `TcpClient`.

Note 4: `byte[] receive = new byte[80];`

We read one line to reverse, so we make the array size 80.

Note 5: `if (count == 0) break;`

If we do not read any bytes from the client, we break and terminate the server. Normally a server would remain in a loop and return to the `AcceptTcpClient` statement to wait for another client to connect. Even better, it would use threads to serve more than one client simultaneously. We consider these improvements later and in the exercises.

Note 6: `char[] c = new char[size];`

We cannot change a `String` object, so we create an array of characters to hold the reverse of the line the client inputs.

Note 7:

```
for (int i = 0; i < size; i++)
  c[i] = s[size-1-i];
```

We reverse the `String` by copying it from its end, starting at the beginning of the `char` array.

Note 8: `byte[] send = Encoding.ASCII.GetBytes(c);`

We convert the `char` array containing the reversed characters to bytes to send to the client.

Note 9: `}catch(Exception e) {`

We handle any exceptions that may be thrown. We just display a message in this example.

Note 10: `}finally {`

The system will execute the code in the `finally` clause whether or not an exception occurs. Had the `Close` statement been at the end of the `try` block an exception might have caused it to be skipped. By putting it here we will be sure to close the file in any case.

Note 11: `server.Stop();`

The `Stop` method closes the listener.

We can run the server on the same machine as the client or on a different machine.[4] The server does not terminate until we abort it, so we should run it in the background in its own thread, and we can do other things while it is waiting for clients to connect.[5] Figures 14.6 and 14.7 show the client and server running on the same machine. The client connects using the address of the host, which we pass as a program argument. The name `localhost` denotes the local machine, so the client connects to the server on the same machine with the command

```
ReverseClient localhost
```

Using two machines, we would have started the server on one machine and let the client connect to it using the server's name or its IP address. We usually refer to machines by their names, as, for example, `www.cecs.csulb.edu`, but underlying each name is a 4-byte IP (Internet Protocol) address, as, for example 134.139.67.68. (The local machine, named localhost, has the IP address 127.0.0.1.) In connecting in a small lab in which the computers are linked to the Internet, we may just use these basic IP addresses. If we start `ReverseServer` on machine 134.139.67.68, we would connect to the server from another machine using the command

```
ReverseClient 134.139.67.68.
```

The client creates a `TcpClient` using the port 5678, on which the server is listening. The client enters a loop, printing a prompt, getting a line from the user, sending it to the server, getting the reversed line from the server, displaying it on the screen, and exiting when the user signals the end of input by entering an empty line. Example 14.6 shows the client program that connects to a server that reverses its input.

EXAMPLE 14.6 ■ ReverseClient.cs

```
/* Connect to a server that reverses whatever
 * the user inputs.  Specifies the host of the
 * server on the command line.
 */

using System;
using System.Text;
using System.IO;
using System.Net.Sockets;
```

---

[4]When running a server on the same machine as the client in Windows, the machine does not need to be connected to the Internet, but the TCP/IP protocol should be installed.

[5]In Windows systems, use the start command to run the server in the background:

```
start ReverseServer.
```

If using an integrated development environment, use separate projects for the server and client, running the server first.

```
public class ReverseClient {
  public static void Main(String[] args) {
    TcpClient client = new TcpClient(args[0], 5678);    // Note 1
    NetworkStream stream = client.GetStream();
    try{
      while(true) {
        Console.Write("#");
        String s = Console.ReadLine();                     // Note 2
        if (s == "")
           break;                                          // Note 3
        byte[] send = Encoding.ASCII.GetBytes(s);
        stream.Write(send, 0, send.Length);                // Note 4
        byte[] bytes = new byte[80];
        stream.Read(bytes, 0, 80);
        String data = Encoding.ASCII.GetString(bytes);
        Console.WriteLine(data);                           // Note 5
      }
    }catch(Exception e) {
       Console.WriteLine(e);
    }finally {
       stream.Close();
    }
  }
}
```

Note 1: `TcpClient client = new TcpClient(args[0], 5678);`

The client creates a socket connection to the server on port 5678, the port on which the server is listening.

Note 2: `String s = Console.ReadLine();`

We display a prompt and read a line from the keyboard.

Note 3: `if (s == "") break;`

If the user enters an empty line we break the loop, which will terminate the client.

Note 4: `stream.Write(send, 0, send.Length);`

We convert the input string to a byte array which we send to the server.

Note 5: `Console.WriteLine(data);`

We read a byte array from the server, convert it to a String, and display it on the screen. It will be the reverse of the string we sent.

The BIG Picture

Using a `TcpClient` to connect gives more flexibility, but both client and server must follow the appropriate protocol. When writing our own server, we can define the protocol by which client and server communicate. The server creates a `TcpListener` and uses an `AcceptTcpClient` statement to wait for a client to connect.

✓ Test Your Understanding

Try It Yourself ➤

5. In Example 14.4, omit sending the blank line at the end of the `GET` request. Describe the result.

Try It Yourself ➤

6. Start the `ReverseServer` of Example 14.5. Connect to it with a client. After sending some strings for the server to reverse, send an empty line to the server. What happens to the client and the server programs? In the exercises we will suggest modifications to the `ReverseServer` to change this behavior.

14.3 BROWSERS AND WEB SERVERS

A browser is an HTTP client, which may use other protocols, and a web server is an HTTP server. In this section we write a very simple browser and a very simple web server, leaving to the exercises many improvements to make them more functional. We conclude with a threaded web server, which can handle multiple clients connected simultaneously.

A Very Simple Browser

An HTTP client sends a request to the server followed by request headers and a blank line. It then reads the status line, response headers, and the requested file from the server. A browser typically can handle several types of files, the most important being HTML files that define web pages. The browser has to interpret the HTML tags to guide it in displaying the page. With so many file types to handle, and such intricate processing necessary for web pages, a useful browser is not a small or simple undertaking. Our very simple browser handles only plain text files.

Figure 14.8 shows `VerySimpleBrowser` connecting to the author's web site to download a file using the command

```
VerySimpleBrowser  www.cecs.csulb.edu  80 /~artg/TryURL.cs
```

where 80 is the standard HTTP port on which the server is running. An alternative approach would pass a URL, as in the command

```
C# VerySimpleBrowser
           http://www.cecs.csulb.edu/~artg/TryURL.cs
```

and break the URL into the parts needed in Example 14.7.

FIGURE 14.8
`VerySimpleBrowser` downloads a file

`VerySimpleBrowser` always sends a `GET` request and a `Host` request header. It ignores the status line and response headers sent by the server, rather than trying to use them to get information that would help it to display the requested resource.

EXAMPLE 14.7 ■ VerySimpleBrowser

```
/* Connects to a web server to download a text file.
 * Exercises suggest extensions to handle other file types.
 */

using System;
using System.Text;
using System.IO;
using System.Net.Sockets;
public class VerySimpleBrowser {
  public static void Main(String [] args) {
    TcpClient client =
          new TcpClient(args[0], int.Parse(args[1]));  // Note 1
    NetworkStream stream = client.GetStream();
    byte[] send = Encoding.ASCII.GetBytes
                ("GET " + args[2] + " HTTP/1.0 \r\n");// Note 2
    stream.Write(send, 0, send.Length);
    send = Encoding.ASCII.GetBytes
     ("Host: " + args[0] + ':' + args[1] + "\r\n\r\n");// Note 3
    stream.Write(send, 0, send.Length);
    int size = (int)client.ReceiveBufferSize;
    byte[] bytes = new byte[size];
    StreamReader reader = new StreamReader(stream);    // Note 4
    while(reader.ReadLine() != "");                    // Note 5
    String s;
    try{
      while((s = reader.ReadLine()) != null)           // Note 6
         Console.WriteLine(s);
    }catch(IOException e) {
    }finally {
```

```
            reader.Close();
            stream.Close();
            client.Close();
        }
    }
}
```

Note 1: `new TcpClient(args[0], int.Parse(args[1]));`

The standard HTTP port is 80, but some servers use 8080. We run our simple web server on port 11111. The user should pass the server port number as the second program argument.

Note 2:
```
byte[] send = Encoding.ASCII.GetBytes
            ("GET " + args[2] + " HTTP/1.0 \r\n");
```

We use the path to the resource, `/~artg/TryURL.cs` in Figure 14.8, sending the host address and port in a separate `Host` header. Alternatively, we could have sent the `GET` command

```
GET  www.cecs.csulb.edu:80/~artg/TryURL.cs  HTTP/1.0
```

Note 3:
```
send = Encoding.ASCII.GetBytes
  ("Host: " + args[0] + ':' + args[1] + "\r\n\r\n");
```

We append "`\r\n\r\n`" to the last header. The first "\r\n" ends the current line, and the second ends a blank line, which signals the end of the request headers.

Note 4: `StreamReader reader = new StreamReader(stream);`

We create a `StreamReader` from the `NetworkStream` so we can read the headers line by line.

Note 5: `while(reader.ReadLine() != "");`

We read and ignore the status line and headers sent by the server, looking for the blank line that signals the end of the headers and the start of the file we requested. We leave it to the exercises to improve the browser to make use of this information.

Note 6:
```
while((s = reader.ReadLine()) != null)
    Console.WriteLine(s);
```

This loop reads the file we requested from the server, displaying it in the command window. Extending this very simple browser to display HTML would use graphics extensively.

A Very Simple Web Server

An HTTP server reads the request from the client, any headers, and in some cases additional data. It sends a status line followed by headers and the requested resource, if any. Web servers often transmit data from the client to other programs for

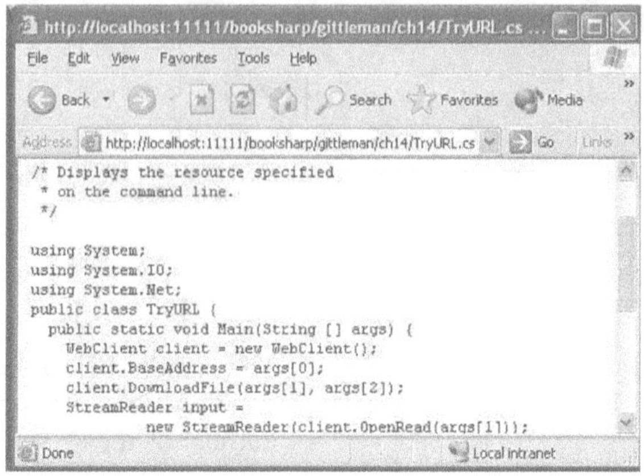

FIGURE 14.9
An Internet Explorer client connecting to `VerySimpleWebServer`

processing before returning results to the client. Our very simple web server responds only to `GET` requests and serves only text files. We leave it to the exercises to add features to make this server more functional.

To start `VerySimpleWebServer` we use the command

```
start VerySimpleWebServer 11111
```

which, on Windows systems, starts the server in a new window. Figure 14.9 shows Internet Explorer connecting to `VerySimpleWebServer` to download a file. We could also have used `VerySimpleBrowser` as the client.

EXAMPLE 14.8 ■ VerySimpleWebServer.cs

```
/* Serves a text file to an HTTP client submitting a GET
 * request.  Exercises suggest extensions to make the
 * server more functional.
 */

using System;
using System.IO;
using System.Text;
using System.Net.Sockets;
public class VerySimpleWebServer {
  public static void Main(String[] args) {
    TcpListener server = new TcpListener(int.Parse(args[0]));
    server.Start();
    TcpClient client = server.AcceptTcpClient();
    NetworkStream stream = client.GetStream();
    StreamReader reader = new StreamReader(stream);
    String s = reader.ReadLine();                       // Note 1
    String[] strings = s.Split();                       // Note 2
    StreamWriter writer;
```

```
    if (strings[0] != "GET") {                          // Note 3
      writer = new StreamWriter(stream);
      writer.WriteLine
                ("HTTP/1.0 501 Not Implemented");
      writer.WriteLine();
    } else {
       String filename = strings[1];                   // Note 4
       while(reader.ReadLine() != "");                 // Note 5
       writer = new StreamWriter(stream);              // Note 6
       writer.WriteLine("HTTP/1.0 200 OK");            // Note 7
       writer.WriteLine("Content-type: text/plain");
       writer.WriteLine();                             // Note 8
       StreamReader file = new StreamReader(filename);
       String z = file.ReadToEnd();                    // Note 9
       writer.WriteLine(z);
       writer.Flush();
       writer.Close();
       file.Close();
    }
    client.Close();
    stream.Close();
    reader.Close();
    writer.Close();
    server.Stop();
  }
}
```

Note 1: `String s = reader.ReadLine();`

We read the first line from the client to find the method and the path to the resource.

Note 2: `String[] strings = s.Split();`

Blanks separate each item of the request. We use the `Split` method to get the method and identifier parts of the request.

Note 3: `if (strings[0] != "GET") {`

If the request method is anything other than `GET`, the server sends a status line with a code of 501 to indicate that the method is not implemented.

Note 4: `String filename = strings[1];`

The file name comes after `GET`, separated by a blank, in the request from the client.

Note 5: `while(reader.ReadLine() != "");`

We read and ignore the request headers from the client, stopping when we reach the blank line that terminates them.

Note 6: `writer = new StreamWriter(stream);`

We create a `StreamWriter` from the `NetworkStream` so we can write lines to the client.

Note 7: `writer.WriteLine("HTTP/1.0 200 OK");`

Having created the file to send, the server sends a status line with code 200, meaning OK, and follows with one header describing the content type to help the client to display it.

Note 8: `writer.WriteLine();`

We write the blank line to terminate the response headers.

Note 9: `String z = file.ReadToEnd();`

We read the entire file requested and write it to the client.

A Threaded Web Server

Our `VerySimpleWebServer` has the very unusual behavior for a server in that it serves one request and terminates. We can easily modify Example 14.8 to put the server code in a loop. After it responds to one request, it can respond to another, and keep serving clients one at a time. Each client has to wait until the server finishes with the preceding client before being served.

Web servers may get requests from many clients at many dispersed locations. Using threads would allow the server to serve many clients simultaneously. The server interacts with one client while others are preparing their requests or displaying responses. It divides its attention among all connected clients so they share the server. Large web sites may have a number of servers sharing the load of serving many, many clients.

Our `ThreadedWebServer` runs in an unending loop. Each time a client connects, the server creates a thread to handle its processing with that client. The client thread creates the files needed to communicate with the server in its constructor and starts itself running. Its `Run` method contains the code from Example 14.8 in which the server responds to the client.

A good test for a threaded server would check how it handles simultaneous requests. We can make a step in that direction by starting two `VerySimpleBrowser` clients, each requesting a large file so the server will give each request some of its attention. We will see both browser windows scrolling the text of the file. The server will alternate, sending some of the first file to the first browser, then some of the second file to the second browser, then returning to the first, and so on until it has satisfied both requests.

We start `ThreadedWebServer` using the command

```
start ThreadedWebServer 11111
```

on Windows systems, and

```
ThreadedWebServer 11111 &
```

on Unix systems. Once the server is running, we start the two clients.

EXAMPLE 14.9 ■ ThreadedWebServer.cs

```
/* When an HTTP client connects, the server creates a thread
 * to respond to the client's request, so multiple
 * clients can be connected simultaneously.
 */

using System;
using System.IO;
using System.Text;
using System.Net.Sockets;
using System.Threading;
public class ThreadedWebServer {
  public static void Main(String[] args) {
    TcpListener server =
              new TcpListener(int.Parse(args[0]));
    server.Start();
    while(true) {                                           // Note 1
      TcpClient client = server.AcceptTcpClient();
      new ClientThread(client);                             // Note 2
    }
  }

  class ClientThread {
    TcpClient client;

    public ClientThread(TcpClient c) {
      client = c;
      Thread t = new Thread(new ThreadStart(Run));
      t.Start();                                            // Note 3
    }
    public void Run() {                                     // Note 4
      NetworkStream stream = client.GetStream();
      StreamReader reader = new StreamReader(stream);
      String s = reader.ReadLine();
      String[] strings = s.Split();
      StreamWriter writer;
      if (strings[0] != "GET") {
        writer = new StreamWriter(stream);
        writer.WriteLine
                ("HTTP/1.0 501 Not Implemented");
        writer.WriteLine();
```

```
            } else {
                String filename = strings[1];
                while(reader.ReadLine() != "");
                writer = new StreamWriter(stream);
                writer.WriteLine("HTTP/1.0 200 OK");
                writer.WriteLine("Content-type: text/plain");
                writer.WriteLine();
                StreamReader file = new StreamReader(filename);
                String z = file.ReadToEnd();
                writer.WriteLine(z);
                writer.Flush();
                writer.Close();
                file.Close();
            }
            client.Close();
            stream.Close();
            reader.Close();
            writer.Close();
        }
    }
}
```

Note 1: `while(true) {`

The server runs in an unending loop, until aborted, continuing to serve clients as they connect.

Note 2: `new ClientThread(client);`

We create a thread in which the server communicates with this client.

Note 3: `t.Start();`

We start the thread running. On a single processor system it will share the processor with other threads.

Note 4: `public void Run() {`

The `Run` method contains the code from Example 14.8 by which the server and client communicate. If several threads are active, then the server will be communicating with several clients who are all connected simultaneously.

The BIG Picture

Browsers and web servers use HTTP to communicate. Our `ThreadedWebServer` spawns a new thread to handle a connection from a client, so many clients may be connected to this server simultaneously. Rather than terminating after a client connects, `ThreadedWebServer` remains in a loop waiting for the next client.

✓ Test Your Understanding

Try It Yourself ➤ **7.** Modify Example 14.7 to use the `HEAD` method, which sends only headers and does not ask for a resource in response. Connect to the very simple web server of Example 14.8. What happens?

Try It Yourself ➤ **8.** Put the server of Example 14.8 into a loop, so that instead of terminating after each connection it waits for another client to connect. Make the loop unending, so the server will have to be aborted to terminate it.

Try It Yourself ➤ **9.** Test the threaded web server of Example 14.9 by connecting to it from two simple web browser clients at close to the same time. Find long text files to request so both clients will be connected to the server at the same time while downloading the requested files. Describe what you observe.

14.4 REMOTING

Remoting takes networking to a higher level, providing distributed computing for C# programs. In distributed computing a program can be composed of parts located on more than one computer. So far we have used input and output streams to communicate between a client and server. These streams transfer data from one machine to another. Using remoting we can distribute our objects on various machines, invoking methods of objects located on remote sites.

Distributed Computing

We use a very simple example, a fortune server, to show how remoting works without introducing the extra complications of an involved example. The fortune server may be running on one machine. Clients from remote sites can request a fortune. In making these requests, clients will invoke a method of an object on the server. A **distributed computing** system must provide the following capabilities:

1. Clients must know what services the fortune server provides.

   Remoting Solution: A `Fortune` interface lists the methods available to remote clients.
2. Clients must find a `Fortune` object on the server.

   Remoting Solution: The fortune server registers an object with a special server, a `TcpServerChannel`, so clients can look it up by name.
3. Clients must be able to pass arguments to and invoke a method of the `Fortune` object located on the server.

   Remoting Solution: The client registers a `TcpChannel` to transport messages to a remote site.

Figure 14.10 shows how Remoting operates.

For our example, which provides a fortune server that will enable clients to request fortunes (the fortune cookie kind, not the billionaire kind), we need to write the following programs:

FIGURE 14.10 **The parts of Remoting**

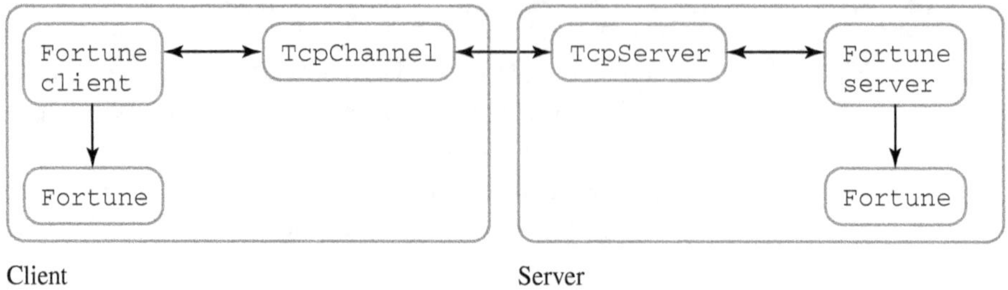

`Fortune`	The interface that shows the client what remote methods it can invoke, the `GetFortune` method in this example.
`FortuneImpl`	The implementation of the `Fortune` interface to define the remote object which is served to clients who wish to use its method to get a fortune.
`FortuneServer`	A server that creates a server channel and registers a `FortuneImpl` object.
`FortuneClient`	A client that gets a reference to a `Fortune` object and invokes its `GetFortune` method remotely.

We run this example on one machine but use two directories, one for the client and one for the server, to simulate the use of a remote site. To compile and run our example we follow these steps:

In the server directory:

1. Compile `Fortune.cs`, `FortuneImpl.cs`, and `FortuneServer.cs`.
2. Start `FortuneServer` (see Figure 14.11).

In the client directory:

3. Compile `Fortune.cs` and `FortuneClient.cs`.
4. Run `FortuneClient` (Figure 14.12).

The Interface

Let us build each part of this Remoting application. The `Fortune` interface specifies the `GetFortune` method.

FIGURE 14.11 **`FortuneServer`**

FIGURE 14.12 **`FortuneClient`**

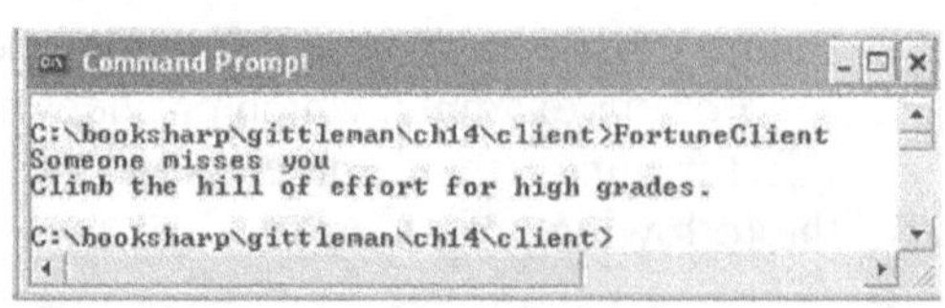

EXAMPLE 14.10 ■ Fortune.cs

```
/* The server implements this interface and clients call
 * its method remotely.
 */

using System;
public interface Fortune {
  String GetFortune(String when);                    // Note 1
}
```

Note 1: Using Remoting, .NET passes arguments and return values across the network.

The Implementation

We define the `FortuneImpl` class, which implements the `Fortune` interface. We will register an object of this class on the server that the client will call remotely.

EXAMPLE 14.11 ■ FortuneImpl.cs

```
/* Implements the Fortune interface.
 */

using System;
using System.Runtime.Remoting;
public class FortuneImpl : MarshalByRefObject, Fortune{// Note 1
  public const int SIZE = 3;
  private String[] now = new String[SIZE];
  private String[] later = new String[SIZE];

  public FortuneImpl() {
    now[0] = "A friend is near";
    now[1] = "Expect a call";
    now[2] = "Someone misses you";
    later[0] = "Wealth awaits -- if you desire it.";
    later[1] = "Climb the hill of effort for high grades.";
    later[2] = "The door to success is open to you.";
  }
  private String[] Find(String when) {               // Note 2
    if (when == "NOW")
       return now;
    else return later;
  }
  public String GetFortune(String when) {
    Random random = new Random();
    int number = random.Next(3);
```

```
    String[] fortunes = Find(when);
    return fortunes[number];                              // Note 3
  }
}
```

Note 1: `public class FortuneImpl : MarshalByRefObject, Fortune{`

`MarshalByRefObject` is a base class for objects that communicate remotely. We want to access a `FortuneImpl` object from a remote site.

Note 2: `private String[] Find(String when) {`

The `Find` method is not part of the `Fortune` interface. We only use it locally. It returns an array of fortunes, either for `NOW` or for `LATER`.

Note 3: `return fortunes[number];`

We use a random index to choose a fortune to return to the caller.

The Server

On the server, we need to create a channel and register an object type so remote users can invoke methods on an object of that type.

EXAMPLE 14.12 ■ FortuneServer.cs

```
/* Creates a channel and registers an object type
 * for remote access.
 */

using System;
using System.Runtime.Remoting;
using System.Runtime.Remoting.Channels;
using System.Runtime.Remoting.Channels.Tcp;
public class FortuneServer {
  public static void Main() {
    TcpServerChannel channel
                       = new TcpServerChannel(7777);  // Note 1
    ChannelServices.RegisterChannel(channel);
    RemotingConfiguration.RegisterWellKnownServiceType(
      typeof(FortuneImpl),
      "Fortune",
      WellKnownObjectMode.SingleCall);                 // Note 2
    Console.WriteLine("Press Any Key");                // Note 3
    Console.ReadLine();
  }
}
```

Note 1:
```
TcpServerChannel channel
                   = new TcpServerChannel(7777);
```

We construct a communication channel that uses port 7777. The channel uses the TCP protocol to transmit messages.

Note 2:
```
RemotingConfiguration.RegisterWellKnownServiceType(
    typeof(FortuneImpl), "Fortune",
    WellKnownObjectMode.SingleCall);
```

The `RegisterWellKnownServiceType` method registers an object with one of two well-known types, `SingleCall` or `Singleton`. Using the `SingleCall` type, a new object gets created at each call of a method. Using the `Singleton` type, an object instance handles all the remote calls. This choice makes no difference in this example. It would matter if the object changed its state as a result of the call.

The first argument is the type of the object we are registering, in this case `FortuneImpl`. The second argument is the name that it will use and by which the client will refer to it. We use the interface name, `Fortune`, in this example. The third argument is a `WellKnownObjectMode`, in this case `SingleCall`.

Note 3:
```
Console.WriteLine("Press Any Key");
```

We are not using a GUI, so the `Main` method will terminate and close the channel. To leave the channel open we add a `Read` statement to pause while it waits for input. Meanwhile, clients can use the channel.

The Client

`FortuneClient` is the last program we need to complete our Remoting example. It creates and registers a channel and activates an object on the server. When the client calls the `GetFortune` method of this remote object, it receives a fortune as the return value. From the client's point of view there is no difference between calling a method of a remote object and a method of a local object.

EXAMPLE 14.13 ■ FortuneClient.cs

```
/* Registers a channel and activates an object on
 * the server. Invokes its GetFortune method remotely
 * to get a fortune for now and for later.
 */

using System;
using System.Runtime.Remoting;
using System.Runtime.Remoting.Channels;
using System.Runtime.Remoting.Channels.Tcp;
public class FortuneClient {
  public static void Main() {
    ChannelServices.RegisterChannel(new TcpChannel()); // Note 1
```

```
      Fortune fortuneTeller = (Fortune)Activator.GetObject(
                   typeof(Fortune),
                  "tcp://localhost:7777/Fortune");       // Note 2

    Console.WriteLine(fortuneTeller.GetFortune("NOW")); // Note 3
    Console.WriteLine(fortuneTeller.GetFortune("LATER"));
  }
}
```

Note 1: `ChannelServices.RegisterChannel(new TcpChannel());`

We register a `TcpChannel`, which can be either a server or a client channel. We do not need to mention the port because we pass it in the URL to the `GetObject` method when we activate an object.

Note 2:
```
Fortune fortuneTeller = (Fortune)Activator.GetObject(
    typeof(Fortune), "tcp://localhost:7777/Fortune");
```

The `GetObject` method activates an object on the server. It is like executing a `new` operation, but it allows us to pass a URL giving the location on the server. In the URL we include the port number and the name, `Fortune`, that we used when registering the object type on the server. The first argument gives the type of the object we wish to construct. We used the interface type name, Fortune, to hide the details of the implementation on the server. Had we used two machines we would replace `localhost` with the address of the server.

Note 3: `Console.WriteLine(fortuneTeller.GetFortune("NOW"));`

This remote method invocation looks like a method call of a local method, but we are invoking an object on the server, which may be at a remote site. Fortunately, `Remoting` handles all the details of communication. We call the `GetFortune` method twice to illustrate the passing of arguments in a remote call.

The BIG Picture

Remoting lets us distribute our program across the network. We can register an object type on the server and activate an object and call its methods from a remote client.

✓Test Your Understanding

Try It Yourself ➤ **10.** In Example 14.12, replace `TcpServerChannel` with `TcpChannel`. Can we still execute the remote call of Example 14.13?

Try It Yourself ➤ **11.** In Example 14.12, change the name used to register the object from `Fortune` to `Seer`. Make the same change in Example 14.13. Rerun the example and describe the result.

SUMMARY

- C# makes it easy to connect to other computers. The `WebRequest` and `WebResponse` classes encapsulate some of the common communication protocols. C# provides implementations for HTTP (Hypertext Transfer Protocol) and the file protocol, and we can define others. We use a URL to locate a resource. Its four parts are the protocol name, the host name, port, and path to the resource.
- The Hypertext Transfer Protocol specifies the messages by which browsers and web servers communicate. A browser or other web client sends a request, then some request headers, and a blank line to the server. The server sends a status line, followed by response headers, a blank line, and the requested resource. The examples show how web clients and servers vary in the headers they choose to send.
- The `WebClient` class provides a simple way to download files and find the HTTP response headers. The `WebRequest` and `WebResponse` classes have methods that allow us to set properties of the connection to customize it or to get information about the connection. The `Header` property lets us get or add headers.
- `TcpClient` and `TcpListener` classes allow us to communicate using standard protocols or to devise protocols of our own for use with clients and servers. A `TcpListener` accepts connections on a numbered port. Standard services have default ports such as 80 for web servers, 25 for sending mail, and 110 for receiving mail. Once we make a connection, we use input and output streams to send data back and forth between the client and the server. The `ReverseClient` example sends strings to the `ReverseServer` which sends them reversed back to the client.
- To display a web page, a browser must interpret all the HTML tags embedded in that page. Our `VerySimpleBrowser` uses HTTP to communicate with web servers. It is a bare outline of a browser, following HTTP but ignoring the response headers and displaying only plain text, not HTML or images. Similarly, our `VerySimpleWebServer` ignores any headers the client sends and puts no effort into accurately sending response headers. Nevertheless, our browser can connect and download files from various web servers and our web server can respond to plain text requests from browsers. The exercises suggest many improvements. Our `ThreadedWebServer` permits several clients to be connected at the same time, each served in its own thread.
- Remoting takes networking to a higher level in which a client can invoke methods of a remote object on the server. An interface specifies the remote methods available to the client. The server and client create a communication channel. The server registers an object type, and the client activates an object of that type.

PROGRAM MODIFICATION EXERCISES

1. Modify Example 14.3 to use the `GetResponseHeader` method rather than properties to find the headers.
2. Example 14.4 uses three program arguments. Add a check that the user passed three arguments and, if not, print a message showing the proper usage and exit the program.
3. Modify Example 14.7 to pass a URL such as

   ```
   http://www.cecs.csulb.edu/TryURL.cs
   ```

   rather than passing the host, port, and resource path program arguments.

4. Modify Example 14.8 to send a status line with code 404 and reason Not Found when the file requested is not available on the server.
5. Modify Example 14.8 so when the server has responded to one client it can accept a request from another.
6. Modify Examples 14.5 and 14.6 to pass the port number as a program argument.
7. Modify Example 14.8 to send a `Content-Length` header giving the length of the file in bytes.
8. Modify Example 14.5 so the server can handle several clients simultaneously. After the server accepts a connection from the client, the server should create a separate thread to handle the communication with that client and loop back to the `accept` statement, waiting for another client to connect.
9. Modify Example 14.5 to put the `accept` statement and the code following it into a nonterminating loop, so the server can accept another client as soon as the current client finishes.
10. Modify Examples 14.10, 14.11, 14.12, and 14.13 to allow the client to request a lucky number. The server will return a number from 1 to 10 at random.
11. Modify Example 14.13 to ask if the user wants another fortune. When testing, let two clients stay connected at the same time.

PROGRAM DESIGN EXERCISES

12. Write a multithreaded server that will pass whatever message line it receives from one client to all the other clients that are connected. Write a client program to connect to this server, which sends its lines and receives the lines sent by the other clients.
13. Write a mail client that will connect to a POP3 server (find the address of your server) and retrieve the first message. Specify the server address, user name, and password as program arguments. The protocol of Figure 14.5 may be helpful.
14. Write a browser that displays a plain text file in a text box, rather than in the command window as `VerySimpleBrowser` does.
15. Write a piece of a browser that will display HTML files. This piece will display text only within header tags, `<h1>` ... `<h6>`. Use the largest point size for text between `<h1>` and `</h1>` tags, and the smallest for text between `<h6>` and `</h6>` tags.
16. Add to the browser of Exercise 14.7 the capability to handle `<em>` and `<strong>` tags.
17. Write a new version of `ReverseClient` in which the user enters the text to be reversed in a text box.
18. Use Remoting to allow clients to connect to a broker to get the price of a stock, or to buy and sell some stock. Use just three stocks, StockA, StockB, and StockC, each with a price that varies randomly within a range. Assume two accounts numbered 1111 and 2222.
    a. For simplicity, do not maintain account information, so no records are kept about buy and sell orders.
    b. Add account information, so each account keeps a record of how many of each stock it contains.

19. Improve the very simple browser of Example 14.7. The browser should properly interpret HTML tags `<h1>`, ..., `<h6>`, `<em>`, `<strong>`, `<ul>`, `<li>`, `<br>`, `<p>`, `<a>`, and `<img>`.

20. Improve the very simple web server of Example 14.8. Use the status codes 200, 301, 400, 404, 406, and 501 appropriately. Send `Date`, `Last-Modified`, `Content-Type`, and `Content-Length` response headers.

21. Implement a chess game in which the server relays moves from one player to the other. Two clients play against one another, with each showing the board and the moves as they are made. Players will use the mouse to drag a piece to its new position. (Alternatively, substitute another game for chess. For example, checkers would be simpler.)

22. Make a user interface for the mail-reading client of Exercise 14.13. The screen will show the message headers and allow the user to choose which message to read. For additional information on the POP3 protocol, search the Internet for RFC 1939, which contains its specification.

23. Implement an SMTP client to send email. Provide a user interface to compose and send the message. Testing requires access to an SMTP server. Port 25 is the default for SMTP servers. An example session follows.

```
Server:     220 charlotte.cecs.csulb.edu ESMTP Sendmail 8.8.4/8.8.4;
                Thu, 11 Feb 1999 15:31:27 -0800 (PST)
Client:     HELO gordian.com                        // sent from
Server:     250 charlotte.cecs.csulb.edu Hello ppool3.gordian.com
                [207.211.232.196], pleased to meet you
Client:     MAIL FROM: artg@csulb.edu               // email address
Server:     250 artg@csulb.edu... Sender ok
Client:     RCPT TO:  artg@csulb.edu                // recipient
Server:     250 artg@csulb.edu... Recipient ok
Client:     DATA                                    // signals message
Server:     354 Enter mail, end with "." on a line by itself
Client:     Subject: test
            To: artg@csulb.edu
            This is                                 // message
            a test.
            .                                       // signals end
Server:     250 PAA27651 Message accepted for delivery
Client:     QUIT
Server:     221 Closing connection.
```

Headers have the form `Name: Value` and are separated from the message body by an empty line.

15 Using a Database

We can use files to store data for small applications, but as the amount of data that we need to save gets larger, the services of a database system become invaluable. A database system allows us to model the information we need while it handles the details of inserting, removing, and retrieving data from individual files in response to our requests.

Of course, each database vendor provides its own procedures for performing database operations. The .NET Framework hides the details of different databases; our programs can work with many different databases on many different platforms. They can be used as part of large-scale enterprise applications. In this chapter we cover the concepts using a small example that allows many extensions, some of which we pursue in the exercises.

The example programs illustrate database access using console applications to avoid obscuring the programs with the details involved in building a GUI. In the last section, our extended case study develops a graphical user interface to a database.

OBJECTIVES

- Introduce relational database tables
- Introduce SQL (Structured Query Language)
- Connect to a database from C#
- Build a database using SQL
- Use C# to query a database
- Obtain the properties of a database

- Introduce selected aggregate functions
- Use stored procedures for efficiency
- Process database transactions
- Provide a GUI for the user to query a database

15.1 DATABASE TABLES AND SQL QUERIES

Database design is best left to other texts and courses. We introduce a few database concepts here to provide an example with which to illustrate the techniques for working with databases using C#. Relational databases provide an implementation-independent way for users to view data. The Structured Query Language (SQL) lets us create, update, and query a database using standard commands that hide the details of any particular vendor's database system.

Relational Database Tables

When designing a database we need to identify the entities in our system. For example, a company might use a database to keep track of its sales and associated information. In our example company, an order includes one customer who can order several items. A salesperson may take several orders from the same customer, but each order is taken by exactly one salesperson.

Using a relational database, we keep our data in tables. In our example, we might have a `Customer` table with fields for the customer id, name, address, and balance due, as shown in Figure 15.1.

Each row of the table represents the information needed for one customer. We assign each customer a unique customer ID number. Customer names are not unique; moreover, they may change. `CustomerID` is a key that identifies the data in the row. Knowing the `CustomerID`, we can retrieve the other information about that customer.

TIP

Do not embed spaces in field names. Use `CustomerID` rather than `Customer ID`. ■

Figures 15.2 and 15.3 show the `Salesperson` and `Item` tables, which we define in a similar manner. A more realistic example would have additional fields.

FIGURE 15.1 The `Customer` table

CustomerID	*CustomerName*	*Address*	*BalanceDue*
1234	Fred Flynn	22 First St.	1667.00
5678	Darnell Davis	33 Second St.	130.95
4321	Marla Martinez	44 Third St.	0
8765	Carla Kahn	55 Fourth St.	0

FIGURE 15.2 **The `Salesperson` table**

SalespersonID	*SalespersonName*	*Address*
12	Peter Patterson	66 Fifth St.
98	Donna Dubarian	77 Sixth St.

FIGURE 15.3 **The `Item` table**

ItemNumber	*Description*	*Quantity*
222222	radio	32
333333	television	14
444444	computer	9

FIGURE 15.4 **The `Orders` table**

OrderNumber	*CustomerID*	*SalespersonID*	*OrderDate*
1	1234	12	4/3/99
2	5678	12	3/22/99
3	8765	98	2/19/99
4	1234	12	4/5/99
5	8765	98	2/28/99

The `SalespersonID` serves as the key for the `Salesperson` table, and we use the `ItemNumber` to identify an item in the Item table. We have to be more careful in designing the `Orders` table, because an order can have multiple items. We use a second table, the `OrderItem` table, to list the items in each order. Figure 15.4 shows the `Orders` table with the fields `OrderNumber`, `CustomerID`, `SalespersonID`, and `OrderDate`. The `OrderNumber` is the key. `CustomerID` and `SalespersonID` are foreign keys that allow us to avoid redundancy by referring to data in other tables. For example, including the `CustomerID` lets us find the customer's name and address from the `Customer` table rather than repeating it in the `Orders` table.

TIP

When choosing field names, avoid names like `Number`, `Value`, `Order`, `Name`, or `Date` that might conflict with reserved names in the database system. ■

The `OrderItem` table uses a compound key consisting of both the `OrderNumber` and the `ItemNumber` to identify a specific item that is part of an order. Figure 15.5 shows that each pair (`OrderNumber`, `ItemNumber`) occurs only

FIGURE 15.5 **The `OrderItem` table**

OrderNumber	*ItemNumber*	*Quantity*	*UnitPrice*
1	222222	4	27.00
1	333333	2	210.50
1	444444	1	569.00
2	333333	2	230.95
3	222222	3	27.00
3	333333	1	230.95
4	444444	1	569.00
5	222222	2	27.00
5	444444	1	725.00

once, identifying a row containing the data for a specific item in a particular order. For example, the first row shows that for order number one, and item 222222, four units were ordered at a price of $27 each.

Now that we have defined our `Sales` database, we want to see how to get information from it and how to make changes as needed.

Structured Query Language (SQL)

The Structured Query Language (SQL) is a standard language with which to get information from or make changes to a database. We can execute SQL statements from within C#. The SQL statements we will use are `CREATE`, `SELECT`, `INSERT`, `DELETE`, and `UPDATE`. We illustrate these statements using the `Sales` database defined in the previous section. The names for the data types may depend on the actual database system used. Our examples work with Microsoft Access.

We could use the `CREATE` statement

```
CREATE TABLE Customer (CustomerID CHAR(4), CustomerName
      VARCHAR(25), Address VARCHAR(25), BalanceDue DECIMAL)
```

to create the `Customer` table, the statement

```
CREATE TABLE Orders (OrderNumber VARCHAR(4), CustomerID
      CHAR(4),  SalespersonID CHAR(2), OrderDate DATE)
```

to create the `Orders` table, and the statement

```
CREATE TABLE OrderItem (OrderNumber VARCHAR(4), ItemNumber
      CHAR(6),  Quantity INTEGER, UnitPrice DECIMAL)
```

to create the `OrderItem` table. We use character fields for `CustomerID`, `OrderNumber`, `SalespersonID`, and `ItemNumber`, even though they use numerical characters, because we have no need to do arithmetic using these values. By contrast, we use the type `INTEGER` for the `Quantity` field because we may wish to compute with it.

FIGURE 15.6 **SQL data types**

Type	*Standard SQL Description*
CHAR(N)	Fixed size string of length N
VARCHAR(N)	Variable size string up to length N
INTEGER	32-bit integer
DATE	Year, month, and day
DECIMAL	Used for dollars and cents

Standard SQL uses various types, which are not all supported in every database system. Figure 15.6 shows the SQL types we use in this text.

The type `DECIMAL(M,N)`, where `M` is the maximum number of digits and `N` is the maximum number of digits after the decimal point, is standard SQL, but is not supported in Access.

To insert the first row in the `Customer` table, we could use the `INSERT` statement

```
INSERT INTO Customer
VALUES (1234, 'Fred Flynn', '22 First St.', 1667.00)
```

TIP Use the single quote, `'`, to enclose strings within an SQL statement.

The statement

```
INSERT INTO Orders VALUES (1,1234,12,'Apr 3, 1999')
```

inserts the first row into the `Order` table. We write dates in the form

```
Month Day, Year
```

to avoid confusion among date formats used in various locales and to indicate the century explicitly. The database system translates this form to its internal representation and can present dates in various formats in its tables.

The `DELETE` statement

```
DELETE FROM OrderItem WHERE OrderNumber = '1'
```

will delete the first three rows of the `OrderItem` table in Figure 15.5. These rows contain the data for the three items comprising the order with an `OrderNumber` of 1.

TIP Use the single equality sign, `=`, in the equality test, OrderNumber = 1, instead of the C# equality symbol, `==`.

To delete just the televisions from that order and leave the order for radios and a computer, we could use the statement

```
DELETE FROM OrderItem
WHERE OrderNumber = '1' AND ItemNumber = '333333'
```

To update an existing row we use the UPDATE statement. For example, to reduce the number of radios in order number 1 to 3, we can use the statement

```
UPDATE OrderItem SET Quantity = 3
WHERE OrderNumber = '1' AND ItemNumber = '222222'
```

When we change an order we will also want to change the balance due in the Customer table, which we can do using

```
UPDATE Customer SET BalanceDue = 1640.00
WHERE CustomerID = '1234'
```

TIP

Because the OrderItem table uses a compound key

```
(OrderNumber, ItemNumber)
```

to identify a row, we need to specify values for both in the WHERE clause. In updating the Customer table we only need to specify the value of the single CustomerID key to identify a row. ■

The CREATE statement creates a table, and the INSERT, DELETE, and UPDATE statements make changes in a table. In many applications, we retrieve information from the database more frequently than we create a table or make changes to a table. To retrieve information we use the SELECT statement.

The simplest query we can make is to retrieve the entire table. For example, the statement

```
SELECT * FROM Customer
```

retrieves the entire Customer table. We use the star symbol, *, which matches every row. To retrieve the names and addresses of the customers we use the statement

```
SELECT CustomerName, Address FROM Customer
```

If we do not want data from the entire table, we can use a WHERE clause to specify a condition that the data of interest satisfy. For example, to retrieve all orders for radios we could use the statement

```
SELECT * FROM OrderItems
WHERE ItemNumber = '222222'
```

The power of database systems becomes evident when we use SQL to get information combined from several tables. For example, suppose we would like to know the names of all customers who placed orders on March 22, 1999. We can find that information using the statement

```
SELECT CustomerName FROM Customer, Orders
WHERE Customer.CustomerID = Orders.CustomerID
AND  OrderDate = #3/22/99#
```

where #3/22/99# is the Microsoft Access format for a date.

TIP When a field such as Address occurs in more than one table, prefix the field name with the table name, as in Customer.Address, to state precisely which Address field you desire. Similarly, use the prefixes Customer and Orders to refer to the CustomerID fields in each of these tables. ■

In finding the names of customers who placed orders on March 22, 1999, the database joins two tables. Customer names occur in the Customer table, but we find order dates in the Orders table, so we list both the Customer and the Orders tables in the FROM part of the query. We want to find which orders each customer placed. CustomerID, the primary key of the Customer table, is also a foreign key of the Orders table. For each CustomerID in the Customer table we want to inspect only the rows of the Orders table that have the same CustomerID, so we include the condition

```
Customer.CustomerID = Orders.CustomerID
```

in our query.

The first row of the Customer table has a CustomerID of 1234. The first and fourth rows of the Orders table have the same CustomerID of 1234, but neither of the OrderDate fields equals 3/22/99. The second row of the Customer table has CustomerID 5678, as does the second row of the Orders table, and the OrderDate is 3/22/99, so the system adds 'Darnell Davis' to the result set of customers placing orders on March 22, 1999. Continuing the search turns up no further matches. A three-line SQL statement can cause many steps to occur in the process of retrieving the requested information. The database handles all the details. We will use other interesting examples of SELECT statements when we develop our C# programs later in this chapter.

Figure 15.7 shows the general pattern for the SQL statements we have introduced so far.

```
CREATE TABLE tablename
     (fieldname1 TYPE1, fieldname2 TYPE2, ... , fieldnameN TYPEn)

INSERT INTO tablename
VALUES (field1value,field2value, ..., fieldNvalue)

DELETE FROM tablename
WHERE fieldname1 = value1 ... AND fieldnameN = valueN

UPDATE tablename SET fieldnameToSet = newValue
WHERE fieldname1ToCheck = value1ToCheck

SELECT fieldname1, ..., fieldnameN FROM table1, ..., tableM
WHERE condition1 ... AND conditionN
```

FIGURE 15.7 **Some patterns for SQL statements**

The BIG Picture

In a relational database we keep our data in tables, making sure not to enter information redundantly. Using SQL, we can write statements to create a table, insert, delete, and update elements, and query the database. Generally, SQL is standardized so queries do not reflect implementation details of specific database systems.

✓Test Your Understanding

1. Why is it a good idea to use `SalespersonID` as the key in the `Salesperson` table rather than the salesperson's name?
2. Write an SQL statement to create the `Salesperson` table with the fields shown in Figure 15.2.
3. Write SQL statements to insert the data shown in Figure 15.2 into the `Salesperson` table.
4. Write an SQL statement to add a new salesman, Paul Sanchez, who lives at 88 Seventh St., and has an ID of 54, to the `Salesperson` table of Figure 15.2.
5. Write an SQL statement to delete Carla Kahn's order of a computer from the `Sales` database.
6. Write an SQL statement to find the names of all salespersons in the `Sales` database.
7. Write an SQL statement to find the order numbers of all orders taken by Peter Patterson.

15.2 CONNECTING TO A DATABASE

After an overview contrasting two-tiered with three-tiered architectures for software systems, we show how to connect to a database using the C#.

Database and Application Servers

In building large systems, a database server may reside on one machine to which various clients connect when they need to access the stored data (Figure 15.8).

In a three-tiered design, business logic resides in a middle machine, sometimes called an application server, which acts as a server to various application clients (Figure 15.9). These clients provide user interfaces to the business applications on the middle machine, which is itself a client of the database server.

FIGURE 15.8
Client–server database access

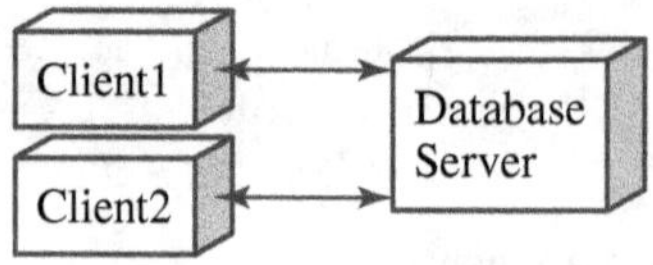

FIGURE 15.9 **A three-tiered system architecture**

For example, a business may have an accounting department that runs a payroll client providing a user interface to the payroll application on the middle machine which itself is a client of the database server. The marketing department might have several client programs running in their sales offices enabling salespersons to get necessary information. Rather than configuring each salesperson's machine to process all the details of the application, the company simply allows the sales staff to interact with the sales application on the middle machine. This sales program gets data from the database server as needed.

The .NET Framework allows us to write C# programs that will work no matter which database system we use. We can work entirely on one machine or use a two-tier, three-tier, or even more complex architecture for our system. Microsoft Access is suitable for work on a single machine, but we can still illustrate a three-tiered architecture because the tiers are logical, not necessarily physical, separations.

Creating the Database

We open Microsoft Access and create a blank database, give it a file name and save it. We will refer to the database in our program by the file name we use to create it. In this chapter we use the name `Sales` and the file `Sales.mdb` to hold our database of five tables.

Connecting from C#

We want our `Sales` database to contain the five tables with the data shown in Figures 15.1 through 15.5. We could create these tables and populate them within Access, but prefer to show how to do this using C#.

The .NET Framework provides an `SqlConnection` class in the `System.Data.SqlClient` namespace to connect to the Microsoft SqlServer database and an `OleDbConnection` class in the `System.Data.OleDb` namespace to connect to Microsoft Access and other database systems. Example 15.1 will connect to the `Sales` database. The code we use will occur at the beginning of all of our examples in this chapter.

EXAMPLE 15.1 ■ Connect.cs

```
/* Connects to a Microsoft Access database.
 */

using System;
using System.Data;
```

```
using System.Data.OleDb;
public class Connect {
 public static void Main () {
   String connect = "Provider=Microsoft.JET.OLEDB.4.0;"
     + @"data source=c:\booksharp\gittleman\ch15\Sales.mdb";
                                                         // Note 1
   OleDbConnection con = new OleDbConnection(connect); // Note 2
   con.Open();                                         // Note 3
   Console.WriteLine
       ("Made the connection to the Sales database");
   con.Close();                                        // Note 4
 }
}
```

Output

```
Made the connection to the Sales database
```

Note 1: `String connect = "Provider=Microsoft.JET.OLEDB.4.0;" + @"data source=c:\booksharp\gittleman\ch15\Sales.mdb";`

We use an OLE DB connection string that includes the provider and the data source, which is the file containing the database we created. The @ character in front of the string signifies that every character is a literal and not a special character such as an escape character. C# calls such a string a *verbatim* string. Normally the backslash is an escape character that combines with the next character to form a special character. For example, '\b' represents a backspace. Had we omitted the @ character we would have to escape the backslashes by writing the string as

```
data source=c:\\booksharp\\gittleman\\ch15\\Sales.mdb
```

Note 2: `OleDbConnection con = new OleDbConnection(connect);`

We pass the connection string to the `OleDbConnection` constructor to connect to the `Sales` database.

Note 3: `con.Open();`

We open the connection to the database.

Note 4: `con.Close();`

We close the database to release any resources used and do any necessary cleanup.

Building the Database

Once we have a connection to the database we can execute SQL statements to create our database. The `CreateCommand` method returns an `OleDbCommand` object that we use to send SQL statements to the database.

Some SQL statements, such as those used to create tables and insert values in a table, change the database but do not return any values to the program. To execute SQL `CREATE` and `INSERT` statements we use the `ExecuteNonQuery` method. We set the `CommandText` property of an `OleDbCommand` with the SQL statement and then invoke `ExecuteNonQuery`. For example,

```
cmd.CommandText =
    "INSERT INTO Item VALUES ('55555', 'CD player', 10)";
cmd.ExecuteNonQuery();
```

would insert a fourth row into the `Item` table.

Example 15.2 uses C# to create and populate the `Sales` database. We create the five tables shown in Figures 15.1 through 15.5, using a `CREATE` statement to create each table and `INSERT` statements to add the rows. Figure 15.10 shows the resulting Access `Sales` database and Figure 15.11 shows the `Customer` table that results from executing Example 15.2.

FIGURE 15.10 The Access `Sales` database created by Example 15.2

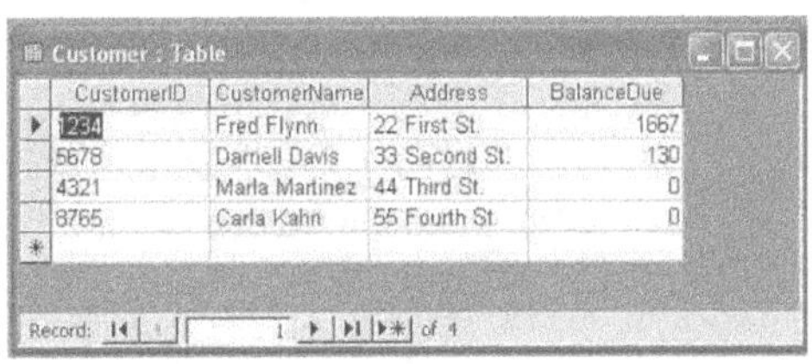

FIGURE 15.11 The `Customer` table created by Example 15.2

TIP

After running this program, the database contains the five tables. Running the program again will cause an error unless the tables are first deleted from the database. ■

EXAMPLE 15.2 ■ Create.cs

```
/* Creates and populates the Sales database
 */

using System;
using System.Data;
using System.Data.OleDb;
public class Create {
 public static void Main () {
   String connect = "Provider=Microsoft.JET.OLEDB.4.0;"
    + @"data source=c:\booksharp\gittleman\ch15\Sales.mdb";
   OleDbConnection con = new OleDbConnection(connect);
   con.Open();
   Console.WriteLine
        ("Made the connection to the Sales database");
   OleDbCommand cmd = con.CreateCommand();

   cmd.CommandText = "CREATE TABLE Customer (CustomerID "
          + "CHAR(4), CustomerName VARCHAR(25), Address "
          + "VARCHAR(25), BalanceDue DECIMAL)";          // Note 1
   cmd.ExecuteNonQuery();
   cmd.CommandText = "INSERT INTO Customer VALUES (1234,'Fred "
                   + "Flynn','22 First St.',1667.00)";
   cmd.ExecuteNonQuery();
   cmd.CommandText = "INSERT INTO Customer VALUES "     // Note 2
             "(5678,'Darnell Davis','33 Second St.',130.95)";
   cmd.ExecuteNonQuery();
   cmd.CommandText = "INSERT INTO Customer VALUES (4321,'Marla "
                     + "Martinez','44 Third St.',0)";
   cmd.ExecuteNonQuery();
   cmd.CommandText = "INSERT INTO Customer VALUES (8765,'Carla "
                      + "Kahn','55 Fourth St.', 0)";
   cmd.ExecuteNonQuery();

   cmd.CommandText = "CREATE TABLE Salesperson (SalespersonID "
                  + "CHAR(2), SalespersonName VARCHAR(25), "
                  + "Address VARCHAR(25))";
   cmd.ExecuteNonQuery();
   cmd.CommandText = "INSERT INTO Salesperson VALUES "
                   + "(12,'Peter Patterson','66 Fifth St.')";
   cmd.ExecuteNonQuery();
```

```
cmd.CommandText = "INSERT INTO Salesperson VALUES "
                 + "(98,'Donna Dubarian','77 Sixth St.')";
cmd.ExecuteNonQuery();

cmd.CommandText = "CREATE TABLE Item (ItemNumber CHAR(6),"
           + "Description VARCHAR(20), Quantity INTEGER)";
cmd.ExecuteNonQuery();
cmd.CommandText =
             "INSERT INTO Item VALUES (222222,'radio',32)";
cmd.ExecuteNonQuery();
cmd.CommandText =
        "INSERT INTO Item VALUES (333333,'television',14)";
cmd.ExecuteNonQuery();
cmd.CommandText =
           "INSERT INTO Item VALUES (444444,'computer',9)";
cmd.ExecuteNonQuery();

cmd.CommandText = "CREATE TABLE Orders (OrderNumber "
          + "VARCHAR(4), CustomerID CHAR(4), SalespersonID "
          + " CHAR(2), OrderDate DATE)";
cmd.ExecuteNonQuery();
cmd.CommandText =
      "INSERT INTO Orders VALUES (1,1234,12,'Apr 3, 1999')";
cmd.ExecuteNonQuery();
cmd.CommandText =
     "INSERT INTO Orders VALUES (2,5678,12,'Mar 22, 1999')";
cmd.ExecuteNonQuery();
cmd.CommandText =
     "INSERT INTO Orders VALUES (3,8765,98,'Feb 19, 1999')";
cmd.ExecuteNonQuery();
cmd.CommandText =
      "INSERT INTO Orders VALUES (4,1234,12,'Apr 5, 1999')";
cmd.ExecuteNonQuery();
cmd.CommandText =
     "INSERT INTO Orders VALUES (5,8765,98,'Feb 28, 1999')";
cmd.ExecuteNonQuery();

cmd.CommandText = "CREATE TABLE OrderItem (OrderNumber "
                + "CHAR(4), ItemNumber CHAR(6), Quantity "
                + "INTEGER, UnitPrice DECIMAL)";
cmd.ExecuteNonQuery();
cmd.CommandText =
  "INSERT INTO OrderItem VALUES (1,222222,4,27.00)";// Note 3
cmd.ExecuteNonQuery();
cmd.CommandText =
        "INSERT INTO OrderItem VALUES (1,333333,2,210.50)";
cmd.ExecuteNonQuery();
```

```
        cmd.CommandText =
                "INSERT INTO OrderItem VALUES (1,444444,1,569.00)";
        cmd.ExecuteNonQuery();
        cmd.CommandText =
                "INSERT INTO OrderItem VALUES (2,333333,2,230.95)";
        cmd.ExecuteNonQuery();
        cmd.CommandText =
                "INSERT INTO OrderItem VALUES (3,222222,3,27.00)";
        cmd.ExecuteNonQuery();
        cmd.CommandText =
                "INSERT INTO OrderItem VALUES (3,333333,1,230.95)";
        cmd.ExecuteNonQuery();
        cmd.CommandText =
                "INSERT INTO OrderItem VALUES (4,444444,1,569.00)";
        cmd.ExecuteNonQuery();
        cmd.CommandText =
                "INSERT INTO OrderItem VALUES (5,222222,2,27.00)";
        cmd.ExecuteNonQuery();
        cmd.CommandText =
                "INSERT INTO OrderItem VALUES (5,444444,1,725.00)";
        cmd.ExecuteNonQuery();
        con.Close();
    }
}
```

Note 1:

```
cmd.CommandText = "CREATE TABLE Customer (CustomerID "
  + "CHAR(4), CustomerName VARCHAR(25), Address "
  + "VARCHAR(25), BalanceDue DECIMAL)";
```

Just as with any string, we need to split the SQL statement over multiple lines using the concatenation operator so that each string constant fits on one line.

Note 2:

```
cmd.CommandText = "INSERT INTO Customer VALUES "
      "(5678,'Darnell Davis','33 Second St.',130.95)";
```

When splitting the SQL statement over multiple lines we must be sure to add spaces to separate identifiers. Without the spaces either after `Customer` or before `VALUES`, the juxtaposition of `CustomerVALUES` would cause an error.

Note 3:

```
cmd.CommandText =
    "INSERT INTO OrderItem VALUES (1,222222,4,27.00)";
```

Using nine statements to insert the nine rows into the `OrderItem` table is cumbersome and would be more so if the table were larger. A better method is to read the data to enter from a file. We leave this improvement to the exercises.

The BIG Picture

We use a connection string that specifies the provider and the data source to connect to a database. Once connected to the database, we can create tables and insert data into them from a C# program. Optionally, we could have created the tables outside of C#.

✓ Test Your Understanding

Try It Yourself ➤ **8.** Rewrite Example 15.1 to omit the @ character in the connection string. What other changes to that string do you need to make?

Try It Yourself ➤ **9.** What happens when you try to run Example 15.2 twice in succession?

Try It Yourself ➤ **10.** Modify Example 15.2, as described in Note 2, to omit the spaces after `Customer` and before `VALUES`. What is the effect of this change?

15.3 RETRIEVING INFORMATION

Now that we have created the `Sales` database we can extract information from it. When executing an SQL statement that returns results, we use the `ExecuteReader` method, which returns an `OleDbDataReader` that allows us to read a stream of data from a data source containing the data that satisfies the query. Executing

```
cmd.CommandText =
       "SELECT CustomerName, Address FROM Customer";
OleDbDataReader reader = cmd.ExecuteReader();
```

provides a reader to obtain the `CustomerName` and `Address` columns from the `Customer` table.

Viewing Query Results

To view the results, the `OleDbDataReader` has `getXXX` methods where `XXX` is the C# type corresponding to the SQL type of the data field we are retrieving. Because `CustomerName` and `Address` both have the `VARCHAR` SQL type, we use the `GetString` method to retrieve these fields. We retrieve fields by field number, starting with zero, as with arrays indexing. The loop

FIGURE 15.12
C# methods for SQL types

C# method	SQL type
GetInt32	INTEGER
GetString	VARCHAR
GetDecimal	DECIMAL
GetDate	DATE

```
while(reader.Read())
  Console.WriteLine("{0}\t{1}",
                  reader.GetString(0), reader.GetString(1));
```

will list the rows of names and addresses from the `Customer` table. We retrieve the `CustomerName` field using its column number 0 and the `Address` field using its column number 1. The `Read()` method returns `true` when another row is available and `false` otherwise. It advances the `OleDbReader` to the next record. Figure 15.12 shows the C# methods corresponding to the SQL types we use.

`SELECT` Statement Options

The `SELECT` statement has additional options. The `ORDER` clause allows us to display the results sorted with respect to one or more columns. The query

```
SELECT CustomerName, Address FROM Customer
ORDER BY CustomerName
```

returns the result set by name in alphabetical order. We could use

```
SELECT CustomerName, Address FROM Customer
ORDER BY 1
```

to achieve the same result using the column number in the `ORDER` clause.

Sometimes a query may return duplicate rows. For example, in selecting customers who ordered computers we would get the result

```
Fred Flynn
Fred Flynn
Carla Kahn
```

because Fred Flynn bought computers in orders 1 and 4. We can remove duplicates by using the `SELECT DISTINCT` variant of the `SELECT` statement. This query,

```
SELECT DISTINCT CustomerName
FROM Customer, Item, Orders, OrderItem
WHERE Customer.CustomerID = Orders.CustomerID
AND Orders.OrderNumber = OrderItem.OrderNumber
AND OrderItem.ItemNumber = Item.ItemNumber
AND Description = 'computer'
```

joins rows from four tables to produce the result.

The UPDATE and DELETE statements change the database, but do not return results, so we use the ExecuteNonQuery method to execute them.

EXAMPLE 15.3 ■ ExtractInfo.cs

```
/* Demonstrates the use of SQL queries from
 * a C# program.
 */

using System;
using System.Data;
using System.Data.OleDb;
public class ExtractInfo {
 public static void Main () {
   String connect = "Provider=Microsoft.JET.OLEDB.4.0;"
    + @"data source=c:\booksharp\gittleman\ch15\Sales.mdb";
   OleDbConnection con = new OleDbConnection(connect);
   con.Open();
   Console.WriteLine
     ("Made the connection to the Sales database");

   OleDbCommand cmd = con.CreateCommand();
   cmd.CommandText = "SELECT CustomerName, Address "
                   + "FROM Customer ORDER BY CustomerName";
   OleDbDataReader reader = cmd.ExecuteReader();
   Console.WriteLine("   Names and Addresses of Customers");
   Console.WriteLine("Name\t\tAddress");                // Note 1
   while(reader.Read())
     Console.WriteLine("{0}\t{1}",
              reader.GetString(0), reader.GetString(1));
   reader.Close();                                       // Note 2

   cmd.CommandText = "SELECT * FROM OrderItem "
            + "WHERE ItemNumber = '222222'";
   reader = cmd.ExecuteReader();
   Console.WriteLine();
   Console.WriteLine("   Order items for radios");
   Console.WriteLine("OrderNumber\tQuantity\tUnitPrice");
   while (reader.Read())
     Console.WriteLine("{0}\t\t{1}\t\t{2}",reader.GetString(0),
           reader.GetInt32(2), reader.GetDecimal(3));  //Note 3
   reader.Close();

   cmd.CommandText = "SELECT CustomerName FROM Customer,Orders "
           + "WHERE Customer.CustomerID = Orders.CustomerID "
           + "AND  OrderDate = #3/22/99#";
   reader = cmd.ExecuteReader();
```

```
Console.WriteLine();
Console.WriteLine
  ("   Customer placing orders on Mar 22, 1999");
while(reader.Read())
  Console.WriteLine(reader.GetString(0));
reader.Close();

cmd.CommandText = "SELECT DISTINCT CustomerName "
         + "FROM Customer, Item, Orders, OrderItem "
         + "WHERE Customer.CustomerID = Orders.CustomerID "
         + "AND Orders.OrderNumber = OrderItem.OrderNumber "
         + "AND OrderItem.ItemNumber = Item.ItemNumber "
         + "AND Description = 'computer'";
reader = cmd.ExecuteReader();
Console.WriteLine();
Console.WriteLine("   Customers ordering computers");
while(reader.Read())
  Console.WriteLine(reader.GetString(0));
reader.Close();

cmd.CommandText =  "SELECT OrderNumber FROM Orders "
          + "WHERE OrderDate BETWEEN #4/1/99# AND #4/30/99#";
reader = cmd.ExecuteReader();
Console.WriteLine();
Console.WriteLine
   ("   Order numbers of orders from 4/1/99 to 4/30/99");
while(reader.Read())
  Console.WriteLine(reader.GetString(0));
reader.Close();

cmd.CommandText = "INSERT INTO Item VALUES ('555555','CD "
                                + "player',10)";      // Note 4
cmd.ExecuteNonQuery();
cmd.CommandText = "UPDATE Item SET Quantity = 12 "
       + "WHERE Description = 'CD player'";
cmd.ExecuteNonQuery();
Console.WriteLine();
Console.WriteLine("   Added and updated a new item");
Console.WriteLine("Description");
cmd.CommandText = "SELECT Description FROM Item";
reader = cmd.ExecuteReader();
while(reader.Read())
  Console.WriteLine(reader.GetString(0));
reader.Close();
cmd.CommandText =
  "DELETE FROM Item WHERE Description = 'CD player'";
cmd.ExecuteNonQuery();
cmd.CommandText = "SELECT Description FROM Item";
```

```
    reader = cmd.ExecuteReader();
    Console.WriteLine();
    Console.WriteLine("   Deleted the new item");
    Console.WriteLine("Description");
    while(reader.Read())
      Console.WriteLine(reader.GetString(0));
    reader.Close();
    con.Close();
  }
}
```

Output

```
Made the connection to the Sales database
   Names and Addresses of Customers
Name            Address
Carla Kahn      55 Fourth St.
Darnell Davis   33 Second St.
Fred Flynn      22 First St.
Marla Martinez  44 Third St.

   Order items for radios
OrderNumber     Quantity        UnitPrice
1               4               27
3               3               27
5               2               27

   Customer placing orders on Mar 22, 1999
Darnell Davis

   Customers ordering computers
Carla Kahn
Fred Flynn

   Order numbers of orders from 4/1/99 to 4/30/99
1
4

   Added and updated a new item
Description
radio
television
computer
CD player

   Deleted the new item
```

```
Description
radio
television
computer
```

Note 1: `Console.WriteLine("Name\t\tAddress");`

We embed tab characters, `\t`, in the string to space the data horizontally.

Note 2: `reader.Close();`

We close the reader after each query to continue using the connection.

Note 3:

```
while (reader.Read())
Console.WriteLine("{0}\t\t{1}\t\t{2}",
    reader.GetString(0),
    reader.GetInt32(2), reader.GetDecimal(3));
```

We omitted field 1, `ItemNumber`, from the display because we selected all results to have `ItemNumber` equal to 222222. We use the `GetInt32` method because field 3, `Quantity`, has SQL type `INTEGER`.

Note 4:

```
cmd.CommandText =
 "INSERT INTO Item VALUES ('555555','CD player',10)";
```

We add a new row to illustrate the `UPDATE` and `DELETE` statements which change the database. We update the new row and then delete it, leaving the database unchanged when we exit the program. This is nice while learning because we can try various `SELECT` statements repeatedly, running the same program without changing the data.

The BIG Picture

When querying the database, a result of the query contains the selected rows. We use methods such as `GetString` to display a value from a resulting row. The SQL types have corresponding C# methods, so the C# `GetInt32` method retrieves `INTEGER` values, for example. We can write our SQL queries to order the results or to eliminate duplicate rows. A query may have to join several tables on common fields to obtain the desired information.

✓Test Your Understanding

11. Write an SQL statement to find names of salespersons and the customers that have placed orders with them. Be sure to eliminate duplicates.

Try It Yourself ➤

12. Modify Example 15.3 to list `CustomerID` in addition to `CustomerName` and `Address`. Arrange the output rows so the `CustomerID` numbers appear in numerical order.
13. Write a `SELECT` statement to find the names and addresses of customers who placed orders with Peter Patterson. Be sure to eliminate duplicates.

15.4 DATABASE INFORMATION AND AGGREGATE FUNCTIONS

.NET allows us to get information about the database with which we are working and about the results of queries. We can use SQL functions to compute with the data.

Database Information

The `GetOleDbSchemaTable` method returns information about the data set. This method has two parameters

```
Guid schema
Object[] restrictions
```

The `Guid` is a 128-bit identifier that is unique across all computers and networks. For this method we use `OleDbSchemaGuid` values. The two we illustrate are `Tables` and `Columns`. Using `Tables` will return a table that describes each table in the data set. Using `Columns` will return a table that describes each column.

The second argument places restrictions on the source data set. Each `OleDbSchemaGuid` has four available restrictions. For `Tables` and `Columns` these restrictions are:

Tables	**Columns**
TABLE_CATALOG	TABLE_CATALOG
TABLE_SCHEMA	TABLE_SCHEMA
TABLE_NAME	TABLE_NAME
TABLE_TYPE	COLUMN_NAME

Microsoft Access does not use a catalog or a schema, so we pass `null` for these restrictions. Example 15.4 shows how to set the last two restrictions.

Creating a Data Set

In this chapter we present a simple introduction to databases using C#. Our examples connect to the `Sales` data, do some processing, and close the connection. More generally, we can create a `DataSet` and process the data offline. We illustrate that in the next example by creating a `DataSet` to represent the results of a query. We can then get information about the data set of query results.

Aggregate Functions

Aggregate functions compute values from the table data, using all the rows to produce the result. For example, the query

```
SELECT SUM(BalanceDue), AVG(BalanceDue),  MAX(BalanceDue)
FROM Customer
```

returns the sum, average, and maximum of all the balances due in the customer table. These functions operate on the `BalanceDue` column for all rows in the `Customer` table. Using a `WHERE` clause, as in

```
SELECT COUNT(*), MIN(Quantity) FROM OrderItem
WHERE ItemNumber = '222222'
```

will limit the computation to the rows of the `OrderItem` table that correspond to orders for radios. The function `COUNT(*)` will return the total number of rows satisfying this condition. `MIN(Quantity)` returns the minimum quantity of radios ordered in one of the three rows of the `OrderItem` table that represent orders for radios (item number 222222).

EXAMPLE 15.4 ■ DatabaseInfo.cs

```
/* Illustrates methods for getting information about
 * the data and SQL aggregate functions.
 */

using System;
using System.Data;
using System.Data.OleDb;
public class DatabaseInfo {
 public static void Main () {
   String connect = "Provider=Microsoft.JET.OLEDB.4.0;"
    + @"data source=c:\booksharp\gittleman\ch15\Sales.mdb";
   OleDbConnection con = new OleDbConnection(connect);
   con.Open();
   Console.WriteLine
    ("Made the connection to the Sales database");

   Console.WriteLine
     ("Information for each Sales table contains:");
   DataTable tables = con.GetOleDbSchemaTable
        (OleDbSchemaGuid.Tables,
              new object[]{null,null,null,"TABLE"});    // Note 1
   foreach(DataColumn col in tables.Columns)
     Console.WriteLine
        ("  {0}\t{1}", col.ColumnName, col.DataType);  // Note 2

   Console.WriteLine("The Sales tables are:");
   foreach(DataRow row in tables.Rows)
     Console.Write("  {0}", row[2]);                     // Note 3
   Console.WriteLine();

   DataTable cols = con.GetOleDbSchemaTable
                         (OleDbSchemaGuid.Columns,
```

```
        new object[]{null,null,"Customer",null});      // Note 4
    Console.WriteLine
      ("The columns describing the Customer table are:");
    foreach(DataColumn col in cols.Columns)
      Console.WriteLine
         ("  {0}\t{1}", col.ColumnName, col.DataType);  // Note 5
    Console.WriteLine("The columns in the Customer table are:");
    foreach(DataRow row in cols.Rows)
      Console.WriteLine("  {0}\t{1}", row[3],
                             (OleDbType)row[11]);     // Note 6
    Console.WriteLine();

    String cmd = "SELECT * FROM Item";                  // Note 7
    OleDbDataAdapter adapter = new OleDbDataAdapter();  // Note 8
    adapter.SelectCommand = new OleDbCommand(cmd, con); // Note 9
    DataSet ds = new DataSet();
    adapter.Fill(ds, "Item");                          // Note 10
    DataTable item = ds.Tables[0];                     // Note 11
    Console.WriteLine("Table name: {0}", item.TableName);
    Console.WriteLine("Its columns are:");
    foreach (DataColumn col in item.Columns)
      Console.WriteLine
         ("  {0}\t{1}", col.ColumnName, col.DataType); // Note 12

    OleDbCommand command = con.CreateCommand();
    command.CommandText =
             "SELECT SUM(BalanceDue) FROM Customer";// Note 13
    Console.WriteLine("Sum of balances: {0:C}",
                 (decimal)command.ExecuteScalar());// Note 14
    command.CommandText =
             "SELECT AVG(BalanceDue) FROM Customer";
    Console.WriteLine("Average of balances: {0:C}",
                       (decimal)command.ExecuteScalar());
    command.CommandText =
             "SELECT MAX(BalanceDue) FROM Customer";
    Console.WriteLine("Max of balances: {0:C}",
                       (decimal)command.ExecuteScalar());
    command.CommandText =
             "SELECT COUNT(*) FROM Customer";
    Console.WriteLine("Number of Customer rows: {0}",
                       (int)command.ExecuteScalar());
    con.Close();
  }
}
```

```
Made the connection to the Sales database
Information for each Sales table contains:
  TABLE_CATALOG System.String
  TABLE_SCHEMA  System.String
  TABLE_NAME    System.String
  TABLE_TYPE    System.String
  TABLE_GUID    System.Guid
  DESCRIPTION   System.String
  TABLE_PROPID  System.Int64
  DATE_CREATED  System.DateTime
  DATE_MODIFIED System.DateTime
The Sales tables are:
  Customer  Item  OrderItem  Orders  Salesperson
The columns describing the Customer table are:
  TABLE_CATALOG System.String
  TABLE_SCHEMA  System.String
  TABLE_NAME    System.String
  COLUMN_NAME   System.String
  COLUMN_GUID   System.Guid
  COLUMN_PROPID System.Int64
  ORDINAL_POSITION      System.Int64
  COLUMN_HASDEFAULT     System.Boolean
  COLUMN_DEFAULT        System.String
  COLUMN_FLAGS  System.Int64
  IS_NULLABLE   System.Boolean
  DATA_TYPE     System.Int32
  TYPE_GUID     System.Guid
  CHARACTER_MAXIMUM_LENGTH      System.Int64
  CHARACTER_OCTET_LENGTH        System.Int64
  NUMERIC_PRECISION     System.Int32
  NUMERIC_SCALE System.Int16
  DATETIME_PRECISION    System.Int64
  CHARACTER_SET_CATALOG System.String
  CHARACTER_SET_SCHEMA  System.String
  CHARACTER_SET_NAME    System.String
  COLLATION_CATALOG     System.String
  COLLATION_SCHEMA      System.String
  COLLATION_NAME        System.String
  DOMAIN_CATALOG        System.String
  DOMAIN_SCHEMA System.String
  DOMAIN_NAME   System.String
  DESCRIPTION   System.String
The columns in the Customer table are:
  Address       WChar
  BalanceDue    Numeric
  CustomerID    WChar
```

```
  CustomerName  WChar

Table name: Item
Its columns are:
  ItemNumber    System.String
  Description   System.String
  Quantity      System.Int32
Sum of balances: $1,797.00
Average of balances: $449.25
Max of balances: $1,667.00
Number of Customer rows: 4
```

Note 1:

```
DataTable tables = con.GetOleDbSchemaTable
(OleDbSchemaGuid.Tables,
      new object[]{null,null,null,"TABLE"});
```

The `GetOleDbSchemaTable` method, with `Tables` as the first argument, returns a `DataTable` containing a row describing each table. We pass null as the third element of the second argument to place no restriction on the names of the tables returned. We restrict the table type to `"TABLE"` in the fourth element so we get only the user-defined tables. The documentation shows others choices of restrictions for specialized uses. The `DataTable` returned has five rows, one for each of the five `Sales` tables.

Note 2:

```
foreach(DataColumn col in tables.Columns)
    Console.WriteLine
      ("  {0}\t{1}", col.ColumnName, col.DataType);
```

The `Columns` property returns a `DataColumnCollection` with one `DataColumn` for each column of the table. The `ColumnName` property gives us the name of the column and the `DataType` property gives us the type. This is a table with five rows, one for each `Sales` table. The nine column names in the output show the nine pieces of information we can get about each `Sales` table if we look at the data in each row.

Note 3:

```
foreach(DataRow row in tables.Rows)
    Console.Write("  {0}", row[2]);
```

The `Rows` property returns a `DataRowCollection` containing the data for each row of the table. From the previous output we see that the third column, with index 2, gives the table name, so we output the third column of the table to get the names of the `Sales` tables.

Note 4:

```
DataTable cols = con.GetOleDbSchemaTable
          (OleDbSchemaGuid.Columns,
             new object[]{null,null,"Customer",null});
```

The `GetOleDbSchemaTable` method, with `Columns` as the first argument, returns a `DataTable` containing a row describing each column. Passing `Customer` as the third element of the second argument restricts the tables to the `Customer` table, so we will get columns of only the `Customer` table. By passing `null` as the fourth element, we place no restrictions on the column names to be returned.

Note 5:

```
foreach(DataColumn col in cols.Columns)
    Console.WriteLine
        ("  {0}\t{1}", col.ColumnName, col.DataType);
```

We use the `ColumnName` and `DataType` properties to display the name and type of each column of this table that has a row for each column of the `Customer` table.

Note 6:

```
Console.WriteLine("  {0}\t{1}", row[3],
                          (OleDbType)row[11]);
```

From the previous output, we know that the column with index 3 contains the column name, and the column with index 11 contains the column type. The type is an integer which we cast to `OleDbType`. The `WChar` type represents a stream of Unicode characters. It maps to the `String` type. The `Numeric` type represents an exact numeric value with fixed precision. It maps to type `Decimal`.

Note 7:

```
String cmd = "SELECT * FROM Item";
```

We just found the names of the five `Sales` tables and the names and types of the four `Customer` columns. We connected to the `Sales` database to process the `Sales` data set. We use this query to illustrate how to build our own `DataSet` and get information about it. The `DataSet` will contain the results of the query.

Note 8:

```
OleDbDataAdapter adapter = new OleDbDataAdapter();
```

The `OleDbDataAdapter` serves as a bridge between the `DataSet` and the data source. We use its `Fill` method to populate the `DataSet` from the data source and the `Update` method to send changes back to the data source.

Note 9:

```
adapter.SelectCommand = new OleDbCommand(cmd, con);
```

We use the `SelectCommand` property to set the SQL statement used to retrieve data from the data source. The first argument to the `OleDbCommand` constructor is a `String` representing the text of the query. The second argument is an `OleDbConnection`.

Note 10:

```
adapter.Fill(ds, "Item");
```

The `Fill` method adds the data resulting from the `SELECT` query to the `DataSet ds`. The second argument is the table name.

Note 11:

```
DataTable item = ds.Tables[0];
```

This data set has only one table. We assign it to a `DataTable` variable.

Note 12:
```
Console.WriteLine
        ("  {0}\t{1}", col.ColumnName, col.DataType);
```

We output the name and type of each column of this table, which because of our query is the same as the `Sales Item` table. By using a `DataSet` we can process data offline and update the data source with the results. Processing offline reduces the load on the connection to the data source.

Note 13:
```
"SELECT SUM(BalanceDue) FROM Customer";
```

The rest of this program illustrates aggregate functions including `SUM`, `AVG`, `MAX`, and `COUNT`.

Note 14:
```
Console.WriteLine("Sum of balances: {0:C}",
            (decimal)command.ExecuteScalar());
```

We use the `ExecuteScalar` method to return a single value. It is easier than using an `OleDbDataReader`. The return type is `Object`, which we cast to `decimal` because currency represents exact values.

> **The BIG Picture**
>
> We use the `GetOleDbSchemaTable` method to obtain properties of the database such as the names of its tables and the names and types of the columns in a table. Aggregate functions compute values from the rows of a table.

✓ Test Your Understanding

Try It Yourself ➤ 14. Modify Example 15.4 to pass `null` as the fourth restriction to the `GetOleDbSchemaTable` method with the `TABLES` as first argument, instead of `"TABLE"` array. This will list all tables in the database, including the system tables.

Try It Yourself ➤ 15. Modify Example 15.4 to find the names of the columns of the `Orders` tables in the `Sales` database.

15.5 STORED PROCEDURES AND TRANSACTIONS

A stored procedure lets us translate a statement to low-level database commands once and execute it many times, thus avoiding the inefficient repetition of the translation process. Using Microsoft Access we illustrate a simple form of stored procedure without named parameters.

When making changes to a database we must be very careful that we complete all steps of the transaction. It would not do to withdraw funds from one account but not have them deposited in another. Transaction processing allows us to explicitly control when changes become final, so we commit changes only when all those desired have completed correctly.

Often we may wish to execute a query repeatedly, using different conditions each time. The query

```
SELECT * FROM OrderItem
WHERE ItemNumber = '222222'
```

selects all order items with number 222222. The Sales database has three types of items. We could repeat the query to find orders for other items. For example, executing the query

```
SELECT * FROM OrderItem
WHERE ItemNumber = '333333'
```

produces the order items for televisions.

We have only three products in our database, but we might have had many more. For each product, the database system must process the SQL query, analyzing how to find the requested data from the database in the most efficient way possible. Our query is quite simple, but it could have been much more complex. Each time we execute the query with a different item number we have to process it, spending the time over and over again to find the best way to find the results that satisfy it.

The stored procedure allows the database system to process an SQL query once, determining the best way to get the results. We can then use this stored procedure over and over again with different data but without the overhead of translating it again.

We use the question mark, ?, to denote the arguments to query that we wish to change from one execution to the next. To make a stored procedure from our previous query, we write it as

```
SELECT * FROM OrderItem WHERE ItemNumber = ?
```

where the question mark stands for the item number that we will pass in. Example 15.5 illustrates how to call this stored procedure with different values. To pass multiple parameters we use additional question marks in the query. In the query

```
SELECT OrderNumber FROM Orders
WHERE OrderDate BETWEEN ? AND ?
```

the parameters represent the starting and ending dates of orders.

EXAMPLE 15.5 ■ Prepare.cs

```
/* Illustrates simple stored procedures with
 * unnamed parameters in the query.
 */

using System;
using System.Data;
using System.Data.OleDb;
public class Prepare {
 public static void Main () {
```

```
String connect = "Provider=Microsoft.JET.OLEDB.4.0;"
 + @"data source=c:\booksharp\gittleman\ch15\Sales.mdb";
OleDbConnection con = new OleDbConnection(connect);
con.Open();
Console.WriteLine
  ("Made the connection to the Sales database");

OleDbCommand cmd = con.CreateCommand();
cmd.CommandText =
 "SELECT Quantity FROM Item WHERE Description = ?";
OleDbParameter param = new OleDbParameter();    // Note 1
cmd.Parameters.Add(param);                      // Note 2
param.Value = "radio";                          // Note 3
OleDbDataReader reader = cmd.ExecuteReader();
Console.WriteLine("   Using a stored procedure
                      to find quantity of radios");
while(reader.Read())
  Console.WriteLine("{0}", reader.GetInt32(0)); // Note 4
reader.Close();

param.Value = "computer";                       // Note 5
reader = cmd.ExecuteReader();
Console.WriteLine
  ("   Using a stored procedure to find "
    + "quantity of computers");
while(reader.Read())
  Console.WriteLine("{0}", reader.GetInt32(0));
reader.Close();

OleDbCommand cmd1 = con.CreateCommand();
cmd1.CommandText = "SELECT OrderNumber FROM Orders "
                 + "WHERE OrderDate BETWEEN ? AND ?";
OleDbParameter p1 = new OleDbParameter();
OleDbParameter p2 = new OleDbParameter();
cmd1.Parameters.Add(p1);
cmd1.Parameters.Add(p2);                        // Note 6
p1.Value = new DateTime(1999,4,1);              // Note 7
p2.Value = new DateTime(1999,4,30);
reader = cmd1.ExecuteReader();
Console.WriteLine
  ("   Using a stored procedure to find April orders");
```

```
    while(reader.Read())
      Console.WriteLine("{0}", reader.GetString(0));
    reader.Close();

    OleDbCommand cmd2 = con.CreateCommand();
    cmd2.CommandText = "SELECT CustomerName FROM Customer "
                          + "WHERE BalanceDue > ?";
                                                    // Note 8
    OleDbParameter p3 = new OleDbParameter();
    cmd2.Parameters.Add(p3);
    p3.Value = new Decimal(0.0);                    // Note 9
    reader = cmd2.ExecuteReader();
    Console.WriteLine("   Using a stored procedure to find "
               + "customers with non-zero balance");
    while(reader.Read())
      Console.WriteLine("{0}", reader.GetString(0));
    reader.Close();

    con.Close();
  }
}
```

Output

```
Made the connection to the Sales database
   Using a stored procedure to find quantity of radios
32
   Using a stored procedure to find quantity of computers
9
   Using a stored procedure to find April orders
1
4
   Using a stored procedure to find customers with non-zero
   balance
Fred Flynn
Darnell Davis
```

■

Note 1: `OleDbParameter param = new OleDbParameter();`

We create an `OleDbParameter` object for each parameter in the query.

Note 2: `cmd.Parameters.Add(param);`

The `Parameters` property keeps an `OleDbParametersCollection` of the parameters. We add the object we just created.

Note 3: `param.Value = "radio";`

We set the value of the parameter to `"radio"` and execute the query.

Note 4: `Console.WriteLine("{0}", reader.GetInt32(0));`

We use the `GetInt32` method to find an integer value.

Note 5: `param.Value = "computer";`

Now we get the benefit of having already processed the query. We do not need to process it again. We just set the parameter to "`computer`" and execute the stored procedure.

Note 6: `cmd1.Parameters.Add(p2);`

When the stored procedure has two parameters, we create a second `OleDbParameter` and add it to the `Parameters` collection.

Note 7: `p1.Value = new DateTime(1999,4,1);`

We pass a `DateTime` instance for a date parameter.

Note 8:
```
cmd2.CommandText = "SELECT CustomerName FROM "
      "Customer WHERE BalanceDue > ?";
```

We use a relational operator in the condition.

Note 9: `p3.Value = new Decimal(0.0);`

We pass `Decimal` to represent a currency value.

Transaction Processing

Often when using a database we need to execute several statements to perform the desired transaction. For example, if a customer places a new order we will update the `Orders` table with another order, the `OrderItem` table with the items ordered, and the `Customer` table with a new `BalanceDue`. We would be unhappy if an error occurred after some but not all of these changes were made. C# allows us to manage transactions so we commit the changes to the database only when they complete without error.

The default is to commit the change as soon as we execute the update. The statement

```
oleDbTransaction trans=con.BeginTransaction();
```

changes from the default behavior to require that we explicitly commit changes using

```
trans.C.commit();
```

If we have already executed some updates and decide we do not want to commit them, we can roll back to the point at which we executed the last commit, undoing these changes using

```
trans.Rollback();
```

For example, if we have begun a transaction, after executing the queries

```
INSERT INTO Item VALUES (555555,'CD player',10)
```

and

```
UPDATE Item SET Quantity = 12
WHERE Description = 'CD player'
```

we can either commit them, making the changes permanent using the `Commit` method, or undo them using the `Rollback` method.

EXAMPLE 15.6 ■ Transact.cs

```
/* Illustrates transaction processing
 */

using System;
using System.Data;
using System.Data.OleDb;
public class Transact {
 public static void Main () {
   String connect = "Provider=Microsoft.JET.OLEDB.4.0;"
    + @"data source=c:\booksharp\gittleman\ch15\Sales.mdb";
   OleDbConnection con = new OleDbConnection(connect);
   con.Open();
   Console.WriteLine
     ("Made the connection to the Sales database");
   OleDbCommand cmd = con.CreateCommand();

   OleDbTransaction trans = con.BeginTransaction();     // Note 1
   cmd.Transaction = trans;                             // Note 2
   cmd.CommandText =
          "INSERT INTO Item VALUES (555555,'CD player',10)";
   cmd.ExecuteNonQuery();
   cmd.CommandText = "UPDATE Item SET Quantity = 12 "
                        + "WHERE Description = 'CD player'";
   cmd.ExecuteNonQuery();
   cmd.CommandText = "SELECT Description FROM Item";
   OleDbDataReader reader = cmd.ExecuteReader();
   Console.WriteLine("   Before commit or rollback"
         + " -- table changed, but can rollback");  // Note 3
   Console.WriteLine("  Description");
   while(reader.Read())
     Console.WriteLine("{0}",
              reader.GetString(0));
   reader.Close();
   trans.Rollback();                                    // Note 4
```

```
    cmd.CommandText = "SELECT Description FROM Item";
    reader = cmd.ExecuteReader();
    Console.WriteLine
      ("    Rolled back insert and update -- table unchanged");
    Console.WriteLine("   Description");                   // Note 5
    while(reader.Read())
      Console.WriteLine("{0}", reader.GetString(0));
    reader.Close();

    trans = con.BeginTransaction();                        // Note 6
    cmd.Transaction = trans;
    cmd.CommandText =
           "INSERT INTO Item VALUES (555555,'CD player',10)";
    cmd.ExecuteNonQuery();
    cmd.CommandText = "UPDATE Item SET Quantity = 12 "
                         + "WHERE Description = 'CD player'";
    cmd.ExecuteNonQuery();
    trans.Commit();                                        // Note 7

    cmd.CommandText = "SELECT Description FROM Item";
    reader = cmd.ExecuteReader();
    Console.WriteLine
      ("    Committed insert and update -- table changed");
    Console.WriteLine("   Description");                   // Note 8
    while(reader.Read())
      Console.WriteLine("{0}",
                 reader.GetString(0));
    reader.Close();

    cmd.CommandText =
     "DELETE FROM Item WHERE Description = 'CD player'";// Note 9
    cmd.ExecuteNonQuery();
       cmd.CommandText = "SELECT Description FROM Item";
    reader = cmd.ExecuteReader();
    Console.WriteLine("    Deleted the new item");
    Console.WriteLine("   Description");
    while(reader.Read())
      Console.WriteLine("{0}",
                 reader.GetString(0));
    reader.Close();

    con.Close();
  }
}
```

Output

```
Made the connection to the Sales database
   Before commit or rollback -- table changed, but can rollback
  Description
radio
television
computer
CD player
   Rolled back insert and update -- table unchanged
  Description
radio
television
computer
   Committed insert and update -- table changed
  Description
radio
television
computer
CD player
   Deleted the new item
  Description
radio
television
computer
```

Note 1: `OleDbTransaction trans = con.BeginTransaction();`

To start a transaction we call the `BeginTransaction` method, which returns an `OleDbTransaction`.

Note 2: `cmd.Transaction = trans;`

We set the `Transaction` property of the command with the transaction we created.

Note 3:

```
Console.WriteLine("   Before commit or rollback"
    + " -- table changed, but can rollback");
```

We will list the descriptions of the items in the database to show that the database system has entered the item `CD player` (with the updated quantity of `12` not shown). We have not yet executed the `Commit` statement, so we still have a chance to rollback this change.

Note 4: `trans.Rollback();`

We rollback the changes made since the beginning of the transaction. Normally we would not call the `Rollback` method here. A call might occur in an exception handler if part of the required processing has failed and we want to rollback the part that completed to maintain consistency of the database.

Note 5: `Console.WriteLine("  Description");`

We display the descriptions to show that after we rollback the updates we find only the original three items in the `Item` table.

Note 6: `trans = con.BeginTransaction();`

We begin another transaction.

Note 7: `trans.Commit();`

Now we make the same updates, this time actually committing them to the database and preventing further rollbacks.

Note 8: `Console.WriteLine("  Description");`

We display the descriptions to show that the table has been augmented again.

Note 9:

```
cmd.CommandText =
  "DELETE FROM Item WHERE Description = 'CD player'";
```

We delete the new row from the database to leave it as we found it in this pedagogical example.

> **The BIG Picture**
>
> A stored procedure lets us translate a query once and substitute values for its parameters to execute it repeatedly. By deciding explicitly when to commit changes to the database, we reserve the option to rollback some changes if the entire transaction cannot be completed.

✓ Test Your Understanding

16. Write a `SELECT` statement to return the names of customers who ordered an item by its description in the Item table, which we pass in as an argument, so we can create a stored procedure from the query.

Try It Yourself ➤ **17.** Modify Example 15.5 to omit the first `reader.Close()` statement. Does any error result? If so, which?

Try It Yourself ➤ **18.** Modify Example 15.5 to find the order numbers of orders placed in March. Use the same stored procedure.

✓

15.6 A GUI FOR DATABASE QUERIES

Our case study builds a graphical user interface for querying our `Sales` database. This example illustrates the techniques covered in this chapter, adding the user interface concepts studied earlier. Even as presented here, it is large for an introductory example. However, most of the code was generated by Visual Studio .NET. It would need many extensions and much polishing to make it a really useful application. Some of these extensions are left to the exercises.

We used Visual Studio .NET to create the interface. Using the concepts of earlier chapters, we could have written all the code using Visual Studio .NET. But when projects get larger, it is much more productive to use a good tool. Some productive features are:

- We drag controls onto the form. Visual Studio .NET writes the code to configure them in the `InitializeComponent` method. We enter property values in Visual Studio .NET, which it reflects in the design and the code.
- When we double-click a control, Visual Studio .NET adds an event handler to it. We need to write only the event handler body and declare any variables these event handlers use. The program allows the user to create a `SELECT` query and executes it, displaying the resulting rows. Figure 15.13 shows the initial screen. The `ListBox` at the upper-right shows the five tables of the `Sales` database. The user selects the tables to search. The names of these tables will appear after `FROM` in the query. The text area at the bottom gives instructions to the user and displays the final results of the search. We disable all buttons except *`Display`*, until we are ready to use them.

Figures 15.14 through 15.18 show the steps in the creation and execution of the query

```
SELECT CustomerName FROM Customer, Orders
WHERE Customer.CustomerID = Orders.CustomerID
AND  OrderDate = {d '1999-03-22'}
```

Figure 15.14 shows the screen after the user has selected the `Customer` and `Orders` tables and pressed the *`Display`* button. We have disabled the *`Display`* button because

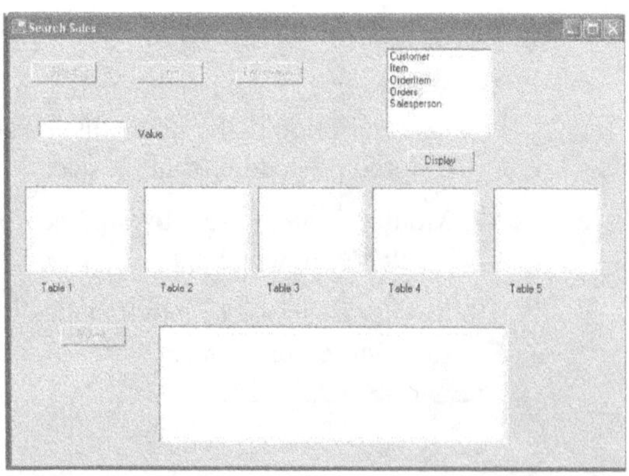

FIGURE 15.13 **The `SearchSales` initial screen**

FIGURE 15.14
Screen to choose columns for the result

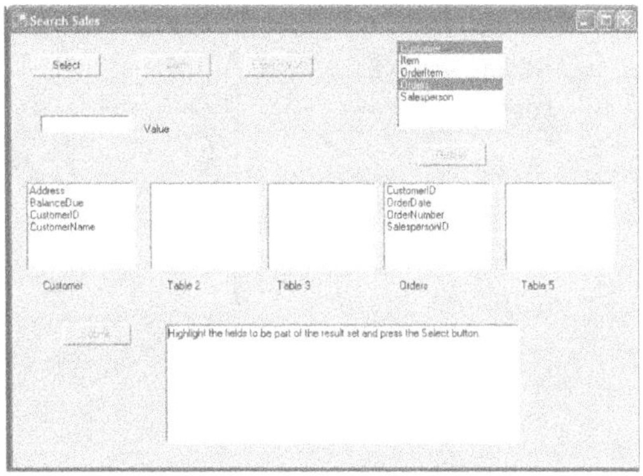

FIGURE 15.15 **After pressing the `Select` button**

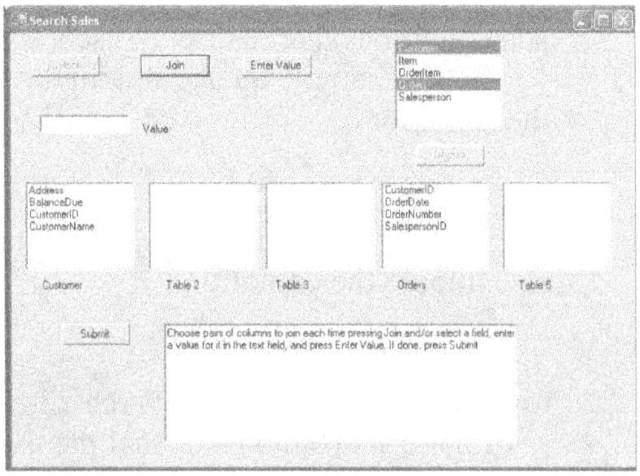

the user has already chosen the tables. The column names for the `Customer` table appear in the left-most `ListBox`, and those for the `Orders` table appear in the fourth `ListBox`. The labels underneath now show the table names. Thus far our query is

```
SELECT  ... FROM Customer, Order.
```

The user now selects the columns to be part of the result set, in this example choosing `CustomerName` and pressing the *`Select`* button. The partially constructed query is now

```
SELECT CustomerName FROM Customer, Order
```

Figure 15.15 shows the next screen in which we disabled the *Select* button, because we select the fields of the result only once. We deselect all fields so the user will not have to deselect the fields before going on to the next step. At this point we enable the *`Join`*, *`Enter Value`*, and *`Submit`* buttons. The user would be ready to execute queries without conditions, such as

```
SELECT CustomerName FROM Customer
```

FIGURE 15.16
Adding a `Join` condition

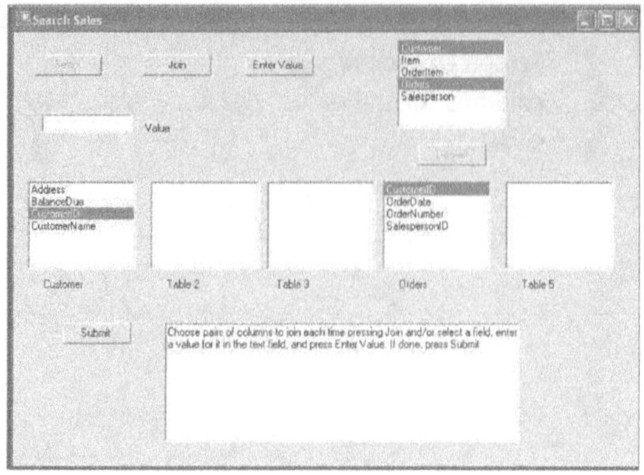

so we enable the *`Submit`* button. The *`Join`* and *`Enter Value`* buttons allow us to add conditions that restrict the scope of the query.

In our example query we join the `Customer` and the `Orders` tables, requiring the condition

```
Customer.CustomerID = Orders.CustomerID.
```

We impose this condition to join the information from the two tables properly, and also impose the condition

```
OrderDate = #3/22/99#
```

to select orders placed on March 22, 1999.

Figure 15.16 indicates that the user has selected the `CustomerID` field in the `Customer` table and the `CustomerID` field in the `Orders` table.

After pressing the *`Join`* button, the partially completed query will be

```
SELECT CustomerName FROM Customer, Order
WHERE Customer.CustomerID = Orders.CustomerID
```

The next screen, Figure 15.17, has the same options as in Figure 15.16, because we can add conditions or submit the completed query. We choose the `OrderDate` column from the `Orders` table and enter the value `#3/22/99#` in the text field. Pressing the *`Enter Value`* button will add to our query the condition that the order

FIGURE 15.17
Entering the `OrderDate` condition

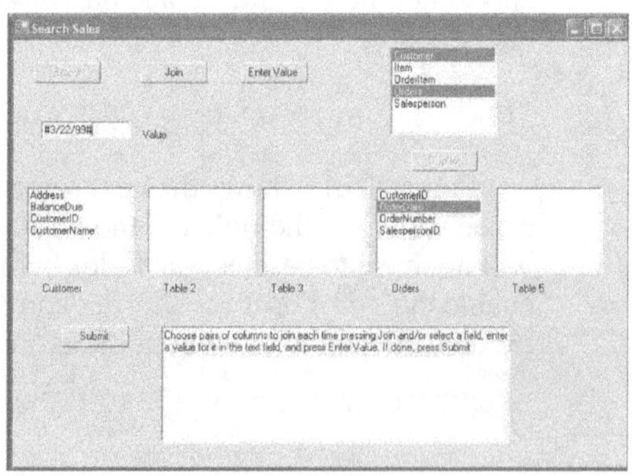

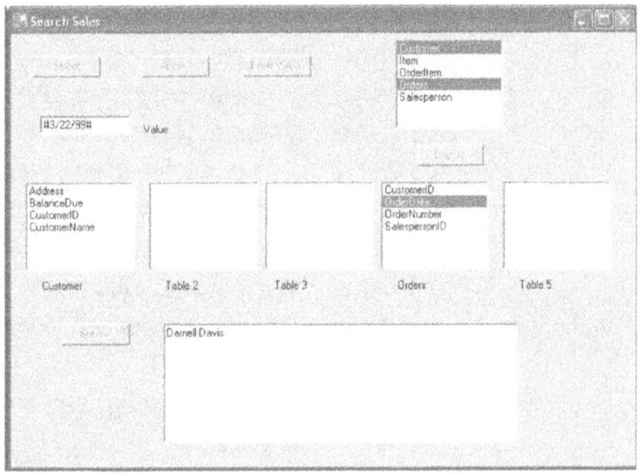

FIGURE 15.18 **The query result**

date be March 22, 1999. We use only the equality relation in our conditions, leaving the extension to less than and greater than to the exercises.

We could add more conditions, but this completes our query, so we press the `Submit` button. Figure 15.18 shows the resulting list (of only one customer, Darnell Davis) displayed in the text area. We disable all buttons, leaving for the exercises the option to continue executing additional queries.

EXAMPLE 15.7 ■ Form1.cs

```
using System;
using System.Drawing;
using System.Collections;
using System.ComponentModel;
using System.Windows.Forms;
using System.Data;
using System.Data.OleDb;

namespace WindowsApplication1
{
     /// <summary>
     /// Summary description for Form1.
     /// </summary>
  public class Form1 : System.Windows.Forms.Form
  {
    private System.Windows.Forms.Button button1;
    private System.Windows.Forms.Button button2;
    private System.Windows.Forms.Button button3;
    private System.Windows.Forms.ListBox listBox1;
    private System.Windows.Forms.TextBox textBox1;
    private System.Windows.Forms.Label label1;
    private System.Windows.Forms.ListBox listBox2;
    private System.Windows.Forms.ListBox listBox3;
    private System.Windows.Forms.ListBox listBox4;
    private System.Windows.Forms.ListBox listBox5;
```

```
private System.Windows.Forms.ListBox listBox6;
private System.Windows.Forms.Label label2;
private System.Windows.Forms.Label label3;
private System.Windows.Forms.Label label4;
private System.Windows.Forms.Label label5;
private System.Windows.Forms.Label label6;
private System.Windows.Forms.Button button4;
private System.Windows.Forms.Button button5;
private System.Windows.Forms.TextBox textBox2;
  /// <summary>
  /// Required designer variable.
  /// </summary>
private System.ComponentModel.Container components = null;
                                                         // Note 1
public const int SIZE = 5;                  // Number of Sales
                                            // tables
String[] tableName = new String[SIZE];      // Table names
int[] indices = null;                       // Selected indices
String resultCols = "";                     // Between SELECT
                                            // and FROM
bool firstJoin = true;                      // First condition?
String joinClauses = "";
String condition = "";
String fromTables = "";                     // Table names after
                                            // FROM
String query = "SELECT ";                   // User builds this
                                            // query
int count = 0;                            // Result column count
ListBox[] columns = new ListBox[SIZE];      // Columns for each
                                  // table
Label[] colLabel = new Label[SIZE];         // Table labels
OleDbConnection con;
OleDbCommand cmd;

public Form1()
{
  //
  // Required for Windows Form Designer support
  //
  InitializeComponent();

  //
  // TODO: Add any constructor code
  //

                                                         // Note 2
String connect = "Provider=Microsoft.JET.OLEDB.4.0;"
+ @"data source=c:\booksharp\gittleman\ch15\Sales.mdb";
```

```
  con = new OleDbConnection(connect);
  con.Open();
  cmd = con.CreateCommand();
  DataTable schema = con.GetOleDbSchemaTable
        (OleDbSchemaGuid.Tables,
         new object[]{null,null,null,"TABLE"});
  int i = 0;
  foreach(DataRow row in schema.Rows)
  listBox1.Items.Add(tableName[i++] = (String)row[2]);
  columns[0] = listBox2;
  columns[1] = listBox3;
  columns[2] = listBox4;
  columns[3] = listBox5;
  columns[4] = listBox6;
  colLabel[0] = label2;
  colLabel[1] = label3;
  colLabel[2] = label4;
  colLabel[3] = label5;
  colLabel[4] = label6;
}

 /// <summary>
 /// Clean up any resources being used.
 /// </summary>
protected override void Dispose( bool disposing )
{
  if( disposing )
  {
  if (components != null)
    {
      components.Dispose();
    }
  }
  base.Dispose( disposing );
}

  #region Windows Form Designer generated code
   /// <summary>
   /// Required method for Designer support - do not modify
   /// the contents of this method with the code editor.
   /// </summary>
private void InitializeComponent()                    // Note 3
{
  this.button1 = new System.Windows.Forms.Button();
  this.button2 = new System.Windows.Forms.Button();
  this.button3 = new System.Windows.Forms.Button();
  this.listBox1 = new System.Windows.Forms.ListBox();
```

```
this.textBox1 = new System.Windows.Forms.TextBox();
this.label1 = new System.Windows.Forms.Label();
this.listBox2 = new System.Windows.Forms.ListBox();
this.listBox3 = new System.Windows.Forms.ListBox();
this.listBox4 = new System.Windows.Forms.ListBox();
this.listBox5 = new System.Windows.Forms.ListBox();
this.listBox6 = new System.Windows.Forms.ListBox();
this.label2 = new System.Windows.Forms.Label();
this.label3 = new System.Windows.Forms.Label();
this.label4 = new System.Windows.Forms.Label();
this.label5 = new System.Windows.Forms.Label();
this.label6 = new System.Windows.Forms.Label();
this.button4 = new System.Windows.Forms.Button();
this.button5 = new System.Windows.Forms.Button();
this.textBox2 = new System.Windows.Forms.TextBox();
this.SuspendLayout();
//
// button1
//
this.button1.Enabled = false;
this.button1.Location
           = new System.Drawing.Point(24, 24);
this.button1.Name = "button1";
this.button1.TabIndex = 0;
this.button1.Text = "Select";
this.button1.Click +=
      new System.EventHandler(this.button1_Click);
//
// button2
//
this.button2.Enabled = false;
this.button2.Location =
           new System.Drawing.Point(144, 24);
this.button2.Name = "button2";
this.button2.TabIndex = 1;
this.button2.Text = "Join";
this.button2.Click +=
      new System.EventHandler(this.button2_Click);
//
// button3
//
this.button3.Enabled = false;
this.button3.Location
           = new System.Drawing.Point(256, 24);
this.button3.Name = "button3";
this.button3.TabIndex = 2;
this.button3.Text = "Enter Value";
```

```
this.button3.Click +=
      new System.EventHandler(this.button3_Click);
//
// listBox1
//
this.listBox1.Location
              = new System.Drawing.Point(424, 8);
this.listBox1.Name = "listBox1";
this.listBox1.SelectionMode =
      System.Windows.Forms.SelectionMode.MultiSimple;
this.listBox1.Size = new System.Drawing.Size(120, 95);
this.listBox1.TabIndex = 3;
//
// textBox1
//
this.textBox1.Location
              = new System.Drawing.Point(32, 88);
this.textBox1.Name = "textBox1";
this.textBox1.TabIndex = 4;
this.textBox1.Text = "";
//
// label1
//
this.label1.Location
            = new System.Drawing.Point(144, 96);
this.label1.Name = "label1";
this.label1.TabIndex = 5;
this.label1.Text = "Value";
//
// listBox2
//
this.listBox2.Location
              = new System.Drawing.Point(16, 160);
this.listBox2.Name = "listBox2";
this.listBox2.SelectionMode =
     System.Windows.Forms.SelectionMode.MultiSimple;
this.listBox2.Size = new System.Drawing.Size(120, 95);
this.listBox2.TabIndex = 6;
//
// listBox3
//
this.listBox3.Location =
            new System.Drawing.Point(152, 160);
this.listBox3.Name = "listBox3";
this.listBox3.SelectionMode =
     System.Windows.Forms.SelectionMode.MultiSimple;
this.listBox3.Size = new System.Drawing.Size(120, 95);
this.listBox3.TabIndex = 7;
```

```
//
// listBox4
//
this.listBox4.Location
            = new System.Drawing.Point(280, 160);
this.listBox4.Name = "listBox4";
this.listBox4.SelectionMode =
      System.Windows.Forms.SelectionMode.MultiSimple;
this.listBox4.Size = new System.Drawing.Size(120, 95);
this.listBox4.TabIndex = 8;
//
// listBox5
//
this.listBox5.Location =
             new System.Drawing.Point(408, 160);
this.listBox5.Name = "listBox5";
this.listBox5.SelectionMode =
      System.Windows.Forms.SelectionMode.MultiSimple;
this.listBox5.Size = new System.Drawing.Size(120, 95);
this.listBox5.TabIndex = 9;
//
// listBox6
//
this.listBox6.Location =
             new System.Drawing.Point(544, 160);
this.listBox6.Name = "listBox6";
this.listBox6.SelectionMode =
      System.Windows.Forms.SelectionMode.MultiSimple;
this.listBox6.Size = new System.Drawing.Size(120, 95);
this.listBox6.TabIndex = 10;
//
// label2
//
this.label2.Location =
             new System.Drawing.Point(32, 264);
this.label2.Name = "label2";
this.label2.TabIndex = 11;
this.label2.Text = "Table 1";
//
// label3
//
this.label3.Location =
             new System.Drawing.Point(168, 264);
this.label3.Name = "label3";
this.label3.TabIndex = 12;
this.label3.Text = "Table 2";
//
// label4
//
```

```
this.label4.Location =
            new System.Drawing.Point(288, 264);
this.label4.Name = "label4";
this.label4.TabIndex = 14;
this.label4.Text = "Table 3";
//
// label5
//
this.label5.Location =
            new System.Drawing.Point(424, 264);
this.label5.Name = "label5";
this.label5.TabIndex = 15;
this.label5.Text = "Table 4";
//
// label6
//
this.label6.Location =
           new System.Drawing.Point(560, 264);
this.label6.Name = "label6";
this.label6.TabIndex = 16;
this.label6.Text = "Table 5";
//
// button4
//
this.button4.Enabled = false;
this.button4.Location =
            new System.Drawing.Point(56, 312);
this.button4.Name = "button4";
this.button4.TabIndex = 17;
this.button4.Text = "Submit";
this.button4.Click +=
     new System.EventHandler(this.button4_Click);
//
// button5
//
this.button5.Location =
           new System.Drawing.Point(448, 120);
this.button5.Name = "button5";
this.button5.TabIndex = 19;
this.button5.Text = "Display";
this.button5.Click += new
      System.EventHandler(this.button5_Click);
//
// textBox2
//
this.textBox2.Location =
           new System.Drawing.Point(168, 312);
this.textBox2.Multiline = true;
this.textBox2.Name = "textBox2";
```

```
    this.textBox2.Size = new System.Drawing.Size(392, 128);
    this.textBox2.TabIndex = 20;
    this.textBox2.Text = "";
    //
    // Form1
    //
    this.AutoScaleBaseSize = new System.Drawing.Size(5, 13);
    this.ClientSize = new System.Drawing.Size(692, 466);
    this.Controls.AddRange
     (new System.Windows.Forms.Control[] {
       this.textBox2, this.button5, this.button4,
       this.label6, this.label5, this.label4,
       this.label3, this.label2, this.listBox6,
       this.listBox5, this.listBox4, this.listBox3,
       this.listBox2, this.label1, this.textBox1,
       this.listBox1, this.button3, this.button2,
       this.button1});
    this.Name = "Form1";
    this.Text = "Search Sales";
    this.ResumeLayout(false);
  }
    #endregion

    /// <summary>
    /// The main entry point for the application.
    /// </summary>
  [STAThread]
  static void Main()
  {
    Application.Run(new Form1());
  }

  /* Combines the selected ListBox items into a string.
   * The start argument is the initial value of the string,
   * while the argument c is the character used to separate
   * the selected items.
   */
  public String Build(String start, char c )
  {
    String s = start;
    ListBox.SelectedObjectCollection colNames;
    for(int i=0; i<indices.Length; i++)
    {
    colNames = columns[indices[i]}.SelectedItems;
    for (int j = 0; j < colNames.Count; j++)
    {
      s += tableName[indices[i]}+ '.' + colNames[j] + ;
    }
    }
```

```
  return s;
}

/* Deselects selected columns.  The arguments are the
 * ListBox array, and the array of indices specifying
 * which tables the user selected.
 */
public void DeselectAll(ListBox[] columns, int[] indices)
{
  for(int i = 0; i < indices.Length; i++)
  columns[indices[i]}.ClearSelected();
}
private void button1_Click
          (object sender, System.EventArgs e)
{
  for(int i=0; i<indices.Length; i++)
  count += columns[indices[i]}.SelectedIndices.Count;
                                                  // Note 4
  resultCols = Build("", ',');                    // Note 5
  resultCols =
     resultCols.Substring(0, resultCols.Length-1);
  textBox2.Text = "Choose pairs of columns to join "
       + "each time pressing Join "
       + "and/or select a field, enter a value for it "
       + "in the text field, and press Enter Value. "
       + "If done, press Submit";
  button2.Enabled = true;
  button3.Enabled = true;
  button1.Enabled = false;
  DeselectAll(columns, indices);                  // Note 6
  query += resultCols + " FROM " + fromTables;    // Note 7
  button4.Enabled = true;
}
private void button2_Click
            (object sender, System.EventArgs e)
{
  String keyword = "";
  if (firstJoin)                                  // Note 8
  {
  keyword = " WHERE ";
  firstJoin = false;
  }
  else
  keyword = " AND ";
  joinClauses = Build(keyword,'=');
  joinClauses =
     joinClauses.Substring(0,joinClauses.Length-1);
  DeselectAll(columns,indices);
  query += joinClauses;
```

```
}
private void button3_Click
            (object sender, System.EventArgs e)
{
  String keyword = "";
  if (firstJoin)
  {
  keyword = " WHERE ";
  firstJoin = false;
  }
  else
  keyword = " AND ";
  condition = Build(keyword,'=');
  condition += textBox1.Text;
  query += condition;
}
private void button5_Click
            (object sender, System.EventArgs e)
{
  indices = new int[listBox1.SelectedIndices.Count];
  listBox1.SelectedIndices.CopyTo(indices, 0);     // Note 9
  for(int i = 0; i < indices.Length; i++)
  {
  colLabel[indices[i]}.Text
          = tableName[indices[i]};                // Note 10
  fromTables += tableName[indices[i]} +',';       // Note 11
  }
  fromTables =
  fromTables.Substring(0,fromTables.Length-1);
                                                  // Note 12
  button5.Enabled = false;
  textBox2.Text =
  "Highlight the fields to be part of the result set "
  + "and press the Select button.";
  for(int i = 0; i < indices.Length; i++)
  {
  DataTable cols = con.GetOleDbSchemaTable
    (OleDbSchemaGuid.Columns,
   new object[]{null,null,tableName[indices[i]},null});
                                                  // Note 13
 foreach(DataRow row in cols.Rows)
   columns[indices[i]}.Items.Add(row[3]);         // Note 14
  }
  button1.Enabled = true;
}
private void button4_Click
        (object sender, System.EventArgs e)
{
  cmd.CommandText = query;
```

```
        OleDbDataReader reader = cmd.ExecuteReader();
        textBox2.Text = "";
        while(reader.Read())
        {
        String s = "";
        for(int i = 0; i < count; i++)
            s += reader.GetString(i) + ' ';              // Note 15
        textBox2.AppendText(s);
        }
        button4.Enabled = false;
        button2.Enabled = false;
        button3.Enabled = false;
      }
    }
  }
```

Note 1: These are the variables we declared to support our event handling code.

Note 2: We added this code to make the connection, get the `Sales` table names, and put the list boxes and labels in arrays.

Note 3: `private void InitializeComponent()`

Visual Studio .NET writes this entire method. We do not touch it because it gets regenerated when we make changes to the form in the designer view.

Note 4: `count += columns[indices[i]}.SelectedIndices.Count;`

We save the total number of columns in the result set for the query, obtaining it by adding up the number of columns selected in each `ListBox`. After executing the query, we use `count` to list the results.

Note 5: `resultCols = Build("", ',');`

The `Build` method combines the selected item into a string, using the second argument as the separator. The first argument is the initial value of the string.

Note 6: `DeselectAll(columns, indices);`

The `DeselectAll` method deselects each of the selected items so the user does not have to manually deselect the previous choices before making selections at the next step toward building the query.

Note 7: `query += resultCols + " FROM " + fromTables;`

We continue to build the query we wish to execute, adding the pieces we have constructed so far.

Note 8: `if (firstJoin)`

The first condition in the query, if any, follows `WHERE`, and the remaining conditions follow `AND`. We use the bool variable `firstJoin` to specify whether or not this is the first condition.

Note 9: `listBox1.SelectedIndices.CopyTo(indices, 0);`

We constructed the tables list to allow the user to select multiple items. The `SelectedIndices` property returns the array of index numbers corresponding to selected items, which we copy to the `indices` array.

Note 10: `colLabel[indices[i]}.Text = tableName[indices[i]};`

Initially, we labeled the five tables, `Table1, . . . , Table5`. We change the labels underneath the selected tables to their actual table names. We could have labeled all five tables correctly, but chose this to differentiate those tables the user selected from the unselected ones.

Note 11: `fromTables += tableName[indices[i]} +',';`

We save the names of the selected tables in a string, separated by commas, to use after `FROM` when we construct the SQL `SELECT` query.

Note 12:
```
fromTables =
        fromTables.Substring(0,fromTables.Length-1);
```

This removes the last comma.

Note 13:
```
DataTable cols = con.GetOleDbSchemaTable
   (OleDbSchemaGuid.Columns,
   new object[]{null,null,tableName[indices[i]},null});
```

For each table the user selected, we get the names of its columns.

Note 14: `columns[indices[i]}.Items.Add(row[3]);`

We add each column name to the `ListBox` representing the selected table.

Note 15: `s += reader.GetString(i) + ' ';`

For simplicity, we have not dealt with the types of each table column. Knowing the column type would allow us to use a more specific method than `GetString`. For example, knowing the column has type `INTEGER` would allow us to use the `GetInt 32` method, but the `GetString` method will also work for every type, although sometimes the formatting will not be as nice.

The BIG Picture

A graphical user interface lets the user compose a query. At each stage the user presses a button that causes some actions to occur and instructions to appear in the text box. The user first selects the tables to be used, and then the fields to be displayed. The user may add conditions by joining tables or requiring a field to have a specific value. After pressing the `Submit` button, the user sees the results in the text box.

Try It Yourself ➤

✓ Test Your Understanding

19. Run Example 15.7 to execute the query that returns the names of customers who placed orders on March 22, 1999, but this time add the condition that the `OrderDate` is March 22, 1999 before the join condition that `Customer.CustomerID = Orders.CustomerID`. This shows we can enter conditions in any order.

SUMMARY

- C# allows us to create database tables; insert, update, and delete data; and query a database from a C# program. Relational databases store data in tables, and each table has a key that uniquely identifies each row. As our example, we use the `Sales` database with five tables. The `Customer` table has `CustomerID` as its key. The `Orders` table has `OrderNumber` as its key, but also includes the foreign keys `CustomerID` and `SalespersonID`, which refer to entries in the `Customer` and `Salesperson` tables to eliminate duplicating the information in the `Orders` table. The `OrderItem` table has a compound key `(OrderNumber, ItemNumber)`; we need both values to identify an order item.
- Structured Query Language (SQL) provides an interface to database systems from different vendors. Users can write statements that each database will translate to process the desired request. In this text we use the `CREATE`, `INSERT`, `UPDATE`, `DELETE`, and `SELECT` statements. The `CREATE` statement defines data in a table. This statement may use data types that are valid in a particular database system. In this text we use `VARCHAR(N)`, a variable size character string of maximum size `N`, `INTEGER`, `DATE`, and `DECIMAL`.
- Once connected to the database, we use the `CreateCommand` method to create a command with an `ExecuteNonQuery` method we can use to execute SQL statements to create a new table or to insert values into a table. We could also create and populate tables using the database system, outside of C#.
- To retrieve information from the database we use the `ExecuteReader` method, which returns a `DataReader` to execute SQL `SELECT` statements. To get the fields in a row we use the `getXXX` method, where `XXX` is the type of the data. We use `GetInt32` for an `INTEGER` field and `GetString` for a `VARCHAR` field.
- The `SELECT` statement has various options, including a `WHERE` clause to add conditions, `SELECT DISTINCT` to remove duplicates, and `ORDER BY` to sort the result. A `SELECT` statement may refer to one table or may join information from several tables.
- The connection class provides a method that gives information about the database. We can find the names of its tables and the names and types of the columns of each table. We can create a `DataSet` and use these techniques to find information about it.
- Aggregate functions compute values using all the rows of the table. We use `SUM`, `MAX`, `MIN`, `AVG`, and `COUNT` in our examples. Stored procedures allow us to pass arguments to a statement to reuse it without having to repeat its translation to an efficient implementation in the database system. Transactions permit us to rollback SQL commands in the event the whole sequence did not complete successfully.

- Our case study builds a graphical user interface for the `Sales` database, allowing users to specify various parts of a `SELECT` statement and execute it.

PROGRAM MODIFICATION EXERCISES

1. Modify Example 15.2 to read the data from a file to insert into the tables.
2. Modify Example 15.7 to use the most appropriate `getXXX` method rather than the `GetString` method referred to in Note 15.
3. Modify Example 15.7 to allow `>=`, `<=`, `>`, and `<` operators in addition to `=`.
4. Modify Example 15.7 to check that exactly two columns, from different tables, have been selected when the user presses the *`Join`* button.
5. Modify Example 15.7 to add a `Checkbox` to require that the query removes duplicates from the result.
6. Modify Example 15.7 to check that exactly one column has been selected when the user presses the *`Enter Value`* button.
7. Modify Example 15.7 to add column headings in the output.
8. Modify Example 15.7 to allow the user to keep executing queries.
9. Modify Example 15.2 to create a `Sales1` database that is like `Sales` except that it has `LastName` and `FirstName` fields, instead of `CustomerName`, in the `Customer` table.

PROGRAM DESIGN EXERCISES

10. Write a graphical user interface for the `Sales` database that lists all customer names in one `ComboBox` and all products in another. When the user selects a customer name and a product and presses the *`Submit`* button, display a list with the customer name, product, quantity, and date of orders by customers with that name for that product. Use stored procedures wherever possible.
11. Write a graphical user interface for a salesperson using the `Sales` database. The salesperson should be able to enter new orders. Rollback the order if, after part of an order has been entered, a part of the order cannot be filled because of insufficient quantity of a product.
12. Develop an `Account` database to use with an electronic banking system. Provide a user interface for a client to transfer funds from one account to another. The user should be able to select the source and target accounts and enter an amount to transfer.
13. Design and populate a database for a car rental system. Allow the client to check availability of a category of car and to make reservations.
14. Design and populate a database for a record collection. Provide a screen for the collection's owner to add and remove items, to change entries, and to search.
15. Design and populate a database for sports records. Use an almanac or search the Web for sample data. Provide a screen for the user to add and remove items, to change entries, and to search.

16 ASP.NET

16.1 HTML
16.2 Web Server Controls and Code Behind
16.3 Three-Tiered Architectures
16.4. Session Tracking

The browser provides access to web sites all over the world. It is the primary mode of computing for many users. Static World Wide Web pages return the same content to every user, but very often users submit information and receive responses based on that information. The web server uses programs running on the server to provide the response tailored to the client. Microsoft includes ASP.NET in the .NET Framework to support dynamic web pages. ASP (Active Server Pages), the previous web technology from Microsoft, in its new form uses the .NET Framework Class Library.

Browsers display HTML documents. HTML (Hypertext Markup Language) is the language used to write web pages, using markup tags to indicate how the browser should present the document. An HTML form can pass information to a C# program running on the server, called the code behind, which processes it and sends results back to the client. This approach separates the presentation in the web form seen by the client using the browser from the content in the code behind run on the server. A web page designer can focus on the presentation while a C# developer prepares the code behind.

With a three-tiered architecture, the client communicates with a code behind on the middle tier, which in turn connects with a database server on the third tier. In this way clients do not have to connect directly to a database.

HTTP connections are stateless, meaning that when a client connects again there is no record of previous connections. Session tracking allows servers to maintain client information from one connection to the next, an essential feature needed for many web applications, including web commerce.

OBJECTIVES

- Introduce HTML
- Use web forms and code behind to provide dynamic web pages
- Add database connectivity in a three-tiered architecture
- Use session tracking to maintain user information

16.1 HTML

The Internet includes many applications, the most used of which is email. The rapidly growing World Wide Web (WWW) allows computers all over the world to explore the enormous web of links from one site to another for educational, commercial, and recreational purposes. We introduce the HTML notation used to write web pages.

Some HTML tags

Web page files often have the `.html` extension. We use **HTML** (Hypertext Markup Language) to create the hypertext files found on the Web. This markup language adds tags to specify the formatting of the text. For example, the tag `<br>` causes a break to a new line. A browser such as Internet Explorer interprets these tags, formatting the page for the client. Using tags allows browsers of different capabilities to interpret the tags differently. For example, the tag `<em>`, requesting emphasis for the text that follows, might cause one browser to display the text in italics, but another browser, without the capability to use italics, might underline that text for emphasis.

The World Wide Web must adapt itself to many computers with differing capabilities. By using HTML tags, web documents can be displayed by a variety of browsers, including those on terminals without graphics capabilities.

Although HTML is not hard to learn to use, we need an introduction to experiment with web forms. To get the flavor of HTML we list a few tags in Figure 16.1 and use them to write a rudimentary web page. Tags are not case sensitive; the tag `<BR>` is the same as `<br>`.

 	Break to the next line
<p>	New paragraph (after a blank line)
<em> ... </em>	Emphasize the text
<strong> ... </strong>	Strongly emphasize the text
<title> ... </title>	Title, displayed separately from text
<h1> ... </h1>	Top-level header
<h3> ... </h3>	Third-level header (lowest is sixth)
<ul> ... </ul>	An unordered list
<li>	Element of a list
<a> ... </a>	An anchor, a hypertext link
<img>	An image

FIGURE 16.1 **Some HTML tags**

We can insert an empty tag such as <br> anywhere to cause a line break. Nonempty tags such as <em> have a closing form using the forward slash that marks the end of the text covered by that tag. Thus

```
<em> .NET is fun. </em>
```

would emphasize the text, *.NET is fun*. The six levels of header tags specify the importance of the header, with `h1` being the most important and `h6` the least. Browsers will try to make the more important headers larger and more impressive. An unordered list includes, between its starting and ending tags, various list elements with tags <li>.

Some tags use attributes embedded in the tag to provide information needed to interpret that tag. The anchor tag uses the `href` attribute to specify the URL of a hypertext link. For example, to link to Microsoft's .NET home page we can use the anchor

```
<a href = "http://www.microsoft.com/net/"> Microsoft's .NET
home page. </a>
```

The `href` attribute gives the URL for Microsoft's .NET home page. The text, *Microsoft's .NET home page* will usually appear underlined and in blue, indicating that a mouse click will cause the browser to request, using HTTP, the Microsoft server to serve up its .NET home page HTML file, which the browser then interprets, displaying Microsoft's .NET home page.

The client must be connected to the Internet to link to other computers. Anchors can also link to files on the same machine using a relative URL. For example, to link to a file `funStuff.html` in the same directory, we could use the anchor

```
<a href = "funStuff.html"> some fun stuff </a>
```

We use the <img> tag to display an image, with an `src` attribute that gives the URL of the source of the picture. For example, to display a picture of the author of the text, found in the same directory as the web page itself, use

```
<img src="gittleman.gif">
```

A browser that cannot display graphics will fill the space with text such as `[IMAGE]`.

Example 16.1 shows an HTML file for a very simple web page, displayed in Figure 16.2, which uses some of the tags from Figure 16.1.

EXAMPLE 16.1 ■ AWebPage.html

```
<!-- Illustrates some html tags in
  -- a simple Web page.
  -->                                          <!-- Note 1 -->

<title> Let's try HTML </title>               <!-- Note 2 -->

<h1> .NET is fun </h1>                         <!-- Note 3 -->
<p>
```

```
<h3> With <em>C# and .NET</em> we can </h3>        <!-- Note 4 -->
<ul> <li> Do object-oriented programming           <!-- Note 5 -->
     <li> Create nifty graphics
     <li> Display dynamic Web pages
     <li> Network to remote computers
     <li> Deploy web services
</ul><p>

<strong>Download the .NET Framework SDK from</strong>
 <a href =
  "http://msdn.microsoft.com/netframework/downloads/">
Downloads for the .NET Framework </a>           <!-- Note 6 -->
<br>

<h2> Get ready -- Here comes the prof
<img src=gittleman.gif><br>                        <!-- Note 7 -->
     who wrote this web page </h2><br>
```

Note 1:

```
<!-- Illustrates some html tags in
  -- a simple Web page.
  -->
```

Comments in HTML documents start with `<!--` and end with `-->`

Note 2:

```
<title> Let's try HTML </title>
```

The title displays at the top of the frame, not in the document itself. Web search engines use the title in their searches.

Note 3:

```
<h1> .NET is fun </h1>
```

The text between the `h1` tags has the largest size.

FIGURE 16.2
Displaying `WebPage.html` in a browser

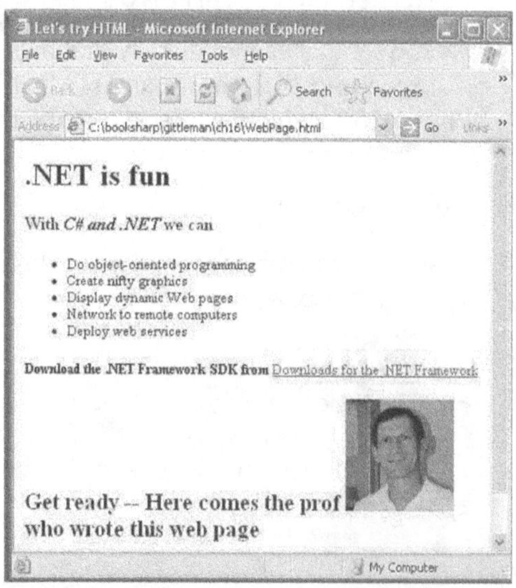

Note 4: `<h3> With <em>C# and .NET</em> we can </h3>`

The `em` tag causes the text to be displayed in italics.

Note 5: `<ul> <li> Do object-oriented programming`

Each item of an unordered list is preceded by a bullet.

Note 6:

```
<a href =
"http://msdn.microsoft.com/netframework/downloads/">
Downloads for the .NET Framework </a>
```

The URL of the anchor does not show up; the text between the <a> and </a> tags is underlined.

Note 7: `<img src=gittleman.gif><br>`

The image is a `.gif` file, a graphics format.

Use a browser to see this page. In Netscape Communicator, click on *`File`*, click on *`Open Page`*, and click on *`Choose File`* to locate the `WebPage.html` file. In Microsoft Internet Explorer, click on *`File`*, click on *`Open`*, and click on *`Browse`* to locate `WebPage.html`. The URL is a file URL, using the `file` protocol. The domain name of the server is just the local host, which can be omitted, so the URL looks like

```
file:///path/WebPage.html
```

where `path` is the path on the local machine to the `WebPage.html` file.

Figure 16.2 shows us browsing a local file, but this is just for testing purposes during development. We deploy web pages on a web site, making them available to anyone who has a browser and is connected to the Internet. Browsing the author's web site at

```
http://www.cecs.csulb.edu/~artg/AWebPage.html
```

will download this web page.

The web site runs a web server that expects web pages to be in a default directory often named *htdocs*. On the author's web site, the files `AWebPage.html` and `gittleman.gif` are in the `htdocs` folder.

The BIG Picture

Using a browser, we can connect to sites anywhere in the World Wide Web to display web pages written using HTML, the Hypertext Markup Language. HTML uses tags enclosed in angle brackets to indicate formatting.

✓Test Your Understanding

1. Which protocol does the browser use to download web pages?

2. Given the URL

```
http://www.cecs.csulb.edu/~artg/AWebPage.html
```

a. What is the protocol?
b. What is the domain name of the server?
c. What is the path to the resource?

3. What language do we use to write web pages?
4. Which header tag, h2 or h5, will most likely cause a more prominent display of the text to which it applies?
5. For what purpose is an HTML anchor tag used?

16.2 WEB SERVER CONTROLS AND CODE BEHIND

Web server controls provide much richer web pages. We use special HTML tags that the server translates into HTML for the particular client. When the user interacts with the control, our event handling code will be called. We first illustrate with the event handling code in the web page, and then put it in a separate code-behind file to separate the C# code from the HTML.

Hosting a Web Page

We need a .NET web server to host our web pages. With Microsoft Windows 2000 or XP operating systems we can install IIS (Internet Information Server) to host our web pages. If IIS is not available in this way, we can use a free hosting service such as `brinkster.com`.

To use IIS on Windows XP, we need to create a virtual directory, which we will use in the URL to enable IIS to locate the requested page. To create a virtual directory, we click on *Start, Control Panel, Administrative Tools, Internet Information Services* to open the Microsoft Management Console. Right-clicking on *Default Web Site, New, Virtual Directory* opens the Virtual Directory Creation Wizard. We click *Next*, enter `ch16` as the alias for our virtual directory, and click *Next*. We browse to find the directory that contains the web pages we want to host in this virtual directory. The examples in this chapter are contained in `C:\booksharp\gittleman\ch16`. We click *Next*, and *Next* again in the Permissions screen, and then click *Finish*.

To view the web page, `GetOrder.aspx`, of Example 16.2 we enter the URL

```
http://localhost/ch16/GetOrder.aspx
```

in the browser, which produces the screen of Figure 16.3. We would change `localhost` to the IP address of a remote host if we were not using the same machine as the host.

Adding Code to a Web Page

The web page shown in Figure 16.3 contains `TextBox`, `Button`, and `Label` web controls. These controls execute on the server, generating the response back to the client using the browser. To place these controls on the page we use tags with the asp prefix to specify server controls. For example, the tag

FIGURE 16.3
A web form

```
<asp:textbox id="Order" Columns="20" runat="server" />
```

represents a `TextBox`. The server will refer to this `id` in its event handling code. We specify 20 columns and use the `runat` attribute to execute this control at the server.

In this simple example, the user enters something to order and clicks the *Submit* button. The server responds by putting a message in a label, echoing the user's order. We include the event handling code inside a `<script>` tag on the web page. Figure 16.4 shows the form after the user clicks `Submit`.

EXAMPLE 16.2 ■ GetOrder.aspx

```
<!-- Illustrates a form with TextBox, Button, and
  -- Label web controls.  Includes event handling code.
  -->

<html>
<head><title>Get Order</title></head>

<script language="c#" runat="server">          <!--  Note 1 -->
  public void Submit_Click(Object Sender, EventArgs e) {
    output.Text = "You ordered " + Order.Text;  <!--  Note 2 -->
  }
</script>

<body>
<h3>Enter an order</h3>
<form method="get" runat="server">              <!-- Note 3 -->
  Order: <asp:textbox id="Order" Columns="20" runat="server" />
         <br/>
         <asp:button id="submit" Text="Submit" runat="server"
                  onclick="Submit_Click" />      <!-- Note 4 -->
         <p/>
         <asp:label id="output" runat="server" />
```

```
</form>
</body>
</html>
```

Note 1: `<script language="c#" runat="server">`

The <script> tag includes C# event handling code. We use the `language` attribute to specify C# and the `runat` attribute to indicate that the server will run this code.

Note 2: `output.Text = "You ordered " + Order.Text;`

When the user clicks the *Submit* button, the server will execute the `Button_Click` method which includes the text from the `Order` `TextBox` in a message in the `output` `Label`.

Note 3: `<form method="get" runat="server">`

The <form> tag creates a form for the user to send information to the server. Using the `GET` method causes the data to be appended to the URL, as we see in Figure 16.4. Before adding the text `food` to the URL, the server adds a coded state field that it keeps in a hidden HTML tag that it writes. When the user connects, the server can read this tag to learn what the user has done previously at this site during this session. We can click on `View, Source` in Internet Explorer to see the HTML file that the server writes, translating the web controls with `asp` prefixes to standard HTML tags. Using the `POST` method will send the form data separately from the URL.

Note 4:
```
<asp:button id="submit" Text="Submit" runat="server"
            onclick="Submit_Click" />
```

For the button, we use the `onclick` attribute to register the `Submit_Click` method to handle the `Click` event for the button.

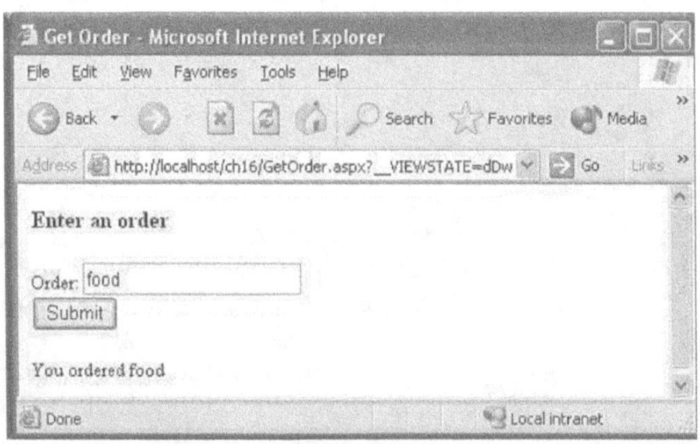

FIGURE 16.4 **The response to the user's entry**

Web designers specialize in creating web pages and may not be qualified or interested in writing C# code. Correspondingly, C# developers specialize in programming and may not be qualified or interested in creating web pages. Using code behind, the web designer can create the web page and refer to code in another file created by a C# developer.

In Example 16.3 we rewrite Example 16.2 to use the code behind of Example 16.4. We use the `.aspx` extension for the web page and the `.aspx.cs` extension for the corresponding code behind program. We put the code-behind file in the host directory along with the web page. Using this form will produce figures like Figures 16.3 and 16.4.

EXAMPLE 16.3 ■ GetOrderBehind.aspx

```
<!-- Uses a code-behind file for event handling.
  -->

<%@ Page Src="GetOrderBehind.aspx.cs"
     Inherits="GetOrderBehind"%>
                                                  <!--Note 1 -->
<html>
<head><title>Get Order</title></head>
<body>
<h3>Enter an order</h3>
<form method="get" runat="server">
  Order:
    <asp:textbox id="Order" Columns="20" runat="server" />
    <br/>
    <asp:button id="submit" Text="Submit" runat="server" />
    <p/>
    <asp:label id="output" runat="server" />
</form>
</body>
</html>
```

■

Note 1:
```
<%@ Page Src="GetOrderBehind.aspx.cs"
                   Inherits="GetOrderBehind"%>
```

The `Page` directive in a `<%@    %>` tag specifies attributes for this page. We use the `Src` attribute to specify the source code-behind file. The `Inherits` attribute defines a code-behind class for the page to inherit. It can be any class derived from the `Page` class in the `System.Web.UI` namespace.

EXAMPLE 16.4 ■ GetOrderBehind.aspx.cs

```
/* Provides a code-behind file for event handling.
 */

using System;
using System.Web.UI;
using System.Web.UI.WebControls;
public class GetOrderBehind : Page {                      // Note 1
  protected Button submit;                                // Note 2
  protected Label output;
  protected TextBox Order;

  private void Page_Init() {                              // Note 3
    submit.Click += new EventHandler(Submit_Click);
  }
  public void Submit_Click(Object Sender, EventArgs e) {
    output.Text= "You ordered " + Order.Text;
  }
}
```

Note 1: `public class GetOrderBehind : Page {`

The code-behind class must inherit from the `Page` class.

Note 2: `protected Button submit;`

We declare the web server controls we used in the form of Example 16.3 using variable names that match the `id` attributes for the corresponding controls used in the form.

Note 3: `private void Page_Init() {`

When we request a page from the server, it compiles the page. ASP.NET uses event-driven processing. An `Init` event occurs when the page is initialized. The `Page_Init` method handles the `Init` event. Here we register an event handler for the button `Click` event.

Posting Data

Using the GET method, the browser appends the data, including the state in the hidden field, to the URL. A better approach uses the POST method to send the data after the request. Posting makes it easier to send larger amounts of data and keeps it out of the very public URL. Example 16.5 simulates an ice cream order using web controls handled by the code behind of Example 16.6. Figure 16.5 shows the form and the response.

EXAMPLE 16.5 ■ PostOrder.aspx

```
<!-- Posts an ice cream order.
  -->

<% @Page Src="PostOrder.aspx.cs" Inherits="PostOrder"%>
<html>
<head><title>Post Order</title></head>
<body>
<form method="post" runat="server">
  <strong>Name:</strong>
    <asp:textbox id="name" columns="20" runat="server"/><br>
  <strong>Password:</strong>
    <asp:textbox id="password" columns="10"
        textmode="password" runat="server"/><br>
                                                <!-- Note 1 -->
  <strong>Flavor:</strong>
    <asp:listbox id="flavor" runat="server">
        <asp:listitem text="Vanilla" />         <!-- Note 2 -->
        <asp:listitem text="Chocolate" />
        <asp:listitem text="Strawberry" />
    </asp:listbox><p>
  <strong>Toppings:</strong>
    <asp:checkboxlist id="toppings" runat="server">
        <asp:listitem value="Hot Fudge"/>       <!-- Note 3 -->
        <asp:listitem value="Butterscotch"/>
        <asp:listitem value="Nuts"/>
        <asp:listitem value="Whipped Cream"/>
    </asp:checkboxlist>
    <asp:radiobuttonlist id="place" runat="server">
        <asp:listitem value="Eat here"/>
        <asp:listitem value="Take out"/>
    </asp:radiobuttonlist>
    <asp:button id="submit" Text="Order" runat="server" />
    <asp:button id="reset" Text="Reset" runat="server" />
    <p/>
    <asp:label id="output" runat="server" />
</form>
</form></body></html>
```

■

FIGURE 16.5
Posting an order

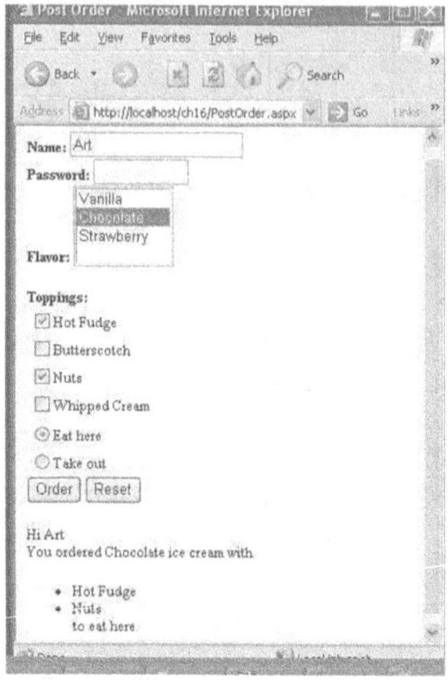

Note 1:

```
<asp:textbox id="password" columns="10"
        textmode="password" runat="server"/>
```

We use the `textmode` attribute to create a `TextBox` to input a password so the text is masked. We do not actually use the password in the code-behind file.

Note 2:

```
<asp:listitem text="Vanilla" />
```

The `text` attribute is displayed in the `ListBox`.

Note 3:

```
<asp:listitem value="Hot Fudge"/>
```

The `value` attribute is displayed next to the `CheckBox`.

EXAMPLE 16.6 ■ PostOrder.aspx.cs

```
/* Provides a code-behind file to handle
 * data posted from the form of Example 16.5.
 */

using System;
using System.Web.UI;
using System.Web.UI.WebControls;
public class PostOrder : Page {
  protected Button submit;
  protected Button reset;
  protected TextBox name;
  protected ListBox flavor;
  protected CheckBoxList toppings;
```

```
  protected RadioButtonList place;
  protected Label output;

  private void Page_Init() {
    submit.Click += new EventHandler(Submit_Click);
    reset.Click += new EventHandler(Reset_Click);
  }
  public void Submit_Click(Object Sender, EventArgs e) {
    output.Text= "Hi " + name.Text + "<br>You ordered "
        + flavor.SelectedItem.Text + " ice cream with <ul>";
    for(int i = 0; i < toppings.Items.Count; i++)
      if(toppings.Items[i].Selected)                    // Note 1
         output.Text += "<li>" + toppings.Items[i].Text;
    if(place.SelectedItem.Value == "Eat here")          // Note 2
      output.Text += "<br> to eat here.";
    else
      output.Text += "<br> to go.";
  }
  public void Reset_Click(Object Sender, EventArgs e) {
    name.Text = "";
    output.Text = "";
    toppings.SelectedIndex = -1;                         // Note 3
    place.SelectedIndex = -1;
    flavor.SelectedIndex = -1;
  }
}
```

Note 1: `if(toppings.Items[i].Selected)`

We can select more than one topping. We go through the list of toppings, adding those that the user selected to the list in the label containing the response.

Note 2: `if(place.SelectedItem.Value == "Eat here")`

We compare the `Value` property of the `ListItem` to the `value` attribute to see which `RadioButton` the user selected.

Note 3: `toppings.SelectedIndex = -1;`

Setting the `SelectedIndex` property to -1 deselects all items.

The BIG Picture

Web controls allow us to divide the web application into a form created by a web designer with events handled by code created by a C# developer. Using the GET method attaches data to the URL. Using the POST method sends the data after the request.

✓Test Your Understanding

Try It Yourself ➤ **6.** Find a web page host, create a virtual directory, and enter the appropriate URL in a browser to browse the `GetOrder` page.

Try It Yourself ➤ **7.** Modify Example 16.2 to use the POST method rather than GET. What changes do you observe?

8. What change to Example 16.4 would we have to make if we changed the `id` attribute in Example 16.3 from `submit` to `sub`?

Try It Yourself ➤ **9.** Omit the `Text` attribute of the `submit` button in Example 16.5. How will Figure 16.5 change as a consequence of this change?

16.3 THREE-TIERED ARCHITECTURES

In a two-tiered client–server application the client connects directly to a database server. The client handles the business logic, the code needed to implement the business model, and the presentation of the data. The inevitably frequent changes in business logic require changes to the programs running on each client. Adding a middle tier to handle business logic simplifies maintenance and does not require as much computational power on client machines.

Using a Database in a Three-Tiered Architecture

We can use a web page to access a database. In a three-tiered architecture, the client tier contains a user interface. The client connects to a middle-tier server that processes the client's request, accessing a database server in the third tier to store and receive information. In this way the business logic resides in middleware and can be changed without reconfiguring the various clients.

Our `Sales` form simply executes the client's SQL query. We leave it to the exercises to design a form to create a query from information supplied by the client. In this example we provide a form with a text box for the user to enter an SQL query, which the code behind executes.

EXAMPLE 16.7 ■ Sales.aspx

```
<!-- Executes a query to the Sales database
  -- entered by the user.
  -->

<%@ Page src="Sales.aspx.cs" Inherits="Sales"%>
<html>
<head><title>Sales</title></head>
<body>
<form method="post" runat="server">
  <strong>Select:</strong>
    <asp:textbox id="select" TextMode= "MultiLine"
```

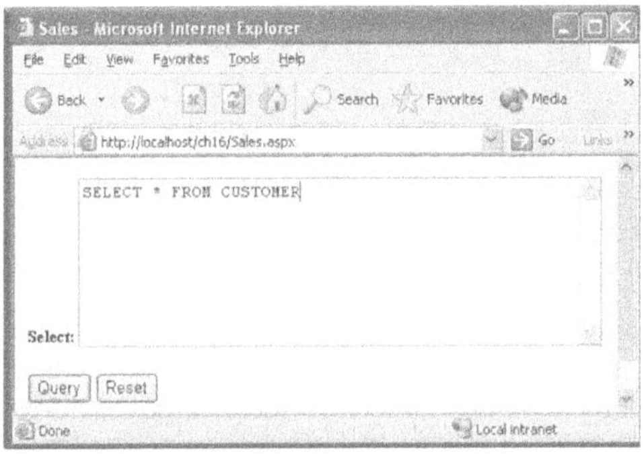

FIGURE 16.6 **Making a `Sales` query**

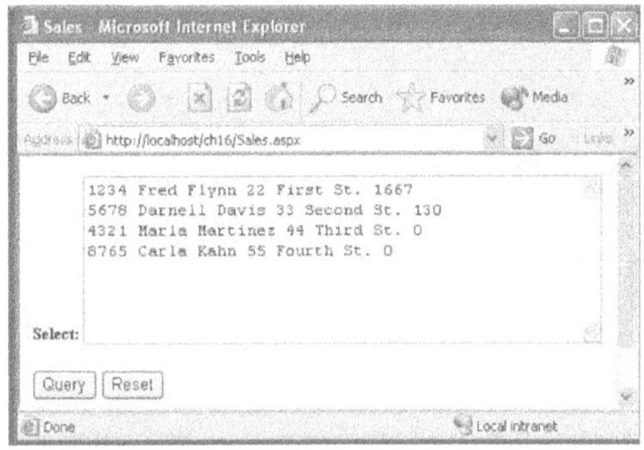

FIGURE 16.7 **The result of the query**

```
        Columns="50" Rows="8" runat="server" /><p> <-- Note 1 -->
      <asp:button id="submit" Text="Query" runat="server" />
      <asp:button id="reset" Text="Reset" runat="server" />
      <p/>
      <asp:label id="output" runat="server" />
</form></body></html>
```

Note 1:

```
<asp:textbox id="select" TextMode= "MultiLine"
          Columns="50" Rows="8" runat="server" /><p>
```

We use the `TextMode` property to specify a multiline text box so the user can enter a longer query.

In the code-behind file, we connect to the database in the constructor. Figure 16.6 shows the query and Figure 16.7 shows the result.

EXAMPLE 16.8 ■ Sales.aspx.cs

```
/* Queries the Sales database.
 */

using System;
using System.Data;
using System.Data.OleDb;
using System.Web.UI;
using System.Web.UI.WebControls;
public class Sales : Page {
  protected OleDbCommand cmd;
  protected TextBox select;
  protected Button submit;
  protected Button reset;
```

```
  protected Label output;

  public Sales() {
    String connect = "Provider=Microsoft.JET.OLEDB.4.0;"
     + @"data source=c:\booksharp\gittleman\ch15\Sales.mdb";
    OleDbConnection con = new OleDbConnection(connect);
    con.Open();
    cmd = con.CreateCommand();
  }
  private void Page_Init() {
    submit.Click += new EventHandler(Submit_Click);
    reset.Click += new EventHandler(Reset_Click);
  }
  public void Submit_Click(Object Sender, EventArgs e) {
    cmd.CommandText = select.Text;
    OleDbDataReader reader = cmd.ExecuteReader();
    output.Text = "" + reader.FieldCount;
    select.Text = "";
    while(reader.Read()) {
      for(int i = 0; i < reader.FieldCount; i++)
        select.Text += reader.GetValue(i) + " ";        // Note 1
      select.Text += "\n";
    }
    reader.Close();
  }
  public void Reset_Click(Object Sender, EventArgs e) {
    select.Text = "";
    output.Text = "";
  }
}
```

Note 1: `select.Text += reader.GetValue(i) + " ";`

The `GetValue` method gets the value of the column in its native format.

The BIG Picture

A three-tiered architecture configures business logic on a middle tier. The client handles the graphic presentation and communicates with the middle tier, which handles the content. The middle tier stores and retrieves data from a database server on the third tier. This architecture keeps business logic in a central location, making it easier and cheaper to perform updates. Powerful middle-tier application servers can scale to meet the demands of serving many clients.

✓ Test Your Understanding

Try It Yourself ➤ **10.** Browse the form of Example 16.7 and enter a query to find the names of all the salespersons. Describe the result.

Try It Yourself ➤ **11.** Change the method in Example 16.7 from POST to GET. Does the example still function properly? Why or why not?

16.4. SESSION TRACKING

Internet commerce will continue to grow in importance. The HTTP protocol does not automatically maintain a connection, so if a customer selects an item and moves to another page, perhaps for an additional item, the connection is lost. The vendor would like to keep the customer's information, including the items ordered, to allow the customer to add items to the order and complete the purchase. The session tracking API lets a servlet keep track of clients from one connection to the next. Session tracking may be implemented using cookies, which are bits of information sent by the web server to the client, and then sent from the client back to the browser when it accesses that page again. A cookie uniquely identifies a client.

The `Session` property of the `Page` class holds an `HttpSessionState` object. We use the key `"items"` to store an `ArrayList` in the `Session` to hold the user's current order. Each time the user connects we update the list of items ordered. Another user will have a different `Session`. Example 16.9 defines a form for the client to place an order.

EXAMPLE 16.9 ■ SessionOrder.aspx

```
<!-- The user enters an order.  The code behind will
  -- maintain a session for each user.
  -->

<%@ Page src="SessionOrder.aspx.cs"
Inherits="SessionOrder"%>
<html>
<head><title>Session Order</title></head>
<body>
<form method="post" runat="server">
  <strong><h3>Choose the items you would like to order.</h3>
  </strong><p>
  <asp:checkboxlist id="order" runat="server">
      <asp:listitem value="C# Book"/>
      <asp:listitem value="Baseball"/>
      <asp:listitem value="Bicycle"/>
      <asp:listitem value="Dress"/>
      <asp:listitem value="Shirt"/>
      <asp:listitem value="Shoes"/>
```

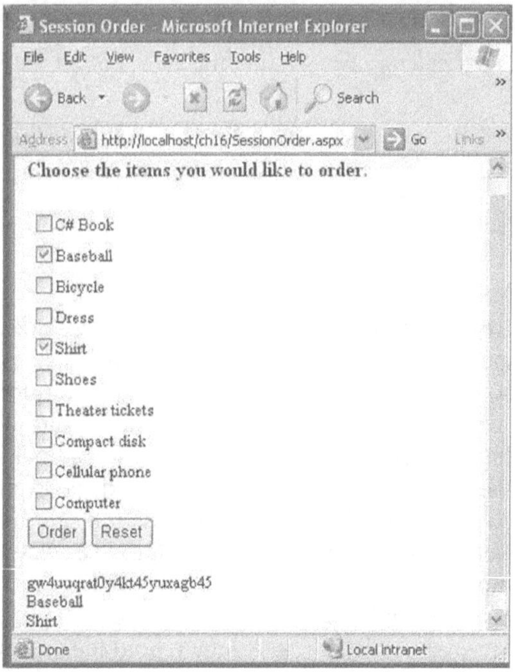

FIGURE 16.8 **Placing an order using a session**

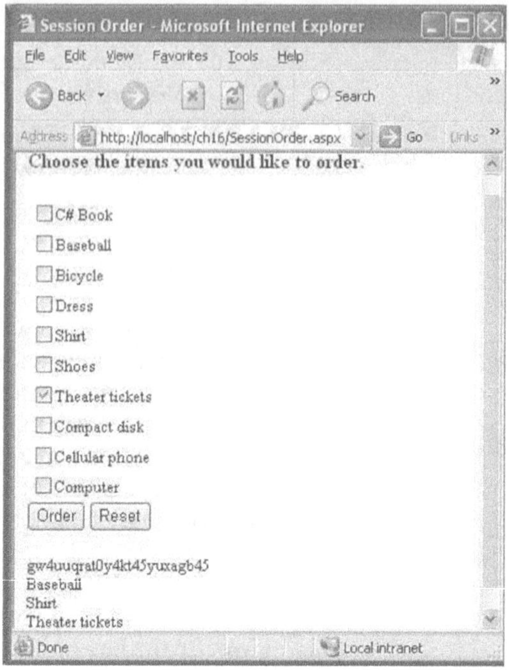

FIGURE 16.9 **Adding to the original order**

```
        <asp:listitem value="Theater tickets"/>
        <asp:listitem value="Compact disk"/>
        <asp:listitem value="Cellular phone"/>
        <asp:listitem value="Computer"/>
    </asp:checkboxlist>
    <asp:button id="submit" Text="Order" runat="server" />
    <asp:button id="reset" Text="Reset" runat="server" />
      <p/>
    <asp:label id="output" runat="server" />
  </form></body></html>
```

Figure 16.8 shows the order form, with the user's choices and the response showing the user's session id and a list of all items ordered so far. If the same user places another order, the session will add the new item to the original order. Figure 16.9 shows the same user ordering another item. The session id is the same and the list includes the items from both connections by this user.

We start Internet Explorer again to simulate another using placing an order. Figure 16.10 shows a new session id and a new list of items. Example 16.10 contains the code behind that makes session tracking work.

FIGURE 16.10
Another customer placing an order

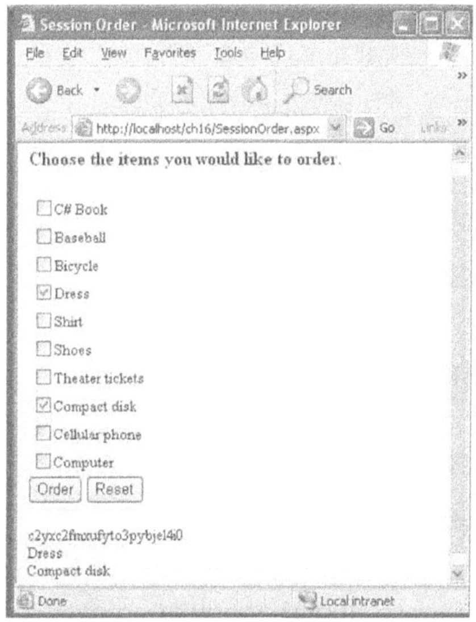

EXAMPLE 16.10 ■ SessionOrder.aspx.cs

```
/* Uses session tracking to maintain a customer's
 * information over multiple connections.
 */

using System;
using System.Web.UI;
using System.Web.UI.WebControls;
using System.Collections;
public class SessionOrder : Page {
  protected Button submit;
  protected Button reset;
  protected Label output;
  protected CheckBoxList order;
  protected ArrayList state;

  private void Page_Init() {
    submit.Click += new EventHandler(Submit_Click);
    reset.Click += new EventHandler(Reset_Click);
  }
  public void Submit_Click(Object Sender, EventArgs e) {
    state = (ArrayList)Session["items"];              // Note 1
    if (state == null)
      state = new ArrayList();                        // Note 2
    for (int i = 0; i < order.Items.Count; i++)
      if (order.Items[i].Selected)
        state.Add(order.Items[i].Value);              // Note 3
    Session.Add("items", state);                      // Note 4
    output.Text = Session.SessionID + "<br>";         // Note 5
```

```
    foreach(String s in state)
      output.Text += s + "<br>";                          // Note 6
  }
  public void Reset_Click(Object Sender, EventArgs e) {
    order.SelectedIndex = -1;
    output.Text = "";
  }
}
```

Note 1: `state = (ArrayList)Session["items"];`

We get the current session object, if any, associated with the `"items"` key.

Note 2: `if (state == null)  state = new ArrayList();`

If there is no current session object, we create a new `ArrayList` to hold the user's order.

Note 3: `state.Add(order.Items[i].Value);`

We add each item selected to the list of all items ordered by this user.

Note 4: `Session.Add("items", state);`

We save the updated list in the current session.

Note 5: `output.Text = Session.SessionID + "<br>";`

We output the session id just to show that a single user maintains the same session id over multiple connections, but a different user has a different session id.

Note 6: We output all items in the current order.

The BIG Picture

Session tracking allows the server to keep track of a client during multiple connections. Information the client sent will be saved so the server can read it the next time the client connects. In HTTP each client request requires a separate connection, so session tracking is essential for e-commerce applications.

✓Test Your Understanding

Try It Yourself ➤ **12.** Browse `SessionOrder.aspx` repeatedly, returning to this page several times and making various choices of items. Describe the results.

Try It Yourself ➤ **13.** Browse `SessionOrder.aspx` placing an order, and then open a new copy of the browser and browse `SessionOrder.aspx` again. Compare the results to those of exercise 12.

SUMMARY

- HTML (Hypertext Markup Language) uses tags to indicate how to present text and images and to provide links to other web sites.
- ASP.NET uses the .NET Framework to enable web applications. Web forms include various types of web controls, including text boxes, list boxes, checkboxes, radio buttons, and buttons. Web controls execute on the server. The web form can include a <script> tag with the C# event handlers or may refer to a code-behind file to better separate C# code from HTML. Clients can send data using either the GET or POST methods. GET appends the data to the URL, and POST sends the data after the request.
- Three-tiered architecture allows the client to concentrate on presentation, connecting to a middle tier to implement the business logic and connect to a database on the third tier.
- Session tracking lets the server keep track of a client who makes multiple requests. Because HTTP is a stateless protocol, not saving information about the client, session tracking is essential to enable electronic commerce applications.

PROGRAM MODIFICATION EXERCISES

1. Modify `SessionOrder.aspx` and `SessionOrder.aspx.cs` to allow the customer to delete items from an order.
2. Modify `Sales.aspx` and `Sales.aspx.cs` to pass the database URL from the form to the code behind.
3. Modify `Sales.aspx` and `Sales.aspx.cs` to create an SQL query from a form the user fills in, rather than having the user enter the query directly.
4. (Putting It All Together ➤) Modify `Sales.aspx` and `Sales.aspx.cs` to use the `SearchSales` program from Chapter 15 to create the query.

PROGRAM DESIGN EXERCISES

5. Write a web form for the user to select a favorite food. Write code behind to save the client's response in a database and output the number of clients who prefer each food.
6. Write a web form for the user to select a favorite sport. Write code behind to save the client's response in a hash table and output the number of clients who prefer each sport.
7. Write a web form for the user to order a pizza with either thick or thin crust and a choice of toppings. Use session tracking so the client can make changes to the order in a second request.

17 XML and Web Services

Web pages use HTML to indicate formatting to a browser. The web has become very popular in part because HTML is relatively simple and easy to use. But HTML focuses on presentation, making it hard to determine the information on a page. XML (Extensible Markup Language) lets us devise our own tags to reflect the information content. We can pass these standard XML files among various applications to transfer information from one program to another. Web services use XML to allow programs to communicate even though they are written in different languages and run on different hardware.

OBJECTIVES

- Learn XML syntax
- Use a schema to specify a valid XML type
- Try DOM (Document Object Model) for processing XML files
- Use XSLT to transform XML to other representations
- Call and create web services

17.1 XML AND INFORMATION

We first illustrate the limitations of HTML for representing content and then introduce XML.

The Limitations of HTML

With HTML we can easily format data for display, but the content is not easy to retrieve. Figure 17.1 shows the web page displayed by the Internet Explorer browser given the HTML file of Figure 17.2.

Most of the tags in Figure 17.2 refer to the display of the file. `<ul>` indicates an unordered list, and `<li>` specifies a list item. A human reader might deduce quickly that a person named Art is listing books he has written, but the word "`books`" is never used. A program processing this file would find it very difficult to determine its content.

Moreover, browsers accept many variations in HTML syntax. In Figure 17.2 the end tag `</ul>` for the unordered list does not appear, and none of the list items have end tags `</li>`. We could have omitted the `<html>` and `</html>` tags. Permitting such variations in syntax makes it hard for programs to extract information from HTML files.

XML Syntax[1]

We can define our own XML tags to indicate the content. For example, we might rewrite (and expand) the HTML file of Figure 17.2 as the XML file of Figure 17.3.

Notice that the `anAuthor.xml` file of Figure 17.3 has content tags such as `<author>` and `<book>`, rather than formatting tags such as `<li>` and `<em>`. The human reader finds it easy to read and understandable. More important, pro-

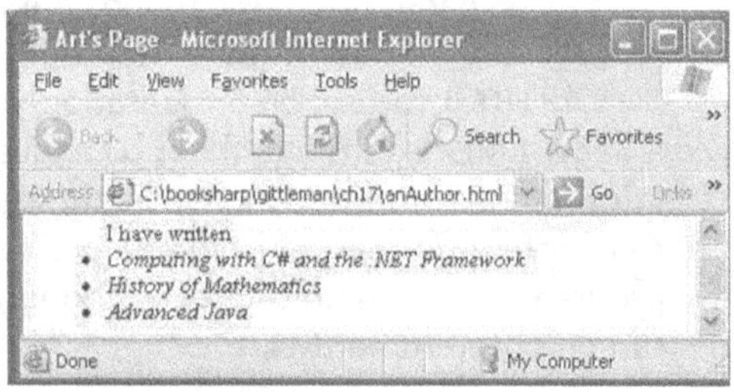

FIGURE 17.1 **Listing an author's books**

```
<html>
<title>Art's Page</title>
<ul>I have written
  <li> <em>Computing with C# and the .NET Framework</em>
  <li> <em>History of Mathematics</em>
  <li> <em>Advanced Java</em>
</html>
```

FIGURE 17.2 **The `anAuthor.html` file for the web page of Figure 17.1**

[1]See `http://www.w3.org/XML` for the XML specification.

```xml
<?xml version="1.0"?>
<!-- Books written by an author -->
<author>
  <name>
    <first> Art </first>
    <last> Gittleman </last>
  </name>
  <age> 39+   </age>
  <books>
     <book type="text">
        <title>Computing with C# and the .NET Framework</title>
        <edition> first </edition>
        <copyright> 2003 </copyright>
        <isbn> xxxxxxxxxx </isbn>
     </book>
     <book type="text">
        <title>History of Mathematics</title>
        <edition> first </edition>
        <copyright> 1975 </copyright>
        <isbn> 0-675-08784-8 </isbn>
     </book>
     <book type="text">
        <title full = "false">Advanced Java</title>
        <edition> second </edition>
        <copyright> 2002 </copyright>
        <isbn> 1-57676-096-0 </isbn>
     </book>
  </books>
</author>
```

FIGURE 17.3 **The `anAuthor.xml` file**

grams can easily find relevant information such as the copyright date or the ISBN number.

Each XML file starts with an optional prolog, which in Figure 17.3 is

```
<?xml version="1.0"?>
```

XML comments use the same HTML syntax, as in

```
<!-- Comments go here. -->
```

Tags may have attributes. For example, the `<book>` tag in Figure 17.3 has the `type` attribute with value `"text"`. Attributes may be optional. For example, the `<title>` tag has a `full` attribute that appears in one title, but not in others.

For programs to easily process XML, the syntax rules are precise.

- Each tag must have an end tag. For example, the `<book>` tag must have a `</book>` tag to mark the end of the `<book>` element. We place the content between the start and the end tags. A tag may be empty, meaning it has no content. For example, in Figure 17.3 we might have used a `<softcover>` tag to indicate that a book has a soft cover. The correct form would be

  ```
  <softcover></softcover>
  ```

  which may be abbreviated as

  ```
  <softcover/>
  ```

- Tags must be nested. For example, if the start tag `<title>` occurs between `<book>` and `</book>`, then its end tag `</title>` must occur before `</book>`.

  Correct: `<book> ... <title> ... </title> ... </book>`

  Incorrect: `<book> ... <title> ... </book> ... </title>`

- Attribute values must be enclosed in quotes.

  Correct: `type = "text"`

  Incorrect: `type = text`

Schemas

A well-formed XML document uses correct XML syntax. A document that had an `<author>` tag without an `</author>` tag would not be well formed. However, a well-formed document may not make sense. For example, the fragment

```
<name>
        <first> George </first>
        <first> John </first>
        <first> Mary </first>
</name>
```

uses correct syntax but does not look appropriate; a name has three `first` entries and no `last`.

We can use an XML schema to specify the form of a valid type of XML document. Figure 17.4 shows a schema for the author type. Before we look at the schema syntax, we show the tree structure of the author type in Figure 17.5. Because XML tags must nest, we can always diagram XML document structure in tree form.

In the schema of Figure 17.4 the top-level schema tag is

```
<xs:schema xmlns:xs="http://www.w3.org/2001/XMLSchema">
```

The schema defines two enumeration types, `typeType` and `fullType`, and the `author` element that defines the usage for the tags in the XML document of Figure 17.3. The enumeration types are restrictions on the base type `xs:string`. Each type has two possible values.

The `author` element is a complex type composed of a sequence of three elements, `name`, `age`, and `books`. The `name` element is a complex type composed of a sequence of two elements, `first` and `last`, which both have type xs:string.

```
<?xml version="1.0"?>
<xs:schema xmlns:xs="http://www.w3.org/2001/XMLSchema">
  <xs:simpleType name="typeType">
    <xs:restriction base="xs:string">
      <xs:enumeration value="text"/>
      <xs:enumeration value="trade"/>
    </xs:restriction>
  </xs:simpleType>
  <xs:simpleType name="fullType">
    <xs:restriction base="xs:string">
      <xs:enumeration value="true"/>
      <xs:enumeration value="false"/>
    </xs:restriction>
  </xs:simpleType>
  <xs:element name="author">
    <xs:complexType>
      <xs:sequence>
        <xs:element name="name">
          <xs:complexType>
            <xs:sequence>
              <xs:element name="first" type="xs:string"/>
              <xs:element name="last" type="xs:string"/>
            </xs:sequence>
          </xs:complexType>
        </xs:element>
        <xs:element name="age" type="xs:string"
                    minOccurs="0" maxOccurs="1"/>
        <xs:element name="books">
           <xs:element name="book" minOccurs="1"
                              maxOccurs="unbounded">
            <xs:complexType>
              <xs:sequence>
                <xs:element name="title" type="xs:string">
                  <xs:attribute name="full" type="fullType"
                                            default="true"/>
                </xs:element>
                <xs:element name="edition" type="xs:string"
                            minOccurs="0" maxOccurs="1"/>
                <xs:element name="copyright" type="xs:string"
                            minOccurs="0" maxOccurs="1"/>
                <xs:element name="isbn" type="xs:string"
                            minOccurs="0" maxOccurs="1"/>
              </xs:sequence>
              <xs:attribute name="type" type="typeType"/>
            </xs:complexType>
           </xs:element>
        </xs:element>
      </xs:sequence>
    </xs:complexType>
  </xs:element>
</xs:schema>
```

FIGURE 17.4 The `author.xsd` schema

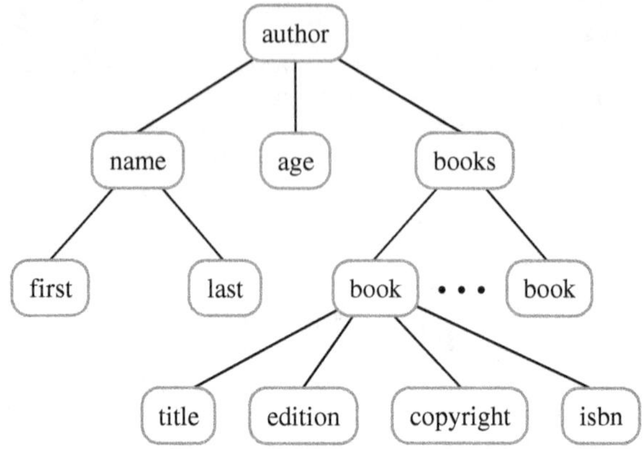

FIGURE 17.5 **The tree structure of the author document type**

The age element has type xs:string and occurs once or may be omitted. The books element is composed of a book element which must occur once and may occur many times.

The book element is a complex type that is a sequence of four elements, title, edition, copyright, and isbn. It has a type attribute of type typeType with values "text" or "trade".

The title element has type xs:string. It has a full attribute that indicates whether it is the full title. This attribute has type fullType and a default value of "true". The edition, copyright, and isbn elements have type xs:string and are optional.

Valid Documents

A valid XML document follows the rules given in its schema. A document can be well formed without being valid. For example, the fragment

```
<name>
      <first> George </first>
      <first> John </first>
      <first> Mary </first>
</name>
```

is not valid. The rule for <name> specifies a single <first> followed by a single <last>. We will associate a schema with an XML document in the next section. We now turn to the processing of XML documents.

> **The BIG Picture**
>
> XML allows us to define a language to represent data. We define tags and their structure. Well-formed XML follows precise rules to make it easier to transfer XML documents between programs. A schema defines the language so we can determine whether an XML document is valid, in that it follows the rules of that language.

✓ Test Your Understanding

1. Which of the following are well-formed XML documents?

   a.
```
<author>
  <name>
    <first> Art </first>
    <last> Gittleman </last>
  </name>
</author>
```

   b.
```
<author>
  <name/>
    <first> Art </first>
    <last> Gittleman </last>
</author>
```

   c.
```
<author/>
```

2. Which of the following are valid XML documents with respect to the schema of Figure 17.4?

   a.
```
<author>
  <name>
    <first> Art </first>
    <last> Gittleman </last>
  </name>
  <books>
     <book>
       <title>Objects to Components with the C#
             Platform
       </title>
     </book>
  </books>
</author>
```

   b.
```
<author>
  <name>
    <last> Gittleman </last>
  </name>
  <age> 39++ </age>
  <books>
    <book>
     <title>Objects to Components with the
          C# Platform</title>
    </book>
  </books>
</author>
```

3. Write an XML document for a record collection.

4. Write a schema to define the type used in Exercise 3.

17.2 DOM (DOCUMENT OBJECT MODEL) PROCESSING

The DOM (Document Object Model) API supports the reading of the entire document to make a tree model in memory. We can access nodes of the tree to locate information contained in the XML document. We use the following classes from the `System.XML` namespace.

Interface	Description
`XmlDocument`	Represents the entire XML document
`XmlElement`	Represents an element in an XML document
`XmlNode`	A superinterface for each node of the DOM tree
`XmlNodeList`	A collection of nodes
`XmlAttribute`	An attribute of an element
`XmlText`	The text of an element or attribute

TIP

Check the documentation for the `System.XML` namespace to see descriptions of each of the methods of these interfaces and for the complete list of interfaces. ■

Building a DOM Tree from an XML File

Example 17.1 produces a DOM tree from an XML file. For example, it will produce a tree with structure like that of Figure 17.5 from the `author.xml` file of Figure 17.3. We then find all `<title>` elements and read the `full` attribute to determine whether or not each is the full title. We can use either a validating or a nonvalidating parser.

EXAMPLE 17.1 ■ Dom.cs

```
/* Uses a DOM parser to identify the parts of an XML
 * document. The user specifies whether to use a
 * validating parser.
 */

using System;
using System.Xml;
using System.Xml.Schema;                                    // Note 1
public class Dom {
  public static void ValidationHandler
          (Object sender, ValidationEventArgs e) {          // Note 2
    Console.WriteLine(e.Message);
  }
  public static void Main(String[] args) {
    XmlValidatingReader reader = new XmlValidatingReader
                     (new XmlTextReader(args[0]));          // Note 3
    if (args[1] == "false")
      reader.ValidationType = ValidationType.None;          // Note 4
    else {
      reader.ValidationType = ValidationType.Schema;
```

```
      reader.ValidationEventHandler +=
        new ValidationEventHandler (ValidationHandler); // Note 5
    }
    XmlDocument doc = new XmlDocument();
    doc.Load(reader);                                   // Note 6
    doc.Normalize();                                    // Note 7
    XmlElement root = doc.DocumentElement;              // Note 8
    XmlNodeList titles
          = root.GetElementsByTagName("title");         // Note 9
    for (int i=0; i < titles.Count; i++) {
      XmlNode title = titles[i];                       // Note 10
      XmlAttribute fullAt = title.Attributes["full"];  // Note 11
      String full;
      if (fullAt == null)
         full = "true";
      else
         full = fullAt.Value;                          // Note 12
      XmlNode text = title.FirstChild;                 // Note 13
      String result
             = (full=="false") ? "is not" : "is";      // Note 14
      Console.WriteLine("{0} {1} the full title.",
                         text.OuterXml, result); // Note 15
    }
  }
}
```

Output

```
Computing with C# and the .NET Framework is the full title.
History of Mathematics is the full title.
Advanced Java is not the full title.
```

Note 1: `using System.Xml.Schema;`

We use the `System.Xml.Schema` namespace because we provide the option to validate the document we are processing.

Note 2:
```
public static void ValidationHandler
       (Object sender, ValidationEventArgs e) {
```

The `ValidationHandler` delegate will be called when the system processes an invalid document.

Note 3:
```
XmlValidatingReader reader = new XmlValidatingReader
                (new XmlTextReader(args[0]));
```

Using an `XmlValidatingReader` gives us the option to validate. We construct it from a basic `XmlTextReader`.

Note 4:
```
if (args[1] == "false")
     reader.ValidationType = ValidationType.None;
```

We set the `ValidationType` property to `None` when we do not want to validate the document.

Note 5:
```
reader.ValidationEventHandler +=
    new ValidationEventHandler (ValidationHandler);
```

We set the `ValidationType` property to `Schema` when we want to validate the document. In this case we register an event handler that will receive a callback when an error occurs.

Note 6:
```
doc.Load(reader);
```

The `Load` method loads the specified XML data.

Note 7:
```
doc.Normalize();
```

The `Normalize` method combines adjacent `XmlText` nodes into one `XmlText` node, otherwise the parser may produce nodes representing whitespace only.

Note 8:
```
XmlElement root = doc.DocumentElement;
```

The `DocumentElement` method returns the `XmlElement` that is the root of the document. It is a child node of the `XmlDocument` node that is the root of the DOM tree.

Note 9:
```
XmlNodeList titles
          = root.GetElementsByTagName("title");
```

The `GetElementsByTagName` method returns an `XmlNodeList` of all descendant elements with the tag name passed to it.

Note 10:
```
XmlNode title = titles[i];
```

The `titles[i]` indexer returns the `XmlNode` with the specified index in the `XmlNodeList`.

Note 11:
```
XmlAttribute fullAt = title.Attributes["full"];
```

The `Attributes` property returns the value of the attribute with the specified name. Attributes are not represented as separate nodes in the DOM tree. They are associated with an `XmlNode`.

Note 12:
```
full = fullAt.Value;
```

The `Value` property gives the value of the attribute.

Note 13:
```
XmlNode text = title.FirstChild;
```

The text in an `XmlNode` is the first child in the DOM tree.

Note 14:
```
String result
       = (full=="false") ? "is not" : "is";
```

We use the value of the `full` attribute to vary the message that we display.

```
<?xml version="1.0"?>
<!-- An author -->
<author xmlns:xsi="http://www.w3.org/2001/XMLSchema-instance"
     xsi:noNamespaceSchemaLocation="authorSimple.xsd">
  <name  gender = "male">
    <first> Art </first>
    <last> Gittleman </last>
  </name>
</author>
```

FIGURE 17.6 **authorSimpleExternal.xml**

Note 15:
```
Console.WriteLine("{0} {1} the full title.",
                    text.OuterXml, result);
```

The `OuterXml` property gets the markup of the node and all its children.

A Simplified Document and Schema

To illustrate validation we simplify the `author.xml` document of Figure 17.3 to the `authorSimpleExternal.xml` shown in Figure 17.6. This XML document refers to a schema that defines the syntax for the tags it uses. The `<name>` element adds a `<gender>` attribute to show attribute processing.

Figure 17.7 shows the schema we use for this XML document.

Checking for Well-Formed and Valid Documents

To check for a well-formed document, we do not need a validating parser or a schema. We use the non-well-formed XML document of Figure 17.8. It has a `<first>` tag, but no matching `</first>` tag. When the parser reaches the `</name>` tag it detects the error, because the `<first>` tag is nested inside `<name>` and must end before `<name>` ends.

Running Example 17.1 using the command

```
Dom authorSimpleError.xml false
```

with the non-well-formed file `authorSimpleError.xml`, which omits the `</first>` tag, produces

```
Unhandled Exception: System.Xml.XmlException: The 'first' start
tag on line '5' doesn't match the end tag of 'name' in file
'file:///C:/booksharp/gittleman/ch17/authorSimpleError.xml'.
Line 7, position 5.
   at System.Xml.XmlTextReader.ParseTag()
   at System.Xml.XmlTextReader.ParseBeginTagExpandCharEntities()
   at System.Xml.XmlTextReader.Read()
   at System.Xml.XmlValidatingReader.ReadNoCollectTextToken()
   at System.Xml.XmlValidatingReader.Read()
```

```
at System.Xml.XmlLoader.LoadCurrentNode()
at System.Xml.XmlLoader.LoadChildren(XmlNode parent)
at System.Xml.XmlLoader.LoadElementNode()
at System.Xml.XmlLoader.LoadCurrentNode()
at System.Xml.XmlLoader.LoadCurrentNode()
at System.Xml.XmlLoader.LoadChildren(XmlNode parent)
at System.Xml.XmlLoader.LoadElementNode()
at System.Xml.XmlLoader.LoadCurrentNode()
at System.Xml.XmlLoader.LoadCurrentNode()
at System.Xml.XmlLoader.LoadChildren(XmlNode parent)
at System.Xml.XmlLoader.LoadElementNode()
at System.Xml.XmlLoader.LoadCurrentNode()
at System.Xml.XmlLoader.LoadCurrentNode()
at System.Xml.XmlLoader.LoadDocSequence(XmlDocument
                                                  parentDoc)
at System.Xml.XmlLoader.Load(XmlDocument doc, XmlReader
     reader, Boolean preserveWhitespace)
at System.Xml.XmlDocument.Load(XmlReader reader)
at Dom.Main(String[] args)
```

```
<?xml version="1.0"?>
<xs:schema xmlns:xs="http://www.w3.org/2001/XMLSchema">
  <xs:simpleType name="genderType">
    <xs:restriction base="xs:string">
       <xs:enumeration value="male"/>
       <xs:enumeration value="female"/>
    </xs:restriction>
  </xs:simpleType>
  <xs:element name="author">
    <xs:complexType>
      <xs:sequence>
       <xs:element name="name">
        <xs:complexType>
          <xs:sequence>
            <xs:element name="first" type="xs:string"/>
            <xs:element name="last" type="xs:string"/>
          </xs:sequence>
          <xs:attribute name="gender" type="genderType"/>
        </xs:complexType>
       </xs:element>
      </xs:sequence>
    </xs:complexType>
  </xs:element>
</xs:schema>
```

FIGURE 17.7 A schema, `authorSimple.xsd`, for `authorSimpleExternal.xml`

FIGURE 17.8
authorSimpleError.xml

```
<?xml version="1.0"?>
<!-- An author -->
<author>
  <name  gender = "male">
    <first> Art
    <last> Gittleman </last>
  </name>
</author>
```

We did not need to use a validating parser to detect a document that is not well formed, nor is a schema necessary.

The invalid document `authorSimpleExternalError.xml` refers to a schema that does not specify a `<middle>` tag, yet it uses one. Checking with a non-validating parser using the command

```
Dom authorSimpleExternalError.xml false
```

produces no errors. Checking with a validating parser using the command

```
Dom authorSimpleExternalError.xml true
```

results in the output

```
Element 'name' has invalid child element 'middle'. Expected
'last'. An error occurred at
file:///C:/booksharp/gittleman/ch17/authorSimpleExternalError.
                                                      xml(8, 6).
The 'middle' element is not declared. An error occurred at
file:///C:/booksharp/
gittleman/ch17/authorSimpleExternalError.xml(8, 6).
```

Building a DOM Tree from Data

In Example 17.2 we build a DOM tree from the customer data in the `Sales` database we created in Chapter 15. We leave the more interesting problem of representing data from several of the `Sales` tables in an XML document for the exercises.

The `XmlDocument` class includes the following methods to create nodes.

```
XmlAttribute CreateAttribute(String name)
XmlComment CreateComment(String data)
XmlElement CreateElement(String tagName)
```

```
XmlText CreateTextNode(String data)
```

The various derived classes of `XmlNode` inherit the

```
XmlNode AppendChild(XmlNode newChild)
```

method to append a new node to the tree.

EXAMPLE 17.2 ■ MakeXml.cs

```
/* Uses the DOM API to create an XML document from
 * Sales database information.
 */

using System;
using System.Xml;
using System.Data;
using System.Data.OleDb;
public class MakeXml {
  public static void Main() {
    String connect = "Provider=Microsoft.JET.OLEDB.4.0;"
      + @"data source=c:\booksharp\gittleman\ch15\Sales.mdb";
    OleDbConnection con = new OleDbConnection(connect);
    con.Open();
    Console.WriteLine
      ("Made the connection to the Sales database");
    OleDbCommand cmd = con.CreateCommand();
    cmd.CommandText = "SELECT * FROM Customer";
    OleDbDataReader reader = cmd.ExecuteReader();
    XmlDocument document = new XmlDocument();
    XmlElement customers
                = document.CreateElement("customers");
                                                        // Note 1
    document.AppendChild(customers);                    // Note 2
    while (reader.Read()) {
      XmlElement customer = document.CreateElement("customer");
      customers.AppendChild(customer);                  // Note 3
      XmlElement name = document.CreateElement("name");
      customer.AppendChild(name);                       // Note 4
      name.AppendChild
           (document.CreateTextNode(reader.GetString(1)));
                                                        // Note 5
      XmlElement address = document.CreateElement("address");
      customer.AppendChild(address);
      address.AppendChild
           (document.CreateTextNode(reader.GetString(2)));
```

```
            XmlElement balance = document.CreateElement("balance");
            customer.AppendChild(balance);
            Decimal b = reader.GetDecimal(3);                  // Note 6
            balance.AppendChild
                        (document.CreateTextNode(b.ToString()));
          }
          document.Save(Console.Out);                          // Note 7
          reader.Close();
        }
      }
```

Output

```
Made the connection to the Sales database
<?xml version="1.0" encoding="IBM437"?>
<customers>
  <customer>
    <name>Fred Flynn</name>
    <address>22 First St.</address>
    <balance>1667</balance>
  </customer>
  <customer>
    <name>Darnell Davis</name>
    <address>33 Second St.</address>
    <balance>130</balance>
  </customer>
  <customer>
    <name>Marla Martinez</name>
    <address>44 Third St.</address>
    <balance>0</balance>
  </customer>
  <customer>
    <name>Carla Kahn</name>
    <address>55 Fourth St.</address>
    <balance>0</balance>
  </customer>
</customers>
```

Note 1:

```
XmlElement customers
          = document.CreateElement("customers");
```

The <customers> tag will be the root of this XML document.

Note 2:

```
document.AppendChild(customers);
```

The customers node will be the only child of the document node.

Note 3: `customers.AppendChild(customer);`

The `customers` tag will contain a `customer` tag for each customer in the Sales database.

Note 4: `customer.AppendChild(name);`

Each `customer` tag will have `name`, `address`, and `balance` nested tags. We do not use the customer ID.

Note 5:

```
name.AppendChild
    (document.CreateTextNode(reader.GetString(1)));
```

We add the data from the Sales database as text nodes in the DOM tree.

Note 6: `Decimal b = reader.GetDecimal(3);`

We use the `Decimal` type to represent money values.

Note 7: `document.Save(Console.Out);`

The `Save` method saves the document in the specified location. We save it to the console screen.

The BIG Picture

The Document Object Model (DOM) builds a tree representing the XML document. The `XmlNode` class represents a single node in the tree. Derived classes identify the components of an XML document. Methods allow us random access to nodes. We can create a DOM tree from an XML document or construct it from data.

✓Test Your Understanding

5. When using a DOM parser, which method, from which class, returns the root element of an XML document?
6. Which is represented as a separate node in the DOM tree, an attribute of an element or the text between the start and end tags of an element?

17.3 XSLT (EXTENSIBLE STYLESHEET LANGUAGE FOR TRANSFORMATIONS)

XSL (Extensible Stylesheet Language) has two parts, one for formatting and the other for transformations. The transformation part, XSLT (Extensible Stylesheet Language for Transformations), was developed first. It allows us to transform one document to another. We can transform an XML document to another XML document or to HTML for display in a browser.

```
<?xml version="1.0"?>
<xsl:stylesheet version="1.0"
    xmlns:xsl="http://www.w3.org/1999/XSL/Transform">

   <xsl:template match="/">
      <html>
        <head>
          <title> An author </title>
        </head>
        <body>
          <xsl:apply-templates />
        </body>
      </html>
   </xsl:template>

   <xsl:template match="name">
      <h1>
         First: <xsl:value-of select="first"/><br/>
         Last: <xsl:value-of select="last"/><br/>
      </h1>

   </xsl:template>
</xsl:stylesheet>
```

FIGURE 17.9 **authorSimple.xsl**

Stylesheets

We specify the transformations in a stylesheet. The stylesheet follows XML syntax. The transformations use templates that a processor matches against the tags in an XML file. Figure 17.9 shows a stylesheet for the `authorSimple.xml` file of Figure 17.10. We use the `.xsl` extension for stylesheets.

Using Internet Explorer

The Internet Explorer browser will apply stylesheet transformations. We add the stylesheet directive

```
<?xml:stylesheet type="text/xsl" href="authorSimple.xsl" ?>
```

to the XML file of Figure 17.10 to create the XML document of Figure 17.11 that refers to a stylesheet. Browsing this document in Internet Explorer displays the web page of Figure 17.12.

Using the .NET Framework

Example 17.3 uses the .NET Framework to apply a stylesheet to an XML document. Using the command

```
XmlToHtml authorSimple.xsl authorSimple.xml
authorSimple.html
```

```
<?xml version="1.0" ?>
<!-- An author -->
<author>
  <name  gender = "male">
    <first> Art </first>
    <last> Gittleman </last>
  </name>
</author>
```

FIGURE 17.10 **authorSimple.xml**

```
<?xml version="1.0" ?>
<?xml:stylesheet type="text/xsl"
     href="authorSimple.xsl" ?>
<!-- An author -->
<author>
  <name  gender = "male">
    <first> Art </first>
    <last> Gittleman </last>
  </name>
</author>
```

FIGURE 17.11 **authorSimpleStyle.xml**

FIGURE 17.12 **Applying a stylesheet**

```
<html><head><title> An author </title></head><body><h1>
         First:  Art <br />
         Last:  Gittleman <br /></h1></body></html>
```

FIGURE 17.13 **authorSimple.html**

produces the web page of Figure 17.12. Figure 17.13 shows the HTML file Example 17.3 generates.

Stylesheet Templates

As with other XML files, we start the stylesheet with the processing instruction

```
<?xml version="1.0"?>
```

Processing instructions occur between `<?` and `?>`. XSLT stylesheets use the XSLT namespace to provide a context for the XSLT commands. Each command uses a tag with the `xsl` prefix, as in `xsl:template`. The `xsl:stylesheet` tag

```
<xsl:stylesheet version="1.0"
    xmlns:xsl="http://www.w3.org/1999/XSL/Transform">
```

indicates the version, `1.0`. The `xmlns:xsl` attribute states that the namespace name is `xsl` and gives the URL where that namespace is defined. As with all XML tags, the `xsl:stylesheet` tag has a closing tag at the end of the stylesheet.

The stylesheet of Figure 17.9 uses two `xsl:template` tags. The first

```
<xsl:template match="/">
```

includes a match attribute with the value "/", which matches the root tag of the XML file, <author> in Figure 17.10. We could have used the tag

```
<xsl:template match="author">
```

When the XSLT processor applies the template to authorSimple.xml, it finds a match with the <author> tag and outputs its body

```
<html>
  <head>
    <title> An author </title>
  </head>
  <body>
    <xsl:apply-templates />
  </body>
</html>
```

The <xsl:apply-templates /> tag applies the templates of the stylesheet to tags nested within the <author> tag. Because it is an empty tag, we use the short form, closing it with a forward slash.

Next the XSLT processor finds a match with the <name> tag, so it fills in its body in the output, giving

```
<html>
  <head>
    <title> An author </title>
  </head>
  <body>
    <h1>
       First: <xsl:value-of select="first"/><br/>
       Last: <xsl:value-of select="last"/><br/>
    </h1>
  </body>
</html>
```

Finally, the <xsl:value-of select="first"/> tag returns the text body of the <first> tag as a String.

Example 17.3 is quite short.

EXAMPLE 17.3 ■ XmlToHtml.cs

```
/* Converts the XML file of args[1] to the HTML file
 * of args[2] using the XSL stylesheet of args[0].
 */

using System;
using System.Xml;
using System.Xml.Xsl;
using System.Xml.XPath;
```

```
public class XmlToHtml {
  public static void Main(String[] args) {
    XslTransform xslt = new XslTransform();                  // Note 1
    xslt.Load(args[0]);                                      // Note 2
    XPathDocument doc = new XPathDocument(args[1]);          // Note 3
    XmlTextWriter writer
              = new XmlTextWriter(args[2], null);            // Note 4
    xslt.Transform(doc, null, writer);                       // Note 5
    writer.Close();
  }
}
```

Output

See Figures 17.12 and 17.13.

Note 1: `XslTransform xslt = new XslTransform();`

An `XslTransform` transforms XML data using an XSLT stylesheet.

Note 2: `xslt.Load(args[0]);`

The `Load` method loads the XSLT stylesheet.

Note 3: `XPathDocument doc = new XPathDocument(args[1]);`

The `XPathDocument` is an optimized form of a DOM representation of an XML document that is used for XSLT processing. We create an `XPathDocument` from our XML file.

Note 4:
```
XmlTextWriter writer
        = new XmlTextWriter(args[2], null);
```

An `XmlTextWriter` represents a `TextWriter` optimized for XML data. We create an `XmlTextWriter` to output our transformed file.

Note 5: `xslt.Transform(doc, null, writer);`

The `Transform` method applies the stylesheet to the document passed as the first argument using any parameters passed as the second argument and using the `XmlWriter` passed as the third argument to write the transformed file.

A Stylesheet for the Author Document

Now that we have seen how XSLT works, we will process the full `author.xml` document of Figure 17.3 using the command

```
XmlToHtml author.xsl author.xml author.html
```

Figure 17.14 shows the stylesheet we will apply. Figure 17.15 shows the resulting HTML file, and Figure 17.16 shows the web page.

```
<?xml version="1.0"?>
<xsl:stylesheet version="1.0"
    xmlns:xsl="http://www.w3.org/1999/XSL/Transform">

   <xsl:template match="/">
      <html>
        <head>
          <title> Books written by an author </title>
        </head>
        <body>
          <xsl:apply-templates />
        </body>
      </html>
   </xsl:template>

   <xsl:template match="name">
      <h3>
         Author: <xsl:value-of select="first"/>
           <xsl:value-of select="last"/><br/>
      </h3>
   </xsl:template>
   <xsl:template match="age">
      <h4>
         Age: <xsl:value-of select="." />
      </h4>
      <hr/>
   </xsl:template>
   <xsl:template match="books">
      <xsl:apply-templates />
   </xsl:template>
   <xsl:template match="book">
      <h4><strong>
           <xsl:value-of select="title"/>
      </strong></h4>
      <table>
        <th>Edition</th>
        <th>Copyright</th>
        <th>ISBN</th>
        <tr>
          <td><xsl:value-of select="edition"/></td>
          <td><xsl:value-of select="copyright"/></td>
          <td><xsl:value-of select="isbn"/></td>
       </tr>
      </table>
      <hr/>
   </xsl:template>
</xsl:stylesheet>
```

FIGURE 17.14 **author.xsl**

```
<html>
  <head> <title>Book written by an author</title> </head>
  <body>
    <h3> Author:  Art  Gittleman <br /> </h3>
    <h4> Age:  39+   </h4><hr />
    <h4><strong> Computing with C# and the .NET Framework
    </strong></h4>
    <table><th>Edition</th><th>Copyright</th><th>ISBN</th>
     <tr>
       <td> first </td><td> 2003 </td><td> xxxxxxxxxx </td>
     </tr>
    </table><hr />
    <h4><strong> History of Mathematics </strong></h4>
    <table><th>Edition</th><th>Copyright</th><th>ISBN</th>
     <tr>
      <td>first</td><td>1975</td><td> 0-675-08784-8 </td>
     </tr>
    </table><hr />
    <h4><strong> Advanced Java </strong></h4>
    <table><th>Edition</th><th>Copyright</th><th>ISBN</th>
     <tr>
      <td>second</td><td>2002</td><td>1-57676-096-0</td>
     </tr>
    </table><hr /></body></html>
```

FIGURE 17.15 **The `author.html` produced by Example 17.3**

FIGURE 17.16 **The resulting web page**

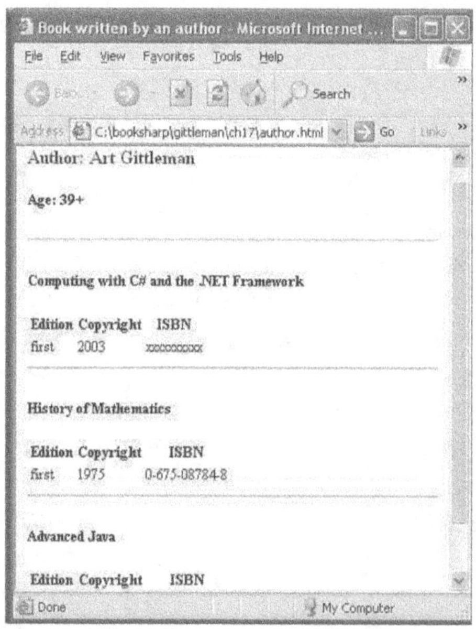

The author.xsl stylesheet uses the <xsl:value-of select="." /> tag inside the age match. The "." in the select attribute refers to the tag of the match containing the value-of command, which in this case is the age tag. Thus the value-of command returns the text of the age tag, which is 39+.

The match for the <books> tag does not directly add any new HTML code, but it specifies the <xsl:apply-templates /> command, which causes the XSLT processor to apply the templates to the tags nested within <books>. When matching <book> we display the title followed by a table containing the book information. The <th> tag indicates a table header, <tr> specifies a table row, and <td> represents the table data in one cell. We follow each table with the empty <hr/> tag to insert a horizontal rule.

Using a Stylesheet

Example 17.1 created a DOM tree from an XML file and then processed it to find the book titles and indicate whether each was the full title. We can use a stylesheet to transform the XML file to give the desired information as a web page. Figure 17.17 shows the stylesheet, Figure 17.18 the resulting HTML file,

```
<?xml version="1.0"?>
<xsl:stylesheet version="1.0"
    xmlns:xsl="http://www.w3.org/1999/XSL/Transform">

   <xsl:template match="/">
      <html>
        <head>
          <title> Book titles </title>
        </head>
        <body>
          <xsl:apply-templates />
        </body>
      </html>
   </xsl:template>
   <xsl:template match="age">
   </xsl:template>
   <xsl:template match="name">
      <h3>
         Author: <xsl:value-of select="first"/>
           <xsl:value-of select="last"/><br/>
      </h3>
   </xsl:template>
   <xsl:template match="books">
      <xsl:apply-templates />
   </xsl:template>
```

FIGURE 17.17 **titles.xsl (continues on next page)**

```
    <xsl:template match="book">
       <xsl:apply-templates select="title"/>
    </xsl:template>

    <xsl:template match="title[@full='false']">
      <h4><strong>
        <xsl:value-of select="."/>
      </strong></h4> is not the full title.
      <hr/>
    </xsl:template>
    <xsl:template match="title">
      <h4><strong>
        <xsl:value-of select="."/>
      </strong></h4> is the full title.
      <hr/>
    </xsl:template>

 </xsl:stylesheet>
```

FIGURE 17.17 **(continued)**

FIGURE 17.18
titles.html

```
<html>
  <head><title> Book titles </title></head>
  <body>
    <h3> Author:  Art  Gittleman <br /></h3>
    <h4> <strong>
       Computing with C# and the .NET Framework
    </strong></h4> is the full title. <hr />
    <h4><strong>
       History of Mathematics
    </strong></h4> is the full title. <hr />
    <h4><strong>
       Advanced Java
    </strong></h4> is not the full title. <hr />
  </body>
</html>
```

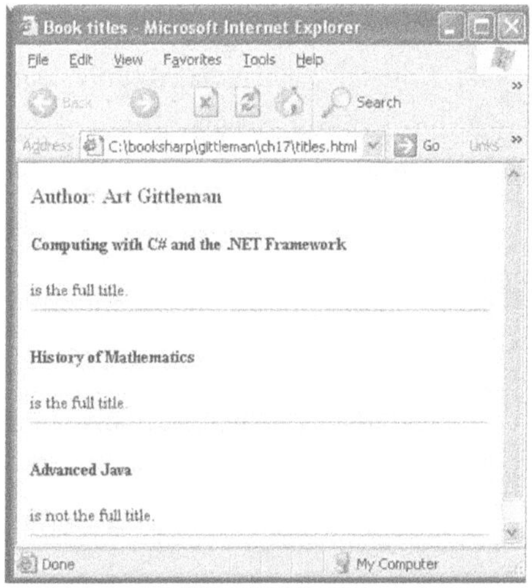

FIGURE 17.19 **The `titles.html` web page**

and Figure 17.19 its corresponding web page. We use the command

```
XmlToHtml titles.xsl author.xml titles.html
```

to do the processing.

We do not want to list the author's age in the output. The `<xsl:apply-templates />` command in the root template will apply to all the nested tags, including `<age>`. If we omit an "`age`" match, the default will be to include the text of the `<age>` tag. To prevent this we include an "`age`" match with an empty body, so no code will be added to the HTML output.

The `<xsl:apply-templates select="title"/>` command will apply templates only to the `<title>` tag, and will ignore the `<edition>`, `<copyright>`, and `<isbn>` tags. When matching the title, we want to distinguish full titles from the others. We use the `full` attribute to indicate which are full titles. It has a default value of `"true"`, so it only appears explicitly when its value is `"false"`.

We match on titles with the `full` attribute set to `false` using the command

```
<xsl:template match="title[@full='false']">
```

The `@` symbol indicates an attribute. We also include a default match for `"title"` that will apply to the `<title>` tags not matched by the previous command when the attribute is `false`. This will cover the cases when the title is the full title.

The BIG Picture

Extensible Stylesheet Language for Transformations (XSLT) allows us to transform an XML document. It is itself an XML file that uses the `xsl` namespace with stylesheet commands. The `template` command matches document tags, building the transformed document with its included code. One application is to transform an XML document, which expresses content, to an HTML document for presentation.

✓Test Your Understanding

7. Write the unabbreviated equivalent of the `<xsl:apply-templates />` tag.
8. Figure 17.17 includes the

   ```
   <xsl:apply-templates select="title"/>
   ```

   tag. Explain the difference between this tag and the tag

   ```
   <xsl:apply-templates />
   ```

9. How would we have to change the tag

   ```
   <xsl:template match="book">
   ```

   in Figure 17.14 to match only textbooks?

17.4 WEB SERVICES

Web applications allow users on diverse platforms to access remote sites using a browser. Web services use a simple protocol with XML to allow programs to communicate. In this way, an application developed on one platform can use methods of another application running on a different platform at a remote site and perhaps written in a different language.

SOAP and WSDL

The Simple Object Access Protocol (SOAP) uses XML to request a web service and to provide the response. Using the .NET Framework, we do not need to code the SOAP request explicitly. Each application has a description of the web services it offers written as an XML document in WSDL, the Web Services Description Language. The .NET Framework provides a tool, `wsdl.exe`, that converts this description to a C# program we can execute to use the web services.

Using a Web Service

To illustrate, we use a periodic table web service found on the XMethods site at

```
http://www.xmethods.com/ve2/ViewListing.po?serviceid=119931
```

This service provides methods by which we can find information about chemical elements. The site provides a link to the WSDL description file given by

```
http://www.webservicex.net/periodictable.asmx?wsdl
```

We shall see that the .NET Framework can automatically generate these WSDL documents. It provides the `wsdl.exe` utility to convert the WSDL description to a library file with executable code for the web services described. We use the command

```
"\Program Files\Microsoft Visual Studio
.NET\FrameworkSDK\Bin\wsdl"
 /o:PeriodicTable.cs
http://www.webservicex.net/periodictable.asmx?wsdl
```

to create `PeriodicTable.cs`, shown in Figure 17.20, from the WSDL description. We compile `PeriodicTable.cs` to a library file containing the web service methods.

```
//-----------------------
// <autogenerated>
//     This code was generated by a tool.
//     Runtime Version: 1.0.3705.0
//
//     Changes to this file may cause incorrect behavior and will
//     be lost if the code is regenerated.
// </autogenerated>
//--------------------------

//
// This source code was auto-generated by wsdl, Version=1.0.3705.0.
//
using System.Diagnostics;
using System.Xml.Serialization;
using System;
using System.Web.Services.Protocols;
using System.ComponentModel;
using System.Web.Services;

/// <remarks/>
[System.Diagnostics.DebuggerStepThroughAttribute()]
[System.ComponentModel.DesignerCategoryAttribute("code")]
[System.Web.Services.WebServiceBindingAttribute
      (Name="PeriodicTableSoap",
       Namespace="http://www.webservicex.net")]
public class PeriodicTable :
        System.Web.Services.Protocols.SoapHttpClientProtocol {

    /// <remarks/>
    public PeriodicTable() {
        this.Url =
            "http://www.webservicex.net/periodictable.asmx";
    }

    /// <remarks/>
    [System.Web.Services.Protocols.SoapDocumentMethodAttribute
       ("http://www.webservicex.net/GetAtoms",
         RequestNamespace="http://www.webservicex.net",
         ResponseNamespace="http://www.webservicex.net",
```

FIGURE 17.20 **`PeriodicTable.cs`** **(continues on next page)**

```
        Use=
         System.Web.Services.Description.SoapBindingUse.Literal,
        ParameterStyle=
      System.Web.Services.Protocols.SoapParameterStyle.Wrapped)]
    public string GetAtoms() {
      object[] results = this.Invoke("GetAtoms", new object[0]);
      return ((string)(results[0]));
    }

    /// <remarks/>
    public System.IAsyncResult BeginGetAtoms
           (System.AsyncCallback callback, object asyncState) {
      return this.BeginInvoke
           ("GetAtoms", new object[0], callback, asyncState);
    }

    /// <remarks/>
    public string EndGetAtoms(System.IAsyncResult asyncResult) {
      object[] results = this.EndInvoke(asyncResult);
      return ((string)(results[0]));
    }

    /// <remarks/>
    [System.Web.Services.Protocols.SoapDocumentMethodAttribute
      ("http://www.webservicex.net/GetAtomicWeight",
        RequestNamespace="http://www.webservicex.net",
        ResponseNamespace="http://www.webservicex.net",
        Use=
          System.Web.Services.Description.SoapBindingUse.Literal,
        ParameterStyle=
      System.Web.Services.Protocols.SoapParameterStyle.Wrapped)]
    public string GetAtomicWeight(string ElementName) {
      object[] results = this.Invoke
          ("GetAtomicWeight", new object[] {ElementName});
      return ((string)(results[0]));
    }

    /// <remarks/>
    public System.IAsyncResult BeginGetAtomicWeight
          (string ElementName, System.AsyncCallback callback,
           object asyncState) {
      return this.BeginInvoke("GetAtomicWeight",
           new object[] {ElementName}, callback, asyncState);
    }
```

FIGURE 17.20 **(continues on next page)**

```
    /// <remarks/>
    public string EndGetAtomicWeight
                            (System.IAsyncResult asyncResult) {
      object[] results = this.EndInvoke(asyncResult);
      return ((string)(results[0]));
    }

    /// <remarks/>
    [System.Web.Services.Protocols.SoapDocumentMethodAttribute
       ("http://www.webservicex.net/GetAtomicNumber",
         RequestNamespace="http://www.webservicex.net",
         ResponseNamespace="http://www.webservicex.net",
         Use=
          System.Web.Services.Description.SoapBindingUse.Literal,
         ParameterStyle=
      System.Web.Services.Protocols.SoapParameterStyle.Wrapped)]
    public string GetAtomicNumber(string ElementName) {
      object[] results = this.Invoke
                 ("GetAtomicNumber", new object[] {ElementName});
      return ((string)(results[0]));
    }

    /// <remarks/>
    public System.IAsyncResult BeginGetAtomicNumber
      (string ElementName, System.AsyncCallback callback,
                                           object asyncState) {
      return this.BeginInvoke("GetAtomicNumber",
            new object[] {ElementName}, callback, asyncState);
    }

    /// <remarks/>
    public string EndGetAtomicNumber
                         (System.IAsyncResult asyncResult) {
      object[] results = this.EndInvoke(asyncResult);
      return ((string)(results[0]));
    }

    /// <remarks/>
    [System.Web.Services.Protocols.SoapDocumentMethodAttribute
       ("http://www.webservicex.net/GetElementSymbol",
         RequestNamespace="http://www.webservicex.net",
         ResponseNamespace="http://www.webservicex.net",
         Use=
          System.Web.Services.Description.SoapBindingUse.Literal,
```

FIGURE 17.20 **(continues on next page)**

```
        ParameterStyle=
      System.Web.Services.Protocols.SoapParameterStyle.Wrapped)]
    public string GetElementSymbol(string ElementName) {
      object[] results = this.Invoke("GetElementSymbol",
                                  new object[] {ElementName});
      return ((string)(results[0]));
    }

    /// <remarks/>
    public System.IAsyncResult BeginGetElementSymbol
        (string ElementName, System.AsyncCallback callback,
                                          object asyncState) {
      return this.BeginInvoke("GetElementSymbol",
             new object[] {ElementName}, callback, asyncState);
    }

    /// <remarks/>
    public string EndGetElementSymbol
                            (System.IAsyncResult asyncResult) {
      object[] results = this.EndInvoke(asyncResult);
      return ((string)(results[0]));
    }
}
```

FIGURE 17.20 **(continued)**

When we click the *Analyze WSDL* link on the XMethods site for the Periodic Table web service we get a link to four operations, `GetAtoms`, `GetAtomicWeight`, `GetAtomicNumber`, and `GetElementSymbol`. Example 17.4 calls the `GetElementSymbol` and `GetAtomicWeight` methods to get the symbol and weight for the element with the name we pass as the argument. We compile it using the command

```
csc /r:PeriodicTable.dll TestWeb.cs
```

The web service sends a SOAP XML response from which the program automatically extracts the return values of the methods we call.

EXAMPLE 17.4 ■ TestWeb.cs

```
/* Calls two methods from the Periodic Table
 * web service.
 */

public class TestWeb {
```

```
  public static void Main(System.String[] args) {
    PeriodicTable t = new PeriodicTable();
    System.Console.WriteLine(t.GetElementSymbol(args[0]));
    System.Console.WriteLine();
    System.Console.WriteLine(t.GetAtomicWeight(args[0]));
  }
}
```

(Using the command `TestWeb Carbon`)

```
<Elements><Atom><ElementName> Carbon</ElementName><Symbol>C<
/Symbol></Atom></Elements>

<Elements><Atom><ElementName> Carbon</ElementName><Symbol>C<
/Symbol><AtomicNumber>6</AtomicNumber><AtomicWeight>12.011</
AtomicWeight></Atom></Elements>
```

Creating a Web Service

The .NET Framework makes it very easy to create and deploy a web service. To illustrate, we create a simple Reverse service that reverses whatever string we send it. Example 17.5 contains the code for this service. We use the .asmx extension. The .NET Framework will compile the code when we deploy it.

EXAMPLE 17.5 ■ ReverseService.asmx

```
<%@ WebService Language="c#" Class="ReverseService" %>  // Note 1

using System.Web.Services;
using System;
public class ReverseService : WebService {               // Note 2

  [WebMethod]                                             // Note 3
  public String Reverse(String s) {                       // Note 4
    int size = s.Length;
    char[] c = new char[size];
    for (int i=0; i<size; i++)
    c[i] = s[size-1-i];
    return new String(c);
  }
}
```

Note 1:

```
<%@ WebService Language="c#" Class="ReverseService" %>
```

The `WebService` directive specifies that the language is C# and the web service class is `ReverseService`.

Note 2:

```
public class ReverseService : WebService {
```

The web service class must derive from `WebService`.

Note 3:

```
[WebMethod]
```

We only need to add this `WebMethod` attribute to enable the annotated method to be called remotely as a web service.

Note 4:

```
public String Reverse(String s) {
```

The `Reverse` method returns the reverse of the string passed to it.

To deploy `ReverseService` we create a `ch17` virtual directory following the steps used in Section 16.2. Browsing

```
http://localhost/ch17/ReverseService.asmx
```

brings up a web page that provides a `Reverse` link to test the `Reverse` method that this web service provides. Clicking on this link produces the web page of Figure 17.21 which provides a text box to enter the string to reverse and a listing of the SOAP request and response (not fully shown in the figure). Entering `"potato"` and clicking on *Invoke* produces the response shown in Figure 17.22.

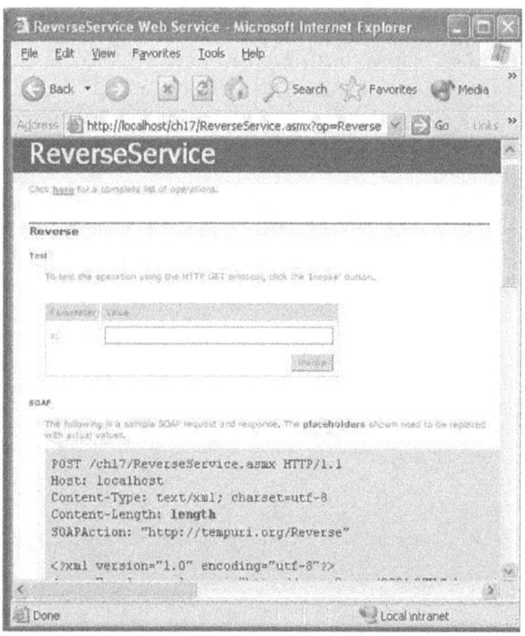

FIGURE 17.21 **Using the `Reverse` method**

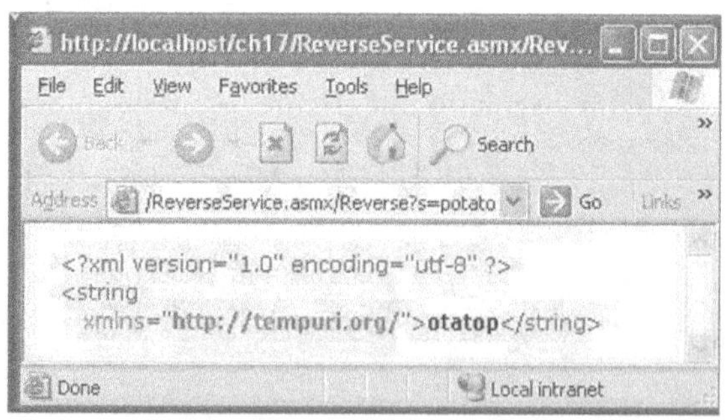

FIGURE 17.22 **The response**

✓ Test Your Understanding

10. How could we use Internet Explorer to test the Periodic Table web service without using the program of Example 17.4?

Try It Yourself ➤

11. Use the approach of Exercise 10 to try three web services from the XMethods web site.

SUMMARY

- HTML tags support the presentation of data. XML tags make it easier to identify the content of a document. The optional prolog

```
<?xml version="1.0"?>
```

is a `processing instruction` tag. Tags may have attributes. XML follows precise syntactical rules to facilitate machine processing of XML files. For example, each tag must have an end tag. Tags must nest properly, and attributes must be enclosed in quotes.
- A schema defines the valid syntax for a document type. A well-formed document conforms to the XML syntax. In addition, a valid document conforms to its schema.
- The Document Object Model (DOM) builds a tree representation of the XML document in memory. The `Load` method builds a DOM tree from an XML file. Methods such as `GetElementsByTagName` let us directly access nodes of the tree. Methods such as `CreateElement` and `AppendChild` let us build a DOM tree from data.
- The Extensible Stylesheet Language for Transformations lets us transform XML documents. For example, we can transform an XML document, which focuses on content, to an HTML document for presentation. We could transform the content to an XML document suitable for a different application. The `xsl` namespace includes commands that implement the transformations. A `template` command matches pieces of the XML documents and specifies the transformed code to use when a match is found. Other commands include `apply-templates` and `value-of`.
- The Simple Object Access Protocol allows us to execute remote procedure calls. HTTP provides wide access and ease of use. An XML message specifies the object on the server, the method to call, and any arguments to that method. The server returns a SOAP XML response. In the .NET Framework we do not need to explicitly write SOAP requests. We obtain the WSDL description from the service and use the `wsdl` tool to create a C# program that we use to execute remote method calls. To create a web service we annotate the method with the `WebService` attribute and deploy the `.asmx` file. Internet Explorer will provide a web page to test the service and users can write programs to access it remotely.

PROGRAM MODIFICATION EXERCISES

1. Modify Example 17.1 to write the output as an HTML file. Write it to the external file `Dom.html`.
2. Modify Example 17.2 to create an XML document with the customer's name and the dates on which that customer placed orders.
3. Modify Example 17.1 to list those titles that contain a word entered on the command line.

4. **a.** Using data from the Sales database of Chapter 15, write a program to create a DOM tree that for each salesperson lists the order number and date of each order handled by that salesperson.

   b. Write a stylesheet to transform the XML document of part a to an HTML file to display the results. Execute Example 17.3 to obtain the HTML file.

5. Write a stylesheet to produce an HTML file from `author.xml`, using Example 17.3, that displays the title and ISBN of each book.
6. Write a stylesheet to produce an HTML file from `author.xml`, using Example 17.3, that displays the author's name and the copyright date of each book.
7. Create and deploy a web service that returns a random lucky number between 1 and 10.
8. Create and deploy a web service that returns the amount that will result if a given initial amount is deposited at a specified interest rate for a specified number of years, if the interest is compounded yearly.
9. Write a stylesheet to transform the XML document created by Example 17.2 to an HTML file to display the results. Execute Example 17.3 to obtain the HTML file.
10. Pick a service from the `www.xmethods.com` site and write a client to access that service.

A Binary and Hexadecimal Numbers

Our familiar decimal number system uses ten digits, 0, 1, 2, 3, 4, 5, 6, 7, 8, and 9, to represent numbers. We can only represent numbers up to nine with one digit. To write the number ten, we use two digits, 10, with the idea that the one in the ten's place represents ten. The number 387 represents 3 x 100 + 8 x 10 + 7 because the three is in the hundred's place, and the eight is in the ten's place. We call this the base ten system because each place represents a power of ten. The unit's place is $10^0 = 1$, the ten's place is $10^1 = 10$, the hundred's place is $10^2 = 100$, and so on.

In the **binary** number system we use two digits, 0 and 1, to represent integers. This is particularly suitable for computers in which each hardware memory **bit** (binary digit) can represent a 0 or a 1. Using only two digits, the largest number we can represent in one digit is one. The first few binary numbers are

Binary	**Decimal equivalent**
0	0
1	1
10	$2 = 1 \times 2 + 0$
11	$3 = 1 \times 2 + 1$
100	$4 = 1 \times 4 + 0 \times 2 + 0 \times 1$
101	$5 = 1 \times 4 + 0 \times 2 + 1 \times 1$
110	$6 = 1 \times 4 + 1 \times 2 + 0 \times 1$
111	$7 = 1 \times 4 + 1 \times 2 + 1 \times 1$
1000	$8 = 1 \times 8 + 0 \times 4 + 0 \times 2 + 0 \times 1$
1001	$9 = 1 \times 8 + 0 \times 4 + 0 \times 2 + 1 \times 1$
1010	$10 = 1 \times 8 + 0 \times 4 + 1 \times 2 + 0 \times 1$

Just as the decimal system is base 10, the binary system is in base 2, and has a unit's place, a two's place, a four's place, an eight's place, and so on as given by the sequence $2^0 = 1$, $2^1 = 2$, $2^2 = 4$, $2^3 = 8$, and so on.

Although the computer hardware uses binary digits, it is hard for human readers to grasp 16 bits of binary, as, for example

```
0010110100110110
```

If we group the bits by fours, as in,

```
0010 1101 0011 0110
```

it's a bit easier to read but still cumbersome. Each group of four represents a number from 0 to 15 in the binary system. If we had a system with 16 digits, we could replace each group of four bits by a single digit. The **hexadecimal** system uses the digits `0`, `1`, `2`, `3`, `4`, `5`, `6`, `7`, `8`, `9`, `a`, `b`, `c`, `d`, `e`, and `f`, where `a=10`, `b=11`, `c=12`, `d=13`, `e=14`, and `f=15`. We can use either lowercase or uppercase letters `A`, `B`, `C`, `D`, `E`, and `F`. To write the above 16-bit number in hexadecimal, replace each group of four by its corresponding hexadecimal digit, giving

```
binary         0010 1101 0011 0110
hexadecimal      2    d    3    6
```

We can specify hexadecimal constants in C# using `0x` or `0X` to prefix the number as, for example, `0x2d36`.

The first 10 hexadecimal digits are the same as the decimal digits. The remaining six have the following binary and decimal equivalents.

Hexadecimal	Binary	Decimal
a or A	1010	10
b or B	1011	11
c or C	1100	12
d or D	1101	13
e or E	1110	14
f or F	1111	15

The main use of hexadecimal numbers is to give a shorter representation for binary numbers which, using only two digits, tend to get long. We could, of course, convert the binary number to base ten, but that takes more work. If you are curious, `0010 1101 0011 0110` converts to

```
8192 + 2048 + 1024 + 256 + 32 + 16 + 4 + 2 = 11,574
```

in base 10.

A Little Extra

Converting Between Base 10 and Binary

As we have just seen, to convert a binary number to decimal, just add the powers of two corresponding to the positions of the 1's in the number. Converting `11001`, we add `16+8+1 = 25` because the `11001` has a one in the sixteen's place, the eight's place, and the one's place.

To convert a base 10 number to binary we use division to get the digits from right to left, starting with the one's digit. To convert 25, divide by two, and the remainder will be the one's digit. Divide the quotient, 12, by two, and the remainder will be the two's digit. Repeat this process until the quotient is zero. The following example shows how the base ten number 25 converts to the base two number `11001`.

```
25 ÷ 2 =  12 r. 1
12 ÷ 2 =   6 r. 0
 6 ÷ 2 =   3 r. 0
 3 ÷ 2 =   1 r. 1
 1 ÷ 2 =   0 r. 1
```

`25 ÷ 2 =  12 r. 1`	so the 1's digit is 1.
`12 ÷ 2 =   6 r. 0`	so the 2's digit is 0.
`6 ÷ 2 =   3 r. 0`	so the 4's digit is 0.
`3 ÷ 2 =   1 r. 1`	so the 8's digit is 1.
`1 ÷ 2 =   0 r. 1`	so the 16's digit is 1.

✓Test Your Understanding

1. Express the value of each base 10 number using powers of 10. For example, 254 has the value `2x100 + 5x10 + 4`.
   - **a.** 38
   - **b.** 4179
   - **c.** 562
   - **d.** 94531
   - **e.** 306
2. Express the value of each base 2 number using powers of 2. For example, 101 has the value `1x4 + 0x2 + 1x1`.
   - **a.** 11
   - **b.** 1101
   - **c.** 101100
   - **d.** 11011
   - **e.** 11101010
3. Give the base 10 value for each of the binary numbers in Exercise 2.
4. Write each of the binary numbers in Exercise 2 in hexadecimal. (Hint: Group by fours and add zeros in front if necessary. For example, `111010` would group as `0011 1010` and convert to `3a`.)
5. Convert each of the following base 10 numbers to binary.
   - **a.** 17
   - **b.** 23
   - **c.** 38
   - **d.** 86
   - **e.** 160
   - **f.** 235
   - **g.** 4444

B Bitwise and Shift Operators

We typically use base 10 integers in our program, which are represented internally as binary numbers. C# `int` values always use 32 bits. Thus C# represents the number 25 internally as

```
0000 0000 0000 0000 0000 0000 0001 1001
```

BITWISE OPERATORS

C# has several **bitwise** operators that operate on each bit of an `int` value.

&	bitwise AND
|	bitwise OR
^	bitwise XOR (exclusive or)
~	bitwise complement

Figure B.1 shows the effects of these operations on corresponding bits of each operand.

To illustrate these operators we use 4-bit values for simplicity, rather than work with the much longer 32-bit `int` values. To evaluate `1010 & 0011` we apply the `&` operator to the bits in corresponding positions in the left and right operands,

FIGURE B.1
The effect of bitwise operators

&	0	1
0	0	0
1	0	1

|	0	1
0	0	1
1	0	1

^	0	1
0	0	0
1	0	1

	~
0	1
1	0

according to the table in Figure B.1. Using the `&` operator on each pair of corresponding bits gives

`1 & 0 = 0` for the leftmost bits of 1010 and 0011

`0 & 0 = 0` for the corresponding bits in the next position

`1 & 1 = 1` for the next bits

`0 & 1 = 0` for the rightmost bits

so that the result is `0010`.

Similarly, using the tables in Figure B.1 we see that

```
1010 | 0011 = 1011
1010 ^ 0011 = 1001
~ 1010      = 0101
```

We can apply the bitwise operators to variables. For example, if

```
int a = 10;
int b =  3;
```

then the 32-bit representations of `a` and `b` are `0000 0000 0000 0000 0000 0000 0000 1010` for a and `0000 0000 0000 0000 0000 0000 0000 0011` for b so that

`a & b =`	`2`	(0010 in binary)
`a	b =`	`11`	(1011 in binary)
`a ^ b =`	`9`	(1001 in binary)

LOGICAL OPERATORS

The operators `&`, `|`, and `^` can also operate on boolean values. The `&` and `|` operators are like the `&&` and `||` operators, except that the logical operators `&` and `|` always evaluate both operands, but the conditional operators `&&` and `||` evaluate both operands only when necessary.

SHIFT OPERATORS

The C# **shift** operators for the `int` type are

`<<` Shift bits left, filling with zero bits on the right-hand side

`>>` Shift bits right, filling with the high bit on the left-hand side

Using 8-bit numbers, rather than 32-bit, to illustrate: `10101010 << 3` evaluates to `01010000`, and `10101010 >> 3` evaluates to `11110101`, where the left-hand operand is the number to shift and the right-hand operand is the number of positions to shift. In evaluating `10101010 << 3`, when we shift `10101010` three positions to the left, the rightmost three bits disappear and we replace the leftmost three bits with zeros.

We can use the shift operator with `int` variables. For example, given

```
int a = 0x00003A7D;
```

evaluating `a << 7` will give `0x001D3E80` since `0x00003A7D` in binary is

```
0000 0000 0000 0000 0011 1010 0111 1101
```

and shifting seven positions to the left gives

```
0000 0000 0001 1101 0011 1110 1000 0000
```

in binary, or `0x001D3E80` in hex.

✓ Test Your Understanding

1. Find

  a. `1100 & 0011`

  b. `1111 & 0101`

  c. `0000 & 1010`

2. Find

  a. `1100 | 0011`

  b. `1111 | 0101`

  c. `0000 | 1010`

3. Find

  a. `1100 ^ 0011`

  b. `1111 ^ 0101`

  c. `0000 ^ 1010`

4. Find

  a. `~0010`

  b. `~1011`

5. Given

```
int a = 27;
int b = 53;
```

find

  a. `a & b`

  b. `a | b`

  c. `a ^ b`

  d. `~a`

6. Evaluate, using 8-bit numbers

  a. `11001011 << 5`

  b. `11001011 >> 4`

C Operator Precedence Table

Highest

Primary	`[ ]   .   ()   ++   --   new`
Unary	`++(prefix) --(prefix) + - ~ ! (T)x`
Multiplicative	`*   /   %`
Additive	`+   -`
Shift	`<<   >>`
Relational	`<   >   <=   >=   is`
Equality	`==   !=`
Bitwise, Logical AND	`&`
Bitwise, Logical XOR	`^`
Bitwise, Logical OR	`|`
Conditional AND	`&&`
Conditional OR	`||`
Conditional	`?:`
Assignment	`= += -= *= /= %= >>= <<= &= ^= |=`

Lowest

D The ASCII Character Set

The first 32 characters and the last are control characters. We label those control characters we use in the text.

0		32	blank	64	@	96	`
1		33	!	65	A	97	a
2		34	"	66	B	98	b
3		35	#	67	C	99	c
4		36	$	68	D	100	d
5		37	%	69	E	101	e
6		38	&	70	F	102	f
7		39	'	71	G	103	g
8	\b	40	(	72	H	104	h
9	\t	41	)	73	I	105	i
10	\n	42	*	74	J	106	j
11		43	+	75	K	107	k
12		44	,	76	L	108	l
13	\r	45	-	77	M	109	m
14		46	.	78	N	110	n
15		47	/	79	O	111	o
16		48	0	80	P	112	p
17		49	1	81	Q	113	q
18		50	2	82	R	114	r
19		51	3	83	S	115	s
20		52	4	84	T	116	t
21		53	5	85	U	117	u
22		54	6	86	V	118	v
23		55	7	87	W	119	w

24		56	8	88	X	120	x
25		57	9	89	Y	121	y
26		58	:	90	Z	122	z
27		59	;	91	[	123	{
28		60	<	92	\	124	|
29		61	=	93	]	125	}
30		62	>	94	^	126	~
31		63	?	95	_	127	

E

Simple Types

Keyword	*Number of Bits*
sbyte	8
byte	8
short	16
ushort	16
int	32
uint	32
long	64
ulong	64
char	16
float	32
double	64
bool	true, false
decimal	128

Answers to Selected Exercises

TEST YOUR UNDERSTANDING EXERCISES

Chapter 1

3. A compiler.

5. managed code

7. C++, Java, and C. One might include Visual Basic and Smalltalk.

9. MSIL code.

11. `public` and `class` are keywords. `Square` is an identifier. `{` is a punctuator.

13. = and *

17. Highest 10 % A, next 20% B, next 40 % C, next 20 % D, last 10 % F, for example

Chapter 2

1. a, b, f, g, and j are valid. c, d, e, and k use invalid characters. h starts with a digit, i is a keyword.

3. name, type

5. add initialization such as int number = 0;

7. The largest value is 2,147,483,647, and the smallest value is −2,147,483,648.

9. The program aborts with the error message

```
Unhandled Exception: System.FormatException: Input string was not in
          a correct format.
at System.Number.ParseInt32(String s, NumberStyles style,
        NumberFormatInfo info)
at InputInteger.Main()
```

11. You owe $8786.00, which is 53 days overdue.

13.
```
x + y = 17     x - y = 7     -y = -5
x * y = 60     x / 7 = 1     x % 7 = 5
```

15. a. 4	**b.** −19	**c.** 4	**d.** 9
e. −2	**f.** 0	**g.** 8	**h.** −3
i. 1			
17. a. 38	**b.** −44	**c.** 8	**d.** 4
e. −2			
19. a. 5	**b.** 13	**c.** 28	**d.** 1
e. 2	**f.** 12		
21. a. −44	**b.** 72	**c.** −20	**d.** −224
e. 136			

Chapter 3

1. a. `234 < 52`

b. `435 != 87`

c. `-12 == -12`

d. `76 >= 54`

3. The left operand is a bool value.

5. `x=5` assigns 5 to x. `x==5` tests whether x is equal to 5.

7. a, b, and **c.** `if (x == 12) y += 7;`

9. a.
```
if (y <= 6)
   z += 5;
```

b.
```
if (x != 0)
   y+=5;
else
   z = y + 9;
```

11. a.

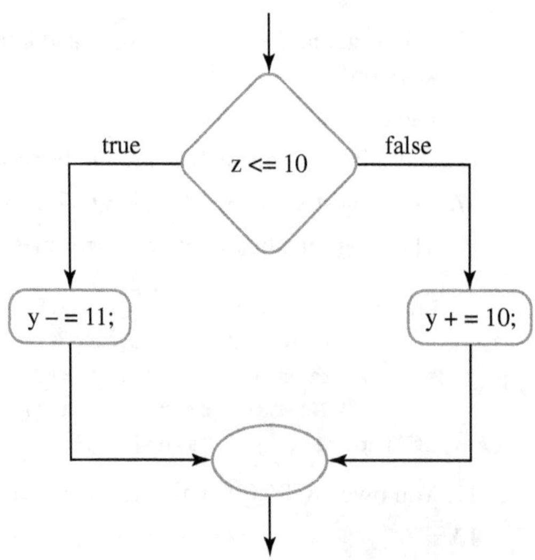

13. a. `3.4522` **b.** `-29876.5` **c.** `9876.5` **d.** `4.35`

15. `a` and `c`

17. a. `3456.789` **b.** `2.3456E-06` **c.** `.09876543` **d.** `1234567890.987`

e. `-234567.765432`

19. correct

21. a. `(double)72+37.5`

b. `23.28/(double)7`

23. a. `}` should be `)`

b. test condition must be **bool** valued

c. `=!` should be `!=`

25. a. does not terminate

b. terminates

27. Look up a number in the telephone directory. (Item 1)

```
Refining Item 1.
     Set start to first page.
     Set end to last page.
     while(listing not found and start <= end) {
       Open the directory to a page between start and end.
       Check for listing.                                   (Item 2)
     }

Refining Item 2.
        if (listing after current page){
          set start to the page after the current page
        else if (listing before current page)
          set end to the page before the current page
        else display listing
```

29. Read 49.23, max = 49.23, 49.23 is nonnegative, read 16.789, `16.789 < 49.23`, 16.789 is non-negative, read 92.145, `92.145 > 49.23`, max = 92.145, 92.145 is nonnegative. read 32.7, `32.7< 92.145`, 32.7 is non-negative, read -1, `-1 < 92.145`, -1 is negative, The max is 92.145.

31. Find the maximum and the minimum of numbers input by the user. (Item 1)

```
Refining item 1.
    Read the quantity of numbers.
    Read first number.
    Set max to first number.
    Set min to first number.
    Set count to one.
    while ( count < quantity)
    Process the rest of the numbers.     (Item 2)
  Display the maximum and minimum.
```

```
Refining Item 2.
     Read the next number.
     if (next number < min) set min to next number
     else if (next number > max) set max to next number.
```

33. 1860

Chapter 4

1. Many correct answers are possible, for example

a. `x=2,y=7`

b. `x=0, y = any integer`

c. `x = 20,y = any integer`

d. `x=11, y =0`

3. Many correct answers are possible, for example

a. 3, false

b. 3, true

c. 13, true

d. 3, false

5. Many correct answers are possible, for example

a. 3

b. 12

c. 3

d. 3

7. a. `a>1 || c==5`

b. `x<y+5 && y>2`

c. `!(x>2 || y!=8)`

9.
```
if (amount >= 1 && amount <= 99) System.out.println("Thanks
     Contributor");
else if (amount >+ 100 && amount < 499)
      System.out.println("Thanks Supporter");
else if (amount >= 500 && amount <= 999)
      System.out.println("Thanks Patron");
else if (amount >= 1000) System.out.println("Thanks Benefactor");
else System.out.println("Please contribute to out charity");
```

11. a. 8 **b.** 7 **c.** 6 **d.** 7

13. a. 9 **b.** 6 **c.** 7 **d.** 9

e. 8 **f.** 9 **g.** 9

15. `for(int i = 1; i <= 10; i++)  System.out.println(i);`

17. `for(int i=9; i>=3; i--)   System.out.println(i);`

19. 28

21. 26

23. 55

25. 0

27. 72

29. a. I like

b. Ali Baba said, "Open, Sesame!" to write C# programs.

c. 67845

d. Find 3\4 of 24

31. 64

The reward on square 64 is 9223372036854775808.

33. a. `Math.Pow(7,4)`

b. `Math.Sqrt(43.0)`

c. `Math.Max(476.22,-608.90)`

d. `Math.Min(58.43,6.32*8.87)`

e. `Math.Abs(-65.234)`

f. `Math.Floor(-43.99)`

g. `Math.Ceiling(-3.01);`

35. `Math.PI * r * r`

37. `Math.Sqrt(x*x) = x;`

39.

```
do {
      Console.WriteLine();
      Console.WriteLine ("Choose from the following list");
      Console.WriteLine ("1.  Convert from British pounds to US dollars");
      Console.WriteLine ("2.  Convert from US dollars to British pounds");
      Console.WriteLine ("3.  Quit");
      int choice = IO.GetInt("Enter your choice, 1, 2 or 3");
          switch (choice) {
              case 1:
                           PoundsToDollars();
                           break;
               case 2:
                           DollarsToPounds();
                           break;
               case 3: Console.WriteLine ("Bye, Have a nice day");
                           break;
           }
      } while (choice != 3);
```

41.

```
public class ConvertMoney {
        public static void DollarsToPounds {
            Console.WriteLine ("Converting from US dollars to British pounds.");
        }
        public static void PoundsToDollars {
            Console.WriteLine ("Converting from British pounds to US dollars");
        }
        public static void Main() {
            int choice;
               do {
                  Console.WriteLine ();
                  Console.WriteLine ("Choose from the following list");
                  Console.WriteLine ("1.  Convert from British pounds to US dollars");
                  Console.WriteLine ("2.  Convert from US dollars to British pounds");
                  Console.WriteLine ("3.  Quit");
                  choice = IO.GetInt("Enter your choice, 1, 2 or 3");
                  switch (choice) {
                       case 1:
                                   DollarsToPounds();
                                   break;
                        case 2:
                                   PoundsToDollars();
                                   break;
                        case 3: Console.WriteLine ("Bye, Have a nice day");
                                   break;
                  }
               } while (choice != 3);
        }
    }
```

Chapter 5

1. `enterMoney` and `selectCandy`
3. `bigRed.enterMoney(50)`. The enterMoney operation refers to a specific vending machine such as bigRed.
5. One possibility is:

   The agent asks the customer to select a car.

   The customer asks the agent to provide a mid-size convertible.

   The agent asks the customer to specify a rental period.

   The customer tells the agent that the rental is for one week.

   The agent checks the computer system for a mid-size convertible.

   The computer checks the inventory for a mid-size convertible.

   The inventory shows a mid-size convertible is available.

   The computer system checks the reservations for a conflict.

The reservations indicate no conflict.

The database tells the agent that such a car is available.

The agent requests a license and credit card from the customer.

The customer provides a license and a credit card.

The agent updates the system.

The system updates the inventory.

The agent provides the car to the customer.

Agent

- Accept request for car.
- Accept result of inquiry to system.

Customer

- Provide rental type.
- Provide license and credit card.
- Accept request for rental.
- Accept update.

Inventory

- Accept request for car availability.
- Accept update.

Reservation List

- Accept request for conflict check

7. We declare instance variables outside of any method. Example 5.1 uses the instance variable `balance`.

11. `BankAccount theAccount = new BankAccount();`

13. The `BankAccount` constructor with no arguments.

15. `TestBankAccount.cs(12,30): error CS0122: 'BankAccount.balance' is inaccessible due to its protection level`

19. After the `serve burger` arrow add a `take burger` arrow from `aWaiter` to `aCustomer`. Similarly, add a `take soda` arrow after `serve soda`, and add a `take fries` arrow after `serve fries`.

Chapter 6

1. a. 27	**b.** h	**c.** 2	**d.** 10
e. three	**f.** THE THREE DID FEED THE DEER		
2. a. 1	**b.** 4	**c.** 4	**d.** −1
e. 6	**f.** −1		
3. a. "9.65"	**b.** "−2.75"		
5. a. −1	**b.** 1	**c.** 0	

7. `Address myAddress = new Address(street, city, state, zip)` where

```
String street = 123 Main St.
String city = Hometown
String state = CA
String zip = 12345
```

9.
```
Name name = new Name("George", "Washington");
myAddress from Question 7.
String id = "12345";
Person person = new Person(id, name, myAddress);
```

11.
```
public void AroundBlock(IDrivable d) {
    d.Start();
    d.Accelerate();
    d.Turn("right");
    d.Turn("right");
    d.Turn("right");
    d.Turn("right");
    d.Decelerate();
    d.Stop();
}
```

Chapter 7

1.
```
int[] intArray = {37,44,68,-12};
intArray[1] = 55;
```

3. `char[] charArray = {'s','y','t','c','v','w'};`

5.
```
21 31 41 51 61 71
L              R

71 31 41 51 61 21
   L        R

71 61 41 51 31 21
      L  R

72 61 51 41 31 21
      R  L
```

7. a. intArray

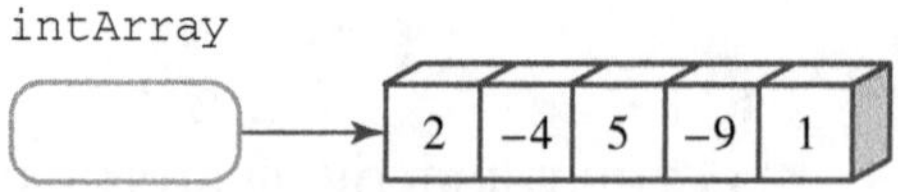

b.

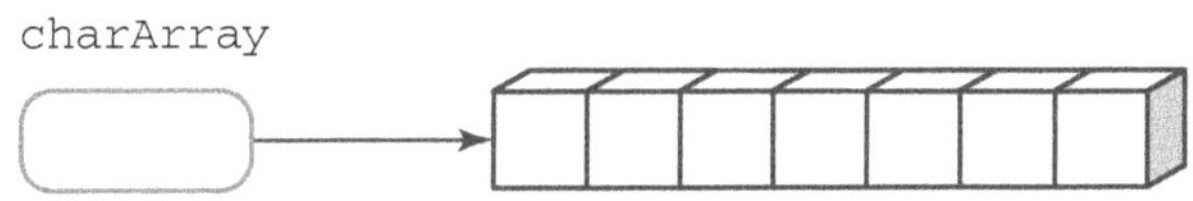

c.

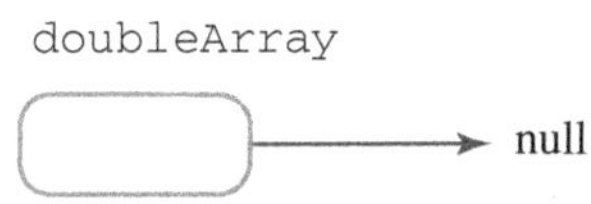

9.
```
int[] b = new int[a.Length];
for(int i=0; i<a.Length, i++)b[i]=a[i];
```

11.

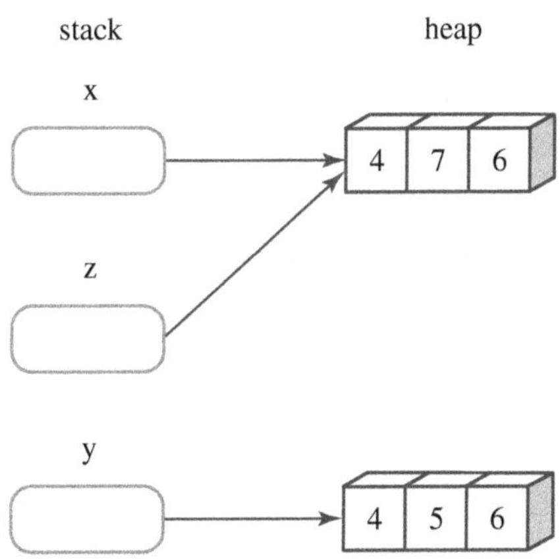

13. Change the call to reverse in `Main` to

```
r.Reverse(1, score.Length-2);
```

15. `random.Next(50, 500)`, where `random` is an instance of the `Random` class.

17.
```
int[ , ] results = {{55,66,87,76},{86,92,88,95}};
```

19. a. b **b.** x **c.** w **d.** c

21. loop, stopping when item i >= item i-1 or index = 0 {
  interchange item i and item i-1;
  decrease i by 1;
}

23.		52 38 6 97 3 41 67 44 15
	Insert 38	38 52 6 97 3 41 67 44 15
	Insert 6	38 6 52 97 3 41 67 44 15
		6 38 52 97 3 41 67 44 15
	Insert 97	
	Insert 3	6 38 52 3 97 41 67 44 15
		6 38 3 53 97 41 67 44 15
		6 3 38 53 97 41 67 44 15
		3 6 38 53 97 41 67 44 15
	Insert 41	3 6 38 53 41 97 67 44 15
		3 6 38 41 53 97 67 44 15
	Insert 67	3 6 38 41 53 67 97 44 15
	Insert 44	3 6 38 41 53 67 44 97 15
		3 6 38 41 53 44 67 97 15
		3 6 38 41 44 53 67 97 15
	Insert 15	3 6 38 41 44 53 67 15 97
		3 6 38 41 44 53 15 67 97
		3 6 38 41 44 15 53 67 97
		3 6 38 41 15 44 53 67 97
		3 6 38 15 41 44 53 67 97
		3 6 15 38 41 44 53 67 97

Chapter 8

3. The upper left corner.
5. `g.DrawLine(Pens.Blue,3,5,15,5);`
7. `g.DrawRectangle(Pens.Blue,30,60,50,50);`
9. `g.DrawArc(Pens.Blue,100,50,200,100,90,120);`
11. `Font f = new Font("Courier New", 30, FontStyle.Italic);`
13. `g.DrawString(s, myFont, Brushes.Blue, 175, h)` where `h` is the vertical position of the string, and `myFont` is a Font.
15. `Color.FromArgb(0,0,255);`
17. 0, 0, 0
19. The triangle does not get redrawn in its new position.
21. Pressing the *R* key generates down, press, and up events. Holding the *Shift* key while pressing *R* generates down, down, press, up, and up events.

Chapter 9

1. A `Click` event.
3. The `Print_Click` method.

5. Add the lines

```
compute = new ComputeDelegate(Math.Floor);
Console.WriteLine(test.Test(5, compute));
```

7. Lines

```
square.CheckedChanged +=
            new EventHandler(Checked_Changed);
circle.CheckedChanged +=
            new EventHandler(Checked_Changed);
```

9. `Selected_Index` and `Check_Changed` represent `EventHandler`. The `OnPaint` method handles Paint events.
11. String is immutable but a `StringBuilder` object may change.

Chapter 10

1. **a.** BankAccount **b.** Object
   c. Object **d.** Object
   e. BankAccount
3. CheckingAccount c = new CheckingAccount(1500.00,0.35);
5. Overloading. To override, the method must have exactly the same parameters as the method of the same name in the superclass. Here we added a boolean parameter not present in the superclass method.
7. c
9. Yes, because the class is still declared using the abstract keyword.
11. It must be public, because we use it in a different file in a class not derived from it.
13. We can use `Get4()` only in the file in which it is declared. We can also use `Get2()` in derived classes.
15. The user asks the teller to accept an ATM card.

    The teller asks the user to enter a PIN.

    The user asks the teller to accept a PIN.

    The teller asks the user to select a transaction type.

    The user asks the teller to accept a withdrawal.

    The teller asks the user to select an account type.

    The user asks the teller to accept a savings account type.

    The teller asks the bank to find the account of the chosen type for the user with the specified PIN. The bank gives the teller a reference to the account.

    The teller asks the user to specify an amount.

    The user asks the teller to accept an amount.

    The teller asks the account to withdraw the specified amount.

    The teller asks the user to select another transaction . . . .

17. The user asks the teller to accept an ATM card.
The teller asks the user to enter a PIN.
The user asks the teller to accept a PIN.
The teller asks the user to select a transaction type.
The user asks the teller to accept a deposit.
The teller asks the user to select an account type.
The user asks the teller to accept a cancellation.

Chapter 11

1. In Examples 11.4 and 11.5 the code in the `catch` block executes.
3. b
5. For example, messages.data might contain
An apple a day keeps the doctor away.
A stitch in time saves nine.
Early to bed, early to rise, makes a person healthy, wealthy, and wise.
7. Using Console.Write("{0} ", input.ReadInt64()); the output becomes
0 1 2 3 4 5 6 7 8 9 0 4607182418800017408 4611686018427387904
4613937818241073152 4616189618054758400 4617315517961601024
4618441417868443648 4619567317775286272 4620693217682128896
4621256167635550208
9. Lines may wrap around, so there is no scroll bar.

Chapter 12

1.
```
int[] data = {8,5,2,7,10,9,3,4};
MergeSort(data,1,8);
    MergeSort(data,1,4);
        MergeSort(data,1,2);
            MergeSort(data,1,1);
            MergeSort(data,2,2);
            Merge(data,1,1,2,2); result {5,8}
        MergeSort(data,3,4);
            MergeSort(data,3,3);
            MergeSort(data,4,4);
            Merge(data,3,3,4,4); result {2,7}
        Merge(data,1,2,3,4);   result {2,5,7,8}
    MergeSort(data,5,8);
        MergeSort(data,5,6);
            MergeSort(data,5,5);
            MergeSort(data,6,6);
            Merge(data,5,5,6,6); result {9,10}
        MergeSort(data,7,8);
            MergeSort(data,7,7);
```

```
            MergeSort(data,8,8);
            Merge(data,7,7,8,8); result {3,4}
        Merge(data,5,6,7,8);   result {3,4,9,10}
    Merge(data,1,4,5,8);       result {2,3,4,5,7,8,9,10}
```

5. Try each list operation with a null list. Try the operations in various orders with a list of length one, and with a list of length greater than one.
7. The stack will be the same. The push operation is the inverse of pop.
11. `ArrayList v = new ArrayList(25);`
13. Running with different data such as

    {"potato","fish","steak","lettuce","pizza","hamburger",

    "hot dog","pie","tuna","candy","cake","ice cream"};

    gives more collisions. Using randomly generated data such as

    {"cnxzcatj","xtzarjex", "vbrtwqve", "unpeecjk", "rdtbkknp", "njkticlb",

    "punojpcj", "jxslnhen", "onoxuyfp", "etlnjisf", "pizwwcut", "payotnwn"}

    gives fewer.
15. We would expect more collisions to occur because there will be less free space in the table and fewer choices for the hash functions.
17. It generates a runtime error because `NewName` does not implement the `IComparable` interface.

Chapter 13

1. 1, Bonnie 1, Clyde 1, Clyde 2, Bonnie 2, Clyde 3, Clyde 4, Bonnie 3, Clyde 5, Bonnie 4, 2, Bonnie 5, 3, 4, 5
3. Main will print its name five times followed first by five Bonnies then by five Clydes, or fives Clydes and five Bonnies. Each thread has more than enough time to print its name five times when it has the processor.
5. Yes, we can edit another program while the animation is running and open another console window to run another Java program.
7. The image flickers.
9. Making the producer sleep a lot longer will cause many `Buffer empty` messages. Making the consumer sleep a lot longer will cause may `Buffer full` messages.

Chapter 14

1. The program displays the author's home page, index.html, with all the HTML tags uninterpreted.
3. The change is:

```
Console.WriteLine("Content type: {0}",
                  response.GetResponseHeader("Content-type"));
```

5. The program deadlocks.
7. The client receives a message that it is connected, but no data because only headers were requested. We could use this to inspect the headers if we modified the program.

9. Clients will be active simultaneously and will alternately receive data.
11. It works as in the original versions.

Chapter 15

1. The ID is unique, but the name may be duplicated.
3.
```
INSERT INTO Salesperson VALUES
    ('12', 'Peter Patterson', '66 FifthSt.')
INSERT INTO Salesperson
    VALUES ('98', 'Donna Dubarian', '77 Sixth St.')
```
5.
```
DELETE FROM OrderItem
WHERE OrderNumber = '5' AND ItemNumber = '444444'
```
7.
```
SELECT OrderNumber FROM Orders, Salesperson
WHERE Orders.SalesPersonID = Salesperson.SalesPersonID
AND SalespersonName = 'Peter Patterson'
```
9. A runtime error indicates that the Customer table already exists.
11.
```
SELECT DISTINCT SalespersonName, CustomerName
FROM Salesperson, Customer, Orders
WHERE  Orders.CustomerID = Customer.CustomerID
AND Orders.SalesPersonID = Salesperson.SalesPersonID
```
13.
```
SELECT DISTINCT CustomerName, CustomerAddress
FROM Customer, Salesperson, Orders
WHERE Customer.CustomerID = Orders.CustomerID
AND Salesperson.SalesPersonID = Orders.SalesPersonID
AND SalespersonName = 'Peter Patterson'
```
15. Change "Customer" to "Orders" in "new object[]{null,null,"Customer",null});"
17. A `System.InvalidOperationException` is thrown.

Chapter 16

1. Hypertext Transfer Protocol (HTTP)
3. Hypertext Markup Language (HTML)
5. To link to another document.
7. Using Post, no data is added to the URL. The data gets sent after the request.
9. The *Order* button has no label.
11. The example still functions correctly. The query appears added to the URL.
13. The session IDs are different.

Chapter 17

1. They are all well formed.

3.
```
<cds>
       <cd>
             <title>Beethoven Violin Concerto</title>
           <artist>Itzhak Perlman</artist>
           <artist>Daniel Barenboim</artist>
           <tracks>5</tracks>
       </cd>
       <cd>
           <title>from broken hearts to blue skies</title>
           <artist>Susannah McCorkle</artist>
            <tracks>14</tacks>
       </cd>
</cds>
```

5. The `DocumentElement` method from the `XmlDocument` class.

7. `<xsl:apply-templates></xsl:apply-templates>`

9. `<xsl:template match="book{[at]type='text']">`

11. Choose services that have an .asmx file in the WSDL link. Click on the link to see the WSDL file and then delete "?wsdl" and hit the *Enter* key to bring up a test page.

Appendix A

1. **a.** $3 \times 10 + 8$ **c.** $5 \times 100 + 6 \times 10 + 2$
   e. $3 \times 100 + 6$

3. **a.** 3 **b.** 13 **c.** 44 **d.** 27
   e. 234

5. **a.** 10001 **b.** 10111 **c.** 100110 **d.** 1010110
   e. 10100000 **f.** 11101011 **g.** 1000101011100

Appendix B

1. **a.** 0000 **b.** 0101 **c.** 0000

3. **a.** 1111 **b.** 1010 **c.** 1010

5. **a.** 17 **b.** 63 **c.** 46 **d.** 4

ANSWERS TO SKILL BUILDER AND CRITICAL THINKING EXERCISES

Chapter 2

1. **a.** int x;
   b. public static void Main () { // code goes here }
   c. z+y cannot occur on the left side of an assignment.
   d. public class MyClass { // put code here }

2. 64

3. a. ii **b.** iii **c.** iv **d.** i

4. b and c

5. a and c

6. a. 3, 4 **b.** 2, 3

7. d

Chapter 3

1. 2

2. a. v **b.** i **c.** iv

3. a. if (x > y) System.out.println("x > y")
else System.out.println("y >= x");

b. while (x > 10) x –=2;

4. c

5. d

6. b

7. c

Chapter 4

1.
```
if (i == 1) j += 2;
else if (i == 3) j-= 5;
else if (i==7 || i==10) j *= 17;
else j = 0;
```

2.
```
int i = 0;
while (i <= 20) {
  sum += i * i;
  i++;
}
```

3.
```
int sum = 0, i;
do {
   int i = IO.GetInt("Enter an integer");
   sum += i;
} while (sum < 100);
```

4. c

5. a

6. d

7. b

Chapter 5

1. a. iii **b.** i **c.** iv **d.** ii

2. value, reference

3. shared
4. a
5. e
6. e
7. b

Chapter 6

1. hack
2. a reference to a String object, an integer value
3. false
4. c
5. a
6. c
7. d

Chapter 7

1. split(0,7) returns 4, nums = { 3, 23, 12, 11, 45, 88, 67, 77}
2. {{21, 21, 21, 21}, {21, 21, 21, 21} {21, 21, 21, 21}}
3. {{34}, {34, 34}, {34, 34, 34}, {34, 34, 34, 34}, {34, 34, 34, 34, 34}}
4. **a.** i **b.** iv **c.** ii **d.** iii
5. c
6. c
7. a

Chapter 8

1. `KeyDown, KeyDown, KeyPress, KeyUp, KeyUp`
2. A centered rectangle whose dimensions are half those of the form
3.
```
new Font(FontFamily.GenericSansSerif, 24,
              FontStyle.Italic);
```
4. c
5. c
6. c
7. d

Chapter 9

1. **a.** ii **b.** i **c.** iii
2. Focus
3. Invalidate
4. a

5. d

6. a

7. c

Chapter 10

1. class, interface, abstract, methods, overriding, class

2. **a.** internal

b. protected internal

c. public

d. private

3. 4, 25

4. b

5. a

6. d

7. d

Chapter 11

1. **a.** iii **b.** i **c.** ii **d.** iii

2.
```
BinaryReader input = new BinaryReader
        (new FileStream(values.data, FileMode.Open));
```

3.
```
BinaryWriter output = new BinaryWriter
        (new FileStream(values.out, FileMode.Create));
```

4. a

5. b

6. b

7. b

Chapter 12

1. 13

2. 243

3. GetHashCode, Equals

4. c

5. a

6. d

7. d

Chapter 13

1. Start

2. a. iii **b.** i **c.** ii

3. Deadlock occurs when threads wait for locks to be freed that cannot be freed.

4. a

5. d

6. b

7. b

Index

D

www.ingramcontent.com/pod-product-compliance
Lightning Source LLC
LaVergne TN
LVHW082001200926
848481LV00010B/2784

9781449614485